THE FIRST

White House Library

THE PENN STATE SERIES IN THE HISTORY OF THE BOOK

James L. W. West III, General Editor

Peter Burke, *The Fortunes of the Courtier:*
The European Reception of Castiglione's Cortegiano

Roger Burlingame, *Of Making Many Books:*
A Hundred Years of Reading, Writing, and Publishing

James M. Hutchisson,
The Rise of Sinclair Lewis, 1920-1930

Julie Bates Dock, ed., *Charlotte Perkins Gilman's*
"The Yellow Wall-paper" and the History of Its Publication and Reception:
A Critical Edition and Documentary Casebook

John Williams, ed., *Imaging the Early Medieval Bible*

James G. Nelson, *Publisher to the Decadents:*
Leonard Smithers in the Careers of Beardsley, Wilde, Dowson

Ezra Greenspan, *George Palmer Putnam:*
Representative American Publisher

Pamela Selwyn, *Everyday Life in the German Book Trade:*
Friedrich Nicolai as Bookseller and Publisher in the Age of Enlightenment

David R. Johnson, *Conrad Richter: A Writer's Life*

David Finkelstein, *The House of Blackwood:*
Author-Publisher Relations in the Victorian Era

Rodger Tarr, ed., *As Ever Yours:*
The Letters of Max Perkins and Elizabeth Lemmon

Randy Robertson, *Censorship and Conflict in Seventeenth Century England:*
The Subtle Art of Division

Catherine M. Parisian, ed., *The First White House Library:*
A History and Annotated Catalogue

THE FIRST
WHITE HOUSE LIBRARY

A History and Annotated Catalogue

edited by

CATHERINE M. PARISIAN

PUBLISHED BY THE PENNSYLVANIA STATE UNIVERSITY PRESS

for the Bibliographical Society of America
and the National First Ladies' Library

Library of Congress Cataloging-in-Publication Data

The first White House library : a history and annotated catalog /
edited by Catherine M. Parisian.
p.   cm. — (Penn State studies in the history of the book)
Includes bibliographical references and index.
Summary: "Examines the founding in 1850 of the first library in the White House
purchased with public funds, which was intended to remain there as a permanent collection.
Documents the contents of the library and considers it within the political, social, and
intellectual milieu of mid–nineteenth-century America"—Provided by publisher.
ISBN 978-0-271-03713-4 (acid-free paper)
1. Libraries—Washington, D.C.—History.
2. Libraries—Washington, D.C.—Catalogs.
3. White House (Washington, D.C.)—History.
4. Fillmore, Millard, 1800–1874—Books and reading.
5. Fillmore, Abigail Powers, 1798–1853—Books and reading.
6. Books and reading—United States—History—19th century.
7. United States—Intellectual life—19th century.
I. Parisian, Catherine M., 1963– .

Z732.W18F57 2010
027.5753—dc22
2009035727

Published by The Pennsylvania State University Press,
University Park, PA 16802-1003

The Pennsylvania State University Press is a member of the
Association of American University Presses.

It is the policy of The Pennsylvania State University Press to use acid-free paper.
Publications on uncoated stock satisfy the minimum requirements of
American National Standard for Information Sciences—Permanence of Paper
for Printed Library Material, ANSI z39.48–1992.

This book is printed on Natures Natural, which contains 50% post-consumer waste.

CONTENTS

ILLUSTRATIONS

PREFACE

In March 2004 I convened a meeting of librarians and bibliographers to consider the feasibility of reconstructing the first permanent White House Library, established in 1850 by President Millard Fillmore and First Lady Abigail Fillmore. What little had been written about that library gave me reason to think that Abigail Fillmore played an important part in designing it and making it a cultural center of the White House during her husband's brief term of office.

It has been my goal to document the historical role and cultural contributions of first ladies ever since I founded the National First Ladies' Library in Canton, Ohio, in 1996. Over the years this organization has restored and renovated a majestic seven-story 1895 bank building, which is the home of the National First Ladies' Library Education and Research Center. This building houses an extensive research library with works about and related to first ladies, museum exhibit rooms, a seminar room, archival storage and processing rooms, and a small Victorian theater open for public presentations. It also has a small library room dedicated to First Lady Abigail Fillmore, in which the books representing those in the first White House Library will be housed. In addition to its scholarly resources on site, the center maintains a Web site with the only available complete bibliography of all publications about first ladies, a biographical entry for each first lady written by renowned historian Carl Sferrazza Anthony, and a wealth of other information about America's first ladies.

But it is one thing to have virtual information about Abigail Fillmore and quite another to show the actual books demonstrating her intellectual influence in the White House and her important role in forming the reading habits of her husband. If it would be possible to determine the contents of the first White House Library, I hoped to acquire equivalent copies of books for display in the Abigail Fillmore Library, where scholars and visitors could see for themselves what books the Fillmores believed were most important for instruction and guidance at a critical juncture in the history of this nation, as well as what books of enduring literary value the Fillmores thought would be used and appreciated by future residents of the White House.

These were the aspirations I had in mind when I discussed this project in the course of the meeting in 2004. At the very beginning of this project, and every step of the way, Jon Lindseth advised me on the bibliographical challenges we would face in identifying these books, which had been dispersed in mysterious circumstances. As far as we could tell, just a few volumes remained in the White House, although some vouchers had come to light that contained a cursory account of the Fillmores' earliest acquisitions. The antiquarian bookseller Jay Dillon delivered a report that encouraged us to think that some books could be identified on the basis of the vouchers.

Also present at the meeting were representatives of the Library of Congress and the Bibliographical Society of America (BSA). They agreed that it would be possible to reconstruct the library and proposed to compile a catalogue with notes and commentary describing the books and explaining their significance in relation to the literary tastes and intellectual outlook of the period. The Librarian of Congress, James H. Billington, offered to provide working space in the Rare Book and Special Collections Division for a project bibliographer, who would be recruited and supervised by BSA. At that time the president of BSA was John Bidwell, and the chair of the Publications Committee was Hope Mayo: they too have been involved in this project every step of the way and have helped to see this catalogue through the press long after they concluded their official responsibilities in the society. They could rely on previous experience at BSA, which organized and supervised the production of the monumental nine-volume *Bibliography of American Literature*, funded by the Lilly Endowment and the National Endowment for the Humanities. Although much smaller in scope, this project required similarly substantial funding, for which I am very grateful to the Institute of Museum and Library Services.

John Bidwell and Hope Mayo invited several individuals active in library and cultural affairs to join them in forming an editorial board: William P. Blair, Mark Dimunation, Jon Lindseth, and Elizabeth Thacker-Estrada. The editorial board proceeded to recruit a project bibliographer, Catherine M. Parisian, who had just received her doctorate at the University of Virginia and, without taking a second breath, immediately went to work in the Library of Congress. She made a number of important discoveries while compiling the catalogue, such as several books in the Library of Congress stacks that still retain traces of having been in the Executive Mansion in 1850 as well as inventories in the Library of Congress archives that have enabled her to identify the exact editions of many books only briefly mentioned in the vouchers. Her prefatory essay on the history of the library reveals what became of it in later administrations and how it served as precedent for the current White House Library, now more of a public institution than a personal collection.

Three other prefatory essays help to put the catalogue in context. Sean Wilentz, the Sidney and Ruth Lapidus Professor in the American Revolutionary Era at Princeton University, has written on the social and political forces underlying the Fillmores' choice of reading matter. Elizabeth Thacker-Estrada, branch manager of the Excelsior Branch of the San Francisco Public Library, has drawn on her research for her forthcoming biography of Abigail Fillmore to recount how the first lady designed the library to be a place for social occasions, cultural events, and leisure activities at the Executive Mansion. William G. Allman, Curator of the White House, has described the decorative scheme and the furnishings the Fillmores selected for the library room. These contributors deserve a special word of thanks.

This catalogue is a co-publication of the Bibliographical Society of America, the National First Ladies' Library, and the Penn State University Press. Patrick Alexander, Director of the press, and his colleagues are to be commended for their editorial expertise and for the handsome design of this volume. I hope that it will inspire people to appreciate the importance of the first White House Library and to learn more about it by viewing the reconstructed version in the Abigail Fillmore Library Room at the National First Ladies' Library's Education and Research Center. Patricia Krider, Executive Director of the National First Ladies' Library, has already started to work with designers to equip the room with bookcases, a fire suppression system, lighting, and humidity control that will meet the highest museum and archival standards.

Finally, I should acknowledge the support of my husband, Ralph Regula, who believes, like I do, that libraries hold a paramount position in the intellectual life of this nation. In 2005 he received the Public Service Award from the Friends of Libraries USA in recognition of his success in implementing government programs to sustain and improve library services. Some libraries grow and prosper; others fade away. After a promising beginning, the first White House Library was neglected and would have been forgotten if not for the collaborative effort that went into this catalogue, which has in its own way grown and prospered to become a valuable record of the ideals, beliefs, concerns, and goals of our nation's leaders at the midpoint of the nineteenth century.

MARY A. REGULA
President and Founding Chair
National First Ladies' Library

ACKNOWLEDGMENTS

The completion of *The First White House Library: A History and Annotated Catalogue* would not have been possible without the generosity, assistance, and cooperation of many institutions and individuals. Mary Regula, founder and director of the National First Ladies' Library, first conceived of the idea; Jay Dillon assessed the feasibility of the project; Jon Lindseth recruited the Bibliographical Society of America to oversee and administer the research and compilation of the *Catalogue;* and the Library of Congress housed the project in its Division of Rare Book and Special Collections. William Allman, Elizabeth Thacker-Estrada, and Sean Wilentz contributed essays that helped to contextualize the library within the historical milieu in which it was formed

I am grateful to the editorial board members, John Bidwell, William Blair, Mark Dimunation, Jon Lindseth, Hope Mayo, and Elizabeth Thacker-Estrada, for their patience, wisdom, and guidance. It has been a privilege and a pleasure to work with this team.

Staff members in numerous divisions of the Library of Congress contributed their expertise to this project. I especially appreciate the support that I received from those of the Division of Rare Book and Special Collections: George Chiassion, Daniel DeSimone, Mark Dimunation, Arthur Dunkleman, Clark Evans, Elizabeth Gettins, Tom Noonan, and Rosemary Plakas. In the Main Reading Room, Emily C. Howie, David Kelly, Thomas Mann, and Evelyn Timberlake provided reference assistance and pointed me to invaluable resources. In the Division of Manuscripts, Lia Apodaca, Jennifer Brathoude, Jeff Flannery, Cheryl Fox, Joseph Jackson, Patrick Kerwin, and Bruce Kirby all assisted in navigating the Library of Congress archives and extensive manuscript collections. In the Law Library, Louis Acosta, James Martin, Meredith Shed-Driskell, Mark Strattner, and Magaret Wood lent their expertise in legal history and documents. Edward J. Redmond in the Geography and Map Division provided expert guidance in researching the maps and atlases that were purchased for the White House. I am grateful to John Cole, Director of the Center of the Book, for his advice and support throughout this project.

Research for this project was conducted at numerous other institutions. I am grateful for the assistance of Stephen Z. Nonack at the Boston Athenaeum; Nancy Johnson, Cynthia

Van Ness, and Patricia Virgil at the Buffalo and Erie County Historical Society; Jennie C. Meade at the Jacob Burns Law Library, George Washington University; David Warrington and Anne Person at the Harvard Law Library; Elizabeth Falsey, Susan Halpert, and Rachael Howarth at the Houghton Library; and John Vandereedt of the National Archives and Records Administration. His knowledge of early American accounting records was invaluable. I am also grateful to Nan Card, Thomas J. Culbertson, and Gil Gonzalez at the Rutherford B. Hayes Presidential Center; to Jeffrey Rankin at the Charles E. Young Research Library, University of California Los Angeles; and to Christian DuPont and Alison White at the University of Virginia. Matthew Schaefer at the Herbert Hoover Presidential Library and Museum provided important information and copies of documents from the President Herbert and First Lady Lou Henry Hoover Papers. William Allman, White House curator, provided access to the books from the first White House Library that remain there and advised on various matters as this project progressed.

The organizations that hosted lectures about the First White House Library provided me with invaluable opportunities to receive feedback on the project as it progressed. Questions from audience members often stimulated further investigation into specific areas. For arranging these forums I thank Monica Higgins John Lannon, Marshall Moriarty, and Richard Wendorf with the Boston Athenaeum; Nan Summer-Mack and Ted Widmer with the John Carter Brown Library; William Higgins and Eric Holzenberg with the Grolier Club; and Sabrina Baron, Eric Lindquist and Eleanor Shevlin with the Washington Area Group for Print Culture Studies.

Several people read and provided feedback on portions of the manuscript. I am especially grateful to John Bidwell, Daniel DeSimone, Thomas Mann, Hope Mayo, Steven L. Snell, Elizabeth Thacker-Estrada, and David Vander Meulen for their careful attention to detail and constructive feedback. I also thank Patrick Alexander, Laura Reed-Morrisson, and Kathryn Yahner of Penn State University Press for their careful handling of all details related to publishing *The First White House Library: A History and Annotated Catalogue*.

Many friends and family members encouraged, supported, and endured with me through this project. I thank John Day, Tessa Muehllehner, Jennie C. Meade, Carlos Rodriguez, Donna Schlosser, and Eleanor Shevlin.

ABBREVIATIONS

ANB	*American National Biography*
AODT	Accounting Offices of the Department of the Treasury
APS	*American Periodical Series*
BEAL	Morris Cohen, *Bibliography of Early American Law*
BECHS	Buffalo and Erie County Historical Society
British Catalogue	Sampson Low, comp., *The British Catalogue of Books Published from October 1837 to December 1852; Containing the Date of Publication, Size, Price, Publisher's Name, and Edition*
(D)	Democrat
DAB	*Dictionary of American Biography*
DFo	Folger Shakespeare Library, Washington, D.C.
DGW	Jacob Burns Law Library, George Washington University, Washington, D.C.
DLC	Library of Congress, Washington, D.C.
Fleeman	J. D. Fleeman, *A Bibliography of the Works of Samuel Johnson*
Greenleaf	Simon Greenleaf, "Greenleaf's Select Law Library"
Harvard	*A Catalogue of the Law Library of Harvard University*
Hoffman	David Hoffman, *A Course of Legal Study, Addressed to Students and the Profession Generally*
Larned	J. N. Larned, *The Literature of American History: A Bibliographical Guide*
L and B	Little and Brown
LC 1816–1851	*The London Catalogue of Books Published in Great Britain with their Sizes, Prices, and Publisher's Names, 1816–1851*

Marvin	J. G. Marvin, *Legal Bibliography or a Thesaurus of American, English, Irish, and Scotch Law Books*
MBA	Boston Athenaeum, Boston, Mass.
MF	Millard Fillmore
MH	Houghton Library, Harvard University, Cambridge, Mass.
NAB	National Archives Building, Washington, D.C.
NACP	National Archives at College Park, Md.
NUC	*National Union Catalog, Pre-1956 Imprints*
ODNB	*Oxford Dictionary of National Biography Online*
OFA	Office of the First Auditor
Putnam	Putnam, *The Book Buyer's Manual*
RCPBG	Records of the Commissioners of Public Buildings and Grounds
RG	Record Group
Roorbach	Orville A. Roorbach, comp., *Bibliotheca Americana: Catalogue of American Publications, Including Reprints and Original Works, from 1820 to 1852, Inclusive*
SMTA	Settled Miscellaneous Treasury Accounts
ViU	University of Virginia, Charlottesville, Va.
(W)	Whig

Millard Fillmore
and His Library

SEAN WILENTZ

Millard Fillmore was the president who established the White House Library. This comes as unexpected news even to professional historians. An earlier, more scholarly president would seem to make more sense—Thomas Jefferson, perhaps, or John Quincy Adams. Compared to those illustrious figures, Fillmore is not simply obscure: his very name, unfairly, has become something of a joke, an emblem of historical irrelevance. Fillmore is half of the correct answer to an unflattering historical trivia question: Which American presidents lost the only time each was a presidential nominee? (The other was Gerald Ford.) It is surprising that Fillmore, along with his cultured wife, Abigail, even found the time to start the library, as he resided in the White House for only two and a half years during a difficult and distracting moment in American history. The Executive Mansion, first occupied in 1800, had to wait fifty years, and for Millard Fillmore's brief presidency, before anyone thought to give it a permanent library. Yet a closer look at the man, his background, and his times dispels the confusion—and shows that Fillmore's distinction as the library's founder makes perfect sense.

Born to hardscrabble rural poverty in Cayuga County, New York, Fillmore prized books and libraries as the chief vehicles of his own ambitions and guarantors of success. A child farm laborer and apprentice to a local manufacturer, he had to struggle for books and book learning. As a teacher (and the doting husband of a teacher) as well as a self-made lawyer, he had a greater appreciation for literature and letters than most presidents have had. An exemplar of the Whig Party's credo of didactic self-improvement, Fillmore saw a permanent, in-house, working library as an essential feature for the most famous residence in the land. By adding the library, he also helped to make the White House into a true home according to the standards of the self-made, genteel middle class of the American Victorian era.

A curious combination of American aristocracy and American democracy precluded the inclusion of a library by the first eleven presidents who lived in the White House. So long as the federal government was located in cosmopolitan New York and then Philadelphia, there were plenty of places to obtain books on loan or for purchase. But when, as a result of sectional bargaining, the government prepared to remove itself to the banks of the Potomac in 1800, it was clear that government officers would require some sort of library. Congress, in particular, needed reliable volumes of laws, statutes, and history, and in 1800, President John Adams approved legislation to purchase $5,000 in books "as may be necessary for the use of Congress."[1] His successor, Thomas Jefferson, widened the library's scope by initiating legislation that established the post of Librarian of Congress (by appointment of the president), gave Congress oversight of the library's budget, and extended borrowing privileges to the president and vice president. (Over the next three decades, those privileges were extended further to include most civil officers as well as the judiciary.) Presidents, in these early years of the republic, were expected to be landed gentlemen who would naturally bring what books they wanted with them from their estates to the Federal City. Anything else they needed could be obtained from the Library of Congress.

The growth of political democracy that preceded the rise of Andrew Jackson and his party destroyed assumptions about gentlemanly, privileged presidents—yet made any suggestion of a White House Library even more far-fetched. The invading British destroyed the existing congressional library when they burned the Capitol in 1814—but the retired Jefferson agreed to sell his own library of 6,487 volumes, the largest private library in the country, to the government as a replacement. Thereafter, there did not seem to be any need for any White House supplement to the Library of Congress (although Jackson and his successors did subscribe to several of the burgeoning number of political newspapers in the 1830s and 1840s). To suggest such a thing would have seemed a manifestation of precisely the kind of corrupt privilege the Jacksonians attacked—spending public monies on duplicate copies of books for the mere convenience of the chief executive.

Fillmore, a bit ironically, was one of those persons of lowly origins whom Jackson claimed to champion—yet he emerged in politics as an anti-Jacksonian, with a very different sense of social and cultural priorities. He was born in 1800 into a dirt farmer's family—literally in a rude log cabin—in the then-frontier Finger Lakes district of western New York, and grew up about ten miles away, on his father's farm in the settlement of Sempronius (now Niles). Like many settlers in the area, the Fillmores were of New England stock (Millard's father, Nathaniel, had been raised in Vermont), lured west by the extravagant descriptions of land speculators. Yet if the land was gorgeous, the living was difficult and isolated. Fillmore later recalled that he spent his early years in obscurity, raised in a house that was in a newly settled area and far from major roads. Unable to support the family with his small farm, Fillmore's father apprenticed him to a cloth maker, in a situation so brutal that some have claimed it came close to slavery.

With only a smattering of formal schooling, Fillmore mastered his letters largely on his own, took to the way of reading, and then became nearly obsessed with educating himself. In 1819, while still working as an apprentice, he enrolled at a new academy opened in nearby New Hope. There, he fell in love with one of his teachers, Abigail Powers, only two years older than himself, the cultivated, red-haired, book-loving daughter of a minister. That same year, Fillmore's father obtained for him a clerkship with a local judge, with whom young Millard began study of the law. After several years of clerking, while he supported himself teaching school, Fillmore was finally admitted to the bar in 1823 and set up in practice, first in the western New York town of East Aurora, then in Buffalo.

Fillmore's political career began in 1826, one year after the completion of the Erie Canal, which quickly turned Buffalo into a major city. Like other enterprising Yankees in western New York, he was caught up in the anti-Masonic movement, a populist cause that resented the Masonic Order as a privileged group that supposedly set itself above the law. But the up-and-coming lawyer, drawn to a popular uprising, would evolve into a model of stolid, pro-business northern conservatism. Led by the master politicians Thurlow Weed and William Henry Seward, the anti-Masons also objected to President Jackson's (and, in time, President Van Buren's) opposition to expansive internal improvements and to Jackson's destruction of the Second Bank of the United States. In the mid-1830s the party merged with the anti-Jacksonian Whig Party. Having established a close friendship with Weed, Fillmore held state office before winning election to Congress in 1832, and then won three successive congressional races beginning in 1836. In 1848 he was serving as New York State comptroller when the Whig national convention, as a sop to the party's northern wing, named him its vice-presidential candidate alongside the military hero and Louisiana slaveholder Zachary Taylor, and the ticket was duly elected.

By then, Fillmore's ties with Weed and Seward had become strained, as he took more moderate positions on the issues of the day. A fervent backer of high tariffs and internal improvements, Fillmore objected to slavery, but not as strenuously as did Seward, who by 1848 was quickly emerging as a leading anti-slavery Whig. Nor was Fillmore deeply offended by advocates of southern rights, as was the new president, "Old Rough and Ready" Taylor. After Taylor's sudden death in July 1850, Fillmore took command and helped engineer passage of the series of bills known as the Compromise of 1850. Believing the compromise had saved the Union once and for all, Fillmore vigorously enforced its provisions, including a Fugitive Slave Law that helped southern planters recapture slaves who had escaped to the North. Angry northern antislavery Whigs denied Fillmore a nomination as president in 1852. Two years later, the Whig Party itself fell apart; two years after that, Fillmore finally was nominated for the presidency by the anti-immigrant Native American Party. Fillmore ran a poor third—but his campaign proved to be the most successful third-party presidential effort until Theodore Roosevelt's run on the "Bull Moose" Progressive Party ticket in 1912.

The foremost proponent of what were known as old-line, "Silver Grey" Whig principles, Fillmore also exemplified a broader Yankee Whig ideal of cultured moderation. A pious Unitarian and a master of self-control, Fillmore refrained from smoking, drinking, and gambling at a time when most American men indulged at least one of these vices. With Abigail—who, from the time they met, had been the single most important influence in his life—he formed a loving, tightly knit nuclear family with their children, son Millard Powers (born in 1828, known as Powers) and daughter Mary Abigail (born four years later, and nicknamed Abbie). In accord with the emerging proper middle-class code of the time, especially in the North, their home was meant to be a place of spiritual and mental uplift, a haven from the raucous demands of a highly competitive and even vulgar outside world. Fillmore was the first American president who, with his wife and children, thoroughly fit this genteel, sentimental American Victorian mold. The impetus behind his request to Congress for a library came in part from Fillmore's desire to turn the White House into the simulacrum of a refined domestic sphere.

The Fillmores had a good deal of work in front of them. Of the six previous White

House occupants, two had died in office (one, William Henry Harrison, only a month after his inauguration), two were widowers, and one, John Tyler, became a widower and then remarried while still president. Although female relatives stepped in to oversee social duties, the White House had not had the constant attention of a First Lady. And with frugal Jacksonians in charge for most of those years, minimal effort or money was expended on White House finery. Two important modernizing projects were, to be sure, completed in the mid-1840s, during James K. Polk's administration: the introduction of a primitive central heating system and the replacement of oil lamps and candles with gas illumination. But if the White House was structurally up-to-date, it was lacking in comfort, let alone gentility. There are accounts from the 1840s of springs in battered furniture stabbing unsuspecting visitors who tried to sit down. When the Fillmores moved in, they found one floor in an upstairs room covered by soiled matting, splattered with tobacco juice. (Beneath it lay an old and somewhat careworn but eminently salvageable Brussels carpet, which they promptly had restored.) At Christmastime in 1850 Fillmore invited his Buffalo law partner to visit, reporting that at least there was one spare room fitted up "in this temple of inconveniences."[2]

By then, Fillmore had set about supplying the White House with a permanent library—an indispensable feature of any proper home in the 1850s, let alone the President's House. The first three books were ordered in August—an atlas, a copy of the Bible, and *Webster's Dictionary*. In September, Fillmore wrote to Congress about the problem of stocking the library, and eventually gained a $2,000 appropriation for the purchase of books—although he still had to overcome abiding Democratic suspicions about presidential munificence. By the end of the year, nearly two hundred titles along with numerous back issues of periodicals had been purchased. (The timing proved fortuitous, as late in 1851, a fire destroyed much of the Library of Congress, including two-thirds of the collection purchased from Jefferson.) Over the next two years, Fillmore and his wife would make more improvements to the White House, but none was more important to the Fillmores' family life than the addition of the library.

The addition was far from mere domestic decoration. Since their courtship, Millard and Abigail's romance had been nourished by books. While on his various business and political journeys, Millard made it a point to bring books back to his wife, carton loads at a time, as presents; and well before he became president, Fillmore had accumulated an impressive library of his own in Buffalo. During the years he was president, the Fillmores entertained several cultural celebrities of the day, including Washington Irving and the visiting English novelist William Makepeace Thackeray. The creation of the White House Library was testimony to the strenuousness of the Fillmores' shared intellectual interests. So was Fillmore's reliance not simply on his own judgment and Abigail's but also on an experienced journalist, author, artist, bookman, Charles Lanman, then serving as librarian for the War Department, in selecting and procuring specific titles.

Created with intelligence and care, the library collection that resulted was notable for its range as well as its seriousness. Not surprisingly for a library intended for presidents, there was a good deal of history, including works by George Bancroft and Richard Hildreth, the major historians to that time of the United States, as well as important histories of modern France (by Guizot, Lamartine, Michelet, and Thiers), Britain, and the classical world. There was an entire subsection for law texts (again, not surprisingly), but also one for books on geography. If a bit weak in poetry (apart from Milton and Robert Burns), the collection did at least include those novels then considered obligatory for any respectable private American library, including the fiction of Sir Walter Scott, Washington Irving, and the then-popular Irish writer Maria Edgeworth (though apparently, and very curiously, no Thackeray and no Charles Dickens). Basic works in natural science, political economy, and moral philosophy (including, interestingly, John Locke's *Essay on Human Understanding* but not his *Two Treatises on Government*) graced the collection, as did several standard reference works and dictionaries. Of contemporary importance was Theresa Pulszky's *Memoirs of a Hungarian Lady*, recounting the failed Hungarian Revolution of 1848 from the vantage point of a liberal aristocratic supporter of the famed revolutionary leader Louis Kossuth. (The Fillmores threw a lavish dinner at the White House for Kossuth during his tumultuous tour of the United States in 1851; Pulszky not only attended but was seated at the president's side.)

The library's ample selection of American political biographies and statesmen's collected papers was similarly broad-minded. Naturally, Jared Sparks's then celebrated collections of the writings of George Washington and Benjamin Franklin made the list, as did the works and biographies of several other heroes of the Revolution and later U.S. presidents. But one might not have expected to see biographies of the rebarbative southern Old Republican John Randolph of Roanoke, or the scandalous Aaron Burr, or the stalwart Jacksonian Democrat (and former New York governor) Silas Wright. Likewise, the library's selection of literary periodicals covered the political spectrum, from the *United States Magazine and Democratic Review* to the *American Whig Review*. Under Fillmore's hand, the White House Library would be built on a firm bipartisan cornerstone, fit for whoever his successors would be.

Still, the library was important not simply as a collection of books but as the chief feature of a redesigned room—the Library proper, with a capital "L." Almost certainly at Abigail's instruction, it was located in the second floor oval room just above the Blue Room—the same room where the tobacco-speckled matting had been found. Three- and five-tiered mahogany bookcases lined the curved walls, interrupted by screens and an ample fireplace. Upholstered, walnut-framed pieces of so-called cottage furniture—a popular, informal domestic style of the time—filled the room.

Thus outfitted, the library, more than a book repository and place for studious contemplation, became the Fillmore family room, for informal entertaining and amusement as well as reading. Mrs. Fillmore is said to have spent most of her days here, with her beloved books. But her own piano and her daughter Mary Abigail's harp were placed here as well—crucial instruments of domestic mirth in any middle-class household of the day. The family is also supposed to have enjoyed playing games of backgammon in the library. Swamped by the chores of the presidency—which then included greeting job seekers and plowing through endless paperwork, enough to fill a six-day week—Fillmore would regularly break off to spend an evening hour with his family in the library.

The library helped enhance Fillmore's image as, in the words of one observer, "the representative of the American gentleman whom his countryman may take pride in."[3] A former schoolmate of Abbie's, visiting from Buffalo, left a fine description of how, after dinner, the family, often with a few intimate friends, usually repaired to the comforts of the library, with its crackling wood fire. "There was reading aloud," she wrote, "interesting conversation and always Miss Fillmore's charming music. Sometimes Powers Fillmore would join his sister in singing such old-time melodies as 'Sweet Vale of Avoca,' 'In the Desert a Fountain is Springing,' or 'Old Folks at Home.'"[4] The latter song—not old at all, but composed by Stephen C. Foster in 1851—was one of the president's favorites, and he would join in the singing. There is no record of it, but a domestic genre-scene print by the New York lithographer Nathaniel Currier (who, in 1852, would first link up with James Merritt Ives) would not have been at all out of place alongside one of the bookcases. Indeed, the family circle inside the original library would have been a fit subject for one of Currier and Ives's enormously popular pictures, today the symbols of a bygone America.

Over the following century and a half, the White House Library evolved with the times. Gradually dispersed during the later nineteenth century, the collection was rejuvenated during the administration of President (and prolific author) Theodore Roosevelt, when the Library of Congress was asked to help enlarge and update the selection. In 1935 the books were relocated to a ground-floor chamber (used as a laundry area in the Fillmores' time), which Theodore Roosevelt had renovated as a gentleman's anteroom. Today's library—furnished in rare Federal and Empire Style antiques dating back to the White House's earliest years, and filled with an entirely new collection of books—bears only the most generic resemblance to the parlor of books that Millard and Abigail Fillmore assembled on the second floor in 1850.[5] But it remains the fine legacy of a too-often ridiculed president, whose love of books and family helped define him as much as they did the era in which he lived.

Basic sources on the White House Library include Francis de S. Ryan, "Centennial of the White House Library" (unpublished ms., prepared for the White House, 1950), and Elizabeth Lorelei Thacker-Estrada, "The Heart of the Fillmore Presidency: Abigail Powers Fillmore and the White House Library," *White House Studies* 1, no. 1 (2001): 83–98. On Fillmore, see Robert J. Rayback, *Millard Fillmore: Biography of a President* (Buffalo, N.Y.: Henry Stewart for the Buffalo Historical Society, 1959), and Robert J. Scarry, *Millard Fillmore* (Jefferson, N.C.: McFarland, 2001). More generally on the politics and Whig culture of the period, see Sean Wilentz, *The Rise of American Democracy: Jefferson to Lincoln* (New York: Norton, 2005), esp. 482–518. The author wishes to thank Catherine Parisian for her encouragement and her help in sifting fact from fancy in the writings on these subjects.

NOTES

1. Library of Congress, About the Library, History, http://www.loc.gov/about/history/ (accessed July 23, 2008).

2. MF letter to S. G. Haven, December 21, 1850, Millard Fillmore Papers, BECHS, qtd. in Robert J. Scarry, *Millard Fillmore* (Jefferson, N.C.: McFarland, 2001), 188.

3. Qtd. in Scarry, *Millard Fillmore,* 196.

4. Qtd. in ibid., 197–98.

5. The only books from the original library that remain in the White House today are the ten volumes of Jared Sparks's *Library of American Biography.* They are kept in an archival box in the curator's office, separate from the rest of the collection.

THE WHITE HOUSE COLLECTION

The Mind of the Common Man

CATHERINE M. PARISIAN

MANY OF THE EARLY UNITED STATES PRESIDENTS AND STATESMEN were avid readers and book collectors. They had to be: books served as their primary means of information, knowledge, and education. Surprisingly, until 1850 no room dedicated to serve as a library could be found in the White House. Before this time, presidents brought their own books to the Executive Mansion and removed them along with their other personal possessions at the end of their terms. After he took office upon the death of Zachary Taylor in July of 1850, President Millard Fillmore, along with First Lady Abigail Fillmore, moved into a White House that was destitute of books. Since both the president and the first lady had been readers and bibliophiles from their youths and as adults became accustomed to having a library in their home for education, entertainment, and relaxation, they found their new home a "temple of inconveniences." Furthermore, the president and his staff members had no library for daily reference as they governed the country. The Fillmores therefore petitioned Congress and received funding to establish a library, redecorate the upstairs oval room, and purchase books that were intended to remain a permanent fixture in the President's House. The collection that they assembled remained nearly intact and available to occupants of the Executive Mansion for the next fifty years. Unlike the libraries of George Washington, John Adams, and Thomas Jefferson, which provide insight into the individual minds of great men, the first White House Library represents the collective mind of an age. While the collections of the founding fathers have been documented and preserved as part of America's intellectual heritage, the White House collection, except for ten lone volumes, has been completely dispersed and its history and contents all but forgotten.

As a self-educated man and one of the first American presidents to have been born in a log cabin, Millard Fillmore—and his wife, Abigail, who was also born into humble circumstances—represented the mid-nineteenth-century American ideal of the "Rise of the Common Man."[1] Both grew up in the western frontier of New York in homes where books were precious commodities. The only books in Millard's childhood home were a Bible, a hymnal, and an almanac. As a child he could attend school only three months out of the year; the rest of the time he was needed to help work the family farm. He would later recall that he learned some arithmetic and geography, but never saw a map or an atlas until he was nine-teen years old. At the age of fourteen he was apprenticed as a wool carder. When he was about seventeen, he purchased a dictionary and a two-dollar share in a small circulating library. While tending the wool-carding machines, Fillmore kept the dictionary open on the desk so that he could glance at it as he passed by and memorize words and their definitions. At the age of eighteen, Fillmore was employed as a schoolteacher during the winter months in New Hope, New York. The following year he returned to school himself and met his teacher Abigail Powers, with whom he spent much of his time after classes studying and who would become the greatest influence in his life. The two married seven years later, when Fillmore became financially secure enough to support the couple. In 1819 Fillmore's family moved to Montville, in Cayuga County, where Millard began to study law and con-tinued to teach school intermittently to pay his living expenses.[2]

Abigail's father died when she was two years old. When Abigail was six, she, along with her mother and six siblings, went to live with her oldest brother, Cyrus Powers, in Sempro-nius, a small town in Cayuga County. Cyrus was a schoolteacher, and Abigail was allowed to attend the district school. By the time she was sixteen, she had begun to teach school her-self during the summers in order to supplement the cost of her own education. By the age of nineteen she was teaching full time, and it is rumored that she may even have helped to establish a library in Sempronius.[3]

As adults Abigail and Millard Fillmore continued to value books as a means of self-education and pleasure. Fillmore's first law office in East Aurora, New York, contained a law library of over 150 volumes as well as the community library for which Fillmore served as the librarian. Although no catalogue survives for this library, records indicate that he purchased forty-five volumes of Walter Scott's Waverley Novels around this time, a title that he and Abigail later selected for the White House Library.[4] After moving to Buffalo in 1830, the Fillmores maintained a personal library in their home, where they were in the habit of receiving guests, reading, and studying together. As a family friend recollected, "Millard never went to New York without bringing home a few books with him, and he was often followed or preceded by a package sent by express." Each time the books overflowed the shelf space, Abigail would have more cases built for the library.[5] When Fillmore took his seat in the New York Assembly in Albany during the winter of 1828, the couple was separated for the first time since their wedding. In a long journal letter, Abigail lamented the loss of her husband's companionship: "Your society is all that I have thought of—have finished study-ing the maps of ancient geography. O, that you could have been here to have studied with me." The next day she added, "I wish you could read to me as you frequently have done after I sit down to sewing."[6]

The Fillmores had catalogues compiled of their personal libraries in 1847, around 1858, and in 1861, which now provide insight into their reading interests and record the growth of their collection. With just under 400 titles in 1847—a substantial size for the time—the library increased to over 2,200 by 1874, the year of Millard's death. It contained works rep-resenting a range of topics, including biography, history, literature, travel, cookery, advice, religion, and reference. The latest catalogue, compiled in 1861, appears to have been con-tinued through the end of his life, with entries added when new books were acquired and annotations made when others were deaccessioned. Usually the entries in this catalogue are written on the verso of the leaf with notes on the facing recto recording changes in a book's location, such as "carried to my office" or "presented to Buffalo Historical Society," always with the date of the transfer recorded. A key in the front of the catalogue explains the library's arrangement, identifying each bookcase with a letter and each shelf on each bookcase with a number. A note directs, "all the letters and numbers go with the sun from left to right, and each set of books is arranged in the case in the same way." Accordingly, the entries in the catalogue include corresponding shelf marks. Although this is the first of Fillmore's catalogues in which he spelled out this system, the same notation appears in the circa 1858 catalogue. All three of the Fillmores' personal catalogues point to their propensity for collecting, organizing, and recording the contents of their library.[7]

Fillmore devoted much of his life, both before and after his presidency, to philanthropic endeavors, many of which helped to promote education and reading. As early as 1838 he had been a member and patron of the Young Men's Association in Buffalo, to which he donated books from his personal library. He founded the University of Buffalo in 1847 and served as its chancellor throughout the rest of his life, even during his presidency. In 1862 he founded and served as the first president of the Buffalo Historical Society, where many of his papers and books are now held, and in 1872 he became president of the board of trustees of the Grosvenor Library, another library to which he donated a number of books.[8] Founding a library in the White House fits integrally with the Fillmores' lifelong concern with books and education.

The White House Library—situated between the private living quarters of the first family and the professional offices of the president and his staff members on the second floor of the White House—functioned as a semi-public/semi-private space where the first family entertained small parties, sometimes public individuals on official visits and sometimes private guests on leisure trips. Cabinet meetings were held in the Cabinet Room, which was conveniently located adjacent to the library (see figure 13). While it supplied a working collection for the president and his staff members, the library also provided a place for the personal instruction and leisure of the first family. By founding a library in the White House, the Fillmores made a public statement about the value of access to knowledge and education to all aspects of American life.

I. The Founding of the First White House Library

President Fillmore began investigating the possibility of establishing a library in the White House shortly after taking office on July 10, 1850. On August 30 he received an estimate for a set of government documents from the Georgetown bookseller George Templeman, an estimate that totaled $2,165, to which Templeman added, "As there may be some other books that the President may select it may be well to say that $2,500 will get a very useful reference Library for the President's House." Although $2,500 may seem like a small sum, in current monetary terms it equals approximately $64,500, an amount large enough to fuel Congressional debates.[9]

The debates prompted by the request for funding the library divided down party lines. John Houston (W) of Delaware first brought the matter before the House of Representatives on September 6, 1850, when he read a resolution to supply the Executive Mansion with

"a complete set of the documents and journals of the two Houses of Congress" and to furnish it with a "suitable library." Thomas Harris (D) of Illinois and others objected, and the
resolution was not received. Houston brought the issue up again just three days later when
he proposed an amendment to an amendment that was up for vote. This time he argued at
greater length for the propriety of furnishing the president with congressional documents.
He had assumed that the president was provided with these, as it was customary to supply
other departments. Houston contended that Congress should grant this request because
the president "had occasion for them for the purpose of daily reference in the discharge of
his official duties," and "is compelled, whenever the necessity of a reference occurs, to send
to some one of the departments." Albert Brown (D) of Mississippi opposed the amendment
on the grounds that it would lay "the foundation for a great Executive library." He complained that "an appropriation for $500 was now asked to furnish the President with the
reports and documents of Congress. Next year there will be $1000 asked for; and the year
following it will be $2000; and so we shall go until we have built up a great Executive
library." The amendment was voted down by the narrow margin of 64 to 63.[10]

Fillmore then enlisted the help of his friend Senator James Pearce (W) of Maryland. On
September 23, two weeks after the amendment had been voted down in the House, Pearce,
by direction of the Joint Committee on the Library of Congress, a committee that he chaired,
proposed in an amendment to a civil and diplomatic appropriations bill that $2,000 be
allocated for the purchase of a library, "to be preserved in the Executive Mansion." This
amendment also authorized the Joint Committee on the Library of Congress to supply the
president with "any duplicates of public documents which can be spared from the public
collections of the Library of Congress or elsewhere."[11] Senator Pearce's argument echoed
Representative Houston's, but was delivered more dramatically: "With regard to the Executive Mansion, not a book, not even a Bible, has been furnished by the Government. And
when the President holds a Cabinet council, there is not even a volume of laws there to
which reference can be had, and the members of it are obliged to run round to their offices
to obtain the books to which they must from necessity be obliged to resort in aid of their
consultations. I hope, therefore, there will be no objection to this amendment."[12] The amendment was adopted, and the bill passed and became law on September 30, 1850. The final
statute also included funding for the establishment of libraries in the Treasury Department
and in the territories of Utah and New Mexico.[13]

An additional $250 was allocated for the library the following year. On February 24
Representative Samuel Vinton (W) of Ohio proposed $1,000 to purchase books for the
Executive Mansion in an amendment to a general appropriation bill. While the amendment
was approved in the House, once it reached the Senate on February 28 Robert Hunter (D)
of Virginia suggested changing that sum from $1,000 to $250. Apparently misremembering
the proceedings from the previous September, he argued that "one thousand" instead of
two thousand "was appropriated last year, and it was supposed by the committee on finance
that two hundred and fifty dollars would be enough for the present year." Hunter's amendment was adopted, and the bill was enacted into law on March 3, 1851. Although Congress
reluctantly granted Fillmore a total of $2,250 for the new library, it readily approved over
$72,000 for rebuilding its own library after it was damaged on Christmas Eve in 1851 by a
fire that President Fillmore himself helped to fight.[14]

Fillmore initially intended to handle purchasing the books for the library in the Executive Mansion himself. In fact, he began purchasing books before congressional funding for the library had been approved. On August 19 he ordered Noah Webster's *Dictionary,* a Bible, and Alexander Keith Johnston's *National Atlas* from George Crosby in Philadelphia and charged them to the account of "furnishing the President's house." These totaled $55.12, with the atlas, at $45.00, making up most of this amount. On September 9 he made another purchase on this account: Samuel Augustus Mitchell's *Universal Atlas* from Franck Taylor for $10.50, including the cost of a spine label, which brought the total that he spent on books from the furnishings account to $65.62.[15]

Fillmore's first official purchases, using the funds allocated by Congress, were made in October and November of 1850 from Franck Taylor and the firm Taylor and Maury, both Washington, D.C., book dealers.[16] These purchases included a number of vital reference sources to which the president and his staff members would have had frequent recourse. Together, Richard S. Fisher's *Book of the World,* Daniel Haskell and J. Calvin Smith's *Gazetteer,* and Edward Waite's *Washington City Directory* contained statistical information for cities, states, and countries throughout the world, as well as the immediate environs of Washington, D.C. William Blackstone's *Commentaries on the Laws of England,* Henry J. Stephen's *New Commentaries on the Laws of England,* and James Kent's *Commentaries on American Law* were the essential legal reference works of the day. Indeed, Blackstone was the first legal work that Fillmore ever read when he began to study law.[17] The *United States Digest* was a seminal work on admiralty, or maritime law, a branch of the law with significant implications for commerce and international affairs, key presidential concerns. In addition, he purchased a volume of Joseph Story's *Commentaries* that has not yet been identified. Story, Dane Professor of Law at Harvard and a Supreme Court justice, was one of America's foremost legal scholars of the time and wrote commentaries on a number of legal subjects. Fillmore would later purchase his commentaries on conflict laws and the constitution. David Hume's *History of England* and Henry Hallam's *Constitutional History of England* were the standard English histories of the day, and Jean Louis de Lolme's *Rise and Progress of the English Constitution* had been the authoritative work that was often cited in debates over the federal constitution. John Paget's *Hungary and Transylvania* was most certainly purchased for its relevance to the Hungarian revolution of 1848, which I will discuss later, and the works of William Shakespeare and Robert Burns were among the standard literary classics of the day. The cost of these early purchases came to a total of $87.90.[18]

Presidential responsibilities must have been too demanding of Fillmore's time for him to continue making purchases for the library. In December of 1850 he commissioned Charles Lanman, the Librarian of the War Department Library, as his purchasing agent. Upon Daniel Webster's recommendation, Fillmore planned to request Lanman's assistance; however, prompted by Charles M. Conrad, Fillmore's secretary of war, Lanman wrote to Fillmore on November 26, "tendering" his services for the job before Fillmore had opportunity to make his request. Lanman claimed to "be extensively acquainted with the booksellers of the north" and that he could save the president $300 out of the $2,000 appropriation. He estimated that his travel expenses to New York and Boston would not exceed $60 and stated that no further compensation to him would be necessary. Fillmore replied that he would be happy to see Lanman in one week, on Wednesday, December 4, at 5:00 P.M.[19]

Lanman took every precaution to ensure that he received this commission. He coordinated his efforts with Joseph Henry, secretary of the Smithsonian Institution, who wrote to the president to recommend his "friend, Mr. Charles Lanman" as a "person well qualified to make the purchases" for the "Presidential Mansion." In his earlier letter Lanman had stated that he would consult Henry for the selection of scientific works unless Fillmore had other preferences. On December 3, the eve of their appointed meeting, Lanman sent the president, for his private library, "a complete set of the American editions" of his own publications, remarking that "they are unpretending in their character, but as they treat principally of the scenery of our beautiful land, and other matters far removed from the cares of state, it occurred to me that they might amuse you during a leisure time."[20] We can only assume that the two men had a pleasant meeting on December 4. As he later recalled, Lanman "duly made out a catalogue, and every book, with one exception, was sanctioned by Mr. Fillmore." Thereafter, Lanman departed for Boston and New York on his buying trip.[21]

Lanman shipped on approval to Washington 134 books, of which the president rejected only 8. The books included 49 titles from Little and Brown in Boston, which totaled $745.87; 72 from Charles Welford in New York, which totaled $351.62; and 13 from George P. Putnam, also in New York, which totaled $176.00. The rejected titles were Joseph Story's *Constitution* at $2.50; Jonathan Swift's *Works* in two volumes at $6.50; an Oxford Bible on fine paper at $8.00; *The Works of Sir Humphry Davy* in seven volumes at $15.00; John Mason Good's *Study of Medicine* in four volumes at $7.00; Matthew Brown's *Geography* at $5.50; Plutarch's *Lives* at $2.00; and Emma Willard's *System of Universal History* at $3.00. When Lanman followed up on December 26 by sending the bills for the books that had been selected for the library, he directed the younger Fillmore, Millard Powers, who served as his father's personal secretary, to "deliver to the bearer" "the rejected books which are by themselves in the north corner of the reading room."[22]

Although the Fillmores left no indication as to why they rejected these books, reasonable conjectures can be made for most of them. At the price of $2.50, Story's *Constitution* was probably the abridged, one-volume edition, which Fillmore either already owned or did not want. He had previously purchased a one-volume book identified on the voucher as Story's *Commentaries* from Franck Taylor on October 24 of 1850 for $3.00. Although the voucher does not specify which of Story's *Commentaries* was purchased, it may have been the one-volume abridgement on the Constitution. Story wrote numerous commentaries on various legal subjects, several of which were single-volume publications. In late December 1850 or early January of 1851 Fillmore requested Story's *Commentaries on the Constitution* from Taylor, who informed Fillmore that it had been out of print for several months with not one "copy remaining in the hands of the Trade." He offered to look for a second-hand copy, but also explained that a new edition was in preparation in Boston and would be available soon. With this letter, Taylor sent a copy of the one-volume abridgement for Fillmore's use, which Fillmore returned upon receiving. The president did, however, purchase the new, two-volume edition from Taylor for $6.50 in June of 1851.[23]

As for the other rejected books, the Fillmores had already purchased one Bible out of the furnishings fund. Swift may have been considered too risqué for mid-Victorian tastes to place in the White House. The Fillmores owned a copy of Plutarch's *Lives* in their personal library, yet did not find it necessary for the White House. Willard's *Universal History* and

Brown's *Geography* were both geographical works, a genre already well represented on the list of books purchased, but Good's *Medicine* would have been the only medical book in the library, and Davy's works would have been the only chemistry text. Good's *Medicine* and Brown's *Geography,* however, do appear in the 1861 catalogue of Fillmore's personal library.[24]

By the 1870s, when he wrote "Presidential Recollections," Lanman must have forgotten about the rejected books. In this essay he recalls that every book he suggested was sanctioned by the president and that the only mistake that he made was purchasing a copy of the *Federalist* without an index. In Lanman's words, "I told him that there was not a better edition then on the market, and that I had done the best I could. He replied with warmth that such a book—that any book indeed, without an index, was worthless." As I discuss later, Lanman was not the first person to learn of Fillmore's predilection for indexes.[25]

In addition to making this buying trip on behalf of the Executive Mansion Library, Lanman also arranged for the transfer of a large number of government documents from the War Department to the White House. Supplying the White House with a set of the congressional documents was, after all, part of the initial appeal to Congress when funding was requested for the library. As Lanman later recalled, the chief clerk to Conrad had "by way of amusement" collected a duplicate set of public documents for the War Department. Lanman suggested to Conrad that these be transferred to the Executive Mansion "as a suitable place for safekeeping." The transfer was made at the expense of $29.25 for the cartage and freight of 894 pounds of documents. The figure of $2,165.00 quoted by Templeman as the cost of a complete set of congressional documents certainly places the value of Lanman's arrangement for the transfer in perspective. The entire sum allocated by Congress for the library could very easily have been spent on these documents alone.[26]

In sum, the Fillmores supervised the purchase of 193 titles, comprising 1,050 volumes, with the addition of government documents bringing the total number of volumes to over 3,500. On his trip Lanman spent $1,555.36 of the $2,000.00 allocated by Congress and acquired 126 of the 193 titles that were purchased for the library during the Fillmore administration. Thus, within the first six months of his tenure in office Fillmore, with Lanman's assistance, had established a substantial library in the Executive Mansion for $1,000.00 less than George Templeman had estimated, with government documents supplied at no charge.[27]

II. The Contents of the First White House Library

The contents of the library reflect its multiple purposes—professional, educational, and leisure. In addition to government documents and legal texts, the Fillmores selected many of the standard works of history, biography, science, and literature that composed the American intellectual landscape of the period. The selections as a whole display a heavy indebtedness to British thought and culture with the inclusion of a number of works by and about British statesmen and politicians, books related to British history, and works by and about British literary authors. This nod to relatives across the Atlantic might be expected since the United States was still close to its British heritage and engaged in ongoing commercial and diplomatic relations with Great Britain. Moreover, the Whig party respected this aspect of America's past more than forward-thinking Democrats, who sought to define a distinctly American national identity.

In many ways the selections also reflect correlative values held by many mid-nineteenth-century Americans: the belief that any white man, regardless of his economic or social background, could attain an elevated position—economic, social, or political—in society and the belief in education as the means to one's advancement. The publishers of a number of the books chosen for the library promoted these core values. For example, the Society for the Diffusion of Useful Knowledge, Henry George Bohn, Jones and Company, and Robert and William Chambers all sought to provide quality literature at an affordable price for the benefit of those with less disposable income. Many publishers produced certain titles and multivolume sets designed for this segment of their consumer market. Usually these were not newly written works, but reprints of older works that were no longer under copyright and were issued in small but often attractive formats. Harper's *Family Classical Library* in thirty-six volumes; Whittaker's *Tales and Novels,* by Maria Edgeworth, in nine volumes; William and Robert Chambers's *Miscellany of Useful and Entertaining Tracts,* twenty volumes in ten books; and Bohn's *British Colonial Library* in ten volumes serve as examples of these sets that were purchased for the White House. While not all of the books purchased for the library were inexpensive reprints, the presence in the White House Library of so many books from these publishing efforts represents the pervasiveness of the movement to provide first-rate reading material to people from a range of social and economic classes. It might also point to frugality on the part of the Fillmores. These reprints served as economical choices for reading copies of older works and allowed them to spend more money to obtain the latest editions of more time-sensitive and costly books such as reference works and legal texts.[28]

Contrary to expectations at the outset of this project, the most recent American edition of a title was not always selected, nor was the least expensive edition available always chosen. Seventy-five of the titles purchased were published in Great Britain, eighty-five in America, and four in France. The least expensive book for the library was *Essays from the London Times* at fifty cents, while the most expensive single title was the Supreme Court Reports, a set of fifty volumes that cost $157.50. The most expensive single-volume title was Johnston's *National Atlas* at $45.00, and the most expensive book, apart from a long serial or plate book, was *The Works of Edmund Burke* at $26.00 in six volumes.

The books that the Fillmores selected for the White House Library can be divided into three categories: standard works that would have been found in most American libraries during the mid-nineteenth century; books that related broadly to law, public affairs, and other presidential concerns in general; and books pertaining to specific issues and events that confronted Fillmore as president. Whereas most of the books purchased through Charles Lanman fall into the first two categories, most of the books that Fillmore purchased apart from Lanman fall into the latter two categories.[29]

i. Books Commonly Found in Antebellum American Libraries

The collection that the Fillmores assembled in the White House is representative of collections that could have been found in many antebellum American circulating and home libraries. The Fillmores' personal library included 90 of the 193 titles that they purchased for the White House. Many of the titles also appear in the records from 1847 to 1856 of books most commonly charged from the New York Society Library. For example, this list includes Sir Walter Scott's Waverley Novels; George Bancroft's *History of the United States;* Archibald Alison's *History of Europe;* William Hickling Prescott's histories of Peru, Mexico, and the reign of Ferdinand and Isabella; James Boswell's *Life of Johnson;* Thomas Babington Macaulay's *History of England;* Louis Adolphe Their's *French Revolution;* the works of Washington Irving and Maria Edgeworth; John Lord Campbell's *Lives of the Lord Chancellors;* Julia Pardoe's *Louis the Fourteenth;* Jared Sparks's *Library of American Biography;* the *American Almanac;* the *North American Review;* and Blackwood's *Edinburgh Magazine,* just to name a few. The content of the White House Library points to a canon of knowledge with which mid-nineteenth-century Americans were expected to be acquainted.[30]

History. Guided by the belief that individuals can learn from the past and from the lives of others, nineteenth-century Americans valued history and biography as a means for moral instruction and intellectual improvement. The educator Caleb Sprague Henry, in a work purchased for the White House Library, advocated reading extensively in history texts. According to him, history "is a necessary part of a thorough education. Aside from its more immediate practical advantages, a full and familiar knowledge of history is requisite to the most liberal cultivation of the mind. Accordingly, the study of history has always had a place in the course of instruction pursued in our higher institutions." Henry contrasted history with science. Unlike science, in which the "leading principles can be systematically exhibited within a moderate compass" and a "complete elementary knowledge can be imparted within a limited time," there is "no short road to a competent knowledge of history." He concluded that "there is really no such thing as an *elementary* study of history. It is not worth while to study it at all, unless it be thoroughly studied. A thorough knowledge of it cannot, however, be imparted in the lecture room; it must be acquired by the student himself in the solitary labor of his closet."[31] The Fillmores must have concurred with this view since they purchased no fewer than sixty history texts for the White House, in contrast to only eight scientific works.

Many of the history texts selected for the White House were mentioned in an anonymous two-part article entitled "A Course of Historical Reading," published in the *Universalist Quarterly and General Review* in January and April 1850. Its author called Thomas Babington Macaulay's *History of England* the "most successful" attempt at historical writing and proceeded to praise Edward Gibbon, George Bancroft, and William H. Prescott. The author chose to include only American publications and, therefore, recommended Connop Thirlwall's *History of Greece* over George Grote's *History of Greece*—the one purchased for the White House—but commented that Thirlwall's "is not greatly surpassed by that of Grote," thus upholding Grote as the standard. With respect to Roman history, the author wrote, "Let the student go to Niebuhr," and then turned to Gibbon, calling his work on the subsequent period in Rome a "stupendous monument of learning, industry and eminent ability." The White House purchased Henry Hart Milman's edition of Gibbon, which retained the notes of the well-known historian François Guizot and was recommended by the *Universalist's* writer above all others. The author maintained, "The student who possesses Niebuhr and Gibbon may be justly said to have as complete a political and civil history of Rome and Roman dominion and power, as it is possible to write out of the materials now in existence." Works recommended for the history of France included Jules Michelet and Louis Adolphe Thiers on the French revolution; for the Restoration, Archibald Alison's *History of Europe* was named "as the most thorough work on the subject"; and for the revolution of 1848, Alphonse de Lamartine—all of which stood on the shelves of the White House Library. Macaulay and Hume were recommended as the best works on English history. William Robertson, Henry Hallam, Washington Irving, James Grahame, Richard Hildreth, and Jared Sparks were also among the White House authors this article endorsed.[32]

Biography. The mid-nineteenth-century American mind valued biographical writing, as it did historical writing, for its salutary and didactic benefits. According to a reviewer of Sparks's *Library of American Biography:*

> Such lives furnish some of our best books. They are the best chapters of history. Biography recognizes human individuality, what the individual is and does; and we esteem the characters and doings of individuals as such, quite as instructive and healthful subjects of contemplation as those of masses and organized bodies of men; less needful indeed in the study of policy and expedients, but more so in that of humanity, and the higher expressions of the moral sentiments.[33]

With biography held in such esteem, it is not surprising that it was given ample space on the White House shelves. Although approximately thirty titles may be classified as biography, these titles constituted at least 130 volumes. Of the biographical monographs selected for the library, eleven focused on American and six on British subjects. With the exception of Samuel Johnson and Walter Scott, all centered on British and American politicians and statesmen, including such notable figures as George Washington, Benjamin Franklin, Thomas Jefferson, Andrew Jackson, Henry Clay, Sir Robert Peel, and John Philpot Curran, among others.

Science. The comparatively sparse selection of scientific works in the library accords with Sprague's view that one can acquire a "complete elementary knowledge" of science within a "moderate compass." Although only eight were included, they were the standard scientific texts of the day in their respective fields: Charles Lyell's *Geology,* John F. W. Herschel's *Astronomy,* Georges Cuvier's *Animal Kingdom,* James Cowles Prichard's *History of Man,* and Asa Gray's *Botany.* Robert Burton's *Anatomy of Melancholy* and Charles Wilkes's *Narrative of the United States Exploring Expedition* may also be considered scientific works; specimens collected on the Wilkes expedition, after all, composed the founding collection for the Smithsonian Institute's National Museum. In addition, Robert and William Chambers's *Miscellany* contained a number of scientific tracts. Although John James Audubon became one of the most notable ornithologists and wildlife artists of the day, his *Birds of America* was not purchased; its price, ranging from $75 to $300, probably made its cost prohibitive.[34]

Literature. Literature was well represented in the first White House Library, with nearly thirty different titles, including reference and biographical works, such as Mary Cowden Clarke's *Complete Concordance to Shakespeare,* James Boswell's *Life of Johnson,* and John Gibson Lockhart's *Memoirs of the Life of Sir Walter Scott.* In many respects the literature that the Fillmores selected for the library underpins mid-nineteenth-century America's celebration of the "Common Man," with the works of authors who took ordinary, every-day people and themes as subjects for their writing and who were from middle-class backgrounds themselves, such as Robert Burns, Maria Edgeworth, Oliver Goldsmith, Washington Irving, Samuel Johnson, Walter Scott, John Milton, and William Shakespeare. The literary selections for the White House also included popular classics of the day, such as Aesop's *Fables*, *The Arabian Nights*, and Tobias Smollett's translation of Alain René La Sage's *Gil Blas*.[35]

American literature was represented by only three separate titles, the works of Washington Irving, and two anthologies from Rufus Wilmot Griswold. There are several possible explanations for the absence of American authors in the library. As I discuss below, much of the current literature first appeared in periodicals. Budgetary concerns were a consideration with all of the purchases, and due to the absence of international copyright, American editions of works by British authors were often less expensive than those by American authors. Publishers were not required to pay copyright fees on works that had first been published abroad; they simply reprinted the text from a foreign edition, usually from London, and only incurred the cost of paper, ink, and labor.[36] It is also possible that the Fillmores chose not to include living authors of literary works to avoid the appearance of showing favoritism to one author over another. If this were the case, Irving would have been an exception, but he was sixty-seven years old and the most popular American author of the first half of the nineteenth century. His age and reputation may have earned him a place in the White House Library.[37]

Many of the authors that one may have expected to find in the library were not present. For example, although First Lady Abigail Fillmore admired Charles Dickens and William Makepeace Thackeray, and the Fillmores even entertained Thackeray at the White House, their works were not purchased for the library, nor were those of Jane Austen; Charlotte, Emily, and Anne Brontë; Nathaniel Hawthorne; Herman Melville; Edgar Allan Poe; or James Fenimore Cooper. However, the most current literature, both British and American, would have been published in the periodicals, of which the Fillmores purchased complete runs and which contained short stories by Poe and Hawthorne as well as the poetry of Walt Whitman, William Cullen Bryant, and John Greenleaf Whittier, among others. It should also be remembered that as avid readers, the Fillmores maintained their own collection—apart from the Executive Mansion's books—which contained a number of literary titles, including Charlotte Brontë's *Jane Eyre*, Charles Dickens's *Sketches by Boz*, Alfred Lord Tennyson's *Lotus Eaters*, Lord Byron's works, and Felicia Hemans's poems.[38]

Periodicals. The periodicals chosen for the library were purchased in complete runs and represent the leading magazines and journals of the day. They offered a balanced perspective on politics with the *Democratic Review* and the *Whig Review*, as well as *Blackwood's Magazine* and the *Edinburgh Review*, reflecting British Tory and Whig ideologies respectively. These four magazines featured not only political views but also current literature and literary news. Together with the *North American Review*, the leading literary periodical of the day, Stryker's *American Register*, Hunt's *Merchant's Magazine*, and *Niles's Weekly Register*, these journals and magazines chronicled events in British and American politics, literature, and news from the beginning of the century through 1850.

Religion. Surprisingly few religious works were selected for the library: only a Bible and the works of William Paley and William Chillingworth. Two other works, however, were written by notable religious leaders, John Lingard's *History of England* and Thomas Rutherforth's *Institutes of Natural Law*.[39] The Fillmores may have thought that it was more appropriate for first families to bring their own devotional works to the White House, since these would vary depending upon one's faith. The president was careful to maintain the separation of church and state and to preserve and respect the religious freedom of individuals. As early as 1832 Fillmore's series of essays entitled "An Examination of the Question, 'Is it Right to Require any Religious Test as a Qualification to be a Witness in a Court of Justice?'" first appeared in the Buffalo *Patriot* and was later collected and published as a pamphlet.[40] Fillmore upheld the separation of the church and the state when he objected to a clause that specified that certain privileges would be extended only to Christians in a convention between the United States and the Swiss Confederation. He sent this convention along with his objections to the Senate for review in February of 1851.[41] Fillmore also went out of his way to learn the faith of Peter Carroll, a porter at the White House, before presenting him with a copy of *St. Vincent's Manual*, a Catholic devotional book, on New Year's Day, 1853. The Fillmores belonged to the Unitarian Church, attended services regularly, and encouraged their children to do the same. The catalogues of their personal libraries show that they owned a number of religious works, including the works of John Bunyan, and works recorded as "Chapel Liturgy," "Biblical Legends," "Bible Biography," and "Bible Pictorial Illustrations," among others.[42]

ii. Books Related to Presidential Concerns

In addition to the standard works that have been discussed thus far, the contents of the library reflect Fillmore's primary concerns as president, which included commerce, both international and domestic; the preservation of the union, as controversy over slavery intensified; peaceable international relations; and faithfulness to the constitution in all affairs of state. With respect to domestic commerce and transportation, Fillmore recommended the federal construction, improvement, protection, and/or maintenance of canals, ports, and harbors on lakes and rivers large enough to bear an "extensive traffic." As Fillmore pointed out, in 1850 all thirty-one states were to some extent bounded by an ocean, the Gulf of Mexico, one of the Great Lakes, or "some navigable river."[43] As for foreign trade, the acquisition of northern California after the Mexican War and the admission of California as a state in 1850 increased the significance and potential for trade between the United States and the Far East. In an effort to establish more efficient trade routes, Fillmore encouraged the construction of a ship canal across Central America and of a railroad across Mexico to connect the Atlantic with the Pacific. Although neither of these projects came to fruition, the president reiterated their importance in each of his three annual addresses to Congress.[44]

Fillmore's efforts to preserve the union and uphold the Constitution with respect to the controversy over slavery brought him into tremendous self-conflict, as it did many of his contemporaries. While he personally opposed slavery, he believed that the Constitution protected it. He was instrumental in engineering the compromise of 1850, with its contradictory measures of abolishing the slave trade in the District of Columbia and authorizing the Fugitive Slave Act, which mandated the return of runaway slaves to their masters regardless of where they were discovered.[45] Although no books purchased for the White House Library directly address the issue of slavery, a number of pamphlets were recorded in the index to Fillmore's pamphlet collection under the subject heading "slavery."[46] From their titles, most of these appear to be pro-abolitionist. A copy of *Uncle Tom's Cabin,* which could have been purchased while Fillmore was president, is recorded in the circa 1858 catalogue of his personal library.[47]

With regard to foreign affairs, Fillmore sought to maintain peaceable relationships with all nations and advocated a policy of nonintervention. In his words it was "an imperative duty not to interfere in the government or internal policy of other nations; and although we may sympathize with the unfortunate or the oppressed everywhere in their struggles for freedom, our principles forbid us from taking any part in such foreign contests."[48] Thus, as revolutions broke out across Europe, the United States might sympathize with the causes of oppressed peoples, but it would not lend forces or material assistance. As I will discuss later, Fillmore had more than one occasion to reiterate this policy during his administration. These concerns that persisted throughout Fillmore's presidency provide a framework in which to consider many of the selections that were made for the first White House Library.

Government Documents. From its inception, Fillmore had conceived of the library—at least in part—as a reference library. It therefore should be no surprise that, volume for volume, government documents outnumbered other books two to one. As a lawyer, statesman, and president, Fillmore relied on government documents and collected them in his personal library.[49] Congressional decisions, like legal decisions, are often based on precedent; therefore, a complete record of congressional proceedings would have been an invaluable resource for the president. Although no itemized list of the documents transferred to the Executive Mansion by Lanman has been discovered, George Templeman's estimate from August of 1850 provides an idea of what was likely to have been included in those 894 pounds. His list reads:

The Journals of the old Congress from 1774 to 1788 in 4 vol.	$ 20.00
House Journals for same period 4 vols.	$ 12.00
Reprints of the Journals of the new Houses of Congress for the first 13 Congresses (or from 1789 to 1815) in 14 vols.	$ 70.00
Journals as printed each Session of Congress from the 14th to the 30th Congress [inclusive] making 72 vols. @ $3.00	$ 226.00
The regular series of Documents from the 9th Congress (1805) to the 30th Congress (1849) will make about 530	<u>$ 1650.00</u>
	$ 1978.00
Then there is Niles Register 76 vols.	$ 170.00
Executive Journals of Senate 3 vols.	$ 15.00
Journal of Federal Convention	<u>$ 2.00</u>
	$2165.00[50]

Law. Law books, with thirty-seven titles, constituted a large component of the library and included standard up-to-date editions of the most widely used texts, as well as the well-known classics that were still considered staples in any law library of quality. Nearly half of the law books that Fillmore chose appear in "Catalogue of a Select Law Library" by the Harvard law professor Simon Greenleaf, which was regularly published in the front of Little and Brown's catalogue of law books.[51] In addition to the commentaries of William Blackstone, Henry J. Stephen, James Kent, and Joseph Story mentioned earlier in this essay, the library included standard legal reference works of the day, such as John Bouvier's *Law Dictionary* and complete sets of the Supreme Court Reports and the *Official Opinions of the Attorneys General.* Legal classics were the oldest books purchased for the library and included Hugo Grotius's *The Rights of War and Peace* (1654), John Gottlieb Heineccius's *A Methodical System of Universal Law* (1738), Samuel Pufendorf's *Law of Nature and Nations* (1703), Thomas Rutherforth's *Institutes of the Natural Law* (1754), Emmerich de Vattel's *Law of Nations* (1758), and Abraham de Wicquefort's *The Embassador and His Functions* (1681).[52]

Like other lawyers and statesmen of his day, Fillmore valued the art of public speaking. David Hoffman, a nineteenth-century legal scholar, underscored this ideal with the inclusion of a section on the importance of eloquence at the bar in his *A Course of Legal Study, Addressed to Students and the Profession Generally.* In addition to the classical orators, Cicero, Aristotle, Quintilian, and so forth, he also recommended the speeches of the British statesmen that were purchased for the first White House Library, those of Thomas Erskine, Edmund Burke, Richard Sheridan, and John Philpot Curran. He called the speeches of Erskine "the best models of Bar eloquence that we possess." Hoffman recommended that the best way for one to be "emulous of clear, correct, and felicitous elocution, is to render himself familiar with the best models of English style, both in prose and verse." He pointed to another work selected for the White House, Hume's *History of England,* as a model of style, calling it "carefully elaborated" and asserting that it "holds, to our view, a desirable medium between the old, natural English style, and the more artificial, stately, antithetical and balanced manner of modern days."[53]

Commerce and Political Economy. Fillmore had a long history of experience with local and federal finances that had prepared him to lead the nation in economic affairs. As a lawyer practicing in Buffalo, he witnessed firsthand the effects of the depression of the late 1830s and early 1840s. One large component of his practice had been representing out-of-town businesses in their dealings with their Buffalo clients. He had vouched for the credit and character of Buffalo's businessmen for years and, when necessary, had sued them for debts owed to his out-of-town clients. When the economy began to falter in the 1830s, Fillmore's practice became much more lucrative but also much more discouraging, as his legal services were called upon for nearly every business failure in Buffalo.[54]

In 1841, during his fourth term in Congress, when the country was in the midst of a depression, Fillmore was appointed chair of the Ways and Means Committee. Thus, the task of directing the finances of a nation in economic crisis fell to his hands. In this position Fillmore formulated several policies that would halt the economy's downward trend: a revenue bill that increased import duties, a bankruptcy act that would clear the past debts of businessmen, and protectionist tariffs that forced importers to either decrease speculative practices and limit their operations or face the same risks as American manufacturers.[55]

After retiring from Congress in 1843 Fillmore found himself once again managing a government's finances, this time for the state of New York. Having lost his bid for the governorship in 1844, Fillmore was elected comptroller of New York in 1847. Although this position lacked the prestige associated with the office of governor, in many ways it wielded more power, because it shaped the economy of the state. Fillmore conducted himself as comptroller of New York, just as he had as the chair of the Ways and Means Committee in Congress, by enacting policies that fostered growth in the state's economy, including enlarging the Erie Canal basin (Buffalo's economy depended on shipping interests that navigated the canal) and revising the banking code. This code included the currency system that would be adopted by Congress sixteen years later as part of the National Banking Act.[56]

Prior to Fillmore's presidential administration, the United States had survived the depression of 1837–44, and by the 1850s the economy was booming. The production of meat, grain, cotton, and coal, which were traded both interregionally and internationally, contributed significantly to the country's economic health. After England repealed its Corn Laws in 1846, American farmers could export their grain to the British Isles, and the demand for it increased 170 percent during the decade that followed.[57] Fillmore purchased thirteen titles for the library that were related to commerce and political economy that represented all pertinent aspects of the subject. His selections included the works of recent economic theorists such as Henry Charles Carey, Calvin Colton, William Torrens McCullagh, John Stuart Mill, and Jean-Charles Léonard de Sismondi, as well the classic economic theorists Thomas Robert Malthus and Adam Smith. He also selected practical reference sources such as John Ramsay McCulloch's *Dictionary, Practical, Theoretical, and Historical of Commerce and Commercial Navigation,* John MacGregor's *Commercial Statistics* and *Progress of America to 1846,* Richard Cowling Taylor's *Statistics of Coal,* and Andrew Ure's *Dictionary of Arts, Manufactures, and Mines.*

Geography. Geographical works were necessary for the library for several reasons. American exploration expeditions flourished during the mid-nineteenth century. Not only had the United States Exploring Expedition led by Charles Wilkes only recently returned in 1842, but during Fillmore's presidency seven other expeditions were underway to regions that included South America, the China Sea, Japan, the Arctic, western Africa, and the North Pacific.[58] At home, the United States was in the midst of westward expansion, having just acquired the American Southwest and northern California with the end of the Mexican War in 1848 and having admitted California to the union as part of the compromise of 1850. Concomitantly, the United States and Mexican Boundary Survey Expedition was underway from 1848 to 1855. Abroad, the revolutions in Europe brought with them the potential renegotiation of international boundaries. In addition, President Fillmore's concern with commerce and trade routes made maps, atlases, and geographical writings indispensable reference sources for himself and his staff members. Furthermore, Fillmore had a lifelong interest in geographical works; as a young man he had been a surveyor, and as an adult he became a map collector. Consequently, nine geographical works, including one terrestrial globe, were purchased for the library.[59]

iii. Books Related to the Fillmore Presidency

While many of the purchases for the library—both ones that Fillmore made on his own and those that he made through Lanman—address topics that would be of concern to any United States president, some of the books that Fillmore selected without Lanman's assistance addressed specific issues that he confronted during his presidency. Interests in the

Amazon, both commercial and civil; the Hungarian Revolution of 1848; and the Cuban fili-buster all prompted the purchase of books.

The Amazon. John Esaias Warren's *Para; Or, Scenes and Adventures on the Banks of the Amazon* was purchased in the midst of the Herndon-Gibbon expedition to this region of the Amazon, an expedition Fillmore approved shortly after taking office. Proponents of the expedition hoped that it would strengthen the American South's economy by opening up trade routes with Brazil and exploring the possibility of establishing agricultural centers there; in addition, they even suggested colonizing the Amazon River basin with slavehold-ers, should slavery be abolished in the United States. While Fillmore would have advo-cated the prospect of improved commercial relations with Brazil, his ideas on colonization differed. As one answer to the controversy over slavery, he considered colonizing the West Indies, Africa, and the Amazon River basin with freed slaves. The Herndon-Gibbon expe-dition departed in January of 1851; in July of the same year, Fillmore purchased Warren's otherwise obscure travel book just after its publication.[60]

The Hungarian Revolution. In addition, Fillmore purchased three books relative to the Hungarian Revolution of 1848: John Paget's *Hungary and Transylvania* (1839), György Klapka's *Memoirs of the War of Independence in Hungary* (1850), and Theresa Pulszky's *Memoirs of a Hungarian Lady* (1850). When Fillmore came to office his administration had to answer charges from the Austrian government that the United States had sided with the revolutionaries. Although he had already expressed his concern personally to adminis-tration officials, Chevalier J. G. Hulsemann, the Austrian chargé d'affaires in Washington, sent a letter on September 30, 1850, to Secretary of State Daniel Webster threatening that interference from the United States in Austria's internal matters could result in a retalia-tion of inciting civil war in America. Webster consulted with President Fillmore and called on his friend and president of Harvard University Edward Everett to help draft a response. The reply, dated December 21, 1850, reiterated the administration's policy of noninterven-tion and offered a paean to American superiority. The president purchased Paget's book on November 27, 1850, in the midst of dealing with this matter.[61]

The following year Fillmore was instrumental in obtaining liberty for the revolution's leader, Louis Kossuth, and invited him to visit the United States. Kossuth, accompanied by Theresa Pulszky and her husband, members of the untitled Hungarian nobility who had supported the revolution, arrived in December 1851. The party dined as the Fillmores' guests at the White House on January 6, 1852; in anticipation of this visit, the Fillmores purchased Klapka's book on December 23, 1851, and Pulszky's work on January 2.[62]

The Cuban Filibuster. The third unauthorized attempt to liberate Cuba from Spain, known as the Cuban filibuster, caused Fillmore to place his largest single order for books apart from those he purchased through Lanman. The filibuster, as illegal expeditions such as this one were labeled, nearly led to a full-scale diplomatic crisis.[63] Narciso Lopez sailed with 450 men, mostly American citizens, from New Orleans in August 1851. Upon landing in Cuba, 52 Americans were executed by a firing squad, more died in jail, and 166 were taken captive and removed to Spain; in September Lopez himself was garroted. Although he had warned those undertaking the invasion that it was unlawful and that if they proceeded with their plan, they would forfeit their right to protection by the United States, Fillmore was nevertheless criticized for not retaliating against Spain or Cuba for its treatment of the filibusterers. Supporters of the filibuster rioted in New Orleans, destroyed property, and attacked the Spanish consul there, forcing him to flee for his life.[64]

Fallout from the filibuster persisted into the next summer. In the fall and winter of 1851, the vessel used in the raid, the *Pampero,* was tried, adjudicated against, and sold at public auction. In November, Spain demanded that the United States invite the Spanish consul back to New Orleans and that his effects and those of other Spanish citizens that were destroyed by the rioters be restored. Should the United States refuse to comply with this demand, Spain threatened to remove its minister from Washington. As a result, Fillmore devoted considerable attention to the filibuster in his December address to Congress. He found the United States laws regarding consuls insufficient and urged Congress to consider revising them. That spring the trial of the filibusterers in New York began on March 20, 1852, and lasted twenty-four days, ending in a hung jury.[65]

In the midst of the filibuster aftermath, Fillmore ordered seventeen books from Little and Brown, an order that totaled $67.61 and nearly doubled the number of law books in the library. Ten of these books related to international law, and seven concerned admiralty law. Clearly, the filibuster raised many issues relating to these branches of the law that Fillmore would not have encountered in his Buffalo practice. The expedition violated the Neutrality Act of 1818, and since United States vessels and citizens were involved, the liability of the ship was in question, as well as the possible claims that Spain could make against the United States for the actions of its citizens against the Spanish sovereignty in Cuba. It was therefore no coincidence that in September, just after the filibuster, Fillmore turned to his friend Edward Everett for help and asked him to recommend books on international law for the White House Library. Fillmore's December order from Little and Brown included fourteen of Everett's recommendations.[66]

The following summer, the Cuban filibuster again became an issue and prompted Fillmore to order more books. Congress approved $6,000.00 "for the relief of *American citizens* then lately imprisoned and pardoned by the Queen of Spain." This amount was intended to provide for their transport back to the United States. Fillmore submitted a claim to Congress for an additional $1,013.34 that had been spent to transport to the United States fifteen foreigners who had participated in the filibuster and had also received pardon from the queen. Although the American consul in Spain had contracted for this expense, apparently with good intention, no provision for this expenditure had been made by law.[67] This additional complication to the resolution of the filibuster must have caused Fillmore to request books specifically on consuls from the local Washington, D.C., bookseller Franck Taylor. Taylor sent four: David Bailie Warden's *Consular Establishments,* John Green's *Consular Service,* Robert Fynn's *British Consuls Abroad,* and *Guide Practique des Consulats.* From these four books Fillmore purchased Warden's and Fynn's works.[68]

The books that Fillmore selected for their relevance to current events, the government documents, and the legal texts all point to the first White House Library's function as a working and reference library for the president and his staff members. Many other titles would have been standard reading fare in most nineteenth-century American home libraries, including the Fillmores' (as the catalogues of their personal libraries indicate). A genteel home would not be complete without its George Bancroft, James Boswell, Edmund Burke, Robert Burns, Edward Gibbon, David Hume, Samuel Johnson, William H. Prescott, Walter

Scott, William Shakespeare, Alexis de Tocqueville, and Daniel Webster; nor would the symbolic American home, the White House. From this perspective the first White House Library reflected the mind of an age—its government and its people. Taken as a whole the library embodied a conservative ideology, one that was still tied to and respectful of America's British origins; one that held to the didactic value of history and biography; one that maintained a continuity with the past, had a respect for tradition, and valued books as a means of self-education through which anyone could better his or her social position. This, however, was not the sole ideological perspective of mid-nineteenth-century America. Competing, emerging, and residual ideologies are ever present, and the "young Americans" of the day, represented by John O'Sullivan's *Democratic Review* in the library, upheld an opposing, progressive philosophy. While they were energized by the revolutions in Europe, supported the Cuban filibuster, and saw the need to break with the past, to start new traditions, and to define a distinctly American voice in literature, law, and politics, they nevertheless had to contend with the specters of earlier times—the Gibbons, the Humes, the Burkes, and the like—who stood on the shelves of libraries and held sway in the American mind.[69]

III. THE USE AND DISPERSAL OF THE FIRST WHITE HOUSE LIBRARY

The collection assembled by the Fillmores in the White House remained mostly intact for over fifty years. The upstairs oval room of the White House served as the library for nearly eighty-five years, until 1935, when President Franklin D. Roosevelt renovated the White House and moved the library to its present location on the ground floor. In addition to serving as a working library for the president and his staff members, the library also served as a parlor for the first family, where they spent time reading, studying, playing backgammon, entertaining friends, and listening to music. The Fillmores moved their piano, harp, and guitar from their Buffalo home to the White House Library; Abbie, as their daughter was known, was an accomplished musician and played for personal enjoyment as well as for the pleasure of company. She was proficient in a broad range of genres, including Irish and Scotch airs, operatic pieces, patriotic tunes, battle hymns, classical waltzes, and other popular songs.[70]

Two longtime friends of the Fillmores later fondly recalled pleasant evenings in the library. Harriet Haven, the wife of Fillmore's former law partner in Buffalo, remembered the Fillmores hosting Daniel Webster and Thomas Corwin, together with some other cabinet members and friends in the library. On this occasion, Abbie played the piano, accompanied by one of the guests, Miss Brook, on the harp for the enjoyment of the entire party. Julia Miller, a childhood friend whom Abbie invited to the White House, also reminisced about delightful time spent in the library, where the family read aloud, engaged in interesting conversation, and enjoyed charming music. She recollected Abbie and Powers singing old-time melodies together, such as "Sweet Vale of Avoca" and "In the Desert a Fountain Is Springing."[71]

Presidents after Fillmore added to the library's holdings, and many first families used the room as a family parlor, where they continued the Fillmores' tradition of reading, entertaining guests, and enjoying musical entertainment. Fillmore's immediate successor, Franklin Pierce (1853–57), held daily family devotions in the library with his servants.[72]

Abraham and Mary Todd Lincoln (1861–65) enjoyed reading in the library, and the president sometimes held private conferences there. While Mary Lincoln was fond of modern English novels, the president preferred poetry and plays. In fact, Shakespeare and Burns, authors whose works the Fillmores had stocked in the library, were among President Lincoln's favorites.[73] On at least three occasions First Lady Lincoln purchased books for the library, spending no less than $478.15. Finding the sets of Scott and Shakespeare that the Fillmores had purchased in poor condition, she selected replacement copies. In addition, she added the works of Cooper. The first lady also purchased poetry by Oliver Goldsmith, Elizabeth Barrett Browning, Edmund Spenser, and Henry Wadsworth Longfellow, although it is unclear whether these were for her personal collection or the White House.[74]

The library played an integral role in the family life of Rutherford B. and Lucy Webb Hayes (1877–81). Lucy Keeler, a second cousin to President Hayes, visited the White House in 1881 when she was seventeen years old and recorded a brief description of the library in her journal; she also sketched accompanying floor plans (see figure 13). Of the second floor she wrote, "The east part of the building is occupied by the business work—secretary's rooms and the elegant Cabinet room, where the President meets with his cabinet on Tuesdays and Fridays. There is a private door leading into the Library. The room is over the Blue Room and is of the same shape. It is furnished in green leather and is a resort for the family. An upright piano is against the wall. Books are in cases and pictures and busts are numerous."[75] It was the Hayeses' family tradition to gather on Sunday evenings around the piano in the library to sing hymns together (see figure 14). Another Hayes relative, Lucy Scott West, a second cousin to First Lady Hayes, visited the White House in February and March of 1878 and wrote journal letters to her family, which include many references to the library. She recalls on one occasion retiring to it after a reception to play whist with friends and family until midnight. President Hayes himself received guests in the library and remembered the family gathering there on Christmas as they waited to open gifts.[76]

Warren G. and Florence King Harding (1920–23) also enjoyed entertaining in the library. Small groups of six to fifteen were often received there, while larger parties were hosted in the central corridor just outside of it. Since his term in office coincided with Prohibition, many of Harding's activities in the library were "wholly illegal." He held poker games there several evenings a week and kept a card table and makeshift bar for serving cocktails, ale, and wine; while the men drank and played cards, the women conversed in other parts of the room.[77]

Long before the Hardings took up residence in the White House, the collection had begun to be dispersed. The first known deaccessioning of books occurred under President Hayes, when, in 1877, he made arrangements with his friend Ainsworth Rand Spofford, the Librarian of Congress, to exchange some of the government documents in the White House for books at the Library of Congress. Hayes must have requested assistance in selecting works to add to the library, because on June 2, 1877, Spofford wrote:

> I return herewith the Catalogue of the Library at the Executive Mansion. . . . On slips enclosed I submit a list of the most necessary reference books desirable for purchase.
>
> There are many hundreds of volumes of State and Congressional Documents in a garret, regarding which I shall take some occasion to say a word.[78]

Apparently, Spofford proposed that he be allowed to select from these documents those that would complete the set at the Library of Congress. Two days later, he wrote that his assistant, Charles Darwin, would make an inventory of the documents for this purpose. The transaction was completed on June 8, when Spofford wrote to one of the president's assistants, Colonel W. K. Rogers, outlining the arrangement. In return for the government documents that he had selected from the Executive Mansion, he had set aside five or six thousand books from which the president could choose. He offered to send Darwin to collect the documents for the Library of Congress and to give a receipt. Thus, on June 8, 1877, the first books were officially deaccessioned from the White House Library. Ironically, in 1850 Congress had resisted supplying the White House with a set of government documents; twenty-seven years later, it drew from the Executive Mansion collection to complete its own set in its own library.[79]

Spofford also assisted Hayes with purchasing some books for the library and wrote to the president on August 6, 1877:

> The reference books and odd volumes ordered for the Executive Mansion Library have been
> picked up by me in N.Y. & Boston and shipped in two parcels by Express marked
>   "Library of Executive Mansion Washington"
> A few remaining books will follow, and some of the broken sets could not be completed in
> either book market. In some cases the odd volumes will need rebinding to match those now
> in the Library.
>   The bills I will bring with me on my return to Washington, & I doubt not you will readily
> excuse the delay in filling the order, in view of the fact that your friend is saved some $25 or
> $30 by personal buying instead of giving out the order. I think the whole will fall within $200.[80]

Unfortunately, no list of the books purchased by Spofford has been found, nor has any record of funding received by Hayes for the library been discovered. It is possible, however, that Spofford purchased these books as part of the exchange for the government documents that he received from Hayes for the Library of Congress.[81]

Although the first books were deaccessioned from the White House Library during the Hayes administration, approximately ninety of the books purchased by the Fillmores remained in the White House until 1903, when Theodore Roosevelt asked the Library of Congress to help update the collection. His request initiated the White House Library Deposit, a program in which books that were no longer desired in the White House were sent to the Library of Congress, which, in turn, placed books on deposit in the White House for the president's use. As M. A. Roberts, superintendent of the Reading Room in 1932, explained, "antiquated and worn books and broken sets" were eliminated and "desirable items in appropriate fields" were added. Those items that were eliminated were taken to the Library of Congress where they were "rebound, catalogued, classified, bookplated," and placed on the shelves at the library for the use of readers.[82]

Herbert and Lou Henry Hoover (1929–33) were avid readers who took a keen interest in the White House Library. Much to their surprise, when they moved in, it had been entirely depleted. Their queries to the Library of Congress initiated the correspondence that has helped to document the dispersal of the library and to reconstruct its history. Calvin

Coolidge (1923–29), Hoover's predecessor, another bibliophilic president, had sent all of the books in the White House to the Library of Congress in order to make room for his personal collection, which he of course took with him when he moved out. The Library of Congress attempted to return the books to their shelves in the White House before Hoover's inauguration, but the necessary approval arrived a few days too late.[83]

When the books were finally returned to the White House, the Hoovers selected the ones that they wished to keep there and sent the others back to the Library of Congress.[84] The books that were returned would have been the ones that Coolidge sent out of the library, not the ones that had been deaccessioned earlier. The books that had been eliminated earlier were brought together in 1932, at the request of Ruth Fessler, one of First Lady Hoover's assistants. At that time, Superintendent Roberts offered to send them back to the White House; no evidence suggests that the Hoovers ever took him up on this offer. In addition, President Hoover requested that the Library of Congress send a "representative collection, for purely working purposes, of the most authentic autobiographic and biographic works relative to former Presidents," a request the library granted. Hoover also transferred multiple copies of the *Presidential Addresses and State Papers of William Howard Taft* and *The Works of Theodore Roosevelt* to the Library of Congress. He neglected, however, to retain a complete set of Roosevelt's works for the White House and had to ask that one be returned.[85]

At the end of their term, the Hoovers had three lists compiled, which they left with the Roosevelt administration, to account for the books that were in the White House: one for the Executive Mansion Collection, one for the White House Library Deposit, and one for books on special loan to the president from the Library of Congress. The Executive Mansion Collection list includes only thirty-nine titles, nine of which were purchased during the Fillmore administration:

> Calvin Colton, *Life and Times of Henry Clay.*
> Benjamin Franklin, *Works.*
> Edward Gibbon, *Decline and Fall of the Roman Empire.*
> Richard Hildreth, *A History of the United States of America.*
> Thomas Jefferson, *Memoirs, Correspondence, and Miscellanies.*
> John P. Kennedy, *Memoirs of the Life of William Wirt.*
> John Stuart Mill, *Principles of Political Economy.*
> Jared Sparks, *Library of American Biography,* first series.
> Jared Sparks, *Library of American Biography,* second series.

The presence of Gibbon's *Decline and Fall of the Roman Empire* on that list and the location of the Executive Mansion copy of it in the Library of Congress stacks in 2006 indicate that the White House was still sending books to the Library of Congress as recently as the 1930s.[86]

Two collections of books from the White House were stored at the Library of Congress, the "Executive Mansion Collection" and the "White House Collection," and remained together, moved in and out of various storage locations, for at least fifty years, until around 1980. While research on this catalogue was under way, several pieces of evidence turned up that referred to these collections. In the process of searching for books from the first White

House Library in the Library of Congress stacks, two dummies were discovered that refer to the Executive Mansion Collection and its location. One, a paper-covered block of wood, is for Grote's *History of Greece* and is undated, but appears to be from the 1930s or '40s. It refers to the "Executive Mansion Collection (Deck 40)" and has "At Pickett Street" written across it in pen. "Pickett Street" was the name of an offsite storage facility used by the Library of Congress during the 1970s and 1980s. The other dummy, for Hallam's *Constitutional History of England,* is dated December 30, 1980, and also refers to the "Executive Mansion Collection Deck 40." A three-by-five-inch typed card with a record for Jean Jacques Barthélemy's *Travels of Anacharsis the Younger in Greece* found in volume 6 of this title has a note penciled in the upper right corner reading "White House Coll. Deck 37 not in rare books." The terms "White House Collection" and "Executive Mansion Collection" most likely refer to two groups of books that were received at the Library of Congress from the White House during two separate periods of time.[87]

A 1977 memo suggests the final fate of the books in these two collections. Written by Earnest Braund, a management analyst, the memo opens "The move to Landover [another Library of Congress offsite storage facility that is still in use today] will provide an excellent opportunity to improve the order of many of our remote collections. This move may well allow us to service collections long considered in 'dead storage.'" The "White House" and the "Executive Mansion" Collections are mentioned later in the memo as among those in dead storage. A "Sequenced Task List for Landover Activities" attached to this memo includes both of these collections and recommends the following tasks for each: "a) arrange (6 man hours) b) make title-author cards c) review for discard (60 man hours)." The memo specifies that the White House Collection contains six hundred books, but does not indicate how many were in the Executive Mansion Collection. It must have contained a similar number of books, since the same amount of time would be needed to service it. Apparently, whatever remained of the Executive Mansion and the White House Collections was then either integrated into the stacks or deaccessioned.[88]

IV. EPILOGUE TO THE HISTORY OF THE FIRST WHITE HOUSE LIBRARY

During the twentieth century several further initiatives were taken to place books in the White House. The first, by the American Booksellers Association in cooperation with *Publisher's Weekly,* began in 1929 after it became public that there were no books in the White House on the Hoovers' arrival. A committee was formed, and five hundred books were selected and purchased with contributions from booksellers and individuals. These were formally presented to the White House on April 25, 1930. Another two hundred books were donated in 1934 and an additional two hundred in 1937. According to Robert C. Gooch, Chief of Book Services at the Library of Congress in 1940, these selections were "the 'best' books of the intervening years. This library, ~~in no sense a reference or research library~~, embraces selections in science, history, biography, travel and adventure, childrens' books, fiction, poetry and drama, current events and the arts. It is meant to be a symbol of the library in the American home, the library to which the household and guests may turn for recreational and cultural reading."[89] The contribution of books to the White House by the American Booksellers Association became a quadrennial event that continues today.

Catalogues of the initial donation of five hundred books were published by Harbor Press in New York and sold for ten cents each. The list of books was also published in the *New York Times* on April 10, 1930. The *Times* article notes that the library included Ernest Hemingway's *A Farewell to Arms,* which had recently been censored in Boston, and mentions the inclusion of Charles A. Lindbergh's *We,* along with works by three former presidents, Theodore Roosevelt, Woodrow Wilson, and Calvin Coolidge.[90]

Another initiative to place books in the White House, "The President's Shelf," began in 1940 as part of the White House Library Deposit. It was "a small library" of detective fiction, primarily, "intended for the personal use of the President." As Archibald MacLeish, the Librarian of Congress, explained, "The Shelf will be a revolving collection in the sense that books will be replaced from time to time as they are read." The writer, theater critic, and wit Alexander Woollcott was appointed by the Library of Congress as the Honorary Consultant for the President's Shelf, in charge of making selections for its content. According to Woollcott, the history of reading detective fiction in the White House dates back to "that critical moment in the 1914–1918 war when Woodrow Wilson—who was too independent of good counsel in this as in some other matters—was discovered relaxing uncritically in the mysteries of an undistinguished specimen called 'The Middle Temple Murder' by an Englishman named Fletcher."[91] Wilkie Collins's *Moonstone,* Arthur Conan Doyle's *The Sherlock Holmes Stories,* Dashiell Hammett's *The Maltese Falcon* and *The Thin Man,* and Dorothy L. Sayers's *The Nine Tailors* and *Gaudy Night* were among the titles selected by Woollcott. The President's Shelf no longer exists, and current White House staff members are unfamiliar with it. It may have been discontinued at Woollcott's death in 1943.

In 1962, as part of her renovation of the White House, First Lady Jacqueline Kennedy took an interest in the library. She even inquired into the Lanman archive at the University of California, Los Angeles.[92] In her effort to build a "new" library in the White House, she requested James Tinkman Babb, librarian of the Yale University Library, to help collect books for it. According to Babb, it was to be "a library of books central to the understanding of the American national experience" and would "include the writings of the Presidents of the United States and their published papers, as well as outstanding titles in American literature, history, biography, religion, philosophy, science, and other works, illuminating the quality of American civilization." Due to limited shelf space in the library, these selections were restricted to 2,500 volumes. Babb noted that the authors would be United States citizens, except for a few writers of classics, and that only deceased writers of creative literature would be included.[93]

An auspicious committee of the leading historians, librarians, and publishing professionals was formed to assist Babb in the selection of books. Chaired by Lyman H. Butterfield, historian and editor of the Jefferson and Adams papers, the committee also included Julian P. Boyd, president of the American Historical Association; Arthur M. Schlesinger Jr., historian and special assistant to President Kennedy; Lawrence Clark Powell, director of the William Andrews Clark Memorial Library at the University of California at Los Angeles; Lawrence W. Towner, librarian at the Newberry Library, Chicago; Dan Lacey, managing director of the American Book Publisher's Council; Rutherford D. Rogers, assistant librarian of Congress; C. Waller Barrett, president of the Bibliographical Society of America; and Joseph A. Duffy, executive director of the American Booksellers Association, Inc. Babb

also enlisted the American Booksellers Association to help pay for the books by incorpo-
rating some of the books selected by the committee for the new library into its quadrennial
donation.[94]

The collection selected by Babb and his committee under the direction of Jacqueline
Kennedy remains the core of the present White House Library (see figure 15). The list of
books included in it was published on August 9, 1963, reprinted in the *New York Times*
on August 16, and reprinted again by the White House Historical Association in 1967.[95] In
his forward to the 1967 printing, Babb added that First Lady Johnson took a great interest
in the library and used it on a regular basis.[96] Only about 125 titles had been added to the
library between 1962 and 1980. The additions included mostly the papers of notable American statesmen, such as John C. Calhoun and Benjamin Franklin, as they continued to be
published, as well as the government-printed papers of the presidents.[97]

The most recent effort to renew the library began in 1998, when the Committee for the
Preservation of the White House recommended, as a "legacy" for the new millennium,
updating the collection with important publications from the previous thirty years. John
Wilmerding, a member of the committee and a professor of art history at Princeton University, agreed to coordinate the selection of five to six hundred new titles, which would
include volumes from the Library of America series. The acquisition and installation of
these books was delayed as time was taken to vet the list, analyze the cost, and determine
which books to weed from the existing collection. Lack of funding delayed the installation
further. The American Booksellers Association declined to help out this time. The Congressional Club, however, donated $2,500 in honor of First Lady Laura Bush; a supporter of the
Library of America contributed 150 current volumes; and the White House Historical Association gave a set of its principal publications. The Annenberg Foundation took care of
the remainder of the expense with a gift of $16,500. A White House bookplate was made
to match the one created in 1963 and was placed in each of the new volumes. Those books
marked for deletion were transferred to storage, and the old and new books were shelved
in the White House Library on October 25 and 26, 2005. Seven years after its initiation, the
completion of the project was announced on October 28 to the Committee for the Preservation of the White House.[98]

Clearly much has changed since the Fillmores established a library in the White House.
Then, and for many years following, it was the center of activity, both professional and personal; staff members and presidents conducted official research there, and many first families read, played board games, conversed with friends, and enjoyed musical performances
in it. Today, staff members' offices no longer occupy the same floor as the first family's living
quarters, and their research and reference needs, along with those of the president, could
not be served by only 3,500 volumes. Instead, they are met by the Executive Office Library
in the Eisenhower Executive Office Building located next to the White House on Pennsylvania Avenue. The upstairs oval room that originally housed the library is now known as
the Yellow Oval Drawing Room and serves as the formal living area for the first family. Bookcase niches in this room have for many years been used to display china and gilded silver.[99]

Today a library as a formal room in the American home may be all but a thing of the
past; however, the values represented by the Fillmores' founding of the first White House
Library endure. Then, Americans relied on books as their primary source of information

and as their means of education that led to individual self-improvement. Present-day Americans rely on new communication media for education and entertainment; televisions, personal computers, and DVD players have replaced the books, pianos, harps, and backgammon boards as fixtures in many American homes. Internet searches, text messaging, and video rental histories may now be the best indicators of the topics that occupy the minds of the age. Nevertheless, just as the Fillmores believed in 1850, education and access to knowledge persist as fundamental ideals of a free and civilized society.

NOTES

1. Edward Pessen, *The Log Cabin Myth: The Social Backgrounds of the Presidents* (New Haven: Yale University Press, 1984), 23; Carl Russell Fish, *The Rise of the Common Man, 1830–1850* (New York: Macmillan, 1929).

2. Robert Scarry, *Millard Fillmore* (Jefferson, N.C.: McFarland, 2001), 17–22.

3. Ibid., 22 (although Scarry gives Abigail's age at the time of moving to Sempronius as six, other historians suggest that she was ten; nevertheless, she moved there at a relatively young age); see Kristin Hoganson, "Abigail (Powers) Fillmore," in *American First Ladies: Their Lives and Their Legacy,* ed. Lewis L. Gould (New York: Garland, 1996), 155.

4. Scarry, *Millard Fillmore,* 27.

5. Ibid., 41; Hiram Day recalls the Fillmores' book-collecting habits in Frank H. Severance, ed., *Millard Fillmore Papers* (Buffalo, N.Y.: Buffalo Historical Society, 1907), 2:506.

6. Abigail Fillmore, letter to Millard Fillmore, January 18–19, 1829, MS3 Millard Fillmore Papers, Special Collections, Penfield Library, SUNY at Oswego, Oswego, N.Y. (hereafter Millard Fillmore Papers, SUNY Oswego); Microfilm Edition of the Millard Fillmore Papers (Buffalo, N.Y.: BECHS, 1975), roll 1 ser. 1.

7. See "Bibliographical Methods," 79–80, for a more extensive discussion of the Fillmores' library catalogues. See also Ronald J. Zboray and Mary Saracino Zboray, "Home Libraries and the Institutionalization of Everyday Practices Among Antebellum New Englanders," *American Studies* 42, no. 3 (2001): 63–86, for more about the size, function, and use of home libraries from this time period. This organization system was commonly employed in nineteenth-century libraries and was used in the catalogue of the Executive Mansion Library that was compiled by the direction of Rutherford B. Hayes in 1877 (see "Bibliographical Methods," 70–71).

8. Scarry, *Millard Fillmore,* 322–26.

9. George Templeman, letter to President Fillmore, August 31, 1850, Millard Fillmore Papers, BECHS, Buffalo, N.Y. (hereafter Millard Fillmore Papers, BECHS). Although Templeman is not listed in Waite's *Washington Directory* for 1850, in 1910 James Croggon, writing for the *Evening Star* about printers in "Old Washington" stated that in the 1840s Templeman was engaged in the book business (see http://www.congressionalcemetery.org/Research/History_Local/Croggon/Croggon_19100709.html, accessed July 6, 2009). For information on calculating monetary values across time, see Samuel H. Williamson, "Six Ways to Compute the Relative Value of a U.S. Dollar Amount, 1774 to Present," MeasuringWorth, 2008, http://www.measuringworth.com/uscompare/ (accessed August 2, 2009). According to Williamson's calculator, $1.00 in 1850 would equal $25.80 in 2005 when measured according to the Consumer Price Index.

10. The only formal record of Congressional Debates from this period is the *Congressional Globe.* If any Democrats supported funding the library in the Executive Mansion, it was not recorded; *Congressional Globe,* 31st Congress, 1st Session, 1761 (1850); *Congressional Globe,* 31st Congress, 1st Session, 1780 (1850), A Century of Lawmaking for a New Nation: U.S. Congressional Documents and Debates, 1774–1875, American Memory, Library of Congress, May 1, 2003, http://lcweb2.loc.gov/ammem/amlaw/lweg.html (accessed July 7, 2009).

11. Scarry, *Millard Fillmore,* 188; according to Scarry, Fillmore wrote a letter to Congress regarding the library on September 23, 1850. This letter has yet to be located. See also Robert J. Rayback, *Millard Fillmore: Biography of a President* (Buffalo, N.Y.: Henry Stewart for the Buffalo Historical Society, 1959), 245; according to Rayback, Fillmore and Pearce's friendship dated back to the 24th–27th Congresses (1835–42), when the two served together in the House. (Both congressmen served nonconsecutive terms. Fillmore did not serve in the 24th Congress and Pearce did not serve in the 26th. Nevertheless, the two still knew one another.) When Fillmore became president, he asked Pearce to serve as Secretary of Interior, but Pearce turned him down, preferring to remain in the Senate.

12. *Congressional Globe,* 31st Congress, 1st Session, 1926 (1850).

13. Act of September 30, 1850, chap. 90, *Statutes at Large,* chap. 32, A Century of Lawmaking for a New Nation: U.S. Congressional Documents and Debates, 1774–1875, American Memory, Library of Congress, May 1, 2003, http://memory.loc.gov/cgi-bin/ampage?collId=llsl&fileName=009/llsl009.db&recNum=6, image 524 (accessed July 6, 2009); according to Henry A. Holmes, state and territorial libraries proliferated between 1850 and 1875. Under the belief that a library was necessary for the "welfare of new communities, that they might be developed and sustained under wise laws" a library had been founded in every state and territory by 1876. These state and territorial libraries were made up primarily of law books; see "State and Territorial Libraries," in *Public Libraries in the United States of America: Their History, Condition, and Management* (1876; repr., Totowa, N.J.: Rowman and Littlefield, 1971), 309–11.

14. *Congressional Globe,* 31st Congress, 2nd Session, 677 (1851); *Congressional Globe,* 31st Congress, 2nd Session, 800 (1851); Act of March 3, 1851, *Statutes at Large,* chap. 32. The appropriations for the library are also recorded in the Appropriation Ledgers for the Treasury and Other Departments, 1807–1945, vol. 10 of 50, Records of the Bureau of Accounts (Treasury), Records Relating to Government Agencies or Functions, Department of the Treasury, RG 39, NACP. *Congressional Globe,* 32nd Congress, 2nd Session, 397 (1853); "Fire in the Capitol at Washington," *Farmer's Cabinet,* December 31, 1851, 2 available at *America's Historical Newspapers,* Readex, NewsBank, http://www.newsbank.com/readex.

15. Sylvanus G. Deeth, letter to President Fillmore, October 23, 1850, Millard Fillmore Papers, BECHS. The New Jersey bookseller Sylvanus G. Deeth wrote to the president asking for the commission to purchase the library for the Executive Mansion and the territories of New Mexico and Utah. Fillmore penciled his response in the right margin: "Have appt. for Utah. Not ready for N. Mexico. & will myself for the Pres. Mansion." See "Bibliographical Methods," 70, for a discussion of the vouchers recording purchases for the Executive Mansion Library. The vouchers are held in Records of the Accounting Offices of the Department of the Treasury, Office of the First Auditor; Settled Miscellaneous Treasury Accounts, September 6, 1790– September 29, 1894, RG 217, NACP. See account 105,579, voucher 1, and account 105,579, voucher 2.

16. See account 105,133, vouchers 6 and 7. I discuss both of these firms at greater length in "Millard Fillmore and His Booksellers."

17. Scarry, *Millard Fillmore,* 23.

18. De Lolme's work was edited by A. J. Stephens and identified as "Stephen's English Constitution" on the voucher; see account 105,133 vouchers 6 and 7.

19. Webster had been a long-time friend of Fillmore. He was one of the first people whom Fillmore met when he came to Washington as a freshman congressman in 1833, and he helped Fillmore gain privileges at the Supreme Court Bar. Webster served as Fillmore's secretary of state, and Charles Lanman left his position in the War Department to become Webster's private secretary. See Rayback, *Millard Fillmore,* passim; Charles Lanman, "Presidential Recollections," box 3, folder 1, Charles Lanman Papers (Collection 728), Charles E. Young Research Library, Department of Special Collections, University of California at Los Angeles. This article has been cut out from its original source and laid down on a heavier stock of paper. Its original source has not yet been identified. Lanman, as a search in *APS Online* (http://www.proquest.com/ products_pq/descriptions/aps.shtml) reveals, was a frequent contributor to periodicals of the day. The opening line of this essay places its writing sometime during Ulysses S. Grant's presidency, from 1869 to 1877, stating, "of the eighteen men who have held the office of President. . . ." It appears that Lanman was revising this article for republication, as it is annotated in pencil with "eighteen" in the first line crossed out and "twenty-three" written in. Lanman also adds, in pencil, anecdotes for presidents after Grant. As it turned out, Lanman's estimate was low; he was actually paid $70 for his expenses. See account 105,133, voucher 1. Charles Lanman, letter to President Millard Fillmore, November 26, 1850, Millard Fillmore Papers, BECHS. Fillmore's letter to Lanman does not survive; he penciled his reply on Lanman's letter.

20. Joseph Henry, letter to President Millard Fillmore, November 26, 1850, Millard Fillmore Papers, BECHS; Charles Lanman, letter to President Millard Fillmore, December 3, 1850, Millard Fillmore Papers, BECHS. Among Lanman's several vocations and avocations, he was a journalist, travel writer, and landscape painter. Before 1850 he had published *Essays for Summer Hours* (1841), *Letters from a Landscape Painter* (1845), *A Summer in the Wilderness* (1847), *A Tour to the River Saguenay, in Lower Canada* (1847), *Adventures of an Angler in Canada, Nova Scotia and the United States* (1848), and *Letters from the Alleghany Mountains* (1849). He had yet to write his well-known *Dictionary of the United States Congress* (1859), which Fillmore would add to his personal collection. See Fillmore Library Catalogue, 1861, p. 61, held in box 2/folder 6, 4/1/Vault, Millard Fillmore Papers, 1833–1874, University Archives, State University of New York at Buffalo.

21. Lanman, "Presidential Recollections."

22. Charles Lanman, letter to Millard P. Fillmore, December 26, 1850, Millard Fillmore Papers, BECHS. This list of rejected books has been generated by comparing the lists of books that Lanman sent on approval with the lists of the books that were actually purchased.

23. The first edition of Story's *Constitution* (1833) was in three volumes; the one-volume abridgement appeared the same year. The second edition, which Fillmore purchased for the White House, was in two volumes. See entries 164–66 in the main catalogue for Joseph Story and a discussion of other commentaries that Story wrote. Franck Taylor, letter to President Millard Fillmore, January 6, 1851, Millard Fillmore Papers, BECHS. Fillmore has penciled, "returned will wait for new edition" in the top margin of Taylor's letter. See account 107,754, voucher number 3.

24. For Plutarch, see Fillmore, 1847 catalogue, p. 14, and 1861 catalogue, p. 172. One might expect that Plutarch's *Lives* would be included in the set of Harper's *Family Classical Library* that was purchased for the White House; however, it was not. See Fillmore, 1861 catalogue, p. 82 for Brown, p. 136 for Good.

25. See "Millard Fillmore and His Booksellers," 62.

26. Lanman "Presidential Recollections"; see account 105,133, voucher 3. George Templeman is the bookseller who provided Fillmore with an estimate for a set of congressional documents, see page 9 of this essay.

27. Apparently, the amounts paid were negotiated further after Lanman sent the bills on December 26, for there are some discrepancies between the amounts he provided and the documented expenditures. While he lists the Little and Brown bill at $707.87, the voucher shows $701.37 as having been paid. Likewise, Lanman lists Welford's charges at $592.00, yet only $584.74 was paid. Lanman's own expenses were billed at $74.38, but only $70.00 was dispensed, and although $30.75 was charged for the freight for transferring the government documents, $29.25 was paid. No record accounting for these discrepancies has been discovered.

28. See entry 128 for the *Penny Cyclopaedia,* 157 for the *Maps for the Society for the Diffusion of Useful Knowledge,* 111 for Montgomery Martin's *British Colonial Library,* 35 for *Chambers Miscellany of Useful and Entertaining Tracts,* 20 for *British Essayists,* 73 for Harper's *Family Classical Library,* and 50 for Edgeworth's *Tales and Novels.*

29. Books that the Fillmores selected apart from Lanman's purchasing trip are marked with a dagger in appendix A, "A List of the Books Purchased for the First White House Library in 1850."

30. For more about the New York Society Library charge records, see Ronald Zboray, *A Fictive People: Antebellum Economic Development and the American Reading Public* (New York: Oxford University Press, 1993), 158–73.

31. Caleb Sprague Henry, preface to François Guizot, *The History of Civilization from the Fall of the Roman Empire to the French Revolution,* trans. William Hazlitt (New York: Appleton, 1846), 1:5–6.

32. "A Course of Historical Reading," *Universalist Quarterly and General Review,* January 1850, and "A Course of Historical Reading Part II: Modern History," *Universalist Quarterly and General Review,* April 1850, both available at *APS Online,* http://www.proquest.com/products_pq/descriptions/aps.shtml.

33. "The Library of American Biography," *Christian Examiner and General Review,* September 1836, available at *APS Online,* http://www.proquest.com/products_pq/descriptions/aps.shtml.

34. These prices found in Putnam's 1852 *Bookbuyer's Manual* and Roorbach's *Bibliotheca Americana;* see "Bibliographical Methods," 78–79, for a discussion of these sources. Although the White House had the funding and could have purchased this set, the cost of such a purchase would have prevented the acquisition of many other books.

35. Although most of Milton's poetical subjects are elevated, his prose topics often champion causes of the people, such as the freedom of the press in *Areopagitica* and divorce rights in *Doctrine and Discipline of Divorce.* Both Milton's prose and poetical works were selected for the library.

36. Rufus Wilmot Griswold address this consequence of copyright law in the preface to both of his anthologies that were purchased for the library, *Prose Writers of America* (Philadelphia: Carey and Hart, 1849), 5–6, and *Poets and Poetry of America* (Philadelphia: Carey and Hart, 1850), 6–7.

37. Since First Lady Jacqueline Kennedy's refurbishment of the library in 1962, it has been the practice not to include works by living literary authors in the White House Library. This decision was made primarily because of space limitations and reasons of tact.

38. Many earlier accounts of the first White House Library state the Fillmores purchased sets of Thackeray and Dickens for it. These accounts probably confuse the Fillmores' personal collection with the White

House collection. No records indicate that the Fillmores purchased any works by Thackeray or Dickens for the White House Library. The invitation to Thackeray to visit the White House, dated February 22, 1853, survives in the Department of Literary and Historical Manuscripts, Pierpont Morgan Library, New York. I am grateful to Anna Lou Ashby, Andrew W. Mellon Curator of Printed Books, for alerting the editorial board of this catalogue to the existence of the Thackeray invitation. Abigail Fillmore had met Charles Dickens when he visited Washington in 1842 (Elizabeth Lorelei Thacker-Estrada, "The Heart of the Fillmore Presidency: Abigail Powers Fillmore and the White House Library," *White House Studies* 1, no. 1 [2001]: 91).

39. I am grateful to Elizabeth Lorelei Thacker-Estrada for calling these two titles to my attention.

40. Severance, *Millard Fillmore Papers,* 1:67–82.

41. James Richardson, ed., *A Compilation of the Messages and Papers of the Presidents 1789–1897* (Washington, D.C.: GPO, 1897), 5:98–99.

42. See Lanman's "Presidential Recollections" for the story of Peter Carroll; for items in the personal library, see Fillmore, ca. 1858 catalogue, 5, 11.

43. Richardson, *Compilation of the Messages and Papers,* 5:78.

44. Ibid., 5:81, 121, 166.

45. Scarry, *Millard Fillmore,* 59.

46. Index to the Fillmore Pamphlet Collection, MS 3, box 51, Millard Fillmore Papers, SUNY Oswego.

47. Fillmore, ca. 1858 catalogue, 65.

48. Richardson, *Compilation of the Messages and Papers,* 5:90–91.

49. A number of volumes of government documents from Fillmore's own library are held by the University Archives, SUNY at Buffalo. These are catalogued under the title "Government publications from the library of Millard Fillmore" in BISON, the library's online catalogue.

50. George Templeman, letter to President Fillmore, August 31, 1850, Millard Fillmore Papers, BECHS. The price that Templeman quoted for *Niles's Register* is considerably higher than what was paid for the copy that was purchased for the Executive Mansion. While Templeman offered seventy-six volumes for $170.00, Little and Brown supplied the White House with fifty-six volumes for $80.00. Only the volumes covering the period from 1811 through 1843 were purchased. Yet the per-volume price from Templeman, $2.24, is still much higher than the $1.43 charged by Little and Brown. A difference in binding or format could account for the disparity; unfortunately, these details were not recorded. No further record of whether Fillmore purchased anything from Templeman survives. If he did, it would most likely have been for his personal library, since only government purchases are recorded in the Treasury Department records.

51. See Little, Brown and Company, *A General Catalogue of Law Books; Including All the Reports* (Boston: Little and Brown, 1853), xv–xxii, for one example of Greenleaf's catalogue. Millard Powers Fillmore had graduated from Harvard Law School just before coming to serve as his father's secretary at the White House and most likely studied under Greenleaf. See "Bibliographical Methods," 81.

52. Most of these were not purchased in first editions; usually an older edition was selected—for Grotius, 1738; Heineccius, 1763; Pufendorf, 1749; Rutherforth, 1754; and de Wicquefort, 1716. Vattel's and Rutherforth's works were the only ones available in modern editions, and Vattel's was the only one purchased in a nineteenth-century edition. In fact, Fillmore purchased two copies of Vattel, one published in 1839 and the other 1852.

53. David Hoffman, *A Course of Legal Study, Addressed to Students and the Profession Generally* (Baltimore: Joseph Neal, 1836), 2:602–22; see especially 602–3 and 621.

54. Rayback, *Millard Fillmore,* 92–93.

55. Ibid., 122–36.

56. Ibid., 169, 172. This system of currency is based on the holdings of United States Treasury securities.

57. Eric Foner and John A. Garraty, eds., *Reader's Companion to American History* (Boston: Houghton Mifflin, 1991), 567; Peter C. Mancall, ed., *American Eras: Westward Expansion 1800–1860* (Detroit: Gale, 1999), 87.

58. Vincent Ponko Jr., *Ships, Seas, and Scientists: U.S. Naval Exploration and Discovery in the Nineteenth Century* (Annapolis: Naval Institute Press, 1974).

59. The Library of Congress acquired Fillmore's personal map collection in 1916. See Richard W. Stephenson, "The Millard Fillmore Map Collection," *Map Collector* 12 (1980): 10–15. I am grateful to Edward Redmond, Reference Librarian, Geography and Map Division, Library of Congress, for bringing this article and the Fillmore Map Collection to my attention.

60. Ponko, *Ships, Seas, and Scientists,* 61–62; Scarry, *Millard Fillmore,* 177. Fillmore had planned to present this proposal in his annual address to Congress in December of 1852, but decided to suppress it. The suppressed portion was preserved in writing and is reprinted in Severance, *Millard Fillmore Papers,* 1:313–24.

61. Scarry, *Millard Fillmore,* 209; Kenneth E. Shewmaker, "Daniel Webster and the Politics of Foreign Policy, 1850–1852," *Journal of American History* 63, no. 2 (1976): 309. Webster also asked a clerk in the Department of State, William Hunter Jr., to draft a reply, but it was Everett's letter that formed the basis for the final draft that Webster sent. A draft of Edward Everett's reply is held in the collection of his papers at the Massachusetts Historical Society, Boston, Edward Everett Papers 1675–1910, Guide to the Microfilm Edition, The Massachusetts Historical Society, http://www.masshist.org/findingaids/doc.cfm?fa=fa0264 (accessed April 22, 2009).

62. See Rayback, *Millard Fillmore,* 327–32, for an account of Kossuth. For an account of this visit see Francis and Theresa Pulszky, *White, Red, Black* (1853; repr. New York: Johnson Reprint Corporation, 1970), 1:179. A second copy of Paget's book was purchased in January of 1852.

63. Sean Wilentz, *The Rise of American Democracy: Jefferson to Lincoln* (New York: Norton, 2005), 669. The term "filibuster," related to the Spanish word for pirate, "filibustero," was commonly used in the nineteenth century to refer to unauthorized military campaigns led by private citizens against a foreign country. The use of the word to refer to obstruction of a legislative assembly through prolonged speechmaking came into currency in the late nineteenth century.

64. Richardson, *Compilation of the Messages and Papers,* 5:111–18.

65. In illegal expeditions like the Cuban filibuster, the ship, as well as the people involved, can be held liable and tried; see Antonio Rafael de la Cova, "Cuban Filibustering in Jacksonville in 1851," *Northeast Florida History* (1996): 17–34, for a full account of the trial of the *Pampero;* and Richardson, *Compilation of the Messages and Papers,* 5:152–53. The trial of the *Pampero* was reported by the *New York Daily Times* in the following articles: "The Steamer Pampero," *New York Daily Times (1851–1857),* October 21, 1851, 3; "Trial of the Steamer Pampero," *New York Daily Times (1851–1857),* October 16, 1851, 2; "The Southern Mails—Arrival of the Isabel from Havana at Charleston—Fatal Railroad Accident—The Steamer Pampero Condemned—Destructive Fire at Charleston, &c." *New York Daily Times (1851–1857),* December 24, 1851, 2 (available through *ProQuest Historical Newspapers The New York Times [1851–2005],* ProQuest, Library of Congress, Washington, D.C., http://www.proquest.com/ [accessed August 5, 2008]). The *New York Daily Times* also reported Spain's threat to recall its minister from the United States in "Front Page 3—No Title," *New York Daily Times (1851–1857),* November 12, 1851, 1 (available through *ProQuest Historical Newspapers The New York Times [1851–2005],* ProQuest, Library of Congress, Washington, D.C., http://www.proquest.com/ [accessed August 5, 2008]).

66. Millard Fillmore, letter to Edward Everett, September 23, 1851, Edward Everett Papers, Massachusetts Historical Society, Boston; Edward Everett, letter to Millard Fillmore, September 29, 1851, Millard Fillmore Papers, BECHS; Fillmore appointed Everett as his secretary of state upon the death of Daniel Webster. The list of recommendations from Everett is provided in appendix C. I am grateful to Steven Snell, attorney at law and legal historian, for consulting with me regarding the Cuban filibuster. I am also grateful to Elizabeth Lorelei Thacker-Estrada for supplying me with a photocopy of Fillmore's letter to Everett.

67. Richardson, *Compilation of the Messages and Papers,* 5:156–57.

68. Franck Taylor, letter to President Fillmore, July 9, 1852, Millard Fillmore Papers, BECHS. No author has been identified for *Guide Practique des Consulats.*

69. O'Sullivan was among the proponents of the filibuster who was charged with violating the neutrality act and tried in New York during the spring of 1852. For more about the "young Americans," see Edward L. Widmer, *Young America: The Flowering of Democracy in New York City* (New York: Oxford University Press, 1999).

70. Elise Kirk, *Music at the White House: A History of American Spirit* (Urbana: University of Illinois Press, 1986), 70–71. The packing lists include eighteen volumes of music as having been packed when the Fillmores moved from the White House. Five bound volumes of music that belonged to Mary Abigail Fillmore are now in the Library of Congress Music Library, M1. A15, vols. 112–15, 118. These were probably among those that she had in the White House, since Mary Abigail died just one year and four months after President Fillmore's term ended; furthermore, the pages in these volumes have been numbered by hand in a dark ink that resembles the ink used to inscribe the "Executive Mansion" books. The packing lists also include a "backgammon board, dice, and men."

71. Thomas Corwin was Fillmore's Secretary of the Treasury and had served with Fillmore in Congress. Laura C. Holloway, *The Ladies of the White House; Or, In the Home of the Presidents* (1869, 1882; repr., New York: AMS, 1976), 469–70. Anne Hollingsworth Wharton, *Social Life in the Early Republic* (1902; repr., New York: Benjamin Blom, 1969), 311.

72. Rev. Dr. Prime, "A Week in the White House," *Farmer's Cabinet,* April 22, 1879, [1], available at *America's Historical Newspapers,* Readex, NewsBank, http://www.newsbank.com/readex.

73. William Seale, *The President's House: A History* (Washington, D.C.: White House Historical Association, 1986), 1:377, 379–80; Douglas Wilson, public lecture delivered at the Library of Congress, February 21, 2007.

74. Louis Warren, "A. Lincoln's Executive Mansion Library," *American Bookman,* February 11, 1950, 569–70. Warren provides lists of the books purchased. An undated, unsigned handwritten note in the Lou Henry Hoover papers indicates that funding had been allocated for the library as follows: $2000.00 in 1850, Fillmore; March 1851, $250.00, Fillmore; March 1855, $250.00, Pierce; August 1856, $17.40, Pierce; March 1857, $239.78, Buchanan; March 1859, $32.35, Buchanan; June 1860, $994.93, Buchanan; and March 1861, $264.00, Lincoln. This note is found in the "White House Library—Book List" folder, box 115, Subject Files, Lou Henry Hoover Papers, Herbert Hoover Presidential Library and Museum, West Branch, Iowa. There is an obvious discrepancy between the information in Warren's article and this note. Warren, however, does not cite sources for his information. Further research would be required to try to reconcile these amounts with the Treasury Department records in order to verify their accuracy. A 1932 letter, cited later in this essay, from M. A. Roberts of the Library of Congress cites the same years and amounts for additional funds received for the library. I am grateful to Matthew Schaefer, Archivist at the Herbert Hoover Presidential Library and Museum, for supplying me with photocopies of the relevant documents in the Hoover papers that are cited in this essay. Ruth Painter Randall, *Mary Lincoln: Biography of a Marriage* (Boston: Little, Brown and Co., 1953), 262; I am grateful to Elizabeth Estrada-Thacker for bringing Randall's book to my attention.

75. Lucy Elliot Keeler, "Excursion to Baltimore, Md. and Washington, D.C. , January 18–February 15, 1881," Rutherford B. Hayes Presidential Center, http://www.rbhayes.org/hayes/onlinetexts/display.asp?id=304&subj=onlinetexts (accessed April 22, 2009).

76. Ibid., n.30. See also Lucy Scott West, "Journal of Lucy Scott West at the White House During the Hayes Administration," Rutherford B. Hayes Presidential Center, http://www.rbhayes.org/hayes/onlinetexts/display.asp?id=694&subj=onlinetexts (accessed April 22, 2009); Rutherford B. Hayes, *Diary and Letters of Rutherford B. Hayes,* vol. 3, http://www.ohiohistory.org/onlinedoc/hayes/Volume03/Chapter38/Christmas1880.txt (accessed April 22, 2009).

77. Seale, *President's House,* 2:842.

78. Ainsworth Rand Spofford, letter to President Hayes, June 2, 1877, Rutherford B. Hayes Papers, Rutherford B. Hayes Presidential Center, Spiegel Grove, Fremont, Ohio.

79. Ainsworth Rand Spofford, letter to President Hayes, June 4, 1877, and Ainsworth Rand Spofford, letter to W. K. Rogers, June 8, 1877, Rutherford B. Hayes Papers, Rutherford B. Hayes Presidential Center, Spiegel Grove, Freemont, Ohio. Itemized lists of the documents transferred survive in the archives at the Rutherford B. Hayes Presidential Center. The transaction was also recorded in the exchange register at the Library of Congress. This register shows very few books being transferred to the White House from the Library of Congress. Those that were transferred to the Library of Congress were primarily government documents. See Library of Congress Archives, Copybooks and Letterbooks Book Exchanges, Container 1, 1870–1890, Manuscript Division Library of Congress. Prior to this date other books may have slipped out of the library, either on loan and never returned, inadvertently packed with a president's personal belongings on the end of his term, or through some other means.

80. Ainsworth Rand Spofford, letter to President Hayes, August 6, 1877, Rutherford B. Hayes Papers, Rutherford B. Hayes Presidential Center, Spiegel Grove, Freemont, Ohio.

81. While the gifts and exchange register shows a credit to Hayes for the documents, it does not place a dollar amount on this credit. It does, however, place a dollar amount of $7.95 on the books given to Hayes by the Library of Congress.

82. M. A. Roberts, letter to Dare Stark McMullin, May 14, 1932, Library of Congress Archives Central File, MacLeish-Evans, box 726, "White House Library 1929–49," Manuscript Division, Library of Congress.

83. Robert C. Gooch, Memo to Archibald MacLeish, August 26, 1940, Library of Congress Archives, Central File, MacLeish-Evans, box 726, "White House Library 1929–49," Manuscript Division, Library of Congress.

84. M. A. Roberts, letter to Lawrence Richey, March 13, 1929, and "Library of Congress" folder, box 194, Subject Files, Presidential Papers, Herbert Hoover Presidential Library and Museum, West Branch, Iowa.

85. Lawrence Richey, letter to M. A. Roberts, March 14, 1929, and Lawrence Richey, letter to M. A. Roberts, March 23, 1929, "Library of Congress" folder, box 194, Subject Files, Presidential Papers, Herbert Hoover Presidential Library and Museum, West Branch, Iowa. The transferred books included fifty-one copies of volume 1 of the *Presidential Addresses and State Papers of William Howard Taft,* published in 1910 by Doubleday; and *The Works of Theodore Roosevelt* in six volumes published by Collier and Son in New York from 1913 to 1918. This set included multiple copies of volumes 2 through 6 as follows: 7 of volume 2; 199 of volume 3; 199 of volume 4; 258 of volume 5; and 254 of volume 6. Linn R. Blanchard, letter to Mr. Webster, June 27, 1929, "Library of Congress" folder, box 194, Subject Files, Presidential Papers, Herbert Hoover Presidential Library and Museum, West Branch, Iowa .

86. These lists are found in the "White House Library-Book List" folder, box 115, Subject Files, Lou Henry Hoover Papers, Herbert Hoover Presidential Library and Museum, West Branch, Iowa.

87. No itemized lists of the books in these two collections have been found. What they contained, and when and how they arrived at the Library of Congress, is unclear. Evidence suggests that both collections contained books that were purchased during the Fillmore administration. A dummy is a marker placed on the shelf when a book has been charged out to a department, removed to another storage area, or discovered missing in an inventory; it refers to the book's new location or identifies it as missing. A numbered "deck" in the Library of Congress lexicon refers to a specific storage area.

88. I am grateful to Steve Herman, chief of Collections Access, Loan and Management Division, for locating this memo in his files and for sharing a copy of it with me. Despite numerous inquiries and searching in the Library of Congress archives, no further information has been found about the fate of these two collections or the books that they contained.

89. Robert C. Gooch, memo to Archibald MacLeish, August 26, 1940, Library of Congress Archives, Central File, MacLeish-Evans, box 726, "White House Library 1929–49," Manuscript Division, Library of Congress. The copy of the memo in this file is a draft. I have reproduced the strikethrough as it appears in the draft.

90. Frederick William Ashley, Chief Assistant Librarian, letter to John T. Harrison, April 17, 1931, Library of Congress Archives, Central File, MacLeish-Evans, box 726 "White House Library 1929–49," Manuscript Division, Library of Congress. "Library Chosen for the White House," *New York Times,* April 10, 1930, 34 col. 2–8.

91. Quoted in draft of press release for the "President's Shelf" written by Archibald MacLeish, Library of Congress Archives, Central File, MacLeish-Evans, box 726 "White House Library 1929–49," Manuscript Division, Library of Congress. The entire history of the President's Shelf is documented in this file, which includes a complete list of the books that were selected to stock it. A version of this press release along with the list of books ran in the April 1940 issue of *Cosmopolitan,* 42–43, and was reprinted in the April 1941 issue of *Reader's Digest,* 59–61.

92. "The First White House Library," *UCLA Librarian* 16, no. 26 (1963): 207.

93. *White House Library List,* August 9, 1963, [3].

94. Ibid., [3]–[4]; *The White House Library: A Short-Title List* (Washington, D.C.: White House Historical Association, 1967), 5.

95. The 1967 edition of the list was designed by Joseph Blumenthal, printed by the Spiral Press in New York City, and issued in three bindings: an encased first edition limited to three hundred copies, all signed by First Lady Johnson and priced at $25.00; a hardcover, priced at $5.00, and a paperback priced at $2.50.

96. See *White House Library,* 6; the publication of this edition was announced in the *Library of Congress Information Bulletin* on June 15, 1967. A copy of this bulletin can be found in the Library of Congress Archives, Central File, MacLeish-Evans, box 726 "White House Library 1929–49," Manuscript Division, Library of Congress.

97. William Allman, White House Curator, e-mail to the author, December 11, 2006.

98. Ibid.

99. Ibid.

ABIGAIL POWERS FILLMORE

First Lady of the Library

ELIZABETH LORELEI THACKER-ESTRADA

ABIGAIL POWERS FILLMORE (1798–1853), a private and reserved woman, played a public role in United States history, serving as first lady from 1850 to 1853. During an age when men and women were expected to inhabit "separate spheres"—the public and professional world of men and the private and domestic realm of women—First Lady Fillmore employed her professional and educational experience, along with her considerable domestic skills, to found a library in the Executive Mansion that afforded a semipublic forum for a semiprivate sphere. In doing so, she provided a means of obtaining public recognition and influence for the feminine domain (see figure 2).

Abigail Fillmore lived during an era now associated with the Cult of Domesticity, when—understandably *and* ironically—the expansion of the public sphere helped bring about the idealization of home life. As a private lady in a paradoxically public position, Abigail Fillmore formed a bond with other notable, and in many ways similarly situated, intellectual women of her era, especially women writers, whose best-selling books shared the subject of "women in and of the home." In the library that Abigail Fillmore created, as well as in other White House rooms, prominent nineteenth-century female intellectuals found a place for themselves—literally and figuratively.[1]

The library that the Fillmores founded served to establish prestige and legitimacy for this presidential couple who rose from humble beginnings and came to office on the unexpected death of President Zachary Taylor in July of 1850. In the new library, Abigail Fillmore wove together many of the intellectual, cultural, and artistic strands of antebellum America. It served not only as the physical center of the first lady's activities, but also as the symbolic center of a cultured administration, where they entertained notable politicians, popular authors, and celebrated divas.

I. EDUCATIONAL AND PROFESSIONAL CONCERNS

Abigail had been familiar with books and loved reading from an early age. Born on March 13, 1798, in Stillwater, New York, Abigail Powers suffered the loss of her father, the Reverend

Lemuel Powers, when she was only two years old. Evidently, the sole legacy the Reverend left to his seven children was a library considered substantial for the time. During the first decade of the nineteenth century, Abigail relocated with her family to central New York, where, during the mid-1810s, she became a schoolteacher and at a young age helped to support her family. At an academy in what is now New Hope or Kelloggsville, Abigail taught and continued her studies.[2] Millard Fillmore, born on January 7, 1800, would later recall that by 1818 he "pursued much of [his] study with, and perhaps was unconsciously stimulated by the companionship of, a young lady whom [he] afterward married."[3] The stimulating young lady was, of course, Abigail Powers. Abigail has also been credited with helping to establish a circulating library close to her home in what is now Kelloggsville, New York. Millard shared her interest in books and purchased a $2.00 share in the small circulating library.[4]

American girls, such as Abigail, who were born in the decades immediately following the American Revolution became the first generation of educated women in the United States. Many pursued careers as writers and teachers; some led nineteenth-century reform movements, standing against slavery and promoting women's rights. Abigail later became acquainted with and expressed interest in the work of many of her contemporary female intellectuals, including the educator Emma Hart Willard and the authors Catharine Sedgwick and Lydia Huntley Sigourney.[5]

Abigail and Millard became engaged in 1819, but the young couple prudently delayed marriage for seven years until they could support a family of their own. Millard eagerly pursued the opportunity to clerk in the law office of his father's landlord and sought upward social mobility as the country passed from the elitist years of the Early Republic to the era of the "common man"; Abigail continued to teach, relocating to Lisle, New York, to become the governess to her cousin's three daughters. There she also founded and superintended a select school from 1824 to 1825, where she garnered such notice for her teaching skills that she received a place in the history books of Broome County.[6]

II. DOMESTIC AND INTELLECTUAL PURSUITS

With Millard on his way to becoming a successful "self-made" man, the couple married on February 5, 1826, in Moravia, New York. In their cottage in what is now East Aurora in western New York, Abigail taught school and gained recognition as one of the "prominent pioneers" of Erie County. This endeavor also earned her place in American history as the first presidential wife to work for wages both before and after marriage. She continued to teach until their first child, Millard Powers, whom they called Powers, was born in 1828.[7]

Domesticity, motherhood, and education were integrally linked during Abigail's lifetime. With her background as a teacher, Abigail achieved an ideal advocated by her contemporary, Catherine Beecher, that every woman be trained as an educator. She possessed the perfect qualifications to fulfill what was then considered a primary maternal function, the education of her own children. Her home served as a school for them, and her instruction prepared them for the classroom as it also supplemented their formal learning.[8]

An up-and-coming attorney, Millard was elected to the New York State Assembly in 1828. While he resided in Albany, Abigail remained at home—nearly the entire length of the state away—to raise their son. There she continued her intellectual pursuits alone, writing to Millard, "Have finished studying the maps of ancient geography. O, that you could have been here to have studied with me."[9] When the town of Erie, New York, required a new name to distinguish it from a town of the same name in Pennsylvania, Abigail supplied one, demonstrating both her influence on her husband and her literary interests. Having recently read the works of Lord George Byron, she suggested the name of his ancestral home, Newstead Abbey; as a result, the name of the town changed to Newstead on April 18, 1831.[10]

In 1830, during Millard's service in the assembly, the Fillmores relocated to Buffalo, New York, where they would maintain a home until the end of their lives. Here, the birth of a daughter, Mary Abigail, known as Abbie (sometimes spelled "Abby"), completed the family in 1832. In Buffalo, Millard and Abigail established the pattern of private intellectual pursuits and cultural leadership that they later brought to the President's House. There they kept a home library that prefigured the one that they would establish in the White House. Abigail indulged her love of books, which Millard purchased for her "by the carton," and their library became a "local attraction."[11] The Fillmores proved true to character by donating a large portion of their private collection to the new library of the Young Men's Association, which opened in Buffalo on April 20, 1836.[12]

While Millard served his first term in the United States House of Representatives from December 1833 through March 1835, Abigail again endured another long-distance separation from her husband. She visited Millard in Washington, D.C., during that term, and, as their children matured, lived part of the time with him there during his three subsequent terms, from September 1837 through March 1843.[13]

Because of teachers like Abigail, 90 percent of native-born Americans were literate, able to read and write, by 1840. This, together with the growth of publishing created by the greater availability of capital, technological developments in printing, the mass production of books, and improved transportation and distribution via railroad, enabled writers to readily reach a large national audience. In 1822 Catharine Maria Sedgwick, with her book *A New England Tale,* became one of the first successful American women novelists and one of the best known prior to Harriet Beecher Stowe.[14]

Despite having fought the British in the Revolutionary War and the War of 1812, Americans still looked to Great Britain for examples of culture and taste. The enormous popularity of the writings of Sir Walter Scott points to this influence.[15] Along with many of her generation, Abigail avidly read Scott's works. Even when far away in Washington, she kept track of the circulation of books from the family library in Buffalo. In a May 1842 letter she urgently charged her son Powers with retrieving a Scott book from their friends, the Mayhews: "I recollect that Mrs. Mayhew borrowed one of Scott's novels you may look at the sett [*sic*] and ascertain if it is missing, if it has not been returned <u>fail not</u> to call and get it <u>immediately</u>." She followed up the next month: "Have you ever got that no. of Scott's novel from Mr. Mayhew's if you have not do not neglect it."[16]

In March 1842, while Millard was chair of the Ways and Means Committee, two popular authors visited Washington, D.C.: Charles Dickens and Samuel G. Goodrich. Abigail met Dickens during his tour of the United States, and wrote to her son, "Mr. Dickens or Boz is now in Washington. We attended a party last evening. . . . I was introduced, and had some conversation with him, he is pleasant and very familiar in his manner—of middling height, dark hair, hanging in profusion about his face with a joyous expression of countenance."[17] Abigail and Millard had used Goodrich's "Peter Parley" books to educate their own children. Millard once wrote from Washington to his son in Buffalo, "You must also read Parley's Universal History very carefully and look out all the places referred to on the Atlas. Your <u>Ma</u> will assist you."[18]

With Millard assuming the office of the state comptroller of New York on January 1, 1848, and accepting the nomination for the vice presidency in June of the same year, Abigail increasingly found herself in the same social circles as then prominent women authors and intellectuals. She wrote to her daughter of her meeting with Ann S. Stephens at the Delevan House in Albany, New York: "Our room has been full—Mrs. Ann L. [sic] Stephens has staid [sic] at this house last night and I obtained her autograph for you & she said also that she would send you Mrs. Sigourney's autograph also."[19] Although largely forgotten today, both of these women were very popular during their own time. Stephens edited the *Portland Magazine* (1834–36) and the periodical *Lady's World* (1843), and she wrote *High Life in New York* (1843) under the pseudonym Jonathan Slick. Lydia Huntley Sigourney of Connecticut wrote popular sentimental and pious verses. In addition, she founded schools for young women and enjoyed a lifelong friendship with the noted educator Emma Willard.[20] Abigail also wrote to her daughter of having tea with the latter: "We met Mrs. Willard. I had some conversation with her. Her musick [sic] teacher is a German. . . . She also has the harp taught, and it occurred to me that you might learn musick there & devote your time to it." Willard advocated women's rights and pioneered higher education for women in America. She founded Troy Academy, among other schools for women, and authored a number of books, including the *History of the United States*.[21] The Fillmores would later consider purchasing Willard's book *A System of Universal History* for the White House Library.

As young adults both of the Fillmore children continued their educations in Massachusetts. While Millard Powers studied law at Harvard in Cambridge, Mary Abigail attended Mrs. Sedgwick's School for Girls in Lenox. Administered by the sister-in-law of the novelist and Lenox resident Catharine Sedgwick, it was considered one of the best schools in the country. According to one historian, there "feminism did not have to be articulated; it was inbred."[22] Elizabeth Buckminster Dwight Sedgwick ran the school for thirty years and was herself an author of several educational texts, including *Lessons Without Books* and *A Talk with My Pupils*. In 1847 Abigail accompanied her daughter safely to the boarding school and then returned to New York. She encouraged Abbie to attend the readings delivered by the celebrated actress Fanny Kemble, observing that to "read well one must enter into [the] spirit of the author and talent is necessary to appreciate the writings of Shakespeare." At Mrs. Sedgwick's Abbie became acquainted with Harriet Hosmer, who later employed the skills she honed at the Sedgwick School to become a renowned sculptor.[23]

The Fillmores enjoyed reading many books together; one of these, *The Neighbors: A Story of Every-Day Life,* was by the Swedish author Fredrika Bremer. Millard, who became vice president in March 1849, met the writer during his tenure in this office. Upon Millard's accession to the presidency in July 1850, she reported, "It is believed that this hasty elevation is not welcome to him. It is said that, when he was told of Taylor's death, he bowed his head and said, 'This is my first misfortune!'"[24]

III. Abigail Fillmore and the White House Library

Upon becoming president, Millard met an unanticipated challenge: the Executive Mansion he and his family would occupy contained no books. Although previous presidents, such as Jefferson and Madison, had brought their own books to the Executive Mansion, these libraries had belonged to them personally and thus were not a permanent fixture of the President's House. Millard had depended upon books for his education, and as president of the United States he needed to refer to them during cabinet meetings. Millard proposed the creation of the library not only for himself but also for Abigail, his wife of twenty-four years, in order to provide for her a more congenial home. As a "distinguished lady of Buffalo," presumably Harriet Haven, recollected:

> When Mr. Fillmore entered the White House, he found it entirely destitute of books. Mrs. Fillmore was in the habit of spending her leisure hours in reading, I might almost say in study-ing. She was accustomed to be surrounded with books of reference, maps, and all the other acquirements of a well-furnished library, and she found it difficult to content herself in a house devoid of such attractions. To meet this want, Mr. Fillmore asked of Congress and received an appropriation.[25]

In Victorian America, which idealized the "Common Man" and the "Cult of Domesticity," a family study or library, as indeed the Fillmores' Buffalo home possessed, was essential to a prosperous middle-class home.

In the White House, both the seat of power for the executive branch of government and the home of the president and his family, the masculine, public sphere united with the feminine, private realm. There the new president and first lady worked together to create a library that would serve both professional and domestic needs. Abigail most certainly would have supported Millard's pursuit of government funding for a library in the White House, although she was occupied during the summer of 1850 with closing their Buffalo home and arranging for the care of her invalid sister, Mary.[26] As an early historian of first ladies wrote, Abigail's "intellectual strength, relieved and sustained [Millard's] every effort."[27] When certain congressional legislators perceived the proposed library as a threat to the power of Congress, the book-loving Fillmores overcame their opposition. The library the Fillmores founded in the Executive Mansion served the president and first lady in their official capacities and their family in their leisure and educational pursuits.

The development of the new library involved the entire Fillmore family. Since in the mid-nineteenth century, American presidents had no large, professional staff, the first family's aid and support became especially crucial.[28] Millard initiated the legislation to fund the library. Abigail inspired, at least in part, the creation of the library; probably selected certain books; transformed and decorated the room that housed the library; and presided over family and social events in this room. Powers, who officially served as the private sec-retary to his father, signed the vouchers allocating funds for the library, and Abbie occasion-ally acted as the White House hostess in her mother's stead and performed in the library on the piano and the harp for the pleasure of her family and White House guests (see figures 3 and 4).[29]

Abigail Fillmore performed and expanded upon the traditional role played by presidential wives as manager of the White House. Ever since another Abigail, Abigail Adams, the wife of the second president, John Adams, famously hung laundry in the unfinished East Room, first ladies had determined the function of White House rooms. Dolley Madison obtained congressional funding to transform the first-floor rooms into magnificent public reception chambers. Unfortunately, British soldiers destroyed her work when they burnt down the White House in 1814. The successors to the Madisons, James and Elizabeth Monroe, the latter known as "la belle americaine," decorated the Executive Mansion with elegant French furnishings.

In contrast to these elite first families of the Early Republic, the Fillmores, the first presidential couple to rise from poverty, brought a middle-class, domestic touch to the Executive Mansion. In the words of one White House historian, "Surviving records suggest that only one room was entirely refurnished and redecorated by the Fillmores."[30] Instead of an ornate public state room, Abigail established a comfortable library. In her choice of library location and furniture, Abigail, the wife of a "common man" president, reflected the taste of many Americans of the time, who often favored, perhaps for greater privacy and quiet, separate libraries on the second floor. The oval room on the second floor—which is now called the Yellow Oval Drawing Room and is directly above the famous Blue Room—became the White House Library. Appropriately, this attractive and pleasant room had long been a favorite of first ladies.[31]

Abigail, credited with being a "good housekeeper, like most intellectual women," employed her ingenuity to create an inviting and functional room. The Fillmores shared with other Americans a partiality for mahogany furniture and fine carpets. For the new White House Library, mahogany bookcases were ordered. Influenced by landscape architect Andrew Jackson Downing, whose book *The Architecture of Country Houses* the Fillmores almost certainly read, Abigail further furnished the library by selecting and purchasing from Washington stores "cottage" furniture constructed with oiled walnut frames. This furniture was probably of the jigsaw or "Swiss" pattern popular at that time in the eastern United States. According to one account, under a filthy straw carpet in the room Abigail "found a good Brussels carpet of the old pattern" that she had taken up, cleaned, and relaid. Portions of the room that she could not make presentable, she screened off.[32]

The library became essential to First Lady Fillmore in her roles as supportive wife, caring mother, and White House hostess. Harriet Haven remembered the library functioning as a reception room for guests, a living room for the family, and a refuge for the president: "Here . . . Mrs. Fillmore, surrounded by her books, spent the greater part of her time, and in this room the family received their informal visitors. The President had but little time to give to this library, but he usually succeeded in leaving the executive chamber at 10:30 at night, and spending a pleasant hour in the library with his family."[33] Abbie's childhood friend Julia Miller fondly recalled "quiet evenings in the Library with the Fillmore family and a few intimate friends." She remembered that "after dinner . . . we sometimes spent a few minutes in the Red Room, but usually went upstairs to the Library." The Fillmores spent many hours in the library reading aloud and conversing.[34]

Abigail transformed the White House Library into a music room as well as a reading room by placing Abbie's piano, harp, and guitar in it. Abbie, gifted at both music and languages, played and sang "old-time melodies" with her brother, Powers.[35]

The library shared the second floor not only with the family living quarters but also with the presidential offices, and the room became, under Abigail Fillmore's direction, more than a private gathering place for friends and family. One biographer even claimed, "Mrs. Fillmore's library became the novelty of social life in Washington. Visitors proclaimed it the most comfortable and cheerful room in the official mansion."[36] The library served as a salon with public influence where cultural and political guests mingled and circulated with the Fillmores.

IV. Celebrated Guests and Literary Lions

In the new library, Abigail Fillmore hosted many of the important figures of her day, including such members of the Cabinet as Daniel Webster, Millard's secretary of state. Harriet Haven recalled, "What Mrs. Fillmore most enjoyed was to surround herself with a choice selection of congenial friends in her own favorite room—the library, where she could enjoy the music she so much loved, and the conversation of the cultivated society which Washington at that time certainly afforded."[37] The Fillmore women particularly delighted in presenting musical events whereby they encouraged a cultural presence for the family in Washington. Haven remembered "with more than ordinary pleasure" one evening in which Abigail arranged musical entertainment for several cabinet officers, their wives, and other "distinguished residents of Washington." "Mr. Webster was there, and Mr. Corwin, and Mrs. A. H. H. Stuart, of Virginia, Judge Hall and his wife, and possibly some other members of the Cabinet." Abbie, accompanied by a singer and a harpist, "played the piano with much skill and exquisite taste. Indeed, few ladies excelled her in this accomplishment. . . . Altogether, the music, the conversation, and the company made it an occasion long and pleasantly . . . remembered."[38] First Lady Fillmore's entertainments brought culture to the White House and highlighted the influence of her husband and family.

During the Fillmore presidency, the Executive Mansion, including the library, became a magnet not only for politicians but for musical and literary celebrities. During the first December of their administration, the Fillmores entertained the celebrated singer Jenny Lind, known as "the Swedish Nightingale," and her famous manager, P. T. Barnum. Barnum observed that Lind, who visited the President's House on December 16 and 17, 1850, "was charmed with the unaffected bearing of the President, and the warm kindnesses expressed by his amiable wife and daughter, and consented to spend the evening with them in conformity with their request. She was accompanied to the 'White House' by Messrs Benedict, Belletti and myself, and several happy hours were spent in the private circle of the President's family."[39] An early biographer of the diva described her reaction to the presidential family: "She was received by [the president] with the greatest kindness and cordiality, and after spending considerably more than an hour in his society, and that of Mrs. Fillmore and her daughter, returned with an even more enthusiastic admiration of the Institutions of the States, than she had previously entertained."[40] When Lind, Barnum, and their entourage toured the White House, the Fillmores would almost certainly have mentioned or shown them the nascent library and music room. Two years later, Australian soprano Anna Bishop garnered an invitation to the White House to sing "On the Banks of the Guadalquivir." Popular during the Mexican War, the song was a favorite of the president.[41]

As first lady, Abigail not only admired the talent of women singers but also acted as a patron to women authors. In one of the few surviving letters written while she was first lady, Abigail expressed a particular interest in a popular book that had been sent to her, *Female Poets of America,* edited by Rufus Wilmot Griswold.[42] Abigail's comments evidence both an appreciation for the poetry and a consciousness of her role as the "President's Lady"—as the wife of the chief executive was then known—in encouraging the literary accomplishments of American women: "It was with great pride and pleasure that I saw these samples of the genius of my fellow-countrywomen." Published in numerous editions, the book featured selections of poetry by such well-known women as Julia Ward Howe, Sarah Josepha Hale, Charlotte Cushman, Catherine Beecher, Elizabeth Ellet, and Lydia H. Sigourney.[43]

A shared interest in literature and women's issues no doubt knit a relationship between Abigail and Frances Calderon de la Barca, the wife of the Spanish minister, Angel Calderon de la Barca, that might well have had political repercussions. Frances wrote *Life in Mexico During a Residence of Two Years in That Country* (2 vols., 1843), based on a series of letters home when her husband had been envoy there. The work described her travels and the lives of those around her, particularly those of the women of Mexico.

Following a summer retreat, Abigail returned to Washington in October of 1851 for the start of the social and political season. The *New York Daily Times* reported that "Mrs. Fillmore and family [were] accompanied by the lady of the Spanish Minister."[44] The timing and public notice of this association between the wives of the president of the United States and the minister of Spain occurred at a politically sensitive and even dangerous time. Only two months earlier Cuba, which was then ruled by Spain, had been the target of a filibustering expedition led by Narciso Lopez to annex the island to the United States. In a reflection of his consistent desire to avoid interference by the United States in foreign lands, President Fillmore condemned the expedition. However, Southerners eager to extend slavery generally supported Lopez and had supplied the majority of the forces for the abortive campaign.

In November 1851, just a month following the return to Washington of First Lady Fillmore and Madame Calderon, the Spanish minister communicated a demand from his government. Spain insisted that the United States government invite back the Spanish consul, who had fled from New Orleans to escape the rioters who had attacked the Spanish inhabitants of the city and vandalized their establishments.[45] The Spanish government also demanded that the consul's property and that of other Spanish subjects whose effects were "destroyed by the mob, be restored. In the event of our Government refusing to make this apology, Señor Calderon de la Barca . . . is instructed by his Government to demand his passports. We learn that Mr. Webster refuses to make the required apology in such a shape."[46] Fortunately this diplomatic crisis was resolved, and Angel and Frances Calderon de la Barca remained in Washington. The following year, evidence that relations between the Fillmores and the Spanish minister and his wife remained amicable arrived in the form of an invitation from Madame Calderon to First Lady Fillmore to share a ride in her carriage to attend a camp meeting—a religious gathering—together.[47] As the wife of the president, Abigail may have served as an unofficial diplomat vis-à-vis the wife of the Spanish minister to assuage relations between the United States and Spain.

Another delicate diplomatic situation brought another female writer into the circle of First Lady Fillmore. First President Taylor, then President Fillmore, had offered asylum in the United States to General Louis Kossuth, a leader of the abortive 1848 Hungarian Revolution. Under international pressure, Austria granted the administration's request for release, allowing Kossuth, his wife, Theresa, their children, and his immediate political followers to leave in August 1851 on the American frigate *Mississippi*.[48]

Practical and realistic like his wife, President Fillmore wished to avoid entangling the United States in European affairs. Although he regarded the Hungarian as more of a showman than a statesman, Millard was well aware of the revolutionary's popularity. The Fillmores did their best to welcome the Kossuths to the President's House when he toured the United States. Millard dispatched his son Powers on a mission to meet privately with Kossuth and invite him to the White House, an invitation Kossuth evidently accepted because he subsequently visited the Executive Mansion on more than one occasion. The Kossuth party arrived in Washington on December 30, 1851.[49]

Abigail hosted the Hungarians in early January when the Fillmores held a large banquet and reception in Kossuth's honor in the Executive Mansion.[50] Historian Elizabeth Ellet noted that thirty-six individual place settings had been ordered: "The Secretaries and the ladies—twelve in all—three of the ladies [presumably Abigail, Abbie, and a sister-in-law or niece] belonging to the President's family—the committees of the Senate and House, the President of the Senate and Speaker of the House, with Kossuth and his suite and a few others, made up the number."[51] Not coincidentally, the Fillmores acquired books about Hungary for the White House Library, including *The Memoirs of a Hungarian Lady,* written by Madame Theresa Pulszky, who visited the White House as a member of the Kossuth entourage.[52]

Abigail formed an especially close emotional bond with another woman author, Susan Helen De Kroyft, a native of Rochester, New York. It was reported that Mrs. De Kroyft, who was known as the "Blind Authoress," was brought to the library one evening in 1852 by a friend of First Lady Fillmore.[53] Pleased with the improvement in her vision that she experienced under the care of a doctor whom Abigail had urged her to consult, Helen thanked "President Fillmore's Lady" in an open and effusive letter published in the *New Orleans Daily Delta.* The letter prompted others to write to the Fillmores requesting information and referrals.[54]

The Fillmore Administration concluded with an appropriately literary flourish as two men who were both politicians and published authors joined the Fillmore cabinet, Edward Everett and John Pendleton Kennedy. Following the death of Daniel Webster in October 1852, President Fillmore offered the position of secretary of state to Everett and invited him to dine at the White house.[55] Everett, an accomplished author, orator, and "conservative" Whig known for "profound learning and persuasive eloquence," served as editor of the *North American Review* from 1820 to 1823 and as president of Harvard University from 1846 to 1849. Everett also recommended books to the president for the new library.[56]

John Pendleton Kennedy, who became the new secretary of the navy, had written several popular political satires. His Baltimore home had long enjoyed distinction as a center of social and literary activity, and Kennedy, who knew most of the country's literary elite, brought the "first American man of letters," Washington Irving, into the Fillmores' social circle. A fellow New Yorker and the author of "The Legend of Sleepy Hollow," Irving had first visited the White House almost forty years earlier when Dolley Madison reigned as "First

Lady."[57] Of the Fillmores, Irving wrote, "I have been much pleased with what I have seen of the President and his family, and have been most kindly received by them. Indeed, I should have a heart like a pebble stone, if I was insensible to the very cordial treatment I experience wherever I go. The only fault I find is, that I am likely to be killed by kindness."[58]

The British author William Makepeace Thackeray visited Washington for three weeks in 1853, during the period when President-Elect Franklin Pierce was in Washington, waiting to assume the presidency.[59] That February, President Fillmore attended with Irving and Pierce one of Thackeray's lectures called the "English Humorists" held at Carusi's Hall. Presumably, the literature-loving first lady attended this or another one of Thackeray's lectures as well. Irving's *Works* and reviews of Thackeray's novels in the periodical literature lined the shelves of the White House Library. Irving, Thackeray, and Pierce attended various events at the White House hosted by President and First Lady Fillmore during their final days in office.[60] Of these days, Irving recalled:

> I was present at the going out of one Administration and the coming in of another; was acquainted with both Presidents and most of the members of both Cabinets, and witnessed the inauguration of General Pierce. It was admirable to see the quiet and courtesy with which this great transition of power and rule from one party to another took place. I was at festive meetings where the members of the opposite parties mingled socially together, and have seen the two Presidents arm in arm, as if the sway of an immense empire was not passing from one to the other.[61]

Irving soon surmised that "poor Mrs. Fillmore must have received her death-warrant while standing by my side on the marble terrace of the Capitol, exposed to chilly wind and snow, listening to the inaugural speech of her husband's successor."[62] Abigail Powers Fillmore died of bronchial pneumonia less than a month after leaving the White House.[63] Yet the library that she and her husband established remained as the heart of the Executive Mansion in the upstairs oval room conveniently situated between the first family's private living quarters and the official offices of the president.

V. CONCLUSION

Abigail Fillmore's lifelong love of books, her professional career as an educator, and her skill as a homemaker culminated in the establishment of a library in the Executive Mansion. By following the historical precedents set by first ladies such as Abigail Adams and Dolley Madison, Abigail fashioned a room in the White House that served as a library, music room, and salon. Family, friends, and other distinguished guests visited this library, where Abigail not only wove together the continuous literary, professional, and domestic threads of life, but where she also knit together separate strands of antebellum society and culture. Events in the library, such as musical entertainment provided by the women of the president's family for his cabinet members and other guests, reflected both the feminine, domestic domain of the first lady and the public, political world of the president. In the library specifically and the White House generally, the all-American, middle-class Fillmore family hosted elite international political, literary, and musical celebrities. Many of the Fillmore guests, including Jenny Lind, P. T. Barnum, William Makepeace Thackeray, and Washington Irving, retain their interest and their fame to the present day. Despite her historical reputation as a passive invalid, in reality Abigail Fillmore actively designed the library, hosted visitors, and brought culture to the White House.

The public, especially women, perceived Abigail as an intellectual and wrote to the former schoolteacher for "advice and assistance" concerning education and schools.[64] The presence of this learned first lady in her library provided other prominent and intellectual women access to the White House and encouraged the recognition of their talents and causes. The Fillmores supported the efforts of the respected mental health care reformer Dorothea Dix, a frequent and welcome guest. In 1852 she won an appropriation to establish the Government Hospital for the Insane, now known as St. Elizabeths Hospital, in Washington, D.C.[65] Abigail nurtured relationships with women authors and praised their writings. In support of the political goals of her husband's administration, Mrs. Fillmore even practiced unofficial diplomacy with two women writers: Frances Calderon de la Barca and Theresa Pulszky. Indeed, a book by Madame Pulszky was purchased for the White House Library, and books by other women found places in the library collection.

First Lady Fillmore established the precedent for subsequent presidents and their wives to maintain a library in the White House. Despite the untimely death of its patron, the Fillmore library survived for decades to serve future first families. To this day, a room in the White House is officially designated as a library. No longer controversial as it was when first proposed in 1850, the library in the White House is a traditional and long-cherished room thanks to the efforts of Millard and Abigail Fillmore.

NOTES

1. Mary Kelley, *Private Woman, Public Stage: Literary Domesticity in Nineteenth-Century America* (New York: Oxford University Press, 1984), ix.

2. Robert J. Scarry, personal conversation, October 11, 2000.

3. Frank H. Severance, ed., *Millard Fillmore Papers* (1907; repr., New York: Kraus Reprint Co., 1970), 1:11.

4. Kristin Hoganson, "Abigail (Powers) Fillmore," *American First Ladies: Their Lives and Their Legacy*, ed. Lewis L. Gould (New York: Garland, 1996), 155; Scarry, personal conversation; Severance, *Millard Fillmore Papers*, 1:9.

5. Mary Beth Norton, *Liberty's Daughters: The Revolutionary Experience of American Women, 1750–1800* (Boston: Little, Brown, 1980), 288.

6. Robert J. Rayback, *Millard Fillmore: Biography of a President* (1959; repr., East Aurora, N.Y.: Henry Stewart for the Buffalo Historical Society, 1972), 7–9; H. Perry Smith, *History of Broome County, with Illustrations and Biographical Sketches of Some of Its Prominent Men and Pioneers* (Syracuse, N.Y.: D. Mason and Co., 1885), 417.

7. H. Perry Smith., ed., *History of the City of Buffalo and Erie County, with Illustrations and Biographical Sketches of Some of Its Prominent Men and Pioneers*, vol. 1, *History of Erie County* (Syracuse, N.Y.: D. Mason and Co., 1884), 547; Karen O'Connor, Bernadette Nye, and Laura Van Assendelft, "Wives in the White House: The Political Influence of First Ladies," *Presidential Studies Quarterly* 26 (1996): 838.

8. Thomas Woody, *A History of Women's Education in the United States* (New York: Science Press, 1929), 1:109; Carl Bode, *American Life in the 1840s* (Garden City, N.Y.: Doubleday, 1967), 89.

9. Abigail Fillmore, letter to Millard Fillmore, January 18, 1830, qtd. in Charles M. Snyder, *The Lady and the President: The Letters of Dorothea Dix and Millard Fillmore* (Lexington: University Press of Kentucky, 1975), 30.

10. Thomas H. McKaig, "Place Names of Western New York," *Niagara Frontier* 1, no. 3 (1954): 65; J. H. French, *Gazetteer of the State of New York: Embracing a Comprehensive View of the Geography, Geology, and*

General History of the State, and a Complete History and Description of Every County, City, Town, Village, and Locality (Syracuse, N.Y.: R. P. Smith, 1860), 292.

11. Sol Barzman, *The First Ladies* (New York: Cowles, 1970), 125; John J. Farrell, ed., *Zachary Taylor, 1784–1850 [and] Millard Fillmore, 1800–1874: Chronology, Documents, Bibliographical Aids* (Dobbs Ferry, N.Y.: Oceana, 1971), 51.

12. Joseph B. Rounds and Michael C. Mahaney, *The Time Was Right: A History of the Buffalo and Erie County Public Library, 1940–1975* (Buffalo, N.Y.: Grosvenor Society, 1985), 3; Rayback, *Millard Fillmore*, 45.

13. Millard Fillmore, letter to Nathan K. Hall, June 7, 1834, and Abigail Fillmore, letter to Mary Powers, June 17, 1834, Millard Fillmore Papers, MS 3, Penfield Library, Special Collections, State University of New York at Oswego, Oswego, N.Y. (hereafter Millard Fillmore Papers, SUNY Oswego). The second letter was microfilmed with 1837 correspondence.

14. Mary P. Ryan, *The Empire of the Mother: American Writing About Domesticity, 1830–1860* (New York: Harrington Park Press, 1985), 14; Kelley, *Private Woman, Public Stage*, 7–8, 14; Russel Blaine Nye, *Society and Culture in America, 1830–1860* (New York: Harper and Row, 1974), 99.

15. Bode, *American Life*, 90.

16. Abigail Fillmore, letter to Millard Powers Fillmore, May 28, 1842, and Abigail Fillmore, letter to Millard Powers Fillmore, June 20, 1842, Millard Fillmore Papers, MS 3, SUNY Oswego.

17. Abigail Fillmore, letter to Millard Powers Fillmore, March 11, 1842, Millard Fillmore Papers, MS 3, SUNY Oswego. Although "[March 4, 1842]" was later written at the top of the letter, the original date on the letter is March 11, 1842.

18. Millard Fillmore, letter to Millard Powers Fillmore, May 5, 1838, Millard Fillmore Papers, MS 3, SUNY Oswego; the work referred to is probably Samuel G. Goodrich, Nathaniel Hawthorne, and Elizabeth Manning Hawthorne, *Peter Parley's Universal History, on the Basis of Geography: For the Use of Families* (Boston: American Stationers' Company, John B. Russell, 1837).

19. Abigail Fillmore, letter to Mary Abigail Fillmore, January 7, 1848, Millard Fillmore Papers, MS 3, SUNY Oswego.

20. Virginia Blain, Patricia Clements, and Isobel Grundy, eds., *The Feminist Companion to Literature in English: Women Writers from the Middle Ages to the Present* (New Haven: Yale University Press, 1990), 983.

21. Abigail Fillmore and Millard Fillmore, letter to Mary Abigail Fillmore, June 20, 1848, Millard Fillmore Papers, MS 3, SUNY Oswego (the quoted portion of the letter was written by Abigail); Carl Bode, *The Anatomy of Popular Culture: 1840–1861* (Berkeley and Los Angeles: University of California Press, 1959), 236.

22. Dolly Sherwood, *Harriet Hosmer: American Sculptor, 1830–1908* (Columbia: University of Missouri Press, 1991), 20.

23. Abigail Fillmore, letter to Mary Abigail Fillmore, November 7, 1847, Millard Fillmore Papers, MS 3, SUNY Oswego; Sherwood, *Harriet Hosmer*, 19.

24. Millard wrote to a friend in 1843: "Mrs. F. has been reading Neighbors since my return and desired me to read with her but I find so little time that I fear we shall never finish it. It is very interesting indeed. I wish you were here to read with her" (Millard Fillmore to Miss Milligan, March 17, 1843, John Story Gulick Collection of American Statesmen, Manuscripts Division, Department of Rare Books and Special Collections, Princeton University Library, Fillmore Papers microfilm, roll 9); Fredrika Bremer, *The Homes of the New World; Impressions of America* (New York: Harper and Brothers, 1853), 449.

25. Harriet Haven was the wife of Millard's law partner in his Buffalo practice, Solomon Haven. Solomon Haven also served in Congress while Fillmore was President. Qtd. in Laura Carter Holloway, *The Ladies of the White House* (New York: U.S. Publishing, 1870), 505.

26. Earlier accounts of the library have asserted that First Lady Fillmore hosted dinners at which she and the president persuaded congressmen to support the proposed legislation to fund the library. However, historians differ as to her whereabouts in mid-September 1850, when the dinner is reported to have taken place. See Francis de S. Ryan, "Centennial of the White House Library," 1950, photocopy, Office of the Curator, the White House, Washington, D.C., 1; William Seale, *The President's House: A History* (Washington, D.C.: White House Historical Association, 1986), 1:289–90; Robert J. Scarry, *Millard Fillmore* (Jefferson, N.C.: McFarland, 2001). One contemporary newspaper reported on October 28, 1850, that "the White House as yet has had no lady tenant under this administration, Mrs. Fillmore not having been in Washington since the death of General Taylor." *Trenton (N.J.) State Gazette*, 2.

27. Holloway, *Ladies of the White House*, 499.

28. According to Benson Lee Grayson, "the support he received from his family made Fillmore's responsibilities as president easier to bear" (*The Unknown President: The Administration of President Millard Fillmore* [Washington, D.C.: University Press of America, 1981], 56).

29. Scarry, *Millard Fillmore*, 323, 375. "To this Christian lady the White House is indebted for the books which to-day make the library one of the most attractive rooms in the presidential mansion" (James Grant Wilson, ed., *The Presidents of the United States* [New York: D. Appleton and Co., 1894], 258). Abigail reportedly ordered "full sets of Dickens and Thackeray" as well as "a broad list of histories and other standard works" ("The First White House Library," *UCLA Librarian* 16, no. 26 [1963]: 207). These sets of works by Thackeray and Dickens were probably purchased by the first lady for the family's personal library; no records indicate that books by Thackeray or Dickens were purchased for the White House Library.

30. Seale, *President's House*, 1:291.

31. William Ryan and Desmond Guinness, *The White House: An Architectural History* (New York: McGraw-Hill, 1980), 183.

32. Elisabeth Donaghy Garrett, *At Home: The American Family, 1750–1870* (New York: Harry N. Abrams, 1990), 64–65; Seale, *President's House*, 1:292, 294; 2:1097; Anne Hollingsworth Wharton, *Social Life in the Early Republic* (Philadelphia: J. B. Lippincott, 1902), 310; Esther Singleton, *The Story of the White House* (New York: McClure, 1907), 2:14–15; Edna M. Colman, *Seventy-Five Years of White House Gossip from Washington to Lincoln* (Garden City, N.Y.: Doubleday, 1925), 233; Ryan, "Centennial of the White House Library," 2.

33. Qtd. in Bess Furman, *White House Profile: A Social History of the White House, Its Occupants, and Its Festivities* (Indianapolis: Bobbs-Merrill, 1951), 156.

34. Qtd. in Wharton, *Social Life in the Early Republic*, 310, 311.

35. Holloway, *Ladies of the White House*, 505; Wharton, *Social Life in the Early Republic*, 311.

36. Mary Ormsbee Whitton, *First First Ladies, 1789–1865: A Study of the Wives of the Early Presidents* (1948; repr., Freeport, N.Y.: Books for Libraries, 1969), 246.

37. Qtd. in Holloway, *Ladies of the White House*, 506.

38. Qtd. in ibid., 506–7; Thomas Corwin served as the Secretary of the Treasury, Alexander Hugh Holmes Stuart served as the Secretary of the Interior, and Nathan Hall served as the Postmaster General.

39. P. T. Barnum, *Struggles and Triumphs: Forty Years' Recollections* (Hartford, Conn.: J. B. Burr & Company, 1869), 310.

40. C. G. Rosenberg, *Jenny Lind in America* (New York: Stringer and Townsend, 1851), 87–88.

41. William Porter Ware and Thaddeus C. Lockard Jr., *P. T. Barnum Presents Jenny Lind: The American Tour of the Swedish Nightingale* (Baton Rouge: Louisiana State University Press, 1980), 53; Elise K. Kirk, "Nightingales at the White House," *Opera News* 45 (1980): 18–19.

42. Thomas H. Bryant, letter to Millard Fillmore, December 26, 1850, Millard Fillmore Papers, MS 3, SUNY Oswego.

43. Abigail Fillmore, letter to Mrs. John Bryant, January 26, 1851, Millard Fillmore Papers, MS 3, SUNY Oswego. The Fillmore White House library contained books by four female authors: Mary Cowden Clarke, Maria Edgeworth, Julia Pardoe, and Theresa Pulszky; it also included Griswold's *The Prose Writers of America* and *The Poets and Poetry of America*. See "Catalogue of the First White House Library" for their entries.

44. "From Washington—The next Presidency—Daniel Webster—Return of Mrs. Fillmore &c.," *New York Daily Times*, October 11, 1851, 2. The Spanish Minister to the United States, Angel Calderon de la Barca, had married the Scottish-born Frances Inglis in 1838. He had served as Spain's first envoy to Mexico after that country had won its independence.

45. Philip S. Foner, *A History of Cuba and Its Relations with the United States*, vol. 2, *1845–1895: From the Era of Annexationism to the Outbreak of the Second War for Independence* (New York: International Publishers, 1963), 61.

46. "Important if True," *New York Daily Times*, November 12, 1851, 1.

47. "Washington: Reconciliation Dinner," *New York Daily Times*, November 25, 1851, 2; Frances Calderon de la Barca, letter to Abigail Fillmore, [1852], Millard Fillmore Papers, MS 3, SUNY Oswego. (The year 1852 has been added in a different handwriting to this letter; no more exact date has been determined for it.)

48. John Robert Irelan, *History of the Life, Administration, and Times of Millard Fillmore, Thirteenth President of the United States*, vol. 13 of *The Republic; or, a History of the United States of America in the*

Administrations, From the Monarchic Colonial Days to the Present Times (Chicago: Fairbanks and Palmer, 1888), 285–86; Scarry, *Millard Fillmore,* 209–10.

49. Scarry, *Millard Fillmore,* 210–11; "Kossuth," *New York Daily Times,* December 9, 1851, 1; Francis and Theresa Pulszky, *White, Red, Black: Sketches of American Society in the United States* (New York: Redfield, 1853), 1:173. I am grateful to Dr. Catherine M. Parisian for bringing this book to my attention.

50. The date of this banquet is uncertain. Theresa Pulszky records it as January 6, yet the *Farmer's Cabinet* reported that it took place January 3. Pulszky and Pulszky, *White, Red, Black,* 178–79; "Presidential Dinner to Kossuth," *Farmer's Cabinet,* January 14, 1852, 2. In his private correspondence Daniel Webster recorded on December 30, 1851: "the President invites him [Kossuth] to dine on Saturday, &c." If Kossuth accepted this invitation the dinner would have occurred on January 3. *The Private Correspondence of Daniel Webster,* ed. Fletcher Webster (Boston: Little, Brown and Co., 1875), 2:501–2.

51. Elizabeth F. Ellet, *Court Circles of the Republic or the Beauties and Celebrities of the Nation* (Hartford, Conn.: Hartford Publishing, 1871), 439. A native New Yorker, Ellet was known as "the first historian of American women" (Lina Mainiero, ed., *American Women Writers* [New York: Frederick Ungar, 1979], 1:581).

52. The Pulszky book was purchased on January 2, 1852; see entry in "Catalogue of the First White House Library." Coincidentally, Melvil Louis Kossuth Dewey, who developed the Dewey Decimal classification system, was born in 1851, during the visit of the popular Hungarian revolutionary to the United States, and was named in his honor.

53. W. J. Burke and Will D. Howe, *American Authors and Books: 1640 to the Present Day,* 3rd rev. ed. (New York: Crown, 1972), 160; Susan Helen De Kroyft, *A Place in Thy Memory* (New York: John F. Trow, 1850), 1; Ryan, "Centennial of the White House Library," 4.

54. Whitton, *First First Ladies,* 245; George Turner, letter to Millard Fillmore, January 5, 1853, and Julia Hart, letter to Abigail Fillmore, March 9, 1853, Millard Fillmore Papers, MS 3, SUNY Oswego. De Kroyft either enjoyed no further improvement in her vision or the improvement was not permanent. In the words of *Appleton's Cyclopaedia of American Biography,* published in 1887, during De Kroyft's lifetime, "She has never recovered her sight" (*Appleton's Cyclopaedia of American Biography* [New York: D. Appleton and Co., 1887], 2:127).

55. Millard Fillmore, letter to Edward Everett, October 25, 1852 ("The President and Mrs. Fillmore request the favor of Mr. Everett's company at dinner on Thursday 18th inst. At 6 o'clock"), and Millard Fillmore and Abigail Fillmore, letter to Edward Everett, November 12, 1852, Edward Everett Papers, Massachusetts Historical Society, Boston. Everett was later the featured speaker at the Gettysburg dedication on November 19, 1863. President Abraham Lincoln delivered brief, follow-up remarks, which later became known as "The Gettysburg Address."

56. Ben Perley Poore, *Perley's Reminiscences of Sixty Years in the National Metropolis* (Philadelphia: Hubbard Brothers, 1886), 1:80; Catherine M. Parisian. "The White House Collection," 23.

57. The Fillmores owned Kennedy's works *Swallow Barn* and *Horseshoe Robinson* in their personal collection; see "Catalogue of the First White House Library," entry 195, for Kennedy's *Life of William Wirt;* Rayback, *Millard Fillmore,* 365; Amy La Follette Jensen, *The White House and Its Thirty-Five Families* (New York: McGraw-Hill, 1970), 72. President Zachary Taylor reportedly was the first to use the term "First Lady," in 1849 during his oration at Dolley Madison's funeral (Robert P. Watson, *The Presidents' Wives: Reassessing the Office of First Lady* [Boulder, Colo.: Lynne Rienner, 2000], 7).

58. Pierre Monroe Irving, *The Life and Letters of Washington Irving* (New York: Putnam, 1869), 3:218.

59. Inauguration day took place in March until 1937.

60. Charles H. Bohner, *John Pendleton Kennedy: Gentleman from Baltimore* (Baltimore: Johns Hopkins University Press, 1961), 208–9; Eyre Crowe, *With Thackeray in America* (London: Cassell, 1893), 116. See the "Catalogue of the First White House Library," entry 82, for Washington Irving and the set of his works that were purchased for the White House. Thackeray dined at the White House on February 24, 1853 (Edgar F. Harden, *A William Makepeace Thackeray Chronology* [Basingstoke, Eng.: Palgrave Macmillan, 2003], 261). Irving was "at the last reception of President Fillmore" on February 25, 1853 (Irving, *Life and Letters of Washington Irving,* 3:221). The Fillmores held a dinner in honor of Pierce on February 28, 1853. A telegraphic dispatch dated February 27 states: "President Fillmore gives an elegant entertainment tomorrow to the President-elect. Messrs. Atchison, Soule and Hunter, of the Senate, and other distinguished Senators, a like number of Representatives, and the prospective Cabinet will be in attendance. On the part of the President, this is a graceful finality of his Administration" (Special Dispatch to the *New York Daily Times,*

"LATEST INTELLIGENCE: By Telegraph to the New-York Daily Times. Presidential Festivities—Marriage of Attorney General Crittenden," *New York Daily Times,* February 28, 1853, 4.

61. Irving, *Life and Letters of Washington Irving,* 3:227.

62. Ibid., 3:229.

63. Coincidentally, on March 30, 1853, the day Abigail Fillmore died, Harriet Beecher Stowe, a major exponent of "literary domesticity," set sail for England, thus extending the international influence of American women writers ("Departure of the Canada—Mrs. Stowe on Board," *New York Daily Times,* March 31, 1853, 1).

64. Charlotte Ward, letter to Abigail Fillmore, January 7, 1852, Millard Fillmore Papers, Buffalo and Erie County Historical Society; Susan Kirkpatrick, letter to Abigail Fillmore, February 20, 1852, Millard Fillmore Papers, MS 3, SUNY Oswego.

65. Dorothy Clarke Wilson, *Stranger and Traveler: The Story of Dorothea Dix, American Reformer* (Boston: Little, Brown, 1975), 197.

Creating a Room for
the Collection

WILLIAM G. ALLMAN

THIS BIBLIOGRAPHIC STUDY is a testament to the efforts of President Millard Fillmore and
First Lady Abigail Fillmore in 1850 to secure a library of books for the President's House.
Although the books that they acquired with a $2,250 congressional appropriation are listed
by title on surviving vouchers, less is known about the setting in which they placed their
new White House Library.[1] In the absence of engraved or photographic depictions of the
room at that time, vouchers and inventories and later images provide what information
can be used to construct a picture, admittedly an incomplete one, of how the Fillmore
"Library" looked.

The books were given a home on the second floor, then the uppermost level of the
house. The room selected was the oval drawing room, the largest room on that floor, something of a buffer between the seven western rooms that served as bedrooms for the first
family and the five rooms to the east that were the presidential offices and waiting rooms
until the 1902 creation of the now famous West Wing. One of the most distinctive architectural features of the White House, as designed by James Hoban in 1792, is the stack of
large elliptical rooms, one on each of the three original floors, at the center of the south side.
The best known of these is the Blue Room, the principal drawing room on the State Floor;
but when John and Abigail Adams moved into the unfinished President's House in 1800, its
second floor counterpart was the handsomely decorated "ladies' drawing room" in which
the first New Year's Day reception was held in 1801. In subsequent decades, that upstairs oval
room was often used as a retreat for women guests after dinners held downstairs, but as
a result of the efforts of the Fillmores in 1850, it acquired the name "Library" that it would
retain until well into the twentieth century.[2]

Some of the original books—a set of ten at the White House, others at the Library of
Congress—still exist, but unfortunately there are no furnishings that can be said with cer-
tainty to have survived from the Fillmore library.[3] In the collection of the Millard Fillmore
House in East Aurora, New York, there is a bookcase said to have been used at the White
House. Although vouchers do document the acquisition of five bookcases, one can only
speculate on the accuracy of the provenance of this particular bookcase. It seems unlikely

that when the Fillmores left in 1853 they would have taken with them one of the bookcases installed for their prized White House Library, created not just for their own use, but for the enjoyment of future families as well. It is possible, however, that when the Fillmore-era bookcases were replaced, some before 1866, all by at least 1869, one could have been disposed of at one of the occasional sales or auctions of old or "decayed" White House property and then found its way to New York state. It is also possible that this bookcase was a family piece Fillmore either brought to the White House from the residence he occupied as vice president or acquired personally while he was president, in either case removable upon the family's departure.

The vouchers tell us something about the bookcases that the Fillmores acquired with government funds for their new library. Washington cabinetmaker William McLean Cripps provided two bookcases in August 1850, even before funds were officially appropriated to buy books, and three more in January 1851. The first purchase consisted of "1 Mahogany Book Case 10 ft $187.50" and "1 Mahogany Book Case $50." The second purchase consisted of "2 circular bookcases and one center $250 [collectively]."[4] None of these appear in the room by the time the earliest photo of it was taken in the late 1870s, one showing a new suite of bookcases acquired in 1869 early in the administration of President Ulysses S. Grant (in place until 1902 [see figure 11]).[5]

The earliest image of the room seems to be an expansive 1866 engraving from *Frank Leslie's Illustrated Newspaper* with identifiable elements indicating that the artist had some firsthand access to the room (see figure 12). That wood engraving shows three bookcases. A tall one with seven shelves in four sections, standing against the east wall north of the fireplace, might be the "10 ft" bookcase of 1850, the stated dimension being height rather than width.[6]

That image also shows a pair of shorter, more architectural bookcases—each with six shelves in four sections—flanking the doorway in the west wall. One of these might have been the less costly bookcase in the 1850 purchase, perhaps with a later mate. If those two depicted bookcases had been made to fit against the curved walls of the room, however, then the 1851 descriptor "circular" might have been used to indicate that they were curved, not in fact round. Otherwise, the depicted pair of cases may have been a post-Fillmore addition.

The walls available for the installation of bookcases were segmented by eight elements—three doors, one fireplace, and, curiously, five windows. Three exterior windows at the south end, sheltered somewhat by the South Portico, looked out onto the South Lawn. At the opposite end of the room, however, the doorway to the transverse Center Hall was flanked by two interior windows. Although these windows (eventually converted to shelf niches in the 1930s) may have been intended to provide light into the central hall, the earliest photos show fabric hanging behind the glazing and doors backing the windows on the hallway side.

Again, in the absence of an image, vouchers help indicate something about what Mrs. Fillmore hung at those five windows. An inventory taken in December 1849, just seven months before the death of President Zachary Taylor catapulted her husband into the presidency, provides timely documentation of what furnishings would have been available to her on her arrival at the White House (the next inventory would not be taken until 1865, after significant post-Fillmore changes to the room). According to the 1849 inventory, curtains hung at all five of the tall windows. These were presumably made of dimity or another fabric of light color, low cost, and ready availability since, during refurbishing work in late 1851, Washington supplier David Baird billed a very modest $3.50 for "making 1 new set of curtains for library," a set that presumably joined four pairs of curtains already in place.[7]

Although there seem to have been no heavy ornamental draperies, Mrs. Fillmore did enliven the window hangings when Baird billed $15 for "making 5 new window valances for library." It would seem these were not soft fabric swags, but of a rigid form, possibly set within the window reveals, made of an undocumented ornamental fabric mounted on pasteboard that Baird also supplied. The only suggestion of color in the room is the "red cambric lining" used by Baird for the valances.[8] Two years later, in 1853, the Franklin Pierces would acquire five new gilded window cornices for the room, which may have replaced or just capped the Fillmore valances. With the acquisition of expensive new curtains for President James Buchanan in 1858, however, any elements of the hangings of the Fillmore library almost certainly vanished. In 1862 a newspaper article reported that "Green is the color that predominates in the room," but it is undetermined if a green palette remained from 1850–51 or had been adopted during the changes made later in the decade.[9]

What else might Mrs. Fillmore have kept from among the furnishings itemized in the 1849 inventory? Seat furniture in 1849 consisted of four "lounges" and ten "gilt chairs," the latter possibly some of the thirty-eight French chairs purchased by James Monroe for the Blue Room in 1817 or possibly the ubiquitous small fancy chairs. The "27 yards Gimp for repairing library chairs at 12½¢ [per yard]" provided by David Baird in 1851 could have been a stockpiling of upholstery supplies, but it would seem more likely that it was intended to repair existing seat furniture. The only room-specific new piece was "1 mahogany tete a tete for library," an S-shaped settee in which two people would sit in opposite directions but could chat "head to head" across the center. Provided by Baird at $60, this piece does not appear, however, in the 1866 engraving.[10]

On the same bill, however, Baird provided an eight-piece suite of seat furniture described as "2 french sofas in hair cloth" at $90, accompanied by two "large arm chairs" at $70, two "small arm chairs" at $50, and two ottomans at $18. That it appears on the same bill with library acquisitions identified by room is not sufficient proof that it was purchased for the library, since the bill also included some bedroom furnishings. The 1866 print, however, shows a pair of oval-back Renaissance-revival sofas, still in the White House collection, that were described in the 1867 inventory as "2 large leather-covered old sofas," while the late-1870s photo shows that there were at least two matching side chairs (none extant) and one matching armchair (two extant) in the room. No ottomans can be seen in either image. Thus one can only wonder if the "old sofas" in 1867, the existing pair, date back to the Fillmores, and if that Baird-supplied suite, described as having two each of large and small armchairs, in fact had two armchairs and two side chairs. If so, the two sofas and two armchairs could be artifacts of the Fillmore library.[11]

Of the tables in the room in 1849—two center tables and two pier tables—all four probably were replaced by the various bookcases acquired by Mrs. Fillmore. Although Baird provided "1 set quartette tables for do. [the Library] 10.00," such a compact nest of four tables, easily separable for use around the room, also does not show in the 1866 engraving.[12]

Cripps and Baird each provided one piece of furniture especially suitable for a library. From Cripps in 1850 came "1 Mahogany Map Stand $12" (no room specified on the voucher), while Baird provided "1 mahogany atlas stand for library" at $12.50 in April 1852. A four-legged book stand and a tripod map rack that might have been these pieces show at the left side in the 1866 print, joining the bookcases depicted as objects that might have been Fillmore acquisitions.[13]

The first globe of the Earth in the White House may be the one acquired in 1851 from the book funds (no globes had been listed in the preceding inventories—1801, 1809, 1825, and 1849). Two globes, one large and one small, were listed in the 1865 inventory and show in the 1866 engraving. The small globe, depicted in a cradle on a tripod pedestal, was possibly the "Terrestrial Globe 18 inches" provided by one of the booksellers, Franck Taylor of Washington, D.C.[14]

Lighting came from a chandelier, powered by gas since 1848, reflected in a pier glass hanging over the mantel, all elements that were presumably retained from prior administrations. In 1853 the mantel and mirror that the Fillmores would have known were replaced when the Pierces installed a statuary marble mantel and a new gilded overmantel mirror that may have complemented the new window cornices provided by the same vendor. That same year the ceilings of the most prominent rooms, including the library, were ornamented with fresco work, as seen in the 1866 print and 1870s photo (eliminated by 1882). In 1858 a new twelve-light "Gothic" gasolier was installed for President Buchanan (in place until 1902).[15]

There was no mention in the 1849 inventory of rugs, carpeting, or other floor covering. Esther Singleton, in her well-researched 1907 book, *The Story of the White House*, included a report about the Fillmores, with the unusual warning "if we may credit the following [unreferenced] account": "The great room over the Blue Room was covered with a star carpet made filthy by tobacco-chewers. Underneath this was found a good Brussels carpet of the old pattern, a basket of roses upset. Mrs. Fillmore had this cleaned." Whatever carpet Mrs. Fillmore had in the room, however, it was replaced by a costly Axminster acquired for the Pierces in 1853 (it would be replaced at least one time more before the late 1870s photo, for the Grants in 1870, and at least three times again before 1902).[16]

The Fillmores purchased from official funds a seven-octave rosewood piano,[17] but it probably replaced the piano traditionally located in the Red Room on the State Floor. The piano that Mrs. Fillmore would have found in the Second Floor oval room may have remained in the house, but it was replaced in the library by Mrs. Fillmore's own piano. As was noted in the conclusion of the description begun above, "She sent to Buffalo for her piano and Abigail's harp, shut off much of the space with screens, and with a wood fire and comfortable surroundings made the place very pleasant [both instruments now located at the Fillmore House in East Aurora]."

In 1862 the above-mentioned article in the *Daily Alta California* reported that "the President's library is chastely and not extravagantly finished."[18] In light of the more elaborate post-Fillmore additions to the room in 1853 (marble mantel, gilded mirror and window cornices, and frescoed ceiling) and in 1858 (draperies and chandelier), one can only wonder how plain the 1862 observer would have found the Fillmores' original library. No matter how the room looked, the new library collection undoubtedly served to improve a house that in December 1850 President Fillmore dubbed "this temple of inconveniences."[19]

NOTES

1. In accordance with Appropriation of September 30, 1850—$2,000 "For the purchase of a library to be preserved in the Executive Mansion"—account 105,133, vouchers 1–7, 1850–51, $1,730.36; account 107,754 ($269.64 remaining from 105,133, plus additional $250 appropriated March 3, 1851), vouchers 1–7, 1851–52, $346.60, and account 109,399, vouchers 1–4, 1851–52, $173.04. Also see account 105,579, vouchers 1–2, 1850, $65.62 of preappropriation book purchases. Records of the Accounting Offices of the Department of the Treasury, Office of the First Auditor, Settled Miscellaneous Treasury Accounts, September 6, 1790–September 29, 1894, RG 217. National Archives at College Park, Md. (hereafter AODT, OFA, SMTA, September 6, 1790–September 29, 1894, RG 217, NACP).

2. William Seale, *The President's House* (Washington, D.C.: White House Historical Association, 1986), 1:291–92. In the annual *Inventory of Property in and Belonging to the Executive Mansion* (Office of the Curator, The White House), the room was called the "Library" (1910–43) or "Library-Study" (1944–49) even after the 1935 creation of a new "Library" on the ground floor. After the Truman renovation it was called "President's Study" (1952–61). Now it is called the Yellow Oval Drawing Room.

3. The ten-volume set that remains in the White House is *The Library of American Biography,* conducted by Jared Sparks, 10 vols. (New York: Harper and Brothers, 1848), purchased from Charles Welford, December 13, 1850, account 105,133, voucher 5, $17—inscribed "Executive Mansion 1850," White House Collection.

4. William McLean Cripps bill of August 30, 1850, account 105,580, voucher 8, December 30, 1850; and bill of January 27, 1851, account 107,778, voucher 4 AODT, OFA, SMTA, September 6, 1790–September 29, 1894, RG 217, NACP.

5. John R. Hunt bill of October 6, 1869, for "2 Walnut winged bookcases in Ebony & oil, french plate glass $480" each and "4 Walnut book cases, Ebony & oil, french plate glass $160" each, account 174,469, voucher 1, AODT, OFA, SMTA, September 6, 1790–September 29, 1894, RG 217, NACP. Room photographs show a pair of larger winged bookcases (two-door wide center with narrow single-door wings), a narrower winged bookcase, and a pair of lower two-door cabinets. Although the bookcases purchased do not fully match the bill voucher description, there is no other room in the house for which such a purchase would have been made.

6. "The President's Library at the White House, Washington, D.C." after a drawing by C. E. H. Bonwill, *Frank Leslie's Illustrated Newspaper,* July 7, 1866. This very wide-angled view shows interior windows at the sides that are in fact opposite the outermost exterior windows at the center rear. Only the north door and the narrow sections of wall between it and the flanking interior windows are not shown.

7. "Inventory of Furniture &c in the President's House [January 21, 1849]," Records of the Commissioners of Public Buildings & Grounds, RG 42, National Archives Building, Washington, D.C. (hereafter RCPBG, RG 42, NAB); David Baird bill of November 1, 1851, account 107,778, unnumbered voucher, April 29, 1852, AODT, OFA, SMTA, September 6, 1790–September 29, 1894, RG 217, NACP.

8. Baird bill of November 1, 1851.

9. L. R. Menger bill of November 17, 1853, for five cornices for the library, account 113,810, voucher 8, AODT, OFA, SMTA, September 6, 1790–September 29, 1894, RG 217, NACP. G. Vollmer bill of December 16, 1858, for "5 Library window curtains Royal Rep lined with silk," account 134,023, voucher 28, February 10, 1859, AODT, OFA, SMTA, September 6, 1790–September 29, 1894, RG 217, NACP. "The Lincolns Redecorate the White House," *Daily Alta California* [San Francisco], May 12, 1862.

10. Baird bill of November 1, 1851.

11. Baird bill of November 1, 1851; "Inventory of furniture &c in the President's House [c. February 28, 1867]," Letters Received, vol. 39, #3,813, RCPBG, RG 42, NAB.

12. Baird bill of November 1, 1851.

13. Cripps bill of August 30, 1850; Baird bill of April 24, 1852.

14. "Inventory Taken at President's House, May 26th, 1865," Letters Received, vol. 38, #3,713, RCPBG; RG 42; NAB. Franck Taylor, for globe, bill of August 6, 1851, account 107,754, voucher 3, AODT, OFA, SMTA, September 6, 1790–September 29, 1894, RG 217, NACP.

15. Ferris & Taber bill of October 12, 1853, for "1 Statuary Marble Mantel for Library," account 113,688, voucher 2; L. R. Menger bill of November 17, 1853, for mirror frame for the library, account 113,810, voucher 8; Cornelius & Baker, bill of December 13, 1858, for a library chandelier, account 134,023, voucher 25, February 8, 1859; AODT, OFA, SMTA, September 6, 1790–September 29, 1894, RG 217, NACP.

16. Esther Singleton, *The Story of the White House* (New York: McClure, 1907), 2:14–15; Seale, *President's House,* 2:318; William S. Mitchell bill of January 8, 1870, for library carpet, account 176,596, voucher 1, January 10, 1870, AODT, OFA, SMTA, September 6, 1790–September 29, 1894, RG 217, NACP.

17. William Hall & Son, account 107,778, voucher 8, March 22, 1851, AODT, OFA, SMTA, September 6, 1790–September 29, 1894, RG 217, NACP.

18. "The Lincolns Redecorate the White House."

19. MF letter to Solomon Haven, December 20, 1850, White House Collection.

Millard Fillmore and His Booksellers

Catherine M. Parisian

THE HISTORY OF ANY LIBRARY would be incomplete without a discussion of the booksellers who helped to acquire and supply its books. Quite naturally, the story of the first White House Library is intimately connected with the history of bookselling in America. Unfortunately, because the letters and personal papers of booksellers from the nineteenth century have often not been collected, much of the documentation of their history has been lost. In fact, very few inside, firsthand accounts of the mid-nineteenth-century American book trade survive. Since their letters were directed to the president, however, some correspondence of the booksellers who supplied the first White House Library has been preserved among Millard Fillmore's personal papers. These letters provide insight into the relationships that Fillmore developed with his booksellers and offer an unusual glimpse into the day-to-day operations of the contemporary book trade, revealing some of the networks in which business was conducted and some of the practices that were customary among trade members.

Although Fillmore purchased books for the White House from ten different booksellers, he spent over 90 percent of the total funding with just five, Little and Brown, Charles Welford, George Putnam, Taylor and Maury, and Franck Taylor; Fillmore made one-time purchases from five other booksellers. The very first books that he bought for the library were from George Crosby of Philadelphia; he ordered a Bible, an atlas, and a dictionary. Fillmore purchased two titles directly from their publishers, a complete run of Stryker's *American Register* from James Stryker of Baltimore and the *Official Opinions of the Attorneys General* from Robert Farnham of Washington, D.C. These were both expensive multivolume sets that might have been obtained at the lowest price by ordering through their publishers. Fillmore also purchased an atlas from William Morrison, a map dealer in Washington, and a map from John Prendon, also of Washington.[1]

I. LITTLE, BROWN AND COMPANY

The Boston firm Little, Brown and Company, founded in 1837 and continuing in business today, supplied the White House with books worth nearly $920—40 percent of the total budget for the library. It was the leading publisher of law books in nineteenth-century America, and accordingly, twenty-nine of the fifty-nine titles that the White House purchased from this firm were legal texts, a genre that tended to be priced higher than others and that often included large, costly multivolume sets. Furthermore, Fillmore purchased from Little and Brown complete runs of the *Edinburgh Review, Niles's Register,* and *Blackwood's Magazine,* which were also expensive sets.[2]

While many of the books purchased from Little and Brown were acquired in December of 1850 by Charles Lanman, the purchasing agent whom Fillmore commissioned to help with the library, Fillmore's relationship with Little and Brown may have begun much earlier. As a lawyer in Buffalo, a statesman in Albany, and a congressman in Washington, Fillmore would have been familiar with the firm's reputation for publishing quality legal works and may even have purchased books from it for his own library. The first correspondence between Fillmore and Little and Brown, however, dates from November of 1850, when, after learning from Asbury Dickens, secretary of the Senate, that Fillmore's copy of the "Statutes at Large" did not contain an index, Little and Brown sent copies of this index to the president. The correspondence that ensued points to Fillmore's meticulous nature and his belief that books should be functional. Upon receiving the index, Fillmore brought what he perceived as an error in it to Little and Brown's attention. The firm replied graciously, thanking Fillmore for "communicating to us what appeared to be an oversight." They directed, however, that "on opening to the head 'President of the U. S., pp. 140–1 Index we find 'to sell certain armed Vessel, II 402,'" acknowledged that it "might have been proper to have indexed the act under several heads," and promised "in our next Ed. we will place it also under that of 'Vessels &.'" Fillmore purchased books from Little and Brown on three more occasions after Lanman's buying trip.[3]

Fillmore's recommendation when it came to books must have carried some clout, since on at least two occasions he endorsed titles for publishers; one of these was for Little and Brown's edition of the *English Law and Equity Reports.* James Brown himself wrote to Fillmore on April 9, 1851, outlining the publication plan for the reports and explaining that "The enterprise is a great one, & at the prices we fix on vols. we shall require a large sale to enable us to carry out our plan. My object in addressing you this note is to ask if you still feel an interest in the success of such a work if you will give me a line in approbation of it which we may use." Fillmore granted Brown's request, and his letter praising the reports appears in several of Little and Brown's advertisements for the publication. In addition, Fillmore endorsed Webster's *Dictionary* for G. and C. Merriam; his praise appeared on the front paper wrapper.[4]

II. CHARLES WELFORD AND SYLVANUS G. DEETH

Charles Welford, an established New York book dealer, supplied $580.74 in books to the White House Library. He had gone into business in 1840 with John Russell Bartlett at 7 Astor House in Manhattan, where their shop became a resort for the literary men of the day, with James Fenimore Cooper and Fitz-Greene Halleck visiting on nearly a daily basis. Operating under the name Bartlett and Welford, the firm dealt mainly in English and foreign books and kept a large stock of inventory. It is possible that Fillmore had become acquainted with Bartlett and Welford during one of his earlier visits to New York City or during the time he spent in Washington as a congressman. The firm had made several contacts in Washington and in 1844 had hoped to become agents for the Library of Congress; although there is no evidence that they ever succeeded, they distributed the publications of the notable Washington printer Peter Force, who was also one of their primary customers. If not Whigs themselves, Bartlett and Welford had Whiggish sympathies, which may have led them to publish their catalogue in the *American Whig Review,* one of the periodicals purchased for the White House Library, a periodical that also reviewed a number of Bartlett and Welford's publications.[5]

Bartlett established a lasting friendship with Fillmore when he was appointed the United States Commissioner on the United States and Mexico Boundary Survey Expedition in 1849. Although the partnership of Bartlett and Welford was dissolved with Bartlett's appointment to the expedition, Welford continued in the bookselling business until 1852, when the entire stock of the firm was sold at an auction by Bangs and Company in New York in October and November of that year. Welford later joined the firm Charles Scribner's Sons and served as their London agent for many years.[6]

Another bookseller, Sylvanus G. Deeth of New Brunswick, New Jersey, became involved with the first White House Library when Welford purchased periodicals from him for the Executive Mansion. Deeth, a self-proclaimed "thorough Whig," also had connections in Washington.[7] He too corresponded with Peter Force and later opened a business in the capital at the former premises of George Templeman, the bookseller who had provided the president with a quote for congressional documents.[8]

A purchase of periodicals for the library, involving Deeth and Welford, demonstrates how dealers sometimes collaborated to supply books to their customers and how these collaborations sometimes went awry. In the fall of 1850 Deeth quoted Fillmore prices for complete runs of the *North American Review, Hunt's Magazine,* the *Whig Review,* and the *Democratic Review.* The president, in turn, gave the estimate to Lanman with the instruction to make the purchase, which Lanman did through Welford. On December 23, 1850, Deeth wrote a confrontational letter to the president insinuating that a 20 percent discount from the prices he had quoted for the periodicals had been demanded in the president's name.[9] In March, Fillmore replied that according to his records he had actually paid slightly more than the price Deeth had originally quoted for these periodicals and that Welford had supplied him with a copy of the receipt from Deeth.[10] Fillmore turned to Lanman for an explanation of this transaction. Lanman, in turn, inquired of Welford, who replied with two letters, one from himself and one from his salesman, A. A. Moore. The two accounts agree that a discount was granted for payment in cash—as was customary among members of the trade—yet they differ on the point of whether Welford and Moore proposed the discount or Deeth offered it. Apparently, no conclusion was ever reached as to whom, if anyone, was at fault in this misunderstanding. The correspondence surrounding this purchase, however, reveals how what appears to be a simple transaction on the vouchers, in fact was a complicated business deal involving three booksellers, one agent, and the president.[11]

The delay between Deeth's confrontational letter in December and Fillmore's reply and investigation of the matter in March and April may be related to the commission to purchase books for the library in the territory of New Mexico. Funding for this library had been approved in September 1850 along with the funding for a library in the territory of Utah and the library in the Executive Mansion. Deeth had petitioned Fillmore in October of 1850 for the commissions to purchase books for all three libraries. He informed the president that he had a thorough knowledge of the "book mart" from Washington to Maine, an expertise that he had gained through twenty-five years of experience in the trade.[12] Along with this petition, Deeth enclosed several letters of recommendation. At that time, Fillmore replied that he had already appointed someone for Utah, was not yet ready to appoint anyone for New Mexico, and planned to handle the purchases for the Executive Mansion himself. In December, Deeth reminded Fillmore of his earlier petition for the post in New Mexico, and on April 26, he visited the president at the White House regarding this matter. Rumors must have been circulating that an appointment was imminent, because within three days, two other agents requested the same commission, Charles Lanman on April 23, and Taylor and Maury on April 26. Who finally received the appointment has not yet been discovered.[13]

III. George P. Putnam

George P. Putnam sold only $174 worth of books to the White House; these were purchased by Lanman on his initial buying trip for the library. Putnam significantly influenced the publishing industry in the United States and had agents in Washington from whom Fillmore purchased a number of books. As a teenager, Putnam worked for various New York firms, and as an adult he became an active member of the trade, encouraging trade journals, arranging dinners, and serving as secretary of the first international copyright association in the United States. One of his trade publications, Putnam's *Bookbuyer's Manual,* may have been used in selecting books for the White House Library.[14] In 1840 he formed a partnership with John Wiley that lasted for nearly seven years. After its dissolution in 1847 Putnam embarked on his first successful independent publishing venture, an edition of Washington Irving's works, which was to be one of the titles purchased from Putnam for the White House Library. Putnam thereafter garnered a reputation for publishing some of the best-known American literary authors. He followed up with President Fillmore on one occasion by offering to procure foreign books or works of art for him in London and Paris. No evidence survives to suggest that the president took him up on this offer. Fillmore was not an art collector, and it certainly would have been more convenient to procure books locally—just down the street in fact—from Putnam's Washington correspondents, Franck Taylor and Taylor and Maury, with whom Fillmore kept running accounts.[15]

IV. Taylor and Maury and Franck Taylor

While the president purchased only $77.35 worth of books from the firm Taylor and Maury, he spent $280.06 with Franck Taylor. It is tempting to assume that Franck Taylor was also the Taylor of the firm Taylor and Maury, however, the two businesses were often referred to as discrete enterprises, and the two Taylors, although possibly related, were probably separate individuals. George P. Putnam named the two separately in his list of Washington correspondents on the front wrapper of his catalogue of April 1850, and at least one published book bears the name of both businesses as distinct entities in its imprint: "Published by

F. Taylor and Taylor & Maury." Furthermore, Franck Taylor mentioned Maury and Taylor in the third person in a letter to Fillmore with which he filled an order and tactfully hinted at some displeasure over being the president's second choice: "I send Paget's work on Hungary by the bearer, understanding from him that he did not find it at Taylor & Maury's." Nevertheless, the two booksellers certainly knew each other; Waite's *Washington City Directory* for 1850 lists both booksellers operating in the northwest quadrant of the city on Pennsylvania Avenue, just a few doors apart, and Franck Taylor mentions borrowing "Mr. Maury's" *London Catalogue* when he had loaned his own to the president.[16]

Although little more is known about Taylor and Maury, Franck Taylor was a prominent bookseller in Washington, D.C., who was known as "a man of culture and judgment, and whose knowledge of books was esteemed by those whose literary tastes brought them into contact with him." He began his career with another Washington bookseller, Pishy Thompson, and succeeded him as proprietor of the Waverly bookshop, which, like Bartlett and Welford's shop in New York, served as a meeting place for the "literary and artistic element" in the city, where many congressmen and politicians—including the prominent Whigs Daniel Webster and Henry Clay—were daily visitors. Taylor and Fillmore may have known one another during Fillmore's terms in Congress (1833–35, 1837–43), and they certainly knew each other while he was vice president.[17] Millard wrote to Abigail in April of 1850 informing her that Taylor notified him that the plays that Abbie wanted were unavailable in Washington. After Fillmore became president, Taylor carried on a regular correspondence with him, sending him books on approval and at times lending books for his use. As the vouchers reveal, Fillmore purchased some of the first books for the White House Library from Taylor and continued to purchase books from him throughout his presidency.[18]

Taylor and Fillmore's relationship proved mutually beneficial. On at least two occasions Taylor requested Fillmore's assistance in gaining government appointments, once for a friend and once for himself. In a letter thanking the president for helping to gain a position for a friend on the United States and Mexico Boundary Survey Expedition, Taylor revealed his own Whiggish inclinations when he congratulated Fillmore on his succession to office: "Nobody has seen you arrive at the Presidency with more pleasure than myself, nor been more glad to see the Whig party standing on its own legs at last for the <u>first</u> time." The following month, on September 11, 1850, Taylor asked the president to mention him favorably to the governor of Utah for the commission to purchase the library for the new territory. Taylor may not have known that when the bill with the proposition for the Utah library would become a law on September 30, it would specify that the president would appoint the purchasing agent. Although it is unknown who finally received this appointment, Fillmore indicated on October 23 that it had already been made. Perhaps Taylor obtained the position if only because he was the first to ask for it.[19]

While Taylor relied upon Fillmore's assistance with these two official appointments, Fillmore, on more than one occasion, sought Taylor's advice on matters related to the library. He turned to Taylor when he needed books relating to consular establishments in the aftermath of the Cuban filibuster.[20] He borrowed Taylor's *London* catalogue when he was reviewing the titles that Lanman sent on approval, and he consulted Taylor regarding the cost of importing works from London while he was making purchases for the library through Lanman. Taylor's response to Fillmore's query about importing books placed the president in a better position to evaluate the prices quoted to him through Lanman. Taylor informed, "A book which costs me in London a pound sterling costs here just about six dollars and a few cents <u>more</u> or <u>less</u> according to circumstances over which I have no control, always however a little more than that when they come by steamer. I speak now of a book which costs <u>me</u> a Pound Sterling, one which <u>retails</u> for that sum in London costing me here less than six dollars by the amount of reduction which I obtain as a bookseller from the retail price."[21] Later in this letter Taylor added, "If you should wish me to import them or any of them. I should charge ten percent on the actual cost to me whatever that might be."[22]

Importing a book from London, therefore, increased its wholesale price by about 20 percent in the United States, since a book that sold wholesale in London for one pound, or $4.87, would have sold wholesale in the United States for $6.00.[23] The dealer would then add another 10 percent to the wholesale value before it reached the consumer. This, at least, was the mark-up that Taylor quoted to the president; it may have been higher for other retail customers. Taylor noted that shipping by steamer was slightly more expensive than by "packet." Steam navigation reduced the time that it took to cross the Atlantic from over a month to just a few days, but the speedier journey did not come without a surcharge.

Fillmore must have inquired about the prices of books that he was contemplating purchasing for the library. Taylor proceeded to inform the president that "this copy of the Edinburgh review therefore would cost me here more than seventy and less than eighty dollars if by packet—Eighty dollars and possibly a portion more if by steamer." He advised, "With regard to the Encyclopedia Americana as mentioned in the letter, it may be said that the price named there is far from the cheapest one. I doubt indeed if the highest price named be not so." When the *Edinburgh Review* and the *Encyclopaedia Americana* were included on the lists that Lanman sent from Boston and New York just a few days later, Fillmore would have known the fair price for these sets from his correspondence with Taylor.[24]

President Fillmore made his final purchase for the library from Frank Taylor on an account that ran from July of 1851 into March of 1853. The book, John MacGregor's *Commercial Statistics* in five volumes, complemented MacGregor's *Progress of America* that had been purchased from Welford by Charles Lanman two years earlier. Entered on the voucher February 12, 1853, it must have arrived at the White House on February 14, the date inscribed in its front pastedown. On March 2, just two days before the inauguration of President Franklin Pierce, Fillmore settled the account.

V. CONCLUSION

By supplying books for the first White House Library Franck Taylor, Taylor and Maury, George P. Putnam, Sylvanus G. Deeth, Charles Welford, and Little and Brown all played significant roles in its founding. Together they collaborated with the president as they quoted prices, lent books, made recommendations for purchase, jockeyed for positions, and plied trade networks that spanned London, Paris, Boston, New Jersey, New York, and Washington, D.C. Through the dynamics of these relationships, we see Fillmore actively engaged in assembling the first White House collection from August of 1850, just after he took office, through to the final days of his presidency.

NOTES

1. The Washington, D.C., booksellers who supplied the first White House Library were located in close proximity to one another on Pennsylvania Avenue in the northwest quadrant of the city. Waite's *Washington Directory* for 1850, a directory that Fillmore purchased for the White House, lists Franck Taylor and William Morrison between 4½ and 6 west Pennsylvania Avenue, Taylor and Maury between 9 and 10 west, and Robert Farnham at the corner of 11 west. Prendon's name does not appear in the Washington directories of the period.

2. The firm established itself in 1837 as Charles C. Little and James Brown; in 1847 it changed its name to Little, Brown and Company; today it is commonly referred to as Little Brown. The firm signed its letters to President Fillmore "Little & Brown," and I hereafter refer to it as Little and Brown.

3. Little and Brown, letter to President Fillmore, November 2, 1850, and Little and Brown, letter to President Millard Fillmore, November 9, 1850, Millard Fillmore Papers, BECHS, Buffalo, N.Y. (hereafter Millard Fillmore Papers, BECHS). Fillmore's letter to Little and Brown has not been located. No closing single quotation mark appears in the original after "President of the U. S."

4. James Brown, letter to President Fillmore, April 9, 1851, Millard Fillmore Papers, BECHS. Fillmore's letter of endorsement was reprinted in an advertisement in *The American Almanac and Repository of Useful Knowledge for the Year 1852* and in other Little and Brown catalogues of the period. See the Smithsonian copy of the 1850 edition of Webster's Dictionary for an example, q PE1625. W382a 1850.

5. John Russell Bartlett, *Autobiography of John Russell Bartlett (1805–1886)*, ed. Jerry E. Mueller (Providence: John Carter Brown Library, 2006), 23–24. I am grateful Nan Summer-Mack, Assistant to the Director for Programs and Development at the John Carter Brown Library, for supplying me with a copy of this book. An announcement for Bartlett and Welford's catalogue bound into the journal appears in *American Whig Review* 4, no. 2 (1846): 213, available at http://cdl.library.cornell.edu/cgi-bin/moa/moa-cgi?notisid= ABL5306-0004&byte=234601251 (accessed May 21, 2009). The catalogue itself, however, was not digitized. For correspondence between Peter Force and Charles Welford see the Peter Force Papers, Series I, Manuscript Division, Library of Congress. John D. Haskell Jr., "John Russell Bartlett: Bookman" (Ph.D. diss., George Washington University, 1977), 36.

6. Bartlett, *Autobiography*, 171 n.37; Haskell, "John Russell Bartlett," 59.

7. Sylvanus G. Deeth, letter to President Fillmore, October 23, 1850, Millard Fillmore Papers, BECHS.

8. See "The White House Collection," 9, 19, for more about Templeman's estimate. When Deeth requested the commission to purchase libraries for the U.S. government, he gave Peter Force as a reference (see letter to President Fillmore, October 23, 1850). Deeth's advertisement in the *Washington and Georgetown Directory* of 1853 gives his location as the "late residence of Geo. Templeman's," and announces that he specializes in Congressional documents, miscellaneous books, and full sets of *Niles's Register;* see *Washington and Georgetown Directory, Stranger's Guide-Book for Washington* (Washington, D.C.: Kirkwood and McGill, 1853), 28, 88. I am grateful to Elizabeth Lorelei Thacker-Estrada for bringing this entry to my attention. By 1860 both men had passed away. Deeth's books were sold by the Washington auction house of James C. Maguire and Company on March 20, of that year. The title page of the auction catalogue advertises the collection as "*belonging to the Estate of the late* SYLVANUS G. DEETH, *and embracing the Collection of the late* GEO. TEMPLEMAN."

9. Sylvanus G. Deeth, letter to President Fillmore, December 23, 1850, Millard Fillmore Papers, BECHS. Deeth closed this letter: "A few offers of essential books for any Public Library are enclosed. New Brunswick N. J. December 23, 1850." No record of what these books were has been discovered.

10. Severance, *Millard Fillmore Papers*, 2:310.

11. W. M. Moore, letter to Charles Lanman, April 22, 1851, and Charles Welford, letter to Charles Lanman, April 22, 1851; both of these are enclosed in Charles Lanman, letter to President Fillmore, April 23, 1851, Millard Fillmore Papers, BECHS.

12. Sylvanus G. Deeth, letter to President Fillmore, October 23, 1850.

13. Although Fillmore's reply to Deeth's October letter does not survive, he penciled his answer across the left-hand margin of Deeth's letter; Sylvanus G. Deeth, letter to President Fillmore, April 26, 1851, Millard Fillmore Papers, BECHS. Lanman may have received the appointment; on November 27, 1852, he wrote to Putnam: "The Spanish Minister has requested me to make out a list of books, suitable for a miscellaneous Library, the purchase of which will be consigned to my hands." He requested from Putnam a copy of

the *Bookbuyer's Manual* to help him in this endeavor. This letter is in the G. P. Putnam Collection, box 10, folder 61, Rare Books and Special Collections at the Princeton University Library. Charles Lanman, letter to President Fillmore, April 23, 1851, and Taylor and Maury, letter to President Fillmore, April 26, 1851, Millard Fillmore Papers, BECHS.

14. See "Bibliographical Methods," 79.

15. Ronald J. Zboray, "Putnam, George Palmer," *American National Biography Online* (Oxford: Oxford University Press, 2000), http://www.anb.org/articles/16/16-02475.html; George P. Putnam, letter to President Fillmore, May 5, 1851, Millard Fillmore Papers, BECHS.

16. The Houghton Library at Harvard University holds a copy of Putnam's April 1850 catalogue in its original wrappers. On February 8, 1851, Putnam wrote to the president acknowledging receipt of payment for the books that Lanman had purchased and directing him to return Plutarch's *Lives* through Taylor and Maury. William Lunt, *A Discourse, Delivered in The City of Washington, in the Unitarian Church, November 30, 1851* (Washington, D.C.: F. Taylor and Taylor and Maury, 1851). Franck Taylor, letter to President Fillmore, December 12, 1851, Millard Fillmore Papers, BECHS. Franck Taylor, letter to President Fillmore, December 27, 1850, Millard Fillmore Papers, BECHS.

17. "Washington Booksellers," *Washington Post (1877–1954)*, February 17, 1895, 15; I am grateful to Stephen Ferguson, Assistant University Librarian for Rare Books and Special Collections and Curator of Rare Books, Princeton University Library, for bringing this article to my attention.

18. Millard Fillmore, letter to Abigail Fillmore, April 1, 1850, Millard Fillmore Papers, MS 3, Special Collections, Penfield Library, SUNY at Oswego, Oswego, N.Y., Microfilm Edition of the Millard Fillmore Papers (Buffalo, N.Y.: BECHS, 1975), roll 17, ser. 1. I am grateful to Elizabeth Lorelei Thacker-Estrada for bringing this letter to my attention.

19. Franck Taylor, letter to President Fillmore, August 22, 1850, and Franck Taylor, letter to President Fillmore, September 11, 1850, Millard Fillmore Papers, BECHS. See above, 64.

20. See "The White House Collection," 23.

21. Franck Taylor, letter to President Fillmore, December 10, 1850, Millard Fillmore Papers, BECHS.

22. Taylor requests the return of his *London Catalogue* in Franck Taylor, letter to President Fillmore, December 27, 1850, Millard Fillmore Papers, BECHS.

23. Lawrence H. Officer, "Dollar-Pound Exchange Rate from 1791," MeasuringWorth, 2008, http://www.measuringworth.com/exchangepound/ (accessed July 7, 2009).

24. Franck Taylor, letter to President Fillmore, December 10, 1850, Millard Fillmore Papers, BECHS; Little and Brown's price on the *Edinburgh Review*, $116 for eighty-three volumes, was considerably higher than that quoted by Taylor, yet without the knowledge of the condition of both sets and the number of volumes for which Taylor provided an estimate, a fair comparison cannot be made.

Bibliographical Methods

CATHERINE M. PARISIAN

WHEN HISTORIANS IN THE LATE NINETEENTH AND EARLY TWENTIETH CENTURIES wrote about the founding of the first White House Library, they usually relied on the recollections of Harriet Haven, a friend of First Lady Abigail Fillmore.[1] She remembered how Abigail regularly spent time reading and studying in the library in her Buffalo home and that, finding no books in the White House, the first lady and the president petitioned Congress for funding to establish a library and thereby make the White House a more comfortable and inviting home. Later historians turned to the debates over the funding for the library as recorded in the *Congressional Globe*. Senator Alfred Pearce's claim that "not even a Bible" had been purchased for the President's House resounds through many narratives of the library. More recently, historians have referred to the Treasury Department records to make generalizations about the contents of the library. While the foregoing scholars have considered First Lady Fillmore's role in the founding of the first White House Library, none have fully accounted for its contents and evaluated its significance in the intellectual milieu of mid-nineteenth-century America. President Millard and First Lady Abigail Fillmore's accomplishment in establishing this library deserves to be better understood. Moreover, until now, the relics of this portion of the United States' cultural and intellectual history have been all but lost, dispersed among various repositories and archives.[2]

All relevant documentary sources have been consulted in order to reconstruct the history of this library and explain its role and importance within the social, political, and intellectual context of mid-nineteenth-century America. This catalogue contains 195 entries that account for 193 books, 1 terrestrial globe, and 1 map that were purchased for the library during the Fillmore administration. Each entry includes annotations that discuss the book's reputation and relevance at midcentury and a bibliographical description of a representative copy of each book that has been identified to have been purchased for the library. These descriptions enable readers to better understand the contents of the library and to identify other copies of editions of the titles that composed the original White House collection. They also provide useful information to scholars of the printing, publishing, and reading history of the period.

I. IDENTIFICATION OF THE CONTENTS OF THE LIBRARY

Vouchers from the Treasury Department archives served as the primary sources for compiling this catalogue. The vouchers provide itemized lists of the books that were purchased and include short titles, the number of volumes (with some exceptions), the price, and the seller (see figure 5). Most of the purchases made by the Fillmores for the library drew on funds allocated by Congress for this purpose and were charged to the "account of the Library in the Executive Mansion." These purchases are filed under three different numbers, one for each year that Fillmore was in office: 105,133; 109,399; and 107,754. The first purchases, however, were made prior to the approval of congressional funding for the library and were charged to the "account of furnishing the President's house," under account number 105,579. Although the Treasury Department records supply substantial information, they identify books only by short titles, without specifying editions.[3]

For 190 titles, it has been possible to determine with varying degrees of certainty the edition that was purchased by consulting sources that supplement the limited information in the vouchers. Two catalogues of the Executive Mansion library have provided publication information for 140 of the books purchased, one dating from 1877 and compiled under the direction of President Rutherford B. Hayes (1877–81), and another dating from circa 1903 and compiled during the presidency of Theodore Roosevelt (1901–9).[4] Other means were used in an effort to ascertain the editions for the remaining 53 titles. The *RLG Union Catalogue* and *WorldCat* databases were consulted along with the *National Union Catalog* (*NUC*) in order to generate a list of the editions that would have been available in 1850 for each title.[5] Booksellers' catalogues and reference sources from the period were also consulted in an attempt to find the editions that most closely match the price indicated on the voucher. The prices, however, usually do not match exactly. Most of the catalogues contain a statement in the front explaining that discounts are offered on large orders.[6] The identification of editions was further complicated by the fact that often the catalogues and trade references of the period do not specify a publisher or date of publication, but only provide the city of publication, and in some cases, just the country. Despite these drawbacks, these resources, used in conjunction with one another, made it possible to reach reasonable conclusions regarding 50 of 53 titles not identified in the two catalogues of the Executive Mansion library.

The Hayes Catalogue. The Hayes Catalogue is the earliest extant catalogue of the Executive Mansion library and contains entries for 140 of the 193 books that were purchased for the White House Library under the Fillmore administration (see figure 6). Bound in calf with red, marbled endpapers, the catalogue consists of 336 pages. The second front free endpaper bears the signature "R. B. Hayes" with the date 1877 written beneath, indicating the year that it was compiled. It probably remained in the White House until at least 1900, the date written next to an entry on page 267. As new books were acquired, they were recorded in it, and changes in location were duly noted. Most books are listed in it by their author; some are also recorded under subject headings and some under their title, all in one alphabet. Sometimes an entry cross-references another entry for the same title. As a result of this organization, there are often several entries for the same book. Shelf marks, consisting of a letter followed by a number, are included for most of the books. In this system, commonly used to arrange libraries in the mid-nineteenth century, the letter referred to the bookcase and the number to the shelf in the case.[7] For some entries the mark has been changed; abrasions can be seen on the paper where old marks were rubbed out and a new mark written in. Sometimes remnants of earlier marks are visible. In these instances, the books were probably moved within the library; however, the person who changed the shelf mark in the catalogue did not change the mark in each entry for that title. As a result, the shelf mark may be different for the same book in separate entries.

The detailed organization of the Hayes Catalogue with its subject headings and cross-references suggests that it may have been compiled by a professional librarian, and Charles Darwin, an assistant librarian at the Library of Congress, stands as the most likely candidate; this attribution, however, must be considered tentative at best. Darwin was involved with arrangements that Hayes made with Ainsworth Rand Spofford, the Librarian of Congress, during the summer of 1877 to exchange some government documents in the Executive Mansion for some books from the Library of Congress. On June 2 Spofford returned the "Catalogue of the Library at the Executive Mansion" to Hayes, and on June 4 he authorized Darwin to make an inventory of the government documents in the White House. Unfortunately, no handwriting sample for Darwin has been located for comparison. The catalogue has been written primarily in one hand, using brown ink with a nib that produced a thin line; entries have been added in a second hand using a darker ink and with a thicker line, produced by a different nib. A third hand, using a pencil, made check marks by most of the entries and took note of missing volumes.[8]

The Roosevelt Catalogue. The Roosevelt Catalogue was probably compiled in 1903, when President Theodore Roosevelt asked the Library of Congress to help update the collection in the White House. His request initiated what became known as the White House Library Deposit, a program in which the Library of Congress placed books on deposit in the Executive Mansion for as long as the president, his family, or staff members needed or wanted them. The White House, in turn, began sending books that it no longer wanted to the Library of Congress. This catalogue exists in two forms, a negative photostat of a typescript (see figure 7) and a positive photocopy of the same typescript, which has a note in pencil across the top of the first page: "Executive Mansion Collection Pre-Hoover" and another written in pencil beneath the title: "i.e. The old library—Not the L.C. deposit." This list was likely compiled to record what was already in the Executive Mansion before the Library of Congress began placing books there. The librarians working on the deposit project would have wanted to know what books were already in the White House in order to avoid sending duplicate titles.[9]

The Roosevelt Catalogue includes entries for 90 of the 193 books that were purchased by the Fillmore administration for the Executive Mansion and measures 245 by 195 millimeters. Like the Hayes Catalogue it lists books by author, sometimes by title, and sometimes by subject, and therefore more than one entry for the same book often appears. Entitled on the first page, "A List of Books in the White House Library," it comprises forty-five unnumbered sheets, typed on only one side. For reference purpose, the sheets have been numbered in sequential order.

The primary differences between the two catalogues are that the Hayes Catalogue identifies editions only by year and city of publication, whereas the Roosevelt Catalogue also names the publishers. In addition, the Roosevelt Catalogue does not include any law books. These books may have been moved prior to 1903 to the new Executive Office Building, now known as the West Wing. This addition to the White House was completed in November of 1902, and the cabinet held its first meeting there on November 6 of that year.[10]

II. COPIES FROM THE EXECUTIVE MANSION COLLECTION

With the information from the Hayes and Roosevelt catalogues, ten of the actual copies from the original Executive Mansion collection were found in the Library of Congress stacks:

> Jean Jacques Barthélemy, *Travels of Anacharsis the Younger,* 6 vols.
> John Lord Campbell, *The Lives of the Lord Chancellors,* 7 vols.
> Richard S. Fisher, *Book of the World,* 2 vols.
> Edward Gibbon, *Decline and Fall of the Roman Empire,* 6 vols.
> George Grote, *History of Greece,* 12 vols.
> Henry Hallam, *Constitutional History of England,* 2 vols.
> John MacGregor, *Commercial Statistics,* 5 vols.
> William Hickling Prescott, *History of the Conquest of Peru,* 2 vols.
> Sir Walter Scott, the Waverley Novels, 20 vols.
> David Bailie Warden, *On the Origin, Nature, Progress and Influence of Consular Establishments.*

These were located by examining all of the books in the Library of Congress that the Hayes and Roosevelt catalogues indicate were in the original Executive Mansion collection. Most of these copies are inscribed on the front pastedown in black ink, "Executive Mansion 1850 [or the year in which they were purchased]," with a shelf mark in pencil consisting of a letter, which probably refers to the specific case, over a number identified as the "shelf no." Some also include the month and even the day of purchase. Barthélemy's *Travels* has no inscription, but a three-by-five-inch typed card with a cataloguing record for the book was found in volume 6. It has a note penciled in the upper right corner that reads: "White House Coll. Deck 37 not in rare books." Fisher's *Book of the World* contains the only example of a spine label, black with gilt stamped letters that read, "Presidential Mansion." Grote's *History of Greece* has been rebound, but the inscription is on the recto of the first leaf of advertisements in volumes 4, 5, and 6. Macgregor's *Commercial Statistics* contains the only example found of an Executive Mansion bookplate (see figure 8). The bookplate measures forty by fifty-eight millimeters and is printed in black ink. A decorative border of type ornaments encloses the text 'EXECUTIVE MANSION LIBRARY. | [thin rule] | *Case* [dotted rule] | *Shelf* [dotted rule] | UNITED STATES OF AMERICA.' The dotted rules in lines 2 and 3 were left for the shelf mark to be added. Although the bookplate appears to be from the mid-nineteenth century and resembles Fillmore's own bookplate in size and style, it cannot be dated precisely to the years of Fillmore's presidency (see figure 9). Warden's *Consular Establishments* is only inscribed "Executive Mansion" across the head of the title page. Other books in the Library of Congress may have been part of the original collection, but the evidence needed to identify them would have been destroyed when they were rebound.[11]

In addition to the books in the Library of Congress, one other copy from the original Executive Mansion collection remains in the White House today, Jared Sparks's *The Library of American Biography,* first series, in ten volumes. It too is inscribed "Executive Mansion 1850" on the front pastedown of each volume (see figure 10). These 11 titles—10 found in the Library of Congress and 1 at the White House—are the only identifiable survivors from the 193 books that were originally purchased for the library.[12]

III. Catalogue Entries

i. Arrangement

This catalogue is arranged alphabetically by author. The possibilities of arranging the entries by the shelf marks from the Hayes Catalogue or by subject were considered but rejected for several reasons. Since President Grant replaced all of the bookcases in the library in 1869, the shelf marks in the Hayes Catalogue could not date to the Fillmore administration.[13] In addition, a trial of this arrangement yielded no consistently logical ordering of the books. Moreover, some books have no shelf mark in the Hayes Catalogue and would have to be arranged arbitrarily. Ordering the entries by subject also proved impractical because a title can often rightly be catalogued under more than one heading. Although cross-referencing can accommodate such circumstances, an index by subject, which has been provided as an appendix to this catalogue, can accomplish the same goal more efficiently.

ii. Headnote and Annotations

Each entry begins with a headnote in bold identifying the book by author, title, city of publication, publisher, and date of publication. Two asterisks (**) precede the headnote of entries that describe one of the eleven Executive Mansion copies that were located. The headnote is followed by annotations that include biographical information about the author, a description of the content of the book, a discussion of the book's significance and relevance to the concerns and policies of the Fillmore presidency, and a justification of the edition selected if it does not appear in either the Hayes or the Roosevelt catalogues. Unless otherwise stated, biographical information has been derived from online editions of *The Dictionary of American Biography* (DAB), *The American National Biography* (ANB), and *The Oxford Dictionary of National Biography* (ODNB). Nineteenth-century book reviews have been consulted and cited to indicate a book's reputation and influence in the mid-nineteenth century. When relevant, reviews that appeared in the periodicals purchased for the library have been cited. The citation of reviews, however, is not, nor is it intended to be, comprehensive. These reviews have been identified primarily through *American Periodical Series* (APS) *Online,* a database that offers the *American Periodical Series Microform Collection* in a digitized, fully searchable format. It provides the full text of over nine hundred periodical titles from the first sixty years of the nineteenth century. Without this database, it would have been impossible to identify as many book reviews as are cited in this catalogue. Additional information in the annotations is sometimes drawn from the preface, advertisements, or introduction to the book itself, and when appropriate the *Encyclopaedia Americana* and the *Penny Cyclopaedia* have been consulted, since these two reference sets were in the first White House Library and might have influenced the reading habits of those who formed it.[14] All citations of these two encyclopedias refer to the editions that were in the library. Numerous cross-references between entries have been footnoted to highlight the relationships between many of the books in the library and demonstrate that collectively these books represent an interconnected body of knowledge.

A transcription of the voucher entry, identification of the bookseller from whom the book was purchased, the date of purchase, and, if applicable, a transcription of either the Hayes or the Roosevelt catalogue entry follows the annotations.[15] The vouchers are not consistent in including a dollar sign before the price or in their abbreviation of "volumes." The transcriptions, therefore, have been standardized to always include the dollar sign and to abbreviate volumes as "vols." The vouchers sometimes include ditto marks referring to the preceding entry; in these instances the references have been spelled out. For most books that appear in both the Hayes and the Roosevelt catalogues, the Roosevelt Catalogue entry is transcribed because it contains more specific publication information. If the information provided in the catalogues varies significantly, transcriptions of the entries from both catalogues are given. Both catalogues usually capitalize only the first word of a title, although there are some exceptions. Capitalization of titles in the transcriptions has been standardized according to the current *Modern Language Association Style Manual* guidelines.

iii. Bibliographical Descriptions

The bibliographical descriptions stand in place for actual copies of the books that they describe. They record a set of physical characteristics in a formulaic manner for each book. Physical features of a book reveal how the publisher packaged its intellectual content. Moreover, these features often influence how a book's readers understand the information it contains. Although some readers may pass over them, scholars who are interested in reading, printing, and publishing history may find much useful information in the bibliographical descriptions.[16]

Bibliographical descriptions have been presented only for those books whose edition has been identified with certainty. If an identification of the edition has not been made, a discussion of the book's content and of the possible editions that could have been purchased has been offered. Usually the most likely edition to have been selected is suggested. It has been impossible to identify even an exact title for three of the voucher entries: *The Jesuit, Index to Review,* and Story's *Commentaries.* In these circumstances discussions of the most likely titles have been supplied.

The bibliographical descriptions presented here represent, as closely as possible, the contents of a specific historical library that has been dispersed. They therefore describe representative copies, not ideal copies. The bibliographical descriptions contain up to seven subsections, labeled as follows: title page, pagination, contents, plates, binding, marks of ownership, and references. If a subsection is not applicable to a book—for example, if a book contains no plates—then that subsection has been omitted.[17]

Format and collation statements have not been furnished because most of the books in the library were printed in the nineteenth century on machine-made paper, which often makes format more difficult to determine than it is for books printed on handmade paper. In addition, most of the copies described here have been rebound and trimmed or cut down to varying degrees, which makes determining format all the more difficult. Had it been possible to determine format and write collation statements for these books, this information would have provided insight into how the books themselves were printed and assembled, which would have offered useful information to scholars interested in printing house, papermaking, and other book trade practices of the period.[18]

An abbreviated description has been provided for periodicals and books published in large multivolume sets, such as the *Annual Biography and Obituary.* For titles in these categories, a title-page transcription has been supplied for the first volume, and significant changes in the title page through the run purchased for the White House have been noted. The subsections "References" and "Copy Described" are also included for periodicals and large sets.

Title Page. The title page can be viewed as a book's "public face," which through the information that it includes and its typographical arrangement can suggest how its publisher designed the edition for a particular reading audience.[19] It may even provide clues— through pictorial vignettes and/or written epigraphs or other devices—as to how readers were encouraged to interpret a book's content. For example, the epigraph on the title page of Matthew Davis's *Memoirs of Aaron Burr,* "I come to bury Caesar, not to praise him," elevates the book's subject matter and author by aligning both with Shakespeare's account of Julius Caesar. It also points to the ambiguity of the lessons to be learned from Burr's life and pleads for the readers' objective consideration of his *Memoirs* at the same time that it defends the biographer's potential bias.[20] The title page may also include other useful information, such as the publisher's address, the price, and/or the location where the book was to be sold.

Each description therefore begins with a quasi-facsimile transcription of the title page following Fredson Bowers's method outlined in *Principles of Bibliographical Description.*[21] For a multivolume work, a full transcription is provided for the title page of volume 1. If the title pages of subsequent volumes vary in ways other than the volume number, only the lines that differ are transcribed; ellipses are used to indicate lines that are the same as those in the first volume. When both letterpress and engraved title pages are present, only the letterpress title page is transcribed in this subsection; the engraved one is described in the subsection "Plates." If the only title page present is engraved, it is identified as such and transcribed here.

Pagination and Contents Statements. Considered together, the pagination and contents statements reveal how a book's intellectual content is distributed across its physical structure. The contents statement indicates the presence of paratextual material such as half titles, tables of contents, advertisements, dedications, appendixes, and indexes, which can reveal more about the book's content than the citation in the headnote and the title-page transcription. For example, the content statement for Nathaniel Atcheson's *Report of a Case Recently Determined in His Majesty's Court at the King's Bench* shows that the list of cases, statutes, and treaties cited takes up only 2 pages, which also include the errata; whereas the appendix "French Laws Now in Force Relative to Maritime Prizes" mentioned on the title page spans 133 pages, which is over twice the length of the text of Atcheson's report.[22] In addition, dedications recorded in the contents statements signify a variety of relationships—admiration, respect, honor, remembrance, and flattery—between the authors and their dedicatees that would otherwise remain hidden. For example, legal scholars often dedicated their works to one another, and their dedications point to a genealogy of knowledge and an interrelated community of minds.

Booksellers' catalogues and publishers' advertisements have often not been included in pagination and contents statements, because they are usually not properly an integral part of the book but were added to it when it was bound. Because they often contain information about availability, price, and binding and thereby provide valuable insight into the book trade practices of the period, they have been included in the pagination statements and identified in the contents statement.

The pagination statement accounts for each page of letterpress material in the book and follows the numeration used by the printer; for example, if lowercase roman numerals appear in the book, then they are used here. No effort has been made to record misprints in pagination or page numbers that have been inferred. However, number sequences that are repeated have been recorded, as in volume 2 of Barthélemy's *Travels of Anacharsis the Younger*. For pages whose numbers cannot be inferred, an italic numeral denoting the total number of pages is given in square brackets in the pagination statement, and an italic numeral corresponding to the page's position in the unnumbered sequence and enclosed in square brackets is used for reference in the contents statement. The pagination and contents statements include only letterpress material. Plates that have been bound into a book are listed under the subsection "Plates," and their position in the copy described is indicated there.

Plates. Plates afford evidence that suggests possible uses and interpretations of a book's intellectual content. For example, the plates bound into the edition of the *Junius Letters* that was purchased for the White House invite the reader to contemplate the mystery of the letters' authorship by providing facsimiles of handwriting samples from the manuscript letters and from the proposed authors. Likewise, the numerous maps and illustrations in Charles Wilkes's *Narrative of the United States Exploring Expedition* help readers to imagine different parts of the world and its inhabitants in new ways.[23]

The "Plates" subsection provides a record of all non-letterpress material that was bound into a book, identified by captions (if present) enclosed in quotation marks. In the absence of a caption, a brief description of the subject has been supplied. If a plate is signed, the signature or signatures are noted along with whether they designate the engraver or the artist of the original work. When such a designation has not been made, the location of the signature is given. It was the convention to place the engraver's signature in the lower right and that of the original artist in the lower left.[24] If evidence suggests that a plate is missing, then that information is noted. For example, in *Biography of the Signers of the Declaration of Independence* offset ghost images of plates that are no longer present appear on pages that they once faced. Sometimes it is impossible to determine that a plate is missing without examining numerous copies of a book. Of the seven copies of Edward Waite's *Washington City Directory* that were consulted, only one contained the fold-out map of Washington, D.C. Unfortunately, multiple copies of the proper edition of a book were usually not available to examine for this catalogue.[25]

Bindings. Bindings often provide clues to the value that the owner placed on a book and indicate the book's anticipated use. Publishers' bindings can also suggest the audience to which a book was marketed. Most of the books that were purchased for the White House

Library were bound in publisher's cloth; eighteen, however, are known to have been bound in either full or half leather.[26] As was customary during this period, most of the law books would have been bound in sheepskin. A letter from Charles Lanman, the purchasing agent for the library, indicates that, where possible, he selected clothbound editions and thereby saved approximately three hundred dollars so that the president could have the volumes uniformly bound.[27] There is no evidence that President Fillmore was interested in a stately array of leather and gilt to impress visitors to the library. Instead, he seems to have been a practical man and selected books that were bound appropriately for their use and content. Publisher's cloth, which can be seen on some of the surviving copies, proved perfectly acceptable for most of the books.

Apparently, Fillmore had initially considered applying custom-made spine labels, like the one on the surviving copy of Fisher's *Book of the World,* to all of the books in the library since charges for spine labels are included for six other early purchases that Fillmore made.[28] He must have abandoned the idea of spine labels for all volumes in the library since no additional charges for them appear after October 1850. This plan may have proved too expensive; at twenty-five cents per volume, it would have cost over $250 to have spine labels made for all of the volumes in the library, not including the government documents. Fillmore probably preferred to spend this amount of money on more books.

Calf or half calf was a more durable binding and would have been preferable on works that would be used frequently or that were expected be of service over a long period of time, such as reference and law books. The Fillmores selected a copy of Mary Cowden Clarke's *Concordance to Shakespeare* bound in calf rather than a less expensive and less durable copy bound in cloth. Likewise, they selected a copy of Fleming and Tibbins's French-English Dictionary bound in half calf instead of one in paper wrappers. Although initially these were more expensive choices, in the long run they proved more economical. Both are large books that would not have held up well with repeated use in the less expensive binding, and re-binding would have been costly.[29]

Descriptions of bindings have been provided only for those books for which the copy described is still in the original publisher's binding or in a period, bespoke binding. When a binding is described, all measurements are given in millimeters, height by width. In addition to a description of the front and back boards and the spine, the binding description includes the head and foot bands, if present, as well as the endpapers. Unfortunately, most of the books described in this catalogue are now bound in library buckram. It is the Library of Congress's practice, as a preservation measure, to rebind books in its general collection as needed, and no exceptions were made for the White House books. Many of the books were in poor condition when they arrived at the Library of Congress, and, at least until 1932, they had been incorporated into the main stacks and made available for readers to use.[30] Moreover, the Library of Congress book stacks were not air conditioned until the 1960s, and many books needed rebinding because of damage suffered from Washington's hot and humid summer climate.[31]

Marks of Ownership. Marks of ownership or provenance help to document the history of a particular copy of a book. Annotations by a previous owner offer insight into how a reader read, responded to, and thought about a book. Unfortunately, Fillmore is known to have written very little in his personal books.[32] Nevertheless from the outset of this project all marks—institutional, personal, pencil, pen, or other—in the books described were recorded in hopes of identifying a pattern that might lead to the discovery of more copies from the original collection. No pattern emerged, and therefore, marks of ownership have been recorded in this catalogue only for copies known to have been in the Executive Mansion collection. Other than the Executive Mansion inscriptions, the most interesting provenance evidence was found in Jared Sparks's *Library of American Biography,* first series, volume 4, in which the *Life of Sir Henry Vane* has been highlighted with pencil markings, and in John MacGregor's *Commercial Statistics,* in which the calling card of General Orville E. Babcock was found in volume 4.[33]

References. This subsection records both primary and secondary sources, with their relevant page numbers, that have been consulted to assist in recovering the content and significance of this library. Primary sources—the vouchers and the Hayes and Roosevelt catalogues discussed earlier in this essay—helped to identify most of the editions. Booksellers' catalogues and book-trade reference works provided further information about price, binding, and format that helped to identify the editions for some titles that would not have been ascertained with certainty otherwise. Subject bibliographies and author bibliographies sometimes supplied more specific information that helped to identify an edition, and specialized legal reference books were consulted for the law books. Finally, the Fillmores' personal library catalogues and the Fillmores' packing lists, compiled when they departed from the White House, allow readers to make comparisons between the Fillmores' own reading preferences and their selections for the White House. Since many of these sources do not supply the city and date of publication for the books that they list, the abbreviation "cf." precedes a reference believed to be relevant to, but not necessarily referring to, the exact edition in the White House Library.

Hayes and Roosevelt Catalogues. These two catalogues are discussed in detail earlier in this essay. Here it should be mentioned that the page number given in reference to these catalogues will be to the main entry only, although many of the books have more than one entry in these catalogues.

Book Trade Reference Sources. Two reference sources used by booksellers in the mid-nineteenth century were consulted for all entries in this catalogue, Orville Roorbach's *Bibliotheca Americana: Catalogue of American Publications, Including Reprints and Original Works, from 1820 to 1852,* which attempts to record all books and their prices published in America within the range of dates given in its title, and Thomas Hodgson's *London Catalogue of Books Published in Great Britain 1816 to 1851,* which endeavors to do the same for books published in Great Britain. The *London Catalogue* has particular relevance to the library because Fillmore borrowed Franck Taylor's copy of it to consult late in 1850 when he was selecting books from those that Lanman sent on approval from Boston and New York. Both of these sources list books by title, price, publisher, and sometimes number of volumes; however, they usually do not cite the year of publication, and they make no effort to account for reprints of a title from the same publisher. Despite their intentions to be comprehensive, Roorbach and Hodgson were unable to account for every book published during the periods that they cover, and some imprints from the first White House Library do not appear in either of these sources.[34]

The editions of Hodgson's and Roorbach's catalogues cited here were chosen for the relevance of their date range and for their ready availability at the Library of Congress. None of Roorbach's catalogues cover the period before 1820, and Hodgson's only extend back to 1814. Only twenty books purchased for the library fall outside the range of dates covered by these two catalogues, and sufficient documentation has been supplied for these titles from other sources.

The *British* and *English* catalogues had a goal similar to that of the *London Catalogue* and were also consulted for most of the entries. Usually they added no additional information to what had already been learned from other sources. These catalogues are cited only when they provide relevant information not found elsewhere. Prices are listed in the *London, British,* and *English* catalogues in pounds and shillings; conversions to United States currency have been provided based on the rate of $4.87 to £1.00.[35]

Booksellers' Catalogues. Useful information regarding prices and editions has also been drawn from the catalogues of two booksellers who supplied the library: Putnam and Little and Brown.[36] Putnam's *Book Buyer's Manual: A Catalogue of Foreign and American Books in Every Department of Literature* proved especially significant to the library because Lanman consulted it for another library for which he was purchasing books and may have used it when selecting books for the Executive Mansion library. In addition, two Washington, D.C., booksellers from whom the Fillmores made purchases, Franck Taylor and Taylor and Maury, were local agents for Putnam, and books in Putnam's catalogue would have been available through them. Although Putnam issued this manual periodically, the 1849, 1850, and 1852 issues all appear to have been printed from the same setting of type. The 1852 issue has been selected for reference in this catalogue because it has the advantages of addenda and a supplement that were not found in the copies of the 1849 and 1850 issues that were consulted. The main catalogue and addenda are in two alphabets but one page numbering sequence—for which only the page number is supplied in the reference—the supplement has a third alphabet and separate pagination sequence—for which the page number followed by an "s" has been provided.[37]

Little and Brown's catalogues served as an important source of information for this catalogue since Fillmore spent 40 percent of the entire congressional allocation with this firm. Surprisingly, only fourteen books published by Little and Brown were purchased for the library, and of those, only seven were acquired from Little and Brown itself. The firm, however, sold books from many publishers and imported numerous titles from London and the continent. The catalogues consulted and cited here include *A Catalogue of An Extensive and Valuable Collection of Books, Ancient and Modern, in Every Department of Literature, for Sale by Little & Brown* (April 1850); *A General Catalogue of Law Books Published During the Present Century: And Including All the Reports from the Earliest Period* (1850); *A Catalogue of Law and Miscellaneous Books, Published and For Sale* (1852); *Little, Brown and Company, General List of Works* (July 1852); *A Complete Catalogue of the Extensive and Valuable Collection of Ancient and Modern Books, in Several Departments of Literature* (1853); and *A General Catalogue of Law Books; Including All the Reports* (1853).

Fillmore Library Catalogues and Packing Lists. The Fillmores' personal library catalogues from 1847, circa 1858, and 1861, in conjunction with the itemized packing lists of books that the Fillmores removed from the White House at their departure, offer insight into their reading preferences and enable present-day readers to make comparisons between what they selected for a collection to remain in the White House and what they purchased for their personal library. These documents reveal significant overlap between their personal collections and the White House collection. Nearly sixty of the titles that the Fillmores purchased for the White House appear in their 1847 catalogue, on their packing lists, or in both. Nearly ninety of the titles appear in the two catalogues of their libraries from Fillmore's post-presidential years. Almost no law books are found in any of the inventories of the Fillmores' personal books. Fillmore sold these in 1847 when he was elected comptroller for the state of New York, the position he left to take the vice presidency. None of the Fillmore catalogues provide publication information for the books that they record, but sometimes a date is present when it is part of the title. For example, *The New York Register of 1858* is the latest book for which a date has been supplied in the circa 1858 catalogue, and it provided the evidence to approximate the year when the catalogue was compiled.[38]

The 1847 catalogue, bound in leather, measures 153 by 100 millimeters and spans forty-eight pages. It reveals much of the contents of the library in the Fillmores' Buffalo home. They planned to sublet this house when Fillmore was elected state comptroller in 1847 and the couple prepared to live in Albany for his tenure in office. Upon their request, William H. Andrews, one of Fillmore's law clerks, compiled a catalogue of the books that were to remain in Buffalo. It includes approximately 395 titles in 1,079 volumes, valued at $889.66. Given their reading habits, the Fillmores presumably took some of their books with them to Albany; those titles would be absent from this catalogue.[39]

The circa 1858 catalogue, recorded in a leatherbound ledger that measures 178 by 114 millimeters, comprises forty-one pages and contains entries for over five hundred titles. It is the first catalogue of Fillmore's library to be compiled after he left the presidency in 1853 and includes books that he and the first lady owned while he was president, as well as books that Millard acquired after Abigail's death.[40]

The 1861 catalogue, bound in calf and measuring 240 by 191 millimeters, records over 2,200 titles on 226 pages. It was continued through the end of Fillmore's life in 1874, with new books added to it as they were acquired and notes recorded when books were deaccessioned. Since Fillmore remarried in 1858, this catalogue includes books that the president and first lady had owned together, books that Millard purchased as a widower, books that his new wife, Caroline McIntosh, owned and added to the family library, and books that Millard and Caroline Fillmore acquired together.

The packing lists, recorded on thirty-six pages in a 178-by-114-millimeter leather bound memorandum book, itemize five hundred titles, some that the Fillmores brought with them to Washington and some that they added to their personal collection while living in the White House.[41] It would be inaccurate to assume that when a book that was purchased for the White House Library appears on the packing lists that the White House copy was packed with the Fillmores' personal possessions; in such instances the same book usually appears in the Hayes and or the Roosevelt catalogue, indicating that it was either returned to or remained in the White House all along. The duplication of a title from the White House Library in the Fillmores' personal collection more likely suggests that the Fillmores considered the book so important that they wanted a personal copy as well as one that would remain in the White House for its future occupants.[42]

Legal Reference Sources. Specialized sources were consulted to identify and annotate the law books in the library. These include Morris Cohen's *Bibliography of Early American Law*

(*BEAL*); J. G. Marvin's *Legal Bibliography, or a Thesaurus of American, English, Irish, and Scotch Law Books;* David Hoffman's *A Course of Legal Study; A Catalogue of the Law Library of Harvard University* from 1846; and Simon Greenleaf's "Select Law Library."[43] *BEAL* is the standard reference source for American law books through 1860 and accounts for all monographic and trial literature of American law that was published in both the United States and abroad. It also includes works on foreign, comparative, and international law published in the United States.

Marvin's *Legal Bibliography* and Hoffman's *A Course of Legal Study* are both reference sources that were used by nineteenth-century lawyers and students of the law. Marvin attempted to list all of the American, English, Irish, and Scottish legal works that had been published prior to the time of his writing in 1847. He did not seek to note peculiarities among editions or to include rarities; rather, he sought to provide a practical manual that listed the best editions available. Hoffman was a law professor at the University of Maryland and published his first edition of *A Course of Legal Study* in 1817. It was widely acclaimed and offered "a comprehensive bibliographical guide to every branch of Anglo-American law, as well as substantial references to Roman law and modern Continental jurisprudence." The expanded second edition, which is cited here, was published in 1836.[44]

A Catalogue of the Law Library of Harvard University (*Harvard*) and Simon Greenleaf's "Select Law Library" have been useful sources because the Fillmores, both father and son, looked to Harvard University for guidance on legal literature. President Fillmore asked his friend Edward Everett, president of Harvard University, to recommend books on international law for the White House Library, and Millard Powers Fillmore graduated from Harvard Law School in 1849, just before coming to serve as his father's personal secretary in the White House, where one of his responsibilities included acting as disbursing agent for the account of the library in the Executive Mansion.[45] The Harvard Law School had been founded in 1817, and by 1846 its library was ranked first among legal libraries in this country. Its 1846 catalogue lists books by author, title, place of publication, year, and sometimes edition. Harvard professor Simon Greenleaf expanded his reading list for his law students to produce his "Select Law Library," which was published in the front of Little and Brown catalogues of legal texts from the period and claimed to list "the books which are useful to every American lawyer, in whatever State he may reside."[46]

Copy Described. For all titles a complete copy of the book was sought for description. Although in some cases it is impossible to know whether a copy is complete, if a plate or leaves were obviously missing from a copy, another one was sought to use for or supplement the description. The specific copy of the book described has been identified by its holding library using the *NUC* library codes and its call number from that library. Most of the copies described are from the Library of Congress (DLC). Books not held by the Library of Congress were requested through interlibrary loan at the University of Virginia. Those that could not be obtained through interlibrary loan were consulted at the University of Virginia (ViU), Harvard University's Houghton Library (MH), the Jacob Burns Law Library at George Washington University (DGW), the Folger Shakespeare Library (DFo), or the Boston Athenaeum (MBA). A leaf measurement, given height by width in millimeters, has been included after the identification of the copy described. This measurement gives the reader an idea of the size of the book; however, since most of the copies described have been rebound and would have been cut down in this process, this measurement does not reflect the book's measurements as issued. The decision to provide leaf measurements was made after the books obtained through interlibrary loan had been returned to their holding libraries. Unfortunately, it has not been possible to provide leaf measurements for five of these books.

NOTES

1. Haven was also the wife of President Fillmore's former partner, Solomon G. Haven, in his Buffalo law firm. She first wrote of the library in 1869 at the request of Laura Holloway, who was collecting material for her book *The Ladies of the White House*. Haven recalled the library again in reminiscences that she wrote for the annual meeting of the Buffalo Historical Society on January 10, 1899, at which an hour was devoted to the memory of Millard Fillmore. Laura C. Holloway, *The Ladies of the White House; Or, In the Home of the Presidents* (1869; Philadelphia: A Gorton, 1882; repr., New York: AMS, 1976), 467–70; Frank H. Severance, ed., *Millard Fillmore Papers* (Buffalo, N.Y.: Buffalo Historical Society, 1907), 2:489–93. For other early references to the library, see Edna M. Colman, *Seventy-Five Years of White House Gossip: From Washington to Lincoln* (Garden City, N.Y.: Doubleday, 1925), 232; Mary Clemmer Ames, *Ten Years in Washington: Life and Scenes in the National Capital, as a Woman Sees Them* (Hartford, Conn., 1873), 228; Mary Ormsbee Whitton, *First First Ladies, 1789–1865: A Study of the Wives of the Early Presidents* (1948; repr., Freeport, N.Y.: Books for Libraries Press, 1969), 246; Anne Hollingsworth Wharton, *Social Life in the Early Republic* (1902; repr., New York: Benjamin Blom, 1969), 310–11.

2. See "The White House Collection," 9–10, for an account of the congressional debates; Elizabeth Lorelei Thacker-Estrada provides the most comprehensive study of the library to date in "The Heart of the Fillmore Presidency: Abigail Powers Fillmore and the White House Library," *White House Studies* 1, no. 1 (2001): 83–98. She surveys previous scholarship on the library and focuses on Abigail Fillmore's role in its founding. Thacker-Estrada also discusses the White House Library and First Lady Fillmore's involvement with it in two subsequent essays, "True Women: The Roles and Lives of Antebellum Presidential Wives Sarah Polk, Margaret Taylor, Abigail Fillmore, and Jane Pierce," in *The Presidential Companion: Readings on the First Ladies*, ed. Robert P. Watson and Anthony J. Eksterowicz (Columbia: University of South Carolina Press, 2003), 77–101, and "Rooms of their Own: First Ladies and Their Impact on Historic White House Rooms," in *Life in the White House: A Social History of the First Family and the President's House*, ed. Robert P. Watson (Albany: SUNY Press, 2004), 49–73. Seale and Scarry also cite the Treasury Department Records: William Seale, *The President's House: A History* (Washington, D.C.: White House Historical Association, 1986), 1:293; Robert J. Scarry, *Millard Fillmore* (Jefferson, N.C.: McFarland, 2001), 187–89.

3. Fiscal years were just beginning to be used at this time and were not used consistently. The closing dates on each of these account numbers correspond with the end of a quarter but not of the fiscal year, which ran from July 1–June 30. The vouchers for the purchases are held in the Records of the Accounting Offices of the Department of the Treasury, Office of the First Auditor, Settled Miscellaneous Treasury Accounts, September 6, 1790–September 29, 1894, RG 217, National Archives at College Park, Md. I am grateful to John Vandereedt, Reference Archivist, Civilian Records, National Archives and Records Administration, College Park Facility, for his assistance in locating these documents.

4. Hereafter, these two catalogues will be referred to as the Hayes and the Roosevelt Catalogue, respectively. I am grateful to William Allman, White House Curator, who informed me of the existence of the Hayes Catalogue. Nan Card, archivist at the Rutherford B. Hayes Presidential Center, helped me locate it on the microfilm of *The Rutherford B. Hayes Papers* (Fremont, Ohio: Rutherford B. Hayes Presidential Center, 1982). I worked with a microfilm copy of the Hayes Catalogue throughout most of this project and later visited the Hayes Presidential Center to verify readings in the original. I am grateful to Cheryl Fox, Program Specialist in the Manuscript Division at the Library of Congress, for her assistance in locating the Library of Congress copy of the Roosevelt Catalogue in the Library of Congress Archives, Central File, MacLeish-Evans, box 726, "White House Library 1929–49." Matthew Schaefer, archivist at the Herbert Hoover Presidential Library and Museum, located another copy of the Roosevelt Catalogue in the "White House Library-Book List" folder, box 115, Subject Files, Lou Henry Hoover Papers, Herbert Hoover Presidential Library and Museum, West Branch, Iowa.

5. Originally two separate online databases, the *RLG Union Catalogue* and *WorldCat* merged while this research was underway.

6. For examples, see the verso of the title leaf in *The Book Buyer's Manual* (New York: Putnam, 1852) and *A General Catalogue of Law Books* (Boston: Little and Brown, 1853), vi.

7. The page numbering begins on the recto of the third leaf with 1 and ends with 332. The front board is gilt stamped with a thin-rule frame that measures 195 × 150 mm with 'CATALOGUE | OF | LIBRARY. | [thin rule] | EXECUTIVE MANSION.' stamped within the frame. The page numbers have been added in pencil, probably at the time that the catalogue was microfilmed. The Hayes Presidential Center did not acquire this catalogue until the 1960s, and the latest books listed in it are dated 1899. A key in the front of the 1861 catalogue of the Fillmores' personal library indicates that they used a similar system to organize their own library.

8. See Ainsworth Rand Spofford, letter to President Hayes, June 2, 1877; Ainsworth Rand Spofford, letter to President Hayes, June 4, 1877; and Ainsworth Rand Spofford, letter to Colonel W. K. Rogers, June 8, 1877, all in Rutherford B. Hayes Papers, Rutherford B. Hayes Presidential Center, Spiegel Grove, Fremont, Ohio; see "The White House Collection," 25–26, for more information about Hayes's and Spofford's involvement in the library.

9. The latest book recorded in the Roosevelt Catalogue is dated 1898; the negative is held in the Library of Congress archives and the positive photocopy is held by the Herbert Hoover Presidential Library and Museum; see n.4, above. Unfortunately, the original typescript has been lost. The Hoovers took a keen interest in the library when they moved into the White House. See "The White House Collection," 26–27, for more about the Hoovers involvement with the library. For further information regarding the White House Library Deposit see "The White House Collection," 26.

10. Seale, *President's House*, 2:681. Law books like many specialized reference sources are time sensitive; it would be unusual for ones purchased in 1850 to remain relevant for fifty years; they therefore may have been deaccessioned, if not moved.

11. I am grateful to Werner Haun, Collection Conservator, Head of the Collections Care Section at the Library of Congress for finding Fisher's *Book of the World* in the Collections Care Section and notifying me of its existence; a numbered "deck" in the Library of Congress lexicon refers to a specific storage area; for more about the spine label, see page 77 in this essay; Fillmore's bookplate is reproduced in Eric Holzenberg and Fernando Peña, eds., *Lasting Impressions: The Grolier Club Library* (New York: Grolier Club, 2004), 194. This is the only example that I have seen of a Fillmore bookplate. It is possible that it had been made and offered to Fillmore but never used. Patricia Virgil, Director of the Library and Archives of the Buffalo Erie County Historical Society, Buffalo, N.Y., has not seen this bookplate in any of the Fillmore books held there. I am grateful to David Vander Meulen for calling my attention to the illustration of Fillmore's bookplate in *Lasting Impressions*.

12. I am grateful to William Allman, the White House curator, for allowing me access to these books. Although they are still in the White House, they are not in the current library; instead, they are stored in an archival box in the curator's office.

13. See William Allman, "Creating a Room for the Collection," 56.

14. See entries 52 and 128.

15. The date of purchase is the date that the book was entered on the voucher, which differs from the date that payment was made to the bookseller. The purchase date is probably closer to the date that the book was actually received at the White House, as the examples of MacGregor's *Commercial Statistics* and Fisher's *Book of the World* indicate. *Commercial Statistics* is inscribed "Executive Mansion February 14, 1853" on the front pastedown and is entered on the voucher on February 12, 1853, but payment was not made for the purchase until March 2, 1853. Likewise *Book of the World* is inscribed on the front pastedown "Presidential Mansion October 21, 1850," the same date that it was entered on the voucher, but payment for it was not made until March 11, 1851.

16. For a discussion of the distinction between a text's physical embodiment and its intellectual content, see G. Thomas Tanselle, *A Rationale of Textual Criticism* (Philadelphia: University of Pennsylvania Press, 1989), 39–43.

17. See Fredson Bowers, *Principles of Bibliographical Description* (1949; repr., New York: Russell and Russell, 1962), 113–23, for a discussion of the distinction between individual and ideal copy.

18. Watermarks and chain lines left by the paper mold are visible on handmade paper and assist with determining format; watermarks appear less frequently on machine-made paper, and the web of the

papermaking machine does not leave markings that are as regular and readily identifiable as the paper mold did. For a thorough discussion of the definition, relevance, and determination of format in books printed on machine-made paper see G. Thomas Tanselle's "The Concept of Format," *Studies in Bibliography* 53 (2000): 67–115.

19. William Proctor Williams and Craig S. Abbott, *An Introduction to Bibliographical and Textual Studies*, 3rd ed. (New York: Modern Language Association, 1999), 38.

20. See entry 45 for Davis's *Memoirs of Aaron Burr.*

21. Bowers, *Principles of Bibliographical Description*, 135–84.

22. See entry 11 for Atcheson's *Report.*

23. See entries 90 and 193 for the *Junius Letters* and Wilkes's *Narrative* respectively.

24. Bamber Gascoigne, *How to Identify Prints* (New York: Thames and Hudson, 1986), 48.

25. See entries 146 for *Biography of the Signers of the Declaration of Independence* and 183 for *The Washington City Directory.*

26. The entries indicate when the vouchers or other evidence suggest that a book was purchased in a leather or partial leather binding.

27. Charles Lanman, letter to President Millard Fillmore, December 12, 1850, Millard Fillmore Papers, Buffalo and Erie County Historical Society, Buffalo, N.Y. (hereafter Millard Fillmore Papers, BECHS).

28. See page 72 in this essay; five other titles purchased from Taylor and Maury in October of 1850 on the same voucher as Fisher's *Book of the World* included charges for "lettering," as did Mitchell's *Universal Atlas*, purchased in September of 1850 from Franck Taylor. See account 105,133, voucher 6, and account 105,579, voucher 2 (Mitchell's *Universal Atlas* is the only title on this voucher).

29. The dictionary in paper wrappers would have been purchased with the intention of having it custom bound. See entries 39 and 55 for Clarke's *Concordance* and Fleming and Tibbins's *Dictionary*, respectively.

30. M. A. Roberts, letter to Dare Stark McMullin, May 14, 1932, Library of Congress Archives, Central File, MacLeish-Evans, box 726, "White House Library 1929–49," Manuscript Division, Library of Congress; Order Division, memo to secretary's office, August 10, 1909, Library of Congress Archives, Central File, MacLeish-Evans, box 726, "White House Library 1929–49," Manuscript Division, Library of Congress. This memo informs the secretary's office that the order division has received a lot of about five hundred pieces of unbound material from the White House. A note in pencil on this memo, signed J. S. F., offers to draft an acknowledgment for the transfer. Another note, with an illegible signature, in pencil, responds, "this stuff is not worth any acknowledgment."

31. Installing air conditioning in the Library of Congress was a multiyear project that began in the 1962 and was probably completed in 1966. See the *Annual Report of the Librarian of Congress for the Fiscal Year Ending June 30, 1965* (Washington, D.C.: Library of Congress, 1966), 72–73. I am grateful to David Kelly, Reference Librarian, main Reading Room, Library of Congress, for locating this information in the *Annual Report.*

32. Lester W. Smith and Arthur C. Detmers, eds., *Guide to the Microfilm Edition of the Millard Fillmore Papers* (Buffalo, N.Y.: BECHS and State University College at Oswego, New York, 1975), 17.

33. For a more detailed account of these marks of ownership, see entry 159 for Sparks and 105 for MacGregor. Babcock had served in the Grant administration.

34. Franck Taylor, letter to President Fillmore, December 27, 1850, Millard Fillmore Papers, BECHS; *The London Catalogue of Books Published in Great Britain with Their Sizes, Prices, and Publisher's Names, 1816– 1851* (London: Thomas Hodgson, 1851); Orville A. Roorbach, comp., *Bibliotheca Americana: Catalogue of American Publications, Including Reprints and Original Works, from 1820 to 1852, Inclusive. Together with a List of Periodicals Published in the United States* (New York: Orville A. Roorbach, 1852).

35. Robert Alexander Peddie and Quintin Waddington, eds. and comps., *The English Catalogue of Books 1801–1836* (London: The Publisher's Circular, 1914); Sampson Low, comp., *The English Catalogue of Books Published from January, 1835, to January, 1863* (London: Sampson Low, Son, and Marston, 1864); Sampson Low, comp., *The British Catalogue of Books Published from October 1837 to December 1852; Containing the Date of Publication, Size, Price, Publisher's Name, and Edition* (London: Sampson Low and Son, 1853); Lawrence H. Officer, "Dollar-Pound Exchange Rate from 1791," MeasuringWorth, 2008, http://www.measuringworth.com/exchangepound/ (accessed July 7, 2009).

36. Other booksellers to the library issued catalogues, but none were found to contain publication data applicable to this project. Some Bartlett and Welford catalogues dating from the early 1840s were consulted, but their dates were considered too early for relevance to the first White House Library.

37. Putnam (firm), *The Book Buyer's Manual* (New York: Putnam, 1852); Lanman wrote to Putnam in November of 1852, when he was purchasing books for a library for the Spanish Minister, and requested a replacement copy of the *Manual* for one that he had lost. Charles Lanman, letter to G. P. Putnam, November 27, 1852, G. P. Putnam Collection, box 10, folder 61, Rare Books and Special Collections, Princeton University Library, Princeton, N.J. Putnam advertised as a commission agent for libraries and offered to procure books from agents in London and Paris as well as Boston and Philadelphia. The paper wrappers on Putnam's April 1850 catalogue name Taylor and Taylor and Maury among the firm's regional agents and encourage readers to place orders through them. The Houghton Library owns a copy of this catalogue in its original wrappers. Pagination is identical among the 1849, 1850, and 1852 issues, and all contain a misprint rendering the date for the publication of Brougham's *Speeches* as 1338 instead of 1838.

38. The 1847 Catalogue is held in the Millard Fillmore Papers, Buffalo Erie County Historical Society, Buffalo, N.Y. The packing lists and the ca. 1858 catalogue are found in MS 3, box 51, Millard Fillmore Papers, Special Collections, Penfield Library, SUNY at Oswego, Oswego, N.Y. I am grateful to Nancy Johnson of Special Collections at the Penfield Library for providing me with digital images of these documents along with the index to the Fillmore Pamphlet Collection. The 1861 catalogue is held in box 2/folder 6, 4/1/Vault, Millard Fillmore Papers, 1833–1874, University Archives, State University of New York at Buffalo. The American Almanac has the year 1859 penciled next to it, but that year appears to have been added some time after the catalogue had been compiled.

39. The 1847 catalogue is the only one of Fillmore's catalogues that records prices for the books and provides a total for the number of volumes in their collection.

40. Abigail died shortly after Fillmore left office in 1853.

41. A note in pencil has been added by the heading of each box indicating the date that it was unpacked—either May 19 or May 20.

42. Since the packing lists and the Fillmores' 1847 catalogue lack page numbers, numbers have been inferred for both, beginning with page 1 on the recto of the first leaf.

43. Morris Cohen, *Bibliography of Early American Law,* 6 vols. (Buffalo, N.Y.: William S. Hein and Co., 1998); J. G. Marvin, *Legal Bibliography or a Thesaurus of American, English, Irish, and Scotch Law Books* (Philadelphia: T. and J. W. Johnson, 1847); David Hoffman, *A Course of Legal Study, Addressed to Students and the Profession Generally,* 2 vols. (Baltimore: Neal, 1836); *A Catalogue of the Law Library of Harvard University* (Cambridge: Metcalf and Co., 1846); I am grateful to James Martin, Law Library Reading Room Operations Officer, Library of Congress Law Library, for calling my attention to these invaluable resources. Greenleaf's "Select Law Library" was published in the front of Little and Brown's catalogues of law books of the period. For an example, see Little, Brown and Company, *General Catalogue of Law Books* (Boston: Little and Brown, 1853), xv.

44. Maxwell Bloomfield, "Hoffman, David," *American National Biography Online* (Oxford: Oxford University Press, 2000), http://www.anb.org /articles/11/11-00416.html.

45. Millard Fillmore, letter to Edward Everett, September 23, 1851, Edward Everett Papers, Massachusetts Historical Society, Boston; Edward Everett, letter to Millard Fillmore, September 29, 1851, Millard Fillmore Papers, BECHS; Scarry, *Millard Fillmore,* 104.

46. Little, Brown and Company, *General Catalogue of Law Books,* xv–xxii. I am grateful to David Warrington, Head of Special Collections at the Harvard Law School Library for supplying me with a copy of the type facsimile "Course of Study" for the Harvard Law School from 1838.

FIGURE 1. President Millard Fillmore. Prints and Photographs Division, Library of Congress.

FIGURE 2. First Lady Abigail Powers Fillmore. White House Collection.

FIGURE 3. Mary Abigail Fillmore.
Buffalo and Erie County Historical
Society.

FIGURE 4. Millard Powers Fillmore.
Buffalo and Erie County
Historical Society.

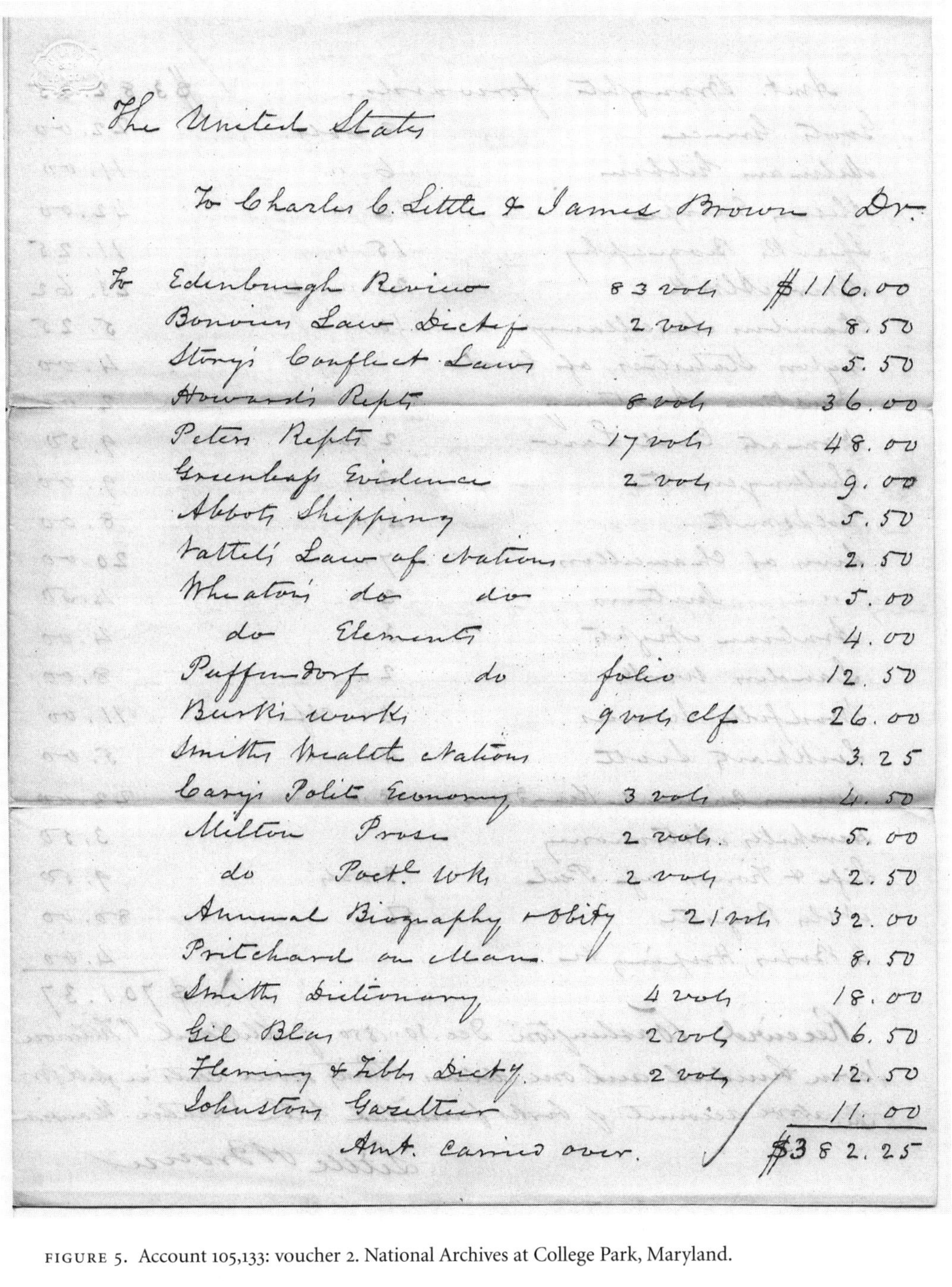

The United States

To Charles C. Little & James Brown   Dr.

To Edenburgh Review	83 vols	$116.00
Bouviers Law Dicty	2 vols	8.50
Storys Conflict Laws		5.50
Howards Repts	8 vols	36.00
Peters Repts	17 vols	48.00
Greenleaf Evidence	2 vols	9.00
Abbots Shipping		5.50
Vattels Law of Nations		2.50
Wheatons do do		5.00
do Elements		4.00
Puffendorf do folio		12.50
Burks works	9 vols clf	26.00
Smiths Wealth Nations		3.25
Carys Polit Economy	3 vols	4.50
Milton Prose	2 vols	5.00
do Poetl Wks	2 vols	2.50
Annual Biography & Obity	21 vols	32.00
Pritchard on Man		8.50
Smiths Dictionary	4 vols	18.00
Gil Blas	2 vols	6.50
Fleming & Tibbs Dicty	2 vols	12.50
Johnstons Gazetteer		11.00
Amt. carried over.		$382.25

FIGURE 5. Account 105,133: voucher 2. National Archives at College Park, Maryland.

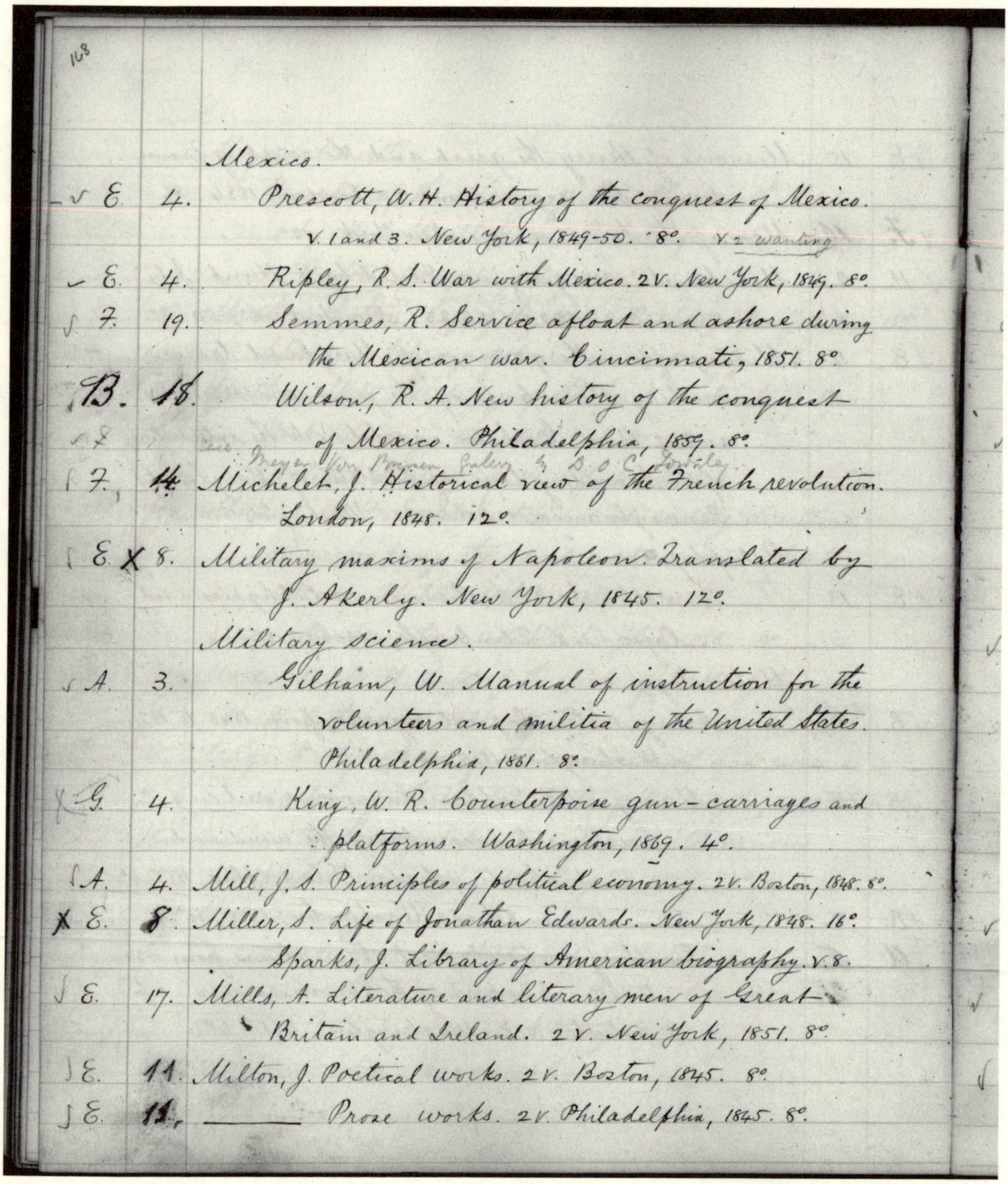

Mexico.

√ E. 4. Prescott, W. H. History of the conquest of Mexico.
  v. 1 and 3. New York, 1849-50. 8°. v. 2 wanting

√ E. 4. Ripley, R. S. War with Mexico. 2 v. New York, 1849. 8°.

√ 7. 19. Semmes, R. Service afloat and ashore during
  the Mexican war. Cincinnati, 1851. 8°.

B. 18. Wilson, R. A. New history of the conquest
  √ E   of Mexico. Philadelphia, 1859. 8°.

7. 14. Michelet, J. Historical view of the French revolution.
  London, 1848. 12°.

E. X 8. Military maxims of Napoleon. Translated by
  J. Akerly. New York, 1845. 12°.

Military science.

√ A. 3. Gilham, W. Manual of instruction for the
  volunteers and militia of the United States.
  Philadelphia, 1861. 8°.

√ G. 4. King, W. R. Counterpoise gun-carriages and
  platforms. Washington, 1869. 4°.

A. 4. Mill, J. S. Principles of political economy. 2 v. Boston, 1848. 8°.

X E. 8. Miller, S. Life of Jonathan Edwards. New York, 1848. 16°.
  Sparks, J. Library of American biography. v. 8.

√ E. 17. Mills, A. Literature and literary men of Great
  Britain and Ireland. 2 v. New York, 1851. 8°.

√ E. 11. Milton, J. Poetical works. 2 v. Boston, 1845. 8°.

√ E. 11. _____ Prose works. 2 v. Philadelphia, 1845. 8°.

FIGURE 6. Hayes Catalogue, page 168. Rutherford B. Hayes Presidential Center, Spiegel Grove, Fremont, Ohio.

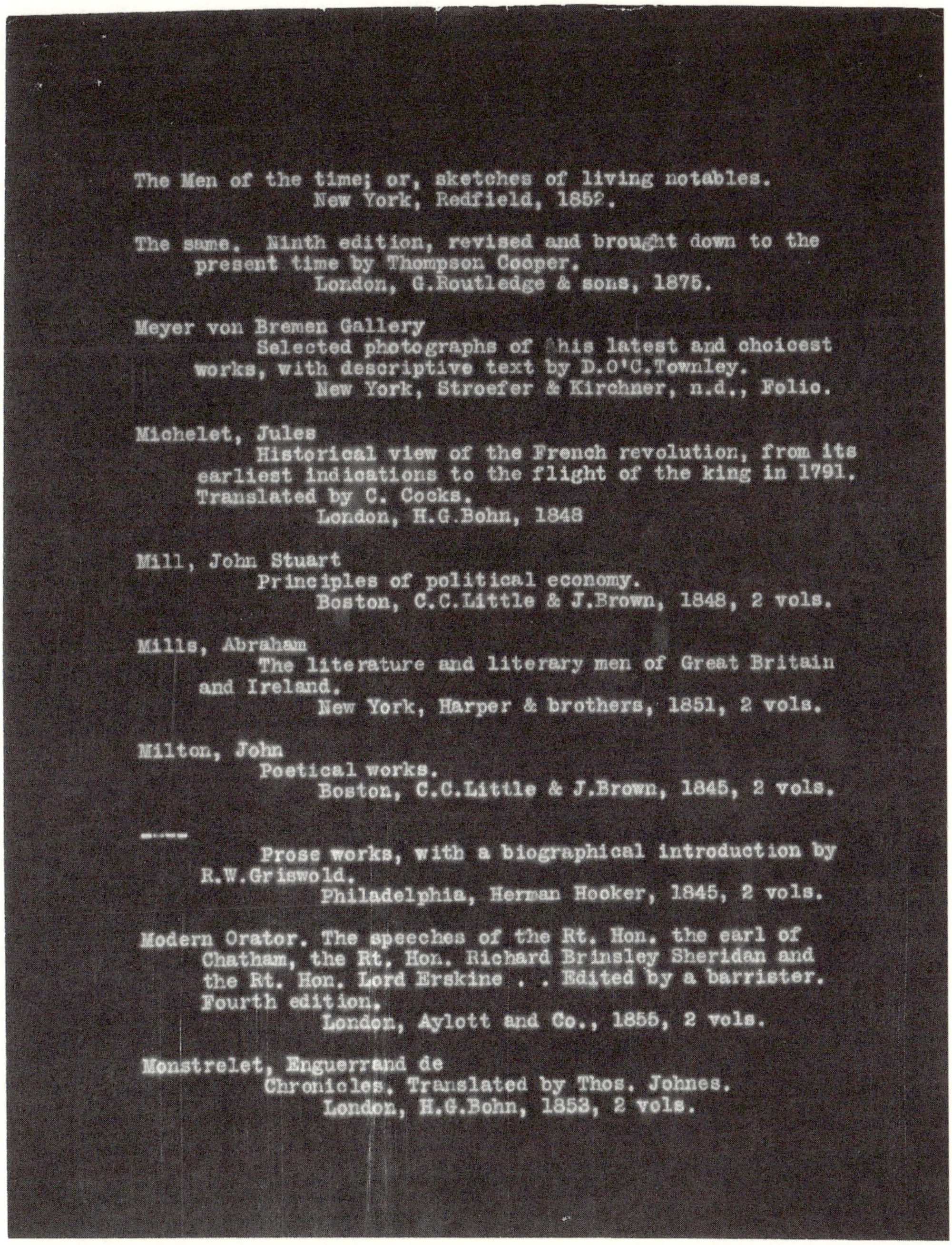

The Men of the time; or, sketches of living notables.
        New York, Redfield, 1852.

The same. Ninth edition, revised and brought down to the
    present time by Thompson Cooper.
        London, G.Routledge & sons, 1875.

Meyer von Bremen Gallery
        Selected photographs of his latest and choicest
    works, with descriptive text by D.O'C.Townley.
        New York, Stroefer & Kirchner, n.d., Folio.

Michelet, Jules
        Historical view of the French revolution, from its
    earliest indications to the flight of the king in 1791.
    Translated by C. Cocks.
        London, H.G.Bohn, 1848

Mill, John Stuart
        Principles of political economy.
        Boston, C.C.Little & J.Brown, 1848, 2 vols.

Mills, Abraham
        The literature and literary men of Great Britain
    and Ireland.
        New York, Harper & brothers, 1851, 2 vols.

Milton, John
        Poetical works.
        Boston, C.C.Little & J.Brown, 1845, 2 vols.

————
        Prose works, with a biographical introduction by
    R.W.Griswold.
        Philadelphia, Herman Hooker, 1845, 2 vols.

Modern Orator. The speeches of the Rt. Hon. the earl of
    Chatham, the Rt. Hon. Richard Brinsley Sheridan and
    the Rt. Hon. Lord Erskine . . Edited by a barrister.
    Fourth edition.
        London, Aylott and Co., 1855, 2 vols.

Monstrelet, Enguerrand de
        Chronicles. Translated by Thos. Johnes.
        London, H.G.Bohn, 1853, 2 vols.

FIGURE 7. Roosevelt Catalogue, page 28. Manuscript Division, Library of Congress.

FIGURE 8. "Executive Mansion Library"
bookplate. Rare Book and Special Collections
Division, Library of Congress.

FIGURE 9. "Millard Fillmore" bookplate. The Grolier Club of New York.

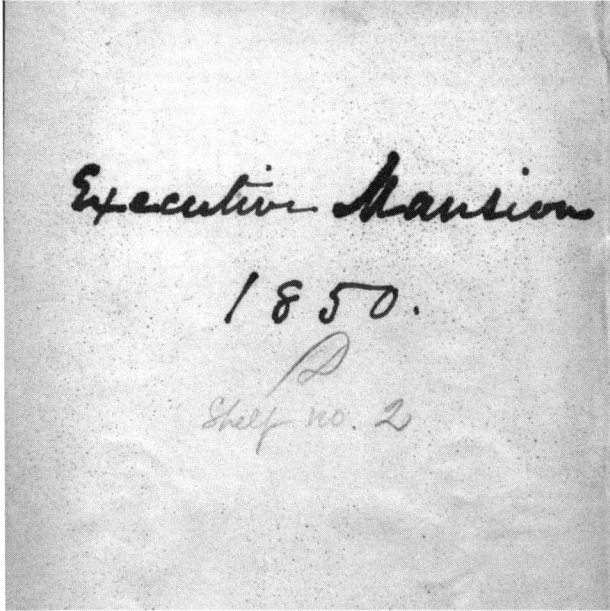

FIGURE 10. Executive Mansion inscription in Jared Sparks, *Library of American Biography,* first series. White House Collection.

FIGURE 11. Earliest photo of the White House Library, stereoview, ca. 1870. White House Collection.

. THE PRESIDENT'S LIBRARY AT THE WHITE HOUSE, WASHINGTON, D. C.

FIGURE 12. "The President's Library at the White House, Washington, D.C.," after a drawing by C. E. H. Bonwill, engraving published in *Frank Leslie's Illustrated Newspaper,* July 7, 1866. Prints and Photographs Division, Library of Congress.

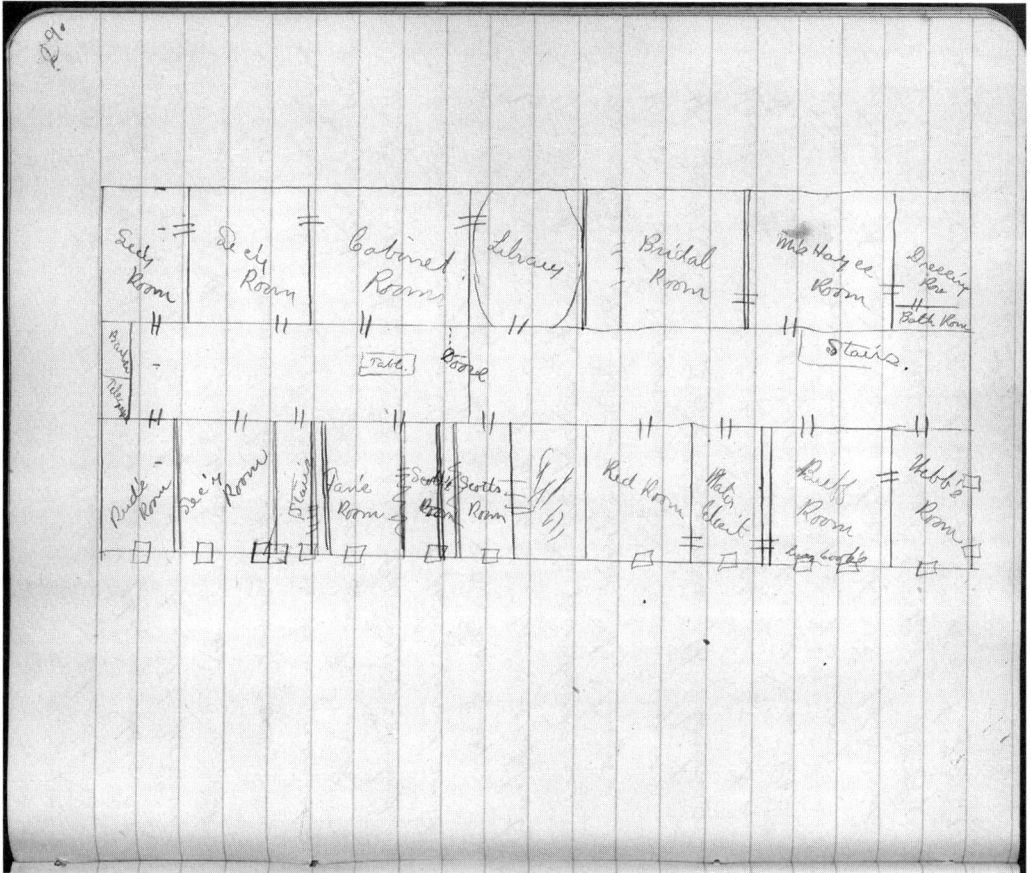

FIGURE 13. Floor plan of the second floor of the White House as sketched by Lucy Keeler, 1881. Rutherford B. Hayes Presidential Center, Spiegel Grove, Fremont, Ohio.

WASHINGTON, D.C.—SOCIAL LIFE IN THE NATIONAL CAPITAL—AN EVENING IN THE PRIVATE PARLORS OF THE EXECUTIVE MANSION.—FROM A SKETCH BY MISS GEORGIE A. DAVIS.—SEE PAGE 71.

FIGURE 14. Hayes family in the White House Library. *Frank Leslie's Illustrated Newspaper,* April 3, 1880. White House Collection.

FIGURE 15. Current White House Library. Photo courtesy White House Historical Association.

Catalogue of the
First White House Library

1. Abbott, Charles. *A Treatise of the Law Relative to Merchant Ships and Seamen.* Ed. J. C. Perkins. [5th or 6th American ed.] Boston: Little and Brown, [1846 or 1850].

Charles Abbott's (1762–1832) *Treatise of the Law Relative to Merchant Ships and Seamen* (1802) was the first English treatise devoted exclusively to the law of shipping. Its publication garnered praise from judges and city attorneys and gained him steady employment in most of the charter party and mercantile cases at Guildhall. It became, according to Marvin, "a legal classic of high character," one on which James Kent based his forty-seventh lecture of his *Commentaries on American Law,* another work purchased for the White House Library.[1]

First published in 1802, Abbott's treatise appeared in an American edition the same year. In 1803 Joseph Story edited the second American edition, which was derived from the third London edition. Marvin cites five American editions of this work and recommended the latest one from Boston, dated 1846, calling it "the most desirable one for the American lawyer." It includes the notes of the English editor, William Shee, those of Story, and those of its most recent editor, J. C. Perkins. Perkins made every effort to identify and cite all cases on the subject that had not been reported in earlier editions and to include all that had been decided since the previous edition. He also added an appendix of all of the statutes respecting the subject of shipping that had been enacted since the year 1829. The sixth American edition was published in 1850. It too contains the notes of the English editor, Shee, as well as those of Story and Perkins. The Executive Mansion probably purchased either the 1846 or the 1850 edition.[2]

105,133 voucher 2: Abbots Shipping $5.50.
Purchased from Little and Brown on December 30, 1850.

REFERENCES
BEAL 1564–65; cf. Greenleaf; cf. Harvard p. 1; cf. Marvin p. 47; cf. Roorbach p. 606; cf. Fillmore Packing Lists p. 21.

---

1. See entry 92 for Kent.
2. See entries 164–66 for Joseph Story.

2. Adams, John. *A Defence of the Constitutions of Government of the United States.* London: John Stockdale, 1794.

John Adams (1735–1826), second president of the United States, diplomat, and political theorist, was prompted to write *A Defence of the Constitutions* (1787) in part by the news of Shay's rebellion—the uprising in western Massachusetts in opposition to high taxes and stringent economic conditions, led by Daniel Shay—and in part by a letter from the former French finance minister Anne Robert Jacques Turgot to the American clergyman Robert Price. In this letter Turgot expressed concern about the new state constitutions in America and suggested that America was still in the need of advice from some "enlightened men."[1] Abigail Adams called the *Defence* an "investigation into the different forms of government, both ancient and modern" and claimed that its purpose was to demonstrate "the superiority of mixed forms over simple ones." Adams began writing the *Defence* in 1786 while he was living in England. It was published the following year just in time to provide theoretical justification of the newly written United States Constitution. The *Defence* won him the favor of the American public, who elected Adams vice president under George Washington shortly after his return to the United States in 1788.[2]

105,133 voucher 5: John Adams Defence Constitution $5.50.
Purchased from Charles Welford on December 13, 1850.
Roosevelt Catalogue: Adams, John. *A Defence of the Constitutions of Government of the U. S. of America against the Attack of M. Turgot in His Letter to Dr. Price, Dated the 22nd Day of March 1788.* London, John Stockdale, 1794, 3 vols.

TITLE PAGE
Vol. I.
A | DEFENCE | OF THE | CONSTITUTIONS OF GOVERNMENT | OF THE | *UNITED STATES* | OF | AMERICA, | AGAINST THE ATTACK OF M. TURGOT | IN HIS | LETTER TO DR. PRICE, | DATED THE TWENTY-SECOND DAY OF MARCH, 1778. | [swelled rule] | By JOHN ADAMS, LL. D. | AND A MEMBER OF THE ACADEMY OF ARTS AND SCIENCES | AT BOSTON. | [swelled rule] | All Nature's Difference keeps all Nature's Peace. POPE. | [swelled rule] | IN THREE VOLUMES. | VOL. I. [II–III.] | *A NEW EDITION.* | [swelled rule] | LONDON: | PRINTED FOR JOHN STOCKDALE, PICCADILLY. | [thin rule] | 1794

Vol. II.
'. . . As for us Englishmen, thank Heaven, we have a better sense of government, | delivered to us from our ancestors. We have the notion of a public, and a | constitution; how legislative, and how executive is moulded. We un- | derstand weight and measure in this kind, and we can reason justly on the ba- | lance of power and property. The maxims we draw from hence are as evi- | dent as those of mathematics. Our increasing knowledge shews us every | day more and more what common sense is in politics. | Shaftesbury's charact. vol. i. p. 108. | 'Tis scarce a quarter of an age since such a happy balance of power was settled | between our prince and people, as has firmly secured our hitherto precarious | liberties, and removed from us the fear of civil commotions, wars, and vio- | lence, either

on account of the property of the subject, or the contending | titles of the crown. | [swelled rule] | VOL. II. . . .'

Vol. III.

'. . . Some philosophers have been foolish enough to imagine, that improvements | might be made in the system of the universe, by a different arrangement | of the orbs of heaven; and politicians, equally ignorant, and equally pre- | sumptuous, may easily be led to suppose, that the happiness of our world | would be promoted by a different tendency of the human mind. | JOHNSON'S ADVENTURER, N° 45. | [swelled rule] | VOL. III. . . .'

PAGINATION

Vol. I. [4] 3–8 i–xxxii 3–392.
Vol. II. [4] 1–452.
Vol. III. [4] 1–564.

CONTENTS

Vol. I. [1] half title, [2] blank, [3] title, [4] blank, 3–8 a short account of the author, i–xxviii preface, xxix–xxxii contents, 3–392 text.
Vol. II. [1] half title, [2] blank, [3] title, [4] blank, 1–451 text, 452 directions to the binder.
Vol. III. [1] half title, [2] blank, [3] title, [4] blank, 1–528 text, 529–64 index.

PLATES

Vol. I.

Portrait frontispiece of John Adams, signed in lower left by Copley and lower right by Hall.
   Note. The frontispiece is missing from the copy described, but is called for in the directions to the binder. It is present in DLC copy 1, which is an incomplete set with only volume 1 present.

REFERENCES

Hayes p. 1; Roosevelt p. 2; L and B 1850 p. 1.

COPY DESCRIBED

DLC: JK171 A2 1794 copy 2

---

1. Carl B. Cone, "Richard Price and the Constitution of the United States," *American Historical Review* 53, no. 4 (1948): 726–47. Turgot's letter is published in Price's *Observations on the Importance of the American Revolution* (1784).

2. Abigail Adams qtd. in William Pencack, "Adams, John," *American National Biography Online* (Oxford: Oxford University Press, 2000; hereafter *ANB Online*), http://www.anb.org/articles/01/01-00007.

∽

3. *Aesop's Fables; A New Version Chiefly from Original Sources.* Trans. Thomas James. Illus. John Tenniel. New York: R. B. Collins, 1850.

By the nineteenth century Aesop's fables were twenty-four hundred years old. The fables, which used animal stories to convey moral truth about political injustice, survived for centuries in the oral tradition, with the first known collected edition dating around 300 B.C. While early rhetoricians used the fables to instruct scholars in grammar and style and to discuss morals and ethics in debates, by the eighteenth century Aesop's fables were widely recognized as children's literature, having been advocated for this purpose by John Locke in *Thoughts Concerning Education* (1693) and *Essay on Human Understanding* (1690). Locke maintained that the stories would delight and entertain children as well as instruct adults. He especially recommended illustrated editions of the fables, because the pictures would amuse children and encourage them to learn to read.[1]

Locke's judgment still held sway in nineteenth-century America, as indicated in a review of Collins's 1850 edition of the fables that casts it as a fondly remembered children's classic. This edition, translated by Thomas James and illustrated by John Tenniel, was a favorite in the nineteenth century, in part because of its illustrations. As one writer for the *Literary World* described, "Wily Reynard looks up from the foot of the page to the grapes gracefully pendent from a trellis at the head, the design framing a few lines of text." Indeed, these wood-engraved illustrations brought Tenniel to the attention of Mark Lennon of *Punch,* the publication where Tenniel would work as a cartoonist for half a century.[2]

The Fillmores may have selected this canonical children's text so as to be able to entertain young guests in the new library in the White House. In addition, the fables were so much a part of the nineteenth-century American mindscape that it may have been consulted as a reference book for allusions to use in essays and speeches.

This title does not appear in either the Hayes or the Roosevelt catalogues, and exactly which edition was selected for the White House cannot be determined. The *NUC* recorded fifty-three separate editions between 1820 and 1850 alone. Roorbach listed five editions published in America (one of these in French), ranging in price from $.38 to $2.00. In addition to the Collins edition, Putnam offered an 1848 London edition for $3.00, and the *London Catalogue* advertised an edition published by Law that sold for 6s. or approximately $1.44. Based on its price and popularity at the time, the $2.00 edition from R. B. Collins is a very likely candidate for purchase by the Executive Mansion.

105,133 voucher 5: Aesop's Fables $1.75.
Purchased from Charles Welford on December 13, 1850.

REFERENCES
cf. L and B 1850 p. 2; cf. L and B 1852 p. 1; cf. *LC 1816–1851* p. 6; cf. Putnam p. 2, 45, 1-s; cf. Roorbach p. 8; cf. Fillmore 1861 p. 66.

---

1. See entry 98 for Locke; Sam Pickering, introduction, and Jack Zipes, afterword to *Aesop's Fables* (New York: Signet, 2004), 4–8 and 277–78; Robert Temple, introduction to *The Complete Fables of Aesop* (New York: Penguin, 1998), ix–xxiii.

2. Joseph Jacobs, ed., *The Fables of Aesop* (New York: Burt Franklin, 1970), 195; "New Version of Aesop's Fables," *Literary World (1847–1853),* August 10, 1850, available at *APS Online,* http://www.proquest.com/products_pq/descriptions/aps.shtml; Simon Houfe, *The Dictionary of British Book Illustrators and Caricaturists 1800–1914,* rev. ed. (Suffolk: Antique Collectors Club, 1981).

≈

4. Aikin, John. *The Works of the British Poets Selected and Chronologically Arranged.* 3 vols. Philadelphia: A. Hart, 1850.

John Aikin's (1747–1822) *Selected Works of the British Poets* (1820) presents the canon of British poets as it was understood in the early nineteenth century. Arranged chronologically, it covers two and a half centuries of poetry and includes biographical and critical prefaces for each author.

The voucher reads "The British Poets 3 vols. 8vo $5.00"; without more information it would be impossible to determine with certainty which book this entry represents, yet the possibilities can be narrowed down based on the number of volumes and price. There were numerous series with "British Poets" in their titles that may have been referred to in short as the "British Poets." Usually these series number fifty or more volumes. Aikin's is one, if not the only one, that was published in three volumes, octavo, as listed on the voucher. It was reprinted in this form twice before the date it was purchased by the White House, once in 1845 by Thomas Wardle and again by Hart in 1850. Roorbach lists the latter edition with the first two volumes priced at $2.00 together and the third at $2.00. The total of $4.00 would be slightly less than the price paid by the White House. Putnam also offered this edition, but priced in cloth at $7.00.

105,133 voucher 5: The British Poets 3 vols. 8vo $5.00.
Purchased from Charles Welford on December 13, 1850.

REFERENCES
cf. Putnam p. 3; cf. Roorbach p. 10; cf. Fillmore 1847 p. 25; cf. Fillmore 1861 p. 20.

❧

5. Alison, Archibald. *History of Europe from the Commencement of the French Revolution to the Restoration of the Bourbons in MDCCCXV.* 14 vols. Edinburgh and London: William Blackwood and Sons, 1849.

Sir Archibald Alison's (1792–1867) monumental *History of Europe* (1833–42) offered the first account of the French Revolution in English. In it, Alison attributed the failure of the *ancien régime* in France to the ruling class's reluctance to stand up to the intimidation tactics of the populace. Alison had proposed this thesis earlier in a series of thirteen articles that link British parliamentary reform with the French Revolution of 1830, written for *Blackwood's Edinburgh Magazine* between January 1831 and January 1832. From Alison's perspective, Whig politics in Britain were analogous to those of the French revolutionaries, and, in his opinion, the era of democracy of the 1830s would be the beginning of a descent into anarchy.[1]

Despite Alison's Tory bias, his *History* was very successful and sold well on both sides of the Atlantic, with translations into French, German, and Arabic. Although at least one American reviewer objected to Alison's Tory views, most lauded Alison's work.[2] William Blackwood and Sons also published an atlas containing 108 plates of maps to accompany Alison's *History*. There is no evidence, however, that the Executive Mansion purchased this atlas. It is not mentioned on the voucher, nor does it appear in the Hayes or the Roosevelt catalogue.

105,133 voucher 2: Alisons Europe 14 vols. $42.00.

Purchased from Little and Brown on December 30, 1850.

Roosevelt Catalogue: Alison, <u>Sir</u> Archibald. *History of Europe from the French Revolution in 1789 to 1815.* Edinburgh, Wm. Blackwood & Sons, 1849–50. 14 vols.

TITLE PAGE

HISTORY OF EUROPE | FROM | THE COMMENCEMENT OF | THE FRENCH REVOLUTION | TO THE | RESTORATION OF THE BOURBONS | IN MDCCCXV | BY | ARCHIBALD ALISON, L. L. D. | F. R. S. E. | New Edition, with Portraits [black letter] | VOL. I. | WILLIAM BLACKWOOD AND SONS | EDINBURGH AND LONDON | MDCCCXLIX

Note. Volumes 10, 11, 12, 13, and 14 are dated MDCCCL.

REFERENCES

Hayes p. 2; Roosevelt p. 2; L and B 1852 p. 1; L and B 1853 p. 4; cf. *LC 1816–1851* p. 10; cf. Putnam p. 2-s; cf. Fillmore 1847 p. 9; cf. Fillmore ca. 1858 p. 2; cf. Fillmore 1861 p. 8.

COPY DESCRIBED

DLC: D 307 A44. *Leaf.* 220 × 131.

---

1. See entry 17 for *Blackwood's Magazine.*

2. For reviews, see "Alison's History of Europe," *Eclectic Museum of Foreign Literature, Science, and Art (1843–1844),* January 1843; "Alison's Modern Europe," *Spirit of the Times: A Chronicle of the Turf, Agriculture and Field Sports,* December 4, 1841; "Alison's History of Europe During the French Revolution," *The Albion: A Journal of News, Politics, and Literature (1822–1876),* October 3, 1835; "Biography," *Prisoner's Friend: A Monthly Magazine Devoted to Criminal Reform Philosophy,* January 11, 1851; and "A Course of Historical Reading Part II Modern History," *Universalist Quarterly and General Review,* April 1850. All of these are available at *APS Online,* http://www.proquest.com/products_pq/descriptions/aps.shtml.

∼

6. *American Almanac and Repository of Useful Knowledge.* 22 vols. Boston: Gray and Bowen, 1830–51.

The *American Almanac,* begun by Jared Sparks in 1830, remained a popular annual in America through 1861. A survey of its contents from the 1843 volume provides an example of the kind of information that it contained. The first part comprises calendars, geographical facts, astronomical information, and other reference material usually found in almanacs. Part two focuses primarily on the United States government, but includes some information related to foreign countries and territories. It lists all of the presidents and their terms and the current government offices for each department. It also provides the names of colleges, medical schools, law schools, theological schools, and religious denominations. In addition, it offers a catalogue of each state's government officials, railroads, and agricultural statistics.

Initially a complete run, from 1830 through 1850, of the *American Almanac* was purchased for the White House Library. The volumes for 1851 and 1852 were added during the Fillmore administration, and subsequent volumes were purchased under later administrations as indicated in the Hayes Catalogue, which records thirty volumes for the years from 1830 through 1859. The Fillmores would have been familiar with this *Almanac* because they owned a complete run in their personal library. In fact the Fillmore copies of the volumes for 1830 and 1831, bound together in one volume of full calf, are held in the Batchelder Collection of the Library of Congress Rare Book and Special Collections Division, inscribed "Millard Fillmore 1830" on the front pastedown.

105,133 voucher 2: Amr. Almk. 21 vols. bd. $23.62.
Purchased from Little and Brown on December 30, 1850.
109,399 voucher 1: American Almanac 1851 bound $1.37.
Purchased from Taylor and Maury on September 2, 1851.
109,399 voucher 1: American Almanac 1852 bound $1.38.
Purchased from Taylor and Maury on November 22, 1851.
Roosevelt Catalogue: *American Almanac and Repository of Useful Knowledge,* for the Years 1830–54, 1857–59. Boston, 1853–59. Vols. for 1855, 1856, missing, 2 copies of 1859.

TITLE PAGE
THE | AMERICAN ALMANAC | AND | REPOSITORY OF USEFUL KNOWLEDGE | FOR THE YEAR | 1830, | COMPRISING | A CALENDAR FOR THE YEAR; ASTRONOMICAL INFORMATION; | MISCELLANEOUS DIRECTIONS, HINTS, AND REMARKS; | AND STATISTICAL AND OTHER PARTICULARS | RESPECTING FOREIGN COUNTRIES AND | THE UNITED STATES. | [thin rule] | VOL. I. [I–XXIII] | [thin rule] | BOSTON: | PUBLISHED BY GRAY AND BOWEN. | NEW YORK: | BY G. AND H. CARVILL.
Note. The imprint changes frequently throughout the run.

REFERENCES
Hayes p. 2; Roosevelt p. 2; L and B 1850 p. 2–3; L and B 1852 p. 1; L and B 1853 p. 4; Putnam p. 4; cf. Roorbach p. 16; cf. Fillmore 1847 p. 6 and p. 18; cf. Fillmore Packing Lists p. 28; Fillmore ca. 1858 p. 1; cf. Fillmore 1861 p. 2.

COPY DESCRIBED
DLC: Batchelder Coll. Ay64 A5 1830–31. *Leaf.* 179 × 105.

7. American Quarterly Register and Magazine. Ed. James Stryker. Philadelphia, 1848–53.

The *American Quarterly Register and Magazine,* founded and edited by James Stryker, ran from 1848 through 1853 and claimed to provide a "comprehensive record of all the events and facts that belong to the history, the improvements, and the progress of the times." Stryker promised to include original articles, biography, and miscellany, along with a statement of the proceedings of Congress at the close of each session, ingredients designed to interest "all classes of readers."[1] For example, volume 2 offered a historical register for the preceding year; "Statistics" on various topics such as education, the navy, the post office, climate, and currency; "Original Communications" on topics such as the press and periodical literature, China and the Chinese, and the education of orphans; "Miscellaneous"; "Poetry"; "Quarterly Chronicle"; "Obituary Notices"; and "Documents," such as the president's annual message, revenue laws of California, and a list of the Acts of the last session of the United States Congress.

Stryker published the *American Quarterly* in Philadelphia from 1848 through 1849 and then moved it to New York in 1850, where it was published until it ceased in 1853. The Executive Mansion purchased the entire run of this periodical from James Stryker. For its contemporary readers, including the first family and their staff members, it provided an up-to-the-moment chronicle of their own time.

107,754 voucher 5: one copy American Register 6 vols. $20.00.
Purchased from James Stryker on March 24, 1852.
Hayes Catalogue: *American Quarterly Register and Magazine.* Conducted by J. Stryker. May
	1848 to 1851. v. 1 to 6. Philadelphia, 1848–53. 8°.

TITLE PAGE
THE | American [black letter] | QUARTERLY REGISTER | AND | MAGAZINE. | Causas rerum videt, earumque progressus.—Cicero. | [thin wavy rule] | Conducted by James Stryker. [black letter] | [thin wavy rule] | MAY, 1848. . . . VOL. No. I. | PHILADELPHIA: | E. C. AND J. BIDDLE, | No. 6 SOUTH FIFTH STREET.

Stryker's [black letter] | AMERICAN REGISTER | AND | MAGAZINE. | Cuasas rerum videt, earumque progressus.—CICERO. | [wavy rule] Conducted by James Stryker. | [wavy rule] | 1851—VOLUME VI. | [decorative rule] | NEW YORK: | PUBLISHED FOR THE PROPRIETORS, | AT 290 BROADWAY.
	Note. The imprint changed several times through the course of publication.

REFERENCES
Hayes p. 265; cf. Fillmore ca. 1858 p. 60.

COPY DESCRIBED
DLC: AP2 S92 3rd set.

---

	1. From an advertisement found on the original wrapper bound into volume one of the Library of Congress copy of this periodical.

～

8. *The American Review: A Whig Journal.* New York: Wiley and Putnam, 1845–47; *A Whig Journal Devoted to Politics and Literature* (1847–50); and *The American Whig Review* (1850–52).

The American Review: A Whig Journal was founded in 1845 to provide a voice for the Whig party that would counterbalance the political agenda of the *Democratic Review.*[1] Fillmore probably joined with other Whig members of the Twenty-Seventh Congress, including his friends Daniel Webster and John Pendleton Kennedy, to sign a resolution in support of this new periodical.[2] The first editor was George H. Colton, who died during the *Review*'s third year of publication. James D. Whelpley succeeded him and continued as editor through 1849, when George W. Peck took the helm and served in this position through 1852.[3]

	Like the *Democratic Review,* the *American Review* offered political news and commentary in combination with literary reviews, original poetry, new prose fiction, and philosophical and moral essays. Edgar Allan Poe's "The Raven" made one of its first public appearances in the *American Review*'s second number. It continued to publish a number of other works by Poe as well as pieces by James Russell Lowell, George P. Marsh, John Quincy Adams, Daniel Webster, Edward Everett, and John C. Calhoun.[4] In content, it sought to offer a balance between political news and other topics, but politics won out, especially during the period preceding the election of 1847, when it endorsed the Taylor-Fillmore ticket. With the demise of the Whig party in 1852, the *American Review* ceased publication.[5] The selection of both the *Democratic Review* and the *American Review* for the Executive Mansion library ensured readers access to essays written from a variety of political perspectives as well as much contemporary American literature.

105,133 voucher 5: Whig Review 12 vols. $18.00.
Purchased from Charles Welford on December 13, 1850.

TITLE PAGE
Vol. I.
THE | AMERICAN | REVIEW: | A WHIG JOURNAL | OF | POLITICS, LITERATURE, ART AND SCIENCE. | [thin rule] | "TO STAND BY THE CONSTITUTION." | [thin rule] | VOL. I. | [thin wavy rule] | Pulchrum est bene facere Republicæ, etiam bene dicere haud absurdum est. | [thin wavy rule] | NEW-YORK: | WILEY AND PUTNAM. | [thin rule] | 1845.

Vol. VII.
THE | AMERICAN REVIEW: | A WHIG JOURNAL, | DEVOTED TO | POLITICS AND LITERATURE. | [thin rule] | "TO STAND BY THE CONSTITUTION." | [thin rule] | NEW SERIES, VOL. I.—WHOLE VOL. VII. | NEW YORK: | PUBLISHED AT 118 NASSAU STREET. | [thin rule] | 1848.

Vol. XI.
THE | AMERICAN | WHIG REVIEW. | "TO STAND BY THE CONSTITUTION." | NEW SERIES, VOL. V.—WHOLE VOL. XI. | NEW YORK: | PUBLISHED AT 118 NASSAU STREET. | 1850.

REFERENCES
Roorbach p. 644.

COPY DESCRIBED
DLC: AP 2 A465. *Leaf.* 220 × 136.

---

1. See entry 176 for the *Democratic Review.*
2. Fillmore would later appoint Webster as his secretary of state and Kennedy as secretary of the navy. See entry 195 for Kennedy's *Memoirs of William Wirt* and entries 184–85 for Webster's works and speeches.
3. Frank Luther Mott, *A History of American Magazines, 1741–1850* (Cambridge: Harvard University Press, 1939), 750–51; Alan Nourie and Barbara Nourie, *American Mass-Market Magazines* (New York: Greenwood Press, 1990), 18–19.
4. See entry 28 for John C. Calhoun; see "White House Collection," 23, for more about Edward Everett and the library; see also appendix C for the list of books that Everett recommended for the library.
5. Mott, *History of American Magazines, 1741–1850,* 752–54; Nourie and Nourie, *American Mass-Market Magazines,* 19–20.

9. *The Annual Biography and Obituary.* 21 vols. London: Longman, et al., 1817–37.

Each volume of this annual provides brief biographical essays about celebrated people who died the year preceding its publication date. In its early years it included sections entitled "Neglected Biographies," "An Analysis of Recent Biographical Works," "General List of Persons Who Have Died," "Chronological Table of Subjects," and "An Alphabetical Table of Subjects." These subsections were discontinued by the eighth volume in order to devote more space to the main entries. Volumes 1 through 5 label the main entries "Memoirs of Celebrated Men Who Have Died in [year]." While volume 1 is devoted entirely to male subjects, beginning with volume 2, which includes Her Royal Highness Princess Charlotte, a few women appear in nearly every installment, including Madame de Staël, Mrs. Garrick, the Duchess of York, and Mrs. Piozzi. In volume 6 "Men" changes to "Persons" in the heading for the main entries.

105,133 voucher 2: Annual Biography obity 21 vols. $32.00.
Purchased from Little and Brown on December 30, 1850.
Roosevelt Catalogue: *Annual Biography and Obituary for the Years 1817–1837.* London, Longman, 1817–37, 21 vols.

TITLE PAGE
THE | ANNUAL | BIOGRAPHY AND OBITURARY, | FOR THE YEAR | 1817. [1818–1837] | [swelled rule] | VOL. I. | [swelled rule] | *LONDON:* | PRINTED FOR LONGMAN, HURST, REES, ORME, AND BROWN, | PATERNOSTER-ROW. | 1817.
> *Notes.*
> Volumes 4 through 10, 12, and 17 through 21 add a thin rule between the imprint and the date.
> Volumes 8 through 21 add Green's name to the imprint.
> Volumes 12 and 14 through 21 change the lineation of the imprint to read, 'LONDON: | PRINTED FOR | LONGMAN, REES, ORME, BROWN, AND GREEN, | . . .'
> Volume 13 reverts back to previous lineation for imprint.
> Volumes 16 through 21 add another Longman to the imprint so that it reads: 'LONGMAN, REES, ORME, BROWN, GREEN, AND LONGMAN.'
> Volumes 17 through 21 change the 'AND' in the imprint to an ampersand.

REFERENCES
Hayes p. 3; Roosevelt p. 3; L and B 1850 p. 4; cf. *LC 1816–1851* p. 16.

COPY DESCRIBED
DLC: CT 100 A6. *Leaf.* 212 × 128.

10. *Arabian Nights.* Ed. Edward Lane. 3 vols. London: Murray, 1850.

The *Arabian Nights* was immensely popular in nineteenth-century England and America among readers of all ages. One American reviewer called it the most celebrated of the "Eastern works" and described the tales as "powerful delineations of national character, seen through a veil of delicately wrought fiction." An 1848 article on children's literature named the *Arabian Nights*, alongside Bunyan and Le Sage, as a work that had become not only part of "the world's poetry, but of its philosophy, the accepted of all languages."[1]

Edward Lane was the first of three major translators of the *Arabian Nights* into English during the nineteenth century; the other two, John Payne and Richard Burton, followed later in the century.[2] Lane first published his translation in monthly parts that appeared from 1838 to 1841 and later issued it as three bound volumes. Background information that he had collected for his earlier work, *Manners and Customs of Modern Egyptians*, enabled him to include many footnotes on subjects such as "cloves, graveyards, gypsum, chess, hippopotami, laws of inheritance, perspiration, polygamy, rubbish tips," and much more in hopes that it would serve instructional purposes for its readers.[3]

Lane designed this edition to occupy a respectable place in the drawing room, expurgating the text and eliminating or rewriting certain sections that he deemed unsuitable for the entire family. He omitted stories that he thought were repetitive and "discarded most of the poetry as irrelevant," not always indicating where material had been cut or altered.[4] His expurgations may have made this edition especially appealing to nineteenth-century readers' sense of propriety and prudence.

Despite (or perhaps because of) these editing procedures, Lane's edition was well received. Leigh Hunt lauded this edition in the *London and Westminster:* "Mr. Lane's version is beyond all doubt a most praiseworthy, painstaking, learned and delightful work; worthy to be received with honour and thanks by all lovers of 'Arabian Nights' and to form an epoch in the history of popular Eastern literature."[5]

While we cannot be certain which edition of the *Arabian Nights* was purchased for the Executive Mansion library, the possibilities can be narrowed down on the basis of the date, the price, the number of volumes, and the bookseller from whom it was purchased. There was a three-volume edition of 1847 from C. S. Francis of New York. However, Roorbach lists this edition as selling for $3.50; therefore, it may be ruled out unless an explanation can be found for the higher price cited in the vouchers, such as evidence that the White House purchased it in an upgraded binding. Several catalogues from Little and Brown, the seller from whom the White House purchased this book, list three-volume Lane editions of *Arabian Nights* but do not name publishers. The firm's 1852 law catalogue places this listing under the category "English editions of Miscellaneous Books at Net prices" and gives its price as $4.50. Since James Brown had a close personal and business relationship with the London publisher John Murray and imported a number of his publications, Murray's three-volume Lane edition of 1850 stands as a likely candidate for purchase by the Executive Mansion.[6] Regardless of the edition selected, the Fillmores were familiar with the *Arabian Nights*, for it appears in all three of the catalogues compiled of their personal libraries.

105,133 voucher 2: Arabian Nights 3 vols. $4.00.
Purchased from Little and Brown on December 30, 1850.

REFERENCES
cf. L and B 1850 p. 52; cf. L and B Law 1852 p. 30; cf. L and B 1853 p. 5; cf. *LC 1816–1851* p. 17; cf. Putnam p. 6; cf. Fillmore 1847 p. 9; cf. Fillmore ca. 1858 p. 2; cf. Fillmore 1861 p. 4.

1. "The Arabian Nights Entertainments, Carefully Revised," *American Quarterly Review,* December 1829, and "Quaint Stories for Children," *Literary World (1847–1853),* October 22, 1848, both available at *APS Online,* http://www.proquest.com/products_pq/descriptions/aps.shtml; see entry 144 for Le Sage.

2. *Arabian Nights,* trans. Husain Haddawy (New York: Norton, 1990), xv.

3. Robert Irwin, *The Arabian Nights: A Companion* (London: Penguin, 1994), 24.

4. Ibid., 25.

5. Qtd. in ibid.

6. James Brown even named his youngest son after Murray; see *One Hundred Years of Publishing, 1837–1937* (Boston: Little, Brown and Co., 1937), 22.

~

11. Atcheson, Nathaniel. *Report of a Case Recently Argued and Determined in His Majesty's Court of the King's Bench.* **London: Butterworth, et al., 1800.**

Nathaniel Atcheson (1771–1825) published this report to provide better documentation for admiralty law, since England's recent engagement in war had drawn attention to a lack of texts related to this topic (v–vi). Fillmore most likely ordered this very specialized book for its relevance to the Cuban filibuster, since it was among a number of other books on admiralty and international law that Fillmore purchased during the aftermath of this event. The case on which Atcheson reports bears similarity to that of the *Pampero,* the ship used in the filibuster, which was seized, tried for libel, condemned, and sold at public auction.[1] Atcheson's report specifically addresses the rights of the ship's owner. Because it included a list of cases, statutes, and treaties cited, it would also have served as a useful reference to additional sources.

107,754 voucher 4: 1 vol. Atchinsons Reports $1.50.
Purchased from Little and Brown on December 31, 1851.
Hayes Catalogue: Atcheson N. *Report of a Case in the Court of King's Bench on the Validity of a Sentence of Condemnation by an Enemy's Consul in a Neutral Port.* London, 1800. 8°.

TITLE PAGE
REPORT | OF A | CASE | RECENTLY ARGUED AND DETERMINED | IN HIS MAJESTY's | Court of the King's Bench, [black letter] | ON | THE VALIDITY OF A SENTENCE OF CONDEMNATION | BY AN ENEMY'S CONSUL IN A NEUTRAL PORT, | AND | THE RIGHT OF THE OWNER OF THE SHIP, TO CALL UPON THE | UNDERWRITERS, TO REIMBURSE HIM THE MONEY PAID | FOR THE PURCHASE OF THE SHIP AT SALE BY | AUCTION, UNDER SUCH SENTENCE. | WITH | AN APPENDIX, | CONTAINING | THE FRENCH LAWS NOW IN FORCE RELATIVE TO | MARITIME PRIZES, &c. | AND | *The Danish Ordinance, of the 20th of April, 1796,* | IMPOSING A DUTY ON FOREIGN SHIPS. | [thick/thin double rule] | By NATHANIEL ATCHESON, F.A.S. Solicitor. | [thin/ thick double rule] | *LONDON:* | PRINTED BY W. AND C. SPILSBURY, SNOWHILL; | AND SOLD BY J. BUTTERWORTH, FLEET-STREET, AND J. HATCHARD, | Nº 173, PICCADILLY. ALSO BY MOTTLEY, PORTSMOUTH; | GRAHAM AND REED, SUNDERLAND; CHARNLEY, | NEWCASTLE- | UPON-TYNE; APPLEBY, NORTH SHEILDS; BROWNE, HULL; | AND BUSH, YARMOUTH. | [thin rule] | 1800.

PAGINATION
i–xii 1–166.

CONTENTS
i title, ii statement: "The profit arising from the sale of this publication will be applied to the fund of 'The Society for Bettering the Condition, and Increasing the Comforts of the Poor,'" iii dedication to "The Right Honourable William Kent Scott," iv blank, v–vi advertisement, vii–x contents, xi–xii lists of cases, statutes, and treaties cited, as well as errrata, 1–52 text, 53–166 appendix.

REFERENCES
Hayes p. 7; cf. Harvard p. 10; Marvin p. 74.

COPY DESCRIBED
DLC: Trials (A + E) Rockwood. *Leaf.* 216 × 127.

---

1. Antonio Rafael de la Cova, "Cuban Filibustering in Jacksonville in 1851," *Northeast Florida History* (1996): 17–34.

∽

12. Bacon, Francis. *The Works of Francis Bacon.* Ed. Basil Montagu. 3 vols. Philadelphia: Carey and Hart, 1848.

During the nineteenth century Francis Bacon (1561–1626) was known as the "founder of modern philosophy" (1:iii) and considered "one of the most remarkable men of whom any age can boast."[1] Basil Montagu (1770–1851), author and legal reformer, edited an edition of Bacon between 1825 and 1837, which was originally published in sixteen volumes in London. In 1841 Carey and Hart began publishing Montagu's text in a three-volume edition in Philadelphia. The *New Yorker*'s announcement of this edition testified further to Bacon's reputation in America when it called his works "the greatest of the British Classics" and remarked, "if the publishers can, by presenting his works in such a form that render them attainable by general readers, make them familiar to our reading community, they will do the country a great service."[2]

105,133 voucher 5: Lord Bacons Works 3 vols. $8.50.
Purchased from Charles Welford on December 13, 1850.
Roosevelt Catalogue: Bacon, Francis. *The Works of Francis Bacon, Lord Chancellor of England.* A New Edition with a Life of the Author, by Basil Montague [*sic*], Esquire. Philadelphia, Carey & Hart, 1848, 3 vols.

TITLE PAGE
[thin double-rule frame enclosing all of the following text] | THE WORKS | OF | FRANCIS BACON | Lord Chancellor of England. [black letter] | A NEW EDITION: | WITH A LIFE OF THE AUTHOR, | BY | BASIL MONTAGU, ESQ. | IN THREE VOLUMES. | VOL. I. [II–III.] | PHILADELPHIA: | CAREY AND HART. | 1848. | *Stereotyped by L. Johnson* [The last line appears outside of the frame.]

PAGINATION

Vol. I. i–cxx 1–456.

Vol. II. i–viii 1–590.

Vol. III. i–xvi 1–584.

CONTENTS

Vol. I. i title, ii printer's imprint, iii–iv "Advertisement of the American Publishers," v–viii
    preface, ix–xiii contents, xiv blank, xv dedication of "this Life of Francis Bacon" to "The
    Reverend and Learned Martin Davy, D. D., Master of Caius College, Henry Bickersteth,
    Clement T. Swanston, George Tuthill, and to the memory of Samuel Romilly," xvi blank,
    xvii–cxvii text of "Life of Bacon," cxviii blank, cxix section title, "Lord Bacon's Works,"
    cxx blank, 1–455 text, 456 blank.

Vol. II. i title, ii printer's imprint, iii–viii contents, 1–589 text, 590 blank.

Vol. III. i title, ii printer's imprint, iii–xv contents, xvi blank, 1–544 text, 545–84 index.

REFERENCES

Hayes p. 11; Roosevelt p. 4; cf. Putnam p. 10; cf. Roorbach p. 36; cf. Fillmore ca. 1858 p. 6; cf.
Fillmore 1861 p. 14.

COPY DESCRIBED

ViU: Phil B128w 1848. *Leaf.* 245 × 152.

---

1. "Francis Bacon," *Encyclopaedia Americana.*
2. "Literary Intelligence," *New-Yorker (1836–1841),* November 21, 1840, available at *APS Online,* http://
www.proquest.com/products_pq/descriptions/aps.shtml.

∾

13. Bancroft, George. *History of the United States.* **4 vols. Boston: Little and Brown, 1850–52.**

George Bancroft's *History of the United States* offered a salutary message in the midst of the
political turmoil of the nineteenth century by assuming "providential guidance, the transi-
tory significance of the individual, popular conservatism, and the durability of the nation's
political institutions."[1] In it Bancroft attempted to document "how divinely ordained natural laws sustained growth," and to articulate "a national consciousness, providing substan-
tiation for an optimistic faith."[2]

Bancroft began publishing his *History* in 1834, and completed the tenth and final volume
in 1874. After the publication of volume 1, Bancroft's work on the history was interrupted
by his acceptance of several government appointments. When his service ended with the
election of the Whig Zachary Taylor in 1848, Bancroft retired to New York, where he continued writing his *History.*

The *History* received a warm reception from reviewers. Edward Everett, writing for the
North American Review, proclaimed "it does such justice to its noble subject, as to supersede
the necessity of any future work of the same kind; and if completed as commenced, will
unquestionably forever be regarded, both as an American and as an English classic."[3] Everett
followed up this review with a letter to Bancroft in which he wrote, "I think you have written a work which will last while the memory of America lasts."[4]

The Executive Mansion purchased the first three volumes of Bancroft's *History* in June of 1851 and added volume 4 in March of 1852. Apparently, the presidents who succeeded Fillmore in the White House continued to purchase volumes of the *History*, for in 1877 the Hayes Catalogue recorded all ten volumes. Although it identifies a Little and Brown edition, it does not specify the imprint year for each volume, only the inclusive years for the set, 1850–70. Volume 4 was certainly dated 1852, since that was the year that it was first published as well as the year that it was purchased; volumes 1 through 3 were probably all dated 1850, the year of the fourteenth edition. By 1840 the first three volumes had been stereotyped, and the 1850 edition was most likely printed from the same set of plates. The White House copy was presumably bound in either half or full calf since Putnam and Little and Brown both list the first three volumes priced at $6.00 in cloth, $8.50 in half calf, and $10.00 in "calf extra."

107,754 voucher 3: Bancroft's History of the U. S. 3 vols. $8.50.

Purchased from Franck Taylor on June 12, 1851.

109,399 voucher 4: Bancroft's vol. 4 $2.25.

Purchased from Franck Taylor on March 26, 1852.

Roosevelt Catalogue: Bancroft, George. *History of the United States, from the Discovery of the American Continent.* Boston, Little and Brown 1850–75, 10 vols.

REFERENCES

Hayes p. 11; Roosevelt p. 4; L and B 1850 p. 6; L and B 1852 p. 1; cf. L and B 1853 p. 33; cf. Putnam p. 11 and p. 3-s; Roorbach p. 39; cf. Fillmore 1847 p. 11; cf. Fillmore Packing Lists p. 23; cf. Fillmore ca. 1858 p. 7; cf. Fillmore 1861 p. 214 and p. 216.

---

1. Lilian Handlin, "Bancroft, George," *ANB Online*, http://www.anb.org/articles/14/14-0034.

2. Ibid.

3. "Bancroft's History of the United States," *North American Review (1821–1940)*, January 1835, available at *APS Online*, http://www.proquest.com/products_pq/descriptions/aps.shtml. Attribution to Everett made by M. A. DeWolfe Howe in *Dictionary of American Biography* Base Set, American Council of Learned Societies, 1928–36 (hereafter *DAB*), reproduced in *Biography Resource Center* (Farmington Hills, Mich.: Thomson Gale, 2007), http://gale.cengage.com/servlet/BiographyRC.

4. Qtd. in "George Bancroft," *DAB*, http://gale.cengage.com/servlet/BiographyRC.

≈

**14. Barthélemy, Jean Jacques. *Travels of Anacharsis the Younger in Greece.* 6th ed. 6 vols. London: Rivington, Clarke, Longman et al., 1825.

————. *Maps, Plans, Views, and Coins, Illustrative of the Travels of Anacharsis the Younger in Greece.* 6th ed. London: Rivington, Clarke, Longman et al., 1825.

Voyage du jeune Anacharsis en Grèce (1788) was the most widely read book in France during the nineteenth century. In it Jean Jacques Barthélemy (1716–95), French archaeologist and author, presented the fictional travel journal of a young Scythian who made a thirty-seven-year journey to Greece. The narrator recounts his impressions of various places, transcribes conversations with different people, and includes letters from correspondents. *Travels* went into numerous English translations and revived interest in Greek culture and ancient erudition. The seventh volume of this work consists of a series of maps constructed by Barbié du Bocage, which, since many of the ancient sites were unknown at the time of Barthelémy's writing, are geographically inaccurate.[1]

  Travels of Anacharsis stood on the White House shelves among a small number of other books related to ancient Greek culture. The copy of *Travels* described here may have been the Executive Mansion copy. A three-by-five-inch typed card containing a cataloguing record for this book was found between pages 73 and 74 of volume 6 with a note, penciled in the upper right corner, that reads: "White House Coll. Deck 37 not in rare books." This copy has been rebound, and any inscription that may have been on the front pastedown to indicate that it had been the Executive Mansion copy has been lost.

105,133 voucher 5: Anacharsis' Travel's in Greece 7 vols. & Atlas $12.00.
Purchased from Charles Welford on December 13, 1850.
Roosevelt Catalogue: Barthélemy, Jean Jacques. *Travels of Anacharsis the Younger in Greece, during the Middle of the Fourth Century before the Christian Era.* Sixth edition, maps etc. London, 1825, 7 vols.

Travels of Anacharsis the Younger in Greece.

TITLE PAGE

TRAVELS | OF | ANACHARSIS THE YOUNGER | IN | GREECE, | DURING | *THE MIDDLE OF THE FOURTH CENTURY* | BEFORE THE CHRISTIAN ÆRA. | [thin rule] | BY THE ABBE BARTHELEMY, | LATE KEEPER OF THE MEDALS IN THE CABINET OF THE KING OF FRANCE, | AND MEMBER OF THE ROYAL ACADEMY OF INSCRIPTIONS | AND BELLES LETTRES. | [thin rule] | *TRANSLATED FROM THE FRENCH.* | [short swelled rule] | IN SIX VOLUMES; | AND A SEVENTH, IN QUARTO, CONTAINING | MAPS, PLANS, VIEWS, AND COINS, [black letter] | *Illustrative of the Geography and Antiquities of ancient Greece.* | [short swelled rule] | THE SIXTH EDITION: | Carefully revised, corrected, and enlarged, by the last improved Paris Edition prepared | for the Press by the Author; with Memoirs of the Life of J. J. Barthelemy, | written by himself, and embellished with his Portrait. | [thin rule] | VOL. I. [II–VI.] | [thin rule] | LONDON: | PRINTED FOR C. AND J. RIVINGTON; J. AND W. T. CLARKE; LONGMAN, | HURST, REES, ORME, BROWN, AND GREEN; T. CADELL; J. AND A. ARCH; | JOHN RICHARDSON; J. MAWMAN; W. GINGER; J. BOOKER; R. SCHOLEY; | T. TEGG; BALDWIN, CRADOCK, AND JOY; J. BOHN; R. SAUNDERS; E. | EDWARDS; J. DUNCAN; G. B. WHITTAKER; SIMPKIN AND MARSHALL; | T. AND J. ALLMAN; HARDING, TRIPHOOK, AND LEPARD; C. TAYLOR; | C. SMITH; J. WICKSTEED; AND F. MASON. | [thin rule] | 1825.

PAGINATION

Vol. I. [4] i–xviii 1–464.
Vol. II. i–iv 1–464 463–94.
Vol. III. [4] 1–472.
Vol. IV. [4] 1–522.
Vol. V. [4] 1–492.
Vol. VI. [4] 1–440.

CONTENTS

Vol. I. [1] title page, [2] printer's imprint, [3]–[4] contents, i–xiii translator's preface, xiv blank, xv–xviii advertisement of the French editors, 1–120 "Memoirs of the Life of J. J. Barthelemy," 121–24 "Advertisement of the Author," 125–26 "Chronological order of the Travels of Anacharsis," 127–453 introduction, 454 blank, 455–63 notes, 464 printer's imprint.

Vol. II. i title page, ii printer's imprint, iii–iv contents, 1–464 text, 465–94 notes.

Vol. III. [1] title page, [2] printer's imprint, [3]–[4] contents, 1–450 text, 451–72 notes.

Vol. IV. [1] title page, [2] printer's imprint, [3]–[4] contents, 1–498 text, 499–522 notes.

Vol. V. [1] title page, [2] printer's imprint, [3]–[4] contents, 1–467 text, 468 blank, 469–91 notes, 492 printer's imprint.

Vol. VI. [1] title page, [2] printer's imprint, [3]–[4] contents, 1–218 text, 219–31 notes, 232 blank, 233 "Advertisement Concerning the Following Tables," 234 "Contents of the Tables," 235–358 tables, 359–440 index.

> *Note.* The text in volume 2 runs through the second page numbered 464.

REFERENCES

Hayes p. 11; Roosevelt p. 4; cf. Fillmore 1861 p. 2; cf. Fillmore ca. 1858 p. 3; cf. Fillmore 1847 p. 20; cf. *LC 1816–1851* p. 13.

COPY DESCRIBED

DLC: DF 28 B4 1825. *Leaf.* 210 × 127.

Maps, Plans, Views, and Coins, Illustrative of the Travels of Anacharsis the Younger in Greece.

TITLE PAGE

Maps, Plans, Views, and Coins, [black letter] | ILLUSTRATIVE OF THE | TRAVELS | OF | ANACHARSIS THE YOUNGER | IN | *GREECE,* | DURING | THE MIDDLE OF THE FOURTH CENTURY | BEFORE THE CHRISTIAN ÆRA. | [thick/thin double rule] | SIXTH EDITION. | ACCURATELY RE-ENGRAVED FROM THOSE OF THE LAST PARIS EDITION. | [thin/thick double rule] | LONDON: | PRINTED FOR C. AND J. RIVINGTON; J. AND W. CLARKE; LONGMAN, HURST, REES, ORME, BROWN, | AND GREEN; T. CADELL; J. AND A. ARCH; JOHN RICHARDSON; J. MAWMAN; W. GINGER; | J. BOOKER; R. SCHOLEY; T. TEGG; BALDWIN, CRADOCK, AND JOY; J. BOHN; R. SAUNDERS; | E. EDWARDS; J. DUNCAN; G. B. WHITTAKER; SIMPKIN AND MARSHALL; T. AND J. ALLMAN; | HARDING, TRIPHOOK, AND LEPARD; C. TAYLOR; C. SMITH; J. WICKSTEED; AND F. MASON. | [thin rule] | 1825.

PAGINATION

i–iv 1–108.

CONTENTS

i title, ii printer's imprint, iii–iv table of the plates, 1–97 "Critical Observations on the Maps of Ancient Greece; Compiled for the Travels of Anacharsis the Younger. By M. Barbié du Bocage," 98 blank, 99–103 "Note Relative to Plate No. XIX.* Representing the Two Pediments of the Parthenon, in the State in which they were in 1674," 104 blank, 105–6 "Explanation of the Plate of Medals and Coins," 107–8 blank.

PLATES

Engraved portrait frontispiece of J. J. Barthelemy, "Published by J. Mawman and the other
    Proprietors 1817."
All thirty-nine plates that are called for to complete the volume are present.

REFERENCES

Hayes p. 11; Roosevelt p. 4; cf. Fillmore 1847 p. 1; cf. Fillmore ca. 1858 p. 1; cf. Fillmore 1861 p. 2.

COPY DESCRIBED

DLC: DF 28 B4 1825. *Leaf.* 273 × 207.

---

1. "Barthélemy, Jean Jacques," *Penny Cyclopaedia;* Merriam Webster, *Encyclopedia of Literature* (Springfield, Mass.: Merriam-Webster, 1995), 109–10.

≈

15. *Bible.*

Nearly every home in nineteenth-century America would have owned a Bible, and the
White House was no exception, at least not after the Fillmores came to office. One can
almost hear Senator Pearce's dramatic declaration: "With regard to the Executive Mansion,
not a book, not even a Bible, has been furnished by the Government," echoing through the
Capitol as he persuaded Congress to fund the new library.[1] As an adult, Millard recalled his
childhood when his family's library was made up of a Bible, an almanac, and a hymn book.[2]
The Fillmores were a devout couple who regularly observed Sunday as a day of rest and
attended church services, and they encouraged their children to do the same. Although
Abigail was the daughter of a Baptist minister, the couple was married by an Episcopal clergyman and later joined a Unitarian church in Buffalo.[3] This Bible was one of the first purchases made for the White House Library, purchased prior to congressional approval of
funding and charged to the account designated "furnishings for the President's house."
Charles Lanman later selected another Bible for the White House, which appears on the list
of books sent on approval from Little and Brown as an "Oxford Bible" on fine paper for
$8.00.[4] The Fillmores must have found the smaller and less expensive duodecimo that they
had initially selected sufficient; this second Bible is not listed on the voucher for the books
actually purchased and must have been returned to the seller.

105,579 voucher 1: 1 Bible 12mo., morocco $2.62.
Purchased from George Crosby on August 19, 1850.

REFERENCES

cf. L and B Law 1852 p. 31; cf. L and B 1853 p. 9; cf. Fillmore 1847 p. 9 and p. 17; cf. Fillmore Packing Lists p. 17; cf. Fillmore ca. 1858 p. 5, p. 45, and p. 47; cf. Fillmore 1861 pp. 16–17 and p. 150.

---

1. See "White House Collection," 10, for Senator Pearce's role in obtaining funding for the library.

2. Robert J. Rayback, *Millard Fillmore: Biography of a President* (Buffalo: Henry Stewart for the Buffalo Historical Society, 1959), 6.

3. Ibid., 45–46.

4. Charles Lanman, letter to President Millard Fillmore, December 12, 1850, Millard Fillmore Papers, Buffalo and Erie County Historical Society, Buffalo, N.Y. (hereafter Millard Fillmore Papers, BECHS).

≈

16. Blackstone, Sir William. *Commentaries on the Laws of England.* Ed. John Wendell. 4 vols. New York: Harper, 1847.

Sir William Blackstone's *Commentaries on the Laws of England* (1765–69) stands as the most influential law book ever published in the English language. Indeed, it was the first legal text that Fillmore read when he began to study law. *Commentaries* grew from a course of lectures on the laws of England that Blackstone had delivered at Oxford in 1753. Setting out to document and elucidate the law of his own time, Blackstone explained legal principles so thoroughly, with reference to their history, that he provided the most complete history of English law to date.

The *Commentaries* began to be published with volume 1 in 1765; three volumes followed over the next four years. By 1854 twenty-three successive British and Irish editions of Blackstone's *Commentaries* had been published. Just as popular in the United States as it was in England, the *Commentaries* appeared in nearly one hundred American editions before 1900. Its widespread use in America fostered the sharing of common legal principles by the two nations and the use of a common language in which to discuss these principles.[1] In addition, translations of the *Commentaries* were published in French, German, Italian, and Russian.

According to Marvin, "not a treaty mentioned in the whole bibliography of common law" has generated as much "contrariety of opinion" as Blackstone's *Commentaries.* It was extensively praised and criticized. In 1847 Marvin noted the absence of a good American edition of Blackstone.[2] Perhaps Wendell, a lawyer, legal editor, and state supreme court reporter in upstate New York, met this need with the edition described here, which includes notes by Joseph Chitty and Edward Christian, with analysis at the beginning of each volume from the third edition of Blackstone's *Tracts* (1771).[3]

105,133 voucher 7: Wendells Blackstone 4 vols. $6.50.
Purchased from Franck Taylor on November 11, 1850.
Hayes Catalogue: Blackstone, Sir W. *Commentaries on the Laws of England.* With notes by
    J. L. Wendell 4 v. New York, 1847 8°.

TITLE PAGE
COMMENTARIES | ON | THE LAWS OF ENGLAND: | IN FOUR BOOKS; | WITH
AN ANALYSIS OF THE WORK. | BY | SIR WILLIAM BLACKSTONE, Knt,. | ONE OF
THE JUSTICES OF THE COURT OF COMMON PLEAS. | WITH THE LAST
CORRECTIONS OF THE AUTHOR, AND NOTES, | From the Twenty=first London
Edition. [black letter] | WITH COPIOUS NOTES EXPLAINING THE CHANGES IN
THE LAW EFFECTED | BY DECISION OR STATUE DOWN TO 1844. | [decorative rule]
| VOL. FIRST, BY J. F. HARGRAVE, | OF LINCOLN'S INN, BARRISTER AT LAW. | VOL.
SECOND, BY G. SWEET, | OF THE INNER TEMPLE, BARRISTER AT LAW. | VOL.
THIRD, BY R. COUCH, | OF THE MIDDLE TEMPLE, BARRISTER AT LAW. | VOL.
FOURTH, BY W. N. WELSBY, | RECORDER OF CHESTER. | [decorative rule] |
TOGETHER WITH THE NOTES ADAPTING THE WORK TO THE AMERICAN
STUDENT. | BY JOHN L. WENDELL, | LATE STATE REPORTER OF NEW YORK. |
IN FOUR VOLUMES. | VOL. I. [II–IV.] | NEW YORK: | HARPER & BROTHERS,
PUBLISHERS, | 82 CLIFF STREET. | 1847.

PAGINATION

Vol. I. i–xlviii [*478*].

Vol. II. i–xx 1–660.

Vol. III. i–xx 1–468.

Vol. IV. i–xxiv 1–482 i–lxx.

> *Note.* The irregular pagination in volume 1 makes actual page numbers beyond the preliminaries irrelevant; therefore, only a page count has been provided.

CONTENTS

Vol. I. i title, ii copyright statement, iii dedication to the Queen, iv blank, v–vi "Preface to the Twenty-First Edition," vii–viii "Preface to the American Edition," ix–x "Sir William Blackstone's Preface" and postscript, xi–xxxv "Life of the Author," xxxvi blank, xxxvii "Contents of the Analysis of Vol. I.," xxxviii blank, xxxix–xlvii "Analysis Introduction of the Study, Nature, and Extent of the Laws of England," xlviii blank, [1] section title, "Commentaries of the Laws of England: In Four Books; With an Analysis of the Work. By Sir William Blackstone, Knt., One of the Justices of the Court of Common Pleas," [2] blank, [3]–[466] text, [467–77] index, [478] blank.

Vol. II. i title, ii copyright statement, iii "Contents of the Analysis of Book II," iv blank, v–xvi "Analysis of Book II Of the Rights of Things," xvii contents of the appendix, xviii blank, xix section title, xx blank, 1–625 text, 626 blank, 627–44 appendix, 645–60 index.

Vol. III. i title, ii copyright statement, iii "Preface to the Third Volume," iv blank, v "Contents of the Analysis of Book III," vi blank, vii–xvi "Analysis of Book III of Private Wrongs," xvii contents of the appendix, xviii blank, xix section title, xx blank, 1–425 text, 426 blank, 427–53 appendix, 454 blank, 455–68 index.

Vol. IV. i title, ii copyright statement, iii "Preface to the fourth volume," iv blank, v–x "Table of Contents, Book IV Public Wrongs," xi "Contents of the Analysis of Book IV," xii blank, xiii–xxii "Analysis Book IV of Public Wrongs," xxiii section title, xxiv blank, 1–482 text, i–x appendix, xi–lxx index.

> *Note.* The section title on 1:[1], 2:xix, 3:xix, and 4:xiii reads the same for all four volumes. A transcription has been provided for volume 1 only.

PLATES

Vol. I.

Portrait frontispiece, "The Honourable Sir William Blackstone, Kt. One of the Justices of the Court of Common Pleas," engraved by C. Phillips, based on a portrait by Gainsborough.

Vol. II.

Facing 237, "Table of Consanguinity."

Facing 276, "Table of Descents," showing maternal and paternal lines with a note reading, "This table exhibits the course of descent prior to the year 1834," engraved by W. Kemble.

Bound after the table above, "Table of Descents," with a note reading, "The order of Descent at the Common Law is indicated by Numerals, that subsequent to the year 1833 by Arabic figures," engraved by W. Kemble.

Vol. III–IV.

None.

BINDING

Vols. III–IV. Law calf, with spine labels, top label red with gilt stamp '[thick/thin rule] | WENDELL'S | BLACKSTONES | COMMENTARIES | [thin/thick rule]'; lower label black with gilt stamp, '[thick/thin double rule] | VOL. III. [IV.] | PRIVATE WRONGS. | [thin/thick double rule]'

> *Notes.* Volume 4 differs only in the text on lower spine label, which reads 'PUBLIC WRONGS.' Volumes 1 and 2 have been rebound.

REFERENCES

Hayes p. 28; *BEAL* 5335; Greenleaf; cf. Harvard p. 23; cf. Marvin p. 122; Roorbach p. 609; cf. Fillmore Packing Lists p. 21; cf. Fillmore ca. 1858 p. 6; cf. Fillmore 1861 p. 16.

COPY DESCRIBED

DLC: Blackstone Collection Eller 102.1. *Leaf.* 231 × 145.

---

1. Sir William Holdsworth, *A History of English Law* (1903; London: Methuen, 1956), 12:712.

2. J. G. Marvin, *Legal Bibliography or a Thesaurus of American, English, Irish, and Scotch Law Books* (Philadelphia: T. and J. W. Johnson, 1847), 123–24.

3. Morris Cohen, *Bibliography of Early American Law* (Buffalo, N.Y.: William S. Hein and Co., 1998), 5335 (hereafter *BEAL*); see entry 38 for Chitty.

∽

17. *Blackwood's Edinburgh Magazine.* Edinburgh: Blackwood, 1817–51.

Blackwood's Edinburgh Magazine was founded in 1817 by William Blackwood as a Tory voice to counterbalance the Whig agenda of the *Edinburgh Review,* which ruled the early nineteenth-century Edinburgh publishing world. Blackwood envisioned a magazine that would offer humor, a variety of articles, and original creative works. Published under the title *Edinburgh Monthly Magazine,* with James Pringle and Thomas Cleghorn as its first editors, the magazine fell short of these goals. After just six months, Blackwood took over the editorship himself and changed the name to *Blackwood's Edinburgh Magazine.* It continued under this title until it ceased publication in 1980. Through the mid-nineteenth century, the editorship remained in the family, with William's son Alexander Blackwood assuming it in 1834 and Alexander's younger brother John Blackwood in 1845.

Blackwood's published new works by a number of important writers, including Thomas De Quincey, George Eliot, and Bulwer Lytton. In fact, George Eliot's first published fiction, *Scenes from Clerical Life,* appeared there. Like the *Edinburgh Review, Blackwood's* cultivated strong loyalty among its authors, with John Gibson Lockhart (Walter Scott's son-in-law), John Wilson, and James Hogg as three of its main contributors. In 1831 the historian Archibald Alison began an association with the magazine that would last a quarter of a century. Articles were published anonymously, a policy that allowed their authors to praise and criticize at will. Although some readers were put off by *Blackwood's* biting satire and often negative criticism, the magazine also ran many favorable reviews. Unlike the *Edinburgh Review,* it found kind words for at least some of the Romantic writers and praised Coleridge's *Rime of the Ancient Mariner* and Wordsworth's poetry.[1]

This is one of the few purchases that is documented beyond its voucher entry in corre-spondence between Fillmore and the bookseller. Little and Brown wrote to the president on April 28, 1851 offering the first sixty volumes of *Blackwood's* to him for the White House at the price of $90.00, plus $3.50 for freight and $0.50 for a packing case. Little and Brown warned, "if this is sold before your order comes to hand we should not be able to supply [another] on the terms named above."[2] In this offer, Little and Brown also promised to pro-cure eight more volumes from London for $24.00, plus $6.00 for binding and $1.25 for freight. Fillmore must have responded promptly, because an invoice, dated May 2, 1851, just four days later, informs him that fifty-nine of the sixty volumes were shipped to him on that day. Little and Brown retained volume 60 as an example for the binder to follow when the subsequent volumes arrived from London.[3]

The prices listed on the invoice differ from those recorded on the voucher. Perhaps Fill-more negotiated to have the shipping and packing charges for the first sixty volumes waived, since he was not charged for any. The additional volumes were not procured until September of 1851, and nine instead of eight volumes are charged on the voucher for the second pur-chase; the price for the volumes and the binding is accordingly higher than what was quoted. During the time between when the offer was made in May and its fulfillment in September, the sixty-ninth volume was issued in June, which accounts for the additional volume.

Although neither the voucher nor the correspondence specify the binding of the White House set, it was most likely in half calf. It would be unusual for the time to custom bind books in cloth. Moreover, Little and Brown and Putnam both list sixty-volume sets for $100.00 in half calf. A 10 percent discount on a large order was often offered by the book-sellers to their customers.

107,754 voucher 2: 1 set Blackwood's Magazine 60 vols. $90.00.
Purchased from Little and Brown on May 2, 1851.
107,754 voucher 2: 9 vol. 61 to 69 mis Blackwood $27.00.
Binding 9 vols. $6.75.
Purchased from Little and Brown on September 26, 1851.
Hayes Catalogue: *Blackwood's Edinburgh Magazine,* April 1817 to June 1851 v. 1 to 69. Edin-burgh, 1817–51. 8°.
Roosevelt Catalogue: *Blackwood's Edinburgh Magazine,* vols. 1 to 68. Edinburgh, 1817–50, vols 20, 64, missing.

TITLE PAGE
BLACKWOOD'S | Edinburgh [black letter] | MAGAZINE. | VOL. I. | APRIL—
SEPTEMBER, 1817. | [portrait in decorative frame] | EDINBURGH: | PRINTED FOR
WILLIAM BLACKWOOD, | NO 17 PRINCE'S STREET, EDINBURGH; AND |
BALDWIN, CRADDOCK, AND JOY, | PATERNOSTER ROW, LONDON. |
[short rule] | 1817.

BLACKWOOD'S | Edinburgh [black letter] | MAGAZINE. | VOL. LXIX. | JANUARY—
JUNE, 1851. | [portrait in decorative frame] | WILLIAM BLACKWOOD & SONS,
EDINBURGH; | AND | 37 PATERNOSTER ROW, LONDON. | [short rule] | 1851.

   Note. The imprint changed several times over the course of the thirty-four years covered
      by these sixty-nine volumes.

REFERENCES

Hayes p. 24; Roosevelt p. 5; Putnam 1850 p. 14; L and B 1850 p. 10; cf. L and B 1853 p. 9.

COPY DESCRIBED

ViU AP4 B6 v.1–69. *Leaf.* 212 × 134.

---

1. Alvin Sullivan, ed., *British Literary Magazines: The Romantic Age, 1789–1836* (Westport, Conn.: Greenwood, 1983), 45–50; see entry 5 for Alison and 99 for Lockhart.

2. Little and Brown, Letter to Millard Fillmore, April 28, 1851, Millard Fillmore Papers, BECHS.

3. Little and Brown, Letter to Millard Fillmore, May 2, 1851, Millard Fillmore Papers, BECHS.

~

18. Boswell, James. *Life of Johnson.* Ed. John Wilson Croker. London: Murray, 1848.

In the nineteenth century, Samuel Johnson was still recognized as one of the most distinguished English men of letters of the eighteenth century, and James Boswell's *Life of Johnson* was regarded as a canonical text.[1] Boswell (1740–95) spent twenty years collecting material and planning this monumental biography before publishing it in 1791. The *Life* was an immediate success, selling eight hundred sets in the first two weeks after its publication.[2] John Wilson Croker's edition first appeared in 1831 and was considered the standard edition until Birckbeck Hill's was published in 1887. Croker's edition included the *Tour to the Hebrides,* a travel narrative from a trip that Boswell and Johnson took together. Boswell published the *Tour* before the *Life* in order to test the market for the full-length biography. A critic for the *Albion* claimed that Croker's edition had "met with greater literary success than any purely literary work might now be fairly expected to enjoy," and the *Museum of Foreign Literature* pronounced it "the best *edition* of an English book that has appeared in our time," calling it the "richest dictionary of wit and wisdom that any language can boast." It also praised Croker's index, a feature that Fillmore would have appreciated.[3]

105,133 voucher 5: Boswell's Life of Johnson by Croker $4.50.

Purchased from Charles Welford on December 13, 1850.

Roosevelt Catalogue: Boswell, James. *Life of Johnson. Including Their Tour to the Hebrides,* by Rt. Hon. John Wilson Croker. London, John Murray, 1845.

> *Note.* The Hayes Catalogue lists this as an 1848 edition. The date in the Roosevelt Catalogue must be a misprint because no record can be found for an edition in 1845 by Murray.

TITLE PAGE

BOSWELL'S | LIFE OF JOHNSON: | INCLUDING THEIR | TOUR TO THE HEBRIDES. | [thin rule] | BY | THE RIGHT HONOURABLE | JOHN WILSON CROKER, LL.D. F.R.S. | [thin rule] | A NEW EDITION, | THOROUGHLY REVISED, WITH MUCH ADDITIONAL MATTER. | With Portraits. [black letter] | LONDON: | JOHN MURRAY, ALBEMARLE STREET. | 1848.

PAGINATION

i–xxiv 1–874.

CONTENTS

i title, ii printer's imprint, iii advertisement to this edition, iv blank, v–x contents, xi–xvii
preface to Mr. Croker's edition, xviii woodcut of James Boswell, xix title page to first edition
of Boswell's Life of Johnson, xx epigraph, xxi dedication to Sir Joshua Reynolds, xxii–xxiii
Mr. Boswell's advertisement, xxiv Mr. Malone's advertisements, 1–846 text, 847–74 index.

PLATES

Frontispiece, "Portraits of Samuel Johnson." (This plate reproduces six portraits of Samuel
    Johnson, four by Reynolds, one by Barry, and one by Nollekins.)
Engraved title page, 'BOSWELL'S | LIFE OF JOHNSON. | *EDITED BY* | The Right Hon.[b]
    John Wilson Croker. | IN ONE VOLUME. | [caricature of James Boswell] | James
    Boswell [script] | *Engraved by F. Holl, from a sketch by Sir Tho.ˢ Lawrence, P.R.A.* |
    LONDON. | JOHN MURRAY, ALBEMARLE STREET. | 1847.'

BINDING

Front and back board. 250 × 165 med. brown ribbed cloth with blind-stamped decorative
frame; the front board has the woodcut of Boswell from p. xviii gilt stamped in the center.
Spine. Gilt stamped in upper third: 'BOSWELL'S | LIFE OF | JOHNSON | [thin rule] |
CROKER.' Blind-stamped decoration beneath, and gilt stamped at the foot: 'LONDON |
JOHN MURRAY.' *Endpapers.* Off-white.

REFERENCES

Hayes p. 24; Roosevelt p. 5; cf. L and B 1850 p. 50; cf. *LC 1816–1851* p. 299; cf. Putnam p. 16
and p. 71; cf. Fillmore 1858 p. 31; cf. Fillmore 1861 p. 114.

COPY DESCRIBED

MH: 6473 10 *Leaf.* 239 × 155.

---

1. "Johnson, Samuel," *Encyclopaedia Americana.*
2. Gordon Turnbull, "Boswell, James (1740–1795)," in *Oxford Dictionary of National Biography*, ed.
H. C. G. Matthew and Brian Hariison (Oxford: Oxford University Press, 2004), online ed., ed. Lawrence
Goldman, May 2006, http://oxforddnb.com/ (hereafter *ODNB*).
3. "Croker's Edition of Boswell's Johnson Part 3," *The Museum of Foreign Literature, Science, Art (1822–
1842)*, February 1832, and "The Right Hon. J. Wilson Croker, L. L. D. F. R. S.," *The Albion: A Journal of News,
Politics, and Literature (1822–1876)*, July 2, 1842, both available at *APS Online*, http://www.proquest.com/
products_pq/descriptions/aps.shtml; see entry 87 for Johnson's *Works.*

～

19. Bouvier, John. *A Law Dictionary.* **3rd ed. 2 vols. Philadelphia: T. and J. W. Johnson, 1848.**

The legal scholar John Bouvier (1787–1851) made his most significant contribution to American law with the publication of this dictionary in 1839. His frustration with using law
dictionaries designed for British lawyers prompted him to design one for American law
students. In his dictionary, he provides extensive definitions of words and phrases that
include all of their potential "shades of meaning." He delineates the "principles and rules as
belong" to each and cites relevant cases. If possible, he also makes comparisons with the
laws of other countries, and, finally, he provides references to "authorities, the abridge-
ments, digests, and the ancient and modern treatises, where the subject is to be found" (vii).

Marvin called Bouvier's *Dictionary* the best book of its kind for the American lawyer: "By means of correspondence with members of the bar in different states, and by a careful examination of local treatises the author has produced not only a good general American Law Dictionary, but one sufficiently local for all purposes."[1]

Although there are two earlier editions of this work, from 1839 and 1843, the Executive Mansion most likely purchased the 1848 edition, the one that the book's seller, Little and Brown, advertised in its 1850 catalogue.

105,133 voucher 2: Bouviers Law Dicty 2 vols. $8.50.
Purchased from Little and Brown on December 30, 1850.

REFERENCES
cf. Greenleaf; cf. Harvard p. 27; cf. Marvin p. 138; cf. Roorbach p. 609.

---

1. Marvin, *Legal Bibliography,* 138.

〜

20. *British Essayists.* London: Jones, 1825–29.
Johnson, Samuel. *The Rambler.* London: Jones, 1825.
Johnson, Samuel. *The Idler.* London: Jones, 1826.
Town, Mr. *The Connoisseur.* London: Jones, 1826.
Addison, Joseph, and Richard Steele. *The Spectator.* London: Jones, [ca. 1825–29].
Hawkesworth, John. *The Adventurer.* London: Jones, 1829.
Steele, Richard, and Joseph Addison. *The Guardian.* London: Jones, 1829.
Steele, Richard, and Joseph Addison. *The Tatler.* London: Jones, 1829.

A number of series entitled *British Essayists* were published during the nineteenth century and usually included the *Tatler,* the *Spectator,* the *Guardian,* the *Rambler,* the *Idler,* the *Adventurer,* the *World,* the *Connoisseur,* the *Mirror,* the *Lounger,* and the *Observer.* These essays had originally been published during the eighteenth century in periodical form and were valued for the pleasure and moral instruction that they afforded readers. They remained popular during the nineteenth century and were frequently reprinted.

Although no three-volume series with the title or one that could reasonably be shortened to *British Essayists* has been identified, this purchase probably refers to a series that Jones was publishing in the 1820s. Although the voucher indicates three volumes, the Hayes Catalogue specifies six volumes in two, published in London in 1829. Those volumes included the *Rambler,* the *Idler,* the *Adventurer,* the *Connoissuer,* the *Tatler,* and the *Guardian.* It is possible that these books had originally been a three-volume set and that a volume had been lost between 1850 and 1877. Putnam lists a three-volume set that includes all of these titles and adds the *Spectator* for a total of $7.00, bound in cloth with portraits. This advertisement names no publisher and cannot be connected with a specific edition. Yet its price is a close match to the $6.50 paid by the White House. It is possible that both the Hayes Catalogue and the Putnam Catalogue refer to the series that Jones was publishing. The Jones edition includes portrait frontispieces as specified by Putnam. In addition, an entry in *WorldCat* designates the *Tatler* volume from Jones as part of a series entitled *British*

Essayists, and the Library of Congress online catalogue indicates that its copies of the *Rambler* and the *Connoisseur* from Jones have *British Essayists* printed on their bindings. These books must have been rebound since the record was made; currently, they do not bear this title and are in newer buckram library bindings. Finally, J. D. Fleeman notes that Jones issued a series entitled the *British Essayists* that could be purchased over time in parts or in bound volumes. The *Idler* and *Rambler* volumes were from the same editions as those that were included in Jones's *Works of Samuel Johnson,* which the White House also purchased.[1]

105,133 voucher 5: British Essayists 3 vol. $6.50.
Purchased from Charles Welford on December 13, 1850.

Hayes Catalogue: *British Essayists.* 6 v. in 2. London, 1825–29. 8°
    v. 1   Rambler. By S. Johnson.
            Idler By S. Johnson.
            Adventurer. By J. Hawkesworth and others.
            Connoisseur. By Mr. Town, pseud.
    v. 2   Tatler.
            Guardian.

REFERENCES

cf. Hayes p. 26; cf. Roosevelt[2] p. 2, p. 9, p. 17, p. 21, p. 34, and p. 41; cf. Putnam p. 17; cf. Fillmore ca. 1858 p. 59, p. 60, and p. 63.

---

1. J. D. Fleeman, *A Bibliography of the Works of Samuel Johnson* (Oxford: Clarendon, 2000), 2:1698–99. See entry 87 for *The Works of Samuel Johnson.*
2. The Roosevelt Catalogue provides an entry for each collection separately, alphabetized by title, all published by Jones.

                        ~

21. Brougham, Henry Lord. *Speeches.* **4 vols. Edinburgh: Adam and Charles Black, et al., 1838.**

22. ———. *Political Philosophy.* **3 vols. London: Knight and Co., 1846.**

Henry Peter Brougham, first Baron Brougham (1778–1868), Lord Chancellor, and journalist, was known for his ability to rouse his listeners to action through passionate speeches. As a social reformer, he took up the causes of the freedom of the press, the abolition of slavery and the slave trade, the extension of popular education, and the reform of laws and the legal system, all issues that were of concern to President Fillmore. Although Brougham's efforts for social reform may not be remembered by many today, in the mid-nineteenth century the American social reformer Henry Brewster Stanton called him "one of the foremost Englishmen of the century."[1]

    Brougham played a significant role in three other publications that were purchased for the White House Library. In 1802 he helped found the *Edinburgh Review,* and for the next thirty years he dominated the *Review*'s editorial policy. In 1826 he helped establish the Society for the Diffusion of Useful Knowledge in order to supply quality texts, such as the *Penny Cyclopaedia* and *Maps for the Society for the Diffusion of Useful Knowledge,* at an inexpensive price for the expanding reading public. Because of their own commitment to education and learning, the Fillmores would have appreciated Brougham's agendas for education and literacy.[2]

Brougham's speeches were considered more informative and argumentative than Burke's and more vigorous and versatile than Webster's, two other orators whose speeches were purchased for the library. Moreover, Brougham's capacity to mold public opinion was believed to surpass even that of Burke.[3] Not only would these two books have provided useful political and legal information for the president and his staff members, but they would also serve as rhetorical models in an age when eloquence was valued as a necessary skill for lawyers, politicians, and statesmen.

155,133 voucher 5:   Lord Brougham's Polit. Philosophy 3 vols. $6.00.
                  Brougham's Speeches 2 vols. $9.00.
Purchased from Charles Welford on December 13, 1850.
Roosevelt Catalogue: Brougham, Henry Lord. *Political Philosophy.* London, Charles Knight & Co., 1846, 4 vols.

————. *Speeches upon Questions Relating to Public Rights, Duties, and Interests; with Historical Introduction, and a Critical Dissertation upon the Eloquence of the Ancients.* Edinburgh, Adam & Charles Black, 1838, 3 vols.

> *Notes.* The compiler of the Roosevelt Catalogue apparently confused the number of volumes for Brougham's *Political Philosophy* with the number for his *Speeches.* It misidentifies *Philosophy* as four volumes and *Speeches* as three, while in fact the editions that it names are of three and four volumes, respectively.
>
> The Roosevelt Catalogue also includes Brougham's *Historical Sketches of Statesmen Who Flourished in the Time of George III* (London: R. Griffin and Co., 1856–58). Obviously, this was purchased after the Fillmore years.

SPEECHES

TITLE PAGE

SPEECHES | HENRY LORD BROUGHAM, | UPON QUESTIONS RELATING TO | PUBLIC RIGHTS, DUTIES, AND INTERESTS; | WITH | HISTORICAL INTRODUCTIONS, | AND | A CRITICAL DISSERTATION | UPON THE ELOQUENCE OF THE ANCIENTS. | [thin rule] | IN FOUR VOLUMES. | [thin rule] | VOL. I. [II.–IV.] | EDINBURGH: | ADAM AND CHARLES BLACK; | LONGMAN, ORME, BROWN, GREEN, AND LONGMAN'S; | RIDGWAY AND SONS; AND CHARLES KNIGHT AND CO. LONDON. | [thin rule] | M.DCCC.XXXVIII.

PAGINATION

Vol. I. i–iv [2] v–x 1–680.
Vol. II. i–iv 1–632.
Vol. III. i–iv 1–626.
Vol. IV. i–iv 1–572.

CONTENTS

Vol. I. i title, ii blank, iii–iv contents, [1] dedication to the "Most Noble Richard Marquess Wellesley," [2] blank, v–x preface, 1–676 text, 677 errata, 678 blank, 679–80 advertisements for other books.

Vol. II. i title, ii blank, iii–iv contents, 1–630 text, 631–32 addenda.

Vol. III. i title, ii blank, iii–iv contents, 1–626 text.

Vol. IV. i title, ii blank, iii–iv contents, 1–519 text, 520 blank, 521–71 index, 572 blank.

> *Notes.* The advertisement on pages 679–80 of volume 1 does not specify a publisher.
> In volume 4 a small errata slip has been inserted after page iv.

REFERENCES

Hayes p. 27; Roosevelt p. 6; L and B 1850 p. 13; cf. *LC 1816–1851* p. 74; cf. Putnam p. 18 (misprints date 1338); cf. Fillmore 1847 p. 4; cf. Fillmore ca. 1858 p. 4; cf. Fillmore 1861 p. 22.

COPY DESCRIBED

DLC: DA 536 B7A3. *Leaf.* 213 × 134.

Political Philosophy.

TITLE PAGE

Vol. I.

UNDER THE SUPERINTENDENCE OF THE SOCIETY FOR | THE DIFFUSION OF USEFUL KNOWLEDGE. | [wavy rule] | POLITICAL PHILOSOPHY. | BY HENRY, LORD BROUGHAM, F. R. S. | MEMBER OF THE NATIONAL INSTITUTE OF FRANCE, | MEMBER OF THE ROYAL ACADEMY OF NAPLES. | PART I. | PRINCIPLES OF GOVERNMENT. | MONARCHICAL GOVERNMENT. | LONDON: | CHARLES KNIGHT & CO., 22, LUDGATE STREET. | [thin rule] | 1846.

Vol. II.

'. . . .PART II. | OF ARISTOCRACY. | ARISTOCRATIC GOVERNMENTS. . . .'

Vol. III.

'. . . PART III. | OF DEMOCRACY. | MIXED MONARCHY. . . .'

PAGINATION

Vol. I. i–xii 1–608 609*–684* 609–64.

Vol. II. i–xiv 1–394.

Vol. III. i–xx 1–426.

> *Note.* In volume 1, 609*–684* has been inserted into the regular numbering scheme.
> Asterisks follow the page numbers on all of the pages in this sequence.

CONTENTS

Vol. I. i half title, ii blank, iii title, iv blank, v–xii contents, 1–644 text, 645–61 index, 662 errata, 663 notes, 664 blank.

Vol. II. i half title, ii blank, iii title, iv blank, v–vi dedication to the Queen, vii–xiv contents, 1–382 text, 383–93 index, 394 blank.

Vol. III. i half title, ii blank, iii title, iv blank, v dedication to Charles Earl Grey, K. G., vi blank, vii preface, viii–xix contents, xx blank, 1–406 text, 407–26 index.

> *Note.* The page numbers for the content of the text of volume 1 include 609*–684*.

REFERENCES

Hayes p. 27; Roosevelt p. 6; cf. *LC 1816–1851* p. 74; cf. Putnam p. 18; cf. Fillmore 1847 p. 3.

COPY DESCRIBED

DLC: JC 223 B85 1846 copy 1. *Leaf.* 213 × 130.

---

1. "Lord Brougham," *The Albion: A Journal of News, Politics, and Literature (1822–1876)*, October 20, 1849, available at *APS Online*, http://www.proquest.com/products_pq/descriptions/aps.shtml.
2. See entries 51, 128, and 157 for the *Edinburgh Review*, the *Penny Cyclopaedia*, and *Maps*, respectively. See also "Lord Brougham," *The Albion*.
3. See entries 24 and 184–85 for Burke and Webster.

~

23. Browne, Arthur. *A Compendious View of the Civil Law, and of the Law of Admiralty.* 2nd ed. 2 vols. London: Butterworth, 1802.

Arthur Browne's (ca. 1756–1805) *Compendious View of Civil Law and the Law of Admiralty* was recognized "the best book in the language showing the connexion between the Common and the Civil Law."[1] Browne based it on a course of lectures that he delivered while Regius Professor of Civil and Canon Law at Trinity College, University of Dublin, the college where he had completed his own studies in 1784. Although some objected to Browne's brevity, Marvin explained that this book was intended as a textbook for students to read after Blackstone's *Commentaries*. Hoffman called Browne's work elementary, but acknowledged that it references enough sources to enable its readers to pursue topics more thoroughly.[2] Fillmore ordered this title from Little and Brown the December following the Cuban filibuster, although it did not appear on Edward Everett's list of recommendations. The second volume, devoted to admiralty law, would have been of particular interest to Fillmore at this time.

107,754 voucher 4: 2 Browne's Civil Law $6.00.
Purchased from Little and Brown on December 31, 1851.
Hayes Catalogue: Browne, A. *Compendious View of the Civil Law.* 2 v. London, 1802, 8°.

TITLE PAGE

A | COMPENDIOUS VIEW | OF THE | CIVIL LAW, | AND OF | THE LAW OF THE ADMIRALTY, | BEING THE SUBSTANCE OF | A COURSE OF LECTURES | READ IN THE | UNIVERISTY OF DUBLIN | BY | *ARTHUR BROWNE, LL.D. S.F.T.C.D.* | PROFESSOR OF CIVIL LAW IN THAT UNIVERSITY, AND | REPRESENTATIVE IN THREE PARLIAMENTS FOR THE SAME. | [thin/thick double rule] | THE SECOND EDITION, WITH GREAT ADDITIONS. | [thick/thin double rule] | VOL. I. [II.] | CONTAINING A VIEW OF THE CIVIL LAW. | [thin/thick double rule] | *LONDON:* | PRINTED FOR J. BUTTERWORTH, FLEET-STREET, | AND JOHN COOKE, DUBLIN; | *By G. Woodfall, No. 22, Paternoster-row,* | [swelled rule] | 1802.

Vol. II.
'. . . | VOL. II. | CONTAINING THE VIEW OF THE ADMIRALTY LAW. | . . .'

Note. Volume 2 uses a period rather than a comma after Paternoster-row in the imprint.

PAGINATION

Vol. I. [4] i–vi iii–vi 1–538.

Vol. II. i–viii i–iv 1–20 [2] 21–572.

CONTENTS

Vol. I. [1] title, [2] blank, [3] dedication to the "Provost Fellows and Scholars of the College of the Holy and Undivided Trinity, near Dublin," [4] blank, i–vi preface, iii–vi contents, 1–508 text, 509 section title, "appendix," 510 blank, 511–25 text, 526–36 index, 537–38 errata and omissa.

     Note. Pages 526–36 are misnumbered as 426–36.

Vol. II. i title, ii blank, iii dedication to "The Right Honourable Sir William Scott, Knt. Judge of the High Court of Admiralty," iv blank, v–vii preface, viii blank, i–iii contents, iv note to the binder, 1–20 introductory chapter, [1] section title, "Law of Admiralty," [2] blank, 21–509 text, 510 blank, 511–57 appendix, 558 blank, 559–67 index, 568 blank, 569–71 errata and omissa, 572 blank.

REFERENCES

Hayes p. p. 28; *BEAL* 5382; Greenleaf; Harvard p. 31; cf. Marvin 155; cf. Hoffman p. 534.

COPY DESCRIBED

DLC: LL KD 720 B76 1802 copy 2. *Leaf.* 225 × 126.

---

1. Marvin, *Legal Bibliography*, 155.
2. David Hoffman, *A Course of Legal Study, Addressed to Students and the Profession Generally* (Baltimore: Joseph Neal, 1836), 535–36.

⁓

24. Burke, Edmund. *Works of Edmund Burke.* 9 vols. Boston: Little and Brown, 1839.

Edmund Burke (1729/30–97), politician, philosopher, and author, served in parliament for eighteen years, from 1766 to 1784, and is remembered today as a social reformer who upheld humanitarian causes over the party line. Because Burke's humanitarian themes transcend the time in which they were written and his arguments are so rich and multifaceted, his works have never gone out of fashion. According to a writer for *Blackwood's Magazine* in 1845, "The great politician of his day, he has become the noblest philosopher of ours. Every man who desires to know the true theory of public morals, and actual causes of which influence the rise and fall of thrones, makes his volumes a study."[1] On the one hand, Burke spoke against England's taxation of the American colonies, its abuse of India, and its oppression of those adhering to the Catholic religion; on the other hand, he opposed the French Revolution, unable to justify the social disorder and violence committed by the revolutionaries.

     This edition claims to comprise "the entire contents of the English edition" and includes two volumes of speeches on the trial of Hastings, published in 1827, which had never been published in the United States.[2] It also reprints "An Account of the European Settlements in America," first published in 1761, but not included in the English edition of Burke's collected works. The publisher's advertisement boasts that although this edition contains a volume more than "the latest and best English one, it is offered at less than one half the price" (1:v). According to Putnam's catalogues, it was "beautifully printed on fine paper" and was available in cloth for $15.00, in neat calf for $22.50, and in full calf, gilt for $28.00. Based on the price paid, the White House most likely purchased a copy in full calf, gilt.

105,133 voucher 2: Burk's works 9 vols. clf. $26.00.
Purchased from Little and Brown on December 30, 1850.
Roosevelt Catalogue: Burke, Edmund. *The Works of Edmund Burke.* Boston, C. C. Little & James Brown, 1839. 9 vols., vols. 1 and 3 missing.

TITLE PAGE
THE | WORKS OF EDMUND BURKE. | IN NINE VOLUMES. | VOL. I. [II–IX] | BOSTON: | CHARLES C. LITTLE AND JAMES BROWN. | MDCCCXXXIX.

PAGINATION
Vol. I. i–xiv 1–4 7–54 [*10*] 57–496.
Vol. II. [*4*] 1–576.
Vol. III. [*4*] 1–532.
Vol. IV. [*4*] 1–554.
Vol. V. i–iv 1–726.
Vol. VI. i–iv 1–690.
Vol. VII. [*4*] 1–644.
Vol. VIII. i–viii 1–574.
Vol. IX. [*4*] i–xvi 17–688.

CONTENTS
Vol. I. i title, ii printer's imprint, iii contents, iv blank, v "Advertisement," vi blank, vii–xi "advertisement to the reader," xii blank, xiii section title, "A Vindication of Natural Society," xiv blank, 1–495 text, 496 blank.
Vol. II. [*1*] title, [*2*] printer's imprint, [*3*] contents, [*4*] blank, 1–575 text, 576 blank.
Vol. III. [*1*] title, [*2*] printer's imprint, [*3*] contents, [*4*] blank, 1–531 text, 532 blank.
Vol. IV. [*1*] title, [*2*] printer's imprint, [*3*] contents, [*4*] blank, 1–554 text.
Vol. V. i title, ii printer's imprint, iii–iv contents, 1–726 text.
Vol. VI. i title, ii printer's imprint, iii–iv contents, 1–690 text.
Vol. VII. [*1*] title, [*2*] printer's imprint, [*3*] contents, [*4*] blank, 1–644 text.
Vol. VIII. i title, ii printer's imprint, iii contents, iv blank, v–vii dedication "To His Most Christian Majesty, Charles Xth King of France and Navarre," viii blank, 1–574 text.
Vol. IX. [*1*] title, [*2*] printer's imprint, [*3*] contents, [*4*] blank, i section title, "An Account of the English Settlements in America," ii blank, iii–v preface, vi blank, vii–xvi contents, 17–650 text, 651–87 index, 688 blank.

PLATES
Vol. I.
Portrait frontispiece of Edmund Burke, "From a picture after Sir Joshua Reynolds in the possession of T. H. Burke Esq.," engraved by C. E. Wagstaff.

REFERENCES

Hayes p. 27; Roosevelt p. 7; L and B 1850 p. 15; Putnam p. 19; cf. Roorbach p. 82; cf. Fillmore 1847 p. 9; cf. Fillmore ca. 1858 p. 5, see also p. 59; cf. Fillmore 1861 p. 24.

COPY DESCRIBED

DLC: DA 506 B8 1839. *Leaf.* 214 × 133.

---

1. "Edmund Burke," *The Eclectic Magazine of Foreign Literature (1844–1898),* January 1845, available at *APS Online,* http://www.proquest.com/products_pq/descriptions/aps.shtml.

2. Warren Hastings served as governor-general of Bengal from 1773 to 1785. The year after his resignation from this position he was accused of and impeached for corrupt activities while in this office. Edmund Burke, Charles James Fox, and Richard Brinsley Sheridan managed the prosecution in an investigation and trial that was protracted over seven years. The early sessions of the trial became a public spectacle, as they were attended by very large crowds and reported about extensively in newspapers and periodicals. Hastings was eventually acquitted of all charges, but only after he had accumulated enormous debt during the trial. He never returned to public life.

~

25. Burns, Robert. *The Works.*

Recognized during his own lifetime as the preeminent Scottish poet, Robert Burns's (1759–96) reputation has never flagged in either Great Britain or America. Written in Scottish dialect, his poetry champions the common people of Scotland and celebrates the country's rustic heritage. Burns's popularity spread rapidly after his death in 1796; clubs formed in honor of his memory, and his works were read enthusiastically throughout Great Britain and America. In 1848 the *Literary World* ranked Burns in the same class of poets as Shakespeare, Homer, Spenser, and Milton.[1] Burns's elevation of the "common people" may have had particular appeal for mid-nineteenth-century Americans who believed in and celebrated the "rise of the common man" in their own country. His works, along with those of Shakespeare, were among the earliest purchases for the new library in the Executive Mansion.

This voucher entry could refer to any one of the many different editions of Burns with illustrations that were available in 1850. J. W. Egerer lists over two hundred editions of Burns's works—both complete and poetical—published between 1830 and 1850, not counting all issues.[2] It would be difficult to know without looking at copies of each edition which ones were illustrated and to what extent. None of the editions that he lists have "illustrated" in the title. A copy of an 1849 Philadelphia edition published by John Locken bears the title "Burns's Works Illustrated" on the spine, yet it is a one-volume, clothbound book that would not have cost $9.00 in 1850. Moreover, the only illustration that it contains is a frontispiece.

Two other charges entered on the voucher for the same date further complicate the identification of the Burns's edition. A seven-volume set for Shakespeare appears first, followed by "Burns Illustrated," and "lettering 8 volumes $2.00." The charge for "lettering" most probably refers to a fee for adding spine labels to each volume like the ones found ones found on Richard S. Fisher's *Book of the World,* which is listed on the same voucher but purchased on a different date. It is unclear, however, whether this charge refers to one volume of Burns and seven of Shakespeare for the total of eight, or to an eight-volume set of

Burns. In another example on this voucher, "Stephens [*sic*] English Constitution 2 vols." and "Hallams [*sic*] Constitutional History of England," which although not specified on the voucher is a two-volume work, were purchased on the October 25, 1850. A charge for lettering two volumes follows these two entries and could refer to either purchase for that date but not both.

Nine dollars would be a high price to pay for one volume in 1850; however, the number and quality of illustrations could account for such a price. The Little and Brown catalogue lists the complete works of Burns in one volume with Cunningham's life and notes by Scott and others, in "full Morocco, gilt," at $8.00. Taylor and Maury's relationship to Putnam as one of their Washington agents lends more weight to items found in Putnam's catalogue as potential purchases. It lists an 1835 eight-volume London edition of Burns with a life by Allan Cunningham for $9.00 in cloth. This listing probably refers to an edition published by Cochrane and McCrone, the only eight-volume set of Burns listed by Egerer between 1830 and 1850.[3] Each volume of this set contains a frontispiece and an engraved title page with a vignette illustrating one of Burns's works. Egerer explains that the Cochrane and McCrone edition was originally planned as six volumes, but in the preface of volume 6 Cunningham announced that he would extend the work to eight volumes. Egerer remarks that the content of this edition is "a baffling mixture of truth and fiction; while many of the statements are certainly true, an equal number probably sprang from gossip or from Cunningham's own fertile imagination."[4]

105,133 voucher 6: Burns Illustrated $9.00.
Lettering 8 volumes $2.00.
Purchased from Taylor and Maury on October 30, 1850.

REFERENCES

cf. *LC 1816–1851* p. 85; cf. Putnam p. 20, p. 5-s; cf. Fillmore Packing Lists p. 1 and p. 18; cf. Fillmore ca. 1858 p. 7; cf. Fillmore 1861 p. 24.

---

1. "Robert Burns: As a Poet and as a Man," *The Literary World (1847–1853),* October 21, 1848, available at *APS Online,* http://www.proquest.com/products_pq/descriptions/aps.shtml. See entries 73 (*Harper's Classical Library*), 117–18, and 151 for Homer, Milton, and Shakespeare.

2. J. W. Egerer, *A Bibliography of Robert Burns* (Edinburgh: Oliver and Boyd, 1964).

3. Ibid., 368.

4. Ibid., 368.

∿

26. Burton, Robert. *The Anatomy of Melancholy.* London: [Blake or Tegg], 1849.

By the mid-nineteenth century Robert Burton's (1577–1640) *Anatomy of Melancholy* was considered a stock item in any library; its owner, however, was not necessarily expected to have read it. The *Boston Miscellany of Literature and Fashion* called it "a book oftener mentioned than read." Another critic characterized it as a "work of established character," one of "the standard works of old authors." Nevertheless, this critic does not advocate that everyone buy a copy; rather, he suggests that the book is gender specific and recommends that "a large number of manly thinkers" should own one.[1]

Burton, a writer and scholar who spent most of his life as a student at Oxford, first published *The Anatomy of Melancholy* in 1621. This popular work went into eight editions during the seventeenth century. Since Burton endeavored to treat his topic thoroughly, the first edition contained 353,368 words; he revised and expanded the text with each subsequent edition during his lifetime so that by the sixth edition he had nearly doubled its length. During the eighteenth century the *Anatomy* fell out of fashion, yet retained at least one notable reader, Samuel Johnson, who suffered from a melancholic disposition himself. Toward the end of the century, John Ferriar's *Illustrations of Sterne* (1798) pointed out the borrowings from *Anatomy* in *Tristram Shandy* and revived interest in Burton. By the end of the eighteenth century several recent editions of *Anatomy* had been published, and Samuel Taylor Coleridge and Charles Lamb, among other Romantic writers, admired it.

Without further information, it is impossible to determine which edition of *Anatomy of Melancholy* the Executive Mansion selected. There were no fewer than fifteen published between 1836 and 1851. Most of these were priced between $2.00 and $2.50. Roorbach lists two American editions, both priced at $2.50, one from John Wiley in New York and the other from J. W. Moore in Philadelphia. The Putnam catalogue lists a New York edition in cloth, octavo for $2.50. It is more likely, however, that the White House bought the London 1849 edition offered for $2.50 by Little and Brown, the seller from whom it was purchased. Two London publishers, Blake and Tegg, brought out editions of *Anatomy* in 1849, and these stand as the most likely candidates for purchase.

105,133 voucher 2: Burton Anatomy $2.00.
Purchased from Little and Brown on December 30, 1850.

REFERENCES
cf. L and B 1850 p. 16; cf. *LC 1816–1851* p. 86; cf. Putnam p. 21; Roorbach.

---

1. "Burton's 'Anatomy of Melancholy,'" *The Boston Miscellany of Literature and Fashion (1842–1843)*, August 1, 1842, and "Editor's Table," *The Journal of Belles Lettres (1832–1842)*, February 23, 1836, both available at *APS Online*, http://www.proquest.com/products_pq/descriptions/aps.shtml.

～

27. *Cabinet Library of Scarce and Celebrated Tracts*. Edinburgh: Thomas Clark, 1837.

Although the voucher entry for this purchase is scant, "3 vols. Law Tracts," it probably refers to the *Cabinet Library of Scarce and Celebrated Tracts*, law series. It is one of the seventeen books that Fillmore ordered from Little and Brown during the aftermath of the Cuban filibuster, an order that included thirteen other books that had been suggested by Edward Everett for the library. Everett recommended "*International Law Tracts* 8vo Edinburgh, 1837." The *Cabinet Library* series is the only title found that meets both the content and the publication criteria for this purchase. Only volume 1 of this series has been available for examination. It contains the following six international law tracts that complement the other books on this order and would have been relevant to the issues Fillmore needed to address:

Sir James MacKintosh, "Discourses on the Law of Nature and Nations."

Joseph Story, "Discourse on the Past History, Present State, and Future Prospects of the Law."

Sir William Scott, "Judgment Pronounced in the Consistory Court in the Case of Dalrymple vs. Dalrymple."[1]

Sir William Scott, "Judgments Pronounced in the High Court of Admiralty in the Cases of the Maria and the Gratitudine."

Lord Liverpool, "Discourse on the Conduct of the Government of Great Britain in Respect of Neutral Nations."

Anonymous, "Controversy Concerning the Law of Nations, Especially Relative to Prussia's Attachment of British Funds, by Way of Reprisal for English Captures."

107,754 voucher 4: 3 vols. Law Tracts $6.00.
Purchased from Little and Brown on December 31, 1851.

---

1. Sir William Scott served as judge of the High Court of Admiralty in England from 1798 to 1828.

⌇

28. Calhoun, John C. *A Disquisition on Government and a Discourse on the Constitution and Government of the United States.* **Ed. Richard K. Cralle. Columbia, S.C.: Johnston, 1851.**

John C. Calhoun (1782–1850) devoted most of his life to public service, serving at different times in both houses of Congress, as secretary of war, and as vice president under two different presidents. In the last years of his life Calhoun drafted two essays in which he set forth his political theory. The first, "A Disquisition on Government," became volume 1 of Calhoun's *Works* (1851), which is how it is designated on the voucher for this purchase.

Richard K. Cralle, Calhoun's intimate friend and personal secretary, revised *A Disquisition on Government and a Discourse on the Constitution and Government of the United States* for its posthumous publication in 1851. The *Disquisition* appeared under three different imprints: one in Columbia "printed by A. S. Johnston," another in Charleston from the "steam-power press of Walker and James," and a third in New York from D. Appleton and Company. Although the pagination of the preliminaries differs slightly between the Johnston and the Walker and James editions, the text of the work itself appears to be printed from the same setting of type.[1] As a writer for the *International Magazine* explained, stereotype plates had been made in New York and the work was printed in Charleston.[2] The *Disquisition* was also issued in large and small paper copies; the five hundred large paper copies, printed for public libraries, were to be sold for the benefit of Calhoun's family.[3]

Since the Hayes Catalogue specifies New York as the place of publication and Roorbach lists the large paper Appleton edition as selling for $2.50, just $0.50 less than the price paid by the Executive Mansion, a large paper Appleton edition was probably purchased for the library. It appears that, unless a typographical error was made, by the time the Roosevelt Catalogue was compiled the original copy had been replaced, because it specifies an 1853–54 set of Calhoun's works.

109,399 voucher 1: 1st volume Calhoun's works $2.50.

Purchased from Taylor and Maury on September 30, 1851.

Hayes Catalogue: Calhoun, J. C. *Works.* 4 v. New York, 1851–54. 8°.

Roosevelt Catalogue: Calhoun, John C. *The Works.* New York, D. Appleton & Co., 1853–54, 4 vols., vol. 2 missing.

REFERENCES

cf. Hayes p. 33; cf. Roorbach p. 88; cf. Fillmore 1861 p. 28; cf. Fillmore ca. 1858 p. 10.

---

1. A DLC copy with the Johnston imprint was compared with online images of the Walker and James imprint found at Hein Online, http://www.heinonline.org. The pagination and signatures of the main body of the text of these two editions match. An Appleton edition has not been available for comparison.

2. It is possible that A. S. Johnston in Columbia partnered on the edition with Walker and James in Charleston and that Walker and James would have printed the entire edition, with some of the copies bearing Johnston's name in the imprint and others bearing that of Walker and James. Alternatively, Johnston operated a press in Columbia, and he therefore may have obtained a set of stereotype plates and printed his own edition.

3. *International Magazine of Literature, Science and Art (1850–1852),* March 1, 1851, available at *APS Online,* http://www.proquest.com/products_pq/descriptions/aps.shtml.

⁓

**29. Campbell, John Lord. *The Lives of the Lord Chancellors and the Keepers of the Great Seal of England.* 3rd ed. 7 vols. London: Murray, 1848.

30. ———. *The Lives of the Chief Justices of England.* 2 vols. Boston: Little and Brown, 1850.

John Campbell, first Baron Campbell (1779–1861), legal biographer, Lord Chief Justice, and Irish Lord Chancellor, garnered a more favorable reputation as a judge than as a biographer. However, even as a judge he was known for "an unworthy love of applause" and an "exalted self-confidence." Nevertheless, his decisions are preserved in thirteen volumes of cases reported by Adolphus and Ellis. Few of his decisions were ever overturned, and some are still cited today as authoritative.[1]

Although highly regarded in their time, both sets of Campbell's *Lives* were also known for blatant plagiarisms and misrepresentations. By Campbell's own admission the *Lives of the Chief Justices* is a selective rather than a comprehensive treatment of the topic: "So many of them as I could not reasonably hope to make entertaining or edifying, I have used the freedom to pass over entirely, or with very slight notice" (1:vi). It was originally published in three volumes that appeared consecutively in 1847, 1848, and 1849. Campbell's *Lives of the Lord Chancellors* was published in three series, totaling seven volumes, the first in 1845, the second in 1846, and the third in 1847.[2]

The inclusion of both of these titles in the Executive Mansion library reflects the interest of the age in biography and the American legal system's debt to its British forebears. The copy of *The Lives of the Lord Chancellors* that is described here is one of the eleven original Executive Mansion copies known to survive today.

105,133 voucher 2: Lives of Chancellors 7 vols. $20.00.

Lives of the Justices 2 vols. $4.50.

Purchased from Little and Brown on December 30, 1850.

Roosevelt Catalogue: Campbell, John <u>Baron Campbell</u>. *The Lives of the Chief Justices of England from the Norman Conquest till the Death of Lord Mansfield.* Boston, C. C. Little & J. Brown, 1850, 2 vols.

————. *The Lives of the Lord Chancellors and Keepers of the Great Seal of England, from the Earliest Times till the Reign of King George IV.* Third Edition. London, John Murray, 1848, 7 vols.

Lives of the Lord Chancellors.

TITLE PAGE

THE | LIVES | OF | THE LORD CHANCELLORS | AND | KEEPERS OF THE GREAT SEAL | OF | ENGLAND, | FROM THE EARLIEST TIMES TILL THE REIGN OF | KING GEORGE IV. | [thin rule] | BY | JOHN LORD CAMPBELL, LL.D. F.R.S.E. | [thin rule] | IN SEVEN VOLUMES. | VOL. I. [II–VII.] | [thin rule] | THIRD EDITION. | [thin rule] | LONDON: | JOHN MURRAY, ALBEMARLE STREET. | 1848.

> *Notes.* Volumes 4, 5, and 7 omit 'IN SEVEN VOLUMES.'; volumes 4 and 5 dated 1849; volumes 6 and 7 add 'CHIEF JUSTICE OF ENGLAND' on separate line after 'JOHN LORD CAMPBELL, LL.D. F.R.S.E.' and are dated 1850.

PAGINATION

Vol. I. i–xxxii 1–660.

Vol. II. i–xx 1–640.

Vol. III. i–xx 1–608.

Vol. IV. [2] i–xxiv 1–662.

Vol. V. [2] i–xx 1–688.

Vol. VI. i–xx 1–680 1–16.

Vol. VII. i–xx 1–712.

> *Notes.* In volume 2, gathering A is unopened; volumes 3, 5, and 7 are mostly unopened; volume 4 is partially unopened.

CONTENTS

Vol. I. i half title, ii printer's imprint, iii title, iv blank, v dedication to the Honorable William Frederick Campbell, the author's son, vi blank, vii preface to the third edition, viii blank, ix–xiii preface to the first edition, xiv blank, xv–xvi preface to the second edition, xvii–xxxii contents, 1–659 text, 660 printer's imprint.

Vol. II. i title, ii printer's imprint, iii–xix contents, xx blank, 1–638 text, 639–40 advertisement for works published by John Murray.

Vol. III. i title, ii–xix contents, xx blank, 1–605 text, 606 blank, 607–8 advertisement for works published by John Murray.

Vol. IV. [1] half title, [2] printer's imprint, i title, ii blank, iii–viii preface to the second series of the *Lives of the Chancellors,* ix–xxiii contents, xxiv blank, 1–661 text, 662 printer's imprint.

Vol. V. [1] half title, [2] blank, i title, ii printer's imprint, iii–xx contents, 1–685 text, 686 printer's imprint, 687–88 advertisement for books published by John Murray.

Vol. VI. i title, ii printer's imprint, iii–vi preface to the third series of the *Lives of the Chancellors,* vii–xx contents, 1–679 text, 680 printer's imprint, 1–16 advertisements for books published by John Murray.

Vol. VII. i half title, ii printer's imprint, iii title, iv blank, v–xx contents, 1–696 text, 697–700 postscript, 701–10 chronological table of chancellors, 711–12 alphabetical table of chancellors.

BINDING

Front board. 228 × 145 blue, ribbed cloth; blind-stamped decorative frame with gilt-stamped scepter and pillow in middle. *Back board.* Blind-stamped decorative frame with decoration in center. *Spine.* Blind-stamped rosette at head with rules and alternating panels down the spine. Gilt-stamped lettering 'LIVES I OF THE I LORD I CHANCELLORS I [thin rule] I VOL. I. [II–VII]I BY I LORD I CAMPBELL. I LONDON. I JOHN MURRAY.' *Endpapers.* Ivory.

 Note. Volumes 2, 6, and 7 have been rebound in Library of Congress bindings.

MARKS OF OWNERSHIP

Inscribed on front pastedown black ink "Executive Mansion I 1850." Shelf mark in pencil beneath "E Shelf no. 9."

REFERENCES

Hayes p. 34; Roosevelt p. 8; L and B 1850 p. 17; L and B 1853 p. 15; cf. *LC 1816–1851* p. 92; Putnam p. 23.

COPY DESCRIBED

DLC: DA28 .4 C35 1848. *Leaf.* 220 × 139.

Lives of the Chief Justices.

TITLE PAGE

THE I LIVES I OF I THE CHIEF JUSTICES I OF I ENGLAND. I FROM THE NORMAN CONQUEST TILL THE DEATH OF I LORD MANSFIELD. I [thin rule] I BY I JOHN LORD CAMPBELL, LL.D. F. R. S. E. I AUTHOR OF I "THE LIVES OF THE LORD CHANCELLORS OF ENGLAND." I [thin rule] I IN TWO VOLUMES. I VOL. I. [II.] I BOSTON: I CHARLES C. LITTLE AND JAMES BROWN. I 1850.

PAGINATION

Vol. I. [2] i–xx 1–590.
Vol. II. [2] i–xii 1–584 1–18.

CONTENTS

Vol. I. [1] advertisement for books lately published by John Murray, [2] blank, i title page, ii blank, iii dedication to the Honorable Dudley Campbell, iv blank, v–vii preface, viii blank, ix–xix contents, xx blank, 1–588 text, 589 blank, 590 advertisement for New Editions of Standard Works.

Vol. II. [1] advertisement for books lately published by John Murray, [2] blank, i title page, ii blank, iii–xii contents, 1–584 text, 1–16 catalogue of works in general literature from John Murray, 17 blank, 18 advertisement for new editions of standard works.

REFERENCES

Hayes p. 34; Roosevelt p. 8; *BEAL* 2173.

COPY DESCRIBED

DLC: DA 28 .4 C3 1850. *Leaf.* 220 × 138.

---

1. Qtd. in *BEAL,* 2173.
2. Ibid.

~

31. **Campbell, William W.** *Life and Writings of De Witt Clinton.* **New York: Baker and Scribner, 1849.**

De Witt Clinton (1769–1828) served in political offices most of his life, first as mayor of New York City, then as a United States Senator, and finally as governor of New York state. The contents of his *Life and Writings* highlight Clinton's civic-minded disposition. In addition to a sketch of the Clinton family, the *Life and Writings* contains Clinton's address to the alumni of Columbia College, his private canal journal of 1810, an address before the New-York Historical Society, speeches in the Senate on the Mississippi question, an address before the Bible Society, an address before the Free School Society in the City of New York, and an address before the Phi Beta Kappa Society of Union College.

The editor William W. Campbell and his family had been close personal friends with the Clinton family for several generations; therefore, he may have been expected to produce a praiseworthy biography of Clinton. A reviewer for the *Literary World,* however, found Campbell's volume disappointing and called it a "meagre and insufficient memoir of a man who has occupied so wide a space in the history of his native state."[1] Nevertheless, Fillmore probably had a special interest in Clinton, since he was governor of Fillmore's home state during Fillmore's young adult years.

Other biographies of Clinton were available for purchase by the White House; yet, based on price, Campbell's from Baker and Scribner is the most likely choice. The Putnam catalogue offered this edition in octavo, bound in cloth for $1.50. Roorbach recorded four different possibilities for this entry. In addition to the Campbell biography, he included one by James Renwick from Harper that sold for $0.45, another anonymous life from G. H. Derby and Co. (no price included), and a memoir of Clinton by David Hosack from Carvill priced at $6.00, too high to qualify for this purchase.

105,133 voucher 5: Lf. Dewitt Clinton $1.50.
Purchased from Charles Welford on December 13, 1850.

REFERENCES

cf. Putnam p. 23; Roorbach p. 90; cf. Fillmore 1858 p. 10; cf. Fillmore 1861 p. 36.

---

1. "The Life and Writings of De Witt Clinton," *Literary World (1847–1853),* June 9, 1849, available at *APS Online,* http://www.proquest.com/products_pq/descriptions/aps.shtml.

~

32. Carey, Henry Charles. *Principles of Political Economy.* 3 vols. Philadelphia: Carey, Lea & Blanchard, 1837–40.

Henry Charles Carey (1797–1857), economist, publisher, and social scientist, was the son of the publisher and economist Matthew Carey. Henry became a partner in his father's firm, Carey and Lea, and under the name Carey, Lea and Carey, it became one of the largest publishing and bookselling houses in the country. After retiring in 1835 Henry devoted his life to studying and writing about political economy. His *Principles of Political Economy* (1837) is an expansion of his first published work on the topic, *Essay on the Rate of Wages* (1835). In it he advocates laissez-faire economic theory and controverts the views of Malthus, Ricardo, McCulloch, and Torrens. He rejects Ricardo's rent theory, while he sets forth his own distribution theory, "which called for progressive dispersal of wealth among the poorest families in society."[1] Especially popular in Europe, *Principles* was translated into Swedish and Italian as well as German, Japanese, Portuguese, and Russian and was reprinted numerous times throughout the nineteenth century. Ironically, Carey renounced his belief in free trade in 1848 and became an ardent protectionist, a position he continued to advocate the rest of his life.[2]

105,133 voucher 2: Carey's Political Economy 3 vols. 4.50.
Purchased from Little and Brown on December 30, 1850.
Hayes Catalogue: Carey, H. C. *Principles of Political Economy.* 3 parts in 3 v. Philadelphia, 1837–40. 8°

TITLE PAGE
PRINCIPLES | OF | POLITICAL ECONOMY. | PART THE FIRST: | OF | THE LAWS OF THE | PRODUCTION AND DISTRIBUTION OF WEALTH. | [thin rule] | BY H. C. CAREY, | AUTHOR OF AN ESSAY ON THE RATE OF WAGES. | [thin rule] | "All discord harmony not understood."—POPE. | "God hath made man upright, but they have sought out many inventions." — | ECCLESIASTES. | [thin rule] | PHILADELPHIA: | CAREY, LEA & BLANCHARD. —CHESTNUT STREET. | 1837.

Vol. II.
'. . . | PART THE SECOND: | OF | THE CAUSES WHICH RETARD | INCREASE | IN | THE PRODUCTION OF WEALTH, | AND | IMPROVEMENT | IN | THE PHYSICAL AND MORAL CONDITION OF MAN. | . . . | 1838.'

Vol. III.
'. . . | PART THE THIRD: | OF | THE CAUSES WHICH RETARD | INCREASE IN THE NUMBERS OF MANKIND. | [thin rule] | PART THE FOURTH: | OF | THE CAUSES WHICH RETARD | IMPROVEMENT IN THE POLITICAL CONDITION OF MAN. | [thin rule] | . . . | LONDON: | JOHN MILLER, | HENRIETTA STREET—COVENT GARDEN. | 1840.'

PAGINATION
Vol. I. [2] i–xvi 1–58 58–59 59–60 60–61 61–62 62–63 63–64 64–65 65–342.

Vol. II. i–vi 9–234 234–35 235–36 236–37 237–38 238–39 239–40 240–41 241–42 242–43 243–44 244–45 245–46 246–47 247–48 248–49 249–50 250–51 251–52 252–53 253–54 254–55 255–56 256–57 257–58 258–59 259–60 260–61 261–466.

Vol. III. [6] 1–112 111–270.

CONTENTS

Vol. I. [1] title, [2] copyright statement, i errata, ii blank, iii contents, iv blank, v–vii preface, viii–xvi introduction, 1–342 text.

Vol. II. i title, ii copyright statement, iii contents, iv errata, v–vi preface, 9–466 text.

Vol. III. [1] title, [2] blank, [3] contents, [4] blank, [5] errata, [6] blank, 1 section title, "Principles of Political Economy Part the Third of the Causes which Retard Increase in the Numbers of Mankind," 2 blank, 3–91 text, 92 blank, 93 section title, "Principles of Political Economy Part the Fourth of the Causes which Retard Improvement in the Political Condition of Man," 94 blank, 95–259 text, 260 blank, 261–70 index.

REFERENCES

Hayes p. 34; L and B 1850 p. 18; cf. Roorbach p. 91; cf. Putnam p. 6-s.

COPY DESCRIBED

DLC: HB 161 C25. *Leaf.* 227 × 125.

---

1. Francesco L. Napa, "Henry Charles Carey," *ANB Online,* http://www.anb.org/articles.
2. See entries 108, 104, 103, for Malthus, McCulloch, and Torrens.

∽

33. Catlin, George. *Illustration of the Manners, Customs, and Condition of the North American Indians.* 2 vols.

George Catlin (1796–1872), lawyer turned artist, was the first to offer a view of Indian life based on personal observation. His portraits, widely exhibited during the mid-nineteenth century throughout the United States, England, and continental Europe, fashioned an image of the American Indian that endures in Western consciousness. His oeuvre included more than three hundred portraits of men, women, and children, representing more than fifty different tribes. Although he petitioned Congress for aid on many occasions—he even wrote to President Fillmore and requested assistance with obtaining funding[1]—Catlin was never rewarded with patronage for his enterprise. When Congress refused to purchase his collection in 1852, it was forfeited to the hands of his creditors. Amazingly, his collection survived intact and is now held by the National Museum of American Art.

Catlin and his reviewers were aware of the eventual decimation of the tribes. While he lamented, "art may mourn when these people are swept from their earth, and the artists of future ages may look in vain for another race so picturesque in their costumes, their weapons, and their colours,"[2] a writer for the *Museum of Foreign Literature and Science* recalled, "it is but a few hundred years since white men first set foot in their country, and when their numbers exceeded, it is believed sixteen million . . . and now, of these sixteen millions, not two [million] remain in all the vast continent! and of these the greater part have been degraded and demoralized by their intercourse with white men."[3]

Nineteenth-century notices and reviews of Catlin's books assume that most readers have seen his work, acknowledge the accuracy of his paintings, and prophesy about the inevitable extinction of the peoples that he documented in his art.[4]

Catlin published several works in conjunction with his portraits, and the voucher entry could refer to any of them, but it most likely refers to *Illustration of the Manners, Customs, and Condition of the North American Indians*. Putnam offered three works by Catlin: the forementioned *Illustration of the Manners* in 2 volumes for $7.25, *Notes on Eight Years in Europe with the American Indians* for $4.00, and *Indian Portfolio* for $20.00. The price of the first is closest to the price paid by the Executive Mansion. In addition, the spine title on three Library of Congress copies as well as several copies in other libraries reads "Catlin's North American Indians," as Welford designated this book on his invoice.[5]

Exactly which edition of *Illustration of the Manners, Customs, and Condition of the North American Indians* the Fillmores purchased cannot be determined without further information. It was issued first as *Letters and Notes on the Manners and Customs of the North American Indians* (1841); with the fifth edition in 1845 the title was changed. Both the London and American editions sold at comparable prices. Roorbach recorded an edition from Wiley and Putnam in two volumes at $7.25, while Putnam and Little and Brown advertised London editions at $7.25 and $8.00, respectively. Although the voucher does not indicate this title was a multivolume set, no single-volume edition of this title dated before 1850 has been located; the bookseller Charles Welford probably neglected to write the number of volumes on his invoice. There were five publishers of *Illustrations* prior to 1850. Catlin published the work himself in London and had it printed by Toswill and Myers, then Tilt and Bogue, and Bogue alone until 1845, when Bohn began to publish it. George Putnam was the only American publisher of this title before 1850.

105,133 voucher 5: Catlins Indians N. America $6.50.
Purchased from Charles Welford on December 13, 1850.

REFERENCES
L and B 1850 p. 18; cf. L and B 1853 p. 14; cf. Roorbach p. 94; cf. Putnam p. 25.

---

1. George Catlin, letter to Millard Fillmore, April 20, 1852, Millard Fillmore Papers, BECHS.
2. George Catlin, *Letters and Notes on the Manners, Customs, and Conditions of North American Indians*, ed. Marjorie Halpin (New York: Dover, 1973), vii–viii.
3. "Review," *The Museum of Foreign Literature, Science, and Art (1822–1842)*, September 1841, available at *APS Online*, http://www.proquest.com/products_pq/descriptions/aps.shtml.
4. *Journal of Belles Lettres (1832–1842)*, February 1842; see also "Review," *The Knickerbocker; Or New York Monthly Magazine (1833–1862)*, August 1841, and "New Puplications," [sic] *Dwights American Magazine and Family Newspaper*, April 5, 1845. All are available at *APS Online*, http://www.proquest.com/products_pq/descriptions/aps.shtml.
5. Cataloguing records in online databases indicate that copies in other libraries bear this title on the spine.

∼

34. Chalmers, George. *Opinions of Eminent Lawyers.* 2 vols. London: Reed and Hunter, 1814.

George Chalmers (*bap.* 1742–*d.* 1825), antiquary and political writer, compiled *Opinions of Eminent Lawyers* because the commentaries of the law of England did not address legal topics related to "colonies, fisheries, and commerce" (1:i). While researching *Annals of the Present United Colonies* (1780) and an *Introduction to the History of the Revolt of the Colonies* (1782), Chalmers took copies of these opinions as he came across them.[1] Urged by his friends to publish this collection, Chalmers digested the opinions that he had compiled and arranged them under the following headings: (1) The King's prerogative abroad, (2) The King's general jurisdiction abroad, (3) How far the King's subjects who emigrate carry with them the English law, (4) Of the colonial constitutions, (5) Of the various modifications which the constituted assembly admits, (6) Of the national fisheries, (7) Of commerce, and (8) Of the law of nations. Edward Everett recommended this book to Fillmore in response to his request for books on international law after the Cuban filibuster.

107,754 voucher 4: 2 vols. Chalmer's Opinions $4.00.

Purchased from Little and Brown on December 31, 1850.

Hayes Catalogue: Chalmer, G. *Opinions of Eminent Lawyers on Various Points of English Jurisprudence.* 2 v. London, 1814 8°.

TITLE PAGE

OPINIONS | OF | EMINENT LAWYERS, | ON VARIOUS POINTS OF | ENGLISH JURISPRUDENCE, | CHIEFLY CONCERNING THE | *COLONIES, FISHERIES, AND COMMERCE,* | OF | Great Britain: [black letter] | COLLECTED, AND DIGESTED, FROM THE ORIGINALS, IN | THE BOARD OF TRADE, AND OTHER DEPOSITORIES. | [thick/thin double rule] | By GEORGE CHALMERS, Esq. F.R.S. and S.A. | [swelled rule] | VOL. I. [II.] | *LONDON:* | PRINTED FOR REED AND HUNTER, LAW BOOKSELLERS, | BELL YARD, LINCOLN'S INN. | [thin rule] | 1814.

PAGINATION

Vol. I. [2] i–lvi 1–364.
Vol. II. [2] 1–532.

CONTENTS

Vol. I. [1] title, [2] blank, i–liii preface, liv–lvi blank, 1–364 text.
Vol. II. [1] title, [2] blank, 1–508 text, 509 postscript, 510 blank, 511–32, index.

REFERENCES

Hayes p. 43; *BEAL* 7390; Harvard p. 41; Marvin p. 181.

COPY DESCRIBED

MH: Law School Storage UK 904 CHA. *Leaf.* 208 × 130.

---

1. These were two of his literary projects designed to arouse opinion against Americans and their British supporters.

35. Chambers, Robert, and William Chambers. *Chambers's Miscellany of Useful and Entertaining Tracts.* 20 vols. in 10. Edinburgh: Chambers, 1847–48.

The brothers Robert (1802–71) and William Chambers (1800–1883) were both Edinburgh publishers and writers who collaborated on a number of projects for producing quality literature at affordable prices. Some of their publishing ventures include *Chambers's Edinburgh Journal* (1832–1956), *Chambers's Historical Newspaper* (1833); *Chambers's Information for the People* (1833–35); *Chambers's Miscellany of Useful and Entertaining Tracts* (1844); *Chambers's Encyclopaedia: A Dictionary of Universal Knowledge* (1860–68); and *Chambers's English Dictionary* (1872). William Chambers mentions the *Miscellany* as one of their publications that furthered the distribution of inexpensive publications among "less affluent" classes; he describes it as having been "adapted for parish, school, regimental, prison, and similar libraries."[1] The contents of the *Miscellany* comprised a mixture of poetry, science, biography, history, and prose fiction.

There were several ten-volume editions of *Chambers's Miscellany of Useful and Entertaining Tracts* that the White House could have purchased in 1850. Roorbach lists an edition from Gould, ten volumes, in cloth, for $7.50, a price too high to make it a candidate. The *British Catalogue* lists a ten-volume edition from Orr, 1845–47 for 20*s.*, or approximately $5.00, a price that makes it a possibility. The most likely, however, is the Chamberses' own Edinburgh edition dated 1847–48, because that is the one that Little and Brown, the seller from whom it was purchased, was advertising in its 1852 and 1853 catalogues for $5.50 in cloth and $10.00 half calf.

105,133 voucher 2: Chambers Miscellany 10 vols. $5.25.
Purchased from Little and Brown on December 30, 1850.

REFERENCES
British Catalogue p. 69; cf. L and B 1850 p. 19; cf. L and B 1852 p. 2; cf. L and B 1853 p. 15; cf. Putnam p. 26.

---

1. William Chambers, *Memoir of Robert Chambers* (New York: Scribner, Armstrong and Co., 1872), 240.

∽

36. Chase, Lucien B. *History of the Polk Administration.* New York: Putnam, 1850.

Under the direction of the Democratic president James K. Polk (1795–1849), the United States fought the Mexican War from 1846 to 1848 and acquired the territories of New Mexico and California. His successor in the White House, Zachary Taylor, garnered the sobriquet "old rough and ready" while serving under Polk as a general in the war. President Fillmore would most certainly have been interested in the recent presidential history, from which he had inherited the escalating division between the North and the South.

Lucien B. Chase (D) (1817–1864) served as a member of the U. S. House of Representatives during the Polk administration from 1845 through 1849. Upon his retirement from Congress, he wrote his lengthy history of Polk's presidency, which received mixed reviews, depending on the reviewer's political persuasion. One writer for the *Literary World* called it "ponderous" and characterized it as an "apotheosis" that could be "safely postponed." In contrast, the *Knickerbocker; or New York Monthly Magazine* praised it as a handsome and clearly-written volume," and, not surprisingly, the *United States Magazine, and Democratic Review* found the subject a "worthy theme for the historian" and remarked that Chase had "ably discharged the trust." From a more objective standpoint, *Graham's American Monthly Magazine of Literature, Art, and Fashion* wrote that "the partisan character of the work prevents it from coming properly under the name of history, but it contains a well arranged statement of a vast mass of facts, that will be valuable both to the intelligent Whig and Democrat."[1]

105,133 voucher 5: Chases History Polks Administration $2.25.
Purchased from Charles Welford on December 13, 1850.
Roosevelt Catalogue: Chase, Lucien B. *History of the Polk Administration.* New York, G. P. Putnam, 1850.

TITLE PAGE
HISTORY | OF THE | POLK ADMINISTRATION. | BY | LUCIEN B. CHASE, | A MEMBER OF THE TWENTY-NINTH AND THIRTIETH | CONGRESSES. | NEW YORK: | GEORGE P. PUTNAM, 155 BROADWAY. | M.DCCC.L.

PAGINATION
i–viii 9–512 1–13 13A 14–17 17A 18–48.

CONTENTS
i title, ii copyright statement and printer's imprint, iii–iv preface, v–viii contents, 9–475 text, 476 blank, 477–512 appendix, 1–43 G. P. Putnam's List of New Publications and Works in Preparation, 44–45 index to G. P. Putnam's publications, 46 blank, 47 1850 prospectus for the *New-York Weekly Mirror*, 48 blank.

REFERENCES
Hayes p. 35; Roosevelt p. 8; Roorbach p. 101.

COPY DESCRIBED
DLC: E 416 C48 copy 2. *Leaf.* 230 × 140.

---

1. *The Literary World (1847–1853)*, July 27, 1850, *The Knickerbocker; or New York Monthly Magazine (1833–1862)*, July 1850, *The United States Magazine, and Democratic Review (1837–1851)*, August 1850, and *Graham's American Monthly Magazine of Literature, Art, and Fashion (1844–1858)*, November 1850, all available at *APS Online*, http://www.proquest.com/products_pq/descriptions/aps.shtml.

~

37. Chillingworth, William. *The Works.* 3 vols. Oxford: Oxford University Press, 1838.

The theologian William Chillingworth (1602–44) earned a reputation for his skill in disputation. The merits of Protestantism in comparison to Catholicism were the subject of much debate during his time as a student at Oxford, and for a brief time Chillingworth even converted to Catholicism. Chillingworth consistently took a stance of rational skepticism. In his major theological work, "Religion of Protestants, a safe way to Salvation," Chillingworth argued that doctrinal differences among Christians who insist on the exclusive possession of truth fracture the unity of Christianity. Later writers read and recommended reading him to learn his art of reasoning. Locke recommended, "If you would have your son to reason well, . . . let him read Chillingworth," and Anthony Wood declared, "if the great Turk or the Devil could be converted, he [Chillingworth] could do it."[1] In addition to purchasing a copy for the Executive Mansion, the Fillmores owned a copy of this book in their personal library.

105,133 voucher 2: Chillingworth 3 vols. $9.00.
Purchased from Little and Brown on December 30, 1850.
Roosevelt Catalogue: Chillingworth, William. *The Works*. Oxford, University Press, 1836–38, 3 vols.

TITLE PAGE
THE | WORKS | OF | WILLIAM CHILLINGWORTH, M. A. | IN THREE VOLUMES. | VOL. I. [II–III.] | [swelled rule] | Rex arbitratur, rerum absolute necessariarum ad salutem non magnum esse numerom. Quare | existimat ejus majestas, nullam ad ineudam concordiam breviorem viam fore, quam si | diligenter separentur necessaria a non necessariis, et ut in necessariis conveniat, omnis | opera insumatur: in non necessariis libertati Christianae locus detur. Simpliciter neces- | saria Rex appellat, quæ vel expresse verbum Dei præcipit credenda faciendave, vel ex verbo | Dei necessaria consequentia vetus ecclesia elicuit.—Si ad decidendas hodiernas contro- | versias hæc distinctio adhiberetur, et jus divinum a positivo seu ecclesiastico candide | separaretur; non videtur de iis quæ sunt absolute neccesaria, inter pios et moderato viros, | longa aut acris contentio futura. Nam et pauca illa sunt, ut modo dicebamus, et fere ex | æquo omnibus probantur, qui se Christianos dici postulant. Atque istam distinctionem | Sereniss. Rex tanti putat esse momenti ad minuendas controversias, quæ hodie Ecclesiam | Dei tantopere exercent, ut omnium pacis studiosorum judicet officium esse, diligentissime | hanc explicare, docere, urgere. | *Isaac. Casaubon. in Epist. ad Card. Perron. Regis Jacobi nomine scripta.* [swelled rule] | OXFORD, | AT THE UNIVERSITY PRESS. | MDCCCXXXVIII.

PAGINATION
Vol. I. i–xxxiv 1–412.
Vol. II. [4] 1–500.
Vol. III. i–vi 1–450.

CONTENTS
Vol. I. i title, ii blank, iii–vi dedication "To the most high and mighty Prince Charles, by the grace of God, King of Britain, France, and Ireland, defender of the faith, &c," vii–ix prefaces, x advertisement, xi–xii contents, xiii–xxxiv "The Life of Mr. Chillingworth," 1–412 text.
Vol. II. [1] title, [2] blank, [3] contents, [4] catchword "Charity Maintained," 1–499 text, 500 blank.
Vol. III. i title, ii blank, iii–v contents, vi blank, 1–438 text, 439–50 "A table of the principal matters in Charity Maintained, &c."

REFERENCES
Hayes p. 36; Roosevelt p. 8; cf. L and B 1850 p. 19; L and B 1853 p. 16; cf. Fillmore 1847 p. 9; cf. Fillmore 1858 p. 10; cf. Fillmore 1861 p. 34.

COPY DESCRIBED
DLC: BX 4809 C45 1838. *Leaf.* 216 × 130.

---

1. Qtd. in "Chillingworth, William," *Penny Cyclopaedia.*

❦

38. Chitty, Joseph. *A Practical Treatise on the Law of Nations.* London: Clarke and Son, 1812.

Joseph Chitty (1775–1841), barrister and legal writer, became England's first and most prolific professional legal writer, publishing more than twenty law books on topics ranging from bills of exchange to apprentices and from game laws to commercial laws. Chitty devoted much of his *Law of Nations* to the effect of the French wars on trade. In it he endeavored to "collect and arrange all the rules and decisions connected with this subject." He believed that "the whole law relative to the foreign commerce of belligerents and neutrals, in the time of war, is peculiarly interesting, as well as to the statesman and the lawyer as to the merchant" and, therefore, extended his "inquiry into the Laws of Nations generally, and of Great Britain in particular, as to the effect of war upon the commerce of belligerents and neutrals" (vii–viii).

Hoffman and Marvin divided in their opinions of this work. While Hoffman praised it and recommended it as "a very proper commencement of the study of the voluntary, customary, and conventional Law of Nations," he nonetheless maintained that "Mr. Chitty has shown in this essay the versatility of his powers, and the ease with which he passes from a consideration of one legal subject to another. There is no depth of learning, but great clearness in the arrangement of his topics, and concinnity of style and thought."[1] In contrast, Marvin found this treatise "superficial and imperfect," claiming that it "does not deserve the title which it bears." According to him, "its chief merit is the arrangement of Sir William Scott's judgments in prize causes, under appropriate titles."[2] Scott had served as judge of the high court of admiralty from 1798 to 1828, and the index of his judgments alone could have been enough for Fillmore to find the book useful. It is among the titles relative to international and admiralty law that Edward Everett recommended to Fillmore after the Cuban filibuster.

107,754 voucher 4: 1 vol. Chitty on Law of Nations $3.06.
Purchased from Little and Brown on December 31, 1851.
Hayes Catalogue: Chitty, J. *Practical Treatise on the Law of Nations. London, 1812. 8°.*

TITLE PAGE
A I PRACTICAL TREATISE I ON THE I LAW OF NATIONS, I RELATIVE TO THE I LEGAL EFFECT OF WAR I ON THE I COMMERCE I OF I Belligerents and Neutrals; [black letter] I AND ON I ORDERS IN COUNCIL I AND I LICENCES. I [thick/thin double rule] I By JOSEPH CHITTY, Esq. I OF THE MIDDLE TEMPLE. I [thin/thick double rule] I *LONDON:* I PRINTED FOR W. CLARKE AND SONS,

PORTUGAL-STREET, LIN- | COLN'S-INN; J. BUTTERWORTH, FLEET-STREET; J. RIDGEWAY, | PICCADILLY; AND J. M. RICHARDSON, CORNHILL. | [thin rule] | 1812.

PAGINATION
i–xii 1–296.

CONTENTS
i half title, ii printer's imprint, iii title, iv blank, v–vi dedication to Thomas Lord Erskine, vii–xii preface, 1–287 text, 288 blank, 289–96 index.

REFERENCES
Hayes p. 43; cf. *BEAL* 7167; cf. Harvard p. 44; Hoffman p. 452; cf. Marvin p. 190.

COPY DESCRIBED
DCGW: KZ6385 C45 1812. *Leaf.* 215 × 125.

---

1. Hoffman, *Course of Legal Study*, 452.
2. Marvin, *Legal Bibliography*, 190.

❧

39. Clarke, Mary Cowden. *The Complete Concordance to Shakespeare.* London: Charles Knight, 1845.

Mary Cowden Clarke's (1809–98) *Complete Concordance of Shakespeare* was the most complete work of its kind to date, superseding Francis Twiss's *A Complete Verbal Index to the Plays of Shakespeare* (1805) and Samuel Ayscough's *An Index to the Remarkable Passages and Words Made Use of by Shakespeare* (1791) and not superseded itself until 1894 by John Bartlett's *New and Complete Concordance.*[1] A literary scholar and writer, Clarke began the concordance in 1829. Its composition alone took twelve years, and its time in the press added another four to its incubation period. Originally it was issued in eighteen monthly parts between 1844 and 1845. Thereafter, it was published as a single volume in both London and Boston.

Clarke's work was so admired in America that a group of literary men decided to take up a subscription for a testimonial to be presented to Clarke. Accordingly, they had a highly ornamented chair with a writing desk made and inscribed:

> TO MRS. MARY COWDEN CLARKE,
> THIS CHAIR IS PRESENTED,
> BY A FEW LADIES AND GENTLEMEN OF AMERICA,
> AS A TRIBUTE OF GRATITUDE FOR THE UNEQUALLED INDUSTRY
> WHICH GAVE THE READERS OF ENGLISH
> THOUGHOUT THE WORLD
> HER CONCORDANCE OF SHAKESPEARE.

NEW YORK.   15 JULY, 1851

Daniel Webster, who would soon become Fillmore's secretary of state, heads the list of subscribers and is accompanied by such notable luminaries as Samuel Eliot, Henry Wadsworth

Longfellow, George Ticknor, William Cullen Bryant, Washington Irving, George P. Putnam, and William Gilmore Simms.

Shakespeare was immensely popular in nineteenth-century America, and Clarke asserts that he was the most frequently quoted "universal-minded genius that ever lived," one from whom an apt quotation on any subject may be drawn. The president and his staff members may have consulted her *Concordance* while they prepared speeches and other public addresses.

By 1877 the original Executive Mansion copy had been replaced by a Boston 1871 copy.[2] Only three or four editions of this work appeared before the time of purchase in 1852, two from Charles Knight in London, dated 1845 and 1847; one from Wiley and Putnam in New York in 1846; and another undated from Little and Brown in Boston that may have been published prior to 1850. While Putnam advertised the 1845 London edition in "Royal 8vo cloth" for $6.00, Little and Brown offered a London 1846 edition in "half Morocco, gilt edges, [$] 9.00." Taylor and Maury, the seller from whom this title was purchased, was one of Putnam's Washington agents, which makes the edition that Putnam offered, the 1845 Knight edition, a likely choice. Purchasing a copy in full calf, as the voucher specifies, could account for the price difference. Even though Putnam does not advertise this edition in full calf, the Library of Congress holds a copy of it in this binding.

109,399 voucher 1: Clarke's Concordance to Shakespeare Calf $7.50.
Purchased from Taylor and Maury on May 15, 1852.

REFERENCES
cf. Hayes p. 43; cf. L and B 1850 p. 21; L and B 1852 p. 2; Putnam p. 29.

----

1. The Fillmores owned Ayscough's work; see p. 190 in their 1861 catalogue.
2. Hayes Catalogue, 43.

~

40. **Colton, Calvin.** *The Life and Times of Henry Clay.* 2 vols. New York: A. S. Barnes and Co., 1846.

41. ———. *Public Economy for the United States.* 2nd ed. New York: A. S. Barnes and Co., 1849.

Henry Clay (1777–1852), a career congressman, was part of the "great triumvirate in the Senate," along with Daniel Webster and John C. Calhoun, that led the Whig Party during the 1830s and 1840s. In 1844 Clay sought the presidency, and Fillmore hoped to be his running mate. These plans were thwarted by Thurlow Weed and William Seward's machinations. Instead, Theodore Freelinghuysen won the second spot on the ticket, and Clay lost the race. As a senator, Clay worked to preserve the Union by helping to engineer the Missouri Compromise in 1820 and later by helping to draft the Compromise of 1850. He died and was laid in state in the Capitol toward the end of Fillmore's term in office.

Calvin Colton (1789–1857), clergyman and author, often employed his pen to promote Whig causes after leaving the ministry. Colton's *Public Economy for the United States* (1848) was admired by mid-nineteenth century American conservatives and won Colton the chair of public economy at Trinity College in Hartford, Connecticut. Not surprisingly, the *American Whig Review* praised Colton along with Henry Carey, Horace Greeley, Henry Clay, Daniel Webster, and George Evans as men "with understandings alike practical, discriminative, and logical," to whom "we are to look for the rescue of political economy." The *American Whig* writer juxtaposed Colton's "eminently original and scientific work" against the "impenetrable chaos of Mr. Mill's last cumbrous octavos."[1] *Political Economy* went into three editions and stood on the White House shelves alongside a host of economic writers, including Adam Smith, John Stuart Mill, Jean-Charles Leonard de Sismondi, Henry Charles Carey, and Thomas R. Malthus.

105,133 voucher 5: Colton's Life of Clay 2 vols. $2.50.
Purchased from Charles Welford on December 13, 1850.
Roosevelt Catalogue: Colton, Calvin. *The Life and Times of Henry Clay.* New York, A. S. Barnes & Co., 1846, 2 vols.
105,133 voucher 5: Colton's Public Economy $2.50.
Purchased from Charles Welford on December 13, 1850.
Hayes Catalogue: Colton, C. *Public Economy of the United States.* New York, 1849. 8°
> *Note.* The title page reads "Public Economy *For* the United States" not "*of* the United States" as the Hayes Catalogue records (italics added).

The Life and Times of Henry Clay.

TITLE PAGE
THE | LIFE AND TIMES | OF | HENRY CLAY. | BY CALVIN COLTON, | AUTHOR OF THE "JUNIUS TRACTS"—"FOUR YEARS IN GREAT BRITAIN"—"TOUR OF | THE AMERICAN LAKES," ETC. | IN TWO VOLUMES, | VOL. I. [II.] | NEW YORK: | PUBLISHED BY A. S. BARNES & CO., | 51 JOHN STREET. | [thin rule] | 1846.

PAGINATION
Vol. I. 1–504.
Vol. II. 1–504.

CONTENTS
Vol. I. 1 title, 2 copyright statement and printer's imprint, 3 dedication to the American people, 4 blank, 5–13 introduction, 14–16 contents, 17–504 text.
Vol. II. 1 title, 2 copyright statement and printer's imprint, 3–4 note, 5–8 contents, 9–488 text, 489–504 index.

PLATES
Vol. I.
None.
Vol. II.
Frontispiece, engraving of a log cabin schoolhouse with the caption 'SCHOOL HOUSE OF THE SLASHERS. | "As far as practice" Vol. I p. 19.'

REFERENCES
Hayes p. 39; Roosevelt p. 9; Putnam p. 167; cf. Roorbach p. 116; cf. Fillmore 1847 p. 23; cf. Fillmore ca. 1858 p. 11; cf. Fillmore 1861 p. 32, 170.

COPY DESCRIBED

DLC: E 340 C6 C74. *Leaf.* 220 × 138.

Public Economy.

TITLE PAGE

PUBLIC ECONOMY | FOR THE | UNITED STATES. | BY | CALVIN COLTON. | SECOND EDITION. | NEW YORK: | PUBLISHED BY A. S. BARNES & CO. | [thin rule] | 1849.

PAGINATION

1–536.

CONTENTS

1 title, 2 copyright statement and printer's imprint, 3 half title, 4 blank, 5 'NOTE. | [thin rule] | All the reasonings of this work on European society, | are based on the *status quo* of its condition before the | convulsions of 1848. It must be seen that these recent | and current events are not sufficiently ripe to be used | as materials in a work of this kind.', 6 blank, 7–15 contents, 16 blank, 17–536 text.

REFERENCES

Hayes p. 39; Putnam p. 30; cf. Roorbach p. 122; cf. Fillmore ca. 1858 p. 10; cf. Fillmore Packing Lists p. 9.

COPY DESCRIBED

DLC: HB161 C72 copy 1. *Leaf.* 230 × 142.

---

1. "Colton's Public Economy," *The American Whig Review: A Journal Devoted to Politics and Literature,* August 1848, available at *APS Online,* http://www.proquest.com/products_pq/descriptions/aps.shtml.

∾

42. Cooper, James Fenimore. *The History of the Navy of the United States of America.* 2 vols. London: Bentley, 1839.

James Fenimore Cooper (1789–1851), one of America's first great novelists, is best remembered today for his *Leatherstocking Tales.* He also wrote in a number of other genres, including short stories, travel literature, history, political pamphlets, editorials, and drama. His *History of the Navy* (1839) remains a valid historical source today. Cooper himself served in the navy from 1808 though 1811 but did not begin researching his *History* until 1838. Upon its publication, reviewers remarked on his experience at sea, his technical knowledge, and his capacity for writing vivid descriptions and captivating adventures. Fillmore took special interest in the navy during his presidency. He supported the abolishment of flogging as a form of discipline in the navy, a practice that was later discontinued during his term in office. Moreover, while Fillmore was president, the navy undertook several important exploring expeditions to the Amazon River Basin, the Arctic, and the Orient, among other destinations.[1]

The *History* was published in both British and American editions, but the American edition lacked an index, a table of contents, and chapter headings, omissions that the *Journal of Belles Lettres* found a "glaring fault" that caused "one half of the value" of the book to be lost. This omission most likely accounts for Fillmore's selection of a British edition.[2] A discrepancy exists between the price paid by the White House and that listed in contemporary book catalogues. While the White House paid only $2.50, Putnam advertised this edition for $5.00, and the *British Catalogue* for 30s., or about $7.30. Since this is an older edition, Welford may have been selling a used copy, passing along a discount that he had received, or discounting an item that had been too long in his inventory.

105,133 voucher 5: Cooper's History Amer. Navy 2 vols. $2.50.
Purchased from Charles Welford on December 13, 1850.
Roosevelt Catalogue: Cooper, James Fenimore. *The History of the Navy of the United States of America.* London, Richard Bentley, 1839, 2 vols.

TITLE PAGE
THE | HISTORY OF THE NAVY | OF | THE UNITED STATES | OF AMERICA. | BY J. FENIMORE COOPER, ESQ. | AUTHOR OF "THE PILOT," "THE RED ROVER," "THE WATER WITCH," &c. | IN TWO VOLUMES. | VOL. I. [II.] | LONDON: | RICHARD BENTLEY, NEW BURLINGTON STREET, | Publisher in Ordinary to her Majesty. [black letter] | 1839.

PAGINATION
Vol. I. i–xxxvi v–xii 1–456.
Vol. II. i–xii 1–560.

CONTENTS
Vol. I. i title, ii printer's imprint, iii dedication to the officers of the Navy of the United States including the Marine Corps, iv blank, v–x preface, xi–xxxv introduction, xxxvi blank, v–xii contents, 1–451 text, 452 blank, 453–56 appendix.
Vol. II. i half title, ii blank, iii title, iv printer's imprint, v–xii contents, 1–558 text, 559 note, 560 blank.

PLATES
Vol. I.
Portrait frontispiece, "Commodore Oliver H. Perry, U. S. N.," signed J. W. Jarvis, artist, and S. Freeman, engraver.
Facing 1, portrait of "Commodore Stephen Decatur, U. S. N.," signed J. W. Jarvis, artist, and J. W. Cooke, engraver.
Vol. II.
Portrait frontispiece, "Commodore Oliver H. Perry, U. S. N.," signed J. W. Jarvis, artist, and S. Freeman, engraver.
    Note. This is the same as the frontispiece in volume 1.
Facing 1, "Map of the Harbour of Tripoli."
Facing 406, portrait of "Commodore Thomas Macdonough, U. S. N.," signed J. W. Jarvis, artist, and S. Freeman, engraver.
Facing 491, "Battle of Plattsburgh Bay."

BINDING

Vol. II. Front and back boards. 225 × 135 blue-ribbed cloth, blind-stamped decorative frame. *Spine.* Gilt-stamped 'UNITED STATES | NAVY | [thin rule] | J. F. COOPER | [thin rule] | VOL. II.'

   Note. Volume 1 has been rebound in library buckram.

REFERENCES

Hayes p. 42; Roosevelt p. 10; *British Catalogue* p. 77; Putnam p. 8-s.

COPY DESCRIBED

DLC: E 182 C78 Copy 2. *Leaf.* 222 × 135.

---

   1. Harold D. Langley, *Social Reform in the United States Navy, 1798–1862* (Chicago: University of Illinois Press, 1967), 192–93, 197; Vincent Ponko Jr., *Ships, Seas, and Scientists: U.S. Naval Exploration and Discovery in the Nineteenth Century* (Annapolis: Naval Institute Press, 1974).

   2. May 28, 1839, available at *APS Online,* http://www.proquest.com/products_pq/descriptions/aps.shtml.

～

43. Curran, John Philpot. *The Speeches of the Right Honorable John Philpot Curran.* Ed. Thomas Davies. London: Bohn, 1847.

John Philpot Curran (1750–1817), Irish politician and lawyer, became one of the most skillful advocates at the Irish bar. Although an author for the *Annual Register* described him as "not particularly distinguished by the depth of his knowledge, or the depth of his researches," this writer maintained that "there was scarcely any on the Irish bench who equaled him addressing a jury." Ironically, Curran had been known as "stuttering Jack Curran" at school, and spent long hours reading aloud and participating in debating societies to overcome this impediment. A fellow Irishman, Wolfe Tone, offered unqualified praise of Curran as a national hero, claiming that his legal accomplishments represented "an imperishable monument to his own and to his country's fame."[1] Memoirs, biographies, and editions of Curran's speeches were published frequently throughout the nineteenth and early twentieth centuries.

   Curran's speeches are among the ones recommended by the nineteenth-century legal scholar David Hoffman. This volume, containing six of his bar speeches and thirty-three of his parliamentary speeches that had never before been published, supplies the context of each one. Arranged chronologically, they provide an outline of the development of Curran's career (i–ii).[2]

105,133 voucher 5: Curran's Speeches 1 vol. $2.25.
Purchased from Charles Welford on December 13, 1850.
Roosevelt Catalogue: Curran, John Philpot. *The Speeches.* Edited with a Memoir . . . by
   Thomas Davis. London, H. G. Bohn, 1847.

TITLE PAGE

THE SPEECHES | OF | THE RIGHT HONORABLE | JOHN PHILPOT CURRAN. | COMPLETE AND CORRECT EDITION. | EDITED, | WITH A MEMOIR AND HISTORICAL NOTICES, | BY | THOMAS DAVIES, ESQ., M. R. I. A., | BARRISTER-AT-LAW. | LONDON: | HENRY G. BOHN, YORK STREET, COVENT GARDEN. | MDCCCXLVII.

PAGINATION
[6] i–ii ix–xliv 1–604.

CONTENTS
[1] half title, [2] blank, [3] title page, [4] blank, [5] dedication to William Elliot Hudson, Esq., [6] blank, i–ii preface, ix–xi contents, xii blank, xiii–xliv memoir, 1–603 text, 604 printer's imprint.

PLATES
Portrait frontispiece of the "Right Honorable John Philpot Curran," painted by Sir Thomas Lawrence, P. R. A., engraved by C. J. Wagstaff.

REFERENCES
Hayes p. 42; Roosevelt p. 10; L and B 1853 p. 19.

COPY DESCRIBED
DLC: DA 948 .3 C9 A35. *Leaf.* 220 × 133.

---

1. The *Annual Register* and Wolfe Tone are both quoted in James Kelly, "Curran, John Philpot (1750–1817)," *ODNB.*
2. The White House also purchased *Curran and His Contemporaries* by Charles Phillips. See entry 129.

∽

44. Cuvier, Georges. *Animal Kingdom*. 8 vols. London: G. Henderson, 1834–37.

Georges Léopold Cuvier's (1769–1832) *Animal Kingdom* (1817) was translated into many languages and became the standard zoological textbook throughout the world in the mid-nineteenth century. As a zoologist and biologist, Cuvier stands among the pioneers of modern scientific study in France. Before his time, it was virtually impossible for one to choose science as a profession. His earlier work, an introductory textbook on natural history, *Tableau élémentaire de l'histoire naturelle des animaux* (1798), became the standard text used in French colleges.[1]

The entries for this work in the Roosevelt and the Hayes Catalogues cannot be reconciled exactly with the eight-volume set entered on the voucher. Both identify the publisher as G. Henderson, but while the Hayes Catalogue gives the date as 1834–36, the Roosevelt Catalogue lists it as 1836–37. Clearly not all volumes were present when either catalogue was compiled, and neither catalogue is clear about how many volumes were supposed to be present. Little and Brown, the seller from whom it was purchased, advertised in its catalogue an 1834 London edition that consists of four volumes of text and four volumes of plates in half morocco with the top edges gilt for $32.00. Putnam offered a similar set bound in cloth for $25.00. Unfortunately, no publisher is named in either catalogue. The *London Catalogue* lists a Henderson edition in eight volumes octavo that sold for £8 8*s.*, which would have been just over $40.00. The Executive Mansion most probably purchased a clothbound set with four volumes of text and four volumes of plates as advertised by Putnam and Little and Brown.

105,133 voucher 2: Cuvier Animal Kingdom 8 vols. $22.00.
Purchased from Little and Brown on December 30, 1850.

Roosevelt Catalogue: Cuvier, Georges L. C. F. D. <u>Baron</u> *The Animal Kingdom.* London, G. Henderson, 1836–37, 4 vols. plates to vols. 2, 4 issued in 8 vols.

Hayes Catalogue: Cuvier, G. L. C. F. D. *Baron Animal Kingdom.* 4 v. with plates v. 1, 2, 4. 7 v. London, 1834–36. 8°. v. 3 plates wanting.

REFERENCES

Hayes p. 43; Roosevelt p. 11; cf. L and B 1850 p. 25–26; cf. L and B 1853 p. 19; cf. *LC 1816–1851* p. 143; cf. Putnam p. 34.

---

1. "Georges Léopold Cuvier, Baron," *Encyclopedia of World Biography,* 2nd ed. (Detroit: Gale Research, 1998), reproduced in *Biography Resource Center* (Farmington Hills, Mich.: Thomson Gale, 2006), http://gale.cengage.com/servlet/BiographyRC.

~

45. Davis, Matthew L. *Memoirs of Aaron Burr.* 2 vols. New York: Harper, 1836.

Aaron Burr (1756–1836), soldier and politician, gained notoriety when he was tried and acquitted in 1804 for the murder of Alexander Hamilton while serving as vice president of the United States under Thomas Jefferson. Matthew Davis's *Memoirs of Aaron Burr* was published just months after Burr's death. Burr had requested Davis, his personal friend, to compile the biography and placed all of his personal papers at Davis's disposal. Davis suppressed those that he deemed improper, especially those relating to Burr's immorality with women (1:v). Despite its bias, a reviewer for the *New-Yorker* acknowledged the didactic value of Burr's biography:

> The fate of Aaron Burr must stand to all time a beacon to the swarm of restless and eager aspirants for fame and power who, reckless of principles and confident in their talents and perfect mastery of the arts of the demagogue, regard success as the almost inevitable result of their experiments on the popular credulity and ignorance. Aaron Burr lacked only integrity to have risen to the highest dignity among his countrymen. . . . But he chose a more venturous path; and the event affords a most impressive commentary on the miserable short-sightedness of sinister policy and vaulting ambition.[1]

Although the Fillmores would have found nothing to admire in Burr's politics or ethics, they would have concurred with the *New-Yorker* regarding the instructive value of his *Memoirs.* Their inclusion of this biography in the library serves as an example of their own egalitarian principles as they selected the lives and works of the American statesmen for the White House.

105,133 voucher 5: Aaron Burr's Life by Davis 2 vols. $3.50.
Purchased from Charles Welford on December 13, 1850.
Roosevelt Catalogue: Davis, Matthew L. *Memoirs of Aaron Burr, with Miscellaneous Selections from His Correspondence.* New York: Harper & Brothers, 1836, 2 vols.

TITLE PAGE
MEMOIRS | OF | AARON BURR. | WITH | MISCELLANEOUS SELECTIONS | FROM | HIS CORRESPONDENCE. | BY MATTHEW L. DAVIS. | "I come to bury Caesar, not to

praise him." | IN TWO VOLUMES. | VOL. I. [II.] | NEW YORK: | PUBLISHED BY HARPER & BROTHERS, | NO. 82 CLIFF-STREET. | [thin rule] | 1836.

PAGINATION

Vol. I. i–xvi 17–436.

Vol. II. i–xii 13–450 1–4 1–30 5–6 31–32.

CONTENTS

Vol. I. i title, ii copyright statement, iii–vi preface, vii–xiv contents, xv section title "Memoirs of Aaron Burr," xvi blank, 17–436 text.

Vol. II. i title, ii copyright statement, iii–x contents, xi section title "Memoirs of Aaron Burr," xii blank, 13–449 text, 450 blank, 1–4 catalogue of "Miscellaneous Works Recently Published by Harper and Brothers," 1–30 catalogue of "Interesting Works Published by Harper and Brothers," 5–6 the final two pages of the "Miscellaneous Works" catalogue, 31–32 the final two pages of the "Interesting Works" catalogue.

PLATES

Vol. I.

Portrait frontispiece, Aaron Burr, signed J. Vanderlyn, artist and G. Parker, engraver.

Facing 61, folding plate "Fac Simile of General Montgomery's Answer to James Duane."

Vol. II.

Portrait frontispiece, Mrs. Theodosia Burr Alston, signed Vanderlyn, artist and Parker, engraver.

REFERENCES

Hayes p. 47; Roosevelt p. 12; Putnam p. 166; Roorbach p. 83; cf. Fillmore 1861 p. 24.

COPY DESCRIBED

DLC: E 302 .6 B9 B9 Copy 2. *Leaf.* 213 × 133.

---

1. "Life of Burr," *The New Yorker (1836–1841)*, December 17, 1836, available at *APS Online*, http://www.proquest.com/products_pq/descriptions/aps.shtml.

∽

46. Dodd, Charles R. *A Manual of Dignities, Privilege, and Precedence.* London: Whittaker, 1844.

Charles Roger Dod [Dodd] (1793–1855) authored several reference works related to British rank and precedence: *The Parliamentary Companion* (1832), *Dod's Peerage, Baronetage and Knightage* (1841), and *A Manual of Dignities* (1842). While the *Parliamentary Companion* provided an annual biographical guide to the members of parliament and peers with notes on parliamentary procedure and other aspects of the London political sphere, the *Peerage* served as a guide to the titled classes and competed with Debrett's *Peerage* into the 1960s. In contrast to a peerage or baronetage that had to be updated annually, the *Manual of Dignities, Privilege, and Precedence* outlines "all that is permanent in titular distinctions" and offers accounts of the institutions themselves (6). The *Manual* describes and illustrates "the nature, characteristics, and extent of the honours" that the titled classes possess (5). It would have been an invaluable reference resource for anyone involved in foreign diplomacy. Copies of the *Manual* were published in 1842, 1843, and 1844, all by Whittaker. Little and Brown advertised the 1844 edition in duodecimo, clothbound, selling for $1.50, and Putnam offered it for $1.25. As the most recent, the 1844 edition is the most likely one to have been selected for the first White House Library.

105,133 voucher 4: Dodd's Man[l]. of Dignities $1.00.
Purchased from George P. Putnam on December 13, 1850.

REFERENCES
Putnam p. 38; L and B 1850 p. 29; cf. *LC 1816–1851* p. 151.

⌇

47. **Domat, Jean.** *The Civil Law in Its Natural Order.* **Ed. Luther S. Cushing. 2 vols. Boston: Little and Brown, 1850.**

In *The Civil Law in Its Natural Order,* Jean Domat (1625–96), French jurist and intimate of Pascal, combined Roman law and French legislation decisions into one system.[1] First published as *Les Lois Civiles dans Leur Ordre Natural* in 1689, it was translated into English by William Strahan in 1721; an improved edition with a supplement was published in 1724. In 1836 David Hoffman still recommended portions of Domat to students of the law: "Great improvements of the present day in the science and study of Roman law, have rendered this work of less importance than formerly; but the general student, and more particularly those who do not possess the means of studying this law in the numerous works we have mentioned under the present title, will find Domat's treatise of great value."[2] Hoffman also advised that the title of this work might be misleading. He explained that it does not refer to the natural order of the Roman law, but to the "Civil Law of France, as far as it is derived from the Roman sources."[3] Little and Brown's advertisement for this title included an endorsement from Joseph Story, who calls Domat's *Civil Law* excellent in method and clear, exact, and comprehensive in matter.[4]

105,133 voucher 2: Domat's Civil Law 2 vols. $9.50.
Purchased from Little and Brown on December 30, 1850.
Hayes Catalogue: Domat, J. *Civil Law in Its Natural Order.* Cushing's ed. 2 v. Boston, 1850. 8°.

TITLE PAGE
THE | CIVIL LAW | IN ITS NATURAL ORDER. | By JEAN DOMAT. | [thin rule] | Translated from the French, [black letter] | By William Strahan, LL.D., | ADVOCATE IN DOCTOR'S COMMONS. | [thin rule] | EDITED, | FROM THE SECOND LONDON EDITION, | By LUTHER S. CUSHING. | [thin rule] | IN TWO VOLUMES. | [thin rule] | VOLUME I. [II.] | CONTAINING THE TREATISE OF LAWS, PRELIMINARY BOOK, AND | PART I. OF ENGAGEMENTS. | [thin rule] | BOSTON: | CHARLES C. LITTLE AND JAMES BROWN. | 1850.

> *Note.* Volume 2 differs in the line after the volume designation as follows: 'CONTAIN-ING PART II. OF SUCCESSIONS.'

PAGINATION
Vol. I. i–xxiv 1–954.
Vol. II. i–viii 1–782.

CONTENTS
Vol. I. i title, ii copyright statement and printer's imprint, iii–x advertisement, xi–xxi contents, xxii blank, xxiii section title, "A Treatise of Laws," xxiv blank, 1–104 text, 105 section
title, "The Civil Law in its Natural Order, Preliminary Book," 106 blank, 107–56 text, 157
section title, "The Civil Law in its Natural Order, Part I, Engagements," 158 blank, 159–
953 text, 954 blank.

Vol. II. i title, ii copyright statement and printer's imprint, iii–viii contents, 1 section title,
"The Civil Law in its Natural Order, Part II, of Successions," 2 blank, 3–681 text, 682
blank, 683 section title, "Appendix," 684 blank, 685–703 text, 704 blank, 705 section title
"Index," 706 blank, 707–81 text, 782 blank.

PLATES
Vol. I.
None.
Vol. II.
Facing 203, a figure showing the succession of descendants, untitled.

REFERENCES
Hayes p. 51; *BEAL* 5364; L and B Law 1853 p. 38; cf. Greenleaf; cf. Harvard p. 72; cf. Marvin
p. 271; cf. Hoffman p. 535.

COPY DESCRIBED
DLC: Law General Law Doma 1850. *Leaf.* 232 × 149.

---

1. David M. Walker, "Domat, Jean," *The Oxford Companion to Law* (Oxford: Clarendon Press, 1980),
no. 372.
2. Hoffman, *Course of Legal Study,* 536.
3. Ibid.
4. See entries 164–66 for Story.

∼

48. Dwight, Theodore. *History of the Hartford Convention.* New York: N. & J. White, 1833.

The History of the Hartford Convention (1833) is the journal that Theodore Dwight (1764–
1846), author, lawyer, and statesman, kept of the proceedings of the Hartford Convention
of 1814 while serving as its presiding secretary. Meeting from mid-December 1814 through
early January 1815, the convention spoke out in opposition to the War of 1812 and sought
to bolster the New England Federalists.[1] Dwight's *History* constitutes a defense of the Federalist Party and of the convention itself. Ironically, the meeting led to the demise of the
Federalist Party, as members of the convention were accused of trying to break up the
Union. Little did they know that the Treaty of Ghent had been signed and brought an end
to the War of 1812 while they met on Christmas Eve 1814; news of the treaty did not reach
the United States until February. Regardless of their bias, Dwight's writings were influential

in shaping the public opinion of early nineteenth-century America and therefore provide insight into the polemics of the period.

155,133 voucher 5: Dwight's History Hartford Convention .88.
Purchased from Charles Welford on December 13, 1850.
Hayes Catalogue: Dwight, T. *History of the Hartford Convention.* New York, 1833. 8°.

TITLE PAGE
HISTORY | OF THE | HARTFORD CONVENTION: | WITH A | REVIEW OF THE | POLICY | OF THE | UNITED STATES GOVERNMENT, | WHICH LED TO THE | WAR OF 1812. | [thin rule] | BY THEODORE DWIGHT, | SECRETARY OF THE | CONVENTION. | [thin rule] | published by N. & J. WHITE, | NEW-YORK; | And RUSSELL, ODIORNE, & Co. | BOSTON. | D. Fanshaw, Printer. | [dotted rule] | 1833.

PAGINATION
1–448.

CONTENTS
1 title, 2 copyright statement, 3–422 text, 422–47 appendix, 448 blank.

REFERENCES
Hayes p. 51; cf. Roorbach p. 167.

COPY DESCRIBED
DLC: E 357.7 D99 copy two. *Leaf.* 198 × 115.

---

1. "Hartford Convention," in *Dictionary of American History,* ed. Stanley I. Kutler, 3rd ed. (New York: Scribner, 2003), 4:101.

~

49. Eaton, John Henry. *The Life of Andrew Jackson.*

Andrew Jackson (1790–1845), soldier and seventh president of the United States, distinguished himself by leading U.S. troops to victory in the Battle of New Orleans in January of 1815. During the nineteenth century his popularity as a national hero surpassed even that of George Washington's, and for many he came to symbolize American democracy. Jackson's biographer John Henry Eaton (1790–1856), politician and diplomat, was a friend of Jackson's who had served under him first during the War of 1812, then as a member of the Tennessee state legislature, and later as secretary of war. Eaton completed the *Life of Andrew Jackson* (1817) after its initial author, John Reid, unexpectedly died. The *Life* appeared in numerous editions prior to 1850, including two campaign versions in 1824 and 1828, and more than one German edition. An abridgment of the *Life* entitled *Memoirs of Andrew Jackson* was also published under several different imprints.

Since pricing information has not been found for most of these editions, it would be difficult to determine which one was selected for the White House. The purchase price, however, suggests that the copy purchased was probably full-length in octavo format. The 1817 Carey and Son and the 1824 Bradford editions both fit this bill. A London edition appeared in 1834, but it is an abridgment and sold for only three shillings, or about $0.75.

The 1828 McCarty and Davis, the 1828 H. Vicary Matchett, and the 1828 Ewer editions are all too small to have cost $1.75. The 1827 Hatch and Nichols, the 1850 Lippincott Grambo and Co., and the 1848 T. K. and P. G. Collins editions have not been available for examination.

105,133 voucher 5: Eaton's Life Gen¹. Jackson $1.75.
Purchased from Charles Welford on December 13, 1850.

REFERENCES
cf. Roorbach p. 284; cf. Fillmore 1847 p. 6; cf. Fillmore ca. 1858 p. 31; cf. Fillmore 1861 p. 112.

～

50. Edgeworth, Maria. *Tales and Novels.* 9 vols. London: Whittaker and Co., et al., 1848.

Maria Edgeworth (1768–1849), novelist and educator, became not only the most important Irish intellectual woman of the nineteenth century, but also the most commercially successful novelist of her age, receiving £2100 for her most lucrative novel, *Patronage* (1814).[1] Edgeworth's writings may be divided into three categories: those depicting Irish life, such as *Castle Rackrent* (1800); those depicting contemporary English life, such as *Belinda* (1801); and those for and about children, such as *Moral Tales* (1801).[2] Her narratives often explore contemporary, social, and political concerns as related to women and the vicissitudes they endured within the sociopolitical constraints of the day. Edgeworth received numerous endorsements from such well-known luminaries as Jeremy Bentham, Sir Humphrey Davy, David Ricardo, and Sir Walter Scott. She, in fact, inspired Scott, who claimed that reading Edgeworth's *The Absentee* prompted him to return to his incomplete manuscript that would become *Waverley,* a debt that he acknowledges in the 1829–33 collected edition of his works.[3] In this way Edgeworth helped to launch the historical novel. Edgeworth also influenced a number of younger writers, including Anthony Trollope and William Makepeace Thackeray, a favorite of the Fillmores.

Edgeworth's popularity remained high well into the nineteenth century. A writer for *Littell's Living Age* testifies to Edgeworth's accomplishment, calling her the "liveliest, shrewdest, most sensible teacher in fiction." Even the historian George Bancroft is said to have turned to reading Scott and Edgeworth as a respite from his theological studies at Harvard.[4] The set of her works selected for the White House included her most notable novels for adults and some of her most favored tales for children. Certainly, Edgeworth, along with Scott and Irving, was a staple in reputable nineteenth-century American home libraries.

105,133 voucher 5: Miss Edgeworth's Works $10.00.
Purchased from Charles Welford on December 13, 1850.
Roosevelt Catalogue: *Tales and Novels.* vol. 4. London, Whittaker & Co., 1848. Published in
    9 vols.

TITLE PAGE
Vol. I.
TALES AND NOVELS | BY | MARIA EDGEWORTH. | [thin rule] | IN NINE VOLUMES. | [thin rule] | VOL. I. [II–IX.] | MORAL TALES. | [thin rule] | LONDON: | WHITTAKER AND CO.; SIMPKIN, MARSHALL, AND CO.; H. WASHBOURNE; | H. G. BOHN;

E. HODGSON; H. RENSHAW; J. BAIN; HOULSTON AND | STONEMAN; J. MURRAY; R. MACKIE; ORR AND CO.; SMITH, ELDER, | AND CO.; ROUTLEDGE AND CO.; TEGG AND CO.; R. S. PARRY; AND | G. AND J. ROBINSON, LIVERPOOL. | [thin rule] | 1848.

Vol. II.
'... | POPULAR TALES. | ...'

Vol. III.
'... | BELINDA. |...'

Vol. IV.
'... | CONTAINING | CASTLE RACKRENT; | AN ESSAY ON IRISH BULLS; | AN ESSAY ON | THE NOBLE SCIENCE OF SELF-JUSTIFICATION; | ENNUI; and THE DUN. | ...'

Vol. V.
'... | MANŒUVRING; | ALMERIA; and VIVIAN. | (TALES OF FASHIONABLE LIFE.) | ...'

Vol. VI.
'... | THE ABSENTEE; | (A TALE OF FASHIONABLE LIFE.) | MADAME DE FLEURRY; EMILIE DE COULANGES; | AND | THE MODERN GRISELDA. | ...'

Vol. VII.
'... | PATRONAGE. | ...'

Vol. VIII.
'... | PATRONAGE, concluded; COMIC DRAMAS; | LEONORA; and LETTERS. | ...'

Vol. IX.
'... | HARRINGTON; THOUGHTS ON BORES; | and | ORMOND. | ...'

PAGINATION
Vol. I. i–viii 1–438.
Vol. II. [2] v–viii 1–486.
Vol. III. [4] 1–464.
Vol. IV. i–viii 1–434.
Vol. V. [2] 1–442.
Vol. VI. [2] 1–470.
Vol. VII. [2] 1–504.
Vol. VIII. [2] 1–486.
Vol. IX. i–iv 1–528.

CONTENTS
Vol. I. i title, ii printer's imprint, iii–vi preface, vii contents, viii blank, 1–438 text.
Vol. II. [1] title, [2] printer's imprint, v–vi preface, vii contents, viii blank, 1–485 text, 486 printer's imprint.
Vol. III. [1] title, [2] printer's imprint, [3] contents, [4] blank, 1–463 text, 464 blank.
Vol. IV. i title, ii epigraph, iii–vi preface, vii contents, viii blank, 1–434 text.

Vol. V. [1] title, [2] printer's imprint, 1–442 text.

Vol. VI. [1] title, [2] printer's imprint, 1–470 text.

Vol. VII. [1] title, [2] printer's imprint, 1 section title, "Patronage," 2 note to the reader from Richard Lovell Edgeworth, 3–4 preface to the third edition, 5–504 text.

Vol. VIII. [1] title, [2] printer's imprint, 1–486 text.

Vol. IX. i title, ii printer's imprint, iii–iv note to the reader from Richard Lovell Edgeworth, 1–528 text.

PLATES

Vol. I.

Frontispiece, "Moral Tales," signed in lower left by W. Harvey and lower right by J. W. Cooke.

Engraved title page, 'MORAL TALES | BY | MARIA EDGEWORTH | [preceding three lines in open face block letters] | [vignette, of a young man escorting a young woman through a garden with another couple looking on] | W. Harvey J. W. Cooke | Mr. Montague gathered three roses, a bud, a half blown and | a full blown rose, and playfully presented them to lady Au- | gusta for her choice." | *Mademoiselle Panache page 389* | LONDON, SIMPKIN, MARSHALL & C⁰· | AND OTHER PROPRIETORS. [preceding two lines in open face block letters.]'

Vol. II.

Frontispiece, "Belinda," signed in lower left by W. Harvey and lower right by F. Bacon.

Engraved title page, 'BELINDA, | BY | MARIA EDGEWORTH. [preceding three lines in open face block letters] | [vignette, man on knees before a lady at a ball] | W. Harvey E. Goodall | Clarence Hervey throwing himself at her feet, addressed her | in that high-flown style which her Majesty was wont to hear | from the gallant Raleigh or the accomplished Essex. | *Belinda Page 106.* | LONDON, SIMPKIN, MARSHALL & C⁰· | AND OTHER PROPRIETORS. [preceding two lines in open face block letters.]'

Vol. III.

Engraved title page, 'POPULAR TALES. | BY | MARIA EDGEWORTH. [preceding three lines in open face block letters] | [vignette, white man with negro in jungle] | W. Harvey F. Engleheart | Cæsar had no knife. "Here is mine for you," said | Mr· Edwards. | *The Grateful Negro Page 412* | LONDON, SIMPKIN, MARSHALL & C⁰· | AND OTHER PROPRIETORS. [preceding two lines in open face block letters.]'

Vol. IV.

Frontispiece, "Castle Rackrent," signed in the lower left by W. Harvey and lower right by H. Robinson.

Engraved title page, 'CASTLE RACKRENT. | IRISH BULLS. | ENNUI A TALE OF FASHIONABLE LIFE. | BY | MARIA EDGEWORTH. [preceding three lines in open face block letters] | [vignette, man standing on a monument in a cemetery preparing to speak to a multitude.] | W. Harvey F. Goodall. | —I stood up on a monument belonging to the Glenthorn family; | and the moment that it was observed that I wished to address the | multitude, the moving waves were stilled, and there was a dead | silence. *Ennui Page 371* | LONDON, SIMPKIN, MARSHALL & C⁰· | AND OTHER PROPRIETORS. [preceding two lines in open face block letters.]'

Vol. V.

Frontispiece, "Tales of Fashionable Life," signed lower left by W. Harvey and lower right by C. Rolls.

Engraved title page, 'MANŒUVRING; | ALMERIA. VIVIAN. | TALES | BY | MARIA EDGEWORTH. [preceding five lines in open face block letters] | [vignette, woman on knees before a man in the woods] | W. Harvey. F. Engleheart. | —In my madness I told him I regarded neither wealth, | nor rank, nor friends,—That I would rather live | with him in obscurity than be the greatest princess up- | on earth— | *Vivian Page 357* | LONDON, SIMPKIN, MARSHALL & C⁰. | AND OTHER PROPRIETORS. [preceding two lines in open face block letters.]'

Vol. VI.

Frontispiece, "Tales of Fashionable Life," signed lower left by W. Harvey and lower right by C. Rolls.

Engraved title page, 'THE ABSENTEE. | MADAME DE FLEURRY. EMILIE DE COULANGES. | THE MODERN GRISELDA. | TALES | BY | MARIA EDGEWORTH. | [vignette, group of beggars, a woman and three children walking in a rural area] | W. Harvey. E. Goodall. | And two girls, one of whom could but just walk, held | her hand and clung to her ragged petticoat; forming al- | together, a complete group of beggars. The woman stopped, | and looked after the man. | *Absentee Page 145.* | LONDON, SIMPKIN, MARSHALL & C⁰. | AND OTHER PROPRIETORS. [preceding two lines in open face block letters.]'

Vol. VII.

Engraved title page, 'PATRONAGE | BY | MARIA EDGEWORTH. [preceding three lines in open face block letters] | [vignette, three woman in dressmaker's shop] | W. Harvey. E. Smith. | "Look, ma'am, a mere strip!—only two breadths of three quar- | ters bare each—which gives no folds in nature, nor dra- | pery, nor majesty." | *page 357.* | LONDON, SIMPKIN, MARSHALL & C⁰. | AND OTHER PROPRIETORS. [preceding two lines in open face block letters.]'

Vol. VIII.

Frontispiece, "Patronage," signed in lower left by W. Harvey and lower right by F. Bacon.

Bound before frontispiece, "Patronage," signed in lower left by W. Harvey and lower right by C. Rolls.

Engraved title page, 'PATRONAGE CONCLUDED. | COMIC DRAMAS. LEONORA. | WITH LETTERS | BY | MARIA EDGEWORTH. [preceding five lines in open face block letters] | [vignette, lady swooning in the midst of a crowd outdoors] | W. Harvey. E. Goodall. | —"O lady Leonora! lady Leonora is ill!" exclaimed | every voice. The consternation was wonderful. | *Leonora Page 305* | LONDON, SIMPKIN, MARSHALL & C⁰. | AND OTHER PROPRIETORS. [preceding two lines in open face block letters.]'

Vol. IX.

Frontispiece, "Harrington," signed W. Harvey in lower left and H. Robinson lower right.

Engraved title page, 'HARRINGTON | AND | ORMOND | BY | MARIA EDGEWORTH | [vignette, injured man with two men attending to him outdoors] | W. Harvey. E. Goodall. | The fowling piece, overloaded had burst, and a large splinter of | the barrel had fractured the skull and had sunk into the brain | *Page 370.* | LONDON, SIMPKIN, MARSHALL & Cᵒ· | AND OTHER PROPRIETORS. [preceding two lines in open face block letters.]'

REFERENCES
Hayes p. 55; Roosevelt p. 14; cf. Putnam 1852 p. 42; cf. *LC 1816–1851* p. 171.

COPY DESCRIBED
Vol. I. MBA: VEF ED3 2.
Vols. II–IX. DLC: PZ3 E23 A2.

---

1. Bertha Coolidge Slade, *Maria Edgeworth, 1767–1849: A Bibliographical Tribute* (London: Constable, 1937), 147.
2. Margaret Drabble, ed., *The Oxford Companion to English Literature,* 6th ed. (Oxford: Oxford University Press, 2000), 306.
3. J. W. McCormack, "Edgeworth, Maria (1768–1849)," *ODNB.* See entry 149 for Scott.
4. "American Works of Fiction," *Littell's Living Age (1844–1896),* October 19, 1844, available at *APS Online,* http://www.proquest.com/products_pq/descriptions/aps.shtml; Lilian Handlin, "Bancroft, George," *ANB Online,* http://www.anb.org/aticles/14/14-00034; See entry 13 in this catalogue for Bancroft.

∼

51. *The Edinburgh Review, or Critical Journal.* Edinburgh: A. and C. Black, 1802–46.

The quarterly *Edinburgh Review, or Critical Journal* was founded in October 1802 as a vehicle for the Whig perspective. Its founders, Sidney Smith, Francis Horner, and Francis Jeffrey, with the assistance of Henry Brougham and others, provided a forum for the discussion of a range of topics. In addition to political views, the *Edinburgh* included literary reviews and essays on science, travel, geography, medicine, and education. During the first half of the nineteenth century, it spoke out on all of the primary political and social concerns. It opposed slavery on all grounds and supported the "reform of the game laws," "higher wages for workers," "the gradual abolition of the poor laws," and "full citizenship for Jews." In foreign affairs the *Edinburgh* advocated free trade, treaties, and the peaceful resolution of conflict. It supported parliamentary reform, but only on a "moderate scale." On the one hand, it agreed that more widespread representation in parliament was needed, but, on the other hand, it opposed universal suffrage.[1]

The *Edinburgh* differed from other British periodicals of this period, which tended to have writers of lesser quality to whom they paid meager sums for contributions. In contrast, the *Edinburgh* chose to have only gentlemen authors who initially were not paid at all for their writings. Soon the *Edinburgh*'s success, with its circulation reaching thirteen thousand by 1818, allowed it to pay handsome sums to its contributors. It encouraged its authors to develop and express their own opinions in their writings. Rather than opting for broad coverage in its book reviews, as its rival the *Monthly Review* did, the *Edinburgh* presented longer reviews of a select number of titles along with lists of other recently published books.[2]

The first quarter of the nineteenth century marked the *Edinburgh*'s heyday and coincided with the Romantic literary movement. At this time Francis Jeffrey wrote most of the literary reviews and condemned the Romantic writers for their choice of common language and common subjects. Thomas Babington Macaulay also made significant contributions to the *Edinburgh*. In 1843 his *Edinburgh* essays were collected, and they have been frequently reprinted ever since.[3]

The Executive Mansion purchased a complete run of the *Edinburgh* through 1846. There is no indication why it stopped short of 1850, and the Hayes and Roosevelt catalogues offer no evidence that subsequent volumes were ever purchased.

105,133 voucher 2: Edinburgh Review 83 vols. $116.00.
Purchased from Little and Brown on December 30, 1850.
Hayes Catalogue: *Edinburgh Review,* Oct. 1802 to April 1846 v. 1–83. Edinburgh 1802–46. 8°
Roosevelt Catalogue: *Edinburgh Review.* Edinburgh, 1803–46, 83 vols., vol. 48, 49, 52, missing.

TITLE PAGE
Vol. I.
THE | EDINBURGH REVIEW, [open face block letters] | OR | *CRITICAL JOURNAL:* | FOR | OCT. 1802. . . . . . . JAN. 1803. | *TO BE CONTINUED QUARTERLY.* | [thick/thin double rule] | JUDEX DAMNATUR CUM NOCENS ABSOLVITUR. | PUBLIUS SYRUS. | [thin/thick double rule] | VOL. I. | *Edinburgh:* | [double rule] | PRINTED BY D. WILLISON, CRAIG'S CLOSE, | FOR ARCHIBALD CONSTABLE, EDINBURGH; | AND T. N. LONGMAN & O. REES, | *LONDON.* | [swelled rule] | 1803.

Vol. LXXXIII.
THE | EDINBURGH REVIEW | OR | *CRITICAL JOURNAL:* | FOR | JANUARY, 1846 . . . . APRIL, 1846. | *TO BE CONTINUED QUARTERLY.* | [thick/thin double rule] | JUDEX DAMNATUR CUM NOCENS ABSOLVITUR. | PUBLIUS SYRUS. | [thin/thick double rule] | VOL. LXXXIII. | EDINBURGH: | PRINTED BY BALLANTYNE AND HUGHES, | FOR LONGMAN, BROWN, GREEN, & LONGMANS, LONDON; | AND ADAM AND CHARLES BLACK, EDINBURGH. | [thin rule] | 1846.

Note. The imprint changed several times during the course of the run that was purchased.

REFERENCES
Hayes p. 55; Roosevelt p. 14; L and B 1850 p. 30; cf. L and B 1853 p. 23; cf. Putnam p. 42; cf. Fillmore 1861 p. 64; cf. Fillmore ca. 1858 p. 17.

COPY DESCRIBED
ViU AP4 E3 Vol. 1–83. *Leaf.* 207 × 132.

1. Sullivan, *British Literary Magazines,* 133–35. See entries 21–22 for Brougham.
2. Ibid.
3. Ibid. See entry 102 for Macaulay.

52. *Encyclopaedia Americana.* Ed. Francis Lieber and E. Wigglesworth. 14 vols. Philadelphia: Lea and Blanchard, 1849.

The Encyclopaedia Americana (1829–1833) was the first encyclopedia to be published in the United States.[1] The brainchild of Francis Lieber (1800–1872), a German-born political scientist and educator, the *Encyclopaedia* began as an English translation of Friedrich Arnold Brockhaus's *Conversations Lexikon* that Lieber proposed to adapt for an American audience. He believed that an American encyclopedia should contain the best topics from the English encyclopedias, address issues of particular interest to Americans, and include subjects of general interest on the continent (1:iv). The *Encyclopaedia Americana* found immediate acceptance, and many notable Americans contributed to its pages, including Joseph Story, who contributed the "longest and most elaborate articles on law" (13:3). Volume 14 of the *Encyclopaedia* is a supplement published fourteen years after the set originally appeared in print and was updated "independently" of the German source. The list of sources that were drawn from for it includes the *Penny Cyclopaedia* and McCulloch's *Geographical, Statistical, and Historical Dictionary* (14:v–vi). The writer confesses that the editor "has not hesitated to use the identical words he found employed by either British, French, or German writers, in a distinct and appropriate manner" (14:vi). Likewise, the *Penny Cyclopaedia* borrowed from the *Encyclopaedia Americana,* as some of its articles read verbatim from the American work.[2]

105,133 voucher 4: Ency. Americana 14 vols. $17.50.
Purchased from George P. Putnam on December 13, 1850.
Roosevelt Catalogue: *Encyclopaedia Americana.* Edited by Frances Lieber, assisted by
    E. Wigglesworth, Philadelphia, Lea & Blanchard, 1849, 14 vols.

TITLE PAGE
Vols. I–XII.
ENCYCLOPÆDIA AMERICANA. | [thin rule] | A | POPULAR DICTIONARY | OF | ARTS, SCIENCES, LITERATURE, HISTORY, POLITICS, AND | BIOGRAPHY, | A NEW EDITION; | INCLUDING | A COPIOUS COLLECTION OF ORIGINAL ARTICLES | IN | AMERICAN BIOGRAPHY; | ON | THE BASIS OF THE SEVENTH EDITION OF THE GERMAN | CONVERSATIONS-LEXICON. | EDITED BY | FRANCIS LIEBER, | ASSISTED BY | E. WIGGLESWORTH. | [thin rule] | Vol. I. [II.–XII.] | [thin rule] | PHILADELPHIA: | LEA & BLANCHARD. | 1849.

Vol. V.
'... | E. WIGGLESWORTH AND T. G. BRADFORD. | ...'

Vol. XII.
Omits "A" on the third line.

Vol. XIV.
ENCYCLOPÆDIA AMERICANA: | SUPPLEMENTARY VOLUME. | [thin wavy rule] | A | POPULAR DICTIONARY | OF | ARTS, SCIENCES, LITERATURE, HISTORY, | POLITICS, AND BIOGRAPHY. | [thin wavy rule] | VOL. XIV. | [thin wavy rule] | EDITED BY | HENRY VETHAKE, LL. D. | VICE-PROVOST AND PROFESSOR OF MATHEMATICS IN THE UNIVERSITY OF PENNSYLVANIA; | MEMBER OF THE AMERICAN PHILOSOPHICAL SOCIETY; AUTHOR OF | "A TREATISE ON POLITICAL ECONOMY," ETC. | PHILADELPHIA: | LEA AND BLANCHARD. | 1849.

REFERENCES

Hayes p. 57; Roosevelt p. 14; cf. Roorbach p. 179; cf. Putnam p. 43; cf. Fillmore Packing Lists p. 8; cf. Fillmore ca. 1858 p. 18; cf. Fillmore 1861 p. 46 and p. 66.

COPY DESCRIBED

DLC: AE 5 E299. *Leaf.* 218 × 124.

---

1. S. Padraig Walsh, *Anglo-American General Encyclopedias: A Historical Bibliography, 1703–1967* (New York: Bowker, 1968), 42.
2. See entry 128 for the *Penny Cyclopaedia.*

~

53. Erskine, Thomas. *The Speeches of the Hon. Thomas Erskine.* 2 vols. New York: Eastburn, Kirk, and Co., 1813.

Thomas Erskine, first Baron Erskine (1750–1823), Lord Chancellor, was known for handling cases involving libel and freedom of the press. Most notably, he defended Thomas Paine in absentia in 1792 when Paine was charged with libel for the publication of part 2 of *Rights of Man.* He also habitually sent his own speeches to the press and promoted their publication as a demonstration of his rhetorical and theatrical skills. According to *Select Reviews, and Spirit of the Foreign Magazine,* Erskine's speeches on the liberty of the press contained a "complete body of the law of libel, and a most perfect history of its progress." Likewise, the nineteenth-century legal scholar David Hoffman recommended Erskine's speeches as the "best models of Bar eloquence that we possess."[1] Erskine's *Speeches* were among a select collection of speeches by eminent statesmen and orators chosen for the first White House Library.

105,133 voucher 5: Lord Erskines Speeches 2 vols. $5.50.

Roosevelt Catalogue: Erskine, Thomas Lord. *The Speeches of the Hon. Thomas Erskine, when at the Bar, on Subjects Connected with the Liberty of the Press; against Constructive Treasons and on Miscellaneous Subjects.* Collected by James Ridgway. New York, Eastburn, Kirk & Co., 1813, 2 vols.

TITLE PAGE

THE | SPEECHES | OF | THE HON. THOMAS ERSKINE, | (NOW LORD ERSKINE,) | WHEN AT THE BAR, | ON | SUBJECTS | CONNECTED WITH | THE LIBERTY OF THE PRESS; | AGAINST | CONSTRUCTIVE TREASONS, | AND ON | MISCELLANEOUS SUBJECTS. | [thick/thin double rule] | COLLECTED BY | *JAMES RIDGWAY.* | [thin/thick double rule] | IN TWO VOLUMES. | [decorative rule] | VOL. I. [II.] | [thick/thin double rule] | *NEW-YORK:* | PRINTED FOR EASTBURN, KIRK, & CO. NO. 86 BROADWAY, | CORNER OF WALL-STREET. | [double dotted rule] | 1813.

> *Note.* The imprint in volume 2 uses an italicized colon after New York and reads 'PRINTED FOR EASTBURN, KIRK, & CO. CORNER OF | NASSAU AND WALL-STREETS.'

PAGINATION

Vol. I. i–xviii 1–602.

Vol. II. i–viii 1–604.

CONTENTS

Vol. I. i half title, ii blank, iii title, iv printer's imprint, v–vi contents, vii dedication to the gentlemen of the American Bar, viii blank, ix–xvi preface to the American edition, xvii–xviii preface to the English edition, 1–602 text.

Vol. II. i half title, ii printer's imprint, iii title, iv blank, v contents, vi blank, vii preface to the second volume, viii blank, 1–604 text.

PLATES

Vol. I.

Portrait frontispiece of the Honorable Thomas Erskine. Signed R. Cosway and P. Maverick, engraver.

REFERENCES

Hayes p. 58; Roosevelt p. 14; cf. Fillmore 1847 p. 26; cf. Fillmore ca. 1858 p. 59; cf. Fillmore 1861 p. 30; Hoffman p. 602.

COPY DESCRIBED

DLC: DA 522 E7A3 1813. *Leaf.* 215 × 130.

---

1. "The Speeches of Thomas Erskine (now Lord Erskine)," *Select Reviews, and Spirit of the Foreign Magazines (1809–1811),* November 1810, available at *APS Online,* http://www.proquest.com/products_pq/descriptions/aps.shtml; Hoffman, *Course of Legal Study,* 602.

◦⌣◦

**54. Fisher, Richard S. *The Book of the World.* 2 vols. New York: J. H. Colton, 1849.

Richard S. Fisher designed *The Book of the World* as a general reference source that would supply scholars and merchants with statistical information about cities, states, and countries throughout the world. He drew from the most reliable sources of the day. For information regarding foreign countries he consulted travelers, writers, and the ministers and consuls of those nations; for the United States he turned to state surveys, periodical censuses, returns of state governments, and federal reports. After reading the proof sheets for Fisher's work, a critic for the *United States Magazine and Democratic Review* predicted, "It cannot but prove highly useful to the mercantile public, and, indeed, to all who wish to extend their sphere of knowledge to other countries." Upon its publication, the *National Era* and the *Merchant's Magazine and Commercial Review* took notice of it, with the former remarking on its usefulness to "editors and politicians" and the latter surveying its contents.[1] *The Book of the World* was among the earliest books purchased for the first White House Library and may have been regarded as a nearly indispensable reference resource.

The copy of *Book of the World* described here is from the original Executive Mansion collection. In addition to the inscription on the front pastedowns, "Presidential Mansion, October 21, 1850," it also has the only examples of a "Presidential Mansion" spine label that has been discovered. The voucher records that two titles totaling three volumes were purchased October 21 and includes a charge for "lettering 3 volumes .75" as the last charge for this day, which probably refers to spine labels like the one on this book. The front pastedown of volume 1 also bears a label for the Washington bookselling firm Taylor and Maury, the seller from whom it was purchased.[2]

105,133 voucher 6: Book of the World, 2 vols. 8vo $5.00.
Purchased from Taylor and Maury on October 21, 1850.
Hayes Catalogue: *Book of the World.* By R. S. Fisher. 2 v. New York, 1849, 8°.

TITLE PAGE

THE | BOOK OF THE WORLD: | BEING AN ACCOUNT OF ALL | REPUBLICS, EMPIRES, KINGDOMS, AND NATIONS, | IN REFERENCE TO THEIR | GEOGRAPHY, STATISTICS, COMMERCE, &c. | TOGETHER WITH A | Brief Historical Outline [black letter] | OF THEIR | RISE, PROGRESS AND PRESENT CONDITION, | &c., &c., &c. | [thin rule] | BY RICHARD S. FISHER, M. D. | [thin rule] | IN TWO VOLUMES. | [thin rule] | VOL. I. [II.] | ILLUSTRATED WITH MAPS AND CHARTS. | [thin double rule] | NEW-YORK: | PUBLISHED BY J. H. COLTON, | No. 86 CEDAR-STREET. | [dotted rule] | 1849.

　　Note. The title page of volume 2 does not include lines 12 through 17.

PAGINATION

Vol. I. i–viii 1–614.
Vol. II. i–vi 1–706.

CONTENTS

Vol. I. i title, ii copyright statement and printer's imprint, iii publisher's advertisement, iv blank, v–viii contents, 1–614 text.
Vol. II. i title, ii copyright statement and printer's imprint, iii–vi contents, 1–705 text, 706 blank.

PLATES

Vol. I.
Bound between front board and front free endpaper, colored Chart of National Flags, published by J. H. Colton, New York.
Bound between rear board and rear free endpaper, "Telegraphic and Railroad map of the United States of America The British Provinces &c.," published by J. H. Colton.
Vol. II.
Bound between front board and front free endpaper, folding colored map of "A Combined View of the Principal Mountains and Rivers in the World," published by J. H. Colton.
Bound between rear board and rear free endpaper, folding colored map of the world, published by J. H. Colton.

BINDING

Front and back board. 245 × 157 med. blue beaded cloth with blind-stamped decorative frame. *Spine.* Blind-stamped decorative bands, gilt stamped between the bands with 'THE | BOOK | [globe] | OF THE | WORLD | VOL. I. [II.]' | black spine label near base of spine gilt stamped '[thin double rule] | PRESIDENTIAL | MANSION. | [thin double rule]'. *End-papers.* Off-white.

Note. The spine of volume 2 is detached, and most of the spine label is missing.

MARKS OF OWNERSHIP

Inscribed on the front pastedown in black ink, "Presidential Mansion | October 21 1850," with the shelf mark, "E shelf no. 11" written in pencil beneath. Presidential Mansion spine label as described in the binding paragraph.

REFERENCES

Hayes p. 66; Roorbach p. 194; cf. Fillmore 1861 p. 82.

COPY DESCRIBED

DLC G121 F53 1849a. *Leaf.* 238 × 149.

---

1. "Notices of New Books," *The United States Magazine, and Democratic Review (1837–1851),* April 1849, "*The Book of the World,*" *National Era (1847–1860),* June 28, 1849, and "The Book of the World, Being an Account of All Republics, Empires, Kingdoms," *The Merchant's Magazine and Commercial Review,* July 1849, all available at *APS Online,* http://www.proquest.com/products_pq/descriptions/aps.shtml.
2. See "Bibliographical Methods," 77, for more information about spine labels on books in the library.

∽

55. Fleming, Charles, and J. Tibbins. *Royal Dictionary English and French and French and English.* 2 vols. Paris: Didot, 1844.

Fillmore himself was not fluent in any foreign language, but his daughter, Mary Abigail, had studied French, German, and Latin and may have used this dictionary.[1] The president and his staff members may have also had occasion to consult it for its selection of technical terms relative to trade, commerce, law, the navy, and the military. It was the standard French–English dictionary, based on and superseding the work of Louis Chambaud.

The White House most likely selected the Paris edition even though the American edition may have been more readily at hand. Putnam offered a two-volume Philadelphia edition, but it sold for only $5.00 while the White House paid $12.50 for its copy. Little and Brown, the seller from whom this dictionary was purchased, advertised a Paris 1844 edition in two large volumes for $10.00 in paper and $13.50 in half calf, prices that match the voucher entry more closely and indicate that the White House copy was probably bound in half calf.

Firmin Didot Frères began publishing this dictionary in 1841 and republished it before the time of the White House purchase in the following years: 1844, 1845, 1846, and 1849. Comparisons between a volume 1 from 1844 and a volume 1 from 1846, and between a volume 2 from 1844 and a volume 2 from 1849, reveal that the dictionary had been stereotyped and that these copies were printed from the same plates; therefore, regardless of the date in the imprint, the content would have been virtually the same.

105,133 voucher 2: Fleming and Tibbs Dicty 2 vols. $12.50.
Purchased from Little and Brown on December 30, 1850.

TITLE PAGE

Vol. I.

ROYAL DICTIONARY | ENGLISH AND FRENCH | AND | FRENCH AND ENGLISH; | COMPILED | FROM THE DICTIONARIES OF JOHNSON, TODD, ASH, WEBSTER, AND CRABB, | FROM THE LAST EDITION OF CHAMBAUD, GARNER, AND J. DESCARRIÈRES, | FROM THE SIXTH EDITION OF THE ACADEMY, THE COMPLEMENT TO THE ACADEMY, | THE GRAMMATICAL DICTIONARY OF LAVEAUX, THE UNIVERSAL LEXICON OF BOISTE, | AND THE STANDARD TECHNOLOGICAL WORKS IN EITHER LANGUAGE, | BY Professors FLEMING and TIBBINS. | [thin decorative rule] | VOL. I.—ENGLISH AND FRENCH. | CONTAINING: | All the Vocables in Common Use, with a Copious Selection of Terms Obsolescent or Obsolete Connected with Polite Literature; | Technical Terms, or such as are in General Use in the Arts, Manufactures, and Sciences, | in Naval and Military Language, in Law, Trade and Commerce; | Geographical and Mythological Terms, with Adjectives or Epithets Elucidating History; | A Literal Pronunciation for the Use of the French; | Accurate and Discriminating Definitions, with Appropriate Examples and Illustrations Tending to Fix as well as Display | the Signification, Import, Rank, and Character of each Individual Word; | Peculiar Constructions, Modes of Speech, Idioms, Sayings, and Proverbs; | Etymology, Exhibiting Words in their Origin and Affinities; | Grammar and Synonymy. | [printer's ornament] | PARIS: | PUBLISHED BY FIRMIN DIDOT FRÈRES, | PRINTERS TO THE KING AND THE INSTITUTE OF FRANCE, | RUE JACOB, N° 56. | 1844.

Vol. II.

GRAND DICTIONNAIRE | FRANÇAIS-ANGLAIS | ET | ANGLAIS-FRANÇAIS, | Rédigé d'après | LA SIXIÈME ÉDITION DU DICTIONNAIRE DE L'ACADÉMIE FRANÇAISE, | LE COMPLÉMENT DE CE DICTIONNAIRE, | LA DERNIÈRE ÉDITION DE CHAMBAUD, GARNIER ET J. DESCARRIÈRES, | LE DICTIONNAIRE GRAMMATICAL DE LAVEAUX ET LE LEXIQUE UNIVERSEL DE BOISTE, | LES DICTIONNAIRE ANGLAIS DE JOHNSON, TODD, ASH, WEBSTER ET CRABB, | ET LES PRINCIPAUX OUVRAGES TECHNOLOGIQUES DE L'UNE ET L'AUTRE LANGUE. | PAR MM. LES PROFESSEURS FLEMING ET TIBBINS. | [thin decorative rule] | TOME II.—FRANÇAIS-ANGLAIS. | CONTENANT: | Tous les mots d'un usage général, avec un choix complet de termes vieux ou vieillis; | Les termes techniques ou consacrés dans les arts, l'industrie, les sciences, la langue militaire et maritime, le droit et le commerce; | Les termes géographiques et mythologiques, avec les épithètes ou adjectifs qui jettent quelques lumières sur l'histoire; | Une prononciation littérale et figurée à l'usage des Anglais. | Les définitions de l'Académie Français, avec des exemples choisis propres à faire connaître le sens, | la valeur, le rang et le caractère de chaque mot; | Les constructions et façons de parler particulières, les idiotismes et les proverbes; | Les difficultés de la grammaire française présentées et résolues en anglais. | [printer's ornament] | PARIS. | LIBRARIE DE FIRMIN DIDOT FRÈRES, ÉDITEURS, | IMPRIMEURS DU ROI ET DE LINSTITUT, | RUE JACOB, N° 56. | [thin rule] | 1845.

PAGINATION

Vol. I. i–ix 10 1–1234.

Vol. II. i–xii 1–1104.

CONTENTS

Vol. I. i half title, ii printer's imprint, iii title, iv blank, v–vii avis, viii specimen, ix explanation, 10 abbreviations, 1–1232 text, 1233–34 an alphabetical list of the most common
Christian names and their abbreviations.

Vol. II. i half title, ii printer's imprint, iii blank, iv notice, v blank, vi–x rules for the pronun-
ciation of the French vowels and diphthongs, xi explanation of the table of simple
sounds, xii blank, 1–1104 text.

REFERENCES

L and B 1850 p. 34; L and B 1853 p. 25; Putnam p. 11-s; Fillmore Packing Lists p. 3; cf.
Fillmore 1861, p. 54.

COPY DESCRIBED

Vol. I. DLC: PC 2640 F6 1844. *Leaf.* 308 × 227.

Vol. II. DLC: PC 2640 F6 1845 copy 2.

---

1. Scarry, *Millard Fillmore*, 104.

❧

Franklin, Benjamin. *The Works of Benjamin Franklin.* 10 vols. Ed. Jared Sparks. Boston:
Tappan, Whittemore, and Mason, n.d.

See Sparks, Jared, entry 162.

❧

56. Fynn, Robert. *British Consuls Abroad.* London: E. Wilson, 1851.

Robert Fynn asserted that his *British Consuls Abroad* (1846) was the first book in the English
language on this subject. He claimed to have visited nearly every British consulate in Europe
and the Levant between 1841 and 1844 before he first published it in 1846. Fynn anticipated
that his book would "prove serviceable and instructive to the trading captains and merchants, by giving them ALL the information which their frequent contact with CONSULS
renders it so indispensable they should possess, and for the want of which, hitherto,
unpleasant misunderstandings have often taken place" (x). Fynn's *British Consuls Abroad* is
among the books that Franck Taylor sent to the president in response to his request for
books related to consuls during the summer of 1852 when he was contending with the aftermath of the Cuban filibuster. The chapter titles provide a guide as to the kind of information found in it: "The Appointment and Qualifications of Consuls," "The Duties of a British
Consul," "The Mode of Payment of Consuls' Salaries," "The Jurisdiction, Privileges, and
Rank of a Consul," and "Consular Fees." The book was republished by Effingham Wilson of
London in 1848, 1850, and 1851. Since it would have been used as a reference source, the most
recent edition available, the third edition dated 1851, was most likely selected for the library.

109,399 voucher 4: Fynn's British Consuls Hand Book $2.75.
Purchased from Franck Taylor on July 8, 1852.

REFERENCES
cf. *LC 1816–1851* p. 208.

~

57. Garland, Hugh A. *The Life of John Randolph of Roanoke.* 2 vols. New York: Appleton, 1850.

John Randolph (1773–1833), United States Congressman, United States Senator, and orator, led a long and controversial public career. Early on he championed Jeffersonian ideals and was one of Fillmore's predecessors as chair of the Ways and Means Committee, in which position he helped to pass the Louisiana Purchase. He later took a proslavery stance, argued against federal power, and advocated the sovereignty of the states, all issues on which Fillmore took a more conservative position. Fillmore would have known Randolph from the brief time that they served together as representatives in Congress. Fillmore first took office in March of 1833, and Randolph died that May. Randolph's biographer, Hugh Garland, had been educated in Randolph's district and observed him among his constituents. Relying on many firsthand accounts of his subject while writing this biography, he became acquainted with some of Randolph's closest friends, interviewed Randolph's surviving family members, and consulted Randolph's personal correspondence.

Contemporary reviews reflect the bias of the periodical in which they appeared. The *Southern Literary Messenger* calls Garland's biography "an interesting and valuable work . . . well worth the attention of the reader," and remarks "that we have no where caught a more entertaining glimpse of a great man, in many scenes of an eventful life, than in Mr. Garland's volumes." In contrast, the *Literary World* speaks with less regard for Randolph:

> the general judgment that he [Randolph] was governed by personal bias, local position, and the indulgence of individual whim, is confirmed in the biography itself. . . .
>
> He was all his life a ruin: where no domestic affection found a steady shelter; and where party, political consanguinity, or public principle, sought in vain a fortress of retreat and defence.[1]

105,133 voucher 5: Garland's Life Jno. Randolph 2 vols. 8vo $3.25.
Purchased from Charles Welford on December 13, 1850.
Roosevelt Catalogue: Garland, Hugh A. *The Life of John Randolph of Roanoke.* New York, D. Appleton & Co., 1850. Vol. 1 only.

TITLE PAGE
THE LIFE | OF | JOHN RANDOLPH | OF ROANOKE. | BY | HUGH A. GARLAND. | VOL. I. [II.] | NEW-YORK: | D. APPLETON & COMPANY, 200 BROADWAY. | PHILADELPHIA: | GEO. S. APPLETON, 164 CHESTNUT-STREET. | M. DCCC.L.

PAGINATION
Vol. I. [4] i–xii 1–320.
Vol. II. 1–384.

CONTENTS

Vol. I. [1]–[4] advertisements for other Appleton publications, i half title, ii blank, iii title, iv copyright statement, v–viii preface, ix–xii contents, 1–311 text, 312 blank, 313–20 advertisements for other Appleton publications.

Vol. II. 1 half title, 2 blank, 3 title, 4 copyright statement, 5–8 contents, 9–375 text, 376 blank, 377–84 advertisements for other Appleton publications.

PLATES

Vol. I.

Portrait frontispiece, "John Randolph," engraved by J. Sartain.

Vol. II.

Frontispiece, caricature entitled "John Randolph in England."

BINDING

Front and back boards. 232 × 150 Brown ribbed cloth, blind-stamped small triple frame inside of large triple frame with decorations at corners between the two. *Spine.* Gilt-stamped 'LIFE I OF I JOHN I RANDOLPH I [decorative rule] I VOL. I [II.]' followed by three blind-stamped decorations.

REFERENCES

Hayes p. 79; Roosevelt p. 16; Roorbach p. 451.

COPY DESCRIBED

ViU: McGreg A 1850 G37. *Leaf.* 225 × 143.

---

1. "The Life of John Randolph of Roanoke," *The Southern Literary Messenger; Devoted to Every Department of Literature,* November 1850, and "Reviews," *The Literary World (1847–1853),* November 9, 1850, both available at *APS Online,* http://www.proquest.com/products_pq/descriptions/aps.shtml.

~

**58. Gibbon, Edward. *The History of the Decline and Fall of the Roman Empire.* Ed. H. H. Milman. 2nd ed. 6 vols. London: Murray, 1846.

In nineteenth-century America, Henry Hart Milman's edition of Edward Gibbon's *The History of the Decline and Fall of the Roman Empire* was considered "indispensable," "one of the most valuable histories in the English language."[1] Gibbon (1737–94) first published this history in six volumes between 1775 and 1788. On the appearance of the first volume, his publisher, William Strahan, wrote that it "will remain a lasting monument of the genius and ability of the writer," and at the completion of the last volume, Adam Smith declared to Gibbon, "it sets you at the very head of the whole literary tribe at present existing in Europe." Controversy over Gibbon's treatment of Christianity, however, tempered this warm reception.[2]

The copy described here represents one of the eleven surviving books from the original Executive Mansion library. It appears, however, that neither Fillmore nor any subsequent occupant of the White House had occasion to consult it, because it remained, in 2006, mostly unopened. Fillmore did, however, own a copy of Gibbon's *Decline and Fall* in his own library both before and after his presidency.

105,133 voucher 2: Milman's Gibbon 6 vols. $11.00.

Purchased from Little and Brown on December 30, 1850.

Roosevelt Catalogue: Gibbon, Edward. *The History of the Decline and Fall of the Roman Empire, with Notes by the Rev. H. H. Milman.* Second edition. London, John Murray, 1846, 6 vols.

TITLE PAGE

THE | HISTORY| OF | THE DECLINE AND FALL | OF THE | ROMAN EMPIRE. | [thin rule] | BY EDWARD GIBBON, ESQ. | [thin rule] | WITH NOTES | BY THE REV. H. H. MILMAN, | PREBENDARY OF ST. PETER'S, AND RECTOR OF ST. MARGARET'S, | WESTMINSTER. | SECOND EDITION. [bold font] | [thin rule] | IN SIX VOLUMES. | VOL. I. [II.–VI.] | [thin rule] | LONDON: | JOHN MURRAY, ALBEMARLE STREET. | 1846.

PAGINATION

Vol. I. i–xxiv 443–46 xxv–xliv 1–600.

Vol. II. i–xii 1–560.

Vol. III. i–xvi 1–544.

Vol. IV. i–xvi 1–524.

Vol. V. i–xvi 1–508.

Vol. VI. i–xvi 1–500.

Note. All volumes are mostly unopened.

CONTENTS

Vol. I. i title, ii printer's imprint, iii–xv preface by the editor, xvi list of maps, xvii–xix preface of the author, xx blank, xxi advertisement to the first octavo edition, xxii blank, xxiii preface to the first volume, xxiv blank, 443–446 preface to the fourth volume of the original quarto edition, xxv–xlii contents, xliii directions to the binder, xliv blank, 1–600 text.

Vol. II. i title, ii printer's imprint, iii–xii contents, 1–559 text, 560 printer's imprint.

Vol. III. i half title, ii blank, iii title, iv blank, v–xv contents, xvi blank, 1–543 text, 544 printer's imprint.

Vol. IV. i half title, ii printer's imprint, iii title, iv blank, v–xv contents, xvi blank, 1–524 text.

Vol. V. i half title, ii printer's imprint, iii title, iv blank, v–xv contents, xvi blank, 1–506 text, 507–8 advertisement for "standard editions printed uniformly with 'Milman's Gibbon.'"

Vol. VI. i half title, ii printer's imprint, iii title, iv blank, v–xv contents, xvi blank, 1–433 text, 434 blank, 435–98 general index, 499 errata, 500 blank.

PLATES

Vol. I.

Facing title, folding map of "Migrations of the Barbarians."

At rear of volume, folding map of the "Western Part of the Roman Empire."

At rear of volume, folding map of the "Eastern Part of the Roman Empire."

Vol. II.

At rear of volume, map of "Propontis, Hellespont, and Bosphorus."

At rear of volume, map of "Constantinople Divided into its Regions."

At rear of volume, folding map of "Western Asia Shewing the Marches of Julian and
    Heraclius."
Vol. III.
At rear of volume, folding map of "Italia."
At rear of volume, folding map of "Europe about the End of the Vth Century."
Vol. IV.
At rear of volume, folding map of "The Eastern Empire Divided into Themes."
At rear of volume, folding map of "Environs of Rome."
Vol. V.
At rear of volume, folding map of "Europe and Part of Asia and Africa at the Time of
    Charlemagne."
At rear of volume, folding map of the "Mahometan Empire."
Vol. VI.
At rear of volume, folding map of the "Crusades."
At rear of volume, folding map of "Ancient Rome."

BINDING

Front and back boards. 228 × 143 brown ribbed cloth. *Spine.* Gilt-stamped 'GIBBONS |
ROMAN | EMPIRE | [thin rule] | Vol. I. [II.–VI.]'

> *Notes.* The spine is missing from volumes 1 and 6. The back board is missing from vol-
> ume 6.

MARKS OF OWNERSHIP

Inscribed on front pastedown in black ink, "Executive Mansion | 1850."
Below inscription in pencil "F | shelf no. 9."

REFERENCES

Hayes p. 81; Roosevelt p. 16; cf. Putnam p. 51; L and B 1850 p. 37; cf. L and B 1852 p. 2; cf. L
and B 1853 p. 27; cf. *LC 1816–1851* p. 214; cf. Fillmore 1847 p. 19; cf. Fillmore ca. 1858 p. 23; cf.
Fillmore 1861 p. 184.

COPY DESCRIBED

DLC: DG311 G54 1846. *Leaf.* 220 × 137.

---

1. *Stryker's American Register and Magazine (1850–1851)*, July 1850, and *The United States Magazine, and
Democratic Review (1837–1851)*, July 1850, both available at *APS Online*, http://www.proquest.com/
products_pq/descriptions/aps.shtml.
2. Strahan and Gibbon are qtd. in David Womersley, *ODNB*. See entry 154 for Smith.

∾

59. Goldsmith, Oliver. *The Miscellaneous Works.* **Ed. James Prior. 4 vols. New York:
Putnam, 1850.**

Oliver Goldsmith's reputation reached its zenith in the Victorian era when William Makepeace Thackeray declared him one of the most beloved writers of the age. Although Goldsmith (ca. 1728–74) wrote in a host of genres, including essays, novels, drama, poetry, history,
and biography, today he is most remembered for his short novel *The Vicar of Wakefield*

(1766), his poems *The Traveller* (1764) and *The Deserted Village* (1770), and his play *She Stoops to Conquer,* which has been in production throughout most of the years since its first performance in 1773.

The Literary World ran reviews of Prior's edition of Goldsmith's works after each volume was published. Regarding volume 1, it praised James Prior as an "industrious and zealous Goldsmith-collector" who has "fairly created the biography of his favorite author." *The Literary World* considered Goldsmith's writings a "treasure": "You see no artificial strugglings, straining of wit, or pumping of emotion in Goldsmith, but in its own limits the clear, natural, limpid, wellspring of genius."[1]

Roorbach recorded this edition in cloth for $5.00 in duodecimo. Putnam, however, offered it in half morocco for $8.00, which, based on price, is most likely the binding of the copy selected for the White House.

105,133 voucher 2: Goldsmith 4 vols. $8.00.
Purchased from Little and Brown on December 30, 1850.
Roosevelt Catalogue: Goldsmith, Oliver. *The Miscellaneous Works of Oliver Goldsmith Including a Variety of Pieces Now First Collected, by James Prior.* New York, G. P. Putnam, 1850, 4 vols. vols 1, 4, missing.

TITLE PAGE

THE | MISCELLANEOUS WORKS | OF | OLIVER GOLDSMITH. | INCLUDING | A VARIETY OF PIECES | NOW FIRST COLLECTED. | BY | JAMES PRIOR, Fellow of the Society of Antiquaries; Member of the Royal Irish Academy; | Author of the Life of Goldsmith, Life of Burke, etc. etc. | [thin rule] | IN FOUR VOLUMES. | VOL. I. [II–IV] | [thin rule] | NEW YORK: | GEORGE P. PUTNAM, 155 BROADWAY. | M.DCCC.L.

PAGINATION

Vol. I. i–x 11–586.
Vol. II. [2] i–x 11–558.
Vol. III. i–xviii 19–518.
Vol. IV. i–xii 13–544.

CONTENTS

Vol. I. i half title, ii blank, iii title, iv printer's imprint, v–viii contents, ix–x advertisement, 11 section title, "The Bee," 12–162 text, 163 section title, "Essays," 164 blank, 165–391 text, 392 blank, 393 section title, "An Inquiry into the Present State of Polite Learning in Europe," 394 textual note, 395–467 text, 468 blank, 469 section title, "Prefaces and Introductions," 470 blank, 471–586 text.

Vol. II. [1] half title, [2] blank, i title, ii printer's imprint, iii–x contents, 11 section title, "Letters of a Citizen of the World," 12 textual note, 13–488 text, 489 section title, "Familiar Introduction to the Study of Natural History In Five Parts," 490 blank, 491–558 text.

Vol. III. i half title, ii blank, iii title, iv printer's imprint, v–viii contents, ix section title, "The Vicar of Wakefield; a Tale," x blank, xi–xvi "opinions of distinguished writers," xvii author's (Goldsmith's) note, xviii blank, 19–209 text of "Vicar of Wakefield," 210 blank, 211 section title, "Biographies," 212 textual note, 213–446 text, 447 section title, "Miscellaneous Criticism," 448 blank, 449–517 text, 518 blank.

Vol. IV. i half title, ii blank, iii title, iv printer's imprint, v–vii contents, viii blank, ix section title, "Poems," x blank, xi section title, "The Traveler," xii blank, 13–121 text, 122 blank, 123 "Miscellanies," 124 blank, 125–78 text, 179 section title, "Dramas," 180 blank, 181–362 text, 363 section title, "Criticism, Relating to Poetry and the Belles-Lettres," 364 blank, 365–528 text, 529 section title, "Index," 530 blank, 531–43 index, 544 blank.[2]

> *Note.* The half title is missing from volume 4 of this copy, but was most likely present before rebinding.

PLATES

Vol. I.

Engraved title page, 'THE | MISCELLANEOUS WORKS | OF | OLIVER GOLDSMITH. M. B. [foregoing lines all in open face block letters] | VOL. 1. | [vignette, people in front of a ruin] | Painted by T. Creswick Engraved by J. N. Gimbrede [script] | LISSOY. [open face block letters] | REMAINS OF THE RESIDENCE OF GOLDSMITH'S FATHER | NEW YORK. | GEO. P. PUTNAM. | 1850. [last three lines in open face block letters.]'

Vol. II.

Engraved title page, same as volume 1 except for vignette '[vignette, people in a village] | Painted by T. Creswick Engraved by J. N. Gimbrede [script] | EDGEWORTHSTOWN. [open face block letters] | IN THE COUNTY OF LONGFORD'

Vol. III.

Frontispiece, '[vignette, people in a village] | Painted by T. Creswick Engraved by J. N. Gimbrede [script] | ARDAGE. [open face block letters] | IN THE COUNTY OF LONGFORD | NEW YORK. | GEO. P. PUTNAM. | 1850. [last three lines in open face block letters.]'

Vol. IV.

Frontispiece, '[vignette, people in a boat in front of an island with windmills] | Painted by C. Stanfield, engraved by J. N. Gimbrede [script] | "OR BY THE LAZY SCHELD." [open face block letters] | THE TRAVELLER | NEW YORK. | GEO. P. PUTNAM. | 1850. [last three lines in open face block letters.]'

REFERENCES

Hayes p. 82; Roosevelt p. 16; Roorbach p. 222; Putnam 12-s; cf. Fillmore ca. 1858 p. 23.

COPY DESCRIBED

NYRU: PR 3481 P95m.

---

1. "Prior's Works of Goldsmith," *The Literary World (1847–1853)*, December 1, 1849, and "Goldsmith," *The Literary World (1847–1853)*, April 6, 1850, both available at *APS Online*, http://www.proquest.com/products_pq/descriptions/aps.shtml.

2. I am grateful to Melissa S. Mead, Digital/Visual Resources Librarian, Rare Books, Special Collections and Preservation, Rush Rhees Library, University of Rochester, for double checking the pagination and contents statement in this book.

60. Goodman, Godfrey. *The Court of King James the First.* 2 vols. London: Bentley, 1839.

Godfrey Goodman (1583–1656), Bishop of Gloucester, wrote his *Court of King James the First* in the 1650s, yet for reasons unknown it was not published until 1839, when its manuscript was found in the Bodleian Library, Oxford (1:v). Initally, Goodman's book appears to be an overflattering account of King James I's reign, one that is "somewhat blind to his vices, and very kind to his virtues" (1:xvi). This favorable presentation of the king may have been influenced by two factors. First, Goodman's tenure as bishop was fraught with controversy; he was accused of popery on several occasions, and King James was tolerant of Catholicism.[1] Second, *The Court of King James the First* may have been originally written in response to a scandalous pamphlet by Sir Anthony Weldon entitled *The Court and Character of King James I.* Rather than a separate, corrective biography, Goodman wrote a "discursive commentary" on Weldon's work.[2] Regardless of Goodman's motivation for writing, John Henry Newman observed that the volumes contain much "gossip of the times to which they relate."[3]

105,133 voucher 5: Goodmans Court James I 2 vols. $2.00.

Purchased from Charles Welford on December 13, 1850.

Roosevelt Catalogue: Goodman, Godfrey. *The Court of King James the First.* London, Richard Bentley, n.d., 2 vols.

> *Note.* Although the Roosevelt Catalogue does not specify a date, the Hayes Catalogue does identify the date as 1839. All recorded Bentley editions of this title are dated 1839.

TITLE PAGE

THE | COURT OF | KING JAMES THE FIRST; [red ink] | BY | DR. GODFREY GOODMAN, | BISHOP OF GLOUCESTER; | TO WHICH ARE ADDED, | LETTERS ILLUSTRATIVE OF THE PERSONAL HISTORY | OF THE MOST DISTINGUISHED CHARACTERS IN | THE COURT OF THAT MONARCH AND HIS PREDECESSORS. | BY JOHN S. BREWER, M. A. | OF QUEEN'S COLLEGE, OXFORD. | IN TWO VOLUMES. | VOL. I. [II.] | LONDON: | RICHARD BENTLEY, NEW BURLINGTON STREET, | Publisher in Ordinary to her Majesty. [black letter, red ink] | 1839.

PAGINATION

Vol. I. [2] i–xxiv 1–422.

Vol. II. i–xii 1–424.

CONTENTS

Vol. I. [1] half title, [2] printer's imprint, i title, ii blank, iii dedication to Joshua Drinkald, Esq., iv blank, v–vi advertisement, vii–xvii introduction, xviii blank, xix–xxiv contents, 1–421 text, 422 blank.

Vol. II. i half title, ii printer's imprint, iii title, iv blank, v–xii contents, 1–410 text, 411–24 index.

PLATES

Vol. I.

Portrait frontispiece, King James I, signed in lower left by G. P. Harding and lower right by W. Greatbatch.

Facing xxiv, full-length portrait of George Villiers, 1st Duke of Buckingham, K. G., signed in lower left by G. P. Harding and lower right by W. Greatbatch.

Vol. II.

Portrait frontispiece, Queen Elizabeth, signed in lower left by G. P. Harding and lower right by W. Greatbatch.

Facing 1, portrait of Count Gondomar, signed in lower left by G. P. Harding and lower right by W. Greatbatch.

BINDING

Front and back boards. 230 × 155 navy straight-grain morocco cloth with blind-stamped decorative frame. *Spine.* Blind stamped with five panels, second panel 'COURT OF | JAMES I | [thin rule] | VOL. II. [gilt stamped]'. *Endpapers.* Pale yellow.

REFERENCES

Hayes p. 82; Roosevelt p. 16; Putnam p. 53.

COPY DESCRIBED

ViU: DA 391 G65. *Leaf.* 230 × 159.

---

1. John Henry Cardinal Newman, "The Court of King James the First," *British Critic* 27 (January 1840), available at Newman Reader, http://newmanreader.org/works/britishcritic/brewer.html (accessed June 20, 2009).

2. Geoffrey Ingle Sodden, *Godfrey Goodman: Bishop of Gloucester 1583–1656* (London: SPCK, 1953), 416–17. I am grateful to Joyce Ransome, Executive Officer, Emerita, at Brown University for bringing Sodden's comments to my attention.

3. Newman, "Court of King James."

~

61. Grahame, James. *The History of the United States of North America.* 2 vols. Philadelphia: Lea and Blanchard, 1850.

James Grahame's *History of the United States* went unrecognized in America until it received notice in the *North American Review* by William Hickling Prescott, who called it "the most thorough work and incomparably the best on the subject, previous to Mr. Bancroft's."[1] Grahame published the first two volumes of his *History* in 1827. He added two more volumes and published all four together in 1836. George Bancroft corrected Grahame and questioned his accuracy and intention in his own *History of the United States.* This questioning initiated a debate that was played out in American periodicals with Grahame and Bancroft trading rejoinders and Josiah Quincy, president of Harvard University, coming to Grahame's defense.[2]

The Lea and Blanchard edition was printed from a "corrected and enlarged copy" of *The History of the United States of North America* that Grahame had left at his death in 1842 with the wish that it be published. Several notable members of the Massachusetts Historical Society of which Grahame had been a corresponding member— Joseph Story, James Savage, Jared Sparks, and William H. Prescott—appointed Josiah Quincy to shepherd the Lea and Blanchard edition through the press and to compile a memoir of Grahame, which was then prefixed to the *History* (1:iii–iv).

Although the American edition of Grahame's work was brought to the public by some of the leading American intellectuals of the day, its reputation did not fare well. In 1902 J. N. Larned commented:

> Grahame never visited this country, and relied wholly on such material as he could collect in Great Britain or find in the library of the University of Göttingen. He does not seem to have made researches, at least to any extent, among the British archives. Pamphlet literature he does not seem to have extensively used. His materials, when compared with those at the command of the historian at present time, were scanty. He wrote too under the influence of the extreme democratic ideas of 1830, and was not sparing in his use of strong expletives. The work then may be regarded as to a large extent superseded. Still it is written in an excellent style and contains passages of great suggestiveness.[3]

107,754 voucher 3: Grahame's Colonial History $4.00.
Purchased from Franck Taylor on May 2, 1851.
Roosevelt Catalogue: Grahame, James. *The History of the United States of North America, from the Plantations of the British Colonies till Their Assumption of National Independence.* Second edition, Philadelphia, Lea & Blanchard, 1850, 2 vols.

TITLE PAGE
THE | HISTORY | OF | THE UNITED STATES | OF | NORTH AMERICA, | FROM THE | PLANTATION OF THE BRITISH COLONIES | TILL | THEIR ASSUMPTION OF NATIONAL INDEPENDENCE. | [thin rule] | By JAMES GRAHAME, LL. D. | [thin rule] | IN TWO VOLUMES. | VOL. I. [II.] | SECOND EDITION, ENLARGED AND AMENDED. | [thin rule] | PHILADELPHIA: | LEA AND BLANCHARD. | 1850.

PAGINATION
Vol. I. i–xlii 25–598.
Vol. II. i–vi 1–620.

CONTENTS
Vol. I. i title, ii copyright statement and printer's imprint, iii–iv preface to the American edition, v–xxviii Memoir of James Grahame, LL. D., xxix Dedication to Robert Grahame, Esq., xxx blank, xxxi–xxxvi preface, xxxvii–xli contents, xlii blank, 25–550 text, 551–66 appendix I, 567–98 notes to the first volume.
Vol. II. i title, ii copyright statement and printer's imprint, iii–vi contents, 1–89 text, 90–108 appendix II, 109–335 text, 336–62 appendix III, 363–556 text, 557–619 notes to the second volume, 620 blank.

PLATES
Vol. I.
Portrait frontispiece of James Grahame, signed in lower left by Healy and lower right by J. Andrews.
Vol. II.
None.

REFERENCES
Hayes p. 82; Roosevelt p. 16; cf. Roorbach p. 227; cf. Putnam p. 53; cf. Fillmore 1847 p. 19; cf. Fillmore ca. 1858 p. 24; cf. Fillmore 1861 p. 214.

COPY DESCRIBED
DLC: E188 G75 1850. *Leaf.* 230 × 139.

---

1. Qtd. in "Grahame, James," in *Appleton's Cyclopaedia of American Biography*, 6 vols., ed. James Grant Wilson and John Fiske, rev. Charles Dick and James E. Homans (New York: The Press Association Compilers, Inc., 1915), vol. 2; See entries 131–33 and 13 for Prescott and Bancroft, respectively.

2. "General Department," *The Historical Magazine, and Notes and Queries Concerning the Antiquities*, August 1865, available at *APS Online*, http://www.proquest.com/products_pq/descriptions/aps.shtml.

3. J. N. Larned, ed., *The Literature of American History; a Bibliographical Guide, in Which the Scope, Character, and Comparative Worth of Books in Selected Lists Are Set Forth in Brief Notes by Critics of Authority* (1902; repr., Columbus, Ohio: Long's College Books Co., 1953), 850.

≈

62. Gray, Asa. *The Botanical Text-book.* **3rd ed. New York: George P. Putnam, 1850.**

Asa Gray's *Botanical Text-book* (1842) introduced "thousands of Americans" to botany and remained the standard text in the field from its publication in 1842 throughout the nineteenth century. Gray (1810–88) is still considered one of the most significant nineteenth-century American scientists. He received his training from the nation's leading botanist of the day, John Torrey, and became one of Charles Darwin's most trusted correspondents. From 1836 through 1838 he served as the botanist for the United States Exploring Expedition under Charles Wilkes; unfortunately, due to numerous delays, he resigned before the expedition actually set sail. In 1842 he became the first American to make a living from botany when he was appointed Fisher Professor of Natural History at Harvard University, where he trained a large number of amateurs and collectors and maintained a large correspondence with them. As Gray explains in the introduction to the *Botanical Text-book,* this "compendious treatise is designed to furnish classes in our schools and colleges with a suitable text-book of Structural and Physical Botany, as well as private students with a convenient introductory manual, adapted to the present condition of the science" (v). His textbooks were widely used and have been credited with making botany the preferred science in many American schools in the nineteenth century.[1]

105,133 voucher 5: Grays Botanical Text Book $1.75.
Purchased from Charles Welford on December 13, 1850.
Hayes Catalogue: Gray, A. *Botanical Text-book.* New York, 1850. 8°

TITLE PAGE
THE | BOTANICAL TEXT-BOOK, | AN | INTRODUCTION TO SCIENTIFIC BOTANY, | BOTH STRUCTURAL AND SYSTEMATIC. | FOR COLLEGES, SCHOOLS, AND PRIVATE STUDENTS. | [thin rule] | THIRD EDITION, | REWRITTEN AND ENLARGED. | Illustrated with twelve hundred Engravings on Wood. [black letter] | [thin rule] | By ASA GRAY, M. D., | FISHER PROFESSOR OF NATURAL HISTORY IN HARVARD UNIVERSITY. | [thin rule] | NEW YORK: | GEORGE P. PUTNAM. | 1850.

PAGINATION

i–xii 13–520.

Note. Pages xi–xii have been misbound in this copy and placed before pages ix–x.

CONTENTS

i title, ii copyright statement and printer's imprint, iii half title, iv blank, v–vi preface, vii–xii contents, 13–504 text, 505–7 appendix, 508–20 index.

REFERENCES

Hayes p. 82; cf. Putnam 13-s; Roorbach p. 228.

COPY DESCRIBED

DLC: QK 45 G75 1850 copy one. *Leaf.* 205 × 125.

---

1. Liz Keeney, "Gray, Asa," *ANB Online,* http://www.anb.org/articles/13/13-00645.html; see entry 193 for Wilkes.

◦◦◦

63. Greenleaf, Simon. *A Treatise on the Law of Evidence.* 3rd ed. 2 vols. Boston: C. C. Little and J. Brown, 1844–46.

Simon Greenleaf's (1783–1853) *Treatise on the Law of Evidence* was one of the first American legal works on this topic. Before its publication, the United States Bar relied on English texts dealing with evidence, and although English decisions were usually relevant to American cases, there were some exceptions. Documentation of the relevant American cases could only be found as addenda to English works on the subject.[1] Greenleaf was appointed Royall Professor of Law at Harvard Law School in 1833, and, in 1846, upon the death of Joseph Story, the Dane Professor of Law. *Law of Evidence* grew out of the need for a textbook to use with his students, yet he designed it for the use of practicing lawyers (1:vii–viii). The demand for it was so great that it went into sixteen editions during the nineteenth century alone and became Greenleaf's most noted work.[2]

Marvin praised Greenleaf's work for its "logical distribution of subjects" and "clear and forcible statement of principles, [all] clothed in a perspicuous Anglo-Saxon style." In addition, the *American Jurist* and the *London Law Magazine* both endorsed Greenleaf's treatise for Little and Brown's 1848 law catalogue. The *London Law Magazine* lauded Greenleaf as one of the "first writers and best esteemed legal authorities of this century," and proclaimed that "more light has shone from the new world than from all the lawyers who adorn the courts of Europe."[3] Greenleaf revised, corrected, and considerably enlarged the third edition (1:ix). Because legal texts are time-sensitive and quickly become obsolete, Fillmore probably selected the latest edition, that of 1844–46, for the White House.

105,133 voucher 2: Greenleafs Evidence 2 vols. $9.00.
Purchased from Little and Brown on December 30, 1850.

REFERENCES

BEAL 5061; cf. Greenleaf; cf. Marvin p. 347; cf. Roorbach p. 617; cf. Harvard[4] p. 99.

---

1. Marvin, *Legal Bibliography,* 347.

2. See entries 164–66 for Joseph Story.

3. *Law Book in Press and Preparing for Publication* (Boston: Little, Brown and Co., 1850), 14. The Library of Congress holds the only recorded copy of this catalogue (call no. Z6459 .Z9 L7 1850a).

4. The *Harvard Law Library Catalogue* notes that in addition to the 2 editions that it lists in its collections, there are 126 copies in its Text Book Library.

∾

64. Griswold, Rufus Wilmot. *The Prose Writers of America.* 3rd ed. rev. Philadelphia: Carey and Hart, 1849.

65. ———. *The Poets and Poetry of America.* Philadelphia: Carey and Hart.

Rufus Wilmot Griswold (ca. 1815–57) attempted to establish a national literature for the United States through compiling and editing anthologies. He made his reputation as an expert in American poetry with his first anthology, *The Poets and Poetry of America* (1842). He added two more American anthologies to his oeuvre, *The Prose Writers of America* (1847) and *The Female Poets of America* (1848), the latter of which helped to promote women's writing before the Civil War and served as a standard reference work on women's poetry for several decades. Although the Fillmores selected only the first two of these three titles for the White House, they owned a copy of the *Female Poets* in their personal collection.[1]

Griswold sets forth his patriotic agenda in the introductions to both of his titles selected for the library. He argues that the absence of international copyright protection has been detrimental to American authors by making it more cost-effective to reprint foreign works, mainly British, which required no payment of copyright fees, instead of publishing new works by American writers. Fillmore became concerned with this issue when it fell to him to consider negotiating an international copyright treaty with England. He even wrote to the publishing firm Harper and Brothers and asked their views on the subject in August of 1852.[2]

In *Poets and Poetry of America* Griswold extolled American subjects for poetry, such as the heroism of Columbus, the settlement of particular regions, the natural beauty of the landscape, and the cultural mythology. Carey and Hart's 1850 edition includes many American poets who are still read today, including Henry Wadsworth Longfellow, Ralph Waldo Emerson, John Greenleaf Whittier, and Edgar Allan Poe; it also contains some who have been all but forgotten, such as Ralph Hoyt, Henry B. Hirst, and Fitz-Greene Halleck.

In *Prose Writers of America* Griswold included writers who, according to his judgment, had influenced the American mind and helped to shape the American character. The volume contains selections from admired statesmen and intellectuals—Benjamin Franklin, Thomas Jefferson, John Quincy Adams, Daniel Webster, William Prescott, George Bancroft, and Josiah Quincy—as well as men of letters, such as Washington Irving, Nathaniel Hawthorne, Ralph Waldo Emerson, and James Fenimore Cooper.[3] A few women are also found in this company, such as Catherine M. Sedgwick, Lydia Maria Child, and S. Margaret Fuller.

The edition of Griswold's *Prose Writers* purchased for the White House is identified in both the Roosevelt and the Hayes catalogues, but that of his *Poets and Poetry* is not. Based upon availability and price, however, the Executive Mansion most likely purchased a Philadelphia, Carey and Hart edition, which, according to Roorbach, sold for $3.00. Carey and Hart published ten editions of this anthology between 1842 and 1850. Without further information, it is impossible to determine which of the ten would have been selected. A comparison of the 1848 and the 1850 Carey and Hart editions reveals that the content was altered with the later edition. Other editions of this title from different publishers were available in 1850, yet their prices do not accord with that listed on the voucher.

105,133 voucher 5: Griswolds Prose Writers America $2.75.
Purchased from Charles Welford on December 13, 1850.
105,133 voucher 5: Griswold Poetical Writers in America $2.75.
Purchased from Charles Welford on December 13, 1850.
Roosevelt Catalogue: Griswold, Rufus Wilmot. Prose writers in America. Third edition.
Philadelphia, Carey & Hart, 1849.

Prose Writers of America.

TITLE PAGE

[double thin rule frame] THE | PROSE WRITERS | OF | AMERICA | WITH | A SURVEY OF THE INTELLECTUAL HISTORY, CONDITION, AND PROSPECTS OF | THE COUNTRY. | BY RUFUS WILMOT GRISWOLD. | ILLUSTRATED WITH PORTRAITS FROM ORIGINAL PICTURES. | THIRD EDITION REVISED. | PHILADELPHIA: | CAREY AND HART. | 1849.

PAGINATION

1–552.

CONTENTS

1 title, 2 copyright statement and printer's imprint, 3 dedication to Horace Binney Wallace, 4 blank, 5–6 preface, 7 list of illustrations, 8 blank, 9–11 contents, 12 index to authors, 13–52 'The Intellectual History, Condition and Prospects of the Country,' 53–552 text.

PLATES

Portrait frontispiece of Washington Irving signed in lower right by G. S. Newton and lower left by J. Sartain.

Engraved title page, 'THE | PROSE WRITERS | OF | AMERICA | BY RUFUS WILMOT GRISWOLD. | [portrait vignette of Joseph Story signed J. E. Johnson in lower left and J. Sartain lower right with a facsimile of Joseph Story's signature centered beneath.] | PHILADELPHIA | CAREY AND HART. | Cousland &. Co. [all lettering is open-faced block style].'

Facing 53, portrait of Jonathan Edwards, signed by G. W. Peale in lower left and by J. Sartain lower right, with a facsimile of Jonathan Edwards's signature centered beneath.

Facing 187, portrait of John J. Audubon, signed in lower left by P. Cruikshanks and lower right by J. Sartain with a facsimile of John J. Audubon's signature centered beneath.

Facing 258, portrait of Richard Henry Wilde, signed in lower left by Johnson and lower right by J. Sartain, with a facsimile of Richard Henry Wilde's signature centered beneath.

Facing 341, portrait of John Pendleton Kennedy, signed in lower left by Wilson and lower right by J. Sartain, with a facsimile of J. P. Kennedy's signature centered beneath.

Facing 369, portrait of William H. Prescott, signed by Ames in lower left and J. Sartain lower right, with a facsimile of William H. Prescott's signature centered beneath.

Facing 440, portrait of Ralph Waldo Emerson, signed by Mrs. Hildreth in lower left and J. Sartain lower right, with a facsimile of Ralph Waldo Emerson's signature centered beneath.

Facing 456, portrait of Charles Fenno Hoffman, signed by Hinman in lower left and J. Sartain lower right with a facsimile of Charles Fenno Hoffman's signature centered beneath.

REFERENCES
Hayes p. 83; Roosevelt p. 17; cf. L and B 1850 p. 39; cf. Putnam p. 55; cf. Roorbach p. 234.

COPY DESCRIBED
DLC: PS362 G7. *Leaf.* 237 × 145.

The Poets and Poetry of America.
REFERENCES
cf. L and B 1850 p. 39; cf. L and B 1853 p. 29; cf. Roorbach p. 234; cf. Putnam p. 55; cf. Fillmore ca. 1858 p. 51; cf. Fillmore 1861 p. 170.

---

1. Griswold also edited the edition of John Milton's *Prose Works* that was purchased for the library (see entry 118). For the *Female Poets,* see Fillmore Catalogue ca. 1858 p. 51.

2. Harper refrained form offering an opinion either for or against international copyright. See Fillmore's letter and the firm's reply reprinted in Eugene Exman, *The Brothers Harper* (New York: Harper and Row, 1965), 390–91.

3. Franklin, Jefferson, Webster, Prescott, Bancroft, and Cooper were all represented in the first White House Library. See entries 162, 83, 184–85, 131–33, 13, and 42.

∽

**66. Grote, George. *History of Greece.* 2nd ed. 12 vols. London: John Murray, 1849.

George Grote's *History of Greece* became the standard text in English on Greek history and was used in universities across England for the fifty years following its initial publication in 1846. Grote (1794–1871) began work on the *History* in 1823, but set it aside to become involved in reform politics, resuming it only after his retirement from parliament in 1841. In the book he described Greek myths and legends and provided historical analysis, focusing primarily on the period from 8 B.C. through 4 A.D., especially on the Periclean Athens of fifth-century B.C. Not only was the *History* a scholarly triumph, it was also a commercial success. From the proceeds of its sales Grote built a home in East Burnham that he named "History Hut."

The first two volumes of *The History* were published in 1846 and the final volume in 1856, with the other nine volumes coming out intermittently during the intervening years. When the Fillmores were selecting books for the first White House Library, they purchased the eight volumes that were available to date. The copy described here represents one of the ten books that survive from the original Executive Mansion library.

105,133 voucher 2: Grotes Greece 8 vols. $22.00.
Purchased from Little and Brown on December 30, 1850.
Roosevelt Catalogue: Grote, George. *History of Greece.* Second edition. London, John Murray, 1849–50. Vols. 1–8 only.

TITLE PAGE

VOLS. I–II.

HISTORY OF GREECE; | I. LEGENDARY GREECE. | II. GRECIAN HISTORY OF THE REIGN OF | PEISISTRATUS AT ATHENS. | BY | GEORGE GROTE, ESQ. | VOL. I. [II.] | *SECOND EDITION.* | LONDON: | JOHN MURRAY, ALBEMARLE STREET. | 1849.

VOLS. III–VIII.

HISTORY OF GREECE. | BY | GEORGE GROTE, ESQ. | VOL. III. [IV–VIII.] | *SECOND EDITION.* | LONDON: | JOHN MURRAY, ALBEMARLE STREET. | 1849.

> *Notes.* Volumes 5 through 8 omit "second edition" from the title page. Volumes 7 and 8 are dated 1850.

PAGINATION

Vol. I. i–xxxvi 1–654.

Vol. II. [2] i–xvi 1–634.

Vol. III. i–xii 1–562.

Vol. IV. [4] i–xvi 1–572.

Vol. V. [6] i–xviii 1–544.

Vol. VI. [6] i–xxii 1–676 1–16 [4].

Vol. VII. [2] i–xvi 1–566 1–16.

Vol. VIII. i–xx 1–676.

> *Note.* A number of pages in volumes 4, 5, and 7 remain mostly unopened.

CONTENTS

Vol. I. i half title, ii blank, iii title, iv printer's imprint, v–xxi preface, xxii blank, xxiii–xxiv names of gods, goddesses, and heroes, xxv–xxxvi contents, 1–654 text.

Vol. II. [1] advertisement for books lately published by John Murray, [2] blank, i title, ii printer's imprint, iii–xvi contents, 1–630 text, 631–33 blank, 634 advertisement for new editions of standard works.

Vol. III. i title, ii printer's imprint, iii–xii contents, 1–562 text.

Vol. IV. [1] blank, [2] advertisement for books for the present season, [3] advertisement for books lately published, [4] blank, i title, ii printer's imprint, iii–xv contents, xvi blank, 1–566 text, 567 a note on the maps, 568–69 blank, 570 advertisement for new editions of standard works, 571 advertisement for Murray's Home and Colonial Library, 572 blank.

Vol. V. [1] blank, [2] advertisement for books for the present season, [3] advertisement for books lately published, [4] blank, [5] title, [6] printer's imprint, i preface to volume 5, ii errata, iii–xviii contents, 1–543 text, 544 blank.

Vol. VI. [1] blank, [2] advertisement for books for the present season, [3] advertisement for books lately published, [4]–[6] blank, i title, ii printer's imprint, iii–xxi contents, xxii blank, 1–675 text, 676 blank, 1–16 catalogue of a list of works in general literature published by John Murray, [1] blank, [2] advertisement for new editions of standard works, [3] advertisement for Murray's Home and Colonial Library, [4] blank.

Vol. VII. [1] blank, [2] blank, i title, ii printer's imprint, iii–xvi contents, 1–566 text, 1–16 catalogue of a list of works published by John Murray.

Vol. VIII. i title, ii printer's imprint, iii–iv preface, v–xix contents, xx blank, 1–676 text.

PLATES

Vol. I.

Bound in at rear of volume, folding map of Extra-Peloponnesian Greece as it stood at the beginning of the Peloponnesian war, by K. O. Muller.

Vol. II.

Bound in at rear of volume, folding map of Peloponnese during the Peloponnesian war.

Bound in at rear of volume, folding map of Boeotia according to Leake and Gell from the "Hellenika" of P. W. Forchhammer, Beslin 1837.

Vol. III.

Bound in at rear of volume, folding map of Grecian colonies in Italy and Sicily at the time of the Peloponnesian war.

Bound in at rear of volume, folding map of Ionic and Aeolic cities in and near Asia Minor.

Vol. IV.

none.

Vol. V.

Facing 96, map of Malic Gulf and Thermopylæ.

Facing 174, map of Battle of Salamis.

Facing 221, map of Battle of Platæa.

Facing 436, folding map of environs of Athens.

Vol. VI.

Facing 634, plan to illustrate the battle of Amphipolis.

Vol. VII.

Bound in at rear of volume, folding plan of Syracuse and adjacent country, Seige of Syracuse before the arrival of Gylippus.

Bound in at rear of volume, folding plan of Syracuse and adjacent country, Syracuse after the additional defenscs provided by Gylippus, and before the arrival of Demosthenes.

Vol. VIII.

None.

BINDING

All volumes have been rebound in Library of Congress bindings.

MARKS OF OWNERSHIP

Vols. I., II., III., and VIII. None.

Vols. IV, V, and VI. Inscribed on first page of advertisements 'Executive Mansion | 1850 [in black ink] | F | shelf no. 9 [in pencil]'.

Vol. VII. Inscribed on first blank page as on the first page of advertisements in vols. 4, 5, and 6.

REFERENCES

Hayes p. 82; Roosevelt p. 17; cf. *LC 1816–1851* p. 233; cf. Putnam p. 55; cf. L and B 1850 p. 39; cf. Fillmore 1861 p. 86.

COPY DESCRIBED

DLC: DF 214 G89. *Leaf.* 215 × 128.

67. Grotius, Hugo. *The Rights of War and Peace.* Ed. J. Barbeyrac. London: W. Innys, et al., 1738.

Hugo Grotius (1583–1645) has been credited with founding modern international law and influencing the entire development of English law. Establishing the law of nations on philosophical principles, he liberated it from theological dominance.[1] Although Grotius's work was banned in both Spain and Italy because of the clergy's influence, the king of Sweden, Gustavus Adolphus, slept with a copy under his pillow while he fought for the liberties of Protestant Europe. Marvin proclaimed that "no legal work ever enjoyed a more widely extended reputation, and none ever exercised such a wonderful influence over the public morals of Europe."[2]

In the nineteenth century Marvin and Hoffman still recommended reading Grotius even though many other works had incorporated his ideas. Hoffman found an acquaintance with both Grotius and Pufendorf essential for students of the law, but named Grotius as the more learned of the two. In 1851 Edward Everett recommended Grotius's *War and Peace* for the White House Library, but Fillmore had already purchased it the previous September.

There were six English editions of *War and Peace* published before 1851, dated 1654, 1655, 1682, 1715, 1738, and 1814. Hoffman mentioned four of these and recommended the one of 1738 for its "valuable notes" by M. Barbeyrac. He warned against the 1814 edition because it had been "newly arranged, and the mass of classical learning, and numerous quotations" that so strongly marked the original had been omitted. Although Everett later recommended the 1814 edition, the White House probably purchased the one from 1738: not only was it Hoffman's choice, but it was also the one that Little and Brown advertised in their 1853 catalogue of law books for $12.00, the price paid by the White House. Although this listing is too late to represent the copy purchased, it still provides a sense of this edition's market value at midcentury.[3]

107,754 voucher 2: 1 Grotius War and Peace $12.00.
Purchased from Little and Brown on September 18, 1851.

REFERENCES
cf. Greenleaf; Hoffman p. 123; cf. Marvin p. 352; cf. Harvard p. 100.

---

1. Holdsworth, *History of English Law*, 5:58.
2. Marvin, *Legal Bibliography*, 353.
3. L and B Law 1853, 56.

∾

68. Guizot, François. *The History of Civilization from the Fall of the Roman Empire to the French Revolution.* Trans. William Hazlitt. Ed. Caleb Sprague Henry. 4 vols. New York: Appleton, 1846.

This edition of François Guizot's (1787–1874) *History of Civilization* was adopted as a textbook by a number of American institutions during the nineteenth century. It is based upon lectures Guizot delivered at the old Sorbonne between 1828 and 1830 and was first published

in French under the title *Histoire de la civilisation en France* (4 vols., 1830). He had established his reputation as a historian earlier with a critical edition of Edward Gibbon's *Decline
and Fall of the Roman Empire,* which secured his appointment in 1812 to the chair of modern
history at the University of Paris. His subsequent works include *History of the Origin of Representative Government* (2 vols., 1821–22), *History of the English Revolution from Charles I to
Charles II* (2 vols., 1826–27), and *General History of Europe* (3 vols., 1828).[1]

Caleb Sprague Henry's edition of *History of Civilization* received generally favorable
reviews in the periodicals. *Brother Jonathan* praised Henry's notes for making the book not
only "valuable as a class book," but also more accessible to the general reader. The *Knickerbocker* recommended that Guizot's history be "carefully perused by every one who desires
to obtain a calm, profound, and philosophical view of the origin, progress, and various
forms of human civilization, and a correct history of the development of the human mind."
Guizot's reputation as a statesman did not fare as well his reputation as a historian, however; he was remembered as "a cold and clever politician whose refusals to grant electoral
reforms precipitated the February Revolution of 1848."[2] A writer for the *American Review*
reminded readers that Guizot was "a despotic minister of the most despotic king in Europe"
and distrusted his historical analysis. This critic argued that "he commits the error of making French civilization the type of civilization in general; a position against which the English historian may advance grave objections. Feudalism in England gave rise to the idea, not
of *popular* liberty under despotism of any kind, but of individual liberty as we have it in
America."[3]

105,133 voucher 5: Guizots Historical Works $3.50.
Purchased from Charles Welford on December 13, 1850.
Hayes Catalogue: Guizot, F.P.G. *History of Civilization.* v. 2 to 4. New York, 1846. 12° v. 1
    wanting.

TITLE PAGE
THE | HISTORY OF CIVILIZATION, | FROM THE | FALL OF THE ROMAN EMPIRE |
TO | THE FRENCH REVOLUTION. | BY F. GUIZOT, | THE PRIME MINISTER OF
FRANCE; | AUTHOR OF "HISTORY OF THE ENGLISH REVOLUTION OF 1640." |
TRANSLATED BY WILLIAM HAZLITT. | VOLUME I. [II–IV.] | NEW YORK: | D.
APPLETON & CO., 200 BROADWAY. | PHILADELPHIA: | GEO. S. APPLETON, 148
CHESNUT STREET. | M DCCC XLVI.

PAGINATION
Vol. I. 1–316 [20] [2] 1–34.
Vol. II. [2] v–vi 1–424.
Vol. III. [2] 7–416.
Vol. IV. [2] 3–392 1–12.

CONTENTS
Vol. I. 1 blank, 2 advertisement for *History of the English Revolution of 1640,* 3 title, 4 blank,
    5–10 "Preface to the Third American Edition," 11–14 contents, 15–306 text, 307–16 "Table
    of Contemporary Sovereigns," [1]–[20] catalogue for Appleton publications, [1] title
    page for another Appleton catalogue, [2] index of subjects, 1–34 text of catalogue.

Vol. II. [1] title, [2] blank, v–vi advertisement, 1–7 contents, 8 blank, 9–424 text.

Vol. III. [1] title, [2] blank, 7–12 contents, 13–414 text, 415–16 advertisements for books published by D. Appleton and Co.

Vol. IV. [1] title, [2] blank, 3–7 contents, 8 blank, 9–370 text, 371–91 index, 392 blank, 1–12 advertisements for books published by D. Appleton and Company.

BINDING

Front and back boards. 195 × 119 med. brown ribbed cloth with blind-stamped triple-rule frame. *Spine.* Blind stamped with six sets of double rules creating five panels with a blind-stamped single rule at base. Gilt stamped in second panel, 'HISTORY | OF | CIVILIZATION', in fourth panel 'GUIZOT | [thin rule] | VOL. I.', and at base 'APPLETON'. *Endpapers.* Off-white.

Note. This description based on volumes 1 and 3 at MH.

REFERENCES

Hayes p. 83; Roosevelt p. 17; cf. Putnam p. 56; cf. Roorbach p. 236; cf. Fillmore 1847 p. 3; cf. Fillmore ca. 1858 p. 23; cf. Fillmore 1861 p. 90.

COPY DESCRIBED

Vol. I. MH: H 5038 28.7B *Leaf.* 182 × 115.

Vol. II–IV. ViU: CB 71 G73 1846. *Leaf.* 187 × 120.

---

1. The edition of Gibbon's *Decline and Fall* that was purchased for the White House retains a translation of Guizot's notes; for biographical information, see "Françoise Pierre Guillaume Guizot," *Encyclopedia of World Biography,* 2nd ed. (Detroit: Gale Research, 1998), reproduced in *Biography Resource Center* (Farmington Hills, Mich.: Thomson Gale, 2006), http://gale.cengage.com/servlet/BiographyRC.

2. "Review 1—No Title," *Brother Jonathan: A Weekly Compend of Belles Lettre and the Fine Arts,* July 23, 1842, and "Review 3—No title," *The Knickerbocker; or New York Monthly Magazine (1833–1862),* May 1840, both available at *APS Online,* http://www.proquest.com/products_pq/descriptions/aps.shtml; "Françoise Pierre Guillaume Guizot."

3. "The History of Civilization, from the Fall of the Roman Empire to the French," *The American Review: A Whig Journal of Politics, Literature, Art and Science,* January 1847, available at *APS Online,* http://www.proquest.com/products_pq/descriptions/aps.shtml.

∽

69. Hallam, Henry. *The Constitutional History of England from the Accession of Henry VII to the Death of George II.* 2 vols. London: Murray, 1846.

70. ———. *View of the State of Europe During the Middle Ages.*

Henry Hallam (1777–1859) may be best known in literary circles as the father of Arthur Henry Hallam, Alfred Lord Tennyson's friend who is immortalized in *In Memoriam A. H. H.* Yet Henry garnered a reputation by his own right as a British historian with *View of the State of Europe During the Middle Ages* (2 vols., 1818) to which he added a set of *Supplemental Notes* (1848), which were incorporated into later editions. He also authored *The Constitutional History of England from the Accession of Henry VII to the Death of George II* (2 vols., 1827); and an *Introduction to the Literature of Europe in the Fifteenth, Sixteenth, and Seventeenth Centuries* (4 vols., 1837–39).

The first two of these three titles were among the purchases for the first White House Library. In *The Middle Ages,* Hallam surveys the political development of Western Europe, with an emphasis on England's Anglo-Saxon and Norman constitutions. He continues his treatment of England's political development in *The Constitutional History* and considers it in relation to events in Scotland and Ireland. Hallam concluded his *Constitutional History* with the accession of George III and thereby avoided the sensitive political debates of the recent past. An 1851 American review of the Harper edition of *The Constitutional History* describes Hallam's work as having achieved "world-wide fame" and as "indispensable for the political student and statesman."[1]

The White House copy of the *Constitutional History* was found in the Library of Congress stacks, but the edition of the *Middle Ages* that was selected remains uncertain. Based on the price paid and the number of volumes, however, a Harper edition was most likely purchased. Murray advertised both the *Constitutional History* and the *Middle Ages* for 24s. each, which would have been approximately $5.85 in 1850.[2] While this price would accord with that paid for the *Constitutional History,* it is too high to account for the *Middle Ages.* Harper advertised their edition of the *Middle Ages* for $2.00, a price closer to the $1.87 paid by the Executive Mansion.[3] Moreover, Harper is among the few publishers who offered this title in a single volume as indicated on the voucher.

105,133 voucher 6: Hallam's Constitutional History of England $6.00.
Purchased from Taylor and Maury on October 25, 1850.
105,133 voucher 5: Hallam's History Middle Ages $1.87.
Purchased from Charles Welford on December 13, 1850.
Roosevelt Catalogue: Hallam, Henry. *The Constitutional History of England from the Accession of Henry VII to the Death of George II.* Fifth edition. London, J. Murray, 1846, 2 vols.

Constitutional History of England.

TITLE PAGE
THE | CONSTITUTIONAL HISTORY | OF | ENGLAND | FROM | THE ACCESSION OF HENRY VII. | TO | THE DEATH OF GEORGE II. | [thin rule] | BY HENRY HALLAM. | [thin rule] | Fifth Edition. [black letter] | IN TWO VOLUMES. | VOL. I. [II.] | LONDON: | JOHN MURRAY, ALBEMARLE STREET. | 1846.

PAGINATION
Vol. I. i–xvi 1–720.
Vol. II. i–viii 1–624.

CONTENTS
Vol. I. i title, ii printer's imprint, iii dedication 'TO HENRY MARQUIS OF LANSDOWNE, | IN TOKEN OF HIGH ESTEEM | AND SINCERE REGARD, | THIS WORK IS RESPECTFULLY INSCRIBED | BY | THE AUTHOR.', iv blank, v–viii preface, viii advertisement to the third edition, ix advertisement to the fifth edition, x reference list, xi–xv contents, xvi blank, 1–719 text, 720 printer's imprint.
Vol. II. i half title, ii printer's imprint, iii title, iv blank, v–viii contents, 1–569 text, 570 blank, 571–624 index.

Note. The advertisement to the third edition appears in volume 1 on page viii after the end of the preface.

BINDING

Front and back boards. 230 × 141 off-white plain paper. *Spine.* Missing from this copy. *Endpapers.* Off-white.

MARKS OF OWNERSHIP

Volume 2 is inscribed on front pastedown in black ink, "Executive Mansion Oct. 1850." Below this inscription "F shelf no. 5" has been written in pencil. Pencil lines appear in the margins of volume 1 on pp. 551 and 553 and volume 2 on pp. 423 and 425.

   Note. Volume 2 apparently carried the Executive Mansion inscription too, but it was lost with the front board; ink from it has offset onto the facing blank page.

REFERENCES

Hayes p. 91; Roosevelt p. 18; Putnam p. 57; cf. L and B 1850 p. 41; cf. L and B 1852 p. 3; cf. L and B 1853 p. 30; cf. *LC 1816–1851* p. 241; cf. Fillmore 1847 p. 9; cf. Fillmore ca. 1858 p. 27; cf. Fillmore 1861 p. 62.

COPY DESCRIBED

DLC: JN 175 H2 1846. *Leaf.* 220 × 133.

View of the State of Europe.

REFERENCES

cf. Fillmore 1847 p. 10; cf. Fillmore ca. 1858 p. 28; cf. Fillmore 1861 p. 96.

---

   1. "Reviews, Magazines, &C," *DeBow's Review of the Southern and Western States* Sept. 1851, available at *APS Online,* http://www.proquest.com/products_pq/descriptions/aps.shtml.

   2. This advertisement is found in a catalogue from Murray that is bound into the sixth volume of the Executive Mansion's copy of Grote's *History of Greece;* see entry 66.

   3. *Harper's Illustrated Catalogue of Standard and Valuable Works* (New York: Harper and Brothers, 1847), 34.

∽

71. Hamilton, Alexander, John Jay, and James Madison. *The Federalist.*

The Federalist was the most widely read of the numerous tracts and pamphlets generated by the debate over the ratification of the United States Constitution. It was lauded by Thomas Jefferson as the "best commentary on the principles of government" and by Alexis de Tocqueville as a work that "should be familiar to statesmen of all countries."[1] *The Federalist* is a collection of eighty-five essays written to persuade New York voters to ratify the Constitution. They were published in several New York newspapers, between 1787 and 1788, signed with the pseudonym "Publius." Alexander Hamilton conceived of and planned the essays, recruiting John Jay, a New York lawyer and politician, and James Madison, the "father of the Constitution," to write some of them. Jay contributed only four essays before becoming ill and leaving the endeavor to his two compatriots. Hamilton penned fifty-five and Madison twenty-nine of the remaining essays. Taken together they outlined how the proposed government would operate. As Terrence Ball summarizes, *The Federalist* explains why the framers of the Constitution found the articles of confederation unsatisfactory; why they sought to separate the powers of the several branches of the government; why they subdivided the national legislature into two houses; why they believed a federal court of final appeal to be both desirable and necessary; why they outlawed titles of nobility; why they believed a bill of rights to be an unnecessary addition—and why many other prescriptions and proscriptions were written into the Constitution or omitted entirely.[2]

This classic commentary on the United States government is an obvious choice for the White House Library, all the more so because throughout his political career Fillmore scrupulously sought to uphold the Constitution regardless of any personal bias he may have had on an issue.

There were no fewer than thirteen English-language editions of the *Federalist* published between 1800 and 1850. Since Lanman's "Recollections" inform that the copy purchased for the White House did not contain an index, all those after 1831 can be ruled out, because the 1831 edition published by Thompson and Homans and printed by Way and Gideon in Washington was the first edition to include an index, and all subsequent editions published prior to 1850 contain an index.[3] The editions that could have been purchased are the 1802 edition from George F. Hopkins in New York; the 1810 edition from Williams and Whiting in New York; the 1817 and 1818 editions from Benjamin Warner in Philadelphia; the 1818 and 1821 editions from Jacob Gideon in Washington; and the 1826 and 1831 editions from Glazier and Co., in Hallowell, Maine.

105,133 voucher 5: The Federalist $1.25.
Purchased from Charles Welford on December 13, 1850.

REFERENCES
cf. Hayes p. 69; cf. Putnam p. 169; cf. Roorbach p. 191; cf. Fillmore 1861 p. 72.

---

1. Qtd. in Alexander Hamilton, James Madison, and John Jay, *The Federalist with Letters of "Brutus,"* ed. Terence Ball (Cambridge: Cambridge University Press, 2003), xiii. See entries 83 and 174 for Jefferson and de Tocqueville.
2. Ibid., xvi–xvii.
3. Paul Leicester Ford, *A List of Editions of "The Federalist"* (Brooklyn, N.Y., 1886), 13; for more about Lanman's "Recollections" see "White House Collection," 13.

≈

72. Hammond, Jabez. *The History of Political Parties in the State of New York.* 4th ed. 2 vols. Cooperstown, N.Y.: Phinney, 1846.

Jabez Hammond's (1778–1855) *History of Political Parties in New York* (1846) was originally planned as a biography of De Witt Clinton; however, the book "took the form of a two-volume collection of biographies of American political movers from the Constitution's framing to 1840." In 1852 he added a third volume, *The Life of Silas Wright* (1848), a book that he had written and published separately several years earlier. Hammond's *History* was well received, with one notable exception, Ambrose Spencer, a former Supreme Court justice, who accused Hammond of criticizing Clinton unfairly and of using the book to promote Van Buren's candidacy for the county judgeship.[1] Fillmore had served in New York's state assembly for two years before his election to Congress and would have taken a keen interest in the political parties of his home state.

There is a discrepancy between the voucher entry, which records this as a three-volume work, and the Hayes Catalogue entry, which only specifies two volumes. Roorbach and Putnam both list this edition as three volumes, $5.00 in Roorbach and $6.00 in Putnam. Their entries probably include Hammond's *Life of Silas Wright*, which was not yet formally issued as part of this set, but may have been added to it by booksellers. Most likely Welford either added this volume to Hammond's *History of Political Parties*, or he may have made a mistake when he wrote the number of volumes on the voucher entry. On this same voucher, Fillmore also purchased a different biography of Silas Wright written by John Jenkins. Since he purchased Jenkins's biography, he may have declined the one by Hammonds and purchased only two of the three volumes that the booksellers offered.[2]

105,133 voucher 5: Hammonds Polit. History N.Y. 3 vols. $3.50.

Purchased from Charles Welford on December 13, 1850.

Hayes Catalogue: Hammond, J. D. *History of Political Parties in New York, to 1840.* 2 v. Cooperstown, 1846. 8°

TITLE PAGE

THE | HISTORY | OF | POLITICAL PARTIES | IN THE | STATE OF NEW-YORK, | FROM THE RATIFICATION OF THE FEDERAL | CONSTITUTION TO DECEMBER, 1840. | IN TWO VOLUMES. | By JABEZ D. HAMMOND, L. L. D. | Fourth Edition, Corrected and Enlarged. [script] | TO WHICH IS ADDED, | NOTES BY GEN. ROOT. | [thin rule] | VOL. I. [II.] | [thin rule] | COOPERSTOWN: | PUBLISHED BY H. & E. PHINNEY. | [thin rule] | 1846.

PAGINATION

Vol. I. i–xiv 1–594.

Vol. II. i–vi 1–556.

CONTENTS

Vol. I. i title, ii copyright statement, iii–iv advertisement, v–vii preface, viii errata, ix–xiv contents, 1–571 text, 572–86 notes, 587–94 index to volume 1.

Vol. II. i title, ii copyright statement, iii–vi contents, 1–537 text, 538–46 notes, 547–53 index to volume 2, 554–56 blank.

PLATES

Vol. I.

Portrait frontispiece, George Clinton, signed in lower right by Ames and lower left by R. Miller.

Facing 89, bust of John Jay, signed beneath in center by F. Michelin, Lith, N.Y.

Facing 210, portrait of Morgan Lewis, signed beneath in center by F. Michelin, Lith, N.Y.

Facing 249, portrait of Daniel D. Tompkins, signed beneath in center by F. Michelin, Lith, N.Y.

Facing 440, portrait of Dewitt Clinton, signed beneath in center by F. Michelin, Lith, N.Y.

Vol. II.

Portrait frontispiece, Martin Van Buren, signed beneath in center by F. Michelin, Lith.

Facing 97, portrait of Joseph C. Yates, signed beneath in center by F. Michelin, Lith, N.Y.

Facing 344, portrait of Enos T. Throop, signed beneath in center by F. Michelin, Lith.

Facing 432, portrait of William L. Marcy, signed beneath in center by F. Michelin, Lith.

Facing 487, portrait of William H. Seward, signed beneath in center by F. Michelin, Lith.

REFERENCES

Hayes p. 92; cf. Putnam p. 58; cf. Roorbach p. 242; cf. Fillmore 1847 p. 23; cf. Fillmore ca. 1858 p. 46.

COPY DESCRIBED

DLC: JK 2295 N71 H24. *Leaf.* 227 × 130.

---

1. Donald M. Roper, "Hammond, Jabez Delano," *ANB Online* http://www.anb.org/articles/14/14-00257.html.

2. See entry 31 for William Campbell's *Life and Writings of De Witt Clinton* and entry 84 for Jenkins's *Life of Silas Wright.*

~

73. *Harper's Classical Library.* 36 vols. New York: Harper, 1844–48.

Harper's *Classical Library,* also known as the *Family Classical Library,* first appeared in 1831, a publication highly recommended at that time as being "cheap, handsome, and uniform size, and embracing correct and elegant translations of the most esteemed authors of Greece and Rome."[1] Subsequent volumes regularly received welcoming notices in the literary periodicals of the day.[2] In addition, the Harper firm ran advertisements with endorsements from the *London Sunday Times,* Dr. Parr, and Dr. Knox, who predicted that it would help readers to "retain a tincture of that elegance and liberality of sentiment which the mind acquires by study of the classics, and which contributes more to form the true gentleman than all the unsubstantial ornament of modern affectation."[3]

While we cannot be certain which *Family Classical Library* the Fillmores selected for the first White House Library, the Harper's series is a very likely choice. According to the *London Catalogue of Books,* J. H. Parker was issuing classical texts in a series titled *Oxford Pocket Editions,* and Parker and Son was issuing similar material without a series title. Both series sold for between one and two shillings per volume and could be candidates for this purchase, yet neither appears to have grown to thirty-six volumes, as stipulated by the voucher. The titles in both of the Parker series and the Harper series are very similar to one another.

The Harper series is probably the one listed in the Hayes Catalogue of 1877, under the title *Classical Library.* Although the Hayes Catalogue does not specify Harper as the publisher, it does indicate New York as the place of publication, and the volumes that it lists by title match those in the Harper series. In 1847 Harper offered its "Family Classical Library" in thirty-seven volumes for $16.30, octodecimo, bound in "muslin," "gilt," and "embellished with portraits."[4] This price is within a reasonable range for this edition to account for the set that the White House purchased for $15.00. A discrepancy exists between the number of volumes purchased as listed on the voucher and that entered in the Hayes Catalogue. While the voucher specified thirty-six volumes, the Hayes Catalogue attempted to account for thirty-seven, but found that some were missing. Since Harpers advertised that these volumes were available for separate purchase, it is possible that the White House elected not to buy one or that Welford simply had a thirty-six-volume set in his inventory in 1850.

105,133 voucher 5: Family Classical Library 36 vols. $15.00.
Purchased from Charles Welford on December 13, 1850.

Hayes Catalogue: *Classical Library*. v. 1–37. New York, 1844–48. 16° vols. 6 and 32 wanting.

v. 1–2. *Xenophon. Anabasis.* Translated by E. Spelman. 2 v.

v. 3–4. *Demosthenes. Orations.* Translated by Leland. 2 v.

v. 5. *Sallust. Catiline Conspiracy Jugurthine War.* Translated by W. Rose.

v. 6.

v. 7. *Caesar Commentaries.* Translated by W. Duncan. v. 2.

v. 8–10. *Cicero. Orations Offices. Cato Laelius.* Translated by various hands. 3 v.

v. 11–12. *Virgil. Ecologues. Georgics. Aeneid.* Translated by various hands. 2 v.

v. 13. *Æschylus. Tragedies.* Translated by R. Potter.

v. 14. *Sophocles. Tragedies.* Translated by T. Francklin.

v. 15–17. *Euripides. Tragedies.* Translated by R. Potter. 3 v.

v. 18–19. *Horace. Odes. Satires. Epistles.* Translated by various hands. 2 v.

v. 19. *Phaedrus. Fables.* Translated by C. Smart.

v. 20–21. *Ovid. Metamorphoses. Epistles.* Translated by various hands. 2 v.

v. 22–23. *Thucydides. Peloponnesian War.* Translated by W. Smith. 2 v.

v. 24–28. *Livy. History of Rome.* Translated by G. Baker. 5 v.

v. 29–31. *Herodotus. History.* Translated by W. Beloe. 3 v.

v. 32.

v. 33–34. *Homer. Iliad. Odyssey.* Translated by A. Pope. v. 2–3.

v. 35. *Juvenal. Satires.* Translated by C. Badham. *Persius. Satires.* Translated by Sir W. Drummond.

v. 36. *Pindar. Odes.* Translated by C. A. Wheelwright. *Anacreon. Odes.* Translated by T. Bourne.

v. 37. *Cicero. Three Dialogues on the Orator.* Translated by W. Guthrie.

4 vols. missing [this note appears to have been added, probably at a later date, by a different hand than the one that wrote the entry].

REFERENCES
Hayes p. 37–38; Roosevelt p. 18; cf. Fillmore 1847 p. 12.

---

1. "Literary." *The New-York Mirror: A Weekly Gazette of Literature and the Fine Arts* June 4, 1831, available at *APS Online*, http://www.proquest.com/products_pq/descriptions/aps.shtml.

2. For examples, see "Literary Notices," *The Family Magazine; or, Monthly Abstract of General Knowledge (1833–1841)*, 1836, and "History of New York," *The American Monthly Magazine (1833–1838)*, May 1837, both available at *APS Online*, http://www.proquest.com/products_pq/descriptions/aps.shtml.

3. *Harper's Illustrated Catalogue of Valuable Standard Works* (New York: Harper and Brothers, 1847), 142.

4. Ibid.

∽

74. Haskell, Daniel, and J. Calvin Smith. *A Complete Descriptive and Statistical Gazetteer of the United States of America.* New York: Sherman and Smith, 1850.

Daniel Haskell and Calvin Smith's *Gazetteer* was compiled to disseminate the information from the census of 1840. It provided the most up-to-date report on the condition of agriculture, commerce, manufacturing, and general improvements in the United States, and it included entries for hundreds of new counties, towns, and post offices. It even listed all existing post offices in the United States at the date of publication and provided the distance from their state capitals and from Washington, D.C. (3–4). In this *Gazetteer* one may look up any state, county, town, or territory of the United States and learn of its geography, climate, commerce, transportation, religious and educational institutions, and demographic facts. For example, the entry for St. Augustine, Florida, informs, among other things, that it is the capital of St. John's County. "It is situated 2 miles back from the Atlantic shore, on the s. point of a peninsula, connected with the main land by a narrow isthmus, protected from the swell of the ocean by Anastasia island, not sufficiently high to obstruct the sea breeze or the view of the ocean" (584). In addition, the entry provides other geographical and demographic information about the city, such as that snow is almost unknown and frost rare; therefore, the city is a favorite for invalids in the winter. It is one mile long and three fourths of a mile wide and has four churches, one Presbyterian, one Episcopal, one Roman Catholic, and one Methodist. It also has 500 dwellings and 2,459 inhabitants. Fillmore must have considered this gazetteer an essential reference source, since it is among the first purchases that he made after receiving funding for the new library.

105,133 voucher 6: Smiths Gazetteer U. States 1 vol. 8vo $3.50.
Purchased from Taylor and Maury on October 21, 1850.
Hayes Catalogue: Haskell, D. and Smith, J. C. *Description and Statistical Gazetteer of the United States.* New York, 1850. 8°.

TITLE PAGE
A COMPLETE I DESCRIPTIVE AND STATISTICAL GAZETTEER I OF THE I UNITED STATES OF AMERICA, I CONTAINING A PARTICULAR DESCRIPTION OF THE I STATES, TERRITORIES, COUNTIES, DISTRICTS, PARISHES, CITIES, TOWNS, AND I VILLAGES—MOUNTAINS, RIVERS, LAKES, CANALS, AND RAILROADS; I WITH AN ABSTRACT OF THE I CENSUS AND STATISTICS FOR 1840, I EXHIBITING A COMPLETE I VIEW OF THE AGRICULTURAL, COMMERCIAL, MANUFACTURING, AND LITERARY I CONDITION AND RESOURCES OF THE COUNTRY. I [thin wavy rule] I BY DANIEL HASKEL, A. M. I Late President of the University of Vermont; I AND I J. CALVIN SMITH, I Geographer, Author of a new Map of the United States, &c. I [thin wavy rule] I [printer's ornament vignette of U. S. Capitol] I NEW YORK: I PUBLISHED BY SHERMAN & SMITH, I 135 BROADWAY. N. W. CORNER OF CEDAR-ST. I 1850.

PAGINATION
1–770.

CONTENTS

1 title, 2 copyright statement, 3–4 preface, 5–6 explanation of abbreviations in this work, 7–747 text, 748–70 appendix.

REFERENCES

Hayes p. 79; cf. Putnam p. 59; cf. Roorbach p. 247.

COPY DESCRIBED

DLC: E154 H34.

∾

75. **Haydn, Joseph.** *Book of Dignities.* **London: Longman, Brown, Green, and Longmans, 1851.**

Joseph Haydn's (1788/93–1856) *Book of Dignities* (1851) is a revised version of Robert Beatson's *Political Index to the Histories of Great Britain and Ireland,* which was riddled with inaccuracies. Haydn's work includes civil, diplomatic, legal, military, naval, and ecclesiastical officials for England, Wales, Scotland, Ireland, and India, as well as the colonial governors, bishops, and the orders of knighthood. Chronologically, it dates as far back as records could be found. For example the kings of Portugal go back to 1093, and the Bishopric of Hereford to 680. Haydn was updated by Horace Ockerby and reissued in a standard edition in 1894, which was reprinted again in 1969. It was and remains a standard reference work for identifying the holders of many British governmental and ecclesiastical posts.[1]

109,399 voucher 4: Haydns Book of Dignities $7.50.
Purchased from Franck Taylor on May 1, 1852.
Hayes Catalogue: Haydn, J. *Book of Dignities.* London, 1851. 8°

TITLE PAGE

BEATSON'S POLITICAL INDEX MODERNISED. | [thin rule] | THE | BOOK OF DIGNITIES; | CONTAINING | ROLLS OF THE OFFICIAL PERSONAGES | OF THE BRITISH EMPIRE, | CIVIL, ECCLESIASTICAL, JUDICIAL, MILITARY, NAVAL, AND MUNICIPAL, | FROM THE EARLIEST PERIODS TO THE PRESENT TIME: | COMPILED CHIEFLY FROM THE RECORDS OF THE PUBLIC OFFICES: | TOGETHER WITH THE | SOVEREIGNS OF EUROPE, | FROM THE FOUNDATION OF THEIR RESPECTIVE STATES; | THE PEERAGE OF ENGLAND AND OF GREAT BRITAIN; | AND NUMEROUS OTHER LISTS. | BY JOSEPH HAYDN, | AUTHOR OF "THE DICTIONARY OF DATES," AND COMPILER OF VARIOUS WORKS. | LONDON: | LONGMAN, BROWN, GREEN, AND LONGMANS. | 1851.

PAGINATION

i–xvi 1–594.

CONTENTS

i title, ii printer's imprint, iii–iv dedication to the "Right Honorable Viscount Palmerston, Her Majesty's Principal Secretary of State for Foreign Affairs," v–vii preface, viii blank, ix–xiii contents, xiv–xv table of the kings and queens of England, xvi addenda, 1–568 text, 569–94 index.

REFERENCES
Hayes p. 105; cf. Putnam p. 15-s; L and B 1853 p. 31.

COPY DESCRIBED
DLC: DA 34 H3. *Leaf.* 207 × 117.

1. "British Biography Officials of the Government," Duke Libraries, March 6, 2007, http://www
.library.duke.edu/ research/subject/guides/british-biography/government.html (accessed July 17, 2007).

∾

76. Heineccius, John Gottlieb. *A Methodical System of Universal Law.* Ed. and trans. George
    Turnbull. 2 vols. London: George Keith, 1763.

During the nineteenth century, John Gottlieb Heineccius (1680–1741) was considered the
most learned jurist that Germany had ever produced. He authored ten separate works on
the topics of logic, jurisprudence, and ethics, including *A Methodical System of Universal
Law.* It was originally written in Latin with the title *Elementa Juris Naturæ et Gentium* and
published in 1738. George Turnbull (1698–1748), British theologian and teacher, translated
and annotated this work in 1741, a translation that Marvin called "accurate," with "learned
and valuable" additions. It is among the works on international law that Edward Everett
recommended to the president after the Cuban filibuster.[1]

107,754 voucher 4: 2 vols. Turnbull's Heineccius $6.48.
Purchased from Little and Brown on December 31, 1851.
Hayes Catalogue: Heineccius, J. G. *Methodical System of Universal Law.* 2 v. London, 1763. 8°.

TITLE PAGE
A METHODICAL | SYSTEM | OF | Universal Law: | OR, THE | Laws OF NATURE AND
NATIONS | DEDUCED | From CERTAIN PRINCIPLES, and applied | to PROPER CASES. |
[thin rule] | Written in *Latin* by the CELEBRATED | *JO. GOT. HEINECCIUS,* | Counsellor
of State to the King of PRUSSIA, | And Professor of Philosophy at *Hall.* | [thin rule] |
TRANSLATED, and illustrated with NOTES and | SUPPLEMENTS, | By GEORGE
TURNBULL, LL.D. | [thin rule] | To which is added, | A DISCOURSE upon the NATURE
and ORIGIN | of MORAL and CIVIL LAWS; in which they are deduced, | by an Analysis
of the Human Mind in the experimental Way, | from our internal Principles and
Dispositions. | [thin rule] | *Natura enim juris ab hominis repetenda natura est.* CIC. |
[thin rule] | VOL. I. [II.] | [double thin rule] | LONDON: | Printed for GEORGE KEITH,
in *Grace Church-Street.* | M.DCC.LXIII.

PAGINATION
Vol. I. [*8*] 1–324.
Vol. II. [*4*] 1–326.
   Note. The title page in volume 2 has been removed and a different one pasted in on the
   stub.

CONTENTS

Vol. I. [*1*] title, [*2*] blank, [*3*]–[*4*] preface, [*5*]–[*8*] contents, 1–323 text, 324 errata.

Vol. II. [*1*] title, [*2*] blank, [*3*] dedication to William Duke of Cumberland, [*4*] blank, 1–244 text, 245 title 'A DISCOURSE | UPON THE | Nature and Origine | OF | Moral *and* Civil Laws. | [thin rule] | By *GEORGE TURNBULL,* L.L.D. | [printer's ornament lyre and horns] | [thick/thin double rule] | *LONDON:* | Printed in the Year MDCCXL.' 246 blank, 247–325 text, 326 errata.

REFERENCES

Hayes p. 153; cf. Harvard p. 108; Marvin p. 380.

COPY DESCRIBED

DCGW: K455 H46 1763. *Leaf.* 192 × 115.

---

1. Marvin, *Legal Bibliography,* 380.

~

77. Herschel, John F. W. *Outlines of Astronomy.* London: Longman, 1849.

Sir John Frederick William Herschel's (1792–1871) *Outlines of Astronomy,* published in 1849, was hailed as the definitive presentation of its kind available in English to date. Herschel devoted his life to scientific and astronomical studies, and, as the leading astronomer of the nineteenth century, he was the first to map the southern skies. By 1871 *Outlines* had gone through eleven editions and been translated into Chinese and Arabic. Although history has recognized the significance of Herschel's work, not all of his contemporary reviewers did. *The Literary World* faulted it for its obscurity, pedantry, and even factual inaccuracies.[1] Herschel, however, had cautioned in his preface that some of the information presented in *Outlines* is addressed to readers with advanced mathematical knowledge (iii–iv). Fillmore may have found this book of interest since the Naval Astronomical Expedition to the Southern Hemisphere was under way from 1846 to 1852, an expedition that sought to measure the solar parallax from the southern hemisphere and set up an observatory for this purpose in Chile.[2]

105,133 voucher 2: Herschel's Astronomy $3.50.

Purchased from Little and Brown on December 30, 1850.

Hayes Catalogue: Herschel, Sir J. F. W. *Outlines of Astronomy,* London, 1849. 8°

TITLE PAGE

OUTLINES | OF | ASTRONOMY: | BY | SIR JOHN F. W. HERSCHEL, BART. K. H. | M.A. D.C.L. F.R.S.L. & E. Hon. M.R.I.A. F.R.A.S. F.G.S. M.C.U.P.S. | Correspondent or Honorary Member of the Imperial, Royal, and National, Academies of Sciences | of Berlin, Brussels, Copenhagen, Göttingen, Haarlem, Massachusetts (U.S.), Modena, | Naples, Paris, Petersburg, Stockholm, Turin, and Washington (U.S.); | the Italian and Helvetic Societies; | the Academies, Institutes, &c., of Albany (U.S.), Bologna, Catania, Dijon, Lausanne, Nantes, Padus, Palermo, Rome, Venice, Utrecht, and Wilna; | the Philomathic Society of Paris; Asiatic Society of Bengal; South African Lit. and Phil.

Society; | Literary and Historical Society of Quebec; Historical Society of New York; | Royal Medico-Chirurgical Soc., and Inst. of Civil Engineers, London; | Geographical Soc. of Berlin; Astronomical and | Meteorological Soc. of British Guiana; | &c. &c. &c. | LONDON: | PRINTED FOR | LONGMAN, BROWN, GREEN, AND LONGMANS, | PATERNOSTER-ROW; | AND JOHN TAYLOR, UPPER GOWER STREET. | 1849.

PAGINATION

i–xvi 1–662.

CONTENTS

i title, ii printer's imprint, iii–vii preface, viii blank, ix–xiv contents, xv errata and addenda, xvi blank, 1–644 text, 645–52 appendix, 653–61 index, 662 printer's imprint.

PLATES

This volume contains six plates, one frontispiece and five additional plates bound at the end of the volume after the index. The plates are all of astronomical bodies, but are untitled. All except for the final one is signed in lower right by H. Adlard. The final one is an unsigned folding plate.

REFERENCES

Hayes p. 93; cf. *LC 1816–1851* p. 257; L and B 1850 p. 43; Putnam p. 61.

COPY DESCRIBED

DLC: QB43 H56. *Leaf.* 214 × 130.

---

1. "Herschel's Astronomy," *Literary World,* October 20, 1849, available at *APS Online,* http://www .proquest.com/products_pq/descriptions/aps.shtml.

2. Ponko, *Ships, Seas, and Scientists,* 93–107.

❧

78. **Hildreth, Richard.** *The History of the United States of America.* **6 vols. New York: Harper and Brothers, 1849–52.**

Richard Hildreth's (1807–65) *History of the United States of America* (1849–51) was known for its faithful relation of unembellished facts. Hildreth rejected "centennial sermons and Fourth-of-July orations . . . in the guise of history"; instead, he offered his audience a well-researched and documented account of historical events (1:iii). Unfortunately, reviewers criticized him for this method. Although an author for the *Literary World* found his work a "valuable contribution to American History and literature" and considered it an important reference book, the writer wished for a "more distinct recognition of the Divine power and guidance in the affairs of men," arguing that "this is the true philosophy of history." A critic for the *North American Review* was not as generous: "The task of the historian is coextensive with that of the astronomer. He must not only chronicle the occurrences, but decipher their meaning, and point out the laws under which they take place. Otherwise his work will have little more value than a collection of old almanacs."[1] After eight years of researching and writing this history, Hildreth published it in six volumes over a three-year period. The first three volumes came out in 1849 with the subtitle *From the Discovery of the Continent to the*

Organization of Government under the Federal Constitution, volumes 4 and 5 followed in 1850 and 6 in 1851, bringing the history up to 1831 under the subtitle *From the Adoption of the Federal Constitution to the End of the Sixteenth Congress.*

109,399 voucher 4: Hildreth's ½ calf *6 vols. + binding $17.50.

Purchased from Franck Taylor on September 27, 1852.

Roosevelt Catalogue: Hildreth, Richard. *The History of the United States of America, from the Discovery of the Continent to the Organization of Government under the Federal Constitution.* New York, Harper & Brothers, 1849, 3 vols.

————. *The History of the United States of America from the Adoption of the Federal Constitution to the End of the Sixteenth Congress.* New York, Harper & Brothers, 1851–52, 3 vols.

TITLE PAGE

Vols. I–III.

THE | HISTORY | OF THE | UNITED STATES OF AMERICA, | FROM THE | Discovery of the Continent [black letter] | TO THE | ORGANIZATION OF GOVERNMENT UNDER THE | FEDERAL CONSTITUTION. | BY RICHARD HILDRETH. | IN THREE VOLUMES. | VOL. I. [II.–III.] | NEW YORK: | HARPER & BROTHERS, PUBLISHERS, | 82 CLIFF STREET. | 1849.

Vol. IV.

THE | HISTORY | OF THE UNITED STATES OF AMERICA, | FROM THE | Adoption of the Federal Constitution [black letter] | BY RICHARD HILDRETH. | IN THREE VOLUMES. | VOL. I. | ADMINSTRATION OF WASHINGTON. | NEW YORK: | HARPER & BROTHERS, PUBLISHERS, | 82 CLIFF STREET. | 1851.

Vol. V.

. . . | VOL. II. | JOHN ADAMS AND JEFFERSON. | . . .

Vol. VI.

. . . | VOL. III. | MADISON AND MONROE. | . . . | 1852.

> *Note.* The half title in volumes 4 through 6 carry the consecutive volume numbers, i.e., 'IV–VI,' while the title pages carry the volume numbers within the three-volume subset, i.e., 'I–III.'

PAGINATION

Vol. I. i–xxvi 33–570.

> *Note.* Although there is a break in the page numbering sequence between pages xxvi and 33, there do not seem to be any pages missing; other copies consulted have the same pagination.

Vol .II. i–xxiv 25–580.

Vol. III. [2] i–xxiv 25–594.

Vol. IV. i–xxiv 25–704.

Vol. V. i–xxiv 25–686.

Vol. VI. i–xxiv 25–742 1–6.

CONTENTS

Vol. I. i title, ii copyright statement, iii–v advertisement, vi blank, vii–xxvi contents, 33–570 text.

Vol. II. i title, ii copyright statement, iii–xxiii contents, xxiv blank, 25–579 text, 580 blank.

Vol. III. [1] title, [2] copyright statement, i–xxiv contents, 25–547 text, 548 blank, 549–64 authorities, 565–92 index, 593 errata, 594 blank.

Vol. IV. i half title, ii blank, iii title, iv copyright statement, v–ix advertisement, x blank, xi–xxiv contents, 25–704 text.

Vol. V. i half title, ii blank, iii title, iv copyright statement, v–xxiii contents, xxiv blank, 25–686 text.

Vol. VI. i half title, ii blank, iii title, iv copyright statement, v–xxiv contents, 25–713 text, 714 blank, 715–20 authorities, 721–39 index, 740 blank, 741 errata, 742 blank, 1–6 "Valuable Standard Works Published by Harper & Brothers, New York."

BINDING

Although this copy, but for volume 6, has been rebound in a Library of Congress buckram bindings, the set purchased for the Executive Mansion library was bound in half calf as specified and charged on the voucher.

REFERENCES

Hayes p. 93; Roosevelt p. 20; cf. Putnam 1852 p. 61, 15-s; Roorbach p. 257; cf. Fillmore ca. 1858 p. 27; cf. Fillmore 1861 p. 214.

COPY DESCRIBED

Vols. I–III. DLC: E 178 H65 copy 2.
Vols. IV–V. DLC: E 178 H66 copy 2 *Vol. VI.* copy 3. *Leaf.* 234 × 140.

---

1. "Mr. Hildreth's History," *The Literary World (184/–1853)*, October 27, 1849, and "A History of the United States of America," *The North American Review (1821–1940)*, October 1851, both available at *APS Online,* http://www.proquest.com/products_pq/descriptions/aps.shtml.

~

79. Hope, Thomas. *Costume of the Ancients.* 2 vols. London: Bohn, 1841.

Thomas Hope's (1769–1831) *Costume of the Ancients* (1809) is a plate book designed to assist practicing artists in rendering the ancients in costume. It includes 321 plates of pen-and-ink drawings of ancients dressed in costumes from various regions, arranged to show their relationship to one another in the following sequence: Egyptian, Asiatic, Grecian, and Roman.

Hope was an art collector and connoisseur who took up the study of classical architecture and civilization. He collected sculpture, vases, and other antiquities as well as Renaissance and baroque paintings, and he exhibited his collection in his town and country houses for the pleasure and instruction of his visitors. *Costume of the Ancients* (1809) is one of three of Hope's instructional books along with *Household Furniture and Interior Decoration* (1807) and *Essay on the Prospects of Man* (1831). *Costume of the Ancients* may have had a particular appeal to the Fillmores' daughter, Abbie, who was interested in sculpture and was preparing to begin instructing herself in this art before her death in 1854.[1]

It was first published in 1809 in London by William Miller; a second edition was issued later in 1809 and a third in 1812. The Miller editions sold for only 21*s.*, or just over $5.00 in octavo, a price too low to qualify for this selection, and for 94*s.*, or about $23.00 in quarto, a price too high to have been chosen.[2] While a French translation was published in Brussels in 1828, another English edition did not appear until 1841, when Henry G. Bohn published it. In 1850 Little and Brown advertised Bohn's edition in cloth for $12.50 and in full calf for $14.00. Based on these prices the Executive Mansion probably purchased the Bohn edition in full calf, perhaps even with gilt edges and spine lettering to account for the dollar that it paid over the advertised price.

105,133 voucher 5: Hopes Costume Ancients 2 vols. $15.00.
Purchased from Charles Welford on December 13, 1850.

REFERENCES
cf. *LC 1816–1851* p. 273; cf. Putnam p. 64; cf. L and B 1850 p. 46; cf. *EC 1801–1836* p. 281.

---

1. Holloway, *Ladies of the White House*, 480.
2. Robert Alexander Peddie and Quintin Waddington, *English Catalogue of Books 1801–1836* (London: Publisher's Circular, 1914), 281.

⁓

80. Hume, David. *The History of England.* 6 vols. New York: Harper, 1850.

By 1850, a century after its first publication, David Hume's *History of England* (1754–61) was universally known in English-speaking countries and ranked among the top two histories of its subject. In it Hume (1711–76) sought to show impartiality between Tory and Whig views and between those of the parliament and the crown. Its initial reception came as a disappointment to Hume, who wrote, "I was assailed by one cry of reproach, disapprobation, and even detestation; English, Scotch, and Irish, Whig and Tory, churchman and sectary, freethinker and religionist, patriot and courtier, united in their rage against the man who had presumed to shed a generous tear for the fate of Charles I and the earl of Strafford" (1:viii).[1] Nineteenth-century American reviewers gave a much warmer reception to new editions of the *History*. The *Universalist Quarterly and General Review* declined to remark on its content because it was already so well known, but noted it among "the very neat and cheap editions of valuable books which the enterprizing publishers [were] putting forth."[2] Another writer for the *Universalist Quarterly* warned that Hume was partisan but predicted that his history would always be the authority on "that portion of English affairs of which it treats."[3]

105,133 voucher 7: Hume's History of England 6 vols. $2.40.
Purchased from Franck Taylor on October 25, 1850.
Hayes Catalogue: Hume, D. *History of England to 1688.* 6 v. New York, 1850. 12°

TITLE PAGE
THE | HISTORY OF ENGLAND | FROM | The Invasion of Julius Caesar [black letter] | TO | THE ABDICATION OF JAMES THE SECOND, | 1688. | By DAVID HUME, Esq. | A NEW EDITION, | WITH THE AUTHOR'S LAST CORRECTIONS AND

IMPROVEMENTS. | TO WHICH IS PREFIXED | A SHORT ACCOUNT OF HIS LIFE, | WRITTEN BY HIMSELF. | VOL. I. [II–VI.] | NEW YORK: | HARPER & BROTHERS, PUBLISHERS, | 82 CLIFF STREET. | 1850.

PAGINATION

Vol. I. i–xxxii 1–484.

Vol. II. i–xii 1–526.

Vol. III. i–xvi 1–466.

Vol. IV. [2] v–xvi 1–572.

Vol. V. [2] v–xvi 1–556.

Vol. VI. [2] v–xvi 1–554 1–6.

CONTENTS

Vol. I. i title, ii blank, iii–xiii "The Life of David Hume, Esq. Written by Himself," xiv–xxi "Letter from Adam Smith, LL. D., to William Strahan, Esq.," xxii blank, xxiii–xxxii contents, 1–474 text, 475–83 notes, 484 blank.

Vol. II. i title, ii blank, iii–xii contents, 1–514 text, 515–26 notes.

Vol. III. i title, ii blank, iii–xv contents, xvi blank, 1–448 text, 449–66 notes.

Vol. IV. [1] title, [2] blank, v–xvi contents, 1–527 text, 528 blank, 529–72 notes.

Vol. V. [1] title, [2] blank, v–xvi contents, 1–533 text, 534 blank, 535–56 notes.

Vol. VI. [1] title, [2] blank, v–xvi contents, 1–377 text, 378 blank, 379–80 notes, 381–554 index, 1–6 advertisement for books published by Harper and Brothers.

PLATES

Vol. I.

Portrait frontispiece of David Hume engraved by W. G. Jackman.

REFERENCES

Hayes p. 98; cf. Fillmore Packing Lists p. 10; cf. Fillmore ca. 1858 p. 27; cf. Fillmore 1861 p. 62.

COPY DESCRIBED

DLC: DA 30 H9 1850. *Leaf.* 190 × 110.

---

1. From Hume's "My Own Life" printed in volume 1 of this edition.

2. "Review 1—No Title," *The Universalist Quarterly and General Review (1844–1891)*, April 1850, available at *APS Online,* http://www.proquest.com/products_pq/descriptions/aps.shtml.

3. "A Course of Historical Reading," *The Universalist Quarterly and General Review (1844–1891)*, April 1850, available at *APS Online,* http://www.proquest.com/products_pq/descriptions/aps.shtml.

~

81. *Index to Review.*

This voucher entry probably refers to *A General Index to the Edinburgh Review.* Little and Brown and Putnam advertise two other titles that could account for this purchase, *An Index of Subjects in Reviews and Periodicals,* which sold for only $1.00 in paper and $1.25 "half bound" and a *General Index to the Quarterly Review* in two parts, which sold for $4.00 in paper. It makes more sense, however, that the Fillmores would have purchased an index for a work already in the White House Library with "review" in the title. There are five of these:

the *Edinburgh Review,* the *North American Review,* the *United States Magazine and Democratic Review,* the *American Review,* and the *Merchants' Magazine and Commercial Review.* Indexes were published to three of these: the *Edinburgh Review* in 1813, 1816, 1832, and 1850; the *North American Review* in 1829; and the *Merchants' Magazine and Commercial Review* in 1846. The *Merchants' Magazine* is the least likely possibility, because it was commonly referred to as "Hunt's Magazine," just as it was listed on the voucher, and not "the Review." The voucher entry for the *North American Review* indicates that seventy-two volumes were purchased, and the Hayes Catalogue entry for it clarifies that the set comprised volumes 1 through 71 of the *Review* and an index for volumes 1 through 25. It is possible that for some reason Fillmore purchase a second copy of the index to the *North American Review;* however, he probably purchased the index to the *Edinburgh Review* since he had not already purchased one for the White House but owned at least one in his personal library.

109,399 voucher 4: Index to Review $3.25.
Purchased from Franck Taylor on April 29, 1852.

REFERENCES
L and B 1853 p. 27; cf. Putnam p. 67; cf. Fillmore 1847 p. 15; cf. Fillmore ca. 1858 p. 45; cf. Fillmore 1861 p. 106.

◀❧▶

82. Irving, Washington. *The Works of Washington Irving.* 15 vols. New York: Putnam, 1849–51.

Washington Irving (1783–1859) was the most popular American writer of the first half of the nineteenth century as well as the first American to make a "comfortable living" as a writer. Today he is most remembered for his *Sketch Book of Geoffrey Crayon,* which includes his well-known stories "The Legend of Sleepy Hollow" and "Rip Van Winkle." Reviews of Putnam's edition of Irving's *Works* highlight his popularity in mid-nineteenth-century America. The *Southern Literary Messenger* found it superfluous to praise Irving: "To praise Hercules was considered an idle task, and equally so is it, at this day, to extol a writer, whose productions are every where regarded as models of English composition." Likewise, the *American Review* commended the Putnam edition: "The Style of this celebrated collection of essays, seems rather to gain in vivacity and richness, like good wine, as it grows older. It is, perhaps, the most perfect example of a pure Addisonian English, produced by an American."[1]

During the winter of 1852–53, Irving visited Washington, D.C., as the guest of John Pendleton Kennedy, the secretary of the navy. He also called at the White House by invitation of President Fillmore. In February of 1853 he joined the president, President-elect Pierce, and members of the cabinet to inspect a new ship in Alexandria, Virginia, and he could have joined Fillmore and Kennedy on a tour of the southern states in 1854. But Irving declined the invitation, probably wishing to avoid the political entanglements such a trip might involve.[2]

Roosevelt Catalogue: Irving, Washington. *The Works of Washington Irving.* New edition revised. New York, G. P. Putnam, 1849–51, 15 vols. Vols. 3, 4, 7, 10, 15 missing.

Hayes Catalogue: Irving, W. *Works.* v. 1 to 14. New York, 1849–51. 12°.

> v. 1. *Knickerbocker's New York;* v. 2. *Sketchbook;* v. 3. wanting; v. 4. wanting; v. 5. *Columbus and His Companions.* v. 3.; v. 6. *Bracebridge Hall;* v. 7. wanting; v. 8. *Astoria;* v. 9. *Crayon Miscellany;* v. 10. *Oliver Goldsmith;* v. 12–13. *Mahomet and His Successors.* 2 v.; v. 14. *Conquest of Granada;* v. 15. wanting.

105,133 voucher 4: Irving's Works 14 vols. $14.40.
Purchased from George P. Putnam on December 13, 1850.

TITLE PAGE
Series Titles.
Vol. I.
THE WORKS | OF | WASHINGTON IRVING. | NEW EDITION, REVISED. | [thin rule] |VOL. I. [II–XV.] | KNICKERBOCKER'S NEW-YORK. | [thin rule] | NEW-YORK: | GEORGE P. PUTNAM. | 1851.

> *Note.* All of the series title pages read the same except for the volume number, title, and variations in the imprint date as follows:
> *Vol. II.* 'THE SKETCHBOOK.', 1851; *Vols. III–IV.* 'LIFE AND VOYAGES OF COLUMBUS.' 1850; *Vol. V.* 'COLUMBUS AND HIS COMPANIONS' 1850; *Vol. VI.* 'BRACEBRIDGE HALL.' 1851; *Vol. VII.* 'TALES OF A TRAVELLER.' 1849; *Vol. VIII.* 'ASTORIA.' 1850; *Vol. IX.* 'CRAYON MISCELLANY.' 1851; *Vol. X.* 'BONNEVILLE'S ADVENTURES.' 1850; *Vol. XI.* 'OLIVER GOLDSMITH.' 1850; *Vols. XII–XIII.* 'MAHOMET AND HIS SUCESSORS.' 1850; *Vol. XIV.* 'CONQUEST OF GRANADA.' 1851; *Vol. XV.* 'THE ALHAMBRA.' 1851.
> *Note.* Volume 15 omits 'NEW EDITION, REVISED.'

Volume Titles.
Vol. I.
A | HISTORY OF NEW-YORK, | FROM THE | BEGINNING OF THE WORLD TO THE END OF | THE DUTCH DYNASTY; | CONTAINING, AMONG MANY SURPRISING AND CURIOUS MATTERS, THE UNUTTERABLE | PONDERINGS OF WALTER THE DOUBTER, THE DISASTEROUS PROJECTS OF WILLIAM | THE TESTY, AND THE CHIVALRIC ACHIEVEMENTS OF PETER THE HEADSTRONG | —THE THREE DUTCH GOVERNORS OF NEW AMSTERDAM: BEING THE ONLY | AUTHENTIC HISTORY OF THE TIMES THAT EVER HATH BEEN OR EVER WILL | BE PUBLISHED. | BY | Diedrich Knickerbocker. [black letter] | [thin rule] | De maarheid die duister lag, | Die fomt met flaarheid aan den dag. | [thin rule] | THE AUTHOR'S REVISED EDITION. | COMPLETE IN ONE VOLUME. | NEW YORK: | GEORGE P. PUTNAM, 155 BROADWAY, | And 142 Strand, London. | 1851.

Vol. II.
SKETCH BOOK | OF | GEOFFREY CRAYON, Gentn. | 'I have no wife nor children, good or bad, to provide for. A mere spectator | of other men's fortunes and adventures, and how they play their parts; | which, methinks, are diversely presented unto me, as from a common theatre or | scene.'—*Burton.* | THE AUTHOR'S REVISED EDITION. |

COMPLETE IN ONE VOLUME. | NEW-YORK: | GEORGE P. PUTNAM, 155 BROADWAY, | And 142 Strand London. | 1850.

Vols. III–V.

THE | LIFE AND VOYAGES | OF | CHRISTOPHER COLUMBUS; | TO WHICH ARE ADDED THOSE OF | HIS COMPANIONS. | BY | WASHINGTON IRVING. | Venient annis | Sæcula seris, quibus Oceanus | Vincula rerum laxet, et ingens | Pateat tellus, Typhisque novos | Detegat Orbes, nec sit terris | Ultima Thule. | Seneca: *Medea.* | AUTHOR'S REVISED EDITION. | VOL. I. [II–III.] | NEW-YORK: | GEORGE P. PUTNAM, 155 BROADWAY, | And 142 Strand, London. | 1850.

> *Note.* Volume 1 of *Columbus* does not have a period after 'AUTHOR'S REVISED EDITION.'

Vol. VI.

BRACEBRIDGE HALL, | OR | THE HUMORISTS. | A Medley. [black letter] | BY | GEOFFREY CRAYON, Gentn. | 'Under this cloud I walk, Gentlemen; pardon my rude assault. I am a traveler, who | having surveyed most of the terrestrial angles of this globe, am hither arrived, to peruse this | little spot.' | Christmas Ordinary. | AUTHOR'S REVISED EDITION. | COMPLETE IN ONE VOLUME. | NEW-YORK: | GEORGE P. PUTNAM, 155 BROADWAY, | And 142 Strand, London. | 1851.

Vol. VII.

TALES OF A TRAVELLER. | BY | GEOFFREY CRAYON, Gentn. | AUTHOR OF "THE SKETCH BOOK," "BRACEBRIDGE HALL," "KNICKERBOCKER'S | NEW-YORK," ETC. | I am neither your minotaure, nor your centaure, nor your satyr, nor your hyæna, nor your babion, but your meer traveller, believe me. | BEN JONSON. | AUTHOR'S REVISED EDITION. | COMPLETE IN ONE VOLUME. | NEW-YORK: | GEORGE P. PUTNAM, 155 BROADWAY, | And 142 Strand, London. | 1849.

Vol. VIII.

ASTORIA | OR, | ANECDOTES OF AN ENTERPRISE | BEYOND THE | ROCKY MOUNTAINS. | BY | WASHINGTON IRVING. | AUTHOR'S REVISED EDITION. | COMPLETE IN ONE VOLUME. | NEW-YORK: | GEORGE P. PUTNAM, 155 BROADWAY. | And 142 Strand, London | 1850.

Vol. IX.

THE | CRAYON MISCELLANY. | BY | WASHINGTON IRVING. | AUTHOR'S REVISED EDITION. | COMPLETE IN ONE VOLUME. | NEW-YORK: | GEORGE P. PUTNAM, 155 BROADWAY, | And 142 Strand, London. 1851.

Vol. X.

THE | ADVENTURES | OF | CAPTAIN BONNEVILLE, U. S. A., | IN THE | ROCKY MOUNTAINS AND THE FAR WEST. | DIGESETD FROM HIS JOURNAL AND ILLUSTRATED | FROM VARIOUS OTHER SOURCES. | BY | WASHINGTON IRVING. | AUTHOR'S REVISED EDITION. | COMPLETE IN ONE VOLUME. | NEW-YORK: | GEORGE P. PUTNAM, 155 BROADWAY, | And 142 Strand, London. | 1850.

Vol. XI.
OLIVER GOLDSMITH: | A BIOGRAPHY. | BY | WASHINGTON IRVING. | NEW-YORK: | GEORGE P. PUTNAM, 155 BROADWAY. | LONDON: JOHN MURRAY. | 1850.

Vols. XII– XIII.
MAHOMET | AND | HIS SUCCESSORS. | BY | WASHINGTON IRVING. | IN TWO VOLUMES. | VOL. I. [II.] | NEW YORK: | GEORGE P. PUTNAM, 155 BROADWAY. | M.DCCC.L.

Vol. XIV.
CHRONICLE | OF THE | CONQUEST OF GRANADA. | FROM THE MSS. OF | FRAY ANTONIO AGAPIDA. | NEW-YORK: | GEORGE P. PUTNAM, 155 BROADWAY. | LONDON: JOHN MURRAY. | 1851.

Vol. XV.
THE ALHAMBRA. | BY | WASHINGTON IRVING. | AUTHOR'S REVISED EDITION. | NEW-YORK: | GEORGE P. PUTNAM, 155 BROADWAY. | M. DCCC. LI.

REFERENCES
Hayes p. 114; Roosevelt p. 22; cf. Putnam pp. 67–68 and p. 17-s; cf. Roorbach p. 282; cf. Fillmore ca. 1858 p. 30; cf. Fillmore 1861 p. 24, p. 88, and p. 110.

COPY DESCRIBED
ViU PS 2050 1849b.

---

1. "The Works of Washington Irving," *The Southern Literary Messenger: Devoted to Every Department of Literature,* September 1848, and "Works of Washington Irving," *The American Review: A Whig Journal Devoted to Politics and Literature,* October 1848, both available at *APS Online,* http://www.proquest.com/products_pq/descriptions/aps.shtml.
2. Scarry, *Millard Fillmore,* 199, 240, and 247.

~

83. Jefferson, Thomas. *Memoir, Correspondence, and Miscellanies, from the Papers of Thomas Jefferson.* Ed. Thomas Jefferson Randolph. 4 vols. Charlottesville, Va.: Carr, 1829.

The *Memoir, Correspondence, and Miscellanies, from the Papers of Thomas Jefferson* is among the collections of published papers of the founding fathers that the Fillmores selected for the White House Library. They also purchased those of Benjamin Franklin, George Washington, and John Adams. This edition of Jefferson's papers contains an account of the events of his life from before the American Revolution through the year 1784; letters dating from 1775 through Jefferson's death; and notes of conversations and memoranda from Jefferson's tenure as secretary of state. A facsimile of a draft of the Declaration of Independence showing corrections by Franklin and Adams is also appended to these volumes.

Since the voucher entry for this title reads only "Jefferson's Works clf," it is difficult to determine the exact title to which it refers. The only book found with "Jefferson" as author and "works" in the title published before 1851 is listed by Roorbach from Thomas Cowperthwait and Company in Philadelphia and priced at $10.00. This record could be a bibliographical ghost since no copy of a book matching Roorbach's entry has been located.

An entry for the *Memoir, Correspondence, and Miscellanies, from the Papers of Thomas Jefferson*, however, appears in the Hayes Catalogue. Moreover, Putnam lists this title, bound in calf for $7.50, a price that makes it a likely candidate for this purchase. Although the voucher does not specify a multivolume work, the price of $6.00 suggests one. Two other editions of this title were available in 1850: one published in London by Colburn and Bentley in 1829 and another published in Boston by Gray and Bowen in 1830.

105,133 voucher 5: Jefferson's Works clf. $6.00.
Purchased from Charles Welford on December 13, 1850.
Hayes Catalogue: Jefferson, T. *Memoirs, Correspondence, and Miscellanies.* 4 v. Charlottesville, 1829. 8°.

REFERENCES

Hayes p. 117; Roosevelt p. 23; cf. Putnam p. 70 and p. 18-s; cf. Roorbach p. 290; cf. Fillmore 1847 p. 24; cf. Fillmore ca. 1858 p. 31; cf. Fillmore 1861 p. 112.

❧

84. Jenkins, John S. *The Life of Silas Wright.* Auburn, N.Y.: Alden and Markham, 1847.
85. ———. *The New Clerk's Assistant, or, Book of Practical Forms.* 4th ed., revised and enlarged. Auburn, N.Y.: Derby and Miller, 1850.

The Life of Silas Wright (1847) was among four eulogistic biographies of Democratic Party leaders written by the lawyer, author, and editor John S. Jenkins (1818–52). In addition to writing biographies Jenkins also compiled abridgments of Jabez Hammond's *History of Political Parties in the State of New York* (1846) and Charles Wilkes's *Narrative of the United States Exploring Expedition* (1845); the full-length version of each was in the White House Library.[1] Wright's biography would have been of particular interest to Fillmore because he had served in the United States Senate from 1833 to 1844 while Fillmore was a member of the House of Representatives. Moreover, he defeated Fillmore for the governorship of New York in 1844.

Jenkins's *New Clerk's Assistant, or, Book of Practical Forms* (1846) was designed for the use of county and town officials, businessmen, farmers, mechanics, and merchants. It includes chapters on auctions, banks and corporations, fees of officers, homestead exemption, mechanics' and laborers' lien, plank roads, supervisors, taxes, town auditors, and town houses. In addition, it provides instruction on how to draw up legal forms, contracts, leases, bills of sale, and other documents. Jenkins anticipated that his book would be useful in the "discharge of public duties" as well as in the "management of private affairs" (iii). It may have proved useful to Millard Powers Fillmore as he carried out the duties of personal secretary to his father. Regardless of how it was used in the White House, the *New Clerk's Assistant* went through numerous editions and sold over thirty thousand copies.

Five editions of Jenkins's *New Clerk's Assistant*, dated 1846, 1847, 1849, and two in 1850, all from Derby and Miller, had been published by 1851 when the White House bought its copy. The preface to the fourth edition (the first of the two editions dated 1850) explains that stereotype plates had been made from it. Without further information, it would be impossible to determine the date on the copy that the White House purchased; however, since it is a reference work, the most recent edition is the obvious choice. Because it had been stereotyped with the first of the 1850 editions, the contents of the two would have been nearly, if not exactly, the same.

105,133 voucher 5: Life Silas Wright .87.
Purchased from Charles Welford on December 13, 1850.
Hayes Catalogue: Wright, Silas. *Life of By J. S. Jenkins,* Auburn, NY, 1847. 12°
109,399 voucher 4: New Clerk's Assistant $2.25.
Purchased from Franck Taylor on November 26, 1851.

Silas Wright.

TITLE PAGE

THE LIFE | OF | SILAS WRIGHT, | LATE GOVERNOR OF THE STATE OF NEW YORK. | WITH AN APPENDIX. | CONTAINING A SELECTION FROM HIS SPEECHES IN THE SENATE | OF THE UNITED STATES, AND HIS ADDRESS READ BEFORE | THE NEW YORK STATE AGRICULTURAL SOCIETY. | BY JOHN S. JENKINS, | AUTHOR OF THE "HISTORY OF POLITICAL PARTIES IN THE STATE OF NEW YORK." | "LIFE OF ANDREW JACKSON," ETC., ETC. | [thin wavy rule] | "The Cato of the American Senate." | THOMAS H. BENTON. | [thin wavy rule] | AUBURN, N. Y.: | ALDEN & MARKHAM, PUBLISHERS, | No. 67 GENESEE St. | 1847.

PAGINATION

i–xii 13–378.

CONTENTS

i title, ii copyright statement and printer's imprint, iii–v preface, vi blank, vii–xi contents, xii blank, 13–264 text, 265 section title, 'APPENDIX', 266 blank, 267–79 Speech relative to the Pressure and the Removal of the Deposits, 280–97 Speech on Mr. Clay's Resolutions of Censure, 298–359 Speech on the Revision and Modification of the Tariff Law of 1842, 360–78 Agricultural Address.

PLATES

Frontispiece, portrait of Silas Wright.

REFERENCES

Hayes p. 117; cf. Roorbach p. 290; cf. Fillmore ca. 1858 p. 70.

COPY DESCRIBED

DLC: E340 W95 J5 copy 1. *Leaf.* 186 × 115.

---

1. Jenkins's other biographies included Andrew Jackson, James Polk, and John Calhoun; see entries 72 and 193 for Hammond and Wilkes, respectively.

❧

86. *The Jesuit.*

No fewer than thirteen books published between 1840 and 1852 have titles that could reasonably be shortened to "The Jesuit." Franck Taylor, the seller from whom this purchase was made, sold very few older books to the White House, which suggests a recent publication for this purchase. Putnam lists no books that would fit with this short title. Roorbach lists "The Jesuit: A Historical Sketch" published by Am. S.S. Union, which sold for $0.21 and another edition of this title, designated as "from the French of Michelet and Quinet," published by Gates & S. for $0.75. The price of the latter makes it a possibility, yet no copies of this book have been located for examination. Carl Spindler published a novel titled *The Jesuit: A Historical Romance* that first appeared in German in 1829; it was translated into English and published in both London and America throughout the 1830s and 1840s. The London editions were in three volumes and sold for just over one pound, which would have made them too expensive to match this purchase. No pricing information has been located for the American editions, which were one-volume books and would have been less expensive than their London counterparts. Another possibility for this purchase is Thomas W. Whitley's play *The Jesuit: A National Melodrama*. It was based on an incident from the war between the United States and Mexico and first published in 1850; Fillmore's interest in a play based on the recent war would not be surprising; however, no pricing information for this play has been discovered.

109,399 voucher 4: The Jesuit .75.
Purchased from Franck Taylor on September 15, 1851.

~

87. Johnson, Samuel. *The Works of Samuel Johnson, LL. D.* Ed. Arthur Murphy. 2 vols. London: Jones, 1825.

Samuel Johnson (1709–84), author and lexicographer, stands as one of the most distinguished men of English letters. As an author he wrote and published in nearly every genre imaginable: criticism, satire, biography, moral essays, prose fiction, poetry, scholarly editions, travel writing, political pamphlets, journalism, and drama. Today he is remembered most for his *Dictionary of the English Language* (1755), his moral tale *Rasselas, Prince of Abissinia* (1759), and his two most enduring poems, *The Vanity of Human Wishes* (1749) and *London* (1738). Johnson was the leading arbiter of taste in London during the second half of the eighteenth century and encouraged and assisted many writers, including Anna Williams, Oliver Goldsmith, James Boswell, Frances Burney, Hester Thrale Piozzi, and Richard Savage, among many others.

Johnson's reputation as a literary giant stood firm through the century after his death, as evidenced by glowing nineteenth-century reviews of his works. One critic characterized his works as "the purest gems from the capacious mine of intellectual treasure," while another referred to Johnson with reverence as the "greatest English master." Sir Walter Scott's biographical essay on Johnson proclaimed, "of all the men distinguished in this or any other age, Dr. Johnson has left upon posterity the strongest and most vivid impression." He declared Johnson the "Jupiter" of eighteenth-century London literary society.[1]

Volume 1 of this edition contains Johnson's essays from his periodicals *The Rambler* and *The Idler,* and his *Lives of Poets,* while volume 2 includes *Rasselas,* the *Lives of Eminent Persons,* poems, prayers and meditations, the *Adventurer* essays, political tracts, and his *Journey to the Western Islands.* J. D. Fleeman notes that the major sections of volume 1 have separate title pages and were designed to be issued separately as well as in this collection. It is possible that these parts are of the same editions or derived from the editions of the *Idler* and the *Rambler* that were included in the *British Essayists,* another collection purchased for the White House. American advertisements for this edition appeared as late as 1839 and offered it for $3.00 folded, $3.50 in cloth, and $4.00 in sheep. Given that Welford charged $4.50 for the White House copy, it may have been bound in either sheep or calf.[2]

105,133 voucher 5: Dr. Johnson Works 2 $4.50.
Purchased from Charles Welford on December 13, 1850.
Roosevelt Catalogue: Johnson, Samuel, *Works. With an Essay on His Life and Genius by Arthur Murphy.* London, Jones & Co., 1825, 2 vols.

TITLE PAGE
THE | WORKS | OF | SAMUEL JOHNSON, LL.D. | WITH | AN ESSAY | ON HIS LIFE AND GENIUS | BY | ARTHUR MURPHY, Esq. | [wavy rule] | IN TWO VOLUMES COMPLETE. | VOL. I. [II.] | LONDON: | PUBLISHED BY JONES & COMPANY, | 3, ACTON PLACE, KINGSLAND ROAD. | [thin rule] | 1825.

PAGINATION
Vol. I. i–xl i–viii 1–352 i–xii 1–112 [4] 1–364.
Vol. II. i–vi 1–688.

CONTENTS
Vol. I. i title, ii printer's imprint, iii–xl "An Essay on the Life and Genius of Samuel Johnson LL. D.," i title for *Rambler,* ii printer's imprint, iii–iv historical preface to *Rambler,* v–viii contents for *Rambler,* 1–351 text of *Rambler,* 352 blank, i title for *Idler,* ii printer's imprint, iii–iv contents for the *Idler,* v–xii historical and biographical preface to *Idler,* 1–111 text of *Idler,* 112 blank, [1] title for *The Lives of the English Poets,* [2] printer's imprint, [3] contents for *The Lives of the English Poets,* [4] blank, 1–363 *The Lives of the English Poets,* 364 blank.
Vol. II. i title, ii printer's imprint, iii–v contents, vi blank, 1–687 text of *The Works of Samuel Johnson,* 688 blank.

PLATES
Vol. I.
Portrait frontispiece, Samuel Johnson, engraved by M. R. Page from the admired painting by Sir Joshua Reynolds.
Engraved title page, '[Decorative cathedral frame] JONES'S | UNIVERSITY EDITION OF | BRITISH CLASSIC AUTHORS [preceding lines incorporated into the design in the top edge of the frame in swash letters] | The | WORKS | OF | SAM^L· JOHNSON, LL. D. | [thin rule] | Vol. I. | [vignette from Rambler No. 65] | AFRAID TO GO FORWARD LEST HE SHOULD GO WRONG $_{No\,65}$ [on bottom edge of frame] | LONDON Published by Jones & Co· June 1, 1825. [beneath frame]'
Facing 78, engraving for *Rambler* no. 44, "Fanaticism and Superstition," engraved by Mr. Lacery from a design by Corbould.
Facing 264, engraving for *Rambler* no. 153, "Treatment Incurred by Loss of Fortune," engraved by Mr. Brown from a painting by Corbould.

Facing 309, engraving for *Rambler* no. 182, "Then Showed Him the Door," engraved by Simmons from a painting by Corbould.

Facing 345, engraving for *Rambler* no. 205, "Segid Interrupted in his Pleasures," engraved by Mr. Halper, from a painting by Corbould.

Vol. II.

Engraved title page. '[Decorative cathedral frame] JONES'S I UNIVERSITY EDITION OF I BRITISH CLASSIC AUTHORS [preceding lines incorporated into the design in the top edge of the frame in swash letters] I The I WORKS I OF I SAM^L· JOHNSON, LL. D. I [thin rule] I Vol. 2. I [vignette from Rasselas] I THE PRINCE & PRINCESS LEAVE THE VALLEY Rasselas [on bottom edge of frame] I Stalker and Neele sc. LONDON Published by Jones & Co· June 1, 1825. 13 Newcastle St. Strand. [beneath frame]'

REFERENCES

Hayes p. 118; Roosevelt p. 23; Fleeman 87.3W/22b; cf. Fillmore ca. 1858 p. 31; cf. Fillmore 1861 p. 114.

COPY DESCRIBED

ViU: PR 3521 M7 1825 *Leaf.* 260 × 130.

<hr>

1. "Literary Notices," *The Family Magazine; or, Monthly Abstract of General Knowledge (1833–1841)*, May 1, 1841, "Literary Review," *The Ladies' Companion, A Monthly Magazine Devoted to Literature and the Fine*, January 1841, and "Life and Character of Dr. Johnson," *The Cincinnati Literary Gazette (1824–1825)*, March 26, 1825, all available at *APS Online*, http://www.proquest.com/products_pq/descriptions/aps.shtml.

2. J. D. Fleeman, *A Bibliography of the Works of Samuel Johnson* (Oxford: Clarendon, 2000), 2:1698–99.

~

88. Johnston, Alexander Keith. *The National Atlas of Historical, Commercial and Political Geography.* Edinburgh: Blackwood, 1850.

89. ———. *Dictionary of Geography, Descriptive, Physical, Statistical, and Historical, Forming a Complete General Gazetteer of the World.* London: Longman, Brown, Green, and Longmans, 1851.

Alexander Keith Johnston (1804–71), geographer and cartographer, formed a publishing partnership with his brothers that would become the most important map-publishing firm of the nineteenth and twentieth centuries. *The National Atlas* (1843) was Johnston's first important work. The product of five years of labor, it contains forty-five maps, most of which were drawn by Johnston himself. Johnston tried to create an atlas that would be an accessible reference work and that would serve as "a guide to the scientific and systematic study of Geography" ([5]). Some features of the maps included sites of important military battles and engagements, along with their dates; fortresses; castles; remarkable ruins; places of historical interest; mountain chains, peaks, and valleys, with heights expressed in English measurements; current and projected railway lines and canals; and tracks of principle voyages of discovery. ([5]).

Johnston sought to produce the most accurate and up-to-date atlas possible. As he explains:

The intimate acquaintance of the Editor with the best methods of engraving, has secured for his drawings more than usual exactness in their transfer to the plates, which have been entirely engraved within the last five years,—a much shorter period of time, it is believed, than has sufficed for the production of any Geographical work of equal extent, and to accomplish which, it required the unremitted labour of many previous years, and latterly the employment of a succession of workmen almost day and night, in order that each Map might contain the most recent information. ([6])

Johnston's "Gazetteer," as his *Dictionary of Geography* (1850) was known, provides geographical facts for cities, states, countries, mountains, rivers, and islands, and so forth throughout the world. For example, from the entry for Suffolk one learns that it is six and one half miles northeast of Bury St. Edmund's, occupying an area of 2,320 acres, with a population of 1,064. "The town is well built, and pleasantly situated on the banks of a small riv." (675).

Johnston received many honors for his geographical work, including being named "geographer at Edinburgh in ordinary to the queen," a fellow of the Royal Society, an honorary doctor of the University of Edinburgh, and a member of most of the world's important geographical societies.

The National Atlas was one of the very first purchases that Fillmore made for the library, made prior to the congressional approval of funds. Fillmore's concern with exploration, commerce, trade, and trade routes as president, as well as his personal interests in maps as a collector, would have prompted him to purchase these two highly acclaimed geographical works for the library.

Putnam advertised Johnston's *National Atlas* bound in half russia for $40.00. Since the White House paid $5.00 more for its copy, it is possible that theirs was bound in full, rather than half russia. The advertised prices for the *Dictionary* however, do not accord with the price of $11.00 specified on the voucher, a discrepancy that may be accounted for by the format of the edition purchased. Putnam advertises the *Dictionary* in octavo format, bound in cloth at only $5.50, while the *London Catalogue* also lists an octavo edition for 36s., which would have been approximately $8.76 in United States currency. The Hayes Catalogue, however, specifies a quarto edition, which would have been more expensive than the octavos that were advertised. Unfortunately, no extant copy of a quarto edition has been located at this time. If the *Gazetteer* were issued in this larger format it most likely would have been in a limited number.

105,579 voucher 11: Johnson's [*sic*] National Atlas $45.00.
Purchased from George Crosby on August 19, 1850.
Hayes Catalogue: Johnston, A. K. *National Atlas*. Edinburgh, 1850. 4°.
105,133 voucher 2: Johnston's gazetteer $11.00.
Purchased from Little and Brown on December 30, 1850.
Hayes Catalogue: Johnston, A. K. *Dictionary of Geography*. London, 1850. 4°.

National Atlas.

TITLE PAGE

Engraved.

THE I NATIONAL ATLAS [decorative open face letters] I OF I HISTORICAL, COMMERCIAL, AND POLITICAL I GEOGRAPHY, [decorative open face letters] I CONSTRUCTED [open face letters] I FROM THE MOST RECENT AND AUTHENTIC SOURCES. I By [decorative open face letters] I ALEXANDER KEITH JOHNSTON, F. R. G. S., [open face letters] I HONORARY MEMBER OF THE GEOGRAPHICAL SOCIETY OF BERLIN, I AND I Geographer at Edinburgh in Ordinary To her Majesty [decorative open face letters] I ACCOMPANIED BY I *MAPS AND ILLUSTRATIONS* [open face letters] I *of the* I Physical Geography of the Globe, [decorative open face letters] I BY I DR HEINRICH BERGHAUS, [open face letters] I Professor of Geography, Berlin. [black letter] I AND AN I ETHNOGRAPHIC MAP OF EUROPE, [decorative open face letters] I By I DR GUSTAF KOMBST, [open face letters] I F. R. N. S. C., M. H. S. P. S., ETC. I [thin rule] I WITH A COPIOUS INDEX CAREFULLY COMPILED I FROM THE MAPS. I [thin rule] I WILLIAM BLACKWOOD & SONS 45 GEORGE STREET, EDINBURGH. I AND 37 PATERNOSTER ROW, LONDON. I MDCCCL. [last five lines in open face letters]

PAGINATION

[*8*] 1–12 1–56.

CONTENTS

[*1*] title, [*2*] blank, [*3*] dedication to The Royal Geographical Society of London, [*4*] quotations regarding the usefulness of maps from the Anniversary Address by the President of the Royal Geographical Society, 1840 and from M. A. M. Perrot, [*5*]–[*6*] Preface to the General Geography, [*7*] contents, [*8*] index to the miscellaneous matter contained in the maps of general geography, 1 section title, "Index to the National Atlas by Alex K. Johnston, F.R.G.S., Geographer to the Queen, Edinburgh and Editor of the Physical Atlas," 2–11 text of index, 12 blank, 1–46 forty-six bifolium plates of maps, 47–56 "Notes on Physical Geography Explanatory of the Maps."

PLATES

Maps:

Map no.	Title
1	World in Hemispheres
2	World on Mercator's Projection
3	Europe
4	England and Wales
5	Scotland
6	Ireland
7	France
8	Spain and Portugal
9	Switzerland
10	Italy
11	Italy, South Part

12	Greece and Hellas, Ionian Islands and Crete
13	Turkey in Europe
14	Empire of Austria
15	Germany, Western States
16	Prussia
17	Belgium
18	Holland
19	Denmark
20	Sweden and Norway
21	Russia in Europe
22	Asia
23	Turkey in Asia
24	Palestine
25	Persia and Cabool
26	India
27	S. E. Peninsula and Malaysia
28	China
29	Islands in the Pacific Ocean
30	Australia
31	Colony of New South Wales and Australia Felix
32	Van Dieman's Land or Tasmania
33	New Zealand
34	Africa
35	Egypt and Arabia Petræa.
36	Nubia and Abyssinia
37	North America
38	Canada
39	United States and Texas
40	West India Islands
41	South America
42	Humboldt's System of Isothermal Lines, or Lines of Annual Mean Temperature over the Globe
43	Geographical Distribution of the Currents of Air or of the Perennial, Periodical and Variable Winds
44	Survey of the Geographical Distribution and Cultivation of the most Important Plants which are used as Food for Man: with indications of the Isotheres & Isochimenes. Or Lines of Equal Summer and Equal Winter Temperature.
45	Mountain Chains in Asia and Europe
46	Ethnographic Map of Europe

BINDING

Half calf.

Front and back boards. 570 × 380 gilt-stamped thick/thin double rule on edges where calf meets cloth. *Spine.* Six panels formed by raised bands, blind-stamped decorations in each panel, gilt stamp decoration on the bands, gilt stamped in second and third panel, 'NATIONAL | ATLAS'; gilt stamped at base of spine 'A. K. JOHNSTON' *Endpapers.* Red, blue, and yellow marbled. Binder's label on verso of second binder's leaf " Bound by Alex^r Banks J^r. 29 North Bridge Edinburgh."

REFERENCES

Hayes p. 118; Putnam p. 18-s.

COPY DESCRIBED

DLC: G1019 J58 1850 fol.

Dictionary of Geography.

REFERENCES

LC 1816–1851 p. 300; Putnam p. 18-s.

≈

90. Junius. *Letters by the Same Writer, Under Other Signatures.* 3 vols. London: Rivington et al., 1812.

Although the Junius letters are notable for their role in the history of the freedom of the press, they are even better known for the unsolved mystery of their authorship. The Junius letters sought to discredit two British prime ministers, first the duke of Grafton and subsequently Lord North, and to question the politics of King George III. In 1770, after Woodfall published an attack on the king, the government unsuccessfully prosecuted Woodfall for seditious libel. Junius was the pseudonym of the still unidentified author of correspondence that was originally published in Henry Sampson Woodfall's *Public Advertiser* between January 21, 1769, and January 21, 1772. Over forty-five candidates have been proposed for authorship, including Jean Louis de Lolme, author of the *Rise and Progress of the English Constitution.* Sir Philip Francis, who was proposed as a possibility in 1816, has gone down in history as the most likely writer of these letters. The plates in this edition invite readers to contemplate the mystery of the *Letters'* author by supplying facsimiles of the handwriting in the manuscript sent to Woodfall and of the handwriting of the proposed authors.[1]

105,133 voucher 2: Woodfall's Junius 3 vols. clf. $11.00.

Purchased from Little and Brown December 30, 1850.

Roosevelt Catalogue: Junius. *Including Letters by the Same Writer, under Other Signatures (Now First Collected) to Which Are Added His Confidential Correspondence with Mr. Wilkes and His Private Letters Addressed to Mr. H. S. Woodfall.* London, F. C. Rivington, 1812, 3 vols. (vol. 2 missing).

TITLE PAGE

JUNIUS: [black letter] | INCLUDING | LETTERS | BY THE SAME WRITER, UNDER OTHER SIGNATURES, | (NOW FIRST COLLECTED.) | TO WHICH ARE ADDED, | HIS CONFIDENTIAL CORRESPONDENCE | WITH | MR. WILKES, | AND HIS | PRIVATE LETTERS | ADDRESSED TO | MR. H. S. WOODFALL. | WITH | A PRELIMINARY ESSAY, NOTES, FAC-SIMILES, &c. | IN THREE VOLUMES. | [thin rule] | VOL. I. [II.–III.] | [thin rule] | STAT NOMINIS UMBRA. | LONDON: | *PRINTED*

BY G. WOODFALL, | FOR F. C. RIVINGTON; T. PAYNE; WILKIE AND ROBINSON; |
LONGMAN, HURST, REES, ORME, AND BROWN; CADELL AND | DAVIES;
J. MURRAY; J. MAWMAN; AND R. BALDWIN. | [thin rule] | 1812.

PAGINATION
Vol. I. iii–xii 1–336 1–248.
Vol. II. iii–xii 1–516.
Vol. III. iii–xvi 1–512.
> *Notes.* Each of these volumes begins with the title page on page iii; there may have been
> a half title that would have accounted for pages i–ii. Some copies of this edition listed
> for sale on the Advanced Book Exchange Web site in January 2006 specify half titles
> as present.

CONTENTS
Vol. I. iii title, iv blank, v–viii contents, ix–xii advertisement, 1–161 preliminary essay, 162
blank, 163 section title, "Private Letters of Junius Addressed to Mr. H. S. Woodfall," 164
blank, 165–259 text of "Private Letters of Junius Addressed to Mr. H. S. Woodfall," 260
blank, 261 section title, "Private Correspondence between Junius and Mr. Wilkes," 262
blank, 263–336 text of "Private Correspondence between Junius and Mr. Wilkes," 1–8
dedication to the English nation, 9–46 preface, 47–248 text of letters of Junius.
Vol. II. iii title, iv blank, v–xi contents, xii blank, 1–516 text.
Vol. III. iii title, iv blank, v–xiii contents, xiv blank, xv section title, "Miscellaneous Letters
of Junius," xvi blank, 1–457 text of "Miscellaneous Letters of Junius," 458 blank, 459–511
index, 512 errata.

PLATES
Vol. I.
Folding plate facing 1, "Fac Similes of the handwriting of Junius in his private Letters to Mr.
H. S. Woodfall."
Folding plate facing xii, "Fac Similes of handwritings of Gentlemen whose names have been
mentioned as the Author of the Letters."
Vol. II.
Folding plate facing 1, "Fac Similes of the handwriting of Junius in his private Letters to Mr.
H. S. Woodfall."
Folding plate facing xii, "Fac Similes of handwritings of Gentlemen whose names have been
mentioned as the Author of the Letters."
Vol. III.
Folding plate facing 1, "Fac Similes of the handwriting of Junius in his private Letters to Mr.
H. S. Woodfall."
Facing xvi, "Seals used by Junius in his correspondence with Mr. H. S. Woodfall.
> *Note.* Although the plates in volume 2 and the first plate in volume 3 have the same titles
> as plates in volume 1, the images differ. The plates are bound into the volumes so that
> they face one another. The location of plates given above indicates the number of the
> page in the book that they would face were the other plate not present.

REFERENCES

Hayes p. 118; Roosevelt p. 23; *LC 1816–1851* p. 305; L and B 1850 p. 51; cf. Fillmore 1847 p. 16; cf. Fillmore 1861 p. 114.

COPY DESCRIBED

DLC: DA 508 A2 1812. *Leaf.* 228 × 133.

---

1. See entry 100 for de Lolme. For historical background, see "Junius," *Encyclopaedia Britannica Online* (2007), http://search.eb.com/eb/article-9044171 (accessed July 23, 2009); John Cannon summarizes the evidence for this proposition as it was understood in 2007 in "Francis, Sir Philip (1740–1818)," *ODNB*.

～

91. Keily, James. *A Map of the City of Washington.* Lloyd Van Derveer: Camden, N.J., 1851.

Maps of Washington, D.C., from the mid-nineteenth century are characterized by a gap between the topography as it existed and the topography as it was represented. According to Robert L. Miller, "the era's commercial maps blended existing conditions and future projections, accurate minutiae and romantic misinformation, to describe a place at best unfinished and at worst raw, stalled and stagnant."[1] James Keily's *Map of the City of Washington* was not alone when it included an inset view of a completed Washington monument that, in fact, remained unfinished for several more decades. Keily's map also included vignettes of the Capitol, President's House, statue of Washington, National Observatory, City Hall, General Post Office, Smithsonian Institution, Treasury, and Patent Office, which may or may not be accurate. Although "numbered blocks, both real and projected," embellished the map, the population statistics printed on the map—divided into "white," "colored," and "slaves" and further subdivided into male and female—are believed to be accurate.[2]

By 1851 many maps of Washington, D.C., had been published, some that included Georgetown and some that did not. It is reasonable to assume, however, that President Fillmore purchased a recent map for the Executive Mansion. The Geography and Map Division at the Library of Congress holds seven maps of Washington, D.C., that were published between 1845 and 1851 and include Georgetown. Most of these are too small to have cost $3.00. Five are derived from the plate that was used to print the one published by Samuel Augustus Mitchell in his *Universal Atlas,* which the White House purchased for the library at the price of $10.50. These maps measure 31 × 38 cm and would not have sold for $3.00 individually. James Keily's map is a likely choice; it measures 73 × 100 cm, is colored, embellished with engraved vignettes, mounted on cloth, and folds in half.[3]

107,754 voucher 1: one map of Georgetown and Washington $3.00.
Purchased from John Prendon on April 23, 1851.

REFERENCES

cf. Fillmore ca. 1858 p. 69.

---

1. Robert L. Miller, "Promoting Washington: Map with Gazette; Amenities, Marred by Racial Profile Chart, The Colton Atlas, " in Iris Miller, *Washington in Maps* (New York: Rizzoli International Publications, 2002), 82.

2. Ibid.

3. P. Lee Phillips, *Maps and Views of Washington and District of Columbia,* 2nd ed. (Norwich, Vt.: Terra Nova Press, 1996), 44. This map is reproduced on the Web site of the Library of Congress's Geography and Map Division at http://memory.loc.gov/cgi-bin/query/D?gmd:1:./temp/~ammem_IGtc:: (accessed June 21, 2009).

～

92. Kent, James. *Commentaries on American Law.* 6th ed. 4 vols. New York: Kent, 1848.

James Kent (1763–1847), lawyer, politician, and professor, made his reputation as a jurist and legal commentator. Although he taught law at Columbia College for many years, he was never considered a successful professor. His lectures, however, made a tremendous impact on the legal profession in America, for it was these lectures that he revised and expanded to become *Commentaries on American Law* (1826), a work that would go through fourteen editions along with numerous abridgments and translations. Kent's *Commentaries* came to stand as "the foremost American institutional legal treatise" of its time.[1] He claimed that the knowledge in these volumes was intended to be "of general application, and is of that elementary kind which is not only essential to every person who pursues the science of the law as a practical profession, but is deemed useful and ornamental to gentlemen of every pursuit, and especially to those who are to assume places of public trust" (1:x). Characterizing Kent's style as "easy, clear, vigorous, and unaffected," Marvin had only the highest praise for Kent. He maintained that this work excelled beyond Blackstone's in "comprehensiveness of research and fullness of illustration" and equaled his in "clearness and cogency of reasoning." He also found Kent's *Commentaries* "a textbook of the highest character for accuracy," and called it "a work which no lawyer thinks of doing without."[2] According to the advertisement printed in volume 1, this edition contains Kent's final revisions, even though he died while it was still in press.

105,133 voucher 7: Kent's Commentaries 4 vols. $13.00.

Purchased from Franck Taylor on October 24, 1850.

Hayes Catalogue: Kent, J. *Commentaries on American Law* 6th ed. 4 v. New York, 1848 8°
    vol. 4 wanting.

TITLE PAGE

COMMENTARIES | ON | AMERICAN LAW. | BY JAMES KENT. | VOLUME I. [II–IV.] | SIXTH EDITION. | NEW-YORK: | PUBLISHED BY WILLIAM KENT, | AND SOLD BY THE PRINCIPAL LAW BOOKSELLERS THROUGHOUT | THE UNITED STATES. | [thin rule] | M DCCC XLVIII.

    Note. The lineation of the imprint in volume 2 differs as follows: 'AND SOLD BY | THE PRINCIPAL LAW BOOKSELLERS THROUGHOUT THE UNITED STATES.'

PAGINATION

Vol. I. i–xxviii [*732*].

Vol. II. i–lii [*980*].

Vol. III. i–xl [*732*].

Vol. IV. i–xxxvi [*752*]

Note. The page numbering for the text beyond the preliminaries of all four volumes is so irregular that it renders the numbers useless; therefore, only a page count has been given above.

CONTENTS

Vol. I. i title, ii copyright statements and printer's imprint, iii advertisement, iv blank, v dedication to William Johnson, Esq., vi blank, vii–viii preface to the first volume of the first edition, ix–x preface to the second volume, xi–xvii contents, xviii blank, xix–xxviii table of cases, [*1*]–[*718*] text, [*719*]–[*732*] index.

Vol. II. i title, ii copyright statements and printer's imprint, iii–ix contents, x blank, xi–li table of cases, lii blank, [*1*]–[*980*] text.

Vol. III. i title, ii copyright statements and printer's imprint, iii–viii contents, ix–xl table of cases, [*1*]–[*732*] text.

Vol. IV. i title, ii copyright statements and printer's imprint, iii–viii contents, ix–xxxv table of cases, xxxvi blank, [*1*]–[*710*] text, [*711*]–[*752*] index.

REFERENCES

Hayes p. 153; *BEAL* 5403; cf. Greenleaf; cf. Harvard p. 127; cf. Marvin p. 437; cf. Roorbach p. 620; cf. Fillmore Packing Lists p. 21; cf. Fillmore 1861 p. 118.

COPY DESCRIBED

DLC: KF 385 K416 copy 2. *Leaf.* 225 × 140.

---

1. *BEAL,* 5403.
2. Marvin, *Legal Bibliography,* 438.

~

93. Klapka, György. *Memoirs of the War of Independence in Hungary.* 2 vols. London: C. Gilpin, 1850.

Gyorgy Klapka's *Memoirs of the War of Independence in Hungary* (1850) was called one of "the most authentic contributions to the history of the Hungarian War" and praised for its portrayal of Artúr Görgey and Louis Kossuth, two leaders of the revolution.[1] Klapka (1820–92), a soldier and nationalist, became a general and led the Northern Hungarian army in the 1848 revolution. Thereafter, he lived in exile until 1867 when he was allowed to return to Hungary. Klapka's book stands alongside Theresa Pulszky's *Memoirs of a Hungarian Lady* and John Paget's *Hungary and Transylvania* as one of three books related to Hungary that was purchased for the first White House Library.[2] This London edition of 1850 from Gilpin is the only English-language edition published of this title. Putnam's advertisement for this book offers an instructive example of how booksellers sometimes drastically reduced prices, as it lists two volumes, octavo, cloth at $6.00 reduced to $2.00.

109,399 voucher 4: Klapka's Hungary $2.00.
Purchased from Franck Taylor on December 23, 1851.

TITLE PAGE
MEMOIRS | OF THE | WAR OF INDEPENDENCE | IN | HUNGARY. | BY GENERAL
KLAPKA, | LATE SECRETARY-AT-WAR TO THE HUNGARIAN COMMONWEALTH,
AND | COMMANDANT OF THE FORTRESS OF KONORN. | TRANSLATED FROM
THE ORIGINAL MANUSCRIPT BY | OTTO WENCKSTERN. | VOL. I. [II.] | LONDON:
| CHARLES GILPIN, 5, BISHOPGATE WITHOUT. | EDINBURGH: ADAM AND
CHARLES BLACK. | DUBLIN: J. B. GILPIN. | [thin rule] | 1850.

PAGINATION
Vol. I. i–lxxxviii 1–232.
Vol. II. i–viii 1–336.

CONTENTS
Vol. I. i half title, ii printer's imprint, iii title, iv blank, v–vii contents, viii blank, ix–lxxxviii
historical introduction, 1–231 text, 232 blank.
Vol. II. i half title, ii printer's imprint, iii title, iv blank, v–viii contents, 1–199 text, 200
blank, 201 section title, "Documentary Appendix and Notes," 202 blank, 203–336 text of
appendix.

PLATES
Vol. I.
Portrait frontispiece of Kossuth.
Bound in rear of volume, folding map of Austrian Empire from Bett's Family Atlas.
Vol. II.
Portrait frontispiece of Klapka.

REFERENCES
Putnam p. 19-s; cf. *LC 1816–1851* p. 313.

COPY DESCRIBED
DLC: DB 935 K63. *Leaf.* 189 × 117.

---

1. "A Comprehensive Lexicon of the Greek Language, adapted to the use of Schools," *The Literary World
(1847–1853),* November 22, 1851, available at *APS Online,* http://www.proquest.com/products_pq/descrip
tions/aps.shtml.

2. *Merriam-Webster's Biographical Dictionary* (N.p.: Merriam-Webster Incorporated, 1995), available at
Biography Resource Center (Farmington Hills, Mich.: Thomson Gale, 2006), http://gale.cengage.com/
servlet/BiographyRC; see entries 136 and 125 for Pulszky and Paget, respectively.

~

94. Lafayette, Marie J. P. Y. G. M., Marquis de. *Memoirs, Correspondence and Manuscripts.*
3 vols. London: Saunders and Otley, 1837.

The French aristocrat Marquis de Layfayette (1757–1834) fought for America in the revolutionary war. Two years into the war, Lafayette arrived in Philadelphia, became friends with
George Washington, and was appointed a major general by the colonists. Lafayette helped
to convince France to send six thousand troops to aid the colonists and was instrumental
in bringing Cornwallis to surrender at Yorktown. Afterward, he returned to France and later

aligned himself with the French bourgeoisie and became one of the most powerful men in France during its revolution. According to the dedicatory statement in the *Memoirs,* these volumes present General Lafayette's personal manuscripts that were collected and arranged by his family, and submitted for publication without any commentary (1:[3]).

105,133 voucher 5: Life La Fayette 3 vols. 8vo hf. cf. $5.50.
Purchased from Charles Welford on December 13, 1850.
Roosevelt Catalogue: Lafayette, Marie J. P. Y. G. M. <u>marquis de</u>. *Memoirs, Correspondence and Manuscripts of General Lafayette Published by His Family.* London, Saunders & Otley, 1837 3 vols.

TITLE PAGE

MEMOIRS I CORRESPONDENCE AND MANUSCRIPTS I OF I GENERAL LAFAYETTE. I PUBLISHED BY HIS FAMILY. I VOL. I. [II–III.] I LONDON I SAUNDERS AND OTLEY, CONDUIT STREET. I MDCCCXXXVII.

PAGINATION

Vol. I. [*4*] vii–xii i–iv 1–470.
Vol. II. i–viii 1–482.
Vol. III. i–viii 1–498.

CONTENTS

Vol. I. [*1*] title, [2] printer's imprint, [3] dedication statement to General Lafayette from his children, [4] blank, vii–xi contents, xii blank, i–ii Notice by the Editors, iii–iv note to the readers, 1–449 text, 450 blank, 451–68 appendix, 469 errata, 470 blank.

Vol. II. i title, ii printer's imprint, iii–vii contents, viii blank, 1–461 text, 462–79 appendixes, 480 blank, 481 errata, 482 blank.

Vol. III. i title, ii printer's imprint, iii–vii contents, viii blank, 1 section title, "French Revolution," 2 blank, 3–465 text, 466 blank, 467–97 appendixes, 498 blank.

PLATES

Vol. I.
Portrait frontispiece, vignette of Lafayette.

REFERENCES

Hayes p. 147; Roosevelt p. 25; cf. *LC 1816–1851* p. 318.

COPY DESCRIBED

DLC: DC146 L2 A3 copy 2. *Leaf.* 210 × 129. (Volume 2 is from DLC copy 1.)

~

95. Lamartine, Alphonse de. *History of the French Revolution of 1848.* **Boston: Phillips Sampson & Co., 1849.**

Since Alphonse Lamartine (1790–1869) led the provisional government of the Second Republic of 1848, his *History of the French Revolution of 1848* (1848) provided a biased narration of its events. As a writer for *Littel's Living Age* pointed out, "If Cromwell had written an account of the protectorate, or if Jefferson had left on record the discussions of the committee who reported the declaration of independence, such narratives would have been egotistical." A critic for the *Southern Literary Messenger* found Lamartine "insufferably vain" and took the skepticism of his history even further, remarking, "It would be a miracle if it were reliable. We are much too near the Revolution of 1848 to judge correctly of its events and personages." Despite this disparagement, an author for the *Methodist Quarterly Review* came to Lamartine's defense and found the *History* "marked by that command of language, spontaneous eloquence, and tenderness of feeling which in Lamartine are so remarkably combined with the power of clear narrative and graphic description." The writer lamented that Lamartine's work has been so criticized, exclaiming, "What then of all this Revolution, most of all, of the repression of violence, wrong, bloodshed, who more truthfully than Lamartine can say, '*Pars magna fui?*'"[1]

Two very similar voucher entries indicate that either this title was purchased twice, or two different titles relative to the French revolution written by Lamartine were purchased: *History of the French Revolution of 1848* and *History of the Girondists; or, Personal Memoirs of the Patriots of the French Revolution* (1847). Most likely two copies of the first title were purchased, because its price matches more closely those listed on the vouchers. Roorbach and Putnam listed both titles. While the *History of the Girondists* was available in editions that range in price from $1.80 to $14.00, the *History of the French Revolution* could have been obtained for $.50 to $.84 in editions from two different publishers, Philips, Sampson and Co. in Boston and Henry Bohn in London. Exactly which editions were purchased for the White House Library will remain uncertain unless more information comes to light.

105,133 voucher 5: Lamartine French Revolution .88.
Purchased from Charles Welford on December 13, 1850.
109,399 voucher 4: Lamartine's Revolution .75.
Purchased from Franck Taylor on September 22, 1851.

REFERENCES
cf. Roorbach p. 310; cf. Putnam p. 76.

----

1. "Lamartine's New History," *Littell's Living Age (1844–1896),* October 27, 1849, "History of the French Revolution of 1848," *The Southern Literary Messenger, Devoted to Every Department of Literature,* November 1849, and "Review 2—No Title," *The Methodist Quarterly Review (1841–1884),* January 1850, all available at *APS Online,* http://www.proquest.com/products_pq/descriptions/aps.shtml.

～

96. **Linden, Johannes van der.** *Institutes of the Laws of Holland.* **Trans. Jabez Henry. London: J. and W. T. Clarke, 1828.**

Johannes van der Linden (1756–1835) practiced law and became a judge in Amsterdam, where he first published his *Rechtsgeleerd Practical en Koopmans-Handboek* in 1806, later translated into English as *Institutes of the Laws of Holland.* As the translator, Jabez Henry, explained in 1828, Dutch law prevailed in Dutch ceded colonies, some of which were in the Caribbean, and an English edition was needed for English settlers in those colonies as well as for students of the law who wished to hold judicial appointments there (xv). According to Henry another English translation of Linden's *Institutes* had been published in 1814 but by 1828 was no longer readily available (x–xi). In 1852 Linden's *Institutes* was adopted as the official law book of the South African Republic.[1]

Fillmore ordered this book in the aftermath of the Cuban filibuster, an event that would have drawn his attention to the nuances of the laws that governed in the Caribbean. In the mid-nineteenth century St. Martin's and Curaçao in the Caribbean and Guiana in South America were governed by the Dutch, and new resources had also opened up for Dutch trade in Brazil, Havana, and Haiti. Furthermore, the Netherlands exported very little to the United States, but it imported from it a considerable amount of tobacco and hides. The legal issues surrounding the filibuster combined with Fillmore's concern with improving trade and commerce may have prompted him to purchase this book.[2]

107,754 voucher 4: 1 vol. Institutes of Laws of Holland $4.00.

Purchased from Little and Brown on December 31, 1851.

Hayes Catalogue: Linden, J. van der. *Institutes of the Laws of Holland*. London, 1828. 8°.

TITLE PAGE

INSTITUTES | OF THE | LAWS OF HOLLAND, | BY | JOHANNES VAN DER LINDEN, LL.D., | AND JUDGE OF THE COURT OF FIRST INSTANCE AT AMSTERDAM. | [thin rule] | AMSTERDAM: | PRINTED IN THE YEAR 1806, | AND NOW TRANSLATED BY ORDER OF THE | RIGHT HONOURABLE | THE EARL OF BATHURST, | LATE | HIS MAJESTY'S PRINCIPAL SECRETARY OF STATE | FOR THE COLONIES, | BY J. HENRY, esq., | OF THE MIDDLE TEMPLE, BARRISTER AT LAW, | AND | SENIOR COMMISSIONER OF LEGAL INQUIRY INTO THE | ADMINISTRATION OF JUSTICE IN THE WEST | INDIAN AND SOUTH AMERICAN COLONIES. | [thin rule] | LONDON: | PRINTED FOR J. AND W. T. CLARKE, PORTUGAL STREET, | LINCOLN'S-INN-FIELDS; J. M. RICHARDSON, | CORNHILL; AND J. RIDGEWAY, PICCADILLY. | [thin rule] | 1828.

PAGINATION

i–xlviii 1–736.

CONTENTS

i half title, ii printer's imprint, iii title, iv blank, v–vii dedication to the Earl of Bathurst, viii blank, ix–xvi preface of the translator, xvii–xviii advertisement, xix–xx abbreviations, xxi–xxvii preface of the author to the reader, xxviii blank, xxix–xlviii contents, 1–697 text, 698 blank, 699–706 "Titles of the Roman Law from the Digest," 707–35 index, 736 blank.

REFERENCES

Hayes p. 153.

COPY DESCRIBED

MH: Neth 905 LIN

---

1. "Linden, Johannes van der," in *Chambers Biographical Dictionary,* ed. Melanie Parry, 6th ed. (Edinburgh: Chambers, 1997), 1135.

2. "Netherlands, Geography and Statistics of," *Encyclopaedia Americana; American Almanac and Repository of Useful Knowledge* (Boston: Gray and Bowen, 1852), 320 (the edition purchased for the White House Library; see entry 6); Rayback, *Millard Fillmore,* 322–26.

⌇

97. Lingard, John. *A History of England from the First Invasion by the Romans.* 5th ed. 8 vols. Paris: Baudry, 1840.

John Lingard's (1771–1851) *A History of England* (1819–30) remained a standard text on English history for Catholics into the twentieth century. It is a revisionist history that answered those scholars who proposed an English church wholly independent of Rome and asserted the "catholicity of the Anglo-Saxon church." Therefore, Lingard's *History* was controversial among Protestants, but once published in French, German, and Italian editions it garnered acclaim for Lingard throughout Europe. With proceeds from the earliest volumes he built a chapel next to the priest's house where he lived in Hornby. Lingard, himself a Catholic priest, wrote several other shorter historical and theological works, including prayers for use by his parishioners, an English translation of the Gospels, and a volume of catechistical instruction. The Little and Brown catalogue from April 1850 lists this edition in paper at $6.00 and in half morocco at $10.00. Given the price paid by the Executive Mansion, its copy may have been full calf or morocco.

105,133 voucher 5: Lingard's History of England 8 vols. $11.00.
Purchased from Charles Welford on December 13, 1850.
Roosevelt Catalogue: Lingard, John. *The History of England from the First Invasion by the Romans to the Accession of William and Mary in 1688.* Fifth edition. Paris, Baudry's European Library, 1840, 8 vols.

TITLE PAGE
A | HISTORY OF ENGLAND, | FROM THE FIRST | INVASION BY THE ROMANS. | BY | JOHN LINGARD, D. D. | [thin rule] | FIFTH EDITION | COMPLETE IN EIGHT VOLUMES. | [thin rule] | VOL. I. [II–VIII.] | [printer's ornament] | PARIS, | BAUDRY'S EUROPEAN LIBRARY, | 3, QUAI MALAQUAIS, NEAR THE PONT DES ARTS; | AND 9, RUE DU COQ, NEAR THE LOUVRE. | SOLD ALSO BY AMYOT, RUE DE LAPAIX; TRUCHY BOULEVARD DES ITALIENS; | GIRARD FRÈRES, RUE RICHELIEU; LEOPOLD MICHELSEN LEIPZIG; AND BY ALL | THE PRINCIPAL BOOKSELLERS ON THE CONTINENT. | [thin rule] | 1840.

PAGINATION
Vol. I. i–xvi 1–446.
Vol. II. i–x 1–376.
Vol. III. i–xii 1–380.
Vol. IV. i–x 1–406.
Vol. V. i–xii 1–388.
Vol. VI. i–xii 1–460.
Vol. VII. i–xii 1–462.
Vol. VIII. i–viii 405–8 ix–xii 1–404 409–12.

> *Notes.* Volume 1 includes a note stating the half title is missing in this set. Volume 5 has the half title. The pagination is given above as if the half title were present in all volumes. Volume 7 was not present in the DLC copy; therefore, its description is based on MH: KE 24746.

CONTENTS

Vol. I. i half title, ii printer's imprint, iii title, iv blank, v–viii preface, ix–xvi contents, 1–445 text, 446 notes.

Vol. II. i half title, ii printer's imprint, iii title, iv blank, v–x contents, 1–374 text, 375–76 notes.

Vol. III. i half title, ii printer's imprint, iii title, iv blank, v–xi contents, xii blank, 1–371 text, 372–80 notes.

Vol. IV. i half title, ii printer's imprint, iii title, iv blank, v–x contents, 1–388 text, 389–406 notes.

Vol. V. i half title, ii printer's imprint, iii title, iv blank, v–xi contents, xii blank, 1–353 text, 354–88 notes.

Vol. VI. i half title, ii printer's imprint, iii title, iv blank, v–xi contents, xii blank, 1–437 text, 438–60 notes.

Vol. VII. i half title, ii printer's imprint, iii title, iv blank, v–xii contents, 1–445 text 446–61 notes, 462 blank.

Vol. VIII. i half title, ii printer's imprint, iii title, iv blank, v–viii contents, 405–8 index, ix conclusion of contents, x blank, xi contents of appendix, xii blank, 1–282 text, 283–91 notes, 292 blank, 293–315 appendix, 316 blank, 317–411 index, 412 blank.

Note. Clearly a binding error occurred when part of the index was bound in with the preliminaries in volume 8. The two misbound leaves were probably printed on the same sheet of paper as the preliminaries with the intention that during binding, the sheet would be cut and these would be bound into their proper position at the rear of the book. It was a common practice to print other items with the preliminaries when they did not require an entire sheet of paper.

PLATES

Vol. I.

Portrait frontispiece of the Reverend John Lingard, from an original painting by James Ramsay, engraved by Hopwood.

REFERENCES

Hayes p. 149; Roosevelt p. 25; L and B 1850 p. 54.

COPY DESCRIBED

DLC: DA 30 L7 1840. *Leaf.* 210 × 127.
MH: KE 24746. Vol. 7 only. *Leaf.* 209 × 127.

∾

98. Locke, John. *Essay on Human Understanding.* **London: Tegg, [1828, 1841, 1846, or 1849].**

In the mid-nineteenth century John Locke (1632–1704) was regarded as one of the "most eminent philosophers and valuable writers of his age and country." Locke's *Essay on Human Understanding* (1690) was considered his greatest and most influential work for its rendering of empirical philosophy. While one critic predicted that it would "ever prove a valuable guide in the acquirement of the science of the human mind,"[1] another writer found the "true value" of Locke's *Essay on Human Understanding* in its "protest against objective philosophy," the philosophical perspective that had "prevailed alike among the ancients" and the scholastics.[2] Locke's subsequent work *Two Treaties on Government* (1690) was a favorite in revolutionary America, where statesmen often appealed to it in their constitutional debates.[3]

By 1850 there were numerous editions of the *Essay* available that the White House could have purchased. Based on price and the number of volumes, a London edition published by Tegg was most likely selected. Tegg may be the only publisher who issued this work in one volume between 1828 and 1850, and he did so in four different years, 1828, 1841, 1846, and 1849. The *London* and *British* catalogues listed the Tegg edition as selling for 7s. to 9s., or between $1.70 and $2.20, which would place it in the proper price range for the Executive Mansion's purchase. Roorbach recorded a Philadelphia edition from Kay and Brothers for $2.00, which is also a possibility for this acquisition.

105,133 voucher 5: Locke's Human Understanding $2.00.
Purchased from Charles Welford on December 13, 1850.

REFERENCES
cf. *LC 1816–1851* p. 341; Roorbach p. 330; cf. Fillmore ca. 1858 p. 6; cf. Fillmore 1861 p. 14.

---

1. "Locke, John," *Encyclopaedia Americana*, 36–38.
2. James Morell as summarized in "An Historical and Critical View of the Speculative Philosophy," *The North American Review (1821–1940)*, April 1849, available at *APS Online*, http://www.proquest.com/products_pq/descriptions/aps.shtml.
3. "Locke, John."

～

99. Lockhart, John Gibson. *Memoirs of the Life of Sir Walter Scott.* 4 vols. Paris: Baudry, 1838.

John Gibson Lockhart's *Memoirs of the Life of Sir Walter Scott* was highly regarded from the moment that it was first published, and its stature as a biography was often compared to that of Boswell's *Life of Johnson*. Lockhart (1794–1854), Sir Walter Scott's son-in-law, also published numerous articles in *Blackwood's Edinburgh Magazine*, wrote several novels, and edited the *Quarterly Review*. Although modern critics have called his vision of Scott idealized and pointed out inaccuracies in the *Memoirs*, Lockhart tried to present Scott by the heroic light in which his contemporaries held him. Maria Edgeworth commended the *Memoirs*, writing to Lockhart, "We thought it impossible any publication could raise Sir Walter Scott's talents or character in public opinion or in private opinion more especially. And yet you certainly have done it without one word of puff or exaggeration or even full-faced eulogy." Scott's popularity in both Great Britain and America cannot be overstated. The American public's esteem for Scott shines through the literary notices for these memoirs. One author referred to Scott as "one who has charmed this age with his magic pen," and another, announcing the completion of the *Memoirs*, dubbed Scott "the Bard of Avon." In addition to this biography, the Executive Mansion purchased Scott's Waverley Novels in twenty volumes.[1]

105,133 voucher 2: Lockharts Scott 4 vols. $5.00.
Purchased from Little and Brown on December 30, 1850.
Roosevelt Catalogue: Lockhart, John Gibson. *Memoirs of the Life of Sir Walter Scott.* Paris, Baudry's European Library, 1838, 4 vols.

TITLE PAGE

MEMOIRS | OF THE | LIFE OF SIR WALTER SCOTT. | BY J. G. LOCKHART, ESQ., | HIS SON-IN-LAW AND LITERARY EXECUTOR. | IN FOUR VOLUMES. | VOL. I. [II–IV] | [Baudry's publisher's ornament] | PARIS, | BAUDRY'S EUROPEAN LIBRARY, | RUE DU COQ, NEAR THE LOUVRE. | SOLD ALSO BY AMYOT, RUE DE LA PAIX; TRUCHY, BOULEVARD DES ITALIENS; | THEOPHILE BARROIS, JUN., RUE RICHELIEU; HEIDELOFF AND CAMPE, | RUE VIVIENNE; AND BY ALL THE PRINCIPAL BOOKSELLERS ON | THE CONTINENT. | [thin rule] | 1838.

PAGINATION

Vol. I. [4] vii–viii i–iv 1–452.

Vol. II. [2] i–iv 1–408.

Vol. III. [2] i–iv 1–370.

Vol. IV. [2] i–viii 1–378.

CONTENTS

Vol. I. [1] title, [2]blank, [3] Dedication to John Bacon Saurey Morritt, of Rokeby Park, Esq., [4] blank, vii–viii preface, i–iii contents, iv blank, 1–452 text.

Vol. II. [1] title, [2] blank, i–iv contents, 1–402 text, 403–8 appendix "The Durham Garland.—In Three Parts."

Vol. III. [1] title, [2] blank, i–iii contents, iv blank, 1–370 text.

Vol. IV. [1] title, [2] blank, i–iv contents, v–viii preface, 1–349 text, 350 blank, 351–54 appendix, "Chronological List of the Publications of Sir Walter Scott," 355–78 index of proper names.

REFERENCES

Hayes p. 149; Roosevelt p. 26.

COPY DESCRIBED

DLC: PR 5332 L6 1838. *Leaf.* 210 × 130.

---

1. See entry 18 for Boswell's *Life of Johnson;* Edgeworth qtd. in Thomas C. Richardson, "Lockhart, John Gibson (1794–1854)," *ODNB;* "The Turf-Seat Shade, Or Notice of Books," *Southern Rose (1835–1839),* December 9, 1837, *The Southern Literary Journal and Magazine of Arts (1835–1838),* May 1838, and "Literary Review." *The Ladies' Companion, a Monthly Magazine; Devoted to Literature,* June 1838, all available at *APS Online,* http://www.proquest.com/products_pq/descriptions/aps.shtml. See entries 50 for Edgeworth, 149 for Scott, and 17 for *Blackwood's Magazine.*

≈

100. Lolme, Jean Louis de. *The Rise and Progress of the English Constitution.* Ed. A. J. Stephens. 2 vols. London: Parker, 1838.

Jean Louis de Lolme's *Rise and Progress of the English Constitution* (1771) remained the authoritative work on the English constitution for several decades. In the United States, both supporters and opponents to the Federal Constitution cited it. In 1768 De Lolme (1741–1806) moved from Geneva to London, where he made a lifelong study of the English government. He began his work *The English Constitution* the following year in 1769. Originally written in French and published in the Netherlands in 1771, it was translated into English and published in London in 1775 where it became a commercial success, reaching a fourth edition by 1784. Curiously, a passage from the 1775 London edition of de Lolme's work on the constitution appeared in the earlier preface to the Junius letters, which was written as early as 1771 and published in 1772. Some conjectured that de Lolme was Junius; Thomas Busby even wrote a pamphlet setting forth this argument.[1]

105,133 voucher 6: Stephen's English Constitution 2 vols. $4.50.
Roosevelt Catalogue: Lolme, Jean Louis de. *The Rise and Progress of the English Constitution: With an Historical and Legal Introduction, and Notes by A. J. Stephens.* London, John W. Parker, 1838, 2 vols.

TITLE PAGE
THE | RISE AND PROGRESS | OF THE | ENGLISH CONSTITUTION: | THE TREATISE OF | J. L. DE LOLME, LL. D. | WITH AN | HISTORICAL AND LEGAL INTRODUCTION, AND NOTES, | BY | A. J. STEPHENS, M. A., F.R.S., | *BARRISTER-AT-LAW.* | IN TWO VOLUMES, | VOL. I. [II.] | LONDON: | JOHN W. PARKER, WEST STRAND. | M.DCCC.XXXVIII.

PAGINATION
Vol. I. i–clxxxiv 1–488.
Vol. II. [2] 489–1148.

CONTENTS
Vol. I. i title, ii blank, iii dedication to the Honourable Sir Edward Hall Alderson, Knight, iv blank, v–xvi preface, xvii–xxviii advertisement, xxix–xxxiii contents of volume 1, xxxiv blank, xxxv–xxxviii contents of volume 2, xxxix–xliv statutes cited, xlv–xlvi cases cited, xlvii–clxxxi index, clxxxii errata and corrigenda, clxxxiii 'Genealogical Tables', clxxxiv lines of descent and contractions, 1–487 text, 488 blank.
Vol. II. [1] title, [2] blank, 489 'THE RISE AND PROGRESS | OF THE | ENGLISH CONSTITUTION.', 490 'THE TREATISE OF DE LOLME.', 491–1139 text, 1140 printer's imprint, 1141–48 advertisement for books published by John Parker in the Strand.

PLATES
Vol. I.
Facing 3, Table I. "Saxon and Danish Kings."
Facing 19, Table II. "Norman Kings of England."
Facing 44, Table III. "The House of Plantagenet."
Facing 129, Table IV. "The Line of Lancaster."
Facing 150, Table V. "The Line of York."
Facing 151, Table VI. "The House of Tudor."
Facing 312, Table VII. "House of Stuart and Brunswick."
Facing 312 following Table VII, Table VIII. "House of Stuart and Brunswick continued."
Vol. II.
None.

REFERENCES
Hayes p. 48; Roosevelt p. 26; cf. Putnam p. 37; Harvard p. 69.

COPY DESCRIBED
DLC: JN 117 l7 1838. *Leaf.* 215 × 130.

---

1. On Junius, see entry 90. G. P. Macdonell, "Lolme, John Louis de (1741–1806)," rev. Adam I. P. Smith, *ODNB.*

∽

101. Lyell, Charles. *Principles of Geology.* 8th ed. London: Murray, 1850.

By 1850 Charles Lyell's *Principles of Geology* (1830) was considered the authoritative work on the subject and referred to as "an encyclopædia of geology." Upon publication Lyell's arguments stirred controversy among two groups: geologists, who found modern causes inadequate for understanding past changes in the earth; and social groups, who treated the biblical narrative as scientifically accurate. Despite these objections, *Principles* received favorable reviews, and at least one reviewer was able to reconcile Lyell's theory with biblical interpretations.[1]

The publication history of *Principles* is not straightforward. Lyell (1797–1875) published the first volume in 1830, the second in 1832, and the third in 1833. By the time the third volume reached the press in 1833, the first two had already gone into second editions. Lyell continued to update and revise his work with each subsequent edition. With the sixth edition in 1840, he divided his work into two separate parts and published the first volume as *Principles of Geology* and the latter two as *Elements of Geology.* The White House purchased only *Principles* for the new library, where it stood on the shelves alongside other standard scientific texts of the day—Asa Gray's *Botanical Text-book,* Georges Cuvier's *Animal Kingdom,* and John F. W. Herschel's *Outlines of Astronomy.*[2]

105,133 voucher 5: Lyell's Geology $3.50.
Purchased from Charles Welford on December 13, 1850.
Hayes Catalogue: Lyell, Sir C. *Principles of Geology.* London, 1850. 8°

TITLE PAGE
PRINCIPLES | OF | GEOLOGY; | OR, | THE MODERN CHANGES OF THE EARTH AND | ITS INHABITANTS | CONSIDERED AS ILLUSTRATIVE GEOLOGY. | BY SIR CHARLES LYELL, M. A. F.R.S. | PRESIDENT OF THE GEOLOGICAL SOCIETY OF LONDON; | AUTHOR OF "A MANUAL OF ELEMENTARY GEOLOGY," "TRAVELS IN | NORTH AMERICA," "A SECOND VISIT TO THE UNITED STATES," | ETC. ETC.| [thin rule] | *EIGHTH AND ENTIRELY REVISED EDITION.* | Illustrated with Maps, Plates, and Woodcuts. [black letter] | LONDON: | JOHN MURRAY, ALBEMARLE STREET. | 1850.

PAGINATION
i–xvi 1–812.

CONTENTS

i title page, ii epigraphs, iii–v preface to the eighth edition, vi list of other works by Sir Charles Lyell, vii–xvi contents (xvi includes list of plates), 1–774 text, 775–811 glossary, 812 printer's imprint.

PLATES

Frontispiece, "View of the Temple of Serapis at Puzzuoli, in 1836."

Facing 110, "Map shewing the present unequal distribution of land and water on the surface of the globe."

Facing 111, folding "Map shewing the position of land and sea which might produce the extremes of heat and cold in the climates of the globe."

Facing 121, folding "Map shewing the extent of surface in Europe which has been covered by the sea since the commencement of the Eocene period."

Facing 223, "Boulders drifted by ice on shores of the St. Lawrence, view taken by Lieut. Bowen, from the N. E., in the Spring of 1835, at Richelieu Rapid, lat. 46. N."

Facing 312, folding map showing the "Line of coast from Ostend to Rugen in which changes have been observed during the historical period."

Facing 337, folding map showing the "Volcanic Band, of the Molucca, and Sunda Islands. Reduced from Maps of Leopold Von Buch," signed J. Gardner in lower right.

Facing 345, plate 7, fig. 1 "Island of Procida," and "Island of Ischia Coast of Misenum"; fig. 2, "Volcanic district of Naples."

Facing 387, "View looking up the Val del Bove, Etna."

Facing 389, "View of the Val del Bove, Etna as seen from above, or from the crater of 1819."

Facing 441, "Map of the Runn of Cutch and Lake of Sindree by Capt. A Burnes."

Facing 442, "Sindree on the Eastern branch of the Indus since submerged by the earthquake of 1819," signed in lower left "Drawn by W. Purser from a sketch by Capt. Grindlay in 1808" and lower right, "Engraved by E. Finden."

BINDING

Front board. 230 × 145 med. green ribbed cloth blind-stamped quadruple-ruled frame with gilt-stamped vignette from "View of the Temple of Serapis at Puzzuoli, in 1836." *Back board.* Blind-stamped quadruple ruled frame with decorative blind stamp in center. *Spine.* Blind-stamped with four bands; gilt stamped in the first panel 'LYELL'S | PRINCIPLES | OF | GEOLOGY.'; blind-stamped decoration in the second panel, and gilt stamped in the third panel, 'LONDON | JOHN MURRAY'. *Endpapers.* Off-white.

> *Note.* The copy described had been rebound in a library binding; therefore the binding description is based on another copy of the same edition: DLC QE26 L96 1850 Batchelder Collection. There is a foil bookseller's stamp from Taylor and Maury on the front pastedown. It identifies their location as "Penn. Ave near 9th St., Washington City."

REFERENCES

Hayes p. 150; cf. Putnam p. 83 and 41-s; cf. L and B 1852 p. 4; cf. *LC 1816–1851* p. 348; cf. Fillmore 1861 p. 84.

COPY DESCRIBED

DLC: QE 26 L96. *Leaf.* 220 × 137.

---

1. "Principles of Geology," *The Museum of Foreign Literature, Science, and Art (1822–1842)*, June 1832, and "Lyell's Geology," *The Literary World (1847–1853)*, March 29, 1851, both available at *APS Online*, http:// www.proquest.com/products_pq/descriptions/aps.shtml.

2. See entries 62 for Gray, 44 for Cuvier, and 77 for Herschel.

◇

102. Macaulay, Thomas Babington. *History of England.* 2 vols. New York: Harper, 1849.

Thomas Babington Macaulay's *History of England* became a bestseller immediately upon the publication of its first two volumes in 1848. These volumes went into two editions and sold six thousand copies in under three months. Both were available in the United States by the end January of 1849 from Harper, who paid Macaulay a hundred guineas per volume. The next two volumes did not appear until 1855, with the fifth and final volume following in 1856. Therefore, only the first two volumes were available to be purchased for the White House Library in 1850.[1]

Notices and reviews in American periodicals testify to the popularity of Macaulay's *History* in the United States. One reviewer predicted it would "create as great a stir as any book published within the last twenty years," while another proclaimed, "All novel-readers have become historical students. The romance of fiction has less attraction, at present, than the romance of fact; and we should not be astonished if the general absorption of society in one book alone, foreclosed, even for some weeks, the demand for the last productions of Dumas and James." The only negative review of the *History* presently located has nothing to do with Macaulay's handling of the subject, but rather Harper's treatment of the text. Its writer complained that Harper had Americanized Macaulay's spelling according to the standards of the late Noah Webster.[2]

The Hayes Catalogue recorded an 1857 New York edition, which must have been a replacement copy for the edition originally purchased. In 1850 the Fillmores probably selected the edition from Harper and Brothers dated 1849. It was the most widely advertised edition of the day, and the Harper Book List from 1853 advertised it in half calf for $1.25 per volume, which closely accords with the $2.25 for two volumes in half calf specified on the voucher. Putnam offered the same edition in two volumes, clothbound for $1.50. The London edition from Longman was also available and was advertised by both Little and Brown and Putnam in their catalogues. However, it sold for $5.50, a price too high to account for this purchase. Other American editions were available and included one from Butler and Company in Philadelphia, dated 1849 and listed for $2.00; one from Phillips in Boston, also dated 1849 and priced at $1.25; one from Applegate and Co., priced at $1.75; and another from Truman in Cincinnati that sold for $1.75.[3]

105,133 voucher 5: Macauley's History England 2 vols. hf. clf. $2.25.
Purchased from Charles Welford on December 13, 1850.

REFERENCES

cf. Hayes p. 163; cf. Putnam p. 83; L and B 1850 p. 57; cf. Roorbach p. 337; cf. Fillmore Packing Lists p. 8; cf. Fillmore ca. 1858 p. 42; cf. Fillmore 1861 p. 62.

1. *Grahame's American Monthly Magazine of Literature, Art, and Fashion (1844–1858)*, December 1848, available at *APS Online*, http://www.proquest.com/products_pq/descriptions/aps.shtml; William Thomas, "Macaulay, Thomas Babbington, Baron Macaulay (1800–1859)," *ODNB*.

2. *Grahame's American Monthly Magazine of Literature, Art, and Fashion (1844–1858)*, December 1848, *The Universalist Quarterly and General Review (1844–1891)*, January 1849, and *Littel's Living Age (1844–1896)*, February 17, 1849; for other reviews of Macaulay's *History* see Literary *World (1847–1853)*, January 13, 1849,and *Literary World (1847–1853)*, January 27, 1849. All these articles are available at *APS Online*, http://www.proquest.com/products_pq/descriptions/aps.shtml. See entry 186 for Noah Webster.

3. See Putnam, *Book Buyer's Manual*, 83, and Roorbach, *Bibliotheca Americana*, 337, for prices.

⌖

103. McCullagh, W. Torrens. *The Industrial History of Free Nations.* 2 vols. London: Chapman and Hall, 1846.

William Torrens McCullagh's (1813–94) *The Industrial History of Free Nations* (1846) stood on the White House shelves alongside a number of other works related to public economy, one of Fillmore's chief concerns as president. McCullagh was an indefatigable social reformer who served twenty years in parliament, was a member of the Anti-Corn Law League, and served on the special commission on relief of the Irish poor. In *The Industrial History* he attempted to prove that "world progress had been achieved only by the industry of urban, non-feudal peoples and that the corn laws were restrictive of independence and self-culture."[1] While volume 1 of McCullagh's book focuses on the industrial history of Greece, volume 2 delineates the industrial history of the Dutch.

105,133 voucher 5: McCulloughs Industrial History Free Nations $4.50.
Purchased from Charles Welford on December 13, 1850.
Hayes Catalogue: McCullagh, W. T. *Industrial History of Free Nations.* 2 vols. London, 1846, 8°.

TITLE PAGE
THE | INDUSTRIAL HISTORY | OF | FREE NATIONS, | CONSIDERED IN RELATION TO | THEIR DOMESTIC INSTITUTIONS AND | EXTERNAL POLICY. | BY | W. TORRENS McCULLAGH. | IN TWO VOLUMES. | VOL. I. [II.] | LONDON: | CHAPMAN AND HALL, 186 STRAND. | [thin rule] | MDCCCXLVI.

PAGINATION
Vol. I. [4] vii–xviii 1–336.
Vol. II. [2] v–xviii 1–398.

CONTENTS
Vol. I. [1] title, [2] blank, [3] dedication to the Marquis of Lansdowne, [4] blank, vii–xviii contents, 1–332 text, 333–34 appendix, "First Commercial Treaty between the Romans and Carthaginians," 335–36 "Second Commercial Treaty between the Romans and the Carthaginians."

Vol. II. [*1*] title, [*2*] blank, v–xviii contents, 1–372 text, 373–76 appendix, 377–97 index, 398 blank.

REFERENCES
Hayes p. 163; cf. Putnam p. 84 (spells name MacCullagh); cf. *LC 1816–1851* p. 351.

COPY DESCRIBED
DLC: HC21 T69 Copy 1. *Leaf.* 213 × 130.

---

1. MacDonagh, "Torrens, (William) Torrens McCullagh (1813–1894)," rev. Matthew Lee, *ODNB*.

⁓

104. McCulloch, John Ramsay. *A Dictionary, Practical, Theoretical, and Historical of Commerce and Commercial Navigation.* Ed. Henry Vethake, LL.D. 2 vols. Philadelphia: Carey and Hart, 1849.

John Ramsay McCulloch (1789–1864) designed *A Dictionary, Practical, Theoretical, and Historical of Commerce and Commercial Navigation* (1832) as a "*vade mecum*" for "merchants, traders, ship-owners, and ship-masters," to assist them in conducting every detail of their respective businesses (1:v). It includes articles, alphabetically arranged, on all aspects of commerce such as manner and place of production, commercial cities, harbors, port regulations, duties, insurance, exchanges, and currency. The edition purchased for the White House Library was reprinted from the latest English edition, to which the editor added information, where appropriate, relating specifically to commerce in the United States. Contemporary reviews lauded the *Dictionary;* one even called it "one of the most valuable reference works on commercial affairs, anywhere to be found."[1]

McCulloch was arguably the first professional economist. He served as the principle economic writer for the *Edinburgh Review* for twenty years, wrote *Principles of Political Economy with a Sketch of the Rise and Progress of the Science* (1825), and edited editions of Adam Smith's *Wealth of Nations* (1828) as well as David Ricardo's works (1845). He also compiled three statistical reference books that reached a substantially larger audience and brought him greater profits than his other publications. This *Dictionary* proved the most financially rewarding. In 1828 he accepted the chair of political economy at the University of London, a post he held until 1837.[2]

McCullochs Com¹ Dictionary 2 vols. $7.50.
Purchased from Charles Welford on December 13, 1850.
Hayes Catalogue: Mc Culloch, J. R. *Dictionary of Commerce and Commercial Navigation.* 2 vols. Philadelphia, 1849, 8°.

TITLE PAGE
A DICTIONARY, | PRACTICAL, THEORETICAL, AND HISTORICAL, | OF | COMMERCE AND COMMERCIAL NAVIGATION. | BY J. R. M'CULLOCH, ESQ. | EDITED BY HENRY VETHAKE, LL.D., | ONE OF THE PROFESSORS IN THE UNIVERSITY OF PENNSYLVANIA; MEMBER OF THE AMERICAN | PHILOSOPHICAL SOCIETY; AUTHOR OF A TREATISE ON POLITICAL ECONOMY,

ETC. | WITH AN APPENDIX CONTAINING | THE NEW TARIFF OF 1846, | TOGETHER WITH | THE TARIFF OF 1842, | REDUCED TO AD VALOREM RATES AS FAR AS PRACTICABLE. | ALSO, | THE SUB-TREASURY, WAREHOUSING, AND | THE CANADIAN TRANSIT BILLS, OF 1846. | LIKEWISE, | THE NEW BRITISH TARIFF | AS AMENDED BY THE PASSAGE OF THE NEW CORN LAW AND SUGAR DUTIES; | WITH | A TABLE OF ALL FOREIGN GOLD AND SILVER COIN, | REDUCED TO FEDERAL CURRENCY, &c. &c. &c. | IN TWO VOLUMES.—VOL. I. [II.] | PHILADELPHIA: | CAREY AND HART. | 1849.

PAGINATION

Vol. I. i–xii 1–768.

Vol. II. 1–804 1–68.

CONTENTS

Vol. I. i title, ii copyright statement and printer's imprint, iii preface of the American editor, iv blank, v–ix "extracts from the preface to the first edition," ix–xi "extracts from the preface to the second edition," xii "advertisement to the last English edition," 1–767 text, 768 blank.

Vol. II. 1 title, 2 copyright statement and printer's imprint, 3–764 text, 765–803 supplement, 804 blank, 1 title 'THE | REVENUE BOOK: | THE NEW TARIFF OF 1846, | TOGETHER WITH | The Tariff of 1842 [black letter] | Reduced to ad valorem rates as far as practicable. | ALSO, | THE SUB-TREASURY, WAREHOUSING, AND | CANADIAN TRANSIT BILLS, OF 1846, | AND THE ACT ALLOWING DRAWBACK ON GOODS EXPORTED TO | SANTA FE, AND OTHER PLACES, PASSED IN 1845. | WITH THE | Treasury Circulars in Relation thereto. | LIKEWISE, | THE NEW BRITISH TARIFF, | AS AMENDED BY THE PASSAGE OF THE NEW CORN LAWS AND SUGAR DUTIES, AT | THE LATE SESSION OF PARLIAMENT; | TOGETHER WITH | A CONDENSED CAMBIST, | OR TABLE OF ALL FOREIGN GOLD AND SILVER COINS, REDUCED TO FEDERAL | CURRENCY. | COMPILED FROM THE MOST AUTHENTIC SOURCES, | BY A. JONES. | [swelled rule] | New York: [black letter] | PUBLISHED BY BELL & GOULD, 158 NASSAU STREET, | BOOKSELLERS AND STATIONERS, | PRINTERS AND LAW BLANK PUBLISHERS, | [thin rule] | 1847.', 2 printer's imprint and copyright statement, 3–67 text, 68 blank.

REFERENCES

Hayes p. 163; cf. Roorbach p. 356; cf. Putnam p. 83; cf. L and B 1853 p. 43; cf. *LC 1816–1851* p. 351; cf. Fillmore Packing Lists p. 9; cf. Fillmore ca. 1858 p. 15; cf. Fillmore 1861 p. 56.

COPY DESCRIBED

CtY: Nf30 832me.

---

1. "Literary Intelligence," *Southern Literary Messenger (1834–1845)*, October 1841, and *DeBow's Review of the Southern and Western States. Devoted to Commerce*, April 1851, both available at *APS Online*, http://www .proquest.com/products_pq/descriptions/aps.shtml.

2. McCulloch's edition of *Wealth of Nations* was purchased for the first White House Library; see entry 154.

**105. MacGregor, John. *Commercial Statistics*. 5 vols. London: Whittaker and Co., 1847.

106. ———. *Progress of America to 1846*. 2 vols. London: Whittaker and Co., 1847.

John MacGregor (1797–1857), civil servant and free trader, published more than thirty books dealing with travel, commerce, and history, many of which were considered essential reference sources for the period. *Commercial Statistics* provided "a comparative view of the natural resources, advantages, capabilities, and power" of Europe, Africa, and "most of Asia." It also included the "commercial treaties which regulate the trade and navigation between the United Kingdom and other nations" as well as tariffs and port, and other local charges related to trade and shipping.[1]

Progress of America complemented *Commercial Statistics* by focusing on the Americas. One reviewer called it "the most valuable store of facts which has ever been collected respecting the commercial and social history of the New Continent." Volume 1 recounts the history of the discovery of North America, along with its more recent political events, and treats the history and geography of British America, Brazil, and Spanish America separately. Volume 2 is devoted entirely to the statistics of the United States.[2] Fillmore's concern with international trade and commerce would have made these two works particularly relevant to the president and his administration.

The copy of *Commercial Statistics* described here is one of the ten titles that survive from the original White House Library. Volumes 2 and 4 have the inscription "Executive Mansion 1850" on their front pastedowns and also bear the only example that has been found of an Executive Mansion bookplate (see figure 8). The card of General Orville E. Babcock was found in volume 4 between pages 26 and 27, on which import duties and port charges for Cuba are discussed. Babcock served with President Ulysses S. Grant (1869–77) during the Civil War as a general and was selected by Grant to deliver the terms of surrender to Robert E. Lee. Later, in 1869, while serving as Grant's private secretary in the White House, Babcock visited Santo Domingo in relation to Grant's attempt to annex the island. Babcock's political career came to an end in 1875 when a grand jury indicted him along with a number of other men for "conspiracy to defraud the revenue" in a scandal known as the Whiskey Ring. He may have consulted MacGregor's book for some reason related to his Caribbean travels.[3]

109,399 voucher 4: McGregor's Coml Statistics [te] 5 vol. $2.04.

Purchased from Franck Taylor on February 12, 1853.

105,133 voucher 5: McGregor's Progress America 2 vols. $10.50.

Purchased from Charles Welford on December 13, 1850.

Hayes Catalogue: Macgregor, J. Commercial Statistics of All Nations. 5 vols. London, 1847–50. 8°

———. Progress of America to 1846 v. 1 London, 1847. 8°

> *Note.* A parenthetical note beneath the entry for *Commercial Statistics* on the voucher reads "(clearing 14.96 due in [or on] same)." It is unclear exactly what this note means; it is possible that Taylor owed Fillmore $14.96 and applied it to the purchase of this book. MacGregor's *Commercial Statistics* in five volumes cost £7 10s. according to the London Catalogue, which would have been almost $27.00. Furthermore, $2.04 is an unusually low price to pay for a five-volume work; $17.00 would be a more likely sum, but still low for this title. It is tempting to assume that Fillmore purchased

only volume 5, if one interprets the "5 vol." in the voucher to mean the fifth volume; however, this is one of the ten titles that survives from the original Executive Mansion collection, and this copy is inscribed in volumes 2 and 4 "Executive Mansion February 14, 1853." "Price $1.25" is also written on the front pastedown of volumes 2 and 4, which further complicates this question. If this price was written by Taylor, the bookseller from whom it was acquired, then he discounted at least these two volumes; yet the total of $2.50 still does not accord with the price on the voucher.[4]

Commercial Statistics.

TITLE PAGE

COMMERCIAL STATISTICS. | A DIGEST | OF THE | PRODUCTIVE RESOURCES, COMMERCIAL LEGISLATION, | CUSTOMS TARIFFS, | NAVIGATION, PORT, AND QUARANTINE LAWS, AND CHARGES, | SHIPPING, IMPORTS AND EXPORTS, | AND | THE MONIES, WEIGHTS, AND MEASURES OF | ALL NATIONS. | INCLUDING ALL | British Commercial Treaties with Foreign States. [black letter] | COLLECTED FROM AUTHENTIC RECORDS, AND CONSOLIDATED WITH ESPECIAL REFERENCE TO | BRITISH AND FOREIGN PRODUCTS, TRADE, AND NAVIGATION. | BY JOHN MACGREGOR, | AUTHOR OF "BRITISH AMERICA," AND ONE OF THE JOINT SECRETARIES OF THE BOARD OF TRADE. | IN FOUR VOLUMES. | VOL. I. [II–V.] | LONDON:—WHITTAKER AND CO., | AVE-MARIA LANE. | 1847.

    Note. The title page of volume 2 is missing.

Vol. IV.

'. . . BY JOHN MACGREGOR, M.P., | LATE SECRETARY OF THE BOARD OF TRADE; AUTHOR OF "THE PROGRESS OF AMERICA, FROM THE | DISCOVERY BY COLUMBUS TO THE YEAR 1847." | . . . | 1848.'

Vol. V.

'. . . | BY JOHN MACGREGOR, M.P., | LATE SECRETARY OF THE BOARD OF TRADE. | IN FIVE VOLUMES. | VOL. V. | . . . | 1850.'

PAGINATION

Vol. I. i–xx 1–1282 1–8.

Vol. II. i–xii 1–1196.

Vol. III. i–x 1–1147 1146–1396.

Vol. IV. i–viii 1–1036.

Vol. V. i–viii 1–400 1–222.

    Note. Volumes 2, 3, and 4 are mostly unopened.

CONTENTS

Vol. I. i title, ii printer's imprint, iii dedication to Queen Victoria, iv blank, v–x preface, xi–xix contents, xx blank, 1–1282 text, 1–7 supplement, 8 errata.

Vol. II. i title, ii printer's imprint, iii–xii contents, 1–1195 text, 1196 blank.

Vol. III. i title, ii printer's imprint, iii–ix contents, x blank, 1–1395 text, 1396 blank.

Vol. IV. i title, ii printer's imprint, iii–viii contents, 1–1036 text.

Vol. V. i title, ii "summary of the contents of the five volumes," iii–iv contents, v–vii contents of supplements, viii blank, 1–399 text, 400 blank, 1–221 supplements, 222 blank.

> *Note.* Since the title page is missing from volume 2, the content for pages i–ii has been inferred.

BINDING

Front and back board. 262 × 165 med. green cloth with blind-stamped decorative frame. *Spine.* Six panels blind stamped, gilt stamped in second and third panels 'MACGREGOR'S | COMMERCIAL | STATISTICS | [thin rule] | VOL. II. [III–IV] | OTTOMAN EMPIRE | GREECE. AFRICAN STATES. | RUSSIAN EMPIRE. | SWEDEN AND NORWAY. | SPAIN AND PORTUGAL.' *Endpapers.* Yellow.

Vol. III. '. . . AMERICA. | SPANISH AMERICAN REPUBLICS | CENTRAL & SOUTH AMERICA. | SPANISH REPUBLICS | OF SOUTH AMERICA.'

Vol. IV. '. . . HAYTI AND | FOREIGN WEST INDIES. | BRAZILS. | ORIENTAL COMMERCE.'

> *Note.* Volumes 1 and 5 have been rebound in Library of Congress buckram bindings.

MARKS OF OWNERSHIP

Volumes 2 and 4 have "Executive Mansion, February 14th 1853" inscribed on the front pastedown, with "E Shelf no. 17" written below in pencil. These two volumes also have an Executive Mansion bookplate with the same shelf mark.

REFERENCES

Hayes p. 163; cf. Putnam p. 84; cf. L and B 1850[5] p. 57; cf. *LC 1816–1851* p. 353.

COPY DESCRIBED

DLC: Volumes I–IV HF 1001 M25 1847; Volume V HF 1001 M25 1850. *Leaf.* 248 × 165.

Progress of America.

TITLE PAGE

THE | PROGRESS OF AMERICA, | FROM THE | DISCOVERY BY COLUMBUS TO THE YEAR 1846. | BY JOHN MAGREGOR, | SECRETARY TO THE BOARD OF TRADE; AUTHOR OF "COMMERCIAL | STATISTICS," &c. &c. | [thin rule] | VOL. I. [II.] | HISTORICAL AND STATISTICAL. | [thin rule] | LONDON: | WHITTAKER AND CO., AVE MARIA-LANE. | [thin rule] | 1847.

> *Note.* In volume 2 the line after the volume number reads 'GEOGRAPHICAL AND STATISTICAL.'

PAGINATION

Vol. I. [4] i–vi v* vi* vii–xii 1–1520.

Vol. II. i–viii 1–1334 1–84.

CONTENTS

Vol. I. [1] title, [2] blank, [3] dedication to Lord John Russell, First Lord of the Treasury, [4] blank, i–vi* introduction, vii–xii contents, 1–1520 text.

Vol. II. i title, ii printer's imprint, iii–viii contents, 1–1334 text, 1–84 supplement.

Note. Some leaves are missing from the preliminaries of volume 1 in DLC: E 18 M14; therefore, the contents statement for volume 1 has been written using DLC: 7416 Toner Collection E 18 M14.

BINDING

Front and back board. 258 × 165 med. green ribbed cloth with blind-stamped decorative frame. *Spine.* '[blind-stamped rule] | [blind-stamped double rule] | [gilt stamped] THE | PROGRESS OF AMERICA. | BY | JOHN MACGREGOR. [thin rule] | VOL. I. [II.] | [blind-stamped double rule] | [blind-stamped double rule] | [blind-stamped double rule] | [blind-stamped double rule]' *Endpapers.* Pale yellow.

    Note. Volume 2 has a blind-stamped diamond shaped decoration in the center of the frame of the front and back boards.

REFERENCES

Hayes p. 163; cf. Putnam p. 84; L and B 1853 p. 43; cf. *LC 1816–1851* p. 353.

COPY DESCRIBED

DLC: E 18 M14.

DLC: 7416 Toner Collection E 18 M14 (binding and contents for volume 1 only). *Leaf.* 235 × 153.

---

    1. "MacGregor's Commercial Statistics," *The Eclectic Magazine of Foreign Literature (1844–1898),* March 1845, available at *APS Online,* http://www.proquest.com/products_pq/descriptions/aps.shtml.

    2. "Review 2—No Title," *Littell's Living Age (1844–1896),* November 27, 1847, available at *APS Online,* http://www.proquest.com/products_pq/descriptions/aps.shtml.

    3. It is also possible that someone other than Babcock placed his card in this book.

    4. I am grateful to Elizabeth Falsey, Reader Service Librarian, and Susan Halpert, Reference Librarian, at the Houghton Library and to Mark Dimunation, Chief of Rare Book and Special Collections at the Library of Congress, for trying to help decipher this puzzling note on the voucher.

    5. This catalogue lists volume 4 only in cloth for $10.00.

∽

107. Machiavelli, Niccolò. *The History of Florence with the Prince.* London: Bohn, 1851.

Niccolò Machiavelli's (1469–1527) *The History of Florence* (1526) stands as one of the earliest historical works of modern times. Beginning with the year 1215, he chronicles Florentine history through the year 1492, concluding with the death of Lorenzo de' Medici. By the nineteenth century Machiavelli's reputation had suffered from a prevailing misunderstanding of the political philosophy that he formulated in *The Prince* (1513). American writers attempted to rehabilitate his reputation. While the *Encyclopaedia Americana* maintained that few men have shown as truly a civic spirit as Machiavelli, the *Yale Literary Magazine* called him no friend of "tyranny or oppression." Writers for both publications assert that he has been misjudged and unfairly cast as an advocate and perpetuator of despotism. Other nineteenth-century American periodicals regarded him as a political genius who championed republicanism and democratic principles. One even named him as the unforgiving enemy of all kinds of tyranny, and the true friend of the people's rights."[1]

    Although the voucher entry provides minimal information, *The History of Florence* is the only title by Machiavelli published in English between 1820 and 1851. While there were two editions, one from Henry G. Bohn in London and another from Paine and Burgess in

New York, Paine and Burgess's edition may be ruled out because it was in two volumes and would have cost more than $0.87. Putnam advertised a London edition in duodecimo for $1.00, and although no publisher is named in this advertisement, it most likely referred to Bohn's edition. Bohn first published this title in 1847 as part of his *Standard Library* series and reprinted it in 1851. Although an 1847 imprint may have been selected for the Executive Mansion, the 1851 is just as likely a choice, and the text of the two would have been same, since Bohn printed subsequent editions from stereotype plates. Titles in Bohn's *Standard Library* ranged from 3s. 6d. to 7s. 6d., or, in United States currency, from about $0.90 to $2.00, with most volumes listed for 5s., or about $1.25. Prior to Bohn's edition, the only editions of Machiavelli's *History of Florence* are from the mid-eighteenth century or earlier, and may be ruled out because they were in two or more volumes and most certainly would have cost more than $0.87.

107,754 voucher 3: Machiavelli $0.87.
Purchased from Franck Taylor on July 1, 1851.

REFERENCES
cf. Putnam p. 84; cf. *LC 1816–1851* p. 353; cf. Fillmore Packing Lists p. 7; cf. Fillmore 1861 p. 74.

---

1. "Machiavelli," *The Yale Literary Magazine. Conducted by the Students of Yale University,* October 1850, and "Times and Life of Machiavelli," *The United States Magazine and Democratic Review (1837–1851),* May 1847, both available at *APS Online,* http://www.proquest.com/products_pq/descriptions/aps.shtml.

~

108. **Malthus, Thomas Robert.** *An Essay on the Principle of Population.* 4th ed. 2 vols. London: J. Johnson, 1807.

In 1798 Thomas Robert Malthus (1766–1834), clergyman and political economist, published his first and best-known book, *Essay on the Principle of Population,* a work that stemmed from discussions with his father regarding the utopian ideals of William Godwin and the French political scientist the Marquis de Condorcet. In his preface to the second edition, Malthus claimed that his *Principle of Population* "account[s] for much of that poverty and misery observable among the lower classes of people in every nation, and for those reiterated failures in the efforts of the higher classes to relieve them" (1:v). In his research for the second edition, Malthus found that others, including Plato, Aristotle, Franklin, and Montesquieu, had made similar observations. Nevertheless, Malthus argued that the "principle had never been sufficiently pursued to its consequences" (1:vii). To the third edition he added an appendix in which he answered objections that had been raised to the *Essay.* In the advertisement to this edition, he suggests that those who have neither the "leisure" nor the "inclination" to read the entire work will find that the appendix provides a sufficient general overview (1:xii–xiii).[1]

The *Principle of Population,* although controversial and often misunderstood, became a central tenet of classical political economy. Some critics accused Malthus of advocating wars and immoral methods of controlling population, but he claimed to only encourage moral restraint as a control. Malthus's *Principle of Population* remained a topic of debate well into the mid-nineteenth century. Even the historian Archibald Alison published a response to it in 1840, which although later judged to be ponderous, was favorably reviewed by the *American Eclectic*.[2]

105,133 voucher 5: Malthus on Population $3.50.
Purchased from Charles Welford on December 13, 1850.
Hayes Catalogue: Malthus, T. R. *Essay on the Principle of Population.* 2 v. London, 1807. 8°.

TITLE PAGE
AN ESSAY | ON THE | PRINCIPLE OF POPULATION; | OR, A | VIEW OF ITS PAST AND PRESENT EFFECTS | ON | HUMAN HAPPINESS; | WITH | AN INQUIRY INTO OUR PROSPECTS RESPECTING | THE FUTURE REMOVAL OR MITIGATION OF | THE EVILS WHICH IT OCCASIONS. | By T. R. MALTHUS, A. M. | LATE FELLOW OF JESUS COLLEGE, CAMBRIDGE, | AND PROFESSOR OF HISTORY AND POLITICAL ECONOMY | IN THE EAST INDIA COLLEGE, HERTFORDSHIRE. | IN TWO VOLUMES. | VOL. I. [II.] | THE FOURTH EDITION. | LONDON: | PRINTED FOR J. JOHNSON IN ST. PAUL'S CHURCH-YARD, | BY T. BENSLEY, BOLT COURT, FLEET STREET. | 1807.

PAGINATION
Vol. I. i–xvi 1–580.
Vol. II. i–viii 1–544.

CONTENTS
Vol. I. i half title, ii blank, iii title, iv blank, v–x preface, xi–xiii advertisement, xiv blank, xv–xvi contents, 1–580 text.
Vol. II. i half title, ii blank, iii title, iv blank, v–vii contents, viii blank, 1–427 text, 428 blank, 429–84 appendix, 485–544 index.

REFERENCES
Hayes p. 164.

COPY DESCRIBED
DLC: HB861 E7 1807 Rare books.

------

1. The preface to the second edition, the appendix, and the advertisement are included in the fourth edition.
2. *The American Eclectic: or, Selections from the Periodical Literature,* November 1841, available at *APS Online,* http://www.proquest.com/products_pq/descriptions/aps.shtml. See entry 5 for Alison.

⮾

109. Manning, William Oke. *Commentaries on the Law of Nations*. London: S. Sweet, 1839.

William Oke Manning's *Commentaries on the Law of Nations* (1839) was the first English book on the principles of international law.[1] At first, Manning's *Commentaries* went unnoticed, but over time the book's usefulness on the topic was recognized by leading American legal scholars. James Kent found Manning's *Commentaries* a "work of great excellence" and recommended it to the American student, calling it the first English treatise "containing a regular and didactic discussion of the science."[2] Marvin called it a "concise and carefully written production, creditable to the author's learning and judgment"; however, he observes that its "utility is considerably diminished for want of an index,"[3] a sentiment that Fillmore surely would have shared. Fillmore purchased this book on the recommendation of Edward Everett.[4]

107,754 voucher 4: 1 vol. Mannings's Commentaries $3.97.
Purchased from Little and Brown on December 31, 1851.
Hayes Catalogue: Manning, W. O. jr. *Commentaries on the Law of Nations.* London, 1839. 8°.

TITLE PAGE
COMMENTARIES | ON | THE LAW OF NATIONS. | [swelled rule] | BY | WM. OKE MANNING, JUN., ESQ. | [thick/thin double rule] | LONDON: | S. SWEET, 1, CHANCERY LANE, | Law Bookseller and Publisher, | MILLIKEN AND SON, DUBLIN; AND CLARK, EDINBURGH. | [thin rule] | 1839.

PAGINATION
i–xxviii 1–390.

CONTENTS
i half title, ii printer's imprint, iii title, iv blank, v–xii preface, xiii–xxviii contents, 1–390 text.

REFERENCES
Hayes p. 153; Harvard p. 147; cf. *LC 1816–1851* p. 361; Marvin p. 496.

COPY DESCRIBED
DLC: JX 2558 C7 1839 copy 2 *Leaf.* 209 × 129.
> *Note.* Copy 1 is missing the half title.

---

1. Holdsworth, *History of English Law,* 15:330.
2. James Kent, *Commentaries on American Law* (New York: Kent, 1848), 4. See entry 92 for Kent.
3. Marvin, *Legal Bibliography,* 496.
4. See "White House Collection," 13, 23. See also "Millard Fillmore and His Booksellers," 62.

~

110. Martens, Georg Friedrich von. *The Law of Nations: Being the Science of National Law.* 4th ed. London: Cobbett, 1829.

The Law of Nations became Georg Friedrich von Martens's (1756–1821) best-known work. Although Manning and Hoffman disagree on its completeness, both extol its usefulness. Despite its shortcomings, Hoffman still found it of "considerable practical value, systematic in its arrangement, [and] accurate in its definitions." He also noted the importance of the added "list of treatise, conventions, compacts, declarations &c. of the modern nations of Europe, from the year 1731 to 1802."[1] William Oke Manning praised Martens's work as "the most complete treatise that exists on the law of nations, as recognised by the states of Europe. It embraces every topic of usual discussion on the subject, and embodies a vast store of information, . . . It is perhaps of more frequent reference than any other treatise, and it is valuable to every student."[2] *The Law of Nations* was originally published in French in 1789; a shorter preliminary Latin version had been published in Göttingen in 1785. In 1792 it was translated into English by William Cobbett, who published his work in several later editions. Edward Everett noted that later editions in the original were much enlarged and that the latest had appeared in Paris in 1831, but recommended an earlier shorter version of this work, *A Summary of the Law of Nations,* London, 1802. Fillmore did not read French and opted for the most current English edition to date.

107,754 voucher 4: 1 vol. Marten's Law of Nations $4.68.
Purchased from Little and Brown on December 31, 1851.
Hayes Catalogue: Martens G. F. [von]. *Law of Nations* London, 1829. 8°.

TITLE PAGE
THE | LAW OF NATIONS: | BEING | THE SCIENCE OF NATIONAL LAW, | COVENANTS, POWER, &c. | FOUNDED UPON THE | TREATIES AND CUSTOMS OF MODERN NATIONS | *IN EUROPE.* | [thin rule] | BY | G. F. VON MARTENS, | *Professor of Public Law in the University of Gottingen.* | TRANSLATED FROM THE FRENCH, BY | WM. COBBETT. | [thin rule] | TO WHICH IS ADDED, | A LIST OF PRINCIPAL TREATIES, DECLARATIONS, AND OTHER | PUBLIC PAPERS, FROM THE YEAR 1731 TO 1738, BY THE | AUTHOR; AND CONTINUED BY THE TRANSLATOR | DOWN TO NOVEMBER, 1815. | *THE FOURTH EDITION.* | [thin/thick double rule] | LONDON: | PUBLISHED BY WILLIAM COBBETT, | 183, FLEET STREET. | [thin rule] | 1829.

PAGINATION
i–xxxii 1–468.

CONTENTS
i title, ii printer's imprint, iii–iv preface to the fourth edition, v advertisement to the first London edition, vi blank, vii–xi author's preface, xii blank, xiii–xxxii contents, 1–354 text, 355 section title, "List of Treaties and Other Public Acts," 356 blank, 357–468 text.

REFERENCES
Hayes p. 153; *BEAL* 7176; cf. Greenleaf; cf. Harvard p. 149; cf. Marvin p. 500; cf. Hoffman p. 452.

COPY DESCRIBED
DLC: JX2814 P7 1829. Copy 2. *Leaf.* 214 × 129.

---

1. Hoffman, *Course of Legal Study,* 452.
2. William Oke Manning, *Commentaries on the Law of Nations* (London: S. Sweet, 1839), 39. See entry 109 for Manning.

∽

111. Martin, Montgomery R. *British Colonial Library.* **10 vols. London: Bohn, 1844.**

With the *British Colonial Library* Montgomery R. Martin (ca. 1801–68) revised and updated his earlier five-volume *History of the British Colonies,* the work that established his reputation as a writer and as an advocate of the British Empire. His work does not confine itself to a description of the colonies but includes his views on colonial policies related to banking, emigration, convict discipline, and parliamentary representation. The most noteworthy characteristics of Martin's work were his "penchant for statistics and mixture of generalizations with very detailed information on a limited range of topics, and his life-long positions on public issues—the concern with religion, and the strictures for better government of the '100 millions of subjects of the British Crown', anti-slavery, fair reciprocal treatment for overseas territories and their products, and suspicion of foreign powers, especially France."[1]

The principal changes from the earlier *History* include the expansion of the work on India to two volumes and the contraction of the volumes on Ceylon, Penang, and so forth and on the African colonies from two to one. Other than the removal of certain tables, documents, and appendixes in the *Colonial Library*, the contents are quite similar.[2]

Apparently the bookseller Charles Welford made a mistake when he wrote "British Classical Library" on this voucher. This would be an easy slip of the pen, since the Executive Mansion purchased another series titled *Family Classical Library* from Welford, which was listed on this same voucher. The list of books sent on approval from Welford identifies this title as *British Colonial Library*, a set that remained in the White House for the next fifty years and is listed in both the Hayes and the Roosevelt catalogues.[3]

105,133 voucher 5: British Classical Library 10 vols. $7.50.
Purchased from Charles Welford on December 13, 1850.

Hayes Catalogue: *British Colonial Library.* By R. M. Martin. 10 vols. London, 1844. 12°.
> v. 1. *Canada*, v. 2. *Austral-Asia*, v. 3. *Southern Africa*, v. 4–5. *West Indies* 2 v., v. 6. *Nova Scotia, Newfoundland*, etc., v. 7. *British Possessions in the Mediterranean*, v. 8–9. *Possessions of the East India Company*, v. 10. *British Possessions in the Indian and Atlantic Oceans.*

Roosevelt Catalogue: *British Colonial Library, Comprising a Popular and Authentic Description of All the Colonies of the British Empire, by R. Montgomery Martin.* London, H. G. Bohn, 1844, 10 vols.

CONTENTS

vol. 1. *The Canadas.*
2. *Austral Asia, Comprising New South Wales, Van Deimen's Island, Swan River, South Australia.*
3. *Cape of Good Hope, Mauritius, Seychelles.*
4, 5. *West Indies.*
6. *Nova Scotia.*
7. *Gibralter, Malta, Gozo, and the Ionian Islands.*
8, 9. *East India Company.*
10. *British Possessions in the Indian and Atlantic Oceans.*

REFERENCES

Hayes p. 165; Roosevelt p. 6; cf. Putnam p. 88; cf. L and B 1850 p. 59; cf. Fillmore ca. 1858 p. 41; cf. Fillmore 1861 p. 20.

---

1. Frank H. H. King, *Survey Our Empire: Robert Montgomery Martin (1801?–1868)* (Hong Kong: Centre of Asian Studies, University of Hong Kong, 1979), 11.

2. Ibid., 12.

3. Welford's list of books sent on approval is enclosed in Charles Lanman, letter to Millard Fillmore, December 13, 1850, Millard Fillmore Papers, BECHS.

❧

112. *The Merchants' Magazine and Commercial Review.* Ed. Freeman Hunt. New York: 1840–50.

Founded by Freeman Hunt, the monthly *Merchants' Magazine and Commercial Review* ran from 1839 through 1870. It sought to provide encyclopedic coverage of commercial subjects, not only for merchants, but also for members of the general public who "feel an interest in promoting information on subjects deeply identified with the wealth, the greatness, and the happiness of our common country" (1:9). After its first decade of publication, Hunt claimed that his journal was "a perfect *vade mecum* to the merchant, the manufacturer, and the Banker, as well as the Statesman, Commercial lawyer, and Political Economist" (20:696). It included articles on statistics, mercantile law, currency, insurance, banking, navigation, treaties, mercantile libraries, and biographies of successful merchants. Earlier volumes had also devoted space to the troubles of the United States Bank.[1] Hunt remained editor of the *Merchants' Magazine* until his death around 1858. In 1860 the magazine was renamed *Hunt's Merchants' Magazine,* in honor of its founder. The Executive Mansion purchased a complete run of this periodical through 1850 for its library, where it would have served as a reference source for information regarding events and developments in trade and commerce during the preceding decade.

105,133 voucher 5: Hunt's Magazine 23 vols. $46.00.
Purchased from Charles Welford on December 13, 1850.
Roosevelt Catalogue: *Hunt's Merchant's Magazine and Commercial Review.* Conducted by Freeman Hunt. New York, 1839–50, vols. 1–23.

TITLE PAGE
Vol. I.
THE | MERCHANTS' MAGAZINE. | AND | Commercial Review. [black letter] | CONDUCTED BY FREEMAN HUNT. | VOLUME I. | [thin rule] | NEW YORK: | PUBLISHED AT 142 FULTON-STREET, (REAR BUILDING) | MDCCCXL.

REFERENCES
Hayes p. 105; Roosevelt p. 21; cf. Fillmore 1861 p. 100.

COPY DESCRIBED
DLC: HF 1 M5. *Leaf.* 218 × 133.

---

1. Mott, *History of American Magazines, 1741–1850,* 696–97.

❧

113. Michelet, Jules. *Historical View of the French Revolution.* Trans. C. Cocks. London: Bohn, 1848.
114. ———. *History of the Roman Republic.* Trans. William Hazlitt. 1847. [Either London: Bogue, or New York: Appleton.]

Jules Michelet (1798–1874) ranked among the greatest nineteenth-century French historians for his *Histoire de France* (1833) and *Histoire de la Révolution Française* (7 vols., 1847–53).[1]

Bohn's *Historical View of the French Revolution* translates only the first two volumes of the latter. In these volumes Michelet provides historical background, beginning in the Middle Ages, and chronicles the revolution through June of 1791.

Michelet wrote his *History of the Roman Republic* (1831) much earlier, after visiting Italy in 1830, but it was not translated into English until 1847, so that the two works became available to the English-speaking public, in both London and America, at approximately the same time. The American edition of his *Roman Republic* received laudatory reviews from all sides. The *American Review* called it "a political history composed in Michelet's peculiarly brilliant and popular style; written, like his other works, to exalt the popular element in government;" and the *Democratic Review* praised "the soundness of his judgement, the extent of his researches, and the faithfulness of his pictures."[2]

While the edition of Michelet's *French Revolution* that was purchased for the library is identified in the Hayes and Roosevelt catalogues, that of his *History of the Roman Republic* is not. Only two editions of the *Roman Republic* were available for purchase by the White House in 1850: the 1847 London edition from Bogue and the 1847 New York edition from Appleton. Roorbach listed the Appleton edition at $1.00, while the *London Catalogue* listed the Bogue edition at 3*s.* 6*d.* or about $0.85. Based on price either one of these editions could have been selected.

105,133 voucher 5: Michelets French Revolution 1.00.

Roosevelt Catalogue: Michelet, Jules. *Historical View of the French Revolution, from Its Earliest Indications to the Flight of the King in 1791.* Translated by Cocks. London, H. G. Bohn, 1848.

105,133 voucher 5: Michelets Roman Republic $0.87.

Purchased from Charles Welford on December 13, 1850.

French Revolution.

TITLE PAGE

HISTORICAL VIEW | OF THE | FRENCH REVOLUTION. | BY J. MICHELET. | [thin swelled rule] | TRANSLATED BY | C. COCKS, B. L. | PROFESSOR (BREVETÉ) OF THE ENGLISH LANGUAGE IN THE COLLEGE ROYAL. | [thin rule] | LONDON: | H. G. BOHN, YORK STREET, COVENT GARDEN. | MDCCCXLVIII.

PAGINATION

i–xxiv 1–606 283–98.

CONTENTS

i title, ii blank, iii–xxiv contents, 1–12 preface, 13–606 text, 283–97 index, 298 blank.

PLATES

Frontispiece, revolutionary battle in front of St. Germain l'Auxerrois, signed T. Allom in lower left and J. B. Allen lower right.

REFERENCES

Hayes p. 168; Roosevelt p. 28; cf. Putnam p. 91; cf. *LC 1816–1851* p. 376; cf. Fillmore 1861 p. 98.

COPY DESCRIBED

ViU: DC 165 M6 1848. *Leaf.* 182 × 120.

Roman Republic.

REFERENCES

cf. Roorbach p. 365; cf. Fillmore 1861 p. 184.

---

1. "Jules Michelet," *Encyclopedia of World Biography,* 2nd ed. (Detroit: Gale Research, 1998), reproduced in *Biography Resource Center* (Farmington Hills, Mich.: Thomson Gale, 2006), http://gale.cengage.com/servlet/BiographyRC.

2. "History of the Roman Republic," *The American Review: A Whig Journal of Politics, Literature, Art and Science,* April 1847, "Notices of new Books," *The Democratic Review(1837–1851),* April 1847, both available at *APS Online,* http://www.proquest.com/products_pq/descriptions/aps.shtml.

❧

115. Mill, John Stuart. *Principles of Political Economy.* 2 vols. Boston: Little and Brown, 1848.

John Stuart Mill (1806–73), political theorist and social philosopher, wrote *Principles of Political Economy* (1848) in response to contemporary debates about working conditions and criticism of "Malthusian determinism and political non-intervention." More readable and "congenial" than earlier economic textbooks, *Principles of Political Economy* became an immediate success and was hailed as a classic. The *North American Review* published an encomium and an extensive discussion of Mill's work. Likewise, the *Democratic Review* suggested that Mill's *Principles* should "be in the hands of all" in the United States, at a time when the study of political economy had been unjustifiably neglected.[1] Mill himself, however, thought that it was nearly out of date before it was even published because the revolutions on the continent in 1848 brought "widespread experimentation in co-operative, socialist, and public works schemes in many parts of Europe." He later reflected that if he and his wife had anticipated such changes, they would have written in more "ambitious socialist terms." Mill continued to revise *Principles* throughout the rest of his life.[2]

105,133 voucher 5: Mills Polit. Economy $4.00.

Purchased from Charles Welford on December 13, 1850.

Roosevelt Catalogue: Mill, John Stuart. *Principles of Political Economy.* Boston, C. C. Little & J. Brown, 1848, 2 vols.

TITLE PAGE

PRINCIPLES | OF | POLITICAL ECONOMY, | WITH | SOME OF THEIR APPLICATIONS TO SOCIAL PHILOSOPHY. | BY | JOHN STUART MILL. | [thin rule] | IN TWO VOLUMES. | VOL. I. [II.] | [thin rule] | BOSTON: | CHARLES C. LITTLE & JAMES BROWN. | 1848.

PAGINATION

Vol. I. i–xvi 1–600.

Vol. II. i–xii 1–560.

CONTENTS

Vol. I. i title, ii printer's imprint, iii–vi preface, vii–xv contents, xvi blank, 1–579 text, 580 blank, 581–99 appendix, 600 blank.

Vol. II. i title, ii printer's imprint, iii–xii contents, 1–560 text.

REFERENCES

Hayes p. 168; Roosevelt p. 28; Putnam p. 92; Roorbach p. 366; L and B 1850 p. 60; L and B 1852 p. 4; L and B 1853 p. 45.

COPY DESCRIBED

DLC: HB 161 M6 1848. *Leaf.* 238 × 145.

----

1. "Principles of Political Economy," *The North American Review (1821–1940),* October 1848, and "Notices of New Books," *The United States Magazine and Democratic Review (1937–1851),* January 1849, both available at *APS Online,* http://www.proquest.com/products_pq/descriptions/aps.shtml.

2. Jose Harris, "Mill, John Stuart, (1806–1873)," *ODNB.*

∽

116. Mills, Abraham. *The Literature and the Literary Men of Great Britain and Ireland.* **2 vols. New York: Harper, 1851.**

In *The Literature and Literary Men of Great Britain and Ireland* (1851), the educator Abraham Mills (1796–1867) collected a series of essays based upon lectures that he had delivered twenty years earlier under the title "A Course of Lectures on English Literature." Each volume treats nearly two hundred authors. Alfred the Great, Thomas Kyd, Edmund Spenser, Jonathan Swift, Joseph Addison, Colley Cibber, Samuel Johnson, Alexander Pope, and Izaak Walton are among those included. Despite its name, this set discusses some women authors, including Lady Mary Wortley Montagu, the Countess of Winchelsea, Aphra Behn, and Clara Reeve. In addition to these lectures, Mills edited and published American revisions of Edmund Burke's "On the Sublime and the Beautiful" (1829), Hugh Blair's "Lectures on Rhetoric and Belles-Lettres" (1829), "Alison on Taste" (1830), and Lord Kames's "Elements of Criticism" (1833). His editions of these titles immediately became popular and were adopted for use as textbooks.[1]

109,399 voucher 4: Literature & Literary Men of Gr. Britain $3.25.

Purchased from Franck Taylor on September 22, 1851.

Roosevelt Catalogue: Mills, Abraham. *The Literature and Literary Men of Great Britain and Ireland.* New York: Harper & Brothers, 1851, 2 vols.

TITLE PAGE

THE | LITERATURE | AND | THE LITERARY MEN | OF | Great Britain and Ireland. [black letter] | BY | ABRAHAM MILLS, A.M., | AUTHOR OF LECTURES ON RHETORIC AND BELLES LETTRES, ETC. ETC. ETC. | IN TWO VOLUMES. | VOLUME THE FIRST. [SECOND.] | NEW YORK: | HARPER & BROTHERS, PUBLISHERS, | 82 CLIFF STREET. | [thin rule] | 1851.

PAGINATION

Vol. I. i–vi i–xvi 17–576.

Vol. II. i–xvi 17–598.

CONTENTS

Vol. I. i title, ii copyright statement, iii dedication to the Hon. Theodore Frelinghuysen, iv blank, v–vi preface, i–ii authors' names, iii–xvi contents, 17–576 text.

Vol. II. i title, ii copyright statement, iii–iv authors' names, v–xvi contents, 17–598 text.

REFERENCES

Hayes p. 168; Roosevelt p. 28; Putnam p. 23-s; Roorbach p. 367.

COPY DESCRIBED

DLC: PR83 M5. *Leaf.* 220 × 135.

---

1. "Mills, Abraham," in *Appleton's Cyclopaedia of American Biography,* ed. James Grant Wilson and John Fiske, facsim. ed. (1888, Detroit: Gale, 1968), 4:331.

∾

117. Milton, John. *The Poetical Works of John Milton with Notes and a Life of the Author.* 2 vols. Boston: Little and Brown, 1845.

118. ———. *The Prose Works of John Milton: With a Biographical Introduction.* Ed. Rufus Wilmot Griswold. 2 vols. Philadelphia: Herman Hooker, 1845.

John Milton's (1608–74) reputation as a "giant" of English literature stood firm throughout the nineteenth century in England and America. His poetry and prose would have been a mainstay in any library assembled at the time. An article in the *Yale Literary Magazine* reflects Milton's mid-nineteenth-century reputation in America. It begins on a laudatory note: "To one who speaks the English language, the name of John Milton needs no eulogy. His fame is coextensive with the empire of letters."[1] The author proceeds in his essay to extol the works of Milton, both his poetry and prose, as well as to praise his moral character. He concludes by claiming Milton as a progenitor of American freedom: "Above all, as American citizens, we honor him for the principles he embraced in youth and always defended, the principles that are to be cherished by us as the natural growth of the mind, and as the foundation of our freedom and happiness . . . shall his works not live on these shores, which he helped make free, and his memory be revered from the rocks of New England to the waters of the Pacific?"[2]

105,133 voucher 2: Milton poet[l.] wks. 2 vols. $2.50.

105,133 voucher 2: Milton Prose 2 vols. $5.00.

Purchased from Little and Brown on December 30, 1850.

Roosevelt Catalogue: Milton, John. *Poetical Works.* Boston, C. C. Little and J. Brown, 1845. 2 vols.

———. *Prose Works with a Biographical Introduction by R. W. Griswold.* Philadelphia, Herman Hooker, 1845, 2 vols.

The Poetical Works.

TITLE PAGE

THE | POETICAL WORKS OF JOHN MILTON. | WITH NOTES, AND A LIFE OF THE
AUTHOR. | A NEW EDITION. | VOL. I. [II.] | [printer's ornament, anchor with fish] |
BOSTON: | CHARLES C. LITTLE AND JAMES BROWN. | [thin rule] | 1845.

PAGINATION

Vol. I. i–cxxxii 1–372.

Vol. II. [2] i–ii 3–300 [2] 301–478.

CONTENTS

Vol. I. i title page, ii blank, iii contents, iv blank, v Sonnet to Charles Lord Bishop of Win-
chester, on His Publication of Milton De Doctrina Christiana, vi–xviii advertisement,
xix–cvii Life of Milton, cviii–cxi addenda, cxii–cxxvi appendix, cxxvii–cxxix compli-
mentary verses, cxxx blank, cxxxi section title "Paradise Lost," cxxxii "The Verse," 1–371
Paradise Lost text, 372 blank.

Vol. II. [1] title page, [2] blank, i–ii contents, 3–300 text, [1] section title, "Minor Poems," [2]
blank, 301–478 text.

PLATES

Vol. I.

Portrait frontispiece, John Milton, engraved by O. Pelton.

REFERENCES

Hayes p. 168 and p. 213; Roosevelt p. 28; Stevens[3] 150; cf. Fillmore ca. 1858 p. 42; cf. Fillmore
1861 p. 138.

COPY DESCRIBED

DLC: PR 3551 M5 1845. *Leaf.* 243 × 137.

The Prose Works.

TITLE PAGE

THE | PROSE WORKS | OF | JOHN MILTON: | WITH A | BIOGRAPHICAL
INTRODUCTION, | BY | RUFUS WILMOT GRISWOLD. | HE WAS IN HIS STYLE |
NAKED AND STERN; AND TO EFFEMINATE EARS | PERCHANCE EVEN
HARSH; BUT WHO WILL DARE DISPUTE | HIS STRENGTH AND GRANDEUR? |
SIR EGERTON BRYDGES. | MILTON! THOU SHOULDST BE LIVING AT THIS
HOUR. | . . . . RETURN TO US AGAIN, | AND GIVE US MANNERS, VIRTUE,
FREEDOM, POWER. | THY SOUL WAS LIKE A STAR, AND DWELT APART | THOU
HADST A VOICE, WHOSE SOUND WAS LIKE THE SEA: | PURE AS THE NAKED
HEAVENS, MAJESTIC, FREE; | SO DIDST THOU TRAVEL ON LIFE'S COMMON
WAY, | IN CHEERFUL GODLINESS, AND YET THY HEART | THE LOWLIEST
DUTIES ON HERSELF DID LAY. | *WORDSWORTH.* | IN TWO VOLUMES. | I. [II.] |
PHILADELPHIA: | HERMAN HOOKER, PUBLISHER, No. 16 SOUTH SEVENTH
STREET. | 1845.

PAGINATION

Vol. I. i– xii 1–548.

Vol. II. i–iv 5–550.

CONTENTS

Vol. I. i title page, ii printer's imprint, iii–xi biographical introduction, xii contents of the first volume, 1–548 text.

Vol. II. i title page, ii printer's imprint, iii contents of the second volume, iv blank, 5–550 text.

REFERENCES

Hayes p. 168; Roosevelt p. 28; L and B 1850 p. 62; Putnam p. 92; Stevens[4] 1191.

COPY DESCRIBED

DLC: PR3569 G7 1845. *Leaf.* 265 × 176.

---

1. G. H. C., "John Milton," *The Yale Literary Magazine: Conducted by the Students of Yale University,* July 1840, available at *APS Online,* http://www.proquest.com/products_pq/descriptions/aps.shtml.
2. Ibid.
3. David Harrison Stevens, *Reference Guide to Milton from 1800 to the Present* (Chicago: University of Chicago Press, 1930).
4. Ibid.

～

119. Mitchell, Samuel Augustus. *New Universal Atlas Containing Maps of the Various Empires, Kingdoms, States and Republics of the World with a Special Map of Each of the United States Plans of Cities &c. Comprehended in Seventy Sheets and Forming a Series of One Hundred and Seventeen Maps Plans and Sections.* Philadelphia: Thomas Cowperthwait and Co., 1850.

Samuel Augustus Mitchell (1792–1868), geographer and publisher, devoted forty years of his life to writing and publishing geographical works. He began his career as a teacher, but his dissatisfaction with the treatment of geography in the textbooks that he was using inspired him to produce his own texts. His maps and atlases became a successful enterprise, and at one time were in such high demand that sales reached over four hundred thousand annually.

Mitchell's *New Universal Atlas* contains 117 maps, including one of each state in the Union; all of North America; Canada, split between two plates; and each country in the world. In 1845 Mitchell acquired the copyright for Henry S. Tanner's *Universal Atlas* from the Philadelphia publishers Carey and Hart, who had previously acquired it from Tanner. Carey and Hart had printed the atlas from copper plates, but when Mitchell began publishing it, he transferred the images to lithographic stones. The maps are in three colors with distinctive decorative borders. After 1849 the color on the borders appears to have been printed using chromolithography, while the maps themselves were still hand colored. Thomas Cowperthwait and Company of Philadelphia purchased the copyright from Mitchell in 1850.[1]

This atlas was one of the Fillmores' earliest selections for the library, purchased in September of 1850, before congressional funding of the plan had been approved. The 1850

Cowperthwaite edition is listed in Roorbach as selling for $12.00 in folio and bound in half russia. The White House most likely selected the most recent edition of this atlas rather than an older one. Although images from the same plates used for the earlier editions were transferred to lithographic stones and used to print newer editions, new maps were added as new states were admitted to the Union and boundaries changed. Books published late in the calendar year were often dated with the following year; September, the month that Fillmore purchased this book, would have been too early to date the *Atlas* 1851; therefore, an 1850 edition was most likely purchased. The voucher entry for the *Atlas* indicates a charge for "lettering." This most likely refers to a spine label similar to the one found on the Executive Mansion copy of Richard S. Fisher's *Book of the World*.[2]

105,579 voucher 2: Mitchell's Universal Atlas and cost of lettering do. $10.50.
Purchased from Franck Taylor on September 9, 1850.

REFERENCES
Roorbach p. 34; cf. Fillmore 1861 p. 4 and p. 12.

----

1. Walter W. Ristow, *American Maps and Mapmakers: Commercial Cartography in the Nineteenth Century* (Detroit: Wayne State University Press, 1985), 311–12.
2. See "Bibliographical Methods," 72.

≈

120. Murray, Hugh. *Encyclopaedia of Geography.* **3 vols. Philadelphia: Lea and Blanchard, 1848.**

Encyclopaedia of Geography (1834) stands as Hugh Murray's magnum opus. Murray (1779–1846), a fellow of the Society of Edinburgh and the Royal Geographical Society of London, wrote prolifically on geography. In his preface to the *Encyclpædia*, he asserted that political and commercial relations with the colonies had made geography a necessity for the "pursuits of commerce and industry, and for much of the ordinary and current business of life" (1:iii–iv). This *Encyclopaedia* contains eighty-two maps and over one thousand woodcuts. While the geographical portion was written by Murray, he retained leading experts to contribute in other fields. For example, in sections relating to commerce, he relied on McCulloch's *Dictionary of Commerce,* another book that the Fillmores selected for the library (1:iv).[1]

The preface to the American edition of Murray's *Encyclopaedia* outlines the alterations that its editors have made as follows: the description of Great Britain that formerly occupied one third of the book devoted to Europe has been abridged; the text has been "carefully revised and corrected" and "recent statistical details have been substituted for those of the original"; and the book relating to America has been expanded "as far as the limits of the work would allow" (1:v).

We cannot be certain which edition of the *Encyclopaedia of Geography* was purchased for the White House. The only publishers for this work up to 1850 had been Lea and Blanchard in America and Longman in London. Based on price Lea and Blanchard's edition is the most likely choice. This firm had revised its edition to make it more relevant to an

American audience. While Putnam advertised the London edition for $18.00, a price too high to accord with the $5.50 purchase recorded on the voucher, it listed the American edition, bound in sheep, for $8.00. Although this price is still greater than the price paid by the White House, a clothbound copy may have been selected and would have been less expensive. Carey, Lea, and Blanchard (later Lea and Blanchard) began publishing the *Encyclopaedia* in 1837 and reprinted it eight times between 1838 and 1850.

105,133 voucher 2: Murrays Encyclopaedia Geography $5.50.
Purchased from Charles Welford on December 13, 1850.

REFERENCES
cf. Putnam p. 96; cf. Roorbach p. 179.

---

1. See entry 104 for McCulloch.

〜

121. Niebuhr, Barthold Georg. *Lectures on the History of Rome.* **Ed. Leonard Schmitz. 3 vols. London: Taylor, Walton, and Maberly, 1850.**

Barthold Georg Niebuhr (1776–1831), historian and statesman, introduced "philological methodology and social history as a new discipline" in his *Lectures of the History of Rome;* thereby, he initiated a new method of historical scholarship. He began his lectures in Berlin while a member of the Berlin Academy of Sciences. After publishing his first two volumes in 1811 and 1812, he accepted an appointment in 1815 as Prussian ambassador to Rome, where he continued his studies in Roman history. Upon becoming a professor at the University of Bohn in 1823, he rewrote and republished his *History of Rome* and completed its third volume, which was published posthumously in 1832.[1]

Most nineteenth-century reviewers found Niebuhr's work cumbersome. One complained, "The style of the whole work is bad: not simply unattractive, but so cumbrous as to be readable only for the matter it contains." It lacks the "beauty of a good narrative" and the "unpretending lucidity of a good disquisition." Furthermore, this writer takes Niebuhr to task for his use and handling of ancient sources. Another, more generous, critic praised Neibuhr's introductory lectures but predicted that his work "can never become popular or classical as a history, though it will always be consulted by the scholar as a vast mine of antiquarian and historical lore. But analysis too far predominates over synthesis in its pages,— there is too much discussion in it,—to permit its ever being regarded as the counterpart to Gibbon."[2] The *Universalist Quarterly,* nevertheless, recommended Niebuhr's work right alongside Gibbon in its article "A Course of Historical Reading."[3]

105,133 voucher 5: Niebuhr's History Rome 3 vols. $5.50.
Purchased from Charles Welford on December 13, 1850.
Roosevelt Catalogue: Niebuhr, Barthold Georg. *Lectures on the History of Rome, from the Earliest Times to the Fall of the Western Empire.* Edited by Leonard Schmitz. Second edition. London, Taylor, Walton & Maberly, 1849, 3 vols.

TITLE PAGE

LECTURES | ON | THE HISTORY OF ROME, | FROM | THE EARLIEST TIMES OF
THE FALL OF THE | WESTERN EMPIRE. | BY | B. G. NIEBUHR. | EDITED BY |
DR. LEONARD SCHMITZ, F. R. S. E., | RECTOR OF THE HIGH SCHOOL OF
EDINBURGH. | Second Edition. [black letter] | WITH EVERY ADDITION DERIVABLE
FROM DR. ISLER'S GERMAN EDITION. | IN THREE VOLUMES. | VOL. I. [II–III] |
LONDON: | TAYLOR, WALTON, AND MABERLY, | UPPER GOWER STREET, AND
IVY LANE, PATERNOSTER ROW. | M.DCCC.L.

> *Note.* Volumes 2 and 3 are dated 1849. Although the Roosevelt Catalogue lists this as an 1849 edition, it is possible that volume 1 was dated 1850, as it is in this copy. A copy of volume 1 dated 1849 was not available for description here.

PAGINATION

Vol. I. i–xvi 1–456.

Vol. II. i–xxiv 1–408.

Vol. III. [2] i–viii 1–358 i–ii i–xcviii 359–86.

CONTENTS

Vol. I. i title, ii printer's imprint, iii–viii preface, ix–xvi contents, 1–440 text, 441–56 index.

Vol. II. i half title, ii printer's imprint, iii title, iv blank, v dedication to "His majesty, Frederic William the Fourth, King of Prussia," vi blank, vii–ix preface to the second edition, x–xvi preface to the first edition, xvii–xxiv contents, 1–408 text.

Vol. III. [1] title, [2] blank, i–viii contents, 1–357 text, 358 blank, i–ii contents of the "Introductory Lectures," i–xcvii text of "Introductory Lectures," xcviii blank, 359–85 index, 386 blank.

PLATES

Vol. I.

Portrait frontispiece, B. G. Niebuhr, "From a portrait by Julius Schnorr, engraved by John Braine."

BINDING

Front and back board. 233 × 146 green ribbed cloth with blind-stamped decorative frame. *Spine.* Blind-stamped six panels; panels 1, 2, and 3 blind stamped with filigree decoration; panels 2, 3, and 6 gilt stamped; panel 1 'NIEBUHR'S | LECTURES | ON THE | HISTORY | OF ROME'; panel 3 'EDITED BY | DR SCHMITZ | [thin rule] | VOL. I. [II.–III.]'; panel 6 'COMPLETE IN 3 VOLS'. *Endpapers.* Pale yellow.

REFERENCES

Hayes p. 188; Roosevelt p. 30; cf. Putnam p. 99, and p. 25-s; L and B 1850 p. 66; cf. L and B 1852 p. 5; L and B 1853 p. 48; cf. *LC 1816–1851* p. 406.

COPY DESCRIBED

ViBlbV: D6 209 N65 1850.

---

1. "Barthold Georg Niebuhr," *Encyclopedia of World Biography,* 2nd ed. (Detroit: Gale Research, 1998), reproduced in *Biography Resource Center* (Farmington Hills, Mich.: Thomson Gale, 2007), http://gale.cengage.com/servlet/BiographyRC.

2. "Charges Against Niebuhr," *The Eclectic Magazine of Foreign Literature (1844–1898)*, April 1844, and "The History of Rome," *The Southern Quarterly Review (1842–1857)*, October 1844, both available at *APS Online,* http://www.proquest.com/products_pq/descriptions/aps.shtml.

3. See "White House Collection," 15.

∿

122. Niles, Hezekiah. *The Weekly Register.* Baltimore: Niles, 1811–49.

Niles' Weekly Register was a staple in libraries of statesmen and politicians from its early days. John Adams received eleven volumes of it; Thomas Jefferson subscribed to it; Andrew Jackson owned a complete set for at least a dozen years, and James Madison and the Marquis de Lafayette each corresponded with Niles about their subscriptions.[1]

Niles' became one of the first truly national publications in America, achieving circulation throughout the United States and its territories as well as in some foreign countries. From its beginnings *Niles'* garnered a reputation as a reliable source of facts and was known for its ethic of publishing all sides of "burning issues."[2] It maintained the dual purpose of "printing significant news for contemporaries and of preserving for posterity speeches, documents, messages, and correspondence of public officials."[3] The motto adopted by Niles himself in 1837, "The Past—The Present—For the Future," succinctly conveys his vision. Each volume's title page describes the "publication as 'Containing Political, Historical, Geographical, Scientific, Astronomical, Statistical and Biographical Documents, Essays and Facts; Together with the Notices of Arts and Manufactures, and a Record of the Events of the Times.'"[4] Back issues were in great demand, and the first thirty-two volumes were later reprinted.

Hezekiah Niles founded and edited the paper in Baltimore from 1811 to 1836. In 1836 his son William Ogden Niles became editor and moved *Niles'* to Washington. Jeremiah Hughes purchased it in 1840 and returned it to Baltimore. He maintained ownership through February of 1848, when *Niles'*s publication was suspended. In July of the same year, George Beatty revived *Niles'* and managed it through its final issue, September 28, 1849.[5]

Niles' was published as a large octavo for its first twenty-five years. When William Ogden Niles took over the publication in 1836, he increased the size to quarto, the format retained for the remainder of the periodical's life. Each issue contained sixteen pages, although the elder Niles was known for frequently issuing free supplements, usually a half sheet, or eight pages each, so that many volumes ran over five hundred pages. The practice of publishing these supplements was discontinued on Hezekiah Niles's retirement.[6]

One notable typographical feature of *Niles'* is the continuation of articles from the last page of one issue to the first page of the subsequent issue without a break. Thus, the first page of an issue sometimes begins without a headline or any identification but with the remainder of a "document, letter, or court decision" that had begun in the previous number.[7] In the early numbers, Niles would continue an article in a subsequent issue with several pages intervening, but he later changed this practice in anticipation that the parts would be bound into volumes for future readers.

With *Niles'* the library deviated from its usual practice of purchasing the entire run of a periodical. The voucher indicates that fifty-six volumes were purchased; the Hayes Catalogue clarifies this total somewhat by recording sixty-four volumes in fifty-seven, but it introduces a new discrepancy between fifty-six and fifty-seven volumes. Regardless, the library apparently only purchased volumes dating from 1811 to 1843, as listed in the Hayes Catalogue. Perhaps an entire run was not available for sale at the time of purchase. Fillmore himself owned all seventy-five volumes in his personal library.

105,133 voucher 2: Niles Register 56 vols. $80.00.

Purchased from Little and Brown on December 30, 1850.

Hayes Catalogue: Niles, H. *Weekly Register from Sep. 1811 to Aug. 26, 1843*. v. 1 to 64 in 57 v. Baltimore, 1811–43. 8° & 4°.

Roosevelt Catalogue: *Niles* [*sic*] *Weekly Register* from Sept 7, 1811–43. Baltimore, 1816–43, 63 vols.

TITLE PAGE

Vol. I.

THE | WEEKLY REGISTER: | CONTAINING | POLITICAL, ASTRONOMICAL | HISTORICAL, STATISTICAL | GEOGRAPHICAL, and | SCIENTIFIC, BIOGRAPHICAL [the last four lines are in two columns divided by a thick/thin vertical rule] | DOCUMENTS, ESSAYS AND FACTS; | TOGETHER WITH | NOTICE OF THE ARTS AND MANUFACTURES, AND A RECORD OF THE | EVENTS OF THE TIMES. | H. NILES, EDITOR. | [thick/thin rule] | "—I wish no other herald, | "No other speaker of *my living actions,* | "To keep mine honor from corruption | "But such an honest chronicler." | *Shakespeare*—HENRY VIII. | [thin/thick double rule] | *FROM SEPTEMBER* 1811 *TO MARCH* 1812.—VOL. I. | [thick/thin double rule] | BALTIMORE: | PRINTED AND PUBLISHED BY THE EDITOR, | At the Franklin Press, [black letter] | WATER-STREET, NEAR THE MERCHANTS' COFFEE-HOUSE.

Vol. LI.

NILES' | WEEKLY REGISTER, | CONTAINING | POLITICAL, HISTORICAL, GEOGRAPHICAL, SCIENTIFICAL, STATISTICAL, | ECONOMICAL AND BIOGRAPHICAL | DOCUMENTS, ESSAYS AND FACTS: | TOGETHER WITH | NOTICES OF THE ARTS AND MANUFACTURES, | AND A RECORD OF THE EVENTS OF THE TIMES. | [thin rule] | WM. OGDEN NILES, EDITOR. | [thin rule] | THE PAST—THE PRESENT—FOR THE FUTURE. | [thin rule] | FROM SEPTEMBER, 1836, TO MARCH, 1837—VOL. LI. OR, VOLUME XV.—FIFTH SERIES. | [thick/thin double rule] | BALTIMORE: | PRINTED BY THE EDITOR, | AT THE FRANKLIN PRESS, WATER-STREET, EAST OF SOUTH STREET.

REFERENCES

Hayes p. 189; Roosevelt p. 30; cf. Fillmore ca. 1858 p. 45; cf. Fillmore 1861 p. 154.

COPY DESCRIBED

DLC: JK1 N5 Set 1. *Leaf.* octavo, 238 × 140; quarto, 305 × 203.

---

1. Noval Neil Luxon, *Niles' Weekly Register: News Magazine of the Nineteenth Century* (Westport, Conn.: Greenwood, 1947), 8. See entries 2, 83, 49, and 94 for Adams, Jefferson, Jackson, and Lafayette, respectively.

2. Mott, *History of American Magazines 1741–1850*, 269; Neal Edgar, *A History and Bibliography of American Magazines 1810–1820* (Metuchen, N.J.: Scarecrow Press, 1975), 15.

3. Luxon, *Niles' Weekly Register*, 1.

4. Qtd. in ibid., 2.

5. Ibid., 3.

6. Ibid.; Mott, *History of American Magazines, 1741–1850,* 269.

7. Luxon, *Niles' Weekly Register,* 5.

~

123. *North American Review and Miscellaneous Journal.* Boston: Wells and Lilly, 1815–50.

Distinguished as America's oldest literary magazine, the *North American Review* is still in publication today. Founded by a group of friends at Harvard in 1815 as a bimonthly publication, the *North American* was a cross between an English review magazine like the *Edinburgh Review* and a miscellany akin to the *Gentlemen's Magazine.* By the end of 1818, it had become more of a review than a magazine, discarding its news, notes, general essays, and poetry, and adopting quarterly publication. The *North American* published few political essays, but made exceptions when a social or economic discussion veered into politics.[1]

The *North American* underwent many changes in its editorship, with each new editor influencing the nature of the periodical in his own way. Jared Sparks served twice as editor, a one-year term from 1817 to 1818 and a six-year term from 1823 through 1830. Perhaps the single most important piece that he published during his first reign as editor was William Cullen Bryant's "Thanatopsis." Like all items in the *North American,* this poem was published anonymously. Edward Everett took the helm in 1820 and remained there until 1823. Under Everett's leadership the circulation is said to have increased from approximately five or six hundred to twenty-five hundred. Everett himself wrote many of the articles that were published and leads the list of contributors with 116 articles in the *North American's* first forty-five years.[2]

Through the mid-nineteenth century a number of other notable men were affiliated with and contributed to the *North American,* including ex-President John Adams, Joseph Story, George Ticknor, Daniel Webster, Caleb Cushing, Henry Wheaton, Theron Metcalf, George Bancroft, Francis Parkman, and William H. Prescott, to name just a few. Most of these authors appear elsewhere on the shelves of the Executive Mansion library, for they were some of the leading intellectuals of the time, and their ideas shaped mid-nineteenth-century American thought and culture. The purchase of a complete run of the *North American* for the library supplied a chronicle of the previous thirty-five years of American intellectual life beyond the realm of politics.[3]

105,133 voucher 5: North American Review 72 vols. $123.37.

Purchased from Charles Welford on December 13, 1850.

Hayes Catalogue: *North American Review.* May 1815 to Oct. 1850 v. 1–71 with Index to v. 1 to 25. 72 v. Boston 1815–50. 8°.

TITLE PAGE

THE | NORTH-AMERICAN REVIEW | AND | MISCELLANEOUS JOURNAL. | VOLUME SECOND. | BOSTON: | PRINTED AND PUBLISHED BY WELLS AND LILLY, | Court-Street. | [dotted rule] | 1816.

THE | NORTH AMERICAN REVIEW. | VOL. XIII. | [thin double rule] | NEW SERIES. | VOL. IV. | [thick/thin double rule] | BOSTON: | PUBLISHED BY OLIVER EVERETT, NO. 6 COURT STREET. | [thin double rule] | University Press—Hilliard & Metcalf. | 1821.

REFERENCES

Hayes p. 189; Roosevelt p. 31; cf. L and B 1852 p. 5; cf. L and B 1853 p. 49; Roorbach p. 649; cf. Fillmore 1847 p. 15; cf. Fillmore ca. 1858 p. 45; cf. Fillmore 1861 p. 154.

COPY DESCRIBED

DLC: AP2 N7. *Leaf.* 214 × 128.

---

1. Mott, *History of American Magazines, 1850–1865*, 219–41.
2. Ibid.; Fillmore sought Everett's advice on purchases for the library and named Everett as secretary of state after the death of Daniel Webster.
3. For Jared Sparks, see entries 159–62; for John Adams, 2; for Joseph Story, 164–66; for Daniel Webster, 184–85; for Henry Wheaton, 188–89; for Theron Metcalf, 175; for George Bancroft, 13; and for William H. Prescott, 131–33.

124. *Official Opinions of the Attorneys General.* 5 vols. Washington: Farnham, 1852.

The *Official Opinions of the Attorneys General* publishes the most important opinions rendered by this office holder. The attorney general is the official legal advisor to the president and department heads; he or she is also solicitor of the treasury and counselor and advocate of the government in all suits pending in the Supreme Court in which the United States is concerned. The *Official Opinions* did not begin to be published until 1852, when the first five volumes were issued. They are retrospective and contain a compilation of opinions dating back to 1789.[1]

While this edition is designed for "Jurists and Statesmen generally," other "officers of the government" may also find it useful (1:iii). Each volume contains an index that groups all of the decisions relating to the same subject under one heading, and each page includes the name of the author of the opinion that appears on it, the person to whom it is addressed, and the subject. Fillmore purchased this set from its publisher immediately after it became available.

109,399 voucher 2: 1 set Opinions Attorney Genl 5 vols. $15.00.

Purchased from R. Farnham on September 21, 1852.

Hayes Catalogue: *Attorney General Official Opinions.* v. 1 to 14. Washington 1852–75. 8°.

TITLE PAGE

OFFICIAL OPINIONS | OF | THE ATTORNEYS GENERAL | OF THE UNITED STATES, | ADVISING THE | PRESIDENT AND HEADS OF DEPARTMENTS, | IN RELATION TO THEIR OFFICIAL DUTIES; | AND EXPOUNDING THE CONSTITUTION, SUBSISTING TREATIES WITH | FOREIGN GOVERNMENTS AND WITH INDIAN TRIBES, AND | THE PUBLIC LAWS OF THE COUNTRY. | [thin rule] | COMPILED WITH NOTES AND REFERENCES, | By BENJAMIN F. HALL, | COUNSELLOR AT LAW, NEW YORK. | [thin rule] | VOLUME I. [II–V.] | PUBLISHED, WITH COPIOUS INDICES AND A DIGEST, | By ROBERT FARNHAM. | [thin rule] | WASHINGTON: | 1852.

Note. In the fourth line from the bottom of volumes 3 and 4, a lower case "y" instead of a small capital is used in "BY."

PAGINATION

Vol. I. i–viii 17–784.

Vol. II. [4] 1–798.

Vol. III. [4] 1–816.

Vol. IV. [4] 1–784.

Vol. V. i–xii 1–64 61–448.

> *Note.* The pagination error here is not simply a duplication of pages. Page 61 seems to be printed twice, but the second series of pages 62–64 has different text from the first.

CONTENTS

Vol. I. i title, ii copyright statement, iii–v advertisement, vi blank, vii list of attorneys general whose opinions are reported in this volume, viii blank, 17–735 text, 736 blank, 737–84 index.

Vol. II. [1] title, [2] copyright statement, [3] list of attorneys general whose opinions are reported in this volume, [4] blank, 1–733 text, 734–36 blank, 737–97 index, 798 blank.

Vol. III. [1] title, [2] copyright statement, [3] list of attorneys general whose opinions are reported in this volume, [4] blank, 1–751 text, 752 blank, 753–816 index.

Vol. IV. [1] title, [2] copyright statement, [3] list of attorneys general whose opinions are reported in this volume, [4] blank, 1–729 text, 730 blank, 731–83 index, 784 blank.

Vol. V. i title, ii copyright statement, iii–v list of attorneys general whose opinions are reported in these volumes, vi blank, vii advertisement, viii blank, ix–xi "Office of the Attorneys General," xii blank, 1–399 text, 400 blank, 401–48 index.

REFERENCES

Hayes p. 301; cf. Harvard p. 94 and p. 180; cf. Roorbach p. 625.

COPY DESCRIBED

MH: KF 5406 A615. *Leaf.* 229 × 142.

---

1. Laurence F. Schmeckebier and Roy B. Eastin, eds., *Government Publications and Their Use*, 2nd rev. ed. (Washington, D.C.: Brookings Institution, 1969), iii–ix.

❧

125. Paget, John. *Hungary and Transylvania.* 2 vols. Philadelphia: Lea and Blanchard, 1850.

The Hungarian war for independence in 1848 drew attention to John Paget's *Hungary and Transylvania* (1839) as a reliable source for information relative to this region. Critics believed that it provided a "clear view of the state of the country, and the reasons which induced the late insurrection." Furthermore, it showed the causes of the revolution's failure and its likely aftermath.[1] Paget (1808–92), agriculturist and writer, wrote this travelogue based on his own excursions in Hungary. First published in 1839, it was well received and soon translated into German. In October of 1850 Fillmore's administration had to answer the charge made by Austria's *chargé d'affaires* in Washington that the United States had been "impatient for the downfall of the Austrian monarchy." Perhaps this accusation prompted

Fillmore to select this book as one of the earliest purchases for the library, made prior to Lanman's purchasing trip. In fact, two copies of this book were purchased, both from Franck Taylor, the first in November of 1850 and the second in January of 1852, just after the leader of the revolution, Louis Kossuth, visited the White House with his entourage. No information has been found to explain the purchase of the second copy; however, in 1877 only one copy was recorded in the Hayes catalogue.[2]

105,133 voucher 7: Hungary & Transylvania by Paget 2 vols. $2.00.
Purchased from Franck Taylor on Nov. 27, 1850.
109,399 voucher 4: Paget's Hungary 2 vols. $2.00.
Purchased from Franck Taylor on January 12, 1852.
Roosevelt Catalogue: Paget, John. *Hungary and Transylvania; with Remarks on Their Condition, Social, Political, and Economical.* Philadelphia: Lea and Blanchard, 1850, 2 vols.

TITLE PAGE

HUNGARY | AND | TRANSYLVANIA; | WITH REMARKS ON THEIR CONDITION, | SOCIAL, POLITICAL AND ECONOMICAL. | BY | JOHN PAGET, ESQ. | Beata Ungheria! Se non si lascia | Più malmenare. | DANTE. | [thin rule] | from the New London Edition, [black letter] | IN TWO VOLUMES. | VOL. I. [II.] | [thin rule] | PHILADELPHIA: | LEA & BLANCHARD. | 1850.

PAGINATION

Vol. I. i–xvi 13–368.
Vol. II. i–vi 13–324.

CONTENTS

Vol. I. i title, ii printer's imprint, iii dedication 'TO HER | FOR WHOSE PLEASURE THIS WORK WAS UNDERTAKEN, | BY WHOSE SMILES ITS PROGRESS HAS | BEEN ENCOURAGED, | AND AT WHOSE DESIRE IT IS NOW PUBLISHED, | I DEDICATE IT, | IN TESTIMONY OF MY AFFECTION | AND ESTEEM. | J. P.', iv blank, v–x preface, xi–xv contents, xvi blank, 13–324 text, 325–68 Lea and Blanchard advertisement.
Vol. II. i title, ii printer's imprint, iii–vi contents, 13–324 text.

> *Note.* Although the pagination jumps from xvi to 13 in volume 1 and vi to 13 in volume 2, there do not appear to be any pages missing. The tables of contents both indicate the text as beginning on page 13.

REFERENCES

Hayes p. 207; Roosevelt p. 32; Putnam p. 102; Roorbach p. 411.

COPY DESCRIBED

DLC: DB 934 P3 1850a. *Leaf.* 187 × 108.

---

1. "New Publications," *The Literary World*, September 7, 1850, available at *APS Online*, http://www.proquest.com/products_pq/descriptions/aps.shtml.

2. Rayback, *Millard Fillmore*, 327–28; see "White House Collection," 22, for more about the Hungarian revolution; see entries 93 and 136 for other books in the White House Library relative to the revolution.

126. Paley, William. *Paley's Works.* London: Bohn, 1847.

This edition of William Paley's (1743–1805) *Works* includes his most important writings: *Principles of Moral and Political Philosophy* (1785), *A View of the Evidences of Christianity* (1794), *Horae Paulinae* (1790), and *Natural Theology* (1802). His works stood in dialogue with other authors found in the first White House Library; while *Principles* was influenced by Thomas Rutherforth's *Institutes of Natural Law* and the writings of John Locke, *A View of the Evidences* attempted to answer David Hume's skepticism. Paley's writings also influenced Thomas Malthus and William Whewell, two other authors whose books were purchased for the White House Library. *Principles* remained on the mandatory reading list for Cambridge University into the early nineteenth century, appeared in ten American editions between 1814 and 1821, and is said to have been the most popular work on moral philosophy in the United States until the Civil War.[1]

105,133 voucher 5: Paleys Works $1.75.
Purchased from Charles Welford on December 13, 1850.
Roosevelt Catalogue: Paley, William. *Paley's Works; Consisting of Evidences of Christianity, Moral and Political Philosophy, Natural Theology, and Horae Pauline.* London, M. G. Bohn, 1847.

TITLE PAGE
PALEY'S WORKS; | CONSISTING OF | EVIDENCES OF CHRISTIANITY, | MORAL AND POLITICAL PHILOSOPHY, | NATURAL THEOLOGY, | AND | HORÆ PAULINÆ. | COMPLETE IN ONE VOLUME. | LONDON: | HENRY G. BOHN, YORK STREET, COVENT GARDEN. | MDCCCXLVII.

PAGINATION
i–vi 1–162 i–viii 9–200 1–138 1–100 103–68.

CONTENTS
i title, ii blank, iii–iv "A Brief Memoir of the Author," v letter to the Honourable and Right Reverend Shute Barrington, LL.D., Lord Bishop of Durham, vi blank, 1 letter to the Honourable and Right Reverend James York, D.D. Lord Bishop of Ely, 2 blank, 3 section title, "A View of the Evidences of Christianity in Three Parts," 4–162 text of *Evidences of Christianity,* i section title, "Moral and Political Philosophy," ii blank, iii–iv letter to the Right Reverend Edmund Law, D.D., Lord Bishop of Carlisle, v–viii preface to *Moral Philosophy,* 9–200 text of *Moral Philosophy,* 1–138 text of *Natural Theology,* 1 section title, "Horæ Paulinæ, Clergymen's Companion, Tracts," 2 blank, 3 Dedication to the Right Reverend John Law D.D., Lord Bishop of Killala and Achony, 4 blank, 5–98 text of *Horæ Paulinæ,* 99 title, "The Clergymen's Companion," 100–152 text of *Clergymen's Companion,* 153–68 text of tracts.

BINDING
Front and back board. 225 × 145 medium blue cloth, with ruled frame surrounding a cartouche frame. *Spine.* Five panels blind stamped with 'PALEY'S | WORKS' gilt stamped in second panel. *Endpapers.* Pale yellow.

REFERENCES

Hayes p. 207; Roosevelt p. 32; cf. Fillmore 1847 p. 15; cf. Fillmore ca. 1858 p. 50; cf. Fillmore 1861 p. 162.

COPY DESCRIBED

MH: *98–976. *Leaf.* 210 × 127.

---

1. For Locke, see entry 98; Rutherforth, see entry 142; Hume, see entry 80; Malthus, see entry 108; and Whewell, see entry 190.

∼

127. **Pardoe, Julia.** *Louis the Fourteenth and the Court of France in the Seventeenth Century.* 3rd ed. 3 vols. London: Bentley, 1849.

Although Julia Pardoe (1804–62) wrote novels, travel literature, and short stories in addition to history, her historical writings are her most enduring and remained in print well into the twentieth century. Pardoe's *Louis the Fourteenth and the Court of France* (1846) focuses on the King's private, domestic life rather than his public, political presence. In her words, "We are not about to offer our readers an *historical* record of the century of Louis XIV, as the term would be understood by statesmen and politicians; for we shall pass lightly over the campaigns, the battles, and the intrigues of the several European Cabinets.... Our aim will simply be to display more fully than has yet been done the domestic life of the 'Great Monarch'; and to pass in review the wits, the beauties, and the poets of his Court" (1:vi). Pardoe was nevertheless criticized for overlooking political matters and for relying too heavily on the work of the acclaimed French historian Alexandre Dumas. She defends herself by reminding readers that she wrote of the man, not the monarch, and that she and Dumas relied on the same sources—personal memoirs and biographies—and therefore produced similar paragraphs.

Pardoe's work received glowing reviews in American periodicals. *The Anglo American* found it a work of "superior order" and suggested that "no book of the day is more suited to please those who seek amusement combined with profit, and certainly much that is new, enticing, and instructive is to be gathered from this work." *Graham's American Monthly Magazine of Literature* praised this book and its author, pointing to Pardoe's gender as a distinct advantage: "Miss Pardoe follows with her keen, patient mind, the manifold turns of court diplomacy, and discerns, with feminine sagacity, all the nicer and finer threads of the complicated web of intrigue. As a woman, she is acute to discover the hand and brain of her own sex in every incident where women took part; and none but a woman could fully unveil many of the events which elevated or disgraced France during the reign of Louis."[1] Although Harper and Brothers brought out an American edition of this work the same year as it was published in England, the White House selected the London edition. While the Harper edition was in two volumes with no index, the London edition was in three volumes and included an index, which may be why it was selected over the American one. Walt Whitman owned a copy of the Harper edition, which is now held by the Rare Book and Special Collection Division of the Library of Congress.[2] Subsequent to the Fillmores' time in the White House, Pardoe's *The Court and Reign of Francis the First, King of France* was also purchased for the library and duly recorded in the Hayes and Roosevelt catalogues.

105,133 voucher 5: Pardoes Louis 14 & His France 3 vols. $5.00.

Purchased from Charles Welford on December 13, 1850.

Roosevelt Catalogue: Pardoe, <u>Miss</u> Julia. *Louis the Fourteenth and the Court of France in the Seventeenth Century.* Third edition. London, Richard Bentley, 1849, 3 vols.

TITLE PAGE

LOUIS THE FOURTEENTH, I AND I THE COURT OF FRANCE [red ink] I IN I THE SEVENTEENTH CENTURY. I BY MISS PARDOE. [red ink] I AUTHOR OF "THE CITY OF THE SULTAN," ETC. I [printer's ornament] I IN THREE VOLUMES. I VOL. I. [II–III] I THIRD EDITION, I WITH AN INDEX NOW FIRST ADDED. I LONDON: I RICHARD BENTLEY, NEW BURLINGTON STREET, I Publisher in Ordinary to Her Majesty [black letter, red ink] I M.DCCC.XLIX.

PAGINATION

Vol. I. [*14*] v–xvi 1–456.

Vol. II. i–x 1–456.

Vol. III. i–x 1–506.

CONTENTS

Vol. I. [*1*] half title, [*2*] printer's imprint, [*3*] title, [*4*] blank, [*5*] dedication to John Hearne, Esq., [*6*] blank, [*7*]–[*13*] preface to the second edition, [*14*] blank, v–viii preface, ix–xv contents, xvi list of illustrations, 1–455 text, 456 printer's imprint.

Vol. II. i title, ii blank, iii–ix contents, x list of illustrations, 1–456 text.

Vol. III. i title, ii blank, iii–viii contents, ix list of illustrations, x blank, 1–457 text, 458 blank, 459–505 index, 506 blank.

PLATES

Vol. I.

Portrait frontispiece, Louis XIV, "from the original in the Versailles Gallery," engraved by J. Cook.

Vol. II.

Portrait frontispiece, Mademoiselle de la Vallère, "from the original in the Versailles Gallery," engraved by J. Cook.

Facing 348, portrait of Louis XIV, "from a rare print by Van Schuppen, after Mignard (1662)," engraved by W. Greatbatch.

Vol. III.

Portrait frontispiece, Madame Maintenon, "from the original in the Versailles Gallery," engraved by J. Cook.

Facing 168, Louis XIV, "from a rare print by Vermeulen after Geuslin," engraved by W. Greatbatch.

REFERENCES

Hayes p. 208; Roosevelt p. 32; cf. *LC 1816–1851* p. 422.

1. "Literary Notices," *Anglo American*, August 14, 1847, and "Review 2—No Title," *Graham's American Monthly Magazine of Literature*, October 1847, both available at *APS Online*, http://www.proquest.com/products_pq/descriptions/aps.shtml.

2. The call number is Feinberg Whitman DC129 p24 1847.

∽

128. *The Penny Cyclopaedia.* 16 vols. London: Charles Knight, 1833–43.

The *Penny Cyclopaedia* was a popular reference work published for the Society for the Diffusion of Useful Knowledge (SDUK), an organization that was established to publish "cheap and accessible works on both scientific and artistic subjects." It was issued for 9*d.* per part or 7*s.* 6*d.* per clothbound volume.[1] The plan for the publication of the *Penny Cyclopædia* can be followed as it was revised and modified in the prefaces of each volume. First issued in six parts per month, it soon accelerated the pace to two parts per week. The publisher anticipated that a new volume would be completed every eight months. Volume 6 promised to complete the *Cyclopædia* in eighteen to twenty volumes and revised the publication plan to issue three rather than two volumes annually. Under this schedule, the *Cyclopædia* would have been completed by 1838; however, the project exceeded its limit by about one fourth; volume 27 projected a completion date of December 20, 1843. In defense of this delinquency, the publisher claimed that the last letters of the alphabet had not been hurriedly abridged and informed that the complete set included over two hundred contributors and that "no less a sum than forty thousand pounds" had been spent "on the literature and engraving alone" (27:iii).

A writer for the *Cincinnati Mirror* took note of the New York reprint of the *Penny Cyclopaedia* and praised it as "one of the most efficient publications" for "rendering knowledge as cheap and as widely diffused as possible." The same writer recommended the *Penny Cyclopaedia* "to all those who wish to procure a large amount of valuable matter for a little of money."[2] While Putnam listed a sixteen-volume set of the *Penny Cyclopædia* in half morocco with cloth sides and marbled leaves for $70.00, Little and Brown advertised a set in half calf for $60.00. Since the White House paid only $40.00 for this title, its copy was probably bound in cloth. The Fillmores purchased both the *Penny Cyclopaedia* and the *Encyclopaedia Americana* for the new library. A comparison between the two sets reveals that some articles in the former read verbatim as they first appeared in the latter.

105,133 voucher 4: Penny Cyclopaedia ~~17~~ 16 vol. $40.00.

Purchased from George P. Putnam on December 13, 1850.

Roosevelt Catalogue: *The Penny Cyclopaedia of the Society for the Diffusion of Useful Knowledge,* London, C. Knight, 1833, 27 vols. in 14 & supplement 2 vols.

TITLE PAGE

THE | PENNY CYCLOPÆDIA | OF | THE SOCIETY | FOR THE | DIFFUSION OF USEFUL KNOWLEDGE. | [thin rule] | VOLUME I. [II–XXVII.] | A—ANDES. | [thin rule] | LONDON: | CHARLES KNIGHT, 22, LUDGATE STREET, AND 13, PALL-MALL

EAST. | [thin rule] | MDCCCXXXIII. | [thin rule] | *Price Seven Shillings and Sixpence, bound in cloth.*

SUPPLEMENT

THE | SUPPLEMENT | TO THE | PENNY CYCLOPÆDIA | OF | THE SOCIETY | FOR THE | DIFFUSION OF USEFUL KNOWLEDGE. | [thin rule] | VOLUME I. [II.] | ABATI— GYROSTEUS. | [thin rule] | LONDON: | CHARLES KNIGHT AND Co., 22, LUDGATE STREET. | [thin rule] | MDCCCLI. | [thin rule] | *Price Twelve Shillings, bound in cloth.*

Note. An early edition of the supplement was not available for description.

REFERENCES

Hayes p. 209; Roosevelt p. 32; L and B 1850 p. 69–70; cf. Putnam p. 106; cf. *LC 1816–1851* p. 431; cf. Fillmore ca. 1858 p. 11; cf. Fillmore 1861 p. 48.

COPY DESCRIBED

DLC: AE 5 P4. *Leaf.* 279 × 175.

---

1. Walsh, *Anglo-American General Encyclopedias,* 142.
2. "The Penny Cyclopedia," *Cincinnati Mirror, and Western Gazette of Literature, Science, and the Arts,* May 30, 1835, available at *APS Online,* http://www.proquest.com/products_pq/descriptions/aps.shtml.

∼

129. Phillips, Charles. *Curran and His Contemporaries.* New York: Harper, 1851.

Harper's edition of *Curran and His Contemporaries* received much critical acclaim. *The Literary World* remarked that "the animated pictures of the wit, humour, social and political relations of the Irish patriots of the opening of the present century . . . have been favorites of the older members of the present generation." *Graham's American Monthly Magazine of Literature, Art, and Fashion* did not stint on praise for this work, which "blazes from beginning to end with eloquence and wit" and "conveys the most accurate as well as the richest and raciest notion of the old orators and statesmen of Ireland, that we have in print."[1]

Although there were several editions of *Curran and His Contemporaries* that had been published before 1850, the Harper edition was most likely the one selected for the White House Library. The reviewer for the *Literary World* remarked that this title had been out of print for some time, and the Harper edition included corrections and revisions by Phillips. Roorbach recorded the Harper edition for just $0.88, which accords more closely with the price of $0.75 paid by the White House. Moreover, the *National Era* advertised that the Harper edition could be purchased in Washington from Franck Taylor, who in fact supplied the Executive Mansion copy.[2] Editions dated 1850 and 1851 were available from Harper, but since these were probably printed on stereotype plates, the content of the two would have been the same.

C. Wiley in New York and T. Hookham in London originally published this work in 1818 under the title *Recollections of Curran and His Cotemporaries* [*sic*], apparently with such success that Simpkin and Marshall published it again in London in 1822. In 1850 Blackwood in London and Edinburgh and Harper in New York began to publish it as just *Curran and His Contemporaries.* The *London Catalogue* listed the Simpkin and Marshall edition at 10*s.* and

6*d.* or approximately $2.50 in United States currency. Although no pricing information has been found for the 1818 editions, Putnam's catalogues advertised the Edinburgh edition at $3.25, which would be too high for it to qualify for this purchase.

107,754 voucher 3: Curran & His Contemporaries $0.75.
Purchased from Franck Taylor on May 10, 1851.

REFERENCES
cf. Roorbach p. 427; cf. Fillmore 1847 p. 14; cf. Fillmore Packing Lists p. 5; cf. Fillmore ca. 1858 pp. 9, 10; cf. Fillmore 1861 p. 46.

---

1. *Literary World*, November 9, 1850, and *Graham's American Monthly Magazine of Literature, Art, and Fashion*, July 1851, both available at *APS Online*, http://www.proquest.com/products_pq/descriptions/aps.shtml. The White House also purchased Curran's *Speeches*. See entry 43.
2. "Review 1—No Title," *National Era*, May 22, 1851, available at *APS Online*, http://www.proquest.com/products_pq/descriptions/aps.shtml.

130. Phillips, Samuel. *Essays from the London Times.* 1st ser. New York: Appleton, 1852.

Essays from the London Times is a collection that addresses historical topics such as the French revolution of 1848, railway novels, ancient Egypt, and sporting in America as well as biographical subjects, including Jonathan Swift, Robert Southey, Samuel Taylor Coleridge, and John Keats. As a justification for this compilation, the publisher claimed that the *London Times* is "among the most accomplished intellectual products of England" and asserted that "its leaders influence opinion throughout the world" (5–6). *Essays* was published in London by Murray and in New York by Appleton. With the exception of two articles, both publishers include the same selection. The White House most likely purchased the New York edition from Appleton. While it sold for only $0.50, the price indicated on the voucher for this purchase, the London edition sold for 8*s.* in two volumes or about $1.00 per volume in United States currency.[1] Appleton issued this title in a "first series" and a "second series"; both series were included in *Appleton's Popular Library of the Best Authors*. The White House must have purchased only the first series. While the publisher's advertisement in it is dated March 1852, one month prior to the date it was purchased, the advertisement in the second series is dated October of 1852 and, therefore, could not have been chosen for the White House the previous April.

109,399 voucher 1: Essays from the London Times $0.50.
Purchased from Taylor and Maury on April 13, 1852.

TITLE PAGE
ESSAYS | FROM | THE LONDON TIMES: | A COLLECTION OF | PERSONAL AND HISTORICAL SKETCHES. | NEW YORK: | D. APPLETON & COMPANY, 200 BROADWAY. | M.DCCC.LII.

PAGINATION
1–6 9–22 [2] 23–302 i–viii.

CONTENTS

1 title, 2 blank, 3 contents, 4 blank, 5–6 publisher's advertisement, 9–22 text [1] series title, "Appleton's Popular Library of the Best Authors. Essays from the London Times." [2] list of titles in series, 23–301 text, 302 blank, i–viii advertisements for *Appleton's Popular Library*.

> *Note.* Clearly the series title has been misbound. It may have been intended to appear at the very front of the volume, or it may have belonged just after page 6, where there is a break in pagination.

REFERENCES

Roorbach p. 181; cf. Fillmore 1861 p. 208.

COPY DESCRIBED

DLC: D210 P5. *Leaf.* 168 × 106.

---

1. Low, *English Catalogue*, 238.

❧

131. Prescott, William H. *The History of the Reign of Ferdinand and Isabella, the Catholic.* 3 vols. New York: Harper, 1849.

132. ———. *History of the Conquest of Mexico.* 3 vols. New York: Harper, 1849.

**133. ———. *History of the Conquest of Peru.* 2 Vols. New York: Harper, 1848.

During the nineteenth century, William Hickling Prescott (1796–1859) became known as the preeminent historian of Spain. He wrote four works on Spanish history, including *The History of the Reign of Ferdinand and Isabella, the Catholic* (1838), *The Conquest of Mexico* (1843), *The Conquest of Peru* (1847), and *The History of the Reign of Philip the Second* (1855 and 1859). The Fillmores included Prescott's first three works in their selections for the White House Library; the fourth was not yet available. The Executive Mansion copy of the *Conquest of Peru* was found in the Library of Congress stacks and is inscribed "Executive Mansion 1850" on the front pastedown.

All three of the titles that were purchased are advertised in the catalogue "Valuable and Standard Works Published by Harper & Brothers," which is bound into volume 6 of a Library of Congress copy of Hildreth's *History of America*.[1] Prices are given for each title in three different bindings as follows. *Peru:* muslin, $4.50; sheep extra, $4.50; and half calf, $5.00. *Mexico:* muslin, $6.00; sheep extra, $6.75; and half calf, $7.50. *Ferdinand and Isabella:* muslin, $6.00; sheep extra, $6.75; and half calf, $7.50. The Executive Mansion copy of *Peru* survives in its original binding of half calf, and it is probable that all three of these titles would have been purchased in similar bindings. All were acquired from the same seller and listed in one line on the voucher. The retail total for all three in half calf would have been $20.00, and a 10 percent discount would have been in keeping with the booksellers' practice of offering discounts on large orders.

105,133 voucher 5: Prescott's Historical Works, Ferdinand & Isabella Conquest. Mexico & Conquest Peru 18.00.
Purchased from Charles Welford on December 13, 1850.

Roosevelt Catalogue: Prescott, William Hickling. *History of the Conquest of Mexico, with a Preliminary View of the Ancient Western Mexican Civilization, and the Life of the Conqueror, Hernando Cortes.* New York: Harper and Brothers, 1849, 3 vols. Vol. 2 missing.

———. *History of the Conquest of Peru, with a Preliminary View of the Civilization of the Incas.* New York: Harper & Brothers, 1848, 2 vols.

———. *History of the Reign of Ferdinand and Isabella the Catholic.* New York: Harper & Brothers, 1849, 3 vols.

Reign of Ferdinand and Isabella.

TITLE PAGE

HISTORY | OF | THE REIGN OF | FERDINAND AND ISABELLA, | THE CATHOLIC. | [thin rule] | By WILLIAM II. PRESCOTT. | [thin rule] | Quæ surgere regna | Conjugio tali! | *Virgil. Æneid.* iv. 47. | Crevere vires, famaque et imperî | Porrecta majestas ab Euro | Solis ad Occiduum cubile. | *Horat. Carm.* iv. 15. | [thin rule] | IN THREE VOLUMES.— VOL. I. [II–III.]| TENTH EDITION. | [printers ornament, armorial shield with crown on top] | HARPER & BROTHERS, PUBLISHERS, | 82 CLIFF STREET, NEW YORK. | 1849.

PAGINATION

Vol. I. [*4*] i–cxxiv 1–412.

Vol. II. i–xviii 1–510.

Vol. III. i–xvi 1–532 1–4.

CONTENTS

Vol. I. [*1*] half title, [*2*] blank, [*3*] title, [*4*] copyright statement, i dedication to William Prescott, LL. D., ii blank, iii–xiii preface to the first edition, xiv blank, xv–xvi preface to the third English edition, xvii–xxvii contents, xxviii illustrations, xxix–cxxxiv introduction, 1–411 text, 412 blank.

Vol. II. i half title, ii blank, iii title, iv copyright statement, v–xviii contents, 1 section title, "Part First, 1406–92 continued," 2 blank, 3–509 text, 510 blank.

Vol. III. i half title, ii blank, iii title, iv copyright statement, v–xvi contents, 1–496 text, 497–531 index, 532 blank, 1–4 advertisement for valuable standard works for libraries, published by Harper & Brothers.

PLATES

Vol. I.

Portrait frontispiece, "Isabella the Catholic, after an engraving of a picture in the Royal Palace at Madrid," engraved by J. Andrews.

Bifolium between xxviii and xxix, "Facsimiles of Autographs for the History of the Reign of Ferdinand and Isabella."

Facing 1, "Genealogy of Ferdinand and Isabella."

Vol. II.

Portrait frontispiece, "Ferdinand the Catholic," signed in lower left, Ximeno and Cameron, and lower right, G. F. Storm.

Facing 1, "Map for the War of Granada."

Facing 401, "Cardinal Ximenes de Cisnero Regent of Castile," signed in lower left, J. Maea, and lower right, G. F. Storm.

Vol. III.

Portrait frontispiece, "Christopher Columbus, from a picture by Parmigiano in the Royal Gallery at Naples." Engraved by W. Greatbatch.

Facing 1, "Map for Consalvo de Cordobas campaigns in Italy."

Facing 368, Gonsalvo Fernandez of Cordova (a medallion), engraved by Freelinirn.

BINDING

Front and back boards. 243 × 152 med. brown ribbed cloth with blind-stamped cartouche frame. *Spine.* '[Decorative blind-stamped band] | PRESCOTT'S | FERDINAND | AND | ISABELLA. [thin rule] | VOL. 1. [2–3.] [all text gilt stamped] | [decorative blind-stamped band] | [decorative blind-stamped band] | [gilt-stamped printers ornament] | [blind-stamped thin rule] | NEW YORK | HARPER & BROTHERS | blind-stamped thin rule]'. *Endpapers.* White.

REFERENCES

Hayes p. 218; Roosevelt p. 33; cf. Roorbach p. 443; cf. Putnam p. 111; cf. L and B 1850 p. 72; cf. Fillmore 1861 p. 78.

COPY DESCRIBED

ViU: F229 C28292 P73H585 1849. *Leaf.* 237 × 147.

Conquest of Mexico.

TITLE PAGE

HISTORY | OF THE | CONQUEST OF MEXICO | WITH A PRELIMINARY VIEW | OF THE | ANCIENT MEXICAN CIVILIZATION, AND THE | LIFE OF THE CONQUEROR, | HERNANDO CORTÉS. | BY | WILLIAM H. PRESCOTT, | AUTHOR OF THE "HISTORY OF FERDINAND AND ISABELLA." | [thin rule] | "Victrices aquilas alium laturus in orbem." | LUCAN, Pharsalia, lib. v., v. 238 | [thin rule] | IN THREE VOLUMES. | VOLUME I. [II.–III.] | EIGHTH EDITION. | NEW YORK: | HARPER AND BROTHERS, 82, CLIFF STREET | MDCCCXLIX.

> *Notes.* Volume 3 of this copy is dated 1850. Volume 2 of DLC: F 1230 P934 is missing. An 1848 copy of volume 2 has been used for this description, DLC: F1230 P933. The two copies appear to have been printed from the same set of stereotype plates as indicated by shared type damage. Despite their difference in dates, the edition statement on the title page of each reads "Eighth Edition."

PAGINATION

Vol. I. i–xxxiv 1–488.

Vol. II. i–xviii 1–480.

Vol. III. i–xviii 1–524.

CONTENTS

Vol. I. i half title, ii blank, iii title, iv copyright statement, v–xvi preface, xvii general contents, xviii blank, xix–xxxii contents, xxxiii–xxxiv maps and illustrations, 1–488 text.

Vol. II. i half title, ii blank, iii title, iv copyright statement, v–xviii contents, 1–480 text.

Vol. III. i half title, ii blank, iii title, iv copyright statement, v–xvii contents, xviii blank, 1–365 text, 366 blank, 367–479 appendix, 480 blank, 481–524 index.

PLATES

Vol. I.

Portrait frontispiece of Hernando Cortes, engraved by G. F. Storm.

Bifolium inserted between xxxiv and 1, "Map of the Country Traversed by the Spaniards on their March to Mexico."

Vol. II.

Portrait frontispiece of Montezuma, II, Emperor of Mexico, engraved by William Greatbach.

Bifolium inserted between xviii and 1, "Map of the Valley of Mexico at the Period of the Conquest."

Vol. III.

Portrait Frontispiece of Hernan Cortes, engraved by W. Greatbach.

Facing 1, facsimile of the signature of Cortes.

BINDING

Front and back boards. 241 × 141, blue ribbed cloth, blind stamped with decorative frame. *Spine.* Blind-stamped decorative rules with gilt-stamped lettering, '[decorative rule] | PRESCOTT's | CONQUEST | OF | MEXICO. | [thin rule, gilt stamped] | VOL. I. [II.–III.] | [decorative rule] | [decorative rule] | [armes of Cortés] | NEW-YORK | HARPER & BROTHERS.'

> *Note.* While F1230 P934 is rebound in a Library of Congress buckram binding, F1230 P933 is in a publisher's binding. The binding of the copy purchased for the Executive Mansion in 1850 was probably very similar to, if not the same as this one found on F1230 P933 and described here.

REFERENCES

Hayes p. 217; Roosevelt p. 33; cf. Putnam p. 111; cf. Roorbach p. 443; cf. L and B 1850 p. 72; cf. Fillmore 1861 p. 138.

COPY DESCRIBED

Vols. I and III. DLC: F 1230 P934. *Leaf.* 230 × 142.

Vols. II. DLC: F 1230 P933.

Conquest of Peru.

TITLE PAGE

HISTORY | OF THE | CONQUEST OF PERU, | WITH A PRELIMINARY VIEW | OF THE | CIVILIZATION OF THE INCAS. | BY | WILLIAM H. PRESCOTT, | CORRESPONDING MEMBER OF THE FRENCH INSTITUTE; OF THE ROYAL ACADEMY | OF HISTORY AT MADRID, ETC. | [thin rule] | "Congestæ cumulantur opes, orbisque rapinas | Accipit." | CLAUDIAN, In Ruf., lib. i., v. 194. | "So color de religion | Van a buscar plata y oro | Del encubierto tesoro." | LOPE DE VEGA, El Nuevo Mundo, Jorn. I. | [thin rule] | IN TWO VOLUMES. | VOLUME I. [II.] | [thin rule] | NEW YORK: | HARPER AND BROTHERS, 82 CLIFF STREET. | M DCCC XLVIII.

PAGINATION

Vol. I. i–xl 1–528.

Vol. II. i–xx 1–548.

CONTENTS

Vol. I. i half title, ii blank, iii title, iv copyright statement, v–xx preface, xxi–xxxvii contents, xxxviii blank, xxxix–xl illustrations, 1–527 text, 528 blank.

Vol. II. i half title, ii blank, iii title, iv copyright statement, v–xix contents, xx blank, 1–474 text, 475–519 appendix, 520–47 index, 548 blank.

PLATES

Vol. I.

Portrait frontispiece, Francisco Pizarro, engraved by Cook.

Facing 1, map of Peru.

Vol. II.

Portrait frontispiece, Pedro de la Gasca, engraved by Cook.

Facing 1, facsimile of two signatures of Francesco Pizarro.

BINDING

Front and back board. 235 × 150 half calf with brown cloth, no decoration. *Spine.* Gilt decoration across cords with black spine labels, gilt stamped, '[thin triple rule] | PRESCOTT. | [thin rule] | VOL. I. [II.] | [thin triple rule]'. *Endpapers.* Marbled.

MARKS OF OWNERSHIP

Vols. I and II. Front pastedown inscribed in black ink "Executive Mansion | 1850."

REFERENCES

Hayes p. 217; Roosevelt p. 33; cf. Putnam p. 111; cf. Roorbach p. 443; cf. Fillmore 1861 p. 164.

COPY DESCRIBED

DLC: F 3442 P914. *Leaf.* 231 × 141.

---

1. This catalogue is found in DLC E178 H66, a copy of the edition of Hildreth that was purchased for the first White House Library (see entry 78).

~

134. Prichard, James Cowles. *The Natural History of Man: Comprising Inquiries into the Modifying Influence of Physical and Moral Agencies on the Different Tribes of the Human Family.* London: H. Baillière, 1848.

James Cowles Prichard (1786–1848), physician and ethnologist, owes his reputation to his ethnological pursuits, which culminated in *The Natural History of Man* (1843). The *Natural History* began as his medical dissertation, written in Latin with the title *Disputatio inauguralis de generis humani varietate* (1808), which he rewrote five times. *The Natural History* became the most popular and biologically oriented version. In it he rejects eighteenth-century notions of environmentalism that were used to explain differences in race as well as the idea that acquired characteristics could become hereditary. By 1830 Prichard was recognized as the foremost authority on ethnological and anthropological matters.

Interest in the "history of man" as a topic was on the rise in the middle of the nineteenth century. An 1850 article surveys five books on the subject, with Prichard's *Researches into the Physical History of Man* (3rd ed., 1846–47) and his *Natural History* heading the list. Of

Prichard its writer claims, "By conjoining the physiological part of the inquiry with its historical and philological relations, they form the most ample and complete text we yet possess on the subject, and one to which all future investigation must be more or less referred."[1] Prichard's *Natural History* stood on the shelves of the White House Library alongside the other standard scientific texts of the time, including Lyell's *Geology,* John F. W. Herschel's *Astronomy,* Asa Gray's *Botany,* and Georges Cuvier's *Animal Kingdom.* The White House most likely selected the 1848 Baillière edition, since Baillière was the only publisher of this work prior to 1850, and the advertised price of $9.00 for its third edition of 1848 closely matches the price on the voucher.

105,133 voucher 2: Pritchard on Man $8.50.
Purchased from Little and Brown on December 30, 1850.

REFERENCES
cf. Putnam p. 111; cf. *LC 1816–1851* p. 450.

---

1. "Reviews," *Literary World 1847,* June 3, 1848, and "Review 13—No Title," *Littel's Living Age (1844–1896),* March 16, 1850, both available at *APS Online,* http://www.proquest.com/products_pq/descriptions/aps.shtml.

∼

135. **Pufendorf, Samuel.** *Law of Nature and Nations.* **5th ed. Trans. Basil Kennet. London: J. and J. Bonwicke, et al., 1749.**

The German legal professor Samuel baron von Pufendorf (1632–89) ranks among the chief exponents of the philosophical school of international law, in the company of Wolff and Vattel.[1] Nineteenth-century legal scholars recognized him as "one of the first and greatest expounders of natural law." Assessing his legacy, the *Encyclopaedia Americana* maintains, "With Grotius, he laid the foundation of law in the social instinct, which is nearly allied to the Christian precept of love of our neighbor, and with Hobbes, he derived law from the state of fallen nature."[2]

Although the voucher entry for this acquisition is scant, reading "Pufendorf ditto folio $12.50," it most likely refers to the 1749 London edition of Pufendorf's *Law of Nature and Nations* translated by Basil Kennet and published by J. and J. Bonwicke. To what the "ditto" in this entry refers is ambiguous. It follows two other entries with dittos:

Vattel's Law of Nations
Wheatons ditto ditto [Wheaton's Law of Nations]
ditto Elements [Wheaton's Elements of International Law]
Puffendorf ditto[3]

The "ditto" following Pufendorf could logically refer to the item immediately preceding it, in which case a work by Pufendorf with "Elements" in the title would be a logical choice; but it could also point back to the dittoless entry for Vattell's *Law of Nations,* and, in that case, Pufendorf's *Law of Nature and Nations* would be a possible choice. Pufendorf published a work entitled *Elementorum Jurisprudentua* in 1660; however, no record has been found of an English translation prior to 1850 for this title. Since Fillmore did not read Latin and he purchased no other titles in foreign languages, it seems unlikely that he would have purchased this one in Latin.

Pufendorf published a number of legal works, but *Law of Nature and Nations* is the only one recommended in the mid-nineteenth century by both Greenleaf and Hoffman.[4] Hoffman maintained that any serious law student must be familiar with Pufendorf and endorsed this, the most recent edition of *Law of Nature and Nations*. Furthermore, Edward Everett recommended this edition of *Law of Nature and Nations* to Fillmore, who by that time had already purchased it. The price paid by the Executive Mansion accords closely with the prices for which Little and Brown, the firm from whom it was purchased, listed this edition in their catalogues of 1850.[5]

105,133 voucher 2: Puffendorf do folio $12.50.
Purchased from Little and Brown on December 30, 1850.

REFERENCES
cf. L and B Law 1850; cf. L and B 1850 p. 73; cf. Harvard p. 198; cf. Hoffman p. 123.

---

1. Holdsworth, *History of English Law,* 12:632; see entry 178 for Vattell.
2. "Pufendorf, Samuel baron von," *Encyclopaedia Americana.* See entry 67 for Grotius.
3. Since the seventeenth century "Pufendorf" has been spelled sometimes with one and sometimes with two "f"s. Today it is usually spelled with only one.
4. Hoffman, *Course of Legal Study,* 123–24.
5. Little and Brown's 1850 law catalogue appears to have transposed the last two numbers in the date. Although it specifies the fifth edition, carefully corrected, London, $13.50, it lists the date as 1794. The title page of the 1749 edition states that it is the fifth, "carefully corrected, " and no 1794 edition appears to have been published. Another Little and Brown catalogue from April of 1850 also lists this edition and specifies, "Translated by Kennet, with notes by Barbeyrac, folio, best edition *old calf neat* $12.50, London, 1749."

~

136. Pulszky, Theresa. *Memoirs of a Hungarian Lady.* **Philadelphia: Lea and Blanchard, 1850.**

Theresa Pulszky (1815–66) and her husband, Francis, were untitled members of the Hungarian nobility who supported the revolutionary leader, Louis Kossuth. They, along with Kossuth, were forced to leave their country after the collapse of free Hungary in 1849, and they accompanied Kossuth to the United States in 1851.[1] Arriving in December, they dined with the president at the White House on January 6, 1852. Pulszky sat next to the president at dinner and recorded her impressions in her diary. Comparing this evening with elaborate ceremonial occasions in Europe she wrote, "At the White House there is nothing of the kind to be seen. There are here no pictures, no statues, no silk tapestry, no costly furniture, scarcely a few prints, and even these are presents of the French artist who engraved them. The appearance of the guests of the President is as simple as his abode."[2] Of the first family, Pulszky recalled:

> Mr. Fillmore has, in his countenance and in his manners, an expression of natural kind-hearted frankness, fully in harmony with that principle: and Mrs. Fillmore resembles him in that respect. Their daughter has likewise imbibed this republican characteristic, and she

unites with it an amiable sincerity, which struck me, when I remarked to her how very well she spoke French; on which she answered to me, that she had had opportunity to practise it in the school where she lately had been a teacher.[3]

Pulszky's *Memoirs* was among the overwhelming "flood of novels, memoirs, 'Impressions'—general accounts and would-be histories of Hungary, which" poured from the presses of London and continental cities during the years following the failed revolution of 1848.[4] Reviewers praised Pulszky's sketches of social life in Hungary as well as the historical introduction that her husband contributed to the book. An endorsement from the *Globe,* often reprinted in advertisements for *The Memoirs,* asserted, "Madame Pulszky was in the habit of direct intercourse with the foremost and most distinguished of the Hungarian generals and statesmen, and has given a complete summary of the political events in Hungary, from the arrival of the Hungarian deputation in 1848, to the treason of General Georgy on the 13th of August, 1849."[5] The Fillmores purchased Pulszky's book just four days before her arrival at the White House. Pulsky's *Memoirs* came out in 1850 in both a two-volume edition in London from Colburn and a one-volume edition in Philadelphia from Lea and Blanchard. The *London Catalogue* listed the London edition for 12*s.*, which would have been approximately $2.92 in United States currency, whereas Putnam advertised the Philadelphia edition for only $1.00. Based on the price and the number of volumes, the Philadelphia edition was most likely selected.

109,399 voucher 1: Madame Pulszky's Hungarian Lady $1.00.
Purchased from Taylor and Maury on January 2, 1852.

TITLE PAGE
MEMOIRS | OF A | HUNGARIAN LADY. | BY | THERESA PULSZKY. | WITH | A HISTORICAL INTRODUCTION, | BY | FRANCIS PULSZKY. | PHILADELPHIA: | LEA AND BLANCHARD. | 1850.

PAGINATION
i–viii 13–376 1–48.

CONTENTS
i title, ii printer's imprint, iii–iv dedication to the Marchioness of Lansdowne, v–vii contents, viii blank, 13–92 "Historical Introduction," 93–323 text of *Memoirs,* 324 blank, 325–75 appendix, 376 blank, 1–48 catalogue of Lea and Blanchard's publications.

REFERENCES
Roorbach p. 447; Putnam p. 27-s.

COPY DESCRIBED
DLC: DB J36 P3. *Leaf.* 193 × 115.

---

1. Marion Tinling, comp. and ed., *With Women's Eyes: Visitors to the New World: 1775–1918* (Hamden, Conn.: Archon, 1993), 70.
2. Francis and Theresa Pulszky, *White, Red, Black* (1853; New York: Johnson Reprint Corporation, 1970), 179.
3. Ibid.

4. "Works on Hungary," *The Southern Literary Messenger; Devoted to Every Department of Literature,* August 1850, available at *APS Online,* http://www.proquest.com/products_pq/descriptions/aps.shtml.

5. Lea and Blanchard's Catalogue, 11, bound into the back of the copy of Pulszky's *Memoirs* described here.

∽

137. Putnam, George P. *The World's Progress: A Dictionary of Dates, with Tabular Views of General History, and a Historical Chart.* New York: Putnam, either 1850 or 1851.

This book debuted in 1833 under the title *Chronology: An Introduction and Index to Universal History,* published by Appleton, the firm for which George P. Putnam worked before setting up business on his own. The *Chronology* offers a digest of Putnam's reading of 150 standard historical texts of the day. After the *Chronology* had been out of print for several years, Putnam updated and revised its text and began publishing it himself in 1850 under the title *World's Progress.*

The table of contents of the 1851 edition of *World's Progress* indicates the kind of information that it contained. It begins with "Tabular Views of Universal History," subdivided into the categories ancient and modern. The ancient section starts with "The Antediluvian" period and ends with the "Fall of Greece to the Christian Era," while the modern section ranges from the beginning of the Christian era through the year 1850. A "Dictionary of Dates" follows these tables and allows the reader to look up a selected word and, if found, discover its origin. For example, one may look up "library" and learn that the first public library for which we have an account was founded at Athens by Pisistratus in 544 B.C. A "Literary Chronology" follows the "Dictionary of Dates." It is organized by country under the categories of "Imagination," "Fact," and "Speculative and Scientific." Putnam then offers an alphabetical listing of "Heathen Deities &c." and concludes the volume with a biographical index organized alphabetically that gives the subject's country of origin as well as the dates of his or her birth and death.

Editions of *World's Progress* appeared in both 1850 and 1851. Putnam listed the 1850 edition but does not give a price, while Roorbach recorded the 1851 edition for $2.00 in cloth. Given that the purchase was made in December of 1850, either one of these could have been selected for the Executive Mansion library. Books published late in the calender year were often dated with the upcoming new year.

105,133 voucher 4: World's Progress $1.60.
Purchased from George P. Putnam on December 13, 1850.

REFERENCES
cf. Putnam p. 181; cf. Roorbach p. 448.

∽

138. Reddie, James. *Inquiries in International Law.* Edinburgh: Blackwood and Sons, 1842.

Inquiries in International Law (1842) stands as one of four works that the jurist James Reddie (1775–1852) wrote on maritime and international law, the others being *Inquiries Elementary and Historical in the Science of Law* (1840), *An Historical View of the Law of Maritime*

Commerce (1841), and *Researches, Historical and Critical, in Maritime International Law* (1844). In *Inquiries* Reddie traces the history and explores the boundaries of his topic (2–3). It is among the books pertaining to international law that Edward Everett recommended to President Fillmore after the Cuban filibuster.

107,754 voucher 4: 1 vol. Reddies International Law $2.88.
Purchased from Little and Brown on December 31, 1851.
Hayes Catalogue: Reddie, J. *Inquiries in International Law.* Edinburgh, 1842. 8°.

TITLE PAGE
INQUIRIES | IN | INTERNATIONAL LAW. | BY | JAMES REDDIE, ESQ., ADVOCATE, | AUTHOR OF "AN HISTORICAL VIEW OF THE LAW OF MARITIME COMMERCE." | [thin rule] | WILLIAM BLACKWOOD & SONS, | EDINBURGH AND LONDON; | AND SAUNDERS & BENNING, LONDON. | [thin rule] | MDCCCXLII.

PAGINATION
[2] i–viii 1–220.

CONTENTS
[1] half title, [2] blank, i title, ii printer's imprint, iii advertisement, iv blank, v–viii contents, 1–220 text.

REFERENCES
Hayes p. 236; cf. Greenleaf; cf. Harvard p. 203; cf. *LC 1816–1851* p. 462; Marvin p. 602.

COPY DESCRIBED
ViU: INT 00 R32i. *Leaf.* 217 × 125.

❧

139. Robertson, William. *The Works.* London: William Ball, 1840.

William Robertson (1721–93), historian and Church of Scotland minister, helped to establish history as one of the leading genres of the Scottish Enlightenment. He wrote four major histories—*The History of Scotland During the Reigns of Queen Mary and James VI* (1759), *The History of the Reign of Charles V* (1769), *The History of America* (1777), and *An Historical Disquisition Concerning the Knowledge Which the Ancients Had of India* (1791)—all of which are included in William Ball's 1840 edition of his works. Although in the twentieth and twenty-first centuries Gibbon and Hume stand as giants among early historians, in the eighteenth century Robertson was regarded as their equal. Robertson's scope surpasses both of his fellow historians. He was the only one to attempt anything close to a global history with his works, which included Scotland, continental Europe, America, and India as their subject matter.

The *Penny Cyclopaedia* recognized Robertson "among the best historical writers" and characterized his style as "easy and flowing," his language as "correct," and his opinions as "enlightened and sober." With respect to Robertson's contemporaries the *Cyclopaedia*'s writer remarked, "Hume who was his intimate friend notwithstanding the difference of their opinions greatly extolled Robertson's 'History of Scotland', and Gibbon has borne ample testimony both to his accuracy and style."[1]

105,133 voucher 5: Robertson's Works $4.50.

Purchased from Charles Welford on December 13, 1850.

Roosevelt Catalogue: Robertson, William. *Works.* London, Wm. Ball, 1840.

TITLE PAGE

THE | WORKS | OF | WILLIAM ROBERTSON, D. D. | FELLOW OF THE ROYAL
SOCIETY, AND PRINCIPAL OF THE UNIVERSITY, | OF EDINBURGH,
HISTORIOGRAPHER TO HIS MAJESTY FOR | SCOTLAND, AND MEMBER OF THE
ROYAL ACADEMY | OF HISTORY AT MADRID. | TO WHICH IS PREFIXED. | AN
ACCOUNT OF HIS LIFE AND WRITINGS, | BY DUGALD STEWART, F. R. S. EDIN. |
WITH A PORTRAIT AFTER SIR JOSHUA REYNOLDS. | LONDON: | WILLIAM BALL,
PATERNOSTER ROW. | STEREOTYPED AND PRINTED BY JOHN CHILDS AND
SON. | MDCCCXL.

PAGINATION

[4] i–lviii 1–1184 1–30.

CONTENTS

[1] half title, [2] blank, [3] title, [4] blank, i section title "Account of the Life and Writings
of William Robertson, D. D. F. R. S. E. Late Principal of the University of Edinburgh and
Historiographer to His Majesty for Scotland. By Dugald Stewart, F. R. S. Edin. [Read before
the Royal Society of Edinburgh]," ii advertisement, iii–xlix text of the Life and Writings of
William Robertson, l blank, li–lviii text of the "Situation of the World at the Time of Christ's
Appearance," 1–1184 text of the *Works,* 1–30 index.

PLATES

Portrait frontispiece, William Robertson after a painting by Sir Joshua Reynolds, engraved
by W. C. Edwards.

REFERENCES

Hayes p. 234; Roosevelt p. 34; cf. Putnam p. 118.

COPY DESCRIBED

DLC: D7 R7 1840. *Leaf.* 251 × 164.

---

1. See entries 80 and 58 for Hume and Gibbon, respectively.

◁∿▷

140. Robinson, Christopher. *Collectanea Maritima.* London: White and Butterworth, 1801.

Sir Christopher Robinson (1766–1833) served as judge of the high court of admiralty from
1828 until just days before his death in 1833. He specialized in maritime law, gained "con-
spicuous success" as an advocate, was knighted in 1809, and, later in the same year, was
appointed king's advocate, a position in which he concentrated on cases relating to prizes
captured on the high seas.

Collectanea Maritima (1801) is one of several works that Robinson authored on the subject of admiralty law. Others include *Report of the High Court of Admiralty in the Swedish*

Convoy (1799) and *Reports of Cases Argued and Determined in the High Court of Admiralty, 1799 to 1808* (6 vols., 1799–1808). *Collectanea* appears on the list of recommendations on international and admiralty law that Edward Everett sent to President Fillmore after the Cuban filibuster.

107,754 voucher 4: 1 vol. Robinson Collectanea Maritima $1.25.
Purchased from Little and Brown on December 31, 1851.
Hayes Catalogue: Robinson C. *Collectanea Maritima; Public Instruments to Illustrate Prize Law*. London, 1801 8°.

TITLE PAGE
COLLECTANEA MARITIMA; | BEING A | COLLECTION [open face block letters] | OF | *PUBLIC INSTRUMENTS,* | *&C. &C.* | TENDING TO ILLUSTRATE THE | HISTORY AND PRACTICE | OF | Prize Law. [black letter] | [thick/thin double rule] | By CHR. ROBINSON, LL.D. | Advocate in Doctor's Commons. | [thick/thin double rule] | NON VIDETUR VIM FACERE, QUI JURE SUO UTITUR, | ET ORDINARIA ACTIONE EXPERITUR. | DIGEST. | [thick/thin double rule] | LONDON: | Printed by W. Wilson, [black letter] | *St. Peter's Hill, Doctor's Commons;* | FOR J. WHITE, AND J. BUTTERWORTH, | FLEET-STREET. | [thin rule] | 1801.

PAGINATION
[*8*] i–viii 1–214.

CONTENTS
[*1*] title, [*2*] blank, [*3*]–[*8*] contents, i–viii advertisement, 1–211 text, 211–13 postscript, 214 errata.

REFERENCES
Hayes p. 234; cf. Harvard p. 209; Marvin p. 615.

COPY DESCRIBED
DLC: JX 5245 R7. *Leaf.* 220 × 130.

～

141. Russell, William. *The History of Modern Europe.* **3 vols. New York: Harper, 1849.**

William Russell (1746–93), historian and miscellaneous writer, gained recognition with the publication of *The History of America, from the First Discovery by Columbus to the Conclusion of the Late War* (1778). His subsequent work *History of Modern Europe* (1779) received a mixed review in "A Course for Historical Reading." The critic found its treatment of the earlier centuries uneven but praised its thorough treatment of modern Europe. The writer recommended Russell's work to students who "hesitate at the expense of the local histories hereafter named" and called these volumes "the best substitute . . . , for the price." The White House probably purchased this book bound in sheep, the binding for which Roorbach recorded the price as $4.50.[1]

105,133 voucher 5: Russell's History Modern Europe 3 vols. $4.50.
Purchased from Charles Welford on December 13, 1850.

Roosevelt Catalogue: Russell, William. *The History of Modern Europe.* New York, Harper & brothers, 1849, 3 vols.

TITLE PAGE

THE | HISTORY | OF | MODERN EUROPE: | WITH | A VIEW OF THE PROGRESS OF SOCIETY FROM THE RISE OF THE MODERN | KINGDOMS TO THE PEACE OF PARIS, IN 1763. | BY WILLIAM RUSSELL, LL.D. | AND | A CONTINUATION OF THE HISTORY TO THE PRESENT TIME | BY WILLIAM JONES, ESQ., | WITH ANNOTATIONS BY AN AMERICAN. | IN THREE VOLUMES. | VOL. I. [II–III.] | NEW YORK: | HARPER & BROTHERS, PUBLISHERS, | 82 CLIFF STREET. | 1849.

PAGINATION

Vol. I. [2] v–xxx 31–552.
Vol. II. [2] ix–xl 41–604.
Vol. III. i–xxxiv 35–670.

CONTENTS

Vol. I. [1] title page, [2] copyright statement, v–xxix contents, xxx blank, 31 section title 'THE HISTORY OF MODERN EUROPE', 32 blank, 33–551 text, 552 blank.
Vol. II. [1] title page, [2] copyright statement, ix–xl contents, 41–603 text, 604 blank.
Vol. III. i title, ii copyright statement, iii–xxxiv contents, 35–670 text.

PLATES

Vol. I.
Engraved title page, '[decorative cathedral frame] | THE | HISTORY | OF | MODERN EUROPE, | BY | D^R. W. RUSSELL. | IN TWO VOLUMES. | VOL. I. | [Engraving of Henry V before the gates of Harfleur] | HENRY V. BEFORE THE GATES OF HARFLEUR [all foregoing type is decorative and within the frame] | NEW YORK: | HARPER & BROTHERS. [preceding two lines are decorative type, outside of frame.]'
Vol. II.
Engraved title page, '. . . | VOL. II. | [Engraving of Solyman besieging Rhodes] | SOLYMAN BESIEGING RHODES [all foregoing type is decorative and within the frame] | Westall pinxit. Gimber sculpsit. | NEW YORK. | Pub. By Harper & Brothers, 82, Cliff Street. [preceding three lines are decorative type, outside of frame.]'
Vol. III.
Engraved title page, '[decorative cathedral frame] | THE | HISTORY | OF | MODERN EUROPE, FROM 1763, | BEING A CONTINUATION OF | D^R. RUSSELL'S HISTORY, | BY W^M. JONES, | AUTHOR OF THE HISTORY OF THE WALDENSES, &c&c. | [engraving of a man on horseback] [all foregoing type is decorative and within the frame] | Prud homme Sc. | Harper & Brothers, 82 Cliff St. [preceding three lines are decorative type, outside of frame.]'

REFERENCES

Hayes p. 235; Roosevelt p. 35; cf. Putnam p. 120; cf. Roorbach p. 474; cf. Fillmore 1847 p. 20.

COPY DESCRIBED

DLC: D 102 R9 1849. *Leaf.* 231 × 140.

1. *The Universalist Quarterly and General Review* (1844–91), April 1850, available at *APS Online,* http://www.proquest.com/products_pq/descriptions/aps.shtml.

～

142. Rutherforth, Thomas. *Institutes of Natural Law.* 2 vols. Cambridge: Thurlborn, Beecroft, and Innys, 1754–56.

Thomas Rutherforth's (1712–71) two-volume work *Institutes of Natural Law* is based on his lectures on natural and moral philosophy that he delivered at St. John's College, Cambridge. It draws on Grotius to consider "morality" "in terms of its social consequences," a form of utilitarianism" that influenced "his younger Cambridge colleague William Paley."[1] Marvin called Rutherforth "one of the ablest commentators upon Grotius" and found that his work is "clearly and logically written, and exhibits great acuteness, sound argument, and learning." In addition, Edward Everett found Rutherforth's *Institutes* appropriate to recommend to the president after the Cuban filibuster.

Although the Hayes catalogue lists a Cambridge 1854–56 edition, this date is most likely an error on the part of the cataloguer. No other record of a Cambridge edition for these years has been located. Moreover, Little and Brown's 1850 law catalogue lists the Cambridge 1754 edition for $5.00, a price close enough to that paid by the Executive Mansion to make it the most probable candidate for purchase.

107,754 voucher 4: 2 vols. Rutherfords Institutes $4.30.[2]
Purchased from Little and Brown on December 31, 1851.
Hayes Catalogue: Rutherforth, T. *Institutes of Natural Law.* 2 v. Cambridge, 1854–56. 8°.

REFERENCES
Hayes p. 236; cf. Greenleaf; Harvard p. 213; Marvin p. 625.

1. John Gascoigne, "Rutherforth, Thomas (1712–1771)," *ODNB;* see entries 126 and 67 for Paley and Grotius.
2. Since the eighteenth century Rutherforth's name has been spelled two ways: "-forth" and "-ford." The latter spelling is used in the the Hayes catalogue and on the voucher for this purchase. It is spelled "-forth" on the title page of *Institutes of Natural Law,* and this spelling is the one most commonly used by scholars today.

～

143. Sabine, Lorenzo. *The American Loyalists.* Boston: Little and Brown, 1847.

The American Loyalists or Biographical Sketches of Adherents to the British Crown (1847) is Lorenzo Sabine's most important historical work. Sabine (1803–77) lived for twenty years in Eastport, Maine, where his proximity to the Canadian border brought him into contact with a number of the descendents of the American loyalists. These relationships inspired him to undertake this book for which he drew on many family records and recollections. In one writer's assessment:

> The subject of this work is both novel and interesting, and one upon which we are too igno-rant. . . . Separated from their homes and kindred, outlaws, wanderers, and exiles, they have

left but few memorials of their posterity. . . . We find among the sketches, notices of many distinguished and influential men, and while some were notorious for their want of principle, there were many who, we cannot doubt, were true and honest in espousing the cause of the mother country. Then, though we cannot justify any, let us not censure all.[1]

Likewise, a writer for the *North American Review* praised Sabine's work, maintaining that its topic belongs to both Great Britain and America and commending Sabine for his careful handling, research, and unbiased treatment of his subjects. The second edition of *American Loyalists,* which Sabine revised and enlarged in 1864, remained in use well into the twentieth century.[2]

The American Loyalists would have complemented the collection of American revolutionary biographies that were purchased for the library that also contained the works of Washington, Franklin, and Jefferson, along with Sabine's counterpart, Sanderson's *Biographies of the Signers of the Declaration of Independence.*[3]

105,133 voucher 5: American Loyalists $2.00.
Purchased from Charles Welford on December 13, 1850.
Hayes Catalogue: *American Loyalists.* By L. Sabine. Boston, 1847. 8°.

TITLE PAGE
THE | AMERICAN LOYALISTS, | OR | BIOGRAPHICAL SKETCHES | OF ADHERENTS TO THE BRITISH CROWN IN | THE WAR OF THE REVOLUTION; | ALPHABETICALLY ARRANGED; | WITH A | PRELIMINARY HISTORICAL ESSAY. | [thin rule] | By LORENZO SABINE. [thin rule] | BOSTON: | CHARLES C. LITTLE AND JAMES BROWN. | [thin rule] | MDCCCXLVII.

PAGINATION
[2] i–vi 1–734.

CONTENTS
[1] half title, [2] blank, i title, ii copyright statement and printer's imprint, iii–v preface, vi blank, 1–114 text of "Preliminary Remarks, or Historical Essay," 115 section title, "Biographical Sketches of American Loyalists," 116 blank, 117–733 text, 734 blank.

REFERENCES
Hayes p. 253; Roosevelt p. 36; Putnam p. 5, 121; Roorbach p. 476; L and B 1850 p. 3; L and B 1852 p. 1; L and B 1853 p. 4.

COPY DESCRIBED
DLC: E277 S11 Copy 2. *Leaf.* 223 × 127.

---

1. "Notices of New Publications," *The New-England Historical and Genealogical Register (1847–1868),* July 1847, available at *APS Online,* http://www.proquest.com/products_pq/descriptions/aps.shtml.

2. "The American Loyalists," *The North American Review (1821–1940),* July 1847, available at *APS Online,* http://www.proquest.com/products_pq/descriptions/aps.shtml. Sabine also contributed a *Life of Commodore Edward Preble* to Jared Sparks's *Library of American Biography* second series, another title that was purchased for the White House.

3. See entries 161 and 162 for Washington and Franklin, 83 for Jefferson, and 146 for Sanderson.

≁

144. Sage, Alain René Le. *The Adventures of Gil Blas of Santillane.* Trans. Tobias Smollett. 2 vols. London: Dubochet, 1836.

Histoire de Gil Blas de Santillane (1715–35) is considered the masterpiece of the French novelist and dramatist Alain René Le Sage (1668–1747). A picaresque novel that "concerns the education and adventures of a young valet as he progresses from one master to the next," it stands as one of the earliest realistic novels and one of the first novels of manners. *Gil Blas* is believed to have influenced Henry Fielding, Laurence Sterne, and Tobias Smollett, who translated it into English in the eighteenth century.[1]

When Fillmore took William H. Andrews, a clerk from his Buffalo office, to his home to compile an inventory of his books, he gave him an extra copy of *Gil Blas,* remarking that "John Quincy Adams once said he had made it a point to read 'Gil Blas' through once a year, and that he never read it through without new delight and increased knowledge."[2]

No fewer than ten two-volume English translations of *Gil Blas* were published between 1800 and 1850. Of these possibilities, Dubochet's 1836 edition is the only one that sold for a price close to that paid by the Executive Mansion. The *British Catalogue* listed it at 32*s.* or approximately $7.68, which makes it the most likely edition chosen for the library. The Putnam and Little and Brown catalogues advertised London editions that are probably from Dubochet. While Putnam offered an 1844 edition, Little and Brown listed one from 1836. Both advertisements describe a two-volume set in royal octavo, with illustrations by Gigoux.

105,133 voucher 2: Gil Blas 2 vols. $6.50.
Purchased from Little and Brown on December 30, 1850.

REFERENCES
cf. Putnam p. 51; cf. Fillmore 1847 p. 7; cf. Fillmore ca. 1858 p. 24; cf. Fillmore[3] 1861 p. 88; L and B 1850 p. 53.

---

1. "Le Sage, Alain-René," *Merriam Webster's Encyclopedia of Literature* (Springfield, Mass.: Merriam-Webster, 1995), 674; "Lesage, Alain-René," in *Benét's Readers Encylopedia,* ed. Bruce Murphy (New York: HarperCollins, 1996), 621.
2. Millard Fillmore, *Millard Fillmore Papers,* ed. Frank H. Severence (Buffalo: Buffalo Historical Society, 1907), 2:504.
3. This catalogue lists three copies of *Gil Blas,* one in French.

≈

145. Sanders, Francis Williams, George Williams Sanders, and John Warner. *An Essay on Uses and Trusts: And on the Nature and Operation of Conveyances at Common Law: And of Those Which Derive Their Effect from the Statute of Uses.* 2 vols. London: A. Maxwell, 1844.

William Francis Sanders's (1769–1831) *An Essay on Uses and Trusts* (1791) was the standard text on this topic during the nineteenth century. Sanders, lawyer and legal writer, wrote *Uses and Trusts* when he was twenty-one years old and continued to revise and expand its text with each subsequent edition during his life. By 1844 it had gone into five separate editions. One reviewer remarked that this work is "so commonly found on the shelves of the lawyer's library" that it "needs no commendation."[1] While Hoffman recommended *Of Uses and Trusts* along with three other titles on the topic, Marvin agreed that the volumes contain "a thorough, comprehensive, and learned discussion," but warned that the work "becomes too abstruse" in places.

The voucher entry simply reads: "Sanders Work 2 vols." This could refer to either *An Essay on Uses and Trusts* or *Orders of the High Court of Chancery and Statutes of the Realm,* both two-volume sets by Sanders. The first of these two titles is the most likely choice for the Executive Mansion because it appears on the list of books recommended by Greenleaf and because its price is closer to the one indicated on the voucher. Both of these titles are advertised by Butterworth. While the 1844 two-volume London edition of *Uses and Trusts* from A. Maxwell sold for £1 12s. in boards, which in 1850 would have been approximately $7.80, a little less than what the Executive Mansion paid, *Orders of the High Court of Chancery* sold for £2 10s., also in boards which would have been about $12.14, a price too high to account for this purchase. Roorbach recorded an 1830 American edition of *Uses and Trusts* from R. H. Small at $3.50, but its price is too low to qualify for this purchase.[2]

105,133 voucher 2: Sanders Work 2 vols. $8.00.
Purchased from Little and Brown on December 30, 1850.

REFERENCES
cf. *LC 1816–1851* p. 486; cf. Harvard p. 216; cf. Marvin p. 628; cf. Hoffman p. 272.

---

1. "Notices of New Books," *American Law Register,* March 1856, 320.
2. *Butterworth's General Catalogue of Law Books Including all Reports* (London: Butterworth, 1850), 179.

~

146. Sanderson, John. *Biography of the Signers of the Declaration of Independence.* **9 vols. Philadelphia: Pomeroy, 1823–27.**

John Sanderson's (1783–1844) *Biography of the Signers of the Declaration of Independence* was recognized as a successful effort to recover and preserve a part of America's history. Sanderson published the first two volumes with his brother Joseph in 1820. Robert Wain Jr. completed the project with seven additional volumes over the next seven years. Anticipating its commencement, *Niles' Weekly Register* patriotically predicted, "If properly conducted . . . we hope the obscurity in which many of those illustrious founders of the American republic have been suffered to remain, will be unveiled, and their actions become the familiar topic of the day. To revere their memories is a debt we in gratitude owe, and as descendents of illustrious parents, we cannot be backward in discharging it."[1] Once the volumes began to appear, the *North American Review* also praised the commemorative nature of this project. Although the reviewer criticized the lengthy introduction in volume 1 as "ill-conceived," it found much to commend about the enterprise as a whole. This work stood on the shelves of the White House Library among a number of biographies of American politicians and statesmen where it served as a counterpart to Lorenzo Sabine's *The American Loyalists or Biographical Sketches of Adherents to the British Crown* (1847).[2]

105,133 voucher 5: Sanderson's Lives Signers Dec^n Independence 9 vols. $12.50.
Purchased from Charles Welford on December 13, 1850.
Roosevelt Catalogue: Sanderson, John. *Biography of the Signers of the Declaration of Independence.* Philadelphia, R. W. Pomeroy, 1822–27, Vols. 1–9, v. 10 missing.

TITLE PAGE
Engraved.
Vol. I.
'BIOGRAPHY | of the Signers to the | DECLARATION of INDEPENDENCE | BY |
JOHN SANDERSON | [vignette of asp on rock] C. A. Le Sueur del. Caveant moniti
J. B. Longacre Sc. | PHILADELPHIA. | Published by R. W. Pomeroy [all preceding lines in
open face fancy lettering] | J. MAXWELL PRINTER. | 1823.'

Vol. II.
. . . | JOHN SANDERSON | VOL. II. | . . . | Published by Joseph M. Sanderson | for the
Proprietor | . . . | 1822.

Vol. III.
Same as vol. 1 except 'VOL III.' has been added.

Vol. IV.
Same as vol. 1 except 'VOL IIII.' has been added.

Vol. V.
Title page missing.

Vol. VI.
Same as vol. 1; no volume number added.

Vols. VII–IX.
'BIOGRAPHY | OF THE | SIGNERS | TO THE | DECLARATION OF INDEPENDENCE |
[decorative rule] | [vignette of walking Lady Liberty] | Drawn by T. Underwood Engd. by
E. Kearny | PHILADELPHIA | PUBLISHED BY R. W. POMEROY | J. MAXWELL
PRINTER. | 1827.'

PAGINATION
Vol. I. [2] i–ccxxiv 1–44.
Vol. II. [4] 1–250.
Vol. III. 1–310.
Vol. IV. [4] 1–288.
Vol. V. [4] 7–382.
Vol. VI. 1–352.
Vol. VII. 1–344.
Vol. VIII. 1–348.
Vol. IX. 1–340.

CONTENTS

Vol. I. [1]–[2] preface, i half title, ii copyright statement, iii–ccxxiv introduction, 1–43 text of Hancock, 44 blank.

Vol. II. [1] half title, [2] copyright statement, [3] contents, [4] blank, 1 section title "Benjamin Franklin," 2 blank, 3–153 text of Franklin, 154 blank, 155 section title, "George Wythe," 156 blank, 157–80 text of Wythe, 181 section title, "Francis Hopkinson," 182 blank, 183–200 text of Hopkinson, 201 section title, "Robert Treat Paine," 202 blank, 203–40 text of Paine, 241–50 notes.

Vol. III. 1 half title, 2 copyright statement, 3 a note from the publisher, 4 blank, 5 contents, 6 blank, 7 section title "Edward Rutledge," 8 blank, 9–47 text of Rutledge, 48 blank, 49 section title, "Lyman Hall," 50 blank, 51–60 text of Hall, 61 section title, "Oliver Wolcott," 62 blank, 63–77 text of Wolcott, 78 blank, 79 section title, "Richard Stockton," 80 blank, 81–115 text of Stockton, 116 blank, 117 section title, "Button Gwinnett," 118 blank, 119–32 text of Gwinnett, 133 section title, "Josiah Bartlett," 134 blank, 135–65 text of Bartlett, 166 blank, 167 section title, "Philip Livingston," 168 blank, 169–95 text of Livingston, 196 blank, 197 section title, "Roger Sherman," 198 blank, 199–306 text of Sherman, 307–10 notes.

Vol. IV. [I] half title, [2] copyright statement, [3] contents, [4] blank, 1 section title, "Thomas Heyward," 2 blank, 3–17 text of Heyward, 18 blank, 19 section title, "George Read," 20 blank, 21–83 text of Read, 84 blank, 85 section title, "William Williams," 86 blank, 87–105 text of Williams, 106 blank, 107 section title, "Samuel Huntington," 108 blank, 109–27 text of Huntington, 128 blank, 129 section title, "William Floyd," 130 blank, 131–50 text of Floyd, 151 section title, "George Walton," 152 blank, 153–69 text of Walton, 170 blank, 171 section title, "George Clymer," 172 blank, 173–246 text of Clymer, 247 section title, "Benjamin Rush," 248 blank, 249–86 text of Rush, 287–88 notes.

Vol. V. [1] section title, "Thomas Lynch, Jr.," [2] blank, [3] contents, [4] blank, 7–32 text of Lynch, 33 section title, "Matthew Thornton," 34 blank, 35–69 text of Thornton, 70 blank, 71 section title, "William Whipple," 72–98 text of Whipple, 99 section title John Witherspoon," 100 blank, 101–86 text of Witherspoon, 187 section title, "Robert Morris," 188 blank, 189–375 text of Morris, 376 blank, 377–82 notes.

Vol. VI. 1 half title, 2 copyright statement, 3 contents, 4 blank, 5 section title, "Arthur Middleton," 6 blank, 7–46 text of Middleton, 47 section title, "Abraham Clark," 48 blank, 49–94 text of Clark, 95 section title, "John Penn," 96 blank, 97–109 text of Penn, 110 blank, 111 section title, "James Wilson," 112 blank, 113–75 text of Wilson, 176 blank, 177 section title, "Carter Braxton," 178 blank, 179–207 text of Braxton, 208 blank, 209 section title, "John Morton," 210 blank, 211–22 text of Morton, 223 section title, "Stephen Hopkins," 224 blank, 225–60 text of Hopkins, 261 section title, "Thomas M'Kean," 262 blank, 263–350 text of M'Kean, 351–52 appendix.

Vol. VII. 1 half title, 2 copyright statement, 3–4 advertisement, 5 contents, 6 blank, 7 section title, "Thomas Jefferson," 8 blank, 9–148 text of Jefferson, 149 section title, "William Hooper," 150 blank, 151–75 text of Hooper, 176 blank, 177 section title "James Smith," 178 blank, 179–236 text of Smith, 237 section title, "Charles Carroll of Carrollton," 238 blank, 239–61 text of Carroll, 262 blank, 263 section title, "Thomas Nelson, Jr." 264 blank, 265–306 text of Nelson, 307 section title "Joseph Hewes," 308 blank, 309–34 text of Hewes, 335–43 appendix, 344 blank.

Vol. VIII. 1 half title, 2 copyright statement, 3 contents, 4 blank, 5 section title, "Elbridge Gerry," 6 blank, 7–77 text of Gerry, 78 blank, 79 section title, "Cæsar Rodney," 80 blank, 81–124 text of Rodney, 125 section title, "Benjamin Harrison," 126 blank, 127–72 text of Harrison, 173 section title, "William Paca," 174 blank, 175–83 text of Paca, 184 blank, 185 section title, "George Ross," 186 blank, 187–99 text of Ross, 200 blank, 201 section title, "John Adams," 202 blank, 203–337 text of Adams, 338 blank, 339–46 appendix 1, 347–48 appendix 2.

Vol. IX. 1 half title, 2 copyright statement, 3 contents, 4 blank, 5 section title, "Richard Henry Lee," 6 blank, 7–65 text of Lee, 66 blank, 67 section title, "George Taylor," 68 blank, 69–89 text of Taylor, 90 blank, 91 section title, "John Hart," 92 blank, 93–115 text of Hart, 116 blank, 117 section title, "Lewis Morris," 118 blank, 119–49 text of Morris, 150 blank, 151 section title, "Thomas Stone," 152 blank, 153–69 text of Stone, 170 blank, 171 section title, "Frs: Lightfoot Lee," 172 blank, 173–84 text of Lee, 185 section title, "Samuel Chase," 186 blank, 187–235 text of Chase, 236 blank, 237 section title, "William Ellery," 238 blank, 239–83 text of Ellery, 284 blank, 285 section title, "Samuel Adams," 286 blank, 287–327 text of Adams, 328 blank, 329–39 appendix, 340 blank.

PLATES

Vol. I.

Bound between ccxxiv and 1, four plates with facsimiles of the signatures of the signers to the Declaration of Independence, all copied from Mr. J. Binns, printed by J. Warr Jr., engraver, 110 Walnut Street Philadelphia.

Vol. II.

Facing 181, engraved portrait of Francis Hopkinson, engraved by J. B. Longacre and J. H. Nesmith, from a picture by Pine.

Facing 201, engraved portrait of Robert Treat Paine, drawn and engraved by J. B. Longacre, from a sketch by Savage.

> *Note.* Portraits appear to be missing of Franklin, between pages [4] and 1, and of George Wythe, between 154 and 155. Offset ink has left ghost images on these section titles.

Vol. III.

Facing 9, engraved portrait of Edward Rutledge, drawn and engraved by J. B. Longacre from a painting by Earle.

Facing 63, engraved portrait of Oliver Wolcott, engraved by J. B. Longacre from a painting in Delaplaine's Gallery.

Facing 169, engraved portrait of Philip Livingston, engraved by J. B. Longacre from an original in the possession of J. T. Jones Esq. of New York.

Facing 199, engraved portrait of Roger Sherman, engraved by S. S. Jocelyn, N. Haven Con. From a painting by Earle.

Vol. IV.

Facing 3, engraved portrait of Thomas Heyward Jr., engraved by J. B. Longacre from a miniature in the possession of Mrs. Heyward.

Facing 21, engraved portrait of George Read, engraved by J. B. Longacre from a painting by Pine.

Facing 131, engraved portrait of William Floyd, engraved by A. B. Durand from a painting in Delaplaine's Gallery.

Facing 173, engraved portrait of George Clymer, engraved by J. B. Longacre from an original miniature by Trott.

Facing 251, engraved portrait of Benjamin Rush, engraved by J. B. Longacre from a painting by Scully.

Vol. V.

Facing 5, engraved portrait of Thomas Lynch, Engraved by J. B. Longacre from an enamel painting in the possession of Miss E. Lynch.

Facing 101, engraved portrait of John Witherspoon, engraved by J. B. Longacre from a painting by C. W. Peale.

> *Note.* An engraved portrait of Robert Morris appears to be missing; a ghost image of it has offset onto page 189.

Vol. VI.

Facing 7, engraved portrait of Arthur Middleton, engraved by J. B. Longacre after a drawing taken by T. Middleton from a group in a family picture by Benjamin West.

Facing 65, engraved portrait of Francis Lewis, engraved by C. C. Wright from an original painting, 1825.

Facing 113, engraved portrait of James Wilson, engraved by J. B. Longacre from a miniature in the possession of Mrs. Hollingsworth.

Facing 265, engraved portrait of Thomas McKean, engraved by J. B. Longacre from the portrait by G. Stuart.

Vol. VII.

Facing 239, an engraved portrait of Charles Carroll or Carrollton, drawn and engraved by J. B. Longacre from a painting by Field.

Facing 309, an engraved portrait of Joseph Hewes, drawn by J. B. Longacre from a painting in the possession of Joseph Hewes Davis Esq., engraved by F. Kearny.

> *Note.* An engraved portrait of Thomas Jefferson appears to be missing; a ghost image of it has offset onto page 9.

Vol. VIII.

Facing 7, an engraved portrait of Elbridge Gerry, engraved by J. B. Longacre from a drawing by Vanderlyn.

Facing 203, an engraved portrait of John Adams, drawn and engraved by J. B. Longacre from a painting by Otis after Stuart.

> *Note.* An engraved portrait of William Paca appears to be missing; a ghost image of it has offset onto page 175.

Vol. IX.

Facing 153, an engraving of Thomas Stone, drawn by J. B. Longacre from a painting by Pine, engraved by G. B. Ellis.

Facing 287, an engraved portrait of Samuel Adams, drawn and engraved by J. B. Longacre from a painting by Copley.

> *Note.* An engraved portrait of Richard Henry Lee appears to be missing; a ghost image of it has offset onto page 5.

REFERENCES

Hayes p. 253; Roosevelt p. 36; cf. Roorbach p. 478; cf. Fillmore ca. 1858 p. 21; cf. Fillmore 1861 p. 128.

COPY DESCRIBED

DLC: E 221 S212. *Leaf.* 211 × 128.

---

1. *Niles' Weekly Register,* December 19, 1818, available at *APS Online,* http://www.proquest.com/products_pq/descriptions/aps.shtml.
2. "Biography of the Signers of the Declaration of Independence," *The North American Review (1821–1940),* January 1823, available at *APS Online,* http://www.proquest.com/products_pq/descriptions/aps.shtml. For Sabine, see entry 143.

∽

147. **Schlegel, Johan Frederik Vilhelm.** *Neutral Rights, or, an Impartial Examination of the Right of Search of Neutral Vessels under Convoy and of a Judgment Pronounced by the English Court of Admiralty, the 11th June, 1799, in the Case of the Swedish Convoy: With Some Additions and Corrections.*

Johan Frederik Vilhelm Schlegel (1765–1836), professor of law at the University of Copenhagen and assessor of the High Court of Justice, entered the controversy over neutral rights with the publication of this pamphlet. In 1780, during the American Revolution, Russia, Denmark, and Sweden entered into an agreement on four articles to govern belligerents and neutrals. Prussia and Naples later joined the alliance. Great Britain did not openly resist these articles, nor did it officially agree to them. The articles fell by the wayside after the Peace of 1783; however, they were renewed in 1800. Great Britain's opposition to this renewal occasioned several pamphlets on the topic, of which Schlegel's *Neutral Rights* is one. Likewise the publication of Nathaniel Atcheson's pamphlet may also have been inspired by this controversy.[1]

Neutral Rights was originally published in Danish in 1800 at Copenhagen in the periodical *Astræa, et Tidsskrift.* It was translated into French the same year and into English the following year, published in London by J. Debrett and in Philadelphia by the Aurora office.[2] No records indicate that it was published separately after 1801; therefore, the White House would have purchased a copy of either the London or the Philadelphia edition. Edward Everett recommended *Neutral Rights* and specified the London edition of 1800, which makes it a likely candidate. Fillmore, however, did not always follow Everett's suggestions.

107,754 voucher 4: 1 vol. Schlegel on Neutral Rights $1.25.
Purchased from Little and Brown on December 31, 1851.

REFERENCES

BEAL 7523; Sabin 77646 and 77648.

---

1. "From the New York Evening Post. Infringement of Neutral Rights. No. IX," *United States Gazette,* January 22, 1806, 3, available at *America's Historical Newspapers,* http://www.newbank.com/readex; see entry 11.
2. Joseph Sabin, *Bibliotheca Americana: A Dictionary of Books Relating to America* (New York: Sabin, 1891), entries 77646 and 77648.

∽

148. Schömann, George Fredrich. *A Dissertation on the Assemblies of the Athenians.* Cambridge: Grant, 1838.

George Fredrich Schömann (1793–1879) taught ancient literature and eloquence at the University of Greifswald, focusing primarily on ancient Greece. The original Latin text, *De Comitiis Atheniensium* (1819), was one of his first works on this topic. The publisher of the Cambridge edition of *Dissertation on the Assemblies* claimed that it had "long been so extensively known, and its value so universally appreciated," that it required "neither comment upon its utility, nor apology for its republication" (iii). Since language had served as an obstacle to the use of *De Comitiis* in public schools, the publisher offered this translation, with its newly added index and notes, for educational use (iv).

105,133 voucher 5: Schomans Athenian Assemblies $2.00.
Purchased from Charles Welford on December 13, 1850.
Roosevelt Catalogue: Schömann, Georg Friedrich. *Dissertation on the Assemblies of the Athenians.* Cambridge, W. P. Grant, 1838.

TITLE PAGE
A DISSERTATION | ON THE | ASSEMBLIES | OF | THE ATHENIANS. | IN THREE BOOKS. | TRANSLATED FROM THE LATIN OF G. F. SCHÖMANN. | TO WHICH IS ADDED, | A NEW AND COMPLETE INDEX. | CAMBRIDGE: | PUBLISHED BY W. P. GRANT. | M DCCCXXXVIII.

PAGINATION
[2] iii–iv i–ii 1–362 i–vi.

CONTENTS
[1] title, [2] blank, iii–iv advertisement, i–ii contents, 1–24 introduction, 25–361 text, 362 blank, i–vi index.

BINDING
Front and back board. 232 × 144 med. brown beaded cloth, blind-stamped decorative frame with diamond shaped filigree ornament in center. *Endpapers.* Pale yellow.
   Note. The spine on both copies available for examination from ViU has been covered with brown book tape.

REFERENCES
Hayes p. 254; Roosevelt p. 36; Putnam p. 123.

COPY DESCRIBED
ViU: DF 83 S36 1838. *Leaf.* 226 × 140.

∾

**149. Scott, Walter. Waverley Novels. 20 vols. Edinburgh: Cadell, 1847–50.

Sir Walter Scott (1771–1832), Scottish lawyer, antiquary, poet, critic, and novelist, was the most generally admired author of his day. His books were bestsellers, and his stellar reputation shone throughout the nineteenth century. Although other authors had published historical novels before Scott, he was the most popular, prolific, and innovative writer in this genre and has been credited with creating the historical novel. Between the publication of *Waverley* in 1814 and his death in 1832, Scott published twenty-three works of fiction.

The Fillmores must have been fond of Scott since they purchased a set of Waverley Novels in 1825, and the title appears in the 1847 and 1861 catalogues of their personal libraries as well as on the packing lists of the belongings that they removed from the White House.[1] Since the Executive Mansion copies of volumes 8 and 10 were found in the Library of Congress stacks, we can be certain that the Fillmores purchased Cadell's 1847–50 Edinburgh edition, which is listed in the Hayes Catalogue; yet by 1903 volumes from two different sets were present in the Executive Mansion library, as recorded in the Roosevelt Catalogue. Mrs. Lincoln also purchased a set of the Waverley Novels while her husband was president, but we cannot be certain whether it was for the White House Library or for their personal library.[2]

105,133 voucher 5: Walter Scotts Novels 20 v. $20.00.

Purchased from Charles Welford on December 13, 1850.

Hayes Catalogue: Scott, Sir W. *Waverley Novels* v. 4, 5, 7, to 12, 14, 15, 22. Edinburgh, 1847–50.
12°. v. 4. *Rob Roy*, v. 5. *Old Mortality*, v. 7. *Heart of Midlothian*, v. 8 *Bride of Lammermoor*, v. 9. *Ivanhoe*, v. 10. *Monastery*, v. 11. *Abbot*, v. xx *Talisman*, v. 12. *Kenilworth*, v. 14. *Fortune of Nigel*, v. 15. *Peveril of the Peak*, v. 22. *Fair Maid of Perth*.

    Note. Talisman has been added to this entry in a different handwriting.

Roosevelt Catalogue: Scott, Sir Walter. *Waverley Novels*. Edinburgh, R. Cadell, 1848–50.
Contents. v. 2 *The Abbot*; 4. *Rob Roy*; 7. *The Heart of Midlothian*. 10. *The Monastery*; 12 *Kenilworth*; 13. *The Bride of Lammermoor*; 15. *Peveril of the Peak*; 20. *The Talisman. The Two Drovers*; 22. *The Fair Maid of Perth*.

The same. Boston S. H. Parker, 1833–39. Contents v. 3 *Guy Mannering*; 33 *Red Gauntlet*; 35 *Tales of the Crusaders*; 37. *Woodstock*; 39. *Chronicles of the Canongate*; 47. *Tales of My Landlord. Castle Dangerous*.

    Note. A complete set of the Edinburgh 1847–50 edition of Waverley Novels from Cadell has not been available for description. Only the surviving volumes from the orginal Executive Mansion library have been described here.

TITLE PAGE

Vol. VIII and X.

WAVERLEY NOVELS. | VOL. VIII. [X.] | [thin rule] | THE BRIDE OF LAMMERMOOR. | [thin rule] | ROBERT CADELL, EDINBURGH. | MDCCCXLIX.

Vol. X.

. . . | THE MONASTERY. | . . . | MDCCCXLVII.

PAGINATION

Vol. VIII. [2] 1–278.

Vol. X. [2] 1–366.

CONTENTS

Vol. VIII. [1] half title, 'TALES OF MY LANDLORD. | [thin rule] | THE BRIDE OF LAMMERMOOR. | [thin rule] | Hear, land o'Cakes and Brither Scots, | Frae Maidenkirk to Johnny Groats', | If there's a hole in a'your coats, | I rede ye tent it; | A chiel's amang you takin' notes. | An' faith he'll prent it!—Burns.', [2] Spanish quotation from *Don Quixote* with an English translation. 1 title, 2, blank, 3–278 text.

Vol. X. [1] half title, 'THE | MONASTERY.', [2] blank, 1 title, 2 printer's imprint, 3–355 text, 356 blank, 357–65 notes, 366 blank.

PLATES

Vol. VIII.

Engraved title between half title and title, 'THE BRIDE OF LAMMERMOOR. [open face block letters] | [vignette, signed Branston Sc in lower right] | RAVENSWOOOD AND LUCY ASHTON. | ROBERT CADELL, EDINBURGH. [open face block letters] | MDCCCXLVII.'

Vol. X.

Engraved title between half title and title, 'THE MONASTERY. | [vignette, signed T. Williams in lower right and Alex Fraser lower left] | ROBERT CADELL, EDINBURGH. [open face block letters] | MDCCCXLVII.'

BINDING

Front board. 176 × 110 med. brown cloth with blind-stamped filigree frame with gilt-stamped bust of Scott in the center. *Back board.* Same frame as front, but with gilt-stamped city gate in the center. *Spine.* Gilt-stamped '[filigree decoration] | WAVERLEY | NOVELS | VOL. VIII. [X.] [enclosed in heart-shaped frame] | BRIDE | OF | LAMMERMOOR [enclosed in decorative frame]' *Endpapers.* Pale yellow.

Note. Volume 10 reads 'MONASTERY'.

MARKS OF OWNERSHIP

Vols. VIII and *X* Inscribed "Executive Mansion 1850" on the front pastedown. A shelf mark has been added in pencil that reads "F shelf no. [number illegible because a Library of Congress bookplate has been affixed over it]."

REFERENCES

Hayes p. 254; Roosevelt p. 36–37; cf. Fillmore 1847 p. 14; cf. Fillmore Packing Lists p. 22; cf. Fillmore ca. 1858 p. 69; cf. Fillmore 1861 p. 196, 222.

COPY DESCRIBED

DLC: PR 5315 1847. *Leaf.* 170 × 101.

---

1. Scarry, *Millard Fillmore*, 27.
2. Louis Warren, "A. Lincoln's Executive Mansion Library," *American Bookman*, February 11, 1950, 569–70.

150. Semmes, Raphael. *Service Afloat and Ashore.* Cincinnati: Moore, 1851.

In *Service Afloat and Ashore* (1851), Raphael Semmes (1809–77), a Confederate rear admiral, offers a popular firsthand account of the Mexican War. Semmes served first in the navy and then in the army for six months in Mexico. He claimed, "The following pages are the result of this joint connection with the army and navy, and of this interesting journey, made in one of the most unique and interesting countries of which we have an account" (v). His book was well received. *The Literary World* reprinted several extracts from *Afloat and Ashore* and concluded that Semmes is "as pleasant a companion as one might desire on a similar journey, and so commends him to the favor of the reading world." *Godey's Lady's Book* called it "the most unprejudiced and truly historical record of those events that has yet been given to the public."[1]

109,399 voucher 4: Service Afloat and Ashore $1.50.
Purchased from Franck Taylor on July 26, 1851.
Hayes Catalogue: Semmes, R. *Service Afloat and Ashore during the Mexican War.* Cincinnati, 1851. 8°

TITLE PAGE
SERVICE | AFLOAT AND ASHORE | DURING THE | MEXICAN WAR: | BY | LIEUT: RAPHAEL SEMMES, U: S: N:, | LATE FLAG-LIEUTENANT OF THE HOME SQUADRON, AND AID-DE-CAMP OF MAJOR | GENERAL WORTH IN THE BATTLES OF THE VALLEY OF MEXICO. | [thin rule] | CINCINNATI: | WM. H. MOORE & CO., PUBLISHERS, | 118 MAIN STREET. | 1851.

PAGINATION
i–xii [2] 7–480.

CONTENTS
i title, ii copyright statement and printer's imprint, iii dedication to the Hon. B. J. Semmes, iv blank, v–vi preface, vii–xii contents, [1] blank, [2] blank, 7–479 text, 480 addendum.

PLATES
Frontispiece, folding map, "Battles of Mexico, survey of the line of operation of the U. S. Army under the command of Major General Winfield Scott on the 19th and 20th of August and 8th 12th and 13th of Sept. 1847 made by Major Turnbull, Captain McClellan and Lieut. Hardcastle, Topo.[1] engineers. Drawn by Lieutenant Hardcastle.
Facing 185, "City of Jalap," signed in lower left, Onken's Lith. Cincinnati.
Facing 288, "Indians of the plain of Puebla," signed in lower left, Onken's Lith. Cincinnati.
Facing 296, "Pyramid of Cholula," signed in lower left, Onken's Lith. Cincinnati.
Facing 344, "Grand Plaza of Mexico," signed in lower left, Onken's Lith. Cincinnati.
Facing 449, "Castle of Chapultepec," signed in lower left, Onken's Lith. Cincinnati.
Facing 457, "Causeway of San Cosmé, Worth's Line of Operations," signed in lower left, Onken's Lith. Cincinnati.

REFERENCES
Hayes p. 255; cf. Putnam p. 30-s; cf. Roorbach p. 490.

COPY DESCRIBED
DLC: E404 S47 copy 1. *Leaf.* 203 × 120.

---

1. Service Afloat and Ashore," *Literary World,* July 19, 1851, and "Literary Notices," *Godey's Lady's Book,* October 1851, both available at *APS Online,* http://www.proquest.com/products_pq/descriptions/aps.shtml.

〜

151. Shakespeare, William. *The Dramatic Works of William Shakespeare.* 7 vols. Boston: Phillips, Samson and Co., 1849.

The ubiquity of Shakespeare's plays in nineteenth-century America cannot be overstated. While Shakespeare's reputation was on a decline in Great Britain at the time, it reached its height in America in the middle of the century. Many editions and adaptations of his plays had been produced so that people from all economic classes would have had access to them and people of all ages could understand them. Shakespeare's plays were a staple in American theater; in May 1849 the notorious Shakespeare riots broke out in New York City over how two rival actors performed their parts. The bard was often quoted in political oratory, and references in the Fillmores' correspondence indicate their familiarity with his plays.[1]

The Phillips Samson edition of Shakespeare's *Dramatic Works* was chosen as one of the first purchases for the White House Library. It is based on an earlier edition edited by Samuel Weller Singer and retains some of his notes, his preliminary remarks for each play, and a parts of Charles Symmons's biography of Shakespeare. The editors for the Phillips Samson edition have added their own notes and new biographical facts. In May 1852 the Fillmores acquired Mary Cowden Clarke's *Complete Concordance to Shakespeare* for the Library, the authoritative concordance throughout the second half of the century.[2]

105,133 voucher 6: Shakespeare 7 vols. 8vo $10.50.

Purchased from Franck Taylor on October 30, 1850.

Roosevelt Catalogue: Shakespeare, William. *The Dramatic Works of William Shakespeare, with a Life of the Poet and Notes, Original and Selected.* Boston, Phillip, Sampson & co., 1849, vols. 3, 4, 5, 6, only.

TITLE PAGE

THE | DRAMATIC WORKS | OF | WILLIAM SHAKESPEARE; | WITH | A LIFE OF THE POET, | AND | NOTES, | ORIGINAL AND SELECTED. | [thin rule] | VOL. I. [II–VII.] | [thin rule] | BOSTON: | PHILLIPS, SAMPSON, AND COMPANY. | 1849.

PAGINATION

Vol. I. 1–8* i–lxxx 1–508.

Vol. II. [4] 1–538.

Vol. III. [4] 1–556.

Vol. IV. [4] 1–538.

Vol. V. [4] 1–572.

Vol. VI. [4] 1–514.

Vol. VII. [4] 1–518.

CONTENTS

Vol. I. 1* half title, 2* blank, 3* title, 4* blank, 5*–6* blank, 7*–8* general table of contents, i contents of volume 1, ii blank, iii–lxxx "The Life of William Shakespeare," 1–507 text, 508 blank.

Vol. II. [1] half title, [2] blank, [3] title, [4] blank, 1 contents, 2 blank, 3–538 text.

Vol. III. [1] half title, [2] blank, [3] title, [4] blank, 1 contents, 2 blank, 3–556 text.

Vol. IV. [*1*] half title, [*2*] blank, [*3*] title, [*4*] blank, 1 contents, 2 blank, 3–538 text.

Vol. V. [*1*] half title, [*2*] blank, [*3*] title, [*4*] blank, 1 contents, 2 blank, 3–572 text.

Vol. VI. [*1*] half title, [*2*] blank, [*3*] title, [*4*] blank, 1 contents, 2 blank, 3–514 text.

Vol. VII. [*1*] half title, [*2*] blank, [*3*] title, [*4*] blank, 1 contents, 2 blank, 3–518 text.

BINDING

Front and back board. 244 × 153 med. brown ribbed cloth with blind-stamped cartouche frame. *Spine.* Seven bands blind stamped, gilt stamped in second panel '[triple thin rule frame] | Shakespeare [black letter] | I. [II–VII.] | [decorative rule] | KING RICHARD III. | KING HENRY VIII. | TROILUS AND CRESSIDA. | TIMON OF ATHENS. | CORIOLANUS. [all foregoing inside of frame] | [gilt-stamped fish and anchor logo at base of spine. *Endpapers.* Off-white.

>*Note.* The endpapers of the Folger copy are in green and white and have advertisements for other Phillip and Sampson books on them; unfortunately, no prices are listed.

Each volume has different titles on its spine as follows:

Vol. I. 'THE TEMPEST. | TWO GENT. OF VERONA. | MERRY WIVES OF WINDSOR. | TWELFTH NIGHT. | MEASURE FOR MEASURE. | MUCH ADO ABOUT NOTHING.'

Vol. II. 'MID. NIGHT'S DREAM. | LOVE'S LABOUR LOST. | MERCHANT OF VENICE. | AS YOU LIKE IT. | ALL'S WELL THAT ENDS WELL. | TAMING OF THE SHREW.'

>*Note.* A part of the spine is missing. The last four titles have been inferred from the contents.

Vol. III. 'WINTER'S TALE. | COMEDY OF ERRORS. | MACBETH. | KING JOHN. | KING RICHARD II. | KING HENRY THE IV, PT. I.'

>*Note.* A part of the spine is missing. The titles have been inferred from the contents.

Vol. IV. 'KING HENRY IV PT. II. | KING HENRY V. | KING HENRY VI. PT. I. | KING HENRY VI. PT. II. | KING HENRY VI. PT. III.'

Vol. V. 'KING RICHARD III. | KING HENRY VIII. | TROILUS AND CRESSIDA. | TIMON OF ATHENS. | CORIOLANUS.'

Vol. VI. 'JULIUS CAESAR. | ANTONY AND CLEOPATRA. | CYMBELINE | PERICLES. | TITUS ANDRONICUS.'

Vol. VII. 'KING LEAR. | ROMEO AND JULIET. | HAMLET. | OTHELLO.'

REFERENCES

Hayes p. 255; Roosevelt p. 37; cf. Putnam p. 125; cf. Roorbach p. 492; cf. Fillmore 1847 p. 14; cf. Fillmore Packing Lists p. 22; cf. Fillmore ca. 1858 p. 60; cf. Fillmore 1861 p. 190, and p. 200.

COPY DESCRIBED

ViU: PR 2753 P4 1849 Vols. II–VII only. *Leaf.* 237 × 147.

DFo: PR 2752 1849f Sh. col. Vol. I only.

---

1. Nigel Cliff, *The Shakespeare Riots: Revenge, Drama, and Death in Nineteenth-Century America* (New York: Random House, 2007); Scarry, *Millard Fillmore*, 38.

2. See entry 39 for Clarke.

152. Sheridan, Richard Brinsley. *The Speeches of the Right Honourable Richard Brinsley Sheridan.* 3 vols. London: Bohn, 1842.

Richard Brinsley Sheridan (1751–1816), dramatist and politician, would have preferred to be known for his political career and to have been interred near the prominent Whig politician Charles James Fox; instead, he has gone down in history as a skilled dramatist and theater manager of the late eighteenth century and was buried at Westminster Abby in Poet's Corner. His best-known plays, *The Rivals* (1775) and *The School for Scandal* (1777), have never gone completely out of fashion and are still performed today. From a character in the latter, Mrs. Malaprop, a woman who chronically confuses the meanings of words, we have coined the term *malapropism*.

No doubt Sheridan's dramatic abilities helped his political career. The *Penny Cyclopaedia* described it as having been "illuminated by a few bright flashes of eloquence and perpetual wit, but he had neither the depth nor the perseverance of a statesman; and consequently, though he sometimes helped his party with a promising effort, 'gradually degenerated into a useless though amusing speaker, familiarly joked at by the public, admired but disesteemed by friends.'"[1] Sheridan supported the impeachment of Hastings and made his most memorable speech, which lasted several days, at the Hastings trial. In his dramatic conclusion to this speech he proclaimed, "My Lords, I have done," as he swooned into the arms of Edmund Burke.[2] Regardless of his shortcomings as a statesman, Sheridan's speeches still proved instructive, and the nineteenth-century American legal scholar David Hoffman found them worthy enough to recommend to students of the law.

105,133 voucher 5: Sheridan's Speeches 3 vols. $5.50.
Purchased from Charles Welford on December 13, 1850.
Roosevelt Catalogue: Sheridan, Richard Brinsley. *The Speeches of the Right Honourable R. B. Sheridan with a Sketch of His Life.* Edited by a constitutional friend. London, H. G. Bohn, 1842, 3 vols. v. 1. missing.

TITLE PAGE
THE | SPEECHES | OF THE | RIGHT HONOURABLE | RICHARD BRINSLEY SHERIDAN. | WITH A SKETCH OF HIS LIFE. [Black letter] | EDITED BY | A CONSTITUTIONAL FRIEND. | [thin decorative rule] | IN THREE VOLUMES. | VOL. I. [II–III.] | [thin rule] | LONDON: | HENRY G. BOHN, YORK STREET, COVENT GARDEN. | [thin rule] | 1842.

PAGINATION
Vol. I. [6] i–xvi 1–548.
Vol. II. iii–viii 1–564.
Vol. III. iii–viii 1–550.

CONTENTS
Vol. I. [1] title page, [2] printer's imprint, [3–6] contents, i–xvi "Memoir of the Right Honorable Richard Brinsley Sheridan," 1–548 text.
Vol. II. iii title, iv printer's imprint, v–viii contents, 1–564 text.
Vol. III. iii title, iv printer's imprint, v–vii contents, viii blank, 1–550 text.

REFERENCES

Hayes p. 256; Roosevelt p. 38; cf. *LC 1816–1851* p. 503; cf. Putnam p. 126; L and B 1853 p. 60.

COPY DESCRIBED

DLC: DA 522 S4A4. *Leaf.* 203 × 125.

---

1. "Sheridan, Richard Brinsley," *Penny Cyclopaedia.*
2. Qtd. in A. Norman Jeffares, "Sheridan, Richard Brinsley (1751–1816)," *ODNB.* For Burke and more on the Hastings trial, see entry 24.

∽

153. Sismondi, Jean-Charles Léonard de. *Political Economy, and the Philosophy of Government.* London: Chapman, 1847.

Jean-Charles Léonard de Sismondi (1773–1842), economist and historian, was an early follower of Adam Smith and a proponent of laissez-faire economics. Later he recognized the growing rift between classes and argued for social reforms to help the working class. It was he who coined the term "class struggle."[1] Sismondi enjoyed a favorable reputation in America. After his death in 1842 many American periodicals published eulogies lauding his contributions to historical and political writing. One writer in 1845 presented a summary of Sismondi's principles, naming Sismondi "one of the most enlightened and candid historians of modern times" and calling his theories "the clear convictions of one of the calmest and brightest minds of the age."[2]

105,133 voucher 5: Sismondi Pol. Economy $1.50.

Purchased from Charles Welford on December 13, 1850.

Roosevelt Catalogue: Simonde de Sismondi, Jean Charles Leonard. *Political Economy, and the Philosophy of Government: Selected from the Works of Sismondi; with Notice of his Life and Writings by M. Mignet.* London, John Chapman, 1847.

TITLE PAGE

POLITICAL ECONOMY, | AND THE | PHILOSOPHY OF GOVERNMENT; | A SERIES OF ESSAYS SELECTED FROM THE WORKS OF | M. DE SISMONDI. | WITH AN | HISTORICAL NOTICE OF HIS LIFE AND WRITINGS | BY M. MIGNET. | TRANSLATED FROM THE FRENCH, | AND ILLUSTRATED BY EXTRACTS FROM AN UNPUBLISHED MEMOIR, AND FROM | M. DE SISMONDI'S PRIVATE JOURNALS AND LETTERS, | WITH A PRELIMINARY ESSAY, | BY THE TRANSLATOR. | LONDON: | JOHN CHAPMAN, 121, NEWGATE STREET. | MDCCCXLVII.

PAGINATION

[8] 1–456.

CONTENTS

[1] title, [2] printer's imprint, [3] dedication to Madame de Sismondi, [4] blank, [5] prefatory notice, [6] blank, [7] contents, [8] blank, 1–455 text, 456 blank.

REFERENCES

Hayes p. 256; Roosevelt p. 38; cf. Putnam p. 128.

COPY DESCRIBED

DLC: HB 163 S59. *Leaf.* 215 × 134.

---

1. "J.-C.-L. Simonde de Sismondi," *Encyclopaedia Britannica Online* (2007), http://search.eb.com/eb/article-9067861 (accessed Aug. 7, 2007). See entry 154 for Smith.

2. "The Harbinger," *Harbinger, Devoted to Social and Political Progress (1845–1849)*, June 28, 1845, available at *APS Online*, http://www.proquest.com/products_pq/descriptions/aps.shtml.

∾

154. Smith, Adam. *An Inquiry into the Nature and Causes of the Wealth of Nations.* Ed. J. R. McCulloch. Edinburgh: Adam and Charles Black, and William Tait. London: Longman and Co., 1846.

Adam Smith's (1723–90) *Wealth of Nations* (1776) laid foundations for modern economic thought that fit perfectly with the democratic and individualistic ideals set forth in the Declaration of Independence. To Smith, "the 'wealth' of a nation wasn't determined by the size of its monarch's treasure or the amount of gold and silver in its vaults. . . . A nation's wealth was to be judged by the total value of all the goods its people produced for all its people to consume."[1] Smith's text served as the starting point for subsequent generations of political economists, including David Ricardo, Thomas Robert Malthus, and John Stuart Mill, and has remained a staple in the canon of economic literature since its publication.[2]

John Ramsay McCulloch's was the best-known edition of Smith's *Wealth of Nations* during the nineteenth century. It was first published in 1828 as a four-volume set and was reissued in one volume in 1838, an edition that was stereotyped and reprinted repeatedly. In his preface McCulloch focuses on the progress that had been made in the science of political economy since Smith's last revisions in 1784. He provides annotations and notes to call the reader's attention to some of Smith's fallacies in order to point to advances in the field.[3] McCulloch addresses the question of what one can learn from Smith and, despite his criticisms, concludes, "Still however, the great and leading merits of Dr. Smith's work continue unimpaired. Nothing of importance has hitherto been added to his full and masterly exposition of the benefits arising from the freedom of industry" ([6]).

105,133 voucher 2: Smith's Wealth Nations $3.25.

Purchased from Little and Brown on December 30, 1850.

Roosevelt Catalogue: Smith, Adam. *An Inquiry into the Nature and the Causes of the Wealth of Nations.* Edinburgh, Adam & Charles Black, 1846.

TITLE PAGE

AN INQUIRY | INTO | THE NATURE AND CAUSES | OF THE | WEALTH OF NATIONS. | BY ADAM SMITH, LL.D. | WITH | A LIFE OF THE AUTHOR, | AN INTRODUCTORY DISCOURSE, NOTES, AND | SUPPLEMENTAL DISSERTATIONS. | BY J. R. M'CULLOCH, Esq. | A NEW EDITION, | CORRECTED THROUGHOUT, AND GREATLY ENLARGED. | EDINBURGH: | ADAM & CHARLES BLACK, AND WILLIAM TAIT. | LONDON: LONGMAN & CO. | MDCCCXLVI.

PAGINATION

[8] i–lxiv 1–648.

CONTENTS

[*1*] half title, [*2*] blank, [*3*] title page, [*4*] printer's imprint, [*5*]–[*8*] editor's preface, i–xiii "Life of Dr. Smith," xiv blank, xv–lv Introductory Discourse, lvi blank, lvii section title, *An Inquiry into the Nature and Causes of the Wealth of Nations,* lviii blank, lix–lxiii contents, lxiv blank, 1–431 text of *The Wealth of Nations,* 432 blank, 433 section title, "Supplemental Notes and Dissertations," 434 blank, 435–621 text of supplement, 622–48 index.

PLATES

Portrait frontispiece of Adam Smith, drawn and engraved by J. Horsburgh.
Facing i, full-length engraving of Adam Smith, "The Author of the Wealth of Nations."

REFERENCES

Hayes p. 256; Roosevelt p. 38; cf. Putnam p. 128; L and B 1850 p. 83; cf. *LC 1816–1851* p. 513; cf. Fillmore 1861 p. 170.

COPY DESCRIBED

DLC: HB 161 S619. *Leaf.* 219 × 135.

---

1. Robert Reich, introduction to Adam Smith, *The Wealth of Nations* (New York: Modern Library, 2000), xv–xx.
2. See entries 108 and 115 for Malthus and Mill, respectively.
3. Keith Tribe and Hiroshi Mizuta, eds., *A Critical Bibliography of Adam Smith* (London: Pickering and Chatto, 2002), 38.

∽

155. Smith, William. *Dictionary of Greek and Roman Antiquities.* Boston: Little and Brown, 1849.
156. ———. *Dictionary of Greek and Roman Biography and Mythology.* 3 vols. Boston: Little and Brown, 1849.

Sir William Smith (1813–93), classical and biblical scholar, gained a reputation for presenting scholarly information in a clear and concise manner through his dictionaries. His *Dictionary of Greek and Roman Antiquities* (1842) and *Dictionary of Greek and Roman Biography and Mythology* (3 vols., 1844–49) were designed for use by scholars studying the classics. Beginning with "Abacus" and ending with "Zophorus," the *Dictionary of Greek and Roman Antiquities* provides entries for terms related to classical culture. It also includes tables of Greek and Roman weights, measures, and money, as well as a topical index. The *Dictionary of Greek and Roman Biography and Mythology* supplies entries for people of significance who are named by Greek and Roman writers through the year 1453. Unlike other classical dictionaries of the day, Smith's includes entries, although brief, for individuals relative to the Byzantine Empire. Smith wrote many of the entries in these books himself, but he also attracted a number of leading scholars as contributors.[1]

Many dictionaries with "Smith" as author were published in the first half of the nineteenth century, yet none appear to be a four-volume work as indicated on the voucher. These two dictionaries most likely account for this entry, because they were advertised by Little and Brown, the seller from whom the purchase was made; they total four volumes, and their combined price matches closely the price that was paid. Little and Brown advertised only the *Dictionary of Greek and Roman Biography and Mythology* for $16.50 in their April 1850 catalogue, yet in their July 1852 catalogue they listed both titles for sale, with the *Dictionary of Greek and Roman Antiquities* at $5.00. The list price for the two together would have been $21.50, an amount close enough to the price paid to account for this purchase, if a 10 percent discount were granted. Furthermore, the Fillmores would have been familiar with these dictionaries, since they owned copies in their personal libraries. These books were also apparently stock titles in government libraries, as provenance marks in Library of Congress copies indicate that the libraries of the navy, the War Department, and the Department of Interior also owned these dictionaries by Smith.

105,133 voucher 2: Smiths Dictionary 4 vols. $18.00.
Purchased from Little and Brown on December 30, 1850.

REFERENCES
cf. Hayes p. 266; cf. Putnam p. 129, 31-s; cf. L and B 1850 p. 83; cf. L and B 1852 p. 5–6; cf. L and B 1853 p. 61; cf. Roorbach p. 507; cf. Fillmore 1847 p. 9; cf. Fillmore Catalogue ca. 1858 p. 14; cf. Fillmore 1861 p. 56.

---

1. "Notices of New Works," *Southern Literary Messenger (1834–1845)*, May 1845, available at *APS Online*, http://www.proquest.com/products_pq/descriptions/aps.shtml. The writer of this review calls Smith's a "most important work."

〜

157. The Society for the Diffusion of Useful Knowledge. *Maps for the Society for the Diffusion of Useful Knowledge.* New ed. 3 vols. London: C. Knight, 1846–47.

The Society for the Diffusion of Useful Knowledge (SDUK) was founded in 1826 by Henry Brougham for the purpose of publishing quality texts at low prices to meet the needs of the ever-increasing reading public. The idea of publishing maps was first suggested in 1827, and a committee for the project was appointed the following year. The maps were originally published in numbers that contained two maps in each issue in a plan that would include more than two hundred maps over fourteen years. Chapman and Hall first collected and published the maps as an atlas in 1844. Charles Knight purchased the plates for the maps from the society in 1846 and continued to publish the atlas through 1852, when he sold the plates to George Cox.[1]

The voucher indicates that the Executive Mansion purchased a three-volume atlas for $33.00. Only two three-volume editions of these maps published prior to 1853 have been discovered, both from Charles Knight. One is dated 1845–47 and the other 1846–51. Just which of these the White House purchased cannot be determined. However, the maps in these atlases would have been practically identical, as they would have been derived from the same plates. Volume 1 contained maps for Europe; volume 2 for Asia, Africa, America, and Australia; while volume 3 offered plans of cities, astronomical maps, and an index to streets.

Putnam included three listings for maps from SDUK, one in a folio, bound in half russia that contained only 112 colored maps and sold for $40.00; a second, also bound in half russia, in large quarto that contained 200 colored maps and also sold for $40.00; and a third, just like the second, except with black and white maps that sold for $35.00. Given that the White House only paid $33.00 for its copy, it most likely purchased one with maps that were in black and white.

107,754 voucher 7: Atlas Published by the Society for the diffusion of useful knowledge.
  3 vols. $33.00.
Purchased from W. M. Morrison on April 6, 1852.

REFERENCES
cf. Putnam p. 8 and p. 87.

---

1. Mead T. Cain, "The Maps for the Society of the Diffusion of Useful Knowledge: A Publishing History," *Imago Mundi: The International Journal for the History of Cartography*, 46 (1994): 163.

∾

158. Southey, Robert. *Common Place Book.* Ed. John Wood Warter. Vol. 1. London: Longman, 1849.

Although today Robert Southey (1774–1843), poet and reviewer, is remembered more for his friendships with William Wordsworth and Samuel Taylor Coleridge than for his own work, during the early nineteenth century, he was popular as a writer and was even named poet laureate in 1813. His *Common Place Book* received favorable reviews from American critics. One found it "highly adaptable for occasional reading" and described Southey as a man of curious taste and habit who had "read everything that nobody else did," and "remembered what other people were sure to forget." Another remarked on his "powerful mind" and its ability to confer "interest upon everything that has been" its object.[1]

Although Southey's *Common Place Book* was available in both a London edition from Longman and an American edition from Harper, the Executive Mansion most likely purchased the London edition. Putnam, the seller from whom this book was purchased, advertised the New York edition for $1.25 and the London edition for $3.75, the amount paid by the White House. The *Common Place Book* was later completed in four volumes, but in 1851 only volumes 1 through 3 were available, and only volume 1 appears in the Putnam and the Little and Brown catalogues of the period. Although $3.75 seems like a high price for a one-volume book of this size, the London edition features an engraved title page with a medallion portrait of Southey, prints the poem on page ii in red, is enhanced by elaborate printer's ornaments, and prints the text in two columns enclosed in a thin rule frame, with the running title separated by another thin rule. These design elements would have increased the production cost of the book. Putnam also lists the "second series" London 1849 edition for $5.25 in cloth, a price that rules it out as a possibility for this purchase.

105,133 voucher 4: Southey's Com. Place Book $3.75.
Purchased from George P. Putnam on December, 13, 1850.

REFERENCES
Putnam p. 130; cf. *LC 1816–1851* p. 522; L and B 1850 p. 84; L and B 1853 p. 62.

1. "Southey's Common Place Book," *Littell's Living Age (1844–1896)*, August 11, 1849, and "Notices of New Books," *The United States Magazine and Democratic Review (1837–1851)*, September 1849, both available at *APS Online,* http://www.proquest.com/products_pq/descriptions/aps.shtml.

❧

**159. Sparks, Jared, ed. *The Library of American Biography.* 1st ser. 10 vols. New York: Harper Brothers, n.d.

160. ———. *The Library of American Biography.* 2nd ser. 15 vols. Boston: Little and Brown, 1848.

161. ———. *The Writings of George Washington.* 12 vols. New York: Harper, 1847.

162. ———. *The Works of Benjamin Franklin.* 10 vols. Boston: Tappan, Whittemore, and Mason, n.d.

Jared Sparks (1789–1866), historian, editor, and clergyman, became one of the leading nineteenth-century American historians, alongside William Hickling Prescott and George Bancroft. Between 1834 and 1840 Sparks worked concomitantly on several projects: ten volumes for the first series of the *Library of American Biography* (1834–38), twelve volumes of *The Writings of George Washington* (1834–37), and ten volumes of the *Works of Benjamin Franklin* (1836–40). He later compiled fifteen volumes of the second series of the *Library of American Biography* (1844–48). His belief in the importance of historical manuscripts and archives to historical writing guided all of his historical endeavors.

Sparks's contributions found great favor with his reviewers, until his reputation as a documentary editor was called into question in the 1850s. One critic proclaimed that "a worthier literary enterprise has not been projected amongst us than this 'American Biography.'"[1] In 1902 J. N. Larned remarked, "this series of biographical essays is still of great interest. Whatever may be said of Sparks' method as an editor of text, he remains one of the greatest of our historical scholars, and this series is edited to as high a level of excellence as such a series in his time could be."[2] To be sure, Sparks's editorial principles differ from those of most twenty-first-century scholars. He believed it was his responsibility to correct "obvious slips of the pen, occasional inaccuracies of expression, and manifest faults of grammar in letters often written hastily and not for publication."[3]

The first series of the *Library* was originally published in ten volumes by Hilliard, Gray and Company in Boston from 1834 through 1838. The second series followed in fifteen volumes from Little and Brown, beginning its publication in 1844 and ending in 1848. Both were reprinted numerous times. Fillmore purchased both series for the White House Library and for his personal library, as indicated in his 1847 and 1861 catalogues.[4]

Sparks's edition of Washington's writings came to be regarded as his greatest accomplishment. He gathered as many of George Washington's manuscripts as he could possibly collect from Mount Vernon, the Department of State, and other public and private archives. He also interviewed survivors of the American Revolution and visited historical sites to gather more material for his work before he began to publish Washington's writings in 1834, completing it in 1837. Thereafter, the set was frequently reprinted and remained the standard edition throughout most of the nineteenth century, until the publication of Worthington Chauncey Ford's edition began in 1889.

The *North American Review* predicted that Sparks's edition of Franklin would supersede all others and lauded Sparks's research for it. According to the reviewer, Francis Bowen, Sparks included twenty-five articles written by Franklin that had never before been published, thirty-three others that had not been included in any other edition of Franklin's works, and numerous letters that had not been previously published.[5]

The volumes of *The Library of American Biography,* first series, described below, are the only books from the original Executive Mansion library that currently remain in the White House. These books were discovered in the late 1970s by the current White House curator, William Allman, on a bookshelf on the third floor. Each volume has "Executive Mansion 1850" inscribed in black ink on the front pastedown. The only other markings that appear in this set are found in volume 4, in the "Life of Sir Henry Vane, Fourth Governor of Massachusetts." Passages concerning the English Revolution have been marked with pencil; in addition to underlining in the text, lines and check marks appear in the margins. No words have been written. One might conjecture that Vane's experiences in the English Civil War could have had striking significance for a mid-nineteenth-century United States president who understood the imminent threat of civil war to his country.

105,133 voucher 5: Spark's American Biography 10 vols. $7.00.
Purchased from Charles Welford on December 13, 1850.
105,133 voucher 2: Sparks Biography 15 vols. $11.25.
Purchased from Little and Brown on December 30, 1850.
Roosevelt Catalogue: ————. *The Library of American Biography, Conducted by Jared Sparks.*
    New York, Harper & Brothers, n.d. 10 vols.
    Second series, vols. 1–15. Boston, Little and Brown, 1848.
105,133 voucher 4: Spark's Washington 12 vols. $17.00.
Purchased from George P. Putnam on December 13, 1850.
Roosevelt Catalogue: Washington, George. *Writings. With a Life of the Author, Notes and Illustrations by Jared Sparks.* New York, Harper & Brothers, 1847–48, 12 vols., vol. 11 missing.
105,133 voucher 2: Spark's Franklin $18.50.
Purchased from Little and Brown on December 30, 1850.
Hayes catalogue: Franklin, B. *Works.* Edited by J. Sparks. 10 vols. Boston, n. d. 8°
    Note. Since the *Library of American Biography,* 1st ser., represents a set that was purchased for the Executive Mansion library in 1850 *and* the books that it contains are the only books from the original library that remain in the White House, a complete description of all ten volumes has been provided. Abbreviated descriptions have been provided for the rest of Spark's works.

Library of American Biography. 1st ser.
SERIES TITLE PAGE
THE | LIBRARY | OF | AMERICAN BIOGRAPHY. | [thin rule] | CONDUCTED | By JARED SPARKS | [thin rule] | VOL. I. [II–X] | [thin rule] | NEW YORK: | HARPER & BROTHERS, PUBLISHERS, | 82 CLIFF STREET.
    Notes. Vol. II. Same as volume 1, except no period follows 'BIOGRAPHY', a period follows 'SPARKS', and the imprint differs as follows: 'NEW YORK: | PUBLISHED BY HARPER AND BROTHERS. | 1848.' *Vol. III.* Same as volume 1, except a period

follows 'SPARKS.' and the imprint differs as follows: 'NEW YORK: PUBLISHED BY
HARPER & BROTHERS, | FOR ALSTON MYGATT. | 1848.' *Vol. IV.* Same as volume
1, except a period follows 'SPARKS' and the imprint is the same as volume 2. *Vol. V.*
Same as volume 1, except the imprint is the same as volume 2. *Vol. VI.* Same as volume 1, except dated 1848. *Vol. VII.* Same as volume 1. *Vol. VIII.* Same as volume 1,
except the imprint is the same as volume 3. *Vol. IX.* Same as volume 1. *Vol. X.* Same
as volume 1, except dated 1848.

VOLUME TITLE PAGE

Vol. I.
LIVES | OF | JOHN STARK, | CHARLES BROCKDEN BROWN | RICHARD
MONTGOMERY, | AND | ETHAN ALLEN. | [thin rule] | NEW YORK: | HARPER &
BROTHERS, PUBLISHERS, | 82 CLIFF STREET.

Vol. II.
LIVES | OF | ALEXANDER WILSON | AND | CAPTAIN JOHN SMITH. | [thin rule] |
NEW YORK: | PUBLISHED BY HARPER AND BROTHERS. | 1848.

Vol. III.
THE | LIFE AND TREASON | OF | BENEDICT ARNOLD. | [thin rule] | By JARED
SPARKS. | [thin rule] | [thin rule] | NEW YORK: | PUBLISHED BY HARPER &
BROTHERS, | FOR ALSTON MYGATT. | 1848.

Vol. IV.
LIVES | OF | ANTHONY WAYNE | AND | SIR HENRY VANE | [thin rule] | NEW YORK:
| PUBLISHED BY HARPER AND BROTHERS. | 1848.

Vol. V.
LIFE | OF | JOHN ELIOT, | APOSTLE TO THE INDIANS | [thin rule] | By CONVERS
FRANCIS | [thin rule] | [thin rule] | NEW YORK: | PUBLISHED BY HARPER &
BROTHERS | FOR ALSTON MYGATT. | 1848.

Vol. VI.
LIVES | OF | WILLIAM PINKNEY, | WILLIAM ELLERY, | AND | COTTON MATHER |
[thin rule] | NEW YORK: | HARPER & BROTHERS, PUBLISHERS, | 82 CLIFF STREET. |
1848.

Vol. VII.
LIVES | OF | SIR WILLIAM PHIPS, | ISRAEL PUTNAM, | LUCRETIA MARIA
DAVIDSON, | AND | DAVID RITTENHOUSE | [thin rule] | NEW YORK: | HARPER &
BROTHERS, PUBLISHERS, | 82 CLIFF STREET.

Vol. VIII.
LIVES | OF | JONATHAN EDWARDS | AND DAVID BRAINERD. | [thin rule] | NEW
YORK: | PUBLISHED BY HARPER & BROTHERS. | FOR ALSTON MYGATT. | 1848.

Vol. IX.

LIVES | OF | BARON STEUBEN, | SEBASTIAN CABOT | AND | WILLIAM EATON. | [thin rule] | NEW YORK: | HARPER & BROTHERS, PUBLISHERS, | 82 CLIFF STREET.

Vol. X.

LIVES | OF | ROBERT FULTON, | JOSEPH WARREN, | HENRY HUDSON, | AND | FATHER MARQUETTE. | [thin rule] | NEW YORK: | HARPER & BROTHERS, PUBLISHERS, | 82 CLIFF STREET. | 1848.

PAGINATION

Vol. I.

[2] i–vi 1–356.

Vol. II.

i–viii 1–408.

Vol. III.

i–xii 1–336.

Vol. IV.

i–x 1–404.

Vol. V.

v–xii 1–360.

> *Note.* The first page bearing a page number is x; the numbers for the preceding pages have been inferred from x, and page numbering in this volume begins with v.

Vol. VI.

i–viii 1–350.

Vol. VII.

i–xii 1–400.

Vol. VIII.

i–xiv 1–374.

Vol. IX.

i–xii 1–360.

Vol. X.

i–xiv 1–388.

CONTENTS

Vol. I.

[1] series title, [2] blank, i volume title, ii copyright statement, iii–v advertisement, vi contents, 1–116 John Stark text, 117 'LIFE | OF | CHARLES BROCKDEN BROWN: | BY | WILLIAM H. PRESCOTT.', 118 blank, 119–80 Charles Brockden Brown text, 181 'LIFE | OF | RICHARD MONTGOMERY; | BY | JOHN ARMSTRONG.', 182 blank, 183–226 Richard Montgomery text, 227 'LIFE | OF | ETHAN ALLEN; | BY | JARED SPARKS.', 228 blank, 229–356 Ethan Allen text.

Vol. II.

i series title, ii blank, iii volume title, iv copyright statement, v–viii contents, 1 'LIFE | OF | ALEXANDER WILSON; | BY | WILLIAM B. O. PEABODY.', 2 blank, 3–169 Alexander Wilson text, 170 blank, 171 'THE | LIFE AND ADVENTURES | OF | CAPTAIN JOHN SMITH; | BY |

GEORGE S. HILLARD.', 172 blank, 173–76 preface, 177–407 Captain John Smith text, 408 blank.

Vol. III.

i series title, ii blank, iii volume title, iv copyright statement, v–viii preface, ix–xii contents, 1 'THE | LIFE AND TREASON | OF | BENEDICT ARNOLD; | BY | JARED SPARKS.', 2 blank, 3–335 Benedict Arnold text, 336 blank.

Vol. IV.

i series title, ii blank, iii volume title, iv copyright statement, v–x contents, 1 'LIFE | OF | ANTHONY WAYNE; | BY | JOHN ARMSTRONG.', 2 blank, 3–84 Anthony Wayne text, 85 'LIFE | OF | SIR HENRY VANE, | FOURTH GOVERNOR | OF | MASSACHUSETTS. | BY | CHARLES WENTWORTH UPHAM.', 86 blank, 87–90 preface, 91–393 Sir Henry Vane text, 394 blank, 395–403 appendix, 404 blank.

Vol. V.

v series title, vi blank, vii volume title, viii copyright statement, ix–xii contents, 1 'LIFE | OF | JOHN ELIOT, | THE | APOSTLE TO THE INDIANS | BY | CONVERS FRANCIS.', 2 blank, 3–343 John Eliot text, 344 blank, 345–57 appendix, 358–60 blank.

Vol. VI.

i series title, ii blank, iii volume title, iv copyright statement, v–viii contents, 1 'LIFE | OF | WILLIAM PINKNEY; | BY | HENRY WHEATON, LL. D.', 2 blank, 3–84 Pinkney text, 85 'LIFE | OF | WILLIAM ELLERY; | BY | EDWARD T. CHANNING.', 86 blank, 87–159 William Ellery text, 160 blank, 161 'LIFE | OF | COTTON MATHER | BY | WILLIAM B. O. PEABODY.', 162 blank, 163–350 Cotton Mather text.

Vol. VII.

i series title, ii blank, iii title, iv copyright statement, v–xii contents, 1 'LIFE | OF | SIR WILLIAM PHIPS; | BY | FRANCIS BOWEN', 2 blank, 3–4 preface, 5–102 Sir William Phips text, 103 'LIFE | OF | ISRAEL PUTNAM; | BY | OLIVER W. PEABODY', 104 blank, 105–218 Israel Putnam text, 219 A | MEMOIR | OF | LUCRETIA MARIA DAVIDSON; | BY | THE AUTHOR OF "REDWOOD," "HOPE LESLIE" | &c., &c.', 220 blank, 221 preface, 222 blank, 223–94 Lucretia Maria Davidson text, 295 'LIFE | OF | DAVID RITTENHOUSE; | BY | JAMES RENWICK, LL. D.', 296 blank, 297–398 David Rittenhouse text, 399–400 blank.

Vol. VIII.

i series title, ii blank, iii volume title, iv copyright statement, v–vii preface to John Eliot, viii blank, ix–xiv contents, 1 'LIFE | OF | JONATHAN EDWARDS, | PRESIDENT OF THE COLLEGE OF NEW JERSEY; | BY | SAMUEL MILLER, D. D., | PROFESSOR OF ECCLESIASTICAL HISTORY AND CHURCH GOVERNMENT IN | THE THEOLOGICAL SEMINARY AT PRINCETON, NEW JERSEY.', 2 blank, 3–256 Jonathan Edwards text, 257 'LIFE OF DAVID BRAINERD | MISSIONARY TO THE INDIANS; | BY | WILLIAM B. O. PEABODY.', 258 blank, 259 preface, 260 blank, 261–373 David Brainerd text, 374 blank.

> *Note.* The preface to John Eliot that appears on pages v–vii of this volume is an obvious binding error in the Executive Mansion copy; it should have been bound into volume 5, in which the Life of John Eliot appears.

Vol. IX.

i series title, ii blank, iii volume title, iv copyright statement, v–xii contents, 1 'LIFE | OF | BARON STEUBEN | BY | FRANCIS BOWEN.', 2 blank, 3 preface, 4 blank, 5–88 Baron

Steuben text, 89 'LIFE | OF | SEBASTIAN CABOT; | BY | CHARLES HAYWARD, Jr.', 90 blank, 91–92 preface, 93–162 Sebastian Cabot text, 163 'LIFE | OF | WILLIAM EATON; | BY | CORNELIUS C. FELTON,' 164 blank, 165–66 preface, 167–358 William Eaton text, 359–60 blank.

Vol. X.

i series title, ii blank, iii volume title, iv copyright statement, v–xiii contents, xiv blank, 1 'LIFE | OF | ROBERT FULTON, | BY | JAMES RENWICK, LL.D.', 2 blank, 3–89 James Renwick text, 90 blank, 91 'LIFE | OF | JOSEPH WARREN, | BY | ALEXANDER H. EVERETT, LL. D', 92 blank, 93–183 Joseph Warren text, 184 blank, 185 'LIFE | OF | HENRY HUDSON, | BY | HENRY R. CLEVELAND.', 186 blank, 187–261 Henry Hudson text, 262 blank, 263 'LIFE | OF | FATHER MARQUETTE, | BY | JARED SPARKS.', 264 blank, 265–99 Father Marquette text, 300 blank, 301–2 list of lives contained in the first ten volumes, 303 'GENERAL INDEX | TO THE | FIRST TEN VOLUMES.', 304 blank, 305–86 general index text, 387–88 blank.

PLATES

Vol. I.

Engraved title page, 'THE LIBRARY | OF | AMERICAN BIOGRAPHY | CONDUCTED BY | JARED SPARKS. | [Portrait Vignette of John Stark] | JOHN STARK. | NEW YORK. | HARPER & BROTHERS.'

> *Notes. Vols. II–X.* Same as volume 1, except for the portrait vignette. These vignettes are as follows by volume: *II.* John Smith; *III.* Benedict Arnold; *IV.* Sir Henry Vane; *V.* John Eliot with Indians signed 'G. G. Smith Sc.'; *VI.* William Pinkney; *VII.* Israel Putnam; *VIII.* Jonathan Edwards; *IX.* Sebastian Cabot; *X.* Joseph Warren.

Facing 1, facsimile note addressed to John Stark.

Facing 117, facsimile note from Charles Brockden Brown.

Facing 181, facsimile note from Richard Montgomery.

Facing 227, facsimile note from Ethan Allen.

Vol. II.

Facing 1, facsimile note from Alexander Wilson.

Vol. III.

Facing 1, facsimile note to British Army.

Facing 162, facsimile manuscript note from John Anderson.

Facing 176, map of Hudson River Valley.

Facing 210, facsimile note from Benedict Arnold.

Facing 280, facsimile of drawing of Arnold made by himself the day before his execution.

Vol. IV.

Facing 1, facsimile note from Anthony Wayne.

Vol. V.

Facing 1, facsimile manuscript note from John Eliot.

Vol. VI.

Facing 1, facsimile manuscript note from William Pinkney.

Facing 85, facsimile manuscript note from William Ellery.

Facing 161, facsimile manuscript of Cotton Mather.

Vol. VII.
Facing 295, facsimile manuscript note from David Rittenhouse.
Vol. VIII.
Facing 1, facsimile manuscript note signed Jonathan Edwards.
Facing 257, facsimile manuscript note signed David Brainerd.
Vol. IX.
Facing 163, facsimile manuscript note signed by William Eaton.
Vol. X.
Facing 263, facsimile of map from Marquette's journal.

BINDING
Vol. I.
Front and back boards. 169 × 111 med. brown ribbed cloth with blind-stamped cartouche frame. Spine. Gilt stamped '[triple thin rule frame 37 × 27] | LIBRARY | OF | AMERICAN | BIOGRAPHY [swelled rule] | I [all foregoing inside of frame] | STARK. | BROWN. | MONTGOMERY. | ALLEN. [all names near base of spine]' *Endpapers.* Off-white.

> *Notes.* All volumes are the same except for the volume number and title, which appear on the spine as follows: *Vol. II.* '. . . II | WILSON. | [thin rule] | SMITH.'; *Vol. III.* '. . . III . . . BENEDICT | ARNOLD. | By | J. SPARKS.'; *Vol. IV.* '. . . IV . . . WAYNE. | [thin rule] | VANE.'; *Vol. V.* '. . . V . . . LIFE OF | JOHN ELIOT. | BY | C. FRANCIS.'; *Vol. VI.* '. . . VI . . . PINKNEY. | ELLERY. | MATHER.'; *Vol. VII.* '. . . VII . . . W. PHIPS. | PUTNAM. | DAVIDSON. | RITTENHOUSE.'; *Vol. VIII.* 'VIII . . . EDWARDS. | [thin rule] | BRAINERD.' *Vol. IX.* 'IX . . . STEUBEN. | CABOT. | EATON.' *Vol. X.* 'X . . . FULTON. | WARREN. | HUDSON. | MARQUETTE.'

MARKS OF OWNERSHIP
All Vols.
Inscribed on front pastedown in black ink, "Executive Mansion | 1850."
Below inscription in pencil "D | shelf no. 2"
Vol. IV. Pencil markings in the "Life of Sir Henry Vane" as discussed in the headnote to this entry.

REFERENCES
Hayes p. 259; Roosevelt p. 39; Larned 2613; cf. Putnam p. 4 and p. 131; cf. Roorbach p. 512; cf. Fillmore 1847 p. 23; cf. Fillmore 1861 p. 1, p. 190, and p. 200.

COPY DESCRIBED
Executive Mansion 1850.

Library of America Biography. **2nd ser.**
SERIES TITLE PAGE
THE | LIBRARY | OF | AMERICAN BIOGRAPHY. | [thin rule] | CONDUCTED | By JARED SPARKS | VOL. XI. [XII–XXV.] | [thin rule] | BOSTON: | CHARLES C. LITTLE AND JAMES BROWN | 1847 [1846, 1848].

TITLE PAGE

Vol. XI.

LIVES | OF | ROBERT CAVELIER DE LA SALLE | AND | PATRICK HENRY. | [thin rule] | BOSTON: | CHARLES C. LITTLE AND JAMES BROWN | 1848.

Vol. XII.

LIVES | OF | JAMES OTIS | AND | JAMES OGLETHORPE. | [thin rule] | BOSTON: | CHARLES C. LITTLE AND JAMES BROWN. | 1847.

Vol. XIII.

LIVES | OF | JOHN SULLIVAN, | JACOB LEISLER, | NATHANIEL BACON, | AND | JOHN MASON. | [thin rule] | BOSTON. | CHARLES C. LITTLE AND JAMES BROWN | 1848.

Vol. XIV.

LIVES | OF | ROGER WILLIAMS, | TIMOTHY DWIGHT, | AND | COUNT PULASKI. | [thin rule] | BOSTON: | CHARLES C. LITTLE AND JAMES BROWN. | 1847.

Vol. XV.

LIVES | OF | COUNT RUMFORD, | ZEBULON MONTGOMERY PIKE, | AND | SAMUEL GORTON. | [thin rule] | BOSTON: | CHARLES C. LITTLE AND JAMES BROWN. | 1848.

Vol. XVI.

LIVES | OF | JOHN RIBAULT, | SEBASTIAN RALE, | AND | WILLIAM PALFREY. | [thin rule] | BOSTON: | CHARLES C. LITTLE AND JAMES BROWN | 1848.

Vol. XVII.

LIVES | OF | EZRA STILES, | JOHN FITCH, | AND | ANNE HUTCHISON | [thin rule] | BOSTON: | CHARLES C. LITTLE AND JAMES BROWN. | 1847.

Vol. XVIII.

LIVES | OF | CHARLES LEE | AND | JOSEPH REED | [thin rule] | BOSTON: | CHARLES C. LITTLE AND JAMES BROWN | 1848.

Vol. XIX.

LIVES | OF | LEONARD CALVERT, | SAMUEL WARD, | AND | THOMAS POSEY. | [thin rule] | BOSTON: | CHARLES C. LITTLE AND JAMES BROWN. | 1846.

Vol. XX.

LIFE | OF | NATHANAEL GREENE, | MAJOR-GENERAL IN THE ARMY OF | THE REVOLUTION. | [thin rule] | BY HIS GRANDSON, | GEORGE W. GREENE, | LATE AMERICAN CONSUL AT ROME | [thin rule] | BOSTON: | CHARLES C. LITTLE AND JAMES BROWN. | 1848.

Vol. XXI.

LIFE | OF | STEPHEN DECATUR, | A COMMODORE IN THE NAVY OF THE UNITED STATES. | [thin rule] | BY | ALEXANDER SLIDELL MACKENZIE, U.S.N. | [thin rule] | PRO LIBERTATE ET PATRIA DULCE PERICULUM. | *Decatur's Motto* | [thin rule] | BOSTON: | CHARLES C. LITTLE AND JAMES BROWN | 1848.

Vol. XXII.
LIVES | OF | EDWARD PREBLE | AND | WILLIAM PENN. | [thin rule] | BOSTON: | CHARLES C. LITTLE AND JAMES BROWN. | 1847.

Vol. XXIII.
LIVES | OF | DANIEL BOONE | AND | BENJAMIN LINCOLN. | [thin rule] | BOSTON: | CHARLES C. LITTLE AND JAMES BROWN. | 1847.

Vol. XXIV.
LIFE | OF | JOHN LEDYARD, | THE AMERICAN TRAVELLER. | [thin rule] | BY | JARED SPARKS. | [thin rule] | BOSTON: | CHARLES C. LITTLE AND JAMES BROWN. | 1847.

Vol. XXV.
LIVES | OF | WILLIAM RICHARDSON DAVIE | AND | SAMUEL KIRKLAND. | [thin rule] | BOSTON: | CHARLES C. LITTLE AND JAMES BROWN. | 1848.

PAGINATION
Vol. XI. [4] vii–xx 1–398.
Vol. XII. i–x 1–406.
Vol. XIII. i–x 1–438.
Vol. XIV. i–xii 1–446.
Vol. XV. i–xii 1–412.
Vol. XVI. i–xiv 1–376.
Vol. XVII. i–xiv 1–448.
Vol. XVIII. i–xiv 1–440.
Vol. XIX. i–x 1–404.
Vol. XX. i–x 1–404.
Vol. XXI. i–xii 1–444.
Vol. XXII. i–xiv 1–408.
Vol. XXIII. i–xii 1–434.
Vol. XXIV. i–x 1–420.
Vol. XXV. i–xii 1–462.

REFERENCES
Hayes p. 260; Roosevelt p. 39; cf. Putnam p. 4 and p. 131; L and B 1850 p. 85; L and B 1852 p. 6; cf. L and B 1853 p. 62–63; cf. Roorbach p. 512; cf. Fillmore 1847 p. 23; cf. Fillmore 1861 p. 190 and p. 200.

COPY DESCRIBED
DLC: E 176 S83 1839. *Leaf.* 170 × 101.

The Writings of George Washington.
TITLE PAGE
THE | WRITINGS | OF | GEORGE WASHINGTON; | BEING HIS | CORRESPONDENCE, ADDRESSES, MESSAGES, AND OTHER | PAPERS, OFFICIAL AND PRIVATE, | SELECTED AND PUBLISHED FROM THE ORIGINAL

MANUSCRIPTS; | WITH | A LIFE OF THE AUTHOR, | NOTES AND ILLUSTRATIONS. | [thin rule] | By JARED SPARKS. | [thin rule] | VOLUME I. [II–XII.] | [thin rule] | HARPER & BROTHERS, PUBLISHERS, | 82 CLIFF STREET, NEW YORK. | 1847.

> *Notes.* Volumes 2 through 12 have a comma after "Notes"; volumes 11 through 12 are dated 1848; volume 12 has no period after "Illustrations."

PAGINATION

Vol. I. [4] vii–xxxii 1–586.
Vol. II. [6] ix–xvi 1–536.
Vol. III. [4] vii–xx 1–542.
Vol. IV. [6] 1–560.
Vol. V. [6] 1–560.
Vol. VI. [6] 1–556.
Vol. VII. [6] 1–566.
Vol. VIII. [6] 1–572.
Vol. IX. [6] 1–560.
Vol. X. [6] 1–564.
Vol. XI. [6] 1–578.
Vol. XII. i–viii 1–592.

REFERENCES

Hayes p. 310; Roosevelt p. 43; cf. Roorbach p. 512; cf. Putnam p. 131 and p. 150; cf. Fillmore 1847 p. 13; cf. Fillmore 1861 p. 222.

COPY DESCRIBED

DLC: E312.7 1847. *Leaf.* 225 × 140.

The Works of Benjamin Franklin.

TITLE PAGE

THE | WORKS | OF | BENJAMIN FRANKLIN; | CONTAINING | SEVERAL POLITICAL AND HISTORICAL TRACTS | NOT INCLUDED IN ANY FORMER EDITION, | AND | MANY LETTERS OFFICIAL AND PRIVATE | NOT HITHERTO PUBLISHED; | WITH | NOTES | AND | A LIFE OF THE AUTHOR. | [thin rule] | By JARED SPARKS. | [thin rule] | VOLUME I. [II–X] | [thin rule] | BOSTON: | TAPPAN, WHITTEMORE, AND MASON. | NEW ORLEANS: | ALSTON MYGATT.

> *Notes.* The title page of volume 3 is missing; volume 4's title page is missing the comma at end of line 7, the semicolon at end of line 10, the period at end of line 16, and the period at end of final line; the title page of volume 6 is missing the period after the volume number; and the title page of volume 9 has a different imprint, which reads 'BOSTON: | CHARLES TAPPAN, PUBLISHER. | LOUISVILLE, KY.: | ALSTON MYGATT. | 1847.'

PAGINATION

Vol. I. i–xl 1–612.
Vol. II. i–xii 1–558.
Vol. III. [4] vii–xvi 1–578.
Vol. IV. [4] vii–xii 1–540.

Vol. V. i–xvi 1–516.

Vol. VI. i–xiv 1–578.

Vol. VII. i–xxiv 1–568.

Vol. VIII. i–xxiv 1–554.

Vol. IX. i–xxiv 1–550.

Vol. X. i–xxii 1–540.

REFERENCES

Hayes p. 67; Roosevelt p. 15; cf. Roorbach p. 512; cf. Putnam p. 48 and p. 131; cf. Fillmore ca. 1858 p. 21; cf. Fillmore Catalogue 1861 p. 72.

COPY DESCRIBED

DLC: E302 F82 1840a *Leaf.* 216 × 123.

---

1. "The Library of American Biography. Conducted by Jared Sparks," *Christian Examiner and General Review (1829–1844),* September 1836, available at *APS Online,* http://www.proquest.com/products_pq/ descriptions/aps.shtml.

2. J. N. Larned, *The Literature of American History: A Bibliographical Guide* (1902; repr., New York: Unger, 1966), 291.

3. Qtd. in Richard N Sheldon, "Editing a Historical Manuscript: Jared Sparks, Douglas Southall Freeman, and the Battle of Brandywine," *William and Mary Quarterly* 3rd ser., 36, no. 2 (1979): 255.

4. In July 2009 Fillmore's set of the first series from Harper and dated 1860–67 was listed for sale by John K. King Used and Rare Books (http://www.rarebooklink.com). According to King, all of the volumes are inscribed and dated on the title pages and front pastedowns: "From the Library of President Millard Fillmore."

5. Francis Bowen, "The Works of Benjamin Franklin," *The North American Review (1821–1940),* October 1844, available at *APS Online,* http://www.proquest.com/products_pq/descriptions/aps.shtml. For more information about Jared Sparks and his work, see Herbert B. Adams, *The Life and Writings of Jared Sparks* (Boston: Houghton, Mifflin, 1893), 334–38.

∾

163. Stephen, Henry J. *New Commentaries on the Laws of England.* 4 vols. New York: Halsted and Voorhies, 1841–46.

With *New Commentaries on the Laws of England* (1841), Henry J. Stephen (1787–1864) sought to update Blackstone's *Commentaries on the Laws of England.* Accordingly, Marvin called it a "compound" of Stephen and Blackstone, explaining that Stephen "drops the obsolete parts of Blackstone altogether, and aims at furnishing an elementary exposition of English Law as it exists at the present day."[1] The notice to the reader in volume 1 of the *Commentaries* informs that portions were taken directly from Blackstone without alteration and that these portions have been marked with brackets (1:xviii). Because the *New Commentaries* had only recently been published at the time of Marvin's writing, he did not recommend that students dispense with Blackstone just yet. Based on Stephen's reputation, he expected no "material inaccuracies" would be found and suggested that the second perusal of Blackstone's *Commentaries* could be through Stephen's. He cautioned, however, that the American reprint contained many verbal errors. Apparently, Marvin was not alone in his regard for Stephen; the *Commentaries* were later adopted as reading for the Law Society's intermediate exam.

105,133 voucher 7: Stephen's Commentaries 4 vols. & extra binding $13.00.

Purchased from Franck Taylor on November 11, 1850.

Hayes Catalogue: Stephen, H. J. *New Commentaries on the Laws of England.* 4 v. New York, 1841–46. 8°.

TITLE PAGE

NEW | COMMENTARIES | ON THE | LAWS OF ENGLAND. | (PARTLY FOUNDED ON BLACKSTONE.) | BY HENRY JOHN STEPHEN, | SERGEANT AT LAW, | AUTHOR OF THE TREATISE ON PLEADING, &c., &c. | [thin rule] | "For hoping well to deliver myself from mistaking, by the order and perspicuous | expressing of that I do propound, I am otherwise zealous and affectionate to recede | as little from antiquity, either in terms or opinions, as may stand with truth, and | the proficience of knowledge."—*Lord Bac. Adv. of Learning.* | [thin rule] | First American Edition [black letter] | VOL. I. [II–IV.] | [thin rule] | NEW YORK: | HALSTED & VOORHIES, LAW BOOKSELLERS, | [thin rule] | 1841.

Note. Volume 2 is dated 1843; lineation and layout differs in volume 3 as follows: '. . . | BY | HENRY JOHN STEPHEN, | SERGEANT AT LAW | "For hoping well to deliver myself from mistaking, by the order and | "perspicuous expressing of that I do propound, I am otherwise zealous and | "affectionate to recede | as little from antiquity, either in terms or opinions, as | "may stand with truth, and the proficience of knowledge."—*Lord Bac.* | *Adv. of Learning.* | [thin wavy rule] | FIRST AMERICAN EDITION | [thin wavy rule] | VOL. III. | [thin wavy rule] | NEW YORK: | JOHN S. VOORHIES, LAW BOOKSELLER. | 1845.'

Note. Lineation and layout differ in volume 4 as follows: '. . . | "For hoping well to deliver myself from mistaking, by the order and perspi- | "cuous expressing of that I do propound, I am otherwise zealous and affection- | "ate to recede as little from antiquity, either in terms or opinions, as may stand | "with truth, and the proficience of knowledge."—*Lord Bac.* | *Adv. of Learning.* | [thin rule] | Vol. IV. | [thin rule] | FIRST AMERICAN EDITION. | [thin rule] | NEW-YORK: | JOHN S. VOORHIES, LAW BOOKSELLER. | [thin rule] | 1846.'

PAGINATION

Vol. I. [2] i–xxvi 1–588.

Vol. II. i–xii 1–620.

Vol. III. i–xii 1–744.

Vol. IV. i–x 1–572.

CONTENTS

Vol. I. [1] blank, [2] advertisement for Law Books published by Halsted and Voorhies, i title, ii printer's imprint, iii–xvii preface, xviii notice to reader, xix–xxv contents, xxvi blank, 1–575 text, 576 blank, 577–88 index.

Vol. II. i title, ii printer's imprint, iii–xii contents, 1–609 text, 610 blank, 611–20 index.

Vol. III. i title, ii printer's imprint, iii–xi contents, xii blank, 1–729 text, 730 blank, 731–44 index.

Vol. IV. i title, ii printer's imprint, iii–x contents, 1–514 text, 515–72 index.

PLATES

Vol. I.

Facing 400, folding table, "Table of Descent," showing paternal and maternal lines.

REFERENCES

Hayes p. 266; *BEAL* 5366; cf. Harvard p. 236; cf. Marvin p. 664; cf. Roorbach p. 630.

COPY DESCRIBED

DLC: LLRBR Blackstone Collection KD 660 S74 1841 Copy 1 (Vols. 1–3 only); ViU: T S8284c 1841 v. 4. *Leaf.* 226 × 140 (measurement from DLC copy).

---

1. Marvin, *Legal Bibliography*, 664. For Blackstone, see entry 16.

∽

164. Story, Joseph. *Commentaries on the Constitution of the United States.* 2nd ed. 2 vols. Boston: Little and Brown, 1851.

165. ———. *Commentaries on the Conflicts of Laws.* Boston: Little and Brown. London: A. Maxwell, 1846.

166. ———. *Commentaries.*

Joseph Story (1779–1845), U.S. Supreme Court justice, legal scholar, law professor, and congressman, shaped American law through his legal writings more than through any of his other positions. He wrote nine legal commentaries between 1832 and 1845, which became the basis for many private legal libraries, and attorneys throughout the United States who had limited or no access to reports of recent cases relied on Story's writings. Story also played a significant role as a professor at Harvard Law School. In 1828, the year before Story arrived, the program had only one student enrolled. The following year Story was named the first Dane Professor of Law at Harvard and helped to attract twenty-eight students. By 1844 the Harvard Law program had 156 students and had become the nation's premier law school, the one from which the president's son Millard P. Fillmore would graduate in 1849.

Story's *Commentaries on the Constitution* (1833) grew out of a series of lectures on the topic that he prepared for his students. Taking the *Federalist* as the basis for his work, Story "advocates a liberal construction of the palladium of our liberalities, in order to attain a proper exercise of the functions of government; and though he sustains his positions with great power of argument, fullness of illustration, and by indisputable authorities, his views have given rise to several works of an opposite character, in which this doctrine is freely canvassed, and ardently combated."[1] In 1840 Story also published a one-volume abridged edition of his *Commentaries on the Constitution*, entitled *A Familiar Exposition of the Constitution.* Two German works based on Story's *Constitution* appeared, one in 1838 and another in 1844. Little and Brown's 1851 edition of Story's *Constitution* is the first two-volume edition of this title to appear and therefore the only one that could match this voucher entry, which is dated June 13, 1851.[2]

In addition to Story on the Constitution, the Executive Mansion purchased two other commentaries by Story, one titled *Conflicts of Laws* and one for which the voucher simply reads "Story's Commentaries." Story's *Conflicts of Laws* stands as the first systematic treatment of its topic. It best exhibited Story's range of "juridical studies, his skill in contrasting and weighing authorities, and his keen perception of government principles to be derived from them."[3] British, European, and American jurists lauded Story's accomplishment in this work. Despite being published posthumously, as stated in the advertisement, this 1846 edition contains Joseph Story's final revisions [3].[4]

The third title of Story's purchased by the White House could be any one of seven other works: *Commentaries on the Law of Bailments* (1832), $5.00; *Commentaries on Equity Pleadings* (1838), $6.00; *Commentaries on the Law of Agency* (1839), $5.00; *Commentaries on the Law of Partnership* (1841), $5.50; *Commentaries on Bills of Exchange* (1843), $5.50; and *Commentaries on the Law of Promissory Notes and Guarantee of Notes* (1845), $5.50; or the abridged commentary on the Constitution, $3.00.[5] Greenleaf recommends *Bailments, Agency, Bills, Partnership,* and *Equity,* yet the purchase price of $3.00 would suggest the abridgment of the Constitution. This title, however, seems an unlikely choice for several reasons. When Fillmore ordered the full-length version from Franck Taylor the following January, Taylor only had the abridgment and sent it for Fillmore's use until he could get the full-length version. Fillmore returned the copy that Taylor had sent and waited for the new two-volume edition to be published. Fillmore had previously returned another copy of the abridgment that had been sent on approval by Charles Lanman in December of 1850. It is possible that Fillmore had purchased the abridgment in October from Taylor and therefore returned the two subsequent copies; yet as a lawyer and statesman, Fillmore would have wanted the unabridged version instead of the abridgment, which was intended for a popular, rather than a professional, audience. The third title by Story will remain unknown unless further information comes to light.[6]

105,133 voucher 7: Story's Commentaries 1 vol. $3.00.
Purchased from Franck Taylor on October 24, 1850.
105,133 voucher 2: Story's Conflict Laws $5.50.
Purchased from Little and Brown on December 30, 1850.
Hayes Catalogue: Story J. *Commentaries on the Conflict of Laws.* 3rd ed. Boston, 1846 8°.
107,754 voucher 3: Story on the Constitution 2 vols. $6.50.
Purchased from Franck Taylor on June 13, 1851.

Commentaries on the Constitution of the United States.
TITLE PAGE
COMMENTARIES | ON THE | CONSTITUTION OF THE UNITED STATES: | WITH | A PRELIMINARY REVIEW | OF | THE CONSTITUTIONAL HISTORY OF THE COLONIES AND STATES, | BEFORE THE ADOPTION OF THE CONSTITUTION. | By JOSEPH STORY, LL.D., | DANE PROFESSOR OF LAW IN HARVARD UNIVERSITY. | IN TWO VOLUMES. | "Magistratibus igitur opus est; sine quorum prudentiâ ac diligentiâ esse civitas non potest; | quorunmque descriptione omnis Reipublicæ moderatio continetur." | CICERO, DE LEG. lib. 3, cap. 2. | "Government is a contrivance of human wisdom to provide for human wants." | BURKE. | SECOND EDITION. | VOLUME I. [II.] | BOSTON: | CHARLES C. LITTLE AND JAMES BROWN. | 1851.

PAGINATION
i–xxxvi 1–734.
[2] 1–632.

CONTENTS
Vol. I. i title, ii copyright statement and printer's imprint, iii advertisement to the second edition, iv blank, v–vi dedication to John Marshall, Chief Justice of the United States, of America, vi–ix preface, x blank, xi–xvii contents, xviii blank, xix–xxxiii the Constitution, xxxiv blank, xxxv section title "Commentaries on the Constitution," xxxvi blank, 1–734 text.
Vol. II. [1] title, [2] copyright statement and printer's imprint, 1–617 text, 618 blank, 619–32 index.

REFERENCES
BEAL 2916; cf. Greenleaf; cf. Harvard[7] pp. 237–38; cf. Marvin 669; cf. Roorbach 630.

COPY DESCRIBED
DLC: JK 211 S7 1851. *Leaf.* 226 × 141.

Commentaries on the Conflicts of Laws.

TITLE PAGE
COMMENTARIES | ON THE | CONFLICTS OF LAWS, | FOREIGN AND DOMESTIC, | IN REGARD TO | CONTRACTS, RIGHTS AND REMEDIES, | AND ESPECIALLY IN REGARD TO | MARRIAGES, DIVORCES, WILLS, SUCCESSIONS, AND JUDGMENTS. | [thin rule] | BY JOSEPH STORY, LL.D. | DANE PROFESSOR OF LAW IN HARVARD UNIVERSITY. | [thin rule] | "Il régnera donc toujours entre les nations une contrariété perpétuelle de loix; peutêtre rég- | nera-t-elle perpétuellement entre nous sur bien des objets. Delà la nécessité de s'instruire | des règles, et des principes, qui peuvent nous conduire dans la décision des questions, que | cette variété peut faire naître."— BOULLENOIS, *Traité de la Personalité, &c. des Loix, Préface.* | [thin rule] | THIRD EDITION. | REVISED, CORRECTED, AND GREATLY ENLARGED. | [swelled rule] | BOSTON: | CHARLES C. LITTLE AND JAMES BROWN. | LONDON: | A. MAXWELL AND SON, 32 BELL YARD, LINCOLN'S INN. | [thin rule] | MDCCCXLVI.

PAGINATION
[4] vii–xxxvi 1–1068.

CONTENTS
[1] title, [2] copyright statement and printer's imprint, [3] advertisement to the third edition, [4] blank, vii–ix advertisement to the second edition, x blank, xi–xii dedication to the Honorable James Kent, LL. D., xiii–xv preface, xvi blank, xvii contents, xviii–xxii list of authors cited, xxiii–xxxv index to cases cited, xxxvi blank, 1–1068 text.

REFERENCES
Hayes p. 154; *BEAL* 2726.; cf. Greenleaf; cf. Harvard[8] p. 238; cf. Marvin 670; Roorbach p. 630; cf. *LC 1816–1851* p. 535.

COPY DESCRIBED

DLC: KF 411 S76 1846 *Leaf.* 231 × 129.

1. Marvin, *Legal Bibliography,* 669. See entry 71 for the *Federalist.*

2. *BEAL,* 2916. The first edition in 1833 was in three volumes, and the abridgement, also from 1833, was one volume.

3. Marvin, *Legal Bibliography,* 669.

4. This advertisement is signed by Story's son, W. W. Story.

5. Prices given are quoted from Little and Brown catalogues of the period.

6. See "White House Collection," 11–12.

7. A note in the *Harvard Law Library Catalogue* indicates that there are an additional 118 copies of this title in their Text Book Library.

8. A note in the *Harvard Law Library Catalogue* indicates that there are an additional ninety-two copies of this title in their Text Book Library.

∽

167. Supreme Court Reports.

These reports are the official source of the opinions of the Supreme Court of the United States. The first ninety volumes of reports were compiled by individuals known as nominative reporters and were commercial ventures for these entrepreneurs. Thus these reports are known by the reporters' surnames, such as Dallas, Cranch, and so forth. The reporter received no compensation other than profit from sales of the reports for his efforts until 1817. In 1816 Congress officially created the office of Supreme Court reporter, and the year following established a salary of $1000.00 per year for the position. This salary supplemented whatever income the reporter received from sales of the published volumes. Editing and publishing the reports was a demanding task, and in the years prior to this additional compensation, long lapses of time often occurred between the announcement of a decision and its publication. Moreover, prices for these books were high and the market limited. Many of the court's decisions were published inaccurately, and some not at all.[1]

The influence of the reported decisions expanded in mid-nineteenth-century America as "the audience for such decisions grew beyond the parties and lawyers in a specific litigation to the legal profession as a whole, to other judges and public officers, and to all who might be affected by or interested in the developing law of the nation."[2]

A complete set of the Supreme Court Reports up to 1850 was included in the initial purchases for the first White House Library, but because the reports were often reprinted a volume at a time, rather than in complete sets, it would be difficult to determine which edition of each volume was purchased. Furthermore, the reports were not all acquired from the same bookseller.[3]

The purchase of Wheaton's reports stands as one of the few examples for which documentation survives in correspondence from the bookseller. Taylor and Maury offered the set to Fillmore on January 3, 1851, when they wrote to the president:

> Wheaton's Reports 12. Volumes we should be pleased to satisfy you with—The regular catalogue price is $48.00.
>
> There is not a copy at present in this city, but we can get one in two or three days, and furnish it at the lowest [*one word illegible*] price as, we can engage to do with any commission you may be pleased to intrust us.[4]

Fillmore must have declined their offer, because the set does not appear on a voucher for purchase until March 31, 1851; the seller is Franck Taylor and the price, $42.00, a reduction of $6.00 from the advertised price quoted by Taylor and Maury.

The reporters through 1850, the number of volumes that each published, and the years for which each served as reporter are as follows:

Reporter	Vols.	Abbr.	Years
Alexander Dallas	4	Dall.	1790–1800
William Cranch	9	Cranch	1801–1815
Henry Wheaton	12	Wheat.	1816–1827
Richard Peters Jr.	16	Pet.	1828–1842
Benjamin Howard	24	How.	1843–1860

105,133 voucher 4: Dallas Reports 4 vols. $13.50.

Purchased from George P. Putnam on December 13, 1850.

105,133 voucher 4: Cranch's Reports 9 vols. $18.00.

Purchased from George P. Putnam on December 13, 1850.

105,133 voucher 7: Wheaton's Reports 12 vols. $42.00.

Purchased from Franck Taylor on March 31, 1851.

105,133 voucher 2: Peters Repts. 17 vols. $48.00.

Purchased from Little and Brown on December 30, 1850.

105,133 voucher 2: Howard's Repts. 8 vols. $36.00.

Purchased from Little and Brown on December 30, 1850, 8 vols.

Hayes catalogue: Cranch, W. *Reports of Cases Argued and Adjudged in the Supreme Court of the United States* Aug. 1801 to Feb. 1815 9 v. New York, 1812–17. 8°

Wheaton, H. *Reports of Cases Argued and Adjudged in the Supreme Court of the United States* Feb. 1816 to January 1827 12 v. Philadelphia. etc. 1827–47. 8°

Peters, R. jr. *Reports of Cases Argued and Adjudged in the Supreme Court of the United States.* Jan. 1828 to Jan. 1843. 17 v. Philadelphia, etc. 1843–46.

Howard, B. C. *Reports of Cases Argued and Adjudged in the Supreme Court of the United States.* Jan. 1843 to Dec. 1860. v. 1 to 24. Philadelphia, etc. 1854–61. 8°

REFERENCES

Hayes pp. 154–55; cf. Roorbach p. 614, p. 619, p. 625, and p. 634; cf. Harvard p. 64, p. 60, p. 274, p. 189, and p. 114; cf. Fillmore Packing Lists p. 8 (Howard); cf. Marvin p. 238, p. 249, p. 728, p. 564, and p. 400.

---

1. Morris Cohen and Robery C. Berring, eds., *How to Find the Law,* 8th ed. (St. Paul, Minn.: West Publishing, 1983), 37; Kermit Hall, James W. Ely Jr., Joel B. Grossman, and William M. Wiecek, eds., *The Oxford Companion to the Supreme Court of the United States* (New York: Oxford, University Press, 1992), 728. In current monetary terms, $1,000 would be about $25,000.

2. Morris Cohen and Sharon Hamby O'Connor, *A Guide to the Early Reports of the Supreme Court of the United States* (Littleton, Colo.: Fred B. Rothman and Co., 1995), 6.

3. Morris Cohen and Sharon Hamby O'Connor provide a bibliography of the reports that outlines their publication history.

4. Taylor and Maury, letter to Millard Fillmore, January 3, 1851, Millard Fillmore Papers, BECHS.

∼

168. Taylor, John. *Summary of the Roman Law.* London: T. Payne, 1772.

John Taylor's (ca. 1704–66) *Summary of the Roman Law* (1772) is a redaction of his *Elements of the Civil Law* (1755), which grew out of notes that Taylor had written for the instruction of two students under his tutelage. *Elements* provided an introduction to the study of Roman law and to legal principles in general. It called attention to the underlying principles of the law, and, for a student grounded in the classics, it offered an excellent study of Roman law and jurisprudence.[1]

In the preface to the *Summary* an anonymous editor explains that he has selected "those parts of Doctor Taylor's Elements of the Civil Law, which especially relate to that subject, from the miscellaneous observations with which it abounds; as these, though very valuable both to the Antiquary and classic Scholar, are not immediately necessary to the young student" ([5]). The editor also added "some passages from Spelman's *Dionisius Halicarnassensis,* which may be serviceable to explain some particular customs" and translated the principal Greek and Latin quotations ([5]–[6]).

107,754 voucher 2: 1 Taylor's Roman Law $1.25.
Purchased from Little and Brown on September 18, 1851.
Hayes Catalogue: Taylor, J. *Summary of Roman Law.* London, 1772. 8°

TITLE PAGE
A | SUMMARY | OF THE | ROMAN LAW, | TAKEN FROM | DR. TAYLOR's | ELEMENTS | OF THE CIVIL LAW. | TO WHICH IS PREFIXED | A DISSERTATION ON OBLIGATION. | LONDON: | Printed for T. Payne, at the Mews Gate. | MDCCLXXII.

PAGINATION
[8] i–lxx 1–360.
    Note. In this copy the leaf containing pages 211–12 has been bound just after page lxx.

CONTENTS
[1] half title, [2] blank, [3] title, [4] blank, [5]–[6] preface, [7] contents, [8] errata, i–lxx text of "A Dissertation on Obligation," 1–328 text of *Summary of Roman Law,* 329–59 index, 360 blank.

REFERENCES
Hayes p. 285; cf. Harvard p. 244; cf. L and B 1853 p. 66.

COPY DESCRIBED
DLC: Law Roman Law 12 Tayl 1772. *Leaf.* 212 × 127.

---

1. Holdsworth, *History of English Law,* 12:644.

～

169. Taylor, Richard Cowling. *Statistics of Coal.* Philadelphia: J. W. Moore, 1848.

Richard Cowling Taylor's (1789–1851) *Statistics of Coal* (1848) had special relevance for the nineteenth-century American economy. The production of coal in America had increased from 356 tons in 1820 to 3 million tons in 1852 as it came to replace wood as a fuel. Coal was used in manufacturing iron as well as in producing steam and gas, and American periodical writers aptly celebrated the nation's rich stores of coal.[1] *The Literary World* announced *Statistics of Coal* as "nearly ready" on May 13, 1848, and predicted that this work is "calculated to be of immense importance to a certain class of readers in this country."[2] A prospectus for it was first issued in 1845, and the massive 754-page volume first appeared in 1848, with a second edition in 1855. Fillmore's concern with economic issues and with promoting commerce both at home and abroad would have commanded his interest in this book.

105,133 voucher 2: Taylors Statistics of Coal $4.00.
Purchased from Little and Brown on December 30, 1850.
Hayes Catalogue: Taylor, R. C. *Statistics of Coal,* Philadelphia, 1848. 8°.

TITLE PAGE
STATISTICS OF COAL. | [thin decorative rule] | THE GEOGRAPHICAL AND GEOLOGICAL DISTRIBUTION | OF | Mineral Combustibles or Fossil Fuel [black letter] | INCLUDING, ALSO, NOTICES AND LOCALITIES OF THE VARIOUS | MINERAL BITUMINOUS SUBSTANCES, | EMPLOYED IN ARTS AND MANUFACTURES, | ILLUSTRATED BY MAPS AND DIAGRAMS; | EMBRACING, | FROM OFFICIAL REPORTS OF THE GREAT COAL-PRODUCING COUNTRIES, THE | RESPECTIVE AMOUNTS OF THEIR | PRODUCTION, CONSUMPTION AND COMMERCIAL DISTRIBUTION, | IN ALL PARTS OF THE WORLD; | TOGETHER WITH THEIR | Prices, Tariffs, Duties and International Regulations. [black letter] | ACCOMPANIED BY NEARLY | Four Hundred Statistical Tables, and Eleven Hundred Analyses of Mineral Combustibles, | WITH | INCIDENTAL STATEMENTS OF THE STATISTICS OF IRON MANUFACTURES, | DERIVED FROM AUTHENTIC AUTHORITIES. | PREPARED BY | RICHARD COWLING TAYLOR, | FELLOW OF THE GEOLOGICAL SOCIETY OF LONDON, MEMBER OF THE AMERICAN PHILOSOPHICAL | SOCIETY, THE HISTORICAL SOCIETY OF PENNSYLVANIA, OF THE ACADEMY OF NATURAL | SCIENCES OF PHILSDELPHIA, OF THE ALBANY INSTITUTE, NEW YORK, | AND OF VARIOUS OTHER SOCIETIES IN EUROPE AND AMERICA. | Author of "INDEX MONASTICUS, in the Ancient Kingdom of East Anglia, 1821." | [thin decorative rule] | PHILADELPHIA: | PUBLISHED BY J. W. MOORE, 193 CHESTNUT STREET. | 1848.

PAGINATION
i–cxlviii 1–754.

CONTENTS
i title, ii copyright statement and printer's imprint, iii preface, iv blank, v "contents of the introduction," vi blank, vii–xi "plan of this work," xii blank, xiii–cxlviii introduction, 1–685 text, 686 blank, 687–709 analytical tables, 710 blank, 711–54 index.

PLATES
Facing iii, folding "Chart shewing the position of the coal fields on the surface of the globe by Richard C. Taylor," signed, "lith. of Wagner and McGuigan 116 Chestnut St. Phil."
Facing 112, folding "Map of the group of anthracite basins in Pennsylvania, compiled by R. C. Taylor," signed, "Lith. of Wagner and McGuigan Phil."

Facing 144, folding "Map illustrative of the coal trade of Pennsylvania showing the relative positions of the various anthracite & bituminous coal fields. Also the railroads, canals, & navigable waters by which they are intersected, forming their respective avenues to market. Prepared by R. C. Taylor, Esq. 1848.," signed, "Lith of T. Sinclair, Phil."

Facing 208, folding "Map of the New Brunswick, Nova Scotia, Cape Breton, and New Foundland Coal Fields, by Rich. C. Taylor, F. G. S. &c.," signed, "lith of Wagner and McGuigam 116 Chestnut St. Ph."

Facing 390, folding "Map of the coals basins in England, Scotland, Wales, & Ireland, by Rich C. Taylor," signed, "lith of Wagner & McGuigan 116 Chestnut St."

Facing 478, folding "General map of the coal & lignite basins and of the ore deposits in France. From official sources By Richard C. Taylor, F. G. S. &c. Philadelphia 1848," signed, "Lith of Wagner and McGuigan, 116 Chestnut St Phil."

REFERENCES
Hayes p. 281; cf. Putnam p. 137; Roorbach p. 535; L and B 1850 p. 89; L and B 1853 p. 66.

COPY DESCRIBED
DLC: TN 800 T24. *Leaf.* 229 × 139.

---

1. "The Coal Industry of the United States," *Scientific American (1845–1908)*, November 11, 1854, "Statistics of Coal," *The American Almanac and the Repository of Useful Knowledge (1850–1861)*, 1851, both available at *APS Online*, http://www.proquest.com/products_pq/descriptions/aps.shtml.

2. *Literary World*, May 13, 1848, available at *APS Online*, http://www.proquest.com/products_pq/descriptions/aps.shtml.

⁓

170. Taylor, W. Cooke. *The Life and Times of Sir Robert Peel.* 3 vols. London: Fisher and Son, [1846].

William Taylor Cooke's (1800–1849) *The Life and Times of Sir Robert Peel* (3 vols., 1846–48) is one of the first substantial studies of the prime minister. Sir Robert Peel (1788–1850) devoted his life to public service, as a member of the House of Commons, as chief secretary in the Irish administration, and twice as prime minister. He may, however, be remembered most for the "Bobbies," a unified police force to patrol and keep the streets of London safe, created by him and named in his honor.

A death notice that appeared in a Massachusetts periodical indicated Peel's reputation in America when it called him one of the "most remarkable men of his time." Its author pointed out that Peel was a son of a manufacturer and reminded readers that Peel refused a peerage more than once, preferring to remain "'the great commoner,' and confident in his ability to do more good in his generation as plain Robert Peel." In these respects, Peel fulfilled the American ideal of the "rise of the common man."[1] His biography fit nicely with the selection of biographies of British statesmen that was purchased for the library.

105,133 voucher 2: Life & Times of Peel 3 vols. $9.50.
Purchased from Little and Brown on December 30, 1850.

Roosevelt Catalogue: Taylor, William Cooke. *Life and Times of Sir Robert Peel.* London: Fisher and Son & Co., n.d., 3 vols. vol. 4 missing.

> *Note.* The Hayes catalogue makes no mention of a fourth volume.

TITLE PAGE

LIFE AND TIMES | OF | SIR ROBERT PEEL. | BY | W. COOKE TAYLOR, LL. D., | OF TRINITY COLLEGE, DUBLIN; | AUTHOR OF "THE NATURAL HISTORY OF SOCIETY," "REVOLUTIONS OF EUROPE," | "THE FACTORY SYSTEM," ETC. | VOL. I. [II–III.]| FISHER, SON, & CO. | ANGEL STREET, ST MARTIN'S-LE-GRAND, LONDON.

> *Note.* Volumes 2 and 3 differ in the first line of the imprint from volume 1. It reads 'PETER JACKSON, LATE FISHER, SON, & CO.'

PAGINATION

Vol. I. [8] 1–524.
Vol. II. [4] 1–452.
Vol. III. [4] 1–620.

CONTENTS

Vol. I. [1] title, [2] blank, [3]–[5] preface, [6]–[7] contents, [8] list of plates, 1–524 text.
Vol. II. [1] title, [2] blank, [3] contents, [4] list of plates, 1–452 text.
Vol. III. [1] title, [2] blank, [3] contents, [4] list of plates, 1–531 text, 532 blank, 533–618 appendix, 619–20 advertisement for books published by Peter Jackson, Late Fisher, Son, & Co.

PLATES

Vol. I.

Portrait frontispiece, Robert Peel, signed in lower left by Sir Thomas Lawrence, P.R.A., and lower right by Francis Holl.

Engraved title page, 'LIFE AND TIME | OF | THE R^T· HON: SIR ROBERT PEEL. BAR^T· [All foregoing text in open-face block letters] | [vignette of Drayton manor] | W. E. Albutt. [script] | Drayton Manor [script] | FISHER, SON & C^O· LONDON & PARIS. [open-face block letters.]'

Facing 6, "The Spinning Jen," engraved by T. E. Nicholson.

Facing 7, portrait "Dorning Rasbotham esq. High Sherrif of the County Palatine of Lancaster in the year 1769," signed in lower left Pickering and lower right H. Robinson.

Facing 9, two vignettes on one plate, the first, "Birth-place of the late Sir Robt· Peel, Fish Lane Blackburn"; the second, "Birth-place of the present Sir Robt· Peel, In the vicinity of Bury."

Facing 13, portrait of Sir Robert Peel Bar^t·, signed in lower left by Sir Thomas Lawrence and lower right by H. Robinson.

Facing 27, portrait of Sir Richard Arkwright, signed in lower left by Jos^h· Wright and lower right by J. Jenkins.

Facing 35, portrait of Lady Peel, signed in lower left by Sir Thomas Lawrence, P.R.A. and lower right by Charles Heath.

Facing 37, portrait of Lord Byron, signed in lower left by T. Phillips, R.A., and lower right by W. H. Mote.

Facing 51, portrait of the Right Honorable William Pitt, signed in lower left by J. Hoppner, Esq. R.A., and lower right by J. Thomson.

Facing 67, portrait of Charles Whitworth, Viscount Whitworth, signed in lower left by Sir Thomas Lawrence, Esq., and lower right by H. Robinson.

Facing 293, portrait of Nicholas Vansittart, Baron Bexley, signed in lower left by Sir Thomas Lawrence, P.R.A., and lower right by T. A. Dean.

Facing 313, portrait of the Right Honorable George Canning, signed in lower left by T. Stewardson and lower right by William Holl.

Facing 365, portrait of Thomas Moore, Esq. signed in lower left by F. Sicurec and lower right by G. Adcock.

Vol. II.

Portrait frontispiece, Charles Grey, Earl Grey, signed in lower left by T. Phillips, Esq., R.A., and lower right by R. Hicks.

Facing 17, portrait of Edmund Burke, signed in lower left by Sir Joshua Reynolds and lower right by H. Robinson.

Facing 133, portrait of the Right Honorable William Huskisson, "Engraved by J. Cochran from an original picture painted for John Gladstone, Esq. of Seaforth House near Liverpool by John Grahame, Esq. of Edinburgh three months previous to Mr. Huskisson's death."

Facing 185, portrait of the Right Honorable Henry Brougham, Baron Brougham & Vaux, signed in lower left by Sir Thomas Lawrence, P.R.A., and lower right by H^y. Robinson.

Facing 191, portrait of William Conyngham Plunket, D. C. L. Baron Plunket, signed in lower left by H. Hamilton and lower right by J. Jenkins.

Facing 205, portrait of Henry William Paget, Marquess of Anglesey K.G. &c. &c. &c., signed in lower left by Sir Thomas Lawrence and lower right by S. Freeman.

Facing 231, "W^m. 4th. Proroguing Parliament. April 1831. House of Lords Destroyed by Fire Octr. 16, 1834." Drawn and engraved by H. Melville.

Facing 233, portrait of the Right Honorable Sir James Mackintosh, signed in lower left by Sir Thomas Lawrence and lower right by J. Cochran.

Facing 257, portrait of the Right Honorable Sir John Wilson Croker, signed in lower left by Sir Thomas Lawrence, P.R.A., and lower right by T. H. Parry.

Facing 325, portrait of the Right Honorable John Robinson, Earl of Ripon, signed in lower left by Sir Thomas Lawrence, P.R.A., and lower right by J. Jenkins.

Facing 431, portrait of the Right Honorable Sir Spencer Perceval, signed in lower left by Sir W. Beechey, R.A., and lower right by Picart.

Facing 435, portrait of the Right Honorable Henry John Temple, Lord Viscount Palmerton, G.C.B., signed in lower left by J. Lucas and lower right by H. Cook.

Vol. III.

Portrait frontispiece, the Right Honorable William Lamb, Baron Melbourne, signed in lower left by Sir Thomas Lawrence and lower right by S. Freeman.

Facing 33, portrait of Sir Francis Burdett, Bar^t. M.P., signed in lower left by Sir Thomas Lawrence and lower right by J. Morrison.

Facing 77, portrait of the Honorable Charles Pelham Villiers, M.P., signed in lower left by C. A. Du Val and lower right by J. Cochran.

Facing 97, portrait of the Right Honorable Constantine Henry Phipps, F.S.A., Marquess of
    Normandy, and Lieutenant General and General Governor of Ireland, 1838, signed in
    lower left by H. P. Briggs, R.A., and lower right by H. Robinson.

Facing 101, portrait of George Hamilton-Gordon, Earl of Aberdeen K.T.-F.A.S., signed in
    lower left by A. Wivell and lower right by T. Woolnoth.

Facing 155, portrait of Thomas Philip Weddell Robinson, Earl de Grey, signed in lower left
    by W. Robinson and lower right by H. Robinson.

Facing 203, portrait of Richard Cobden, Esq. M.P., signed in lower left C. A. Du Val and
    lower right G. Adcock.

Facing 277, portrait of the Right Honorable Edward Geoffrey Stanley, Lord Stanley, signed
    in lower left by G. Harlow, Esq., and lower right by H. Robinson.

Facing 425, portrait of the Right Honorable Charles Lennox, Duke of Richmond, signed in
    lower left by E. Wilkin, Esq., and lower right by H. Cook.

Facing 497, portrait of the Right Honorable Lord John Russell, M.P.

REFERENCES

Hayes p. 281; Roosevelt p. 41; cf. Fillmore Packing Lists p. 27.

COPY DESCRIBED

DLC DA 536 P3 T2 1846. *Leaf.* 221 × 135.

---

1. "The Late Robert Peel," *Massachusetts Ploughman and New England Journal of Agriculture (1842–1906)*, August 10, 1850, available at *APS Online,* http://www.proquest.com/products_pq/descriptions/aps.shtml.

〜

171. Terrestrial Globe.

Globes were very popular during the nineteenth century, when they were often found in home libraries and commonly used for educational purposes. Franck Taylor wrote to President Fillmore regarding the purchase of this globe, "I ordered the Globe at once, but it did not seem to be ready on the instant, and when it was so they sent it by sea—which I had not ordered—as a cheaper and <u>softer</u> mode of travel. I have no knowledge of it since, but it needs—'the dangers of the seas only excepted'—to be here within a few days."[1] The globe must have arrived shortly, as Taylor anticipated, because its purchase by the White House is recorded nine days later. It had probably been shipped from Boston or New York by sea to avoid any damage that it could have incurred on a rough train or carriage ride. It would have been made of colored paper gores over papier mâché and mounted in a wooden stand with a brass meridian ring. This may be the globe depicted in the illustration of the library that was published in *Frank Leslie's Illustrated Newspaper* (see figure 12.). Ena L. Yonge lists only twelve terrestrial globes measuring forty-six centimeters (eighteen inches) in diameter, the size specified on the voucher. The two published closest in date to this purchase are from Malby and Sons in London, 1846, and J. W. Carey in London, 1835. All others are dated earlier.[2]

107,754 voucher 3: Terrestrial Globe 18 inches $50.00.

Purchased from Franck Taylor on August 6, 1851.

---

1. Franck Taylor, letter to President Fillmore, July 28, 1851, Millard Fillmore Papers, BECHS.

2. "Globes and Terrain Models," Library of Congress: An Illustrated Guide, Geography and Maps, available at http://www.loc.gov/rr/geogmap/guide/gmillgtm.html (accessed July 19, 2009); Ena L. Yonge, *A Catalogue of Early Globes* (New York: American Geographical Society, 1968), 46, 21. Although Yonge claims to list only globes published in 1850 or earlier, at least one entry is dated ca. 1851.

⸎

172. Thiers, Louis Adolphe. *The History of the French Revolution.* London: Whittaker and Co., n.d.

173. ———. *The History of the Consulate and the Empire of Napoleon.* London: Bohn, 1850.

Louis Adolphe Thiers (1797–1877), garnered respect in both his home country of France and the United States for his historical writings. By 1850 his *History of the French Revolution* (1823–27) had become one of the standard works on the topic and was recommended in the essay "A Course of Historical Reading." The writer praised Thiers's thorough use of his sources and his rendering of every "minute and faithful detail of the course of events, from the opening to the close of the fearful tragedy."[1] Thiers began publishing his *History of the French Revolution* in 1823 and finished the ten-volume work in 1827. In 1840 *Burton's Gentleman's Magazine and American Monthly Review* announced that an English translation of "this celebrated work" would soon be available in America from Carey and Hart.[2]

In 1842 the *Southern Quarterly Review* anticipated that the first volume of the *History of the Consulate* (1845) would be completed within the year and announced that Thiers would receive five hundred thousand francs for the copyright. The reviewer lauded him as the most qualified living writer for the task and asserted "from the extensive popularity of his 'History of the French Revolution,' none could be found more acceptable to the public."[3] When the *History of the Consulate* finally began to appear in 1845, the *Anglo American* reported that the first edition, in a print run of ten thousand copies, sold out in Paris within hours of publication and that a new edition of six thousand was in press.[4]

155,133 voucher 5: Thiers French Rev. & History Empire $5.00.

Purchased from Charles Welford on December 13, 1850.

Roosevelt Catalogue: Thiers, Louis Adolphe. *The History of the Consulate and the Empire of Napoleon. Translated from the Last Paris Edition, with Notes.* London, H. G. Bohn, 1850.

———. *The History of the French Revolution.* Translated from the last Paris edition, with notes. London, Whitaker & Co., n.d.

History of the French Revolution.

TITLE PAGE

THE | HISTORY | OF THE | FRENCH REVOLUTION. | BY | M. A. THIERS. | [thin rule] | TRANSLATED FROM THE LAST PARIS EDITION, | WITH NOTES. | [thin rule] | LONDON: WHITTAKER AND CO., AVE MARIA LANE. [all foregoing enclosed in thin rule frame]

PAGINATION

[4] 1–972.

CONTENTS

[1] title, [2] blank, [3] preface, [4] translator's advertisement, 1–868 text, 868–921 appendix, 922 blank, 923–72 index.

REFERENCES

Hayes p. 282; Roosevelt p. 41; cf. *LC 1816–1851* p. 554.

COPY DESCRIBED

DLC: DC 148 T43 1845. *Leaf.* 231 × 150.

History of the Consulate and the Empire.

TITLE PAGE

THE | HISTORY | OF THE | CONSULATE AND THE EMPIRE | OF | NAPOLEON; | FORMING A SEQUEL TO | "THE HISTORY OF THE FRENCH REVOLUTION." | BY | M. A. THIERS, | LATE CHIEF MINISTER OF FRANCE, &C.| [thin rule] | TRANSLATED FROM THE LAST PARIS EDITION, | WITH NOTES. | [thin rule] | LONDON: | HENRY G. BOHN, YORK STREET, COVENT GARDEN. | 1850. [all foregoing enclosed in a thin rule frame]

PAGINATION

[4] 1–658 1–316.

CONTENTS

[1] title, [2] printer's imprint, [3] contents, [4] blank, 1–657 text of volume 1, 658 blank, 1–314 text of volume 2, 315 advertisement for Thiers's *History of the French Revolution,* 316 blank.

REFERENCES

Hayes p. 282; Roosevelt p. 41.

COPY DESCRIBED

DLC: DC 201 T43 1850. *Leaf.* 235 × 150.

---

1. "A Course of Historical Reading Part II: Modern History," *Universalist Quarterly and General Review,* April 1850, available at *APS Online,* http://www.proquest.com/products_pq/descriptions/aps.shtml. See "White House Collection," 15–16.

2. "Review 1—No Title," *Burton's Gentlemen's Magazine and American Monthly Review (1839–1840),* February 1840, available at *APS Online,* http://www.proquest.com/products_pq/descriptions/aps.shtml.

3. *Southern Quarterly Review,* January 1842, available at *APS Online,* http://www.proquest.com/products_pq/descriptions/aps.shtml.

4. *Anglo American,* April 26, 1845, available at *APS Online,* http://www.proquest.com/products_pq/descriptions/aps.shtml.

∽

174. Tocqueville, Alexis de. *Democracy in America.*

With *Democracy in America* (1835–40), Alexis de Tocqueville (1805–59) offered the first classic commentary on American government written by a foreigner. In it de Tocqueville made many predictions that later proved true, such as that American literature would break free of European influence and depict common people, that democracy would emancipate women and change parent-child relations, and that the dominance of American politics by lawyers could be dangerous.[1] *Democracy in America* was translated into English by Henry Reeves and published in London simultaneous with its appearance in Paris.

It received considerable attention from reviewers in the United States, where it immediately became a bestseller. Critics praised de Tocqueville's even-handed and just treatment of his topic and credited him as the first writer to investigate the effects of democracy on both communal and individual character. One proclaimed that "no author of our age has looked deeper, or with a more prophetic eye, into the destinies of mankind, and mighty causes which are now in progress to change the future political and social condition of our race."[2] The reputation of de Tocqueville's work remained high in the United States through the 1850s. When A. S. Barnes and Company republished volume 1 in 1851 under the title *American Institutions and Their Influence,* the *American Whig Review* recommended that it "ought to be read carefully by all who wish to know this country, and to trace its power, position, and ultimate destiny from the true source of philosophic government, Republicanism—the people."[3]

The exact edition that the Fillmores selected for the White House Library remains unclear. There were no fewer than eight publishers of English translations of *Democracy in America* prior to 1851. The London editions from Saunders and Otley may be ruled out since the *London Catalogue* listed these for 49s., or approximately $12.00, and the White House paid only $2.00 for its copy. The other seven publishers for *Democracy in America* were located in New York. While Putnam advertised a New York edition that sold for $3.00, Roorbach recorded the Barnes edition for $1.25, a price too low for it to have been chosen. Unfortunately, no pricing information has been available for the remaining candidates.

105,133 voucher 5: De Tocqueville's Democracy Amer. $2.00.
Purchased from Charles Welford on December 13, 1850.

REFERENCES
cf. Putnam p. 37, p. 141, p. 9-s; cf. Fillmore 1847 p. 24; cf. Fillmore ca. 1858 p. 14; cf. Fillmore 1861 p. 50.

---

1. "Alexis Charles Henri Maurice Clerel de Tocqueville," *World of Sociology* (Detroit: Gale Group, 2001), *Biography Resource Center* (Farmington Hills, Mich.: Thomson Gale, 2006), http://gale.cengage.com/servlet/BiographyRC.
2. "Review 14—No Title," *The New York Review (1837–1842),* July 1840, available at *APS Online,* http://www.proquest.com/products_pq/descriptions/aps.shtml.
3. "American Institutions and Their Influence," *American Whig Review,* April 1851; see also "Review 14—No Title," and "Tocqueville's Democracy in America," *The Museum of Foreign Literature, Science, and Art (1822–1842),* June 1836. All are available at *APS Online,* http://www.proquest.com/products_pq/descriptions/aps.shtml.

175. *United States Digest: Digest of the Decisions of the Courts of Common Law and Admiralty in the United States.* Vols. 1–11. Boston: Little and Brown, 1840–52.

The *United States Digest* digests and indexes cases in the courts of common law and admiralty. As Marvin explains about digests, "All that can be reasonably expected of works of this kind, is, that they contain the general Titles of the law, with appropriate subdivisions, properly arranged, and correct abstracts or references to all the cases embraced in the reports in the period contemplated." With respect to the compilers and their responsibility he adds, "It is very well known, that none of the more comprehensive Digests are wholly prepared for the press, by those persons whose names appear on the title pages, who only stand as vouchers for the substantial accuracy of the volumes, and if this is attained, their legitimate object is accomplished, and the profession receives all that the editors assume to perform."[1] *The Law Reporter* endorsed the *United States Digest* in an advertisement on the back wrapper of at least one Little and Brown catalogue. It estimates that the *Digest* contains between fifty and sixty thousand cases and testifies to the serial's accuracy and completeness.

Hilliard and Gray published volume 1 in 1840; thereafter, Little and Brown published this title.[2] Several compilers worked on the *Digest,* beginning with Theron Metcalf and J. C. Perkins in 1840 for volume 1. George T. Curtis continued with volumes 2 and 3 in 1845 and 1846. Volumes 4 and 5, compiled by John Phelps Putnam, a Massachusetts judge, provide a supplement to the foregoing volumes of the *Digest,* while volume 6, compiled by George Partridge Sanger, supplies a table of cases to the previous volumes. Volume 7 begins the first of the annual volumes and accounts for the year 1847. With that volume's publication the name changed to the *Annual Digest* and the serial began to include equity reports. Putnam continued as the compiler at least through volume 11, the latest one purchased for the White House.

The Executive Mansion purchased a complete set of the *Digest* through 1851, purchasing the first nine volumes in November of 1850 and adding volumes 10 and 11 later. This serial would have complemented the collection of texts related to admiralty and international law that were also chosen for the library.

105,133 voucher 7: United States Digest & Supplement 9 vols. $48.00.
Purchased from Franck Taylor on November 11, 1850.
107,754 voucher 6: 1 vol. 10 U.S. Digest $4.50.
Purchased from Little and Brown on March 26, 1852.
109,399 voucher 4: U. S. Annual Digest vol. 11. $5.00.
Purchased from Franck Taylor on October 12, 1852.
Hayes Catalogue: Metcalf, T. and J. C. Perkins. *Digest of the Decisions of the Courts of Common Law and Admiralty of the United States.* 3 v. Boston, 1847–49. 8°.
———Same. Supplement. By J. P. Putnam. 2 v. Boston, 1849. 8°.
Putnam, J. P. United States digest. Annual digest, 1847 to 1852. 6 v. Boston, 1850–53. 8°.
Sanger, G. P. Tables of the cases contained in the vols. of the United States digest and the two volumes of the supplement. Boston, 1849. 8°.
> *Note.* The compiler for Hayes catalogued these entries by author rather than under the serial title.

TITLE PAGE

Vol. I.

DIGEST | OF | THE DECISIONS | OF THE | Courts of Common Law and | Admiralty [black letter] | IN THE | UNITED STATES. | BY | THERON METCALF | AND | JONATHAN C. PERKINS. | VOL. I. | BOSTON: | HILLIARD, GRAY, AND COMPANY. | 1840.

Vol. III.

'. . . VOL. III. | By GEORGE T. CURTIS. | [thick/thin double rule] | BOSTON: | CHARLES C. LITTLE AND JAMES BROWN. | 1846.'

Note. Only these two volumes were available for examination for this project.

PAGINATION

Vol. I. [4] 1–700.

Vol. III. i–iv 1–724.

CONTENTS

Vol. II. [1] title, [2] copyright statement and printer's imprint, [3] notice to the reader, 'This volume is supposed to contain one third of the matter | which will compose "The United States' Digest." The second | and third volumes will be prepared with all the dispatch which | is consistent with the compilers' views concerning their duty to | the publishers and to the profession.', [4] contents, 1–700 text.

Vol. III. i title, ii copyright statement and printer's imprint, iii–iv contents, 1–724 text.

REFERENCES

Hayes p. 153 and p. 155; *BEAL* 5554–55; cf. Greenleaf; Marvin p. 702; cf. Roorbach p. 633; cf. Harvard p. 162; L and B Law 1850 back wrapper.

COPY DESCRIBED

DLC: KF 148 M48. *Leaf.* 253 × 157.

---

1. Marvin, *Legal Bibliography,* 702.

2. The two firms had been closely affiliated since 1818 and in 1837 merged many of their assets. See *One Hundred Years of Publishing 1837–1937* (Boston: Little, Brown, and Co., 1937), 13–14.

∼

176. *United States Magazine and Democratic Review.* Washington, D.C.: Langtree and O'Sullivan, 1837–50.

The *United States Magazine and Democratic Review* was one of the leading periodicals in nineteenth-century America. Published monthly, it ran from October of 1837 through June of 1859. Founded as a voice for the Democratic Party, the *Democratic Review,* as it was commonly known, not only published articles on a range of political issues, but also published literary reviews, original prose fiction, and poetry. The success of the *Democratic Review* has been attributed to its founder and long-time editor John O'Sullivan, who saw the magazine as an opportunity to advance Jacksonian democratic principles.[1] He expressed his political idealism in the introductory essay of the first issue, where he promised to advocate "that high and holy DEMOCRATIC PRINCIPLE which was designed to be the fundamental element of the new social and political system created by the 'American experiment'" (1:1).

The *Democratic Review* also sought to establish a national literature. Among the many American literary luminaries who contributed to the *Democratic Review* were Nathaniel Hawthorne, John Greenleaf Whittier, William Cullen Bryant, Francis Scott Key, William Gilmore Simms, James Russell Lowell, Walt Whitman, and Edgar Allan Poe. In fact, Hawthorne and O'Sullivan became very good friends, and the *Democratic Review* published more of Hawthorne's stories than any other periodical of the nineteenth century. Many eminent essayists also published their opinions there, including George Bancroft, Henry David Thoreau, Lewis Cass, and Samuel J. Tilden.[2]

In 1842 the *Boston Quarterly Review* merged with the *Democratic Review,* yet the *Democratic Review* underwent no title change until 1852, when it dropped "*United States Magazine*" from its title. Although O'Sullivan was the driving force behind the periodical, the editorship changed hands several times, as listed below. By offering a steady supply of intelligent political commentary in combination with quality American literature, a complete run of the *Democratic Review* up to 1850 chronicled a large segment of the nation's intellectual development for the thirteen years preceding Fillmore's presidency.[3]

Editors of the *Democratic Review* through 1850:

> 1837–39 J. L. O'Sullivan and S. D. Langtree
> 1839–40 S. D. Langtree
> 1841–46 J. L. O'Sullivan
> 1846–51 Thomas Prentice Kettell

105,133 voucher 5: Democratic Review 27 vols. $40.50.

Purchased from Charles Welford on December 13, 1850.

Roosevelt Catalogue: *United States Magazine and Democratic Review,* v. 1–27. Washington, 1838–50.

Hayes Catalogue: *United States Magazine and Democratic Review.* Oct. 1837 to Dec. 1850. v. 1 to 27 in 26 v. Washington and New York, 1838–50. 8°.

> *Note.* Both catalogues cross-list this title with an entry for "Democratic Review."

TITLE PAGE

Vol. I.

THE | UNITED STATES MAGAZINE | AND | DEMOCRATIC REVIEW. | [printer's ornament, silhouette bust of Thomas Paine] | THE BEST GOVERNMENT IS THAT WHICH GOVERNS LEAST. | [thin rule] | VOLUME ONE, | CONTAINING THE POLITICAL AND LITERARY PORTIONS OF | THE NUMBERS PUBLISHED IN OCTOBER, 1837, AND | JANUARY, FEBRUARY AND MARCH, 1838. | [thin rule] | WASHINGTON, D. C. | PUBLISHED BY LANGTREE AND O'SULLIVAN. | 1838.

REFERENCES

Hayes p. 300; Roosevelt p. 42.

COPY DESCRIBED

DLC: AP 2 U6. *Leaf.* 215 × 125.

1. Nourie and Nourie, *American Mass-Market Magazines,* 100; see Edward L. Widmer, *Young America: The Flowering of Democracy in New York City* (New York: Oxford University Press, 1999), for more about O'Sullivan and the influence of the *Democratic Review.*

2. Nourie and Nourie, *American Mass-Market Magazines,* 100; Mott, *History of American Magazines, 1741–1850,* 679. See entry 13 for Bancroft.

3. Mott, *History of American Magazines, 1741–1850,* 680, 683; Nourie and Nourie, *American Mass-Market Magazines,* 101.

∿

177. Ure, Andrew. *A Dictionary of Arts, Manufactures, and Mines.* 11th American ed. New York: D. Appleton and Co., 1848.

One critic called Andrew Ure's (1778–1857) *Dictionary of Arts, Manufactures, and Mines* (1839) "one of the most valuable works republished in this country for years." Another ranked it alongside McCulloch's *Dictionary, Practical, Theoretical, and Historical of Commerce and Commercial Navigation,* which Fillmore also selected for the White House. Indeed, Ure's work contains a wealth of information designed for the use of manufacturers, metallurgists, tradesmen, brokers, drysalters, druggists, revenue officers, students of chemistry and physics, capitalists, lawyers, legislators, and general readers (3). Its treatment of gold mining proved especially relevant to the California gold rush underway from 1848 to 1855. It provides detailed, in-depth entries on a range of topics. From its seven-page entry on the "printing machine," one could build a nineteenth-century steam-powered printing press. It treats "daguerrotype" with similar detail in five pages and has shorter entries for more obscure topics such as "dragon's blood," which is slang for the resinous substance brought from the East Indies, Africa, and South America that was used for tingeing spirit and turpentine varnishes.[1]

Based on price, the Executive Mansion most likely purchased the 1848 Appleton edition, which Putnam, the seller from whom it was acquired, advertised for $5.00. Appleton first published Ure's *Dictionary* in serial form and, in 1843, began issuing it as a single octavo volume. According to its title page, this edition includes a supplement that runs almost three hundred pages. Another New York publisher, Sunderland, issued this title only in two-volume sets, which would disqualify it for this selection, and a London edition, published by Longman, sold for anywhere from 50 to 80s., or approximately $12.00 to $16.00, a price too high to qualify it for the White House purchase.[2]

105,133 voucher 4: Ures Dicty. Arts and Manufacturers $4.25.
Purchased from George P. Putnam on December, 13, 1850.

REFERENCES

cf. Roorbach p. 558; Putnam p. 146; cf. *LC 1816–1851* p. 576; cf. Fillmore 1847 p. 7; cf. Fillmore Packing Lists p. 8; cf. Fillmore ca. 1858 p. 15; cf. Fillmore 1861 p. 54.

1. *Graham's Magazine of Literature and Art (1843–1843),* April 1843, and *The Literary World (1847–1853),* January 13, 1849, both available at *APS Online,* http://www.proquest.com/products_pq/descriptions/aps .shtml. See entry 104 for McCulloch's *Dictionary.*

2. See *London Catalogue,* Low, *British Catalogue,* and Low, *English Catalogue.*

∿

178. Vattel, Emmerich de. *The Law of Nations.* 5th American ed. Philadelphia: T. & J. W.
   Johnson, 1839.
————. *The Law of Nations.* Ed. Edward D. Ingraham. Philadelphia: T. & J. W. Johnson,
   1852.

By the mid-nineteenth century Emmerich de Vattel's (1714–67) *Law of Nations* had become
a classic text on international law. Originally published in French at Neuchâtel in 1758 under
the title *Le Droit des Gens ou Principes de la Loi Naturelle,* Vattel's text was translated into
English and published in London in 1760. This frequently reprinted treatise "succeeded in
modernizing international law and relating it to contemporary issues."[1] Although Hoffman
condemned Vattel's opinions in *Law of Nations* on "religion and religious establishments"
as unorthodox, he found much merit in the work otherwise. According to him it was "universally read" and "to be unacquainted with it would indicate either want of industry, or an
unwarranted fastidiousness of opinion."[2]

   The Executive Mansion purchased two copies of this book, one in December of 1850 and
a second in October of 1852. The first copy was probably the 1839 edition that Little and
Brown listed for sale in its 1850 catalogue of law books. Although there were later editions
available, it is reasonable to assume that Little and Brown would sell what they had in stock.
The second copy would have been the 1852 edition that appears in the Hayes catalogue,
which is based on the 1797 London edition but contains notes added by Edward Ingraham,
along with his preface and an index.

105,133 voucher 2: Vattel's Law of Nations $2.50.
Purchased from Little and Brown on December 30, 1850.
109,399 voucher 4: Vattel's Law of Nations $4.00.
Purchased from Franck Taylor on October 12, 1852.
Hayes Catalogue: Vattel, E. de. *Law of Nations,* Philadelphia, 1852, 8°.

TITLE PAGE
THE | LAW OF NATIONS; | OR, | PRINCIPLES OF THE LAW OF NATURE, | APPLIED
TO THE | CONDUCT AND AFFAIRS | OF | NATIONS AND SOVEREIGNS. | [thin rule]
| FROM THE FRENCH | OF | MONSIEUR DE VATTEL. | [thin rule] | Nihil est enim illi
principi Deo qui omnem hunc mundum regit, quod quidem in terris fiat, acceptius, |
quam concilia cœtusque hominum jure sociati, quæ civitates appellantur." CICERO, SOM. |
SCIP. | (thin rule] | FROM THE NEW EDITION, | BY | JOSEPH CHITTY, ESQ. |
BARRISTER AT LAW. | [thin rule] | WITH ADDITIONAL NOTES AND REFERENCES, |
BY EDWARD D. INGRAHAM, ESQ. | [thin rule] | PHILADELPHIA: | T. & J. W.
JOHNSON, LAW BOOKSELLERS, | NO. 197 CHESTNUT STREET. | 1852.

PAGINATION
i–xlviii 49–656.

CONTENTS
i title, ii copyright statement, iii "preface to this edition," iv advertisement to the edition of
A.D. 1797, v–vi "preface to the present edition," vii–xvii "preface," xviii blank, xix–xlviii contents, 49–623 text, 624 blank, 625–56 index.

Note. This edition retains the irregular pagination in the top outer corners of each page, as found in earlier editions. Correct page numbers have been added in the lower outer corners. Those sections added, such as the index, have the correct pagination in the usual location, the upper outer corners.

REFERENCES

Hayes p. 305; *BEAL* 7196; cf. Harvard p. 262; cf. Hoffman p. 453; cf. Marvin p. 706; cf. Roorbach p. 633; cf. Putnam p. 147; cf. Fillmore 1861 p. 218.

COPY DESCRIBED

DLC: JX 2414 E5 1852. *Leaf.* 227 × 132.

---

1. *BEAL*, 7196.
2. Hoffman, *Course of Legal Study*, 453.

~

179. Walpole, Horace. *Memoirs of the Reign of King George the Third.* Ed. Denis le Marchant. 4 vols. London: Bentley, 1845.

The circumstances of the publication of Horace Walpole's (1717–97) *Memoirs of the Reign of King George the Third* (1845) are as surprising as the its contents are controversial. Upon his death, Walpole left a trunk with instructions that it not be opened until the grandson of his niece and heiress, the sixth Earl of Waldegrave, attained the age of thirty-five. When he opened the trunk, the earl, expecting to find great family treasures, instead found to his dismay the manuscripts for Walpole's *Memoirs of the Last Ten Years of the Reign of King George II* and *Memoirs of the Reign of King George III*. The volumes covering the reign of George II were published in 1822 in an expurgated form. Those containing the memoirs of George III did not go to press until 1845, when they too appeared in an expurgated form.[1]

Upon its publication, the *Memoirs* was widely reviewed and greatly criticized as inaccurate and malevolent. American periodicals reprinted the review from the *London Quarterly*, which asserted that the *Memoirs* contained "a few, and but a few new facts and lights scattered through a very intricate mass of political intrigues—with an overbalancing proportion of prejudice, partiality, misrepresentation, and inconsistency—trivial and variable, but always rancorous, resentments—and general and constitutional proclivity to slander and calumny."[2] While the belletrist Anne Grant of Laggan condemned the *Memoirs* as "a 'Pandora's box' that poured forth its pernicious and very malicious contents upon the devoted heads of the sons and successors of all the great characters," the politician and reviewer John Wilson Croker, who devoted his energies to exposing Walpole's errors and malevolence, asserts that they were "written in even more than his usual spirit of malignity."[3]

105,133 voucher 5: Walpole's Reign Geo 3rd. $6.00.
Purchased from Charles Welford on December 13, 1850.
Roosevelt Catalogue: Walpole, Horace. *Memoirs of the Reign of King George the Third.* London, Richard Bentley, 1845, 4 vols.

TITLE PAGE

MEMOIRS | OF THE REIGN OF | KING GEORGE THE THIRD. | By HORACE
WALPOLE | YOUNGEST SON OF SIR ROBERT WALPOLE, EARL OF ORFORD. |
NOW FIRST PUBLISHED FROM THE ORIGINAL MSS. | EDITED, WITH NOTES, |
BY SIR DENIS LE MARCHANT, BART. | VOL. I. [II–IV] | LONDON: | RICHARD
BENTLEY, NEW BURLINGTON STREET, | Publisher in Ordinary to her Majesty.
[black letter] | 1845.

PAGINATION

Vol. I. [2] v–xxiv 1–422.
Vol. II. [2] v–xii 1–456.
Vol. III. i–xii 1–408.
Vol. IV. i–viii 1–424.

CONTENTS

Vol. I. [1] title, [2] printer's imprint, v–xii preface, xiii–xxii contents, xxiii errata, xxiv blank,
1–422 text.
Vol. II. [1] title page, [2] printer's imprint, v–xi contents, xii blank, 1–456 text.
Vol. III. i title, ii printer's imprint, iii–vi advertisement, vii–xii contents, 1–408 text.
Vol. IV. i title, ii printer's imprint, iii–viii contents, 1–365 text, 366 blank, 367–424
appendixes.

PLATES

Vol. I.
Portrait frontispiece of George III, from artwork of Houston, engraved by G. Cook.
Vol. II.
Portrait frontispiece of Queen Charlotte from artwork by Benjamin West, engraved by
J. Cook.
Vol. III.
Portrait frontispiece of the Honorable Charles Townsend from the original by Sir Joshua
Reynolds, engraved by J. Cook.
Vol. IV.
Portrait frontispiece of Augustus Henry, Third Duke of Grafton, from artwork by P. Battoni,
engraved by J. Cook.

REFERENCES

Hayes p. 309; Roosevelt p. 43; cf. *LC 1816–1851* p. 589; cf. Fillmore 1847 p. 4 (Walpole's
letters).

COPY DESCRIBED

DLC: DA 506 W2 A15. *Leaf.* 211 × 130.

---

1. Paul Langford, "Walpole, Horatio, Fourth Earl of Orford (1717–1797)," *ODNB.*

2. "Walpoles Memoirs of the Reign of George III," *The Eclectic Magazine and Foreign Literature (1844–1898),* April 1846, available at *APS Online,* http://www.proquest.com/products_pq/descriptions/aps.shtml.

3. J. P. Grant, ed., *Memoir and Correspondence of Mrs. Grant* (London: Longman, 1845), 2:306; L. J. Jennings, ed., *The Croker Papers: The Correspondence and Diaries of the Late Right Honourable John Wilson Croker* (London: Murray, 1884), 1:270–71, 3:24.

〜

180. Ward, Robert. *An Enquiry into the Foundation and History of the Law of Nations in Europe.* 2 vols. London: Butterworth, 1795.

Robert Plumer Ward (1765–1846) provided a foundational text on international law with his *An Enquiry into the Foundation and History of the Law of Nations in Europe* (1795). When he published this book, legal scholars had only recently distinguished international law from other branches of law and recognized that its concerns extended beyond warfare. Ward attempted to explain the nature and source of the authority of international law and to document its history in Europe down to the time of Hugo Grotius (1583–1645). In the first part of his work, Ward devoted much space to "proving that men's ethical ideas at different times and in different places are so divergent that there can be no universal law of nations; but that the similarities in the ethical and religious ideas of European nations made a law of nations possible as between them." He devoted the second part of his work to a "historical exposition of the rules which these nations have actually observed in their intercourse with one another."[1] Fillmore purchased this book upon the recommendation of Edward Everett.

107,754 voucher 4: 1 vol. Ward's Law of Nations $6.00.

Purchased from Little and Brown on December 31, 1851.

Hayes Catalogue: Ward, R. *Enquiry into the Foundation and History of the Law of Nations in Europe.* 2 v. London 1795. 8°.

TITLE PAGE

AN | ENQUIRY | INTO THE | FOUNDATION AND HISTORY | OF THE | LAW OF NATIONS IN EUROPE, | FROM THE | TIME OF THE GREEKS AND ROMANS, | TO | THE AGE OF GROTIUS. | [swelled rule] | By ROBERT WARD, | OF THE INNER TEMPLE, ESQ. BARRISTER AT LAW. | [swelled rule] | Semina nobis Scientiæ dedit Natura, Scientiam non dedit.—SENECA. | [thin double rule] | IN TWO VOLUMES. | VOL. I. [II.] | [thick/thin double rule] | LONDON: | PRINTED BY A. STRAHAN AND W. WOODFALL, | LAW PRINTERS TO THE KING'S MOST EXCELLENT MAJESTY, | FOR J. BUTTERWORTH, FLEET-STREET. | [thin rule] | 1795.

PAGINATION

Vol. I. i–cviii 1–396.

Vol. II. [4] 1–628.

CONTENTS

Vol. I. i title, ii blank, iii–lix preface, lx blank, lxi–cviii "Alphabetical Table of the Principal Matters," 1–395 text, 396 errata.

Vol. II. [1] title, [2] blank, [3] errata, [4] blank. 1–628 text.

REFERENCES

Hayes p. 313; cf. Greenleaf; Harvard p. 269; Marvin p. 717.

COPY DESCRIBED
ViU: Int 002 w27e copy 1. *Leaf.* 212 × 127.

---

1. Holdsworth, *History of English Law,* 12:638–39. See entry 67 for Grotius.

181. Warden, David Bailie. *On the Origin, Nature, Progress and Influence of Consular Establishments.* **Paris: Smith, 1813.

David Bailie Warden's (1772–1845) *On the Origin, Nature, Progress and Influence of Consular Establishments* (1813) became a classic text on its subject. A writer for the *Analectic Magazine* remarked that the topic "could not have fallen into better hands" and proclaimed that while de Wicquefort may be known as the champion of ambassadors, Warden deserves the title "champion of consuls."[1] Warden was a diplomat and scholar who had served as the American consul in Paris from 1811 to 1814. After his removal from this position, he remained there and worked to bridge American and European intellectual communities.

    Consular Establishments is among the books that Edward Everett recommended to Fillmore and that the president purchased in response to the Cuban filibuster. The copy described here is one of the ten surviving books from the original White House Library and is inscribed on the title page "Executive Mansion."

109,399 voucher 4: Warden on Consuls $3.25.
Purchased from Franck Taylor on July 8, 1852.
Hayes Catalogue: Warden, D. B. *On Consular Establishment.* Paris, 1813. 8°

TITLE PAGE
ON | THE ORIGIN, NATURE, PROGRESS AND INFLUENCE | OF | CONSULAR ESTABLISHMENTS, | BY D. B. WARDEN, | CONSUL GENERAL OF THE UNITED STATES OF AMERICA, AT | PARIS; D.ʳ MED. COLL. NOV. EBOR.; MEMBER OF THE | PHILOSOPHICAL SOCIETY OF PHILADELPHIA; OF THE PHILOMATIC SOCIETY, AND OF THE SOCIETY FOR THE | ENCOURAGEMENT OF ARTS AND MANUFACTURES, AT PARIS; | OF THE BELFAST LITERARY SOCIETY, ETC. ETC. ETC. | [decorative rule] | PARIS: | PRINTED AND SOLD BY SMITH, RUE MONTGOMERY, n.° 16. | [decorative rule] | 1813.

PAGINATION
[6] 5–332.

CONTENTS
[1] half title, [2] blank, [3] title, [4] blank, [5] dedication to the President of the United States, [6] blank, 5–11 preface, 12 blank, 13–331 text, 332 blank.

MARKS OF OWNERSHIP
"Executive Mansion" inscribed on the top of the title page.

REFERENCES
Hayes p. 309.

COPY DESCRIBED

DLC: JX 1694 W3 copy 2. *Leaf.* 201 × 117.

---

1. "Domestic Literary Intelligence," *Analectic Magazine*, June 1815, available at *APS Online*, http://www.proquest.com/products_pq/descriptions/aps.shtml. See entry 191 for de Wicquefort.

∽

182. Warren, John Esaias. *Para; Or, Scenes and Adventures on the Banks of the Amazon.* New York: G. Putnam, 1851.

John Esaias Warren (1826–96), attorney, diplomat, real estate operator, and travel writer, published two travel books, *Para; Or, Scenes and Adventures on the Banks of the Amazon* (1851) and *Vagamundo, or, The Attaché in Spain: Including a Brief Excursion into the Empire of Morocco* (1851). *Para* received mixed reviews upon its publication. A writer for the *Knickerbocker; Or New York Monthly Magazine* offered effusive praise: "Like an oasis in the desert the relation of these scenes and adventures on the banks of the Amazon stands among the many books of travel constantly issuing from the press. Such a brilliant description, such a luxuriance of bright coloring, such an amount of positive information, are rarely embodied under one cover."[1] In contrast, a reviewer for *Littel's Living Age* found "no great value," in *Para* and claimed that Warren had given his reader no evidence that he possessed "more than an elementary acquaintance with the subject."[2]

The Amazon region related to Fillmore's concerns with economics, trade, and slavery. In October of 1850 he approved the Herndon-Gibbon expedition to the Amazon, which had been proposed as a way to open up trade routes with Brazil, establish agricultural centers there, and possibly even colonize the Amazon River Basin with slaveholders if slavery were discontinued in the United States. The expedition departed for Peru the following January, not to return until July of 1852. During this time, as a solution to the escalating controversy over slavery, Fillmore considered colonizing the Amazon River Basin, not with slaveholders as leaders of the expedition had suggested, but with freed slaves. Fillmore had planned to present this proposal in his annual address to Congress in December of 1852, but decided to suppress it.[3]

Account 109,399 voucher 4: Warren's Para $0.75.

Purchased from Franck Taylor on July 26, 1851.

Roosevelt Catalogue: Warren, John Esaias Para; *Or, Scenes and Adventures on the Banks of the Amazon.* New York, G. P. Putnam, 1851.

TITLE PAGE

PARA; | OR, | Scenes and Adventures [black letter] | ON THE BANKS OF THE AMAZON. | BY | JOHN ESAIAS WARREN. | "Regions immense, unsearchable, unknown | Bask in the splendor of the solar zone." | MONTGOMERY. | NEW YORK: | G. P. PUTNAM, 155 BROADWAY. | [thin rule] | 1851.

PAGINATION

i–iv 5–272.

CONTENTS

i title, ii copyright statement and printer's imprint, iii–iv preface, 5–271 text, 272 blank.

REFERENCES

Hayes p. 310; Roosevelt p. 43; Putnam p. 35-s; Roorbach p. 571.

COPY DESCRIBED

DLC: F2585 W28. *Leaf.* 164 × 117.

---

1. "Rev. of *Para*," *Knickerbocker; Or New York Monthly Magazine,* July 1851, available at *APS Online,* http://www.proquest.com/products_pq/descriptions/aps.shtml.

2. "Rev. of *Para*," *Littel's Living Age,* September 13, 1851, available at *APS Online,* http://www.proquest.com/products_pq/descriptions/aps.shtml.

3. Scarry, *Millard Fillmore,* 177; Ponko, *Ships, Seas, and Scientists,* 61–62; the suppressed part of Fillmore's address was preserved in writing and is reprinted in Severance, *Millard Fillmore Papers,* 1:313–24.

∽

183. *The Washington City Directory and Congressional, and Executive Register, for 1850.* Comp. Edward Waite. Washington, D.C.: Columbus Alexander, 1850.

Edward Waite's *Washington City Directory* is the only recorded directory for Washington, D.C., dated 1850.[1] It includes the names and addresses of all private residences and businesses in Washington; a congressional directory with addresses for all members of the Senate and House, listing the officers of both; an executive register, listing all officials in the executive branch of the government along with their salaries, the cabinet members, consuls, and the officers for each department; a list of officers in the navy; and a list of city officials and offices. The booksellers from whom it was purchased, Taylor and Maury, are among the advertisers in the directory (226).

105,133 voucher 6: Washington City Directory $0.75.
Purchased from Taylor and Maury on December 9, 1850.

TITLE PAGE

THE | WASHINGTON DIRECTORY, | AND | CONGRESSIONAL, | AND | EXECUTIVE REGISTER, | FOR | 1850. | [wavy rule] |COMPILED AND PUBLISHED | BY EDWARD WAITE. | [wavy rule] | WASHINGTON: | COLUMBUS ALEXANDER, PRINTER. | [thin rule] | 1850. [All enclosed in decorative frame]

PAGINATION

i–xii 1–96 [2] 101–242.

CONTENTS

i title page, ii blank, iii preface, iv–vi contents and index, vii–xi index to advertisers, xii "omissions, corrections, and removals" and "abbreviations explained," 1–96 text of directory, [1] "numerical index to diagram of the Senate chamber," [2] "numerical index to diagram of the house of representatives," 101–242 text of directory.

PLATES

Facing title, folding "Map of the City of Washington," engraved by D. McClelland, Washington.

Facing [1], "Plan of the Senate Chamber 1st Session, 31st Congress," engraved by D. McClelland, Washington.

Facing [2], "Plan of the House of Representatives, 1st Session, Thirty-First Congress," engraved by D. McClelland, Washington.

BINDING

Front boards. 195 × 114 med. brown cloth. *Back board.* Same as front. *Spine.* Black spine labels, gilt stamped 'WASHINGTON | DIRECTORY | 1850' *Endpapers.* white.

REFERENCES

cf. Fillmore Packing Lists p. 25; cf. Fillmore 1861 p. 56.

COPY DESCRIBED

DLC: Toner F192.5 A 1850 copy 4 *Leaf:* 188 × 114.

---

1. Dorothea N. Spear, *Bibliography of American Directories Through 1860* (1961; Westport, Conn.: Greenwood, 1978), 373.

❧

Washington, George. *The Writings of George Washington.* Ed. Jared Sparks. 12 vols. New York: Harper, 1847.

See entry 161 for Jared Sparks.

❧

184. **Webster, Daniel.** *Speeches and Forensic Arguments.* 8th ed. 3 vols. Boston: Tappan, Whittemore, and Mason, 1850.

185. ———. *The Works of Daniel Webster.* Ed. Edward Everett. 6 vols. Boston: Little and Brown, 1851.

Daniel Webster (1782–1852), politician and lawyer, dedicated the last forty years of his life to public service as a member of Congress and as the secretary of state under presidents Harrison and Fillmore. After establishing himself as a skilled orator during college at Dartmouth, he cultivated this talent the rest of his life. He delivered a dedication speech for the Bunker Hill monument and funeral speeches upon the deaths of Thomas Jefferson and John Adams. As a senator he employed his oratorical skills in early 1850 on behalf of compromise measures, and after becoming secretary of state in July of that year, he supported what became known as the Compromise of 1850.

Not only was he a distinguished statesman, speaker, and cabinet member, Webster was among the first friends that Fillmore made when he arrived in Washington as a freshman congressman in 1833, and it was Webster who, shortly thereafter, arranged for Fillmore's admission to the Supreme Court bar. In 1852 Fillmore faced Webster in friendly rivalry for the Whig presidential nomination. Both were defeated by Winfield Scott after interminable balloting at the convention.[1]

Webster's *Speeches* began to be published in Boston in 1830 by Perkins and Marvin. Upon their publication, they received laudatory reviews. The *North American Review* maintained that these speeches should be considered among the best of American literature, remarking that the words of Daniel Webster "have a value and interest apart from the time and occasion of their delivery, they are storehouses of thought and knowledge."[2]

Webster's *Works* were first published in 1851, edited and with a biographical memoir by Edward Everett. The editions of the *Speeches* and the *Works* that were purchased for the White House overlap considerably in content. While the speeches contain no material after 1840, the *Works* include documents dated as late as 1850. Reviews of the *Works* indicate that Webster's reputation had not flagged during the ten years since the publication of his *Speeches*. According to a writer for the *Literary World,* "Mr. Webster will owe his permanent hold upon reputation—in the hearts and on the lips of the people, above the perishing names of other men great in their own day and generation, to two circumstances—his clear enunciation of great moral truths as the laws of Providence, Duty, Patriotism, and the literary skill with which he has arrayed them."[3] Likewise the *Knickerbocker; Or New York Monthly Magazine* commended the Little and Brown edition of Webster's *Works* and recommended it to "every American reader, without distinction of party or sect," as worthy example of a style "such as no statesman, of any country beside ours on earth, can at this moment boast."[4] Not only did critics laud the content of the *Works,* but they also praised the physical aspects of this edition: "The publishers seem to have been aware of what they were doing for posterity, and have accordingly performed their duty to the public in the most liberal manner. The type upon which the volumes were printed is large and clear, the paper is good, and the binding elegant and tasteful."[5] The *Works* was available in both large and small paper formats, and a large paper copy was purchased for the White House, as indicated on the voucher. The copy described here bears Webster's signature on a leaf at the front of volume 1, which also has 'SUBSCRIBER'S COPY' printed on it, the only indication that this title was sold by subscription.

105,133 voucher 5: Webster's Speeches 3 vols. $6.00.
Purchased from Charles Welford on December 13, 1850.
109,399 voucher 1: Websters Works 6 vols. [large] 8vo $18.00.
Purchased from Taylor and Maury on April 3, 1852.
Roosevelt Catalogue: Webster, Daniel. *The Works.* Boston: C. C. Little & J. Brown, 1851, 4 vols. vol. 2 missing.
———. *Speeches and Forensic Arguments.* Eighth edition. Boston, Tappan, Whittemore & Mason, 1850, 3 vols.

SPEECHES

TITLE PAGE

SPEECHES | AND | FORENSIC ARGUMENTS. | [thin rule] | BY DANIEL WEBSTER. | [thin rule] | VOL. I. [II–III.] | EIGHTH EDITION. | BOSTON: | TAPPAN, WHITTEMORE, AND MASON. | [thin rule] | 1850.

Note. Volume 3 is missing the periods after "Arguments" and the edition statement.

PAGINATION

Vol. I. i–viii 25–520.

Vol. II. 1–20 17–482.

Vol. III. 1–564.

Note. The page numbers 17–20 are duplicated in volume 2.

CONTENTS

Vol. I. i title page, ii copyright statement, iii–vi preface, vii–viii contents, 25–520 text.

Vol. II. 1 title page, 2 copyright statement, 3–18 "To the Second Volume," 19–20 contents, 17–482 text.

Vol. III. 1 title page, 2 copyright statement, 3–14 preface, 15–16 contents, 17–563 text, 564 blank.

PLATES

Vol. I.

Engraved portrait frontispiece of Daniel Webster, signed by R. M. Staigg, artist and J. Cheney and R. W. Dodson engravers.

REFERENCES

Hayes p. 310; Roosevelt p. 43; Putnam p. 152; cf. Roorbach p. 576; cf. L and B 1850 p. 96; cf. L and B 1852 p. 7; cf. Fillmore 1847 p. 4.

COPY DESCRIBED

DLC: E337 8 W388. *Leaf.* 218 × 131.

Works.

TITLE PAGE

Vol. I. THE | WORKS | OF | DANIEL WEBSTER. | VOLUME I. [II–VI] | [thin rule] | BOSTON: | CHARLES C. LITTLE AND JAMES BROWN. | 1851.

PAGINATION

Vol. I. [2] i–clx 1–458.

Vol. II. i–viii 1–622.

Vol. III. i–viii 1–552.

Vol. IV. i–viii 1–558.

Vol. V. i–viii 1–546.

Vol. VI. i–x 1–634.

CONTENTS

Vol. I. [1] 'SUBSCRIBER'S COPY. | Daniel Webster [autograph signature]', [2] blank, i title, ii copyright statement and printer's imprint, iii dedication to Alice Bridge Whipple and Mary Ann Sanborn, Webster's nieces, iv blank, v–x contents, xi section title, "Biographical Memoir of the Public Life of Daniel Webster by Edward Everett," xii blank, xiii–clx text, 1–457 text of *Works,* 458 blank.

Vol. II. i title, ii copyright statement and printer's imprint, iii dedication to Isaac P. Davis, iv blank, v–vii contents, viii blank, 1–622 text.

Vol. III. i title, ii copyright statement and printer's imprint, iii dedication to Caroline Le Roy Webster, (Webster's wife), iv blank, v–vii contents, viii blank, 1–551 text, 552 blank.

Vol. IV. i title, ii copyright statement and printer's imprint, iii dedication to Fletcher Webster (Webster's son), iv blank, v–viii contents, 1–558 text.

Vol. V. i title, ii copyright statement and printer's imprint, iii dedication to J. W. Paige, iv blank, v–viii contents, 1–545 text, 546 blank.

Vol. VI. i title, ii copyright statement and printer's imprint, iii dedication to Webster's two deceased children, Julia Webster Appleton and Major Edward Webster, iv blank, v–x contents, 1–601 text, 602 blank, 603 section title, 'INDEX', 604 blank, 605–33 index, 634 'GENERAL DIVISION. | [thin rule] | BIOGRAPHICAL MEMOIR, BY EDWARD EVERETT. VOL. I. pp. xi.–clx. | SPEECHES DELIVERED ON VARIOUS PUBLIC OCCASIONS.— Vols. I. and II | SPEECHES IN THE CONVENTION TO AMEND THE CONSTITUTION OF | MASSACHUSETTS.—Vol. III. pp. 1–32. | SPEECHES IN CONGRESS.—From Vol. III. p. 33 to Vol. V. p. 438. | LEGAL ARGUMENTS AND SPEECHES TO THE JURY.—From Vol. V. p. 439 | to Vol. VI. p. 242. | DIPLOMATIC AND OFFICIAL PAPERS.—Vol. VI. pp. 243–530. | MISCELLANEOUS LETTERS.—Vol. VI. pp. 531–601.'

PLATES

Vol. I.

Portrait frontispiece of Daniel Webster, "From the Powers Bust," engraved by S. A. Schoff.

Facing 1, vignette "Birth Place of Daniel Webster, Salisbury, N.H." signed in lower left by H. Billings and lower right by E. A. Fowle.

Vol. II–VI.

None.

REFERENCES

Hayes p. 310; Roosevelt p. 43; Putnam p. 35-s; cf. Roorbach p. 576; cf. Fillmore Packing Lists p. 4; cf. Fillmore ca. 1858 p. 69; cf. Fillmore 1861 p. 224.

COPY DESCRIBED

DLC: E 337 .8 W24 1851. *Leaf.* 246 × 150.

---

1. Scarry, *Millard Fillmore,* 234.

2. *North American Review,* July 1844, available at *APS Online,* http://www.proquest.com/products_pq/descriptions/aps.shtml.

3. "Literature," *Literary World,* May 8, 1852, available at *APS Online,* http://www.proquest.com/products_pq/descriptions/aps.shtml.

4. *Knickerbocker; Or New York Monthly Magazine,* June 1852; see also "Intelligence," *Christan Examiner and Religious Miscellany (1844–1857),* March 1852. Both available at *APS Online,* http://www.proquest.com/products_pq/descriptions/aps.shtml.

5. *Knickerbocker; Or New York Monthly Magazine (1833–62),* June 1852, available at *APS Online,* http://www.proquest.com/products_pq/descriptions/aps.shtml.

186. Webster, Noah. *A Dictionary of the English Language.* Springfield, Mass.: G. and
   C. Merriam, 1850.

The lexicographer Noah Webster's (1758–1843) spellers, readers, and grammars went into
numerous editions and were mainstays in American school curricula during the nineteenth
century. Webster, however, devoted most of his efforts as lexicographer and literary entre-
preneur to his dictionary, first published in two volumes in 1828. His dictionary was an
instant success, although its size precluded it from selling as well as his earlier texts. G. and
C. Merriam acquired the rights and reprinted it numerous times beginning in 1843. The
"preface to the revised edition," dated 1847, explained that it had been updated and reduced
to one volume and that stereotype plates had been made for printing future editions. It
also acknowledged that it relied on *The Penny Cyclopaedia, The Encyclopaedia Americana,*
Bouvier's *Law Dictionary,* Blackstone's *Commentaries,* McCulloch's *Commercial Dictionary,*
and Ure's *Dictionary of Arts, Manufacturers, and Mines,* all works that were purchased for
the library.[1]

Dictionaries had long been essential to Fillmore's intellectual development. When
apprenticed to a wool carder as a teenager, he had purchased one that he kept open on his
desk so that he could learn new words as he tended the wool carding machines. Throughout
his life, his libraries contained numerous dictionaries. It is therefore no surprise that this
dictionary stands as one of the very first books purchased for the White House Library; it,
along with a Bible and Johnston's *National Atlas,* was acquired in August of 1850 before
Congress had approved the plan for the library and allocated any funding for it. Fillmore
endorsed Merriam's edition of Webster's *Dictionary* with a signed blurb that appeared on
the front of its printed paper wrapper. Although the publication date of the copy purchased
for the first White House Library is unknown, it was probably the most recent printing
of 1850.[2]

105,579 voucher 1: 1 Webster's Dictionary $6.00.
Purchased from George Crosby on August 19, 1850.

REFERENCES
cf. Hayes p. 51; cf. Roosevelt p. 43; cf. Roorbach p. 576; cf. Putnam p. 153; cf. Fillmore 1847
p. 9; cf. Fillmore Packing Lists p. 3 and p. 23; cf. Fillmore ca. 1858 p. 15; cf. Fillmore 1861 p. 52.

---

1. See entry 128 for *Penny Cyclopaedia,* 52 for *Encyclopaedia Americana,* 19 for Bouvier's *Law Dictionary,*
16 for Blackstone's *Commentaries on the Laws of England,* 104 for McCulloch's *Dictionary, Practical, Theoretical, and Historical of Commerce and Commercial Navigation,* and 177 for Ure's *Dictionary of Arts, Manufacturers, and Mines.*
2. The Smithsonian Institution copy is still in the original paper wrappers, with Fillmore's endorsement, q PE1625 .W382a 1850.

⟿

187. Wharton, Francis. *State Trials of the United States During the Administrations of
   Washington and Adams.* Philadelphia: Carey and Hart, 1849.

Francis Wharton (1820–89), Yale graduate and attorney general for Pennsylvania, became
known as a legal writer and authority on criminal law. *State Trials of the United States* (1849)

is among Wharton's several early works, which include *A Treatise on the Criminal Law of the United States* (1846), *Precedents of Indictment and Pleas* (1849), and *A Treatise on the Law of Homicide in the United States* (1855). *State Trials* contains seventeen trials, including four for seditious libel, two for libel, one for seditious riot, and two for insurrection with preliminary notes on the Washington and Adams administrations.[1]

109,399 voucher 4: Wharton's State Trials $4.50.
Purchased from Franck Taylor on October 15, 1851.
Hayes Catalogue: Wharton, F. *State Trials of the United States during the Administration of Washington and Adams.* Philadelphia, 1849. 8°.

TITLE PAGE
STATE TRIALS | OF THE | UNITED STATES | DURING THE |ADMINISTRATIONS OF WASHNGTON AND ADAMS. | WITH | REFERENCES, | HISTORICAL AND PROFESSIONAL, | AND | PRELIMINARY NOTES ON THE POLITICS OF THE TIMES. | BY FRANCIS WHARTON, | AUTHOR OF "A TREATISE ON AMERICAN CRIMINAL LAW," ETC. | PHILADELPHIA: | CAREY AND HART, | 126 CHESTNUT STREET. | 1849.

PAGINATION
[4] 1–732.

CONTENTS
[1] title, [2] copyright statement and printer's imprint, [3]–[4] contents, 1–721 text, 722 blank, 723–27 index, 728 errata, 729–32 advertisements for books recently published by Carey and Hart.

REFERENCES
Hayes p. 313; *BEAL* 12117; cf. Putnam p. 154.

COPY DESCRIBED
DLC: LLRBR LL Trials KF 220 W43 1849 copy three. *Leaf.* 221 × 137.

---

1. *BEAL,* 12117.

∾

188. Wheaton, Henry. *Elements of International Law.* Philadelphia: Lea and Blanchard, 1846.
189. ———. *History of the Law of Nations in Europe and America.* New York: Gould, Banks, and Co., 1845.

Henry Wheaton (1785–1848), scholar, diplomat, and Supreme Court reporter, helped to lay the foundation for American law along with John Marshall, James Kent, and Joseph Story. He originally published *Elements of International Law* (1836) and *History of the Law of Nations in Europe and America* (1841) in French while he was posted in Berlin, where both works received warm receptions, were reissued several times, and were translated into English, Italian, Spanish, and Chinese. *Elements* originally included *A Sketch of the History of the Science.* The *Sketch* was dropped from *Elements* upon the publication of his landmark treatise, *History of the Law of Nations,* which is an expansion of his earlier *Sketch* and became the authoritative work on the law of nations. Marvin praised Wheaton's works for their sound views and the learning and research that they displayed. James Reddie also extolled Wheaton's works as "the best of their kind in the English language."[1]

The edition of *History of the Law of Nations* purchased by the White House is identified in the Hayes Catalogue, but the edition of the *Elements of International Law* that was purchased remains unknown.[2] In 1850 there were three editions available that could have been selected, two from Lea and Blanchard in Philadelphia, dated 1836 and 1846, and one from Fellowes in London, dated 1836.[3] Based on price, any of these three editions could account for this purchase. The *English Catalogue* listed the Fellowes edition for 21s., which would have been approximately $5.00 in 1850, and Roorbach listed the 1846 Lea and Blanchard edition at $5.50.[4] The 1846 edition stands as the most likely choice because it is revised and corrected and drops the *Sketch of the History of the Science.* Since legal reference books, such as this one, were time sensitive, Fillmore would have wanted the most up to date edition.

105,133 voucher 2: Wheaton's Law of Nations $5.00.

Wheaton's Elements $4.00.

Purchased from Little and Brown on December 30, 1850.

Hayes Catalogue: Wheaton, H. *History of the Law of Nations,* New York, 1845. 8°.

History of the Law of Nations in Europe and America.

TITLE PAGE

HISTORY | OF THE | LAW OF NATIONS | IN EUROPE AND AMERICA; | FROM THE EARLIEST TIMES TO THE | TREATY OF WASHINGTON, 1842. | [wavy rule] | BY HENRY WHEATON, L. L. D. | MINISTER OF THE UNITED STATES AT THE COURT OF BERLIN, CORRESPONDING | MEMBER OF THE ACADEMY OF MORAL AND POLITICAL | SCIENCES IN THE INSTITUTE OF FRANCE. [wavy rule] | NEW YORK: | PUBLISHED BY GOULD, BANKS & Co. | LAW BOOKSELLERS, NO. 144 NASSAU STREET; | WM. & A. GOULD & Co. ALBANY; | AND ANDREW MILLIKEN, DUBLIN, IRELAND. | [thin rule] | 1845.

PAGINATION

i–vi ix–xiv 1–800.

Note. Pages vii and viii have been skipped in the numbering of the preliminaries.

CONTENTS

i title page, ii copyright statement and printer's imprint, iii–v preface, vi blank, ix–xiv contents, 1–760 text, 761–97 index, 798 blank, 799–800 list of books to be published by Gould and Banks.

REFERENCES

Hayes p. 313; *BEAL* 7208; Harvard p. 274; Marvin p. 728; Roorbach p. 634; Putnam p. 154.

COPY DESCRIBED

DLC: JX 2495 H2 1845. *Leaf.* 239 × 145.

Elements of International Law.
REFERENCES
cf. Roorbach p. 634; cf. Harvard p. 274; Marvin p. 728.

———————

1. Reddie quoted in Marvin, *Legal Bibliography,* 728. See entry 138 for Reddie.
2. By 1877 a new copy had been purchased, for the Hayes catalogue lists an 1855 Boston edition.
3. In *BEAL,* Cohen notes that in the preface to the 1848 French edition published in Leipzig, Wheaton identifies the 1836 London edition from Fellowes as the first.
4. Peddie and Waddington, *English Catalogue of Books 1801–1836,* 632.

∽

190. Whewell, William. *The Elements of Morality.* 2 vols. London: John W. Parker, 1848.

William Whewell (1794–1866), master of Trinity College, Cambridge, was recognized in his own time as a man of tremendous intellectual ability and learning, yet he has been all but forgotten today. Better known for his writings on the philosophy of science, he published two works on moral philosophy, *The Elements of Morality* (1845) and *Lectures on Systematic Morality* (1846), which were not well received. Utilitarian thinkers of the day, such as John Stuart Mill, found these works ponderous and conservative. Even the conservative *North American Review* offered only lukewarm praise for *Elements.* It praised Whewell's distinctive definitions, his accuracy, and his minute and thorough "analysis of moral ideas and conceptions," but asserted that his book could be considerably shorter, calling it "needlessly minute and tediously prolix."[1] Nevertheless, Edward Everett, recommended *Elements* to Fillmore in the aftermath of the Cuban filibuster.

107,754 voucher 4: 2 vols. Whewells Elements of Morality $6.48.
Purchased from Little and Brown on December 31, 1851.
Hayes Catalogue: Whewell, W. *Elements of Morality.* v. 1. London, 1848. 12°.

TITLE PAGE
THE | ELEMENTS OF MORALITY, | INCLUDING | POLITY. | BY | WILLIAM WHEWELL, D.D., | MASTER OF TRINITY COLLEGE, AND PROFESSOR OF MORAL PHILOSOPHY | IN THE UNIVERSITY OF CAMBRIDGE. | *AUTHOR OF THE HISTORY AND THE PHILOSOPHY OF THE INDUCTIVE SCIENCES.* | IN TWO VOLUMES. | [vignette the passing of the torch] |Λαμπάδια ἔχοντες διαδώσονσιν| A NEW EDITION, REVISED AND CORRECTED. | VOLUME I. [II.] | LONDON: | JOHN W. PARKER, WEST STRAND. | [thin rule] | M.DCCC.XLVIII.

PAGINATION
Vol. I. i–lvi 1–396.
Vol. II. i–xxiv 1–288.

CONTENTS
Vol. I. i title, ii printer's imprint, iii dedication to William Wordsworth, iv blank, v–xxviii preface to the second edition, xxix–liii contents, liv "Errata, Vol. I.," lv section title, 'BOOK I. | [thin rule] | *INTRODUCTION.* | ELEMENTARY NOTIONS AND | DEFINITIONS.', lvi blank, 1–388 text, 389–96 advertisements for books published by John W. Parker.

Vol. II. i title, ii printer's imprint, iii–xxi contents, xxii blank, xxiii "Errata Vol. II.," xxiv blank, 1–286 text, 287–88 advertisements for books by William Whewell.

BINDING

Front board. 163 × 118 med. brown ribbed cloth with blind-stamped triple-rule frame, surrounding a filigree decoration with a gilt-stamped torch passing between two hands in the center. *Back board.* Same as front except without the gilt-stamped ornament. *Spine.* Black spine labels, gilt stamped '[thin rule] | ELEMENTS | OF | MORALITY | [thin rule]', volume number gilt stamped on cloth below spine label. *Endpapers.* Pale yellow.

REFERENCES

Hayes p. 311; cf. *LC 1816–1851* p. 602; cf. Putnam p. 154; cf. L and B 1850 p. 97; cf. Fillmore ca. 1858 p. 69; cf. Fillmore 1861 p. 166.

COPY DESCRIBED

MBA 1M W57 *Leaf.* 178 × 109.

―――――――

1. *North American Review* 63 (July 1846), 27, available at *APS Online,* http://www.proquest.com/ products_pq/descriptions/aps.shtml.

~

191. Wicquefort, Abraham de. *The Embassador and His Functions.* London: Lintott, 1716.

Abraham de Wicquefort's (1598–1682) *The Embassador and His Functions* (1681) became the "most highly regarded manual of diplomacy in the eighteenth century."[1] A massive practical work intended for use by working ambassadors, it was first translated from Dutch into English by John Digby in 1716, which is the edition purchased for the Executive Mansion, and was frequently reprinted thereafter. De Wicquefort, a Dutch diplomat and historian, published one other treatise, *The History of the United Provinces from the Peace of Munster* (1719). Edward Everett recommended de Wicquefort's treatise on ambassadors for the library, where it stood among several older but classical legal works.[2]

107,754 voucher 4: 1 vol. De Wicquefords [*sic*] Rights of Ambassadors $2.88.
Purchased from Little and Brown on December 31, 1851.
Roosevelt Catalogue: Wicquefort, Abraham de. *The Embassador and His Functions: With an Historical Discourse Concerning the Election of the Emperor and his Electors.* Translated by John Digby. London, Bernard Lintot, 1716.

TITLE PAGE

[double thin rule frame enclosing all text] | THE | EMBASSADOR | AND HIS | FUNCTIONS: | Written by | Monsieur de *WICQUEFORT,* | Privy-Counsellor to the Duke of *Brunswick* | and *Lunenburg, Zell,* &c. | In Two BOOKS. | I. Shewing, The Right of Sovereigns to send Embassadors: | The several Orders of Publick Ministers: Of the Birth, Learning, and Age | if Embassadors, and the Trust reposed in them: Their Instructions, Let- | ters of Credence, Powers, Passports, Entries, Audiences, Ceremonies, Vi- | sits, Apparel, Expences, Domesticks, Privileges, &c. The Competition | between *France* and *Spain,* and several other Princes and States about | Rank. | II. Treating of the Functions of Embassadors: Their Manner | of Negotiating: Their Liberty of Speech: Their secret

Services, Letters, | Dispatches: Of their Mediatory Treaties: Of the Treaty of *Westphalia,* | and all other Treaties in the last Century: Of Ratifications: The Lives | and Characters of the most Illustrious Embassadors, and of several splendid | Embassies; *viz.* | I. That of Sir *Francis Walsingham* from Q. *Elizabeth* to *France.* | II. The Duke of *Buckingham* to *Spain* and *France.* | III. Sir *Robert Shirley,* Embassador from the K. of *Persia* to K. *James* 1*st.* | IV. Mr. *Lockhart* Minister of *England* at the *Pyrenean* Treaty. | V. The Lord *Falconbridge* to the *French* King at *Dunkirk.* | VI. The Duke of *Crequi* to *Cromwell.* | VII. Sir *John Trevor* to *France.* | VIII. The Lord *Hollis* to *France.* | IX. The Earl of *Essex* to *Denmark.* | X. Sir *William Temple* to the *Hague* and *Nimeguen.* | With many other Embassies from *England, France, Spain,* which afford | Useful Historical Relations no where else to be found. | Also, A large Account of the Constitution of the *German* Empire, the Manner of | Electing their Emperors, of the Electoral College, of the *Golden Bull,* of the E- | lection of the King of the *Romans,* the Rights and Prerogatives of the several Ele- | ctors, and Laws and Usages of the Empire. | [thin rule] | Translated into *English* by Mr. *DIGBY.* | [thin rule] | *LONDON:* | Printed for BERNARD LINTOTT between the *Temple-Gates* in *Fleet street:* And sold by | CHARLES KING in *Westminster-Hall,* EDWARD FLEETWOOD at the Foot of the | *Parliament Stairs,* and WILLIAM TAYLOR at the *Ship* in *Pater-Noster-Row.* 1716. | Price 25s. small, and 35s. large Paper.

ADDITIONAL TITLE PAGE

[thin double-rule frame] | THE | EMBASSADOR | AND HIS | FUNCTIONS. | To which is added, | An Historical Discourse, | Concerning the | ELECTION of the EMPEROR, | AND THE | ELECTORS. | [thin rule] | BY | Monsieur de *WICQUEFORT,* | Counsellor in the Councils of State, and Privy-Counsellor to the | Duke of *Brunswick* and *Lunenburg, Zell,* &c. | [thin rule] | *Translated into* English *by Mr.* Digby. | [thin rule] | [printer's ornament] | *LONDON:* | Printed for BERNARD LINTOTT, at the *Cross-Keys* between the | *Temple-Gates.*

PAGINATION

[*12*] 1–598.

CONTENTS

[*1*] blank, [*2*] royal licence, [*3*] title, [*4*] blank, [*5*] additional title, [*6*] blank, [*7*]–[*8*] dedication to Lord Digby, [*9*]–[*10*] author's epistle to George William, [*11*]–[*12*] contents, 1–430 text of the *Embassador and His Functions,* 431 section title, "An Historical Discourse of the Election of the Emperor, and of the Electors of the Empire," 432 blank, 433–34 dedication to the Lord Seguier, 435–36 note to the reader, 437–570 text of *Election of the Emperor,* 571–98 index.

REFERENCES

Hayes p. 311; Roosevelt p. 44; Harvard p. 276.

COPY DESCRIBED

DFo JX 1652 W6 Cage Fo. *Leaf.* 343 × 215.

---

1. G. R. Berridge, ed., *Diplomatic Classics: Selected Texts from Commynes to Vattel* (New York: Palgrave, 2004), 123.

2. "Wicquefort, Abraham de," *Penny Cyclopaedia.*

192. Wildman, Richard. *Institutes of International Law.* 2 vols. London: Benning, 1849–50.

Richard Wildman (1802–81) provides a useful summary of international law in his two-volume treatise, *Institutes of International Law* (1849–50). Volume 1, subtitled *International Rights in Time of Peace,* deals with "the nature and source of international law, independent states and their territories, public ministers and consuls, treaties, arbitration and reprisals, and offences against the law of nations." Volume 2, *Time of War,* focuses on "the state of war, the national character of persons and things, search and capture, blockade, contraband, licences, ransom, recapture and salvage, prize, . . . jurisdiction and practice of prize courts."[1] Both volumes address the legal issues surrounding the Cuban filibuster, and Edward Everett aptly recommended them to the president. For whatever reason, Fillmore initially purchased only volume 1 in December of 1851 and added volume 2 the following March. Perhaps Little and Brown did not have the complete set in stock in December.

107,754 voucher 4: 1 vol. Wildman's International Law $2.88.
Purchased from Little and Brown on December 31, 1851.
107,754 voucher 6: 1 vol. 2 Wildman's Internat[l] Law $4.62.
Purchased from Little and Brown on March 22, 1852.
Hayes Catalogue: Wildman, R. *Institutes of International Law.* 2 v. London, 1849–50. 8°.

TITLE PAGE

INSTITUTES | OF | INTERNATIONAL LAW. | [thin rule with diamond in center] | BY | RICHARD WILDMAN, Esq., | OF THE INNER TEMPLE BARRISTER AT LAW; | RECORDER OF NOTTINGHAM, &c. | [thin rule] | VOL. I. [II.] | [thin rule] | INTERNATIONAL RIGHTS | IN | TIME OF PEACE. | [thin/thick double rule] | LONDON: | WILLIAM BENNING & CO., LAW BOOKSELLERS, | 43, FLEET STREET. | [thin rule] | 1849.

> *Note.* Volume 2 differs in its sub title and imprint date as follows: 'TIME OF WAR | . . . | 1850.'

PAGINATION
Vol. I. [4] iii–viii 1–204.
Vol. II. i–iv 1–436.

CONTENTS
Vol. I. [1] title, [2] printer's imprint, [3] dedication to Lord Denman, Late Chief Justice of England, [4] blank, iii–viii contents, 1–203 text, 204 blank.
Vol. II. i title, ii printer's imprint, iii–iv contents, 1–378 text, 379–411 appendix, 412 blank, 413–36 index.

REFERENCES
Hayes p. 157; *LC 1816–1851* p. 607.

COPY DESCRIBED
DLC: JX 2592 A3 I57 1849. *Leaf.* 211 × 130.

---

1. Holdsworth, *History of English Law,* 15:330.

193. Wilkes, Charles. *Narrative of the United States Exploring Expedition, During the Years 1838, 1839, 1840, 1841, and 1842.* 5 vols. Philadelphia: Lea and Blanchard, 1845.

The United States Exploring Expedition was the first large-scale scientific exploring mission that the United States undertook and became a model for future expeditions. Charles Wilkes (1798–1877), naval officer and explorer, was appointed commander of the expedition, which departed in six naval vessels from Norfolk, Virginia, in 1838 and traveled 85,000 miles before returning in 1842. It "surveyed 280 islands, including the Tuamotu, Society, Samoan, and Fiji islands; charted 800 miles of rivers and coastline in the Oregon Territory and 1,500 miles of coastal Antarctica; and established that Antarctica is a continent."[1] The reports that followed this expedition raised the stature of the United States in the international scientific community, and the tens of thousands of specimens that were collected on the expedition became the basis for the Smithsonian Institute's National Museum.[2]

Soon after the expedition returned, Congress appointed the Joint Committee on the Library to direct the publication of an account of it. A law limited the number of copies that could be printed of this work to one hundred and delineated how they would be distributed. After considerable expense, the first five volumes and an atlas, written and compiled by Wilkes, were published in 1844. Nineteen volumes written by various people associated with the expedition were added to the narrative; some of these, however, remained unpublished. Although a bill that would have allowed Wilkes to copyright the work was voted down in Congress, Wilkes registered the copyright anyway to prevent his work from being "garbled" by others. He then published editions which, although the same in content, were unauthorized by the government.[3]

Based on price, the Executive Mansion purchased a large paper, or "imperial octavo," edition, the second "unauthorized" issue. An advertisement bound into a regular octavo 1845 copy of a Lea and Blanchard edition in the Library of Congress lists the large paper edition for $25.00, just $1.50 over the price paid by the White House.[4] With a print run of one thousand copies, it was estimated to cost $20,500 to produce. Wilkes commented in a letter to a Congressional committee in January of 1845, "The Imperial 8vo has been got up in beautiful style, and stereotyped—the paper and execution fully equal, and in some respects as a library and reading book, to be preferred to the 4to edition."[5]

105,133 voucher 4: U. S. Explo. Expedition $23.50.
Purchased from George P. Putnam on December 13, 1850.
Roosevelt Catalogue: Wilkes, Charles <u>admiral</u> U. S. N. *Narrative of the United States Exploring Expedition in the Years 1838–42.* With an atlas. Philadelphia, Lea & Blanchard, 1845, 5 vols. and Atlas.

Narrative.

TITLE PAGE

NARRATIVE | OF THE | UNITED STATES | EXPLORING EXPEDITION. | DURING THE YEARS | 1838, 1839, 1840, 1841, 1842. | BY | CHARLES WILKES, U. S. N. | COMMANDER OF THE EXPEDITION, | MEMBER OF THE AMERICAN PHILOSOPHICAL SOCIETY, ETC. | IN FIVE VOLUMES, AND AN ATLAS. | VOL. I. [II–V.] | [thin rule] | PHILADELPHIA: LEA AND BLANCHARD. | 1845.

PAGINATION

Vol. I. i–lx 1–434.

Vol. II. i–xvi 1–476.

Vol. III. i–xvi 1–438.

Vol. IV. i–xvi 1–540.

Vol. V. i–xvi 1–558.

> *Note.* There is a binding error in this copy of volume 3. Gathering 27 is bound before gathering 26.

CONTENTS

Vol. I. i half title, ii blank, iii title, iv copyright statement and printer's imprint, v–xii contents, xiii–xxiii introduction, xxiv blank, xxv–xxxi instructions, xxxii blank, xxxiii–lvi list of officers and men, lvii–lx list of illustrations, 1–345 text, 346 blank, 347 section title, "Appendix," 348 blank, 349–50 contents of appendix, 351–434 text of appendix.

Vol. II. i half title, ii blank, iii title, iv copyright statement and printer's imprint, v–xi contents, xii blank, xiii–xv list of illustrations, xvi blank, 1–414 text, 415 section title, "Appendix," 416 blank, 417–18 contents of appendix, 419–76 text of appendix.

Vol. III. i half title, ii blank, iii title, iv copyright statement and printer's imprint, v–xi contents, xii blank, xiii–xv list of illustrations, xvi blank, 1–394 text, 395 section title, "Appendix," 396 blank, 397 contents of appendix, 398 blank, 399–438 text of appendix.

Vol. IV. i half title, ii blank, iii title, iv copyright statement and printer's imprint, v–xiii contents, xiv blank, xv–xvi list of illustrations, 1–496 text, 497 section title, "Appendix," 498 blank, 499 contents of appendix, 500 blank, 501–39 text of appendix, 540 blank.

Vol. V. i half title, ii blank, iii title, iv copyright statement and printer's imprint, v–xii contents, xiii–xv list of illustrations, xvi blank, 1–502 text, 503 section title, "Appendix," 504 blank, 505 contents of appendix, 506 blank, 507–39 text of appendix, 540 blank, 541 section title, "General Index," 542 blank, 543–58 text of index.

PLATES

Vol. I.

Portrait frontispiece of "Charles Wilkes Commander, U. S. N." painted by T. Sully and engraved by R. W. Dodson.

Facing 3, "Estroza Pass, Madeira," signed in lower left by Drayton and lower right by J. A. Rolph.

Facing 14, "Heath Forest, Madeira," drawn by Drayton and engraved by Jordan and Halpin.

Facing 93, "Patagonian," drawn by A. T. Agate and engraved by Rawdon, Wright, and Hatch.

Facing 119, "Native of Terra del Fuego," signed beneath in center "engraved by Jordan and Halpin from a sketch by J. Drayton."

Facing 229, "Lima Gate Way," drawn by A. T. Agate and engraved by A. Halbert.

Facing 258, "La Vinda Mountain, Peru," drawn by A. T. Agate and engraved by Rawdon, Wright, and Hatch.

Facing 263, "Ba os, Peru," drawn by A. T. Agate and engraved by Rawdon, Wright, and Hatch.

Between 306 and 307, bifolium Map of "Low Archipelago or Paumotu Group."

Vol. II.

Portrait frontispiece of "Wm. L. Hudson," signed in lower left by A. T. Agate and lower right by Jordan and Halpin.

Facing 31, "Broom Road, Tahiti," signed in lower left by A. T. Agate and lower right by Sherman and Smith.

Between 38 and 39, bifolium map, "Island of Tahiti," signed in lower right by Sherman and Smith, N.Y.

Between 62 and 63, bifolium map, "Samoan or Navigator Islands," signed in lower right by Sherman and Smith, N.Y.

Facing 87, "Emma Malietoa," signed beneath in the center, "engraved by F. Halpin from a sketch by A. T. Agate."

Facing 117, "Malietoa," signed in lower left by A. T. Agate and lower right F. Halpin.

Facing 134, "Samoan Dance," drawn by A. T. Agate and engraved by A. Jones.

Facing 157, "Sydney," drawn by A. T. Agate and engraved by Rawdon, Wright, and Hatch.

Facing 188, "Corrobory (Dance) N. H.," drawn by A. T. Agate and engraved by E. G. Dunnell.

Between 200 and 201, bifolium map, "Settled Part of New South Wales 1840,"engraved by E. Tappan.

Facing 241, "Forest Illawara N. S. W.," drawn by A. T. Agate and engraved by J. A. Rolph.

Facing 302, vignette of "Peacock in Contact with Ice-berg," painted by A. T. Agate and engraved by M. Osborne.

Facing 310, "Vincennes in Disappointment Bay," from sketch by C. Wilkes and engraved by C. A. Jewett.

Facing 325, "View of the Antarctic Continent," from a sketch by C. Wilkes and engraved by Jorban [*sic*] and Halpin.

Facing 369, "View in New Zealand," drawn by A. T. Agate and engraved by G. H. Cushman.

Facing 387, vignette, "Tomb of a New Zealand Chief," signed in lower left by A. T. Agate and lower right by Jordan and Halpin.

Facing 396, "Ko-Towa-Towa, A New Zealand Chief," drawn by A. T. Agate and engraved by V. Balch.

Vol. III.

Facing 3, "Town of Nukwalota, Tonga," Drawn by A. T. Agate and engraved by C. A. Jewett.

Facing 56, "Tanga, King of Ambau," drawn by A. T. Agate and engraved by Rawdon, Wright, and Hatch.

Facing 109, "Town of Rewa," drawn by A. T. Agate and engraved by W. G. Armstrong.

Facing 119, "Interior of Garaningiou's House, Feejee," drawn by A. T. Agate and engraved by J. F. E Prudhomme.

Facing 127, "Queen of Rewa," drawn by A. T. Agate and engraved by Welch and Walter.

Facing 136, "Vendovi," drawn by A. T. Agate and engraved by J. W. Paradise.

Facing 190, "Club Dance, Feejee," drawn by J. Drayton and engraved by Rawdon, Wright, and Hatch.

Facing 220, "Biche-de-Mar House," drawn by A. T. Agate and engraved by J. F. E. Prud-homme.

Facing 231, "Tombs at Muthuata I. Feejee," drawn by A. T. Agate and engraved by J. Smillie.

Facing 239, "Observatory Peak, Feejee, Is.," drawn by A. T. Agate and engraved by Jordan and Halpin.

Facing 292, "Valley of Voona Feejee Is.," sketched by A. T. Agate and engraved by Jordan and Halpin.

Facing 391, "Pali, Oahu," sketched by A. T. Agate and engraved by J. B. Neagle.

Vol. IV.

Before title, folding map, "Hawaiian Group, or Sandwich Islands," engraved by W. H. Dougal, N.Y.

Facing 3, "Kamehameha," drawn by A. T. Agate and engraved by Welch and Walter.

Facing 51, "Hanapepe Valley," drawn by A. T. Agate and engraved by J. Andrews.

Facing 69, "Grove of Kukui Trees, Kauai," drawn by A. T. Agate and engraved by J. A. Rolph, N.Y.

Facing 100, "Temple of Kaili, Island of Hawaii," drawn by T. R. Peale and engraved by F. Humphrys.

Facing 111, "Crater of Moku-A-Weo-Weo on the top of Mouna-Loa Hawaii," drawn by C. Wilkes and engraved by J. Andrews and J. Duthie.

Facing 125, "View of the Crater Kilauea," signed in lower left by J. Drayton and lower right by Jordan and Halpin.

Facing 145, "Camp of Pendulum Park," sketched by C. Wilkes and engraved by J. N. Gimbrede.

Facing 159, "Crater of Moku-A-Weo-Weo," sketched by C. Wilkes and engraved by J. Andrews and J. Duthie.

Facing 165, "Crater of Kilauea, Hawaii."

Facing 171, "Wall of Crater, Kilauea," J. Drayton, del. J. F. E. Prudhomme, sc.

Facing 235, "Kekauluohi," drawn by A. T. Agate and engraved by Welch and Walter.

Facing 254, "Crater on East Maui, called by the natives Haleakala," drawn by J. Drayton, engraved by J. Andrews and J. Duthie.

Facing 321, "Concomely's Tomb, Astoria," drawn by A. T. Agate and engraved by W. E. Tucker.

Facing 341, "Chinook Lodge," drawn by A. T. Agate and engraved by R. W. Dodson.

Facing 493, "Wreck of the Peacock," drawn by A. T. Agate and engraved by T. House.

Vol. V.

Before title, bifolium map, "Groups in the Western Part of the Pacific Ocean," not signed.

Facing 3, "Scene at Oatafu Island," sketched by A. T. Agate and engraved by W. E. Tucker.

Facing 14, "Cocoanut Grove at Fakaafo or Bowditch I.," sketched by A. T. Agate and engraved by J. Smillie.

Facing 26, "Ficus or Banyan, Tree, Upolu," sketched by A. T. Agate and engraved by Rawdon, Wright, and Hatch.

Facing 52, "Utiroa," sketched by A. T. Agate and engraved by T. House.

Facing 56, "Interior of Mariapa, Drummond's I.," sketched by A. T. Agate and engraved by Rawdon, Wright, and Hatch.

Facing 79, "Chief of Eta," sketched by A. T. Agate and engraved by J. W. Paradise.

Facing 113, "Astoria, Columbia River," sketched by A. T. Agate and engraved by Rawdon, Wright, and Hatch.

Facing 116, "Pine Forest, Oregon," sketched by J. Drayton and engraved by W. E. Tucker.

Between 150 and 151, bifolium "Map of Upper California, by the U. S. Ex. Ex. and Best Authorities 1841."

Facing 240, "Shasty Peak," sketched by A. T. Agate and engraved by by G. B. Ellis.

Facing 245, "Encampment of the Sacramento," sketched by A. T. Agate and engraved by J. W. Steel.

Facing 275, "City of Manilla," sketched by J. A. Rolph and engraved by A. T. Agate.

Facing 292, "Manilla Cottage," sketched by A. T. Agate and engraved by J. Smillie.

Between 322 and 323, bifolium "Map of the Sooloo Sea and Archipelago by the U. S. Ex. Ex. 1842."

Facing 333, "Masque in the Town of Sooloo," sketched by A. T. Agate and engraved by J. B. Neagle.

Facing 337, "Son of the Sultan Sooloo," sketched by A. T. Agate and engraved by Halpin.

Facing 371, "Chinese Temple, Singapore," sketched by A. T. Agate and engraved by J. A. Rolph.

Between 456 and 457, bifolium, "Map Illustrative of the Currents and Whaling Grounds by the U. S. Ex. Ex.," not signed.

BINDING

Front and back board. 289 × 189 med. brown ribbed cloth with ornate blind-stamped frame and a gilt-stamped vignette of an eagle and shield in the middle. *Spine.* Blind stamped with five bands and ornaments in panels 1 and 3, gilt stamped in the second panel 'UNITED | STATES | EXPLORING | EXPEDITION | [thin rule] | VOL. 1. [2–5]', gilt stamped in fourth panel with vignette of explorer holding map with a ship in the background. *Endpapers.* Pale yellow.

REFERENCES

Hayes p. 311; Roosevelt p. 44; Roorbach p. 584; Putnam p. 155; cf. Fillmore 1861 p. 226.

COPY DESCRIBED

ViU Q115 W66 1845 *Leaf.* 228 × 180.

Atlas.

TITLE PAGE

ATLAS. | NARRATIVE | OF THE | UNITED STATES | EXPLORING EXPEDITION. | DURING THE YEARS | 1838, 1839, 1840, 1841, 1842. | BY | CHARLES WILKES, U. S. N., | COMMANDER OF THE EXPEDITION, | MEMBER OF THE AMERICAN PHILOSOPHICAL SOCIETY, ETC. | IN FIVE VOLUMES, AND AN ATLAS. | [thin rule] | PHILADELPHIA: LEA & BLANCHARD. | 1845.

PAGINATION

[4] (followed by five folding maps)

CONTENTS

[1] title, [2] copyright statement and printer's imprint, [3] contents, [4] blank.

PLATES

Five large folded maps:

> *Note.* The plates in this copy are too fragile to unfold. The descriptions below are transcribed from the contents page in the volume.

Track Map (colored).

This map shows the tracks of the vessels of the exploring Squadron, combined and acting separately; the direction of the winds; the currents, their direction and velocity; the isothermal lines for every five degrees of temperature, from the point of perpetual congelation to the Torrid Zone. (See explanation on Map.)

Map of the Antarctic Continent.

This map exhibits the daily tracks of the vessels along the land discovered by the Expedition,—the winds, currents, temperature, lines of variation, and icy barrier by which Antarctica is bounded.

Map of the Feejee Group.

This Map embraces the Viti or Feejee Group, consisting of one hundred and fifty-four islands, with numerous coral reefs, &c.

Map of the Oregon Territory.

This embraces the United States possessions west of the Rocky Mountains, between the parallels of 42° and 54° 40' N., and also shows Fremont's Pass through the Rocky Mountains.

Map of the Southeast Portion of Hawaii.

This Map exhibits the two remarkable volcanic mountains visited by the Expedition, with their numerous craters, together with the great eruption of 1840, and the track of the party to and from the crater of Moku-a-weo-weo, on the top of Mauna Loa.

BINDING

Same as the first five volumes except for the front board and the spine. *Front board.* Not gilt stamped with the eagle; instead it is gilt stamped with 'ATLAS I U. S. I EXPLORING EXPEDITION'. *Spine.* Blind-stamped decoration at head and foot, gilt-stamped 'U. S. EXPLORING EXPEDITION VOL. 6. [reads from foot to head.]'

REFERENCES

(same as *Narrative* above)

COPY DESCRIBED

ViU Q115 W66 1845 *Leaf.* 280 × 175.

---

1. "Wilkes Expedition," in *The Oxford Companion to United States History,* ed. Paul Boyer (Oxford: Oxford University Press, 2001), 830.

2. Ibid.

3. Daniel C. Haskell, *The United States Exploring Expedition, 1838–1842 and Its Publications 1844–1874* (New York: The New York Public Library, 1942), 9, 17–18. Haskell provides a thorough account of the complex publication history of the *Narrative.*

4. DLC: Q115 W66 1845.

5. Qtd. in Haskell, *United States Exploring Expedition,* 39–40.

～

194. Wilks, Washington. *The Half Century: Its History, Political and Social.* London: Gilpin, 1852.

In the *Half Century* (1852) Washington Wilks (1826–64) chronicles British history from 1800 to 1850. He claims to provide a "history of opinions, rather than of events" and to subordinate "even the narration of legislative proceedings to the exhibition of what the people felt and did" (iv). A reviewer for the *London Athenaeum* characterized the *Half Century* as a "free and spirited account of the troubles, organization, and progress borne and achieved" during the previous fifty years. The same writer, however, also faulted the *Half Century* as too general but recommended it as "a convenient compilation for classes of readers who have not many books of reference near at hand."[1]

109,399 voucher 4: Wilkes Half Century $1.50.
Purchased from Franck Taylor on March 25, 1852.
Hayes Catalogue: Wilks, W. *The Half Century, Its History.* London, 1852. 12°

TITLE PAGE
THE | HALF CENTURY: | ITS HISTORY, POLITICAL AND SOCIAL. | BY WASHINGTON WILKS. | [thin rule] | "HISTORY MAY BE DEFINED AS THE BIOGRAPHY OF NATIONS."—*Dr. Arnold.* | [thin rule] | LONDON: | C. GILPIN, 5, BISHOPGATE STREET WITHOUT, | AND ALL BOOKSELLERS. | [thin rule] | MDCCCLII.

PAGINATION
i–xvi i–iv 1–348.

CONTENTS
i title, ii printer's imprint, iii–iv preface, v–xvi contents, i–iv proem, 1–344 text, 345–48 "A tabular and chronological arrangement of the principal officers of the state, 1800 to 1850."

REFERENCES
Hayes p. 311; cf. Putnam p. 14-s.

COPY DESCRIBED
DLC D358 W68. *Leaf.* 182 × 117.

---

1. *London Athenaeum,* June 12, 1852, 652.

～

195. Wirt, William. *Memoirs of the Life of William Wirt.* Ed. John P. Kennedy. 2 vols. Philadelphia: Lea and Blanchard, 1849.

William Wirt (1772–1834), known for his rhetorical skill and charisma, achieved fame as a prosecutor in the trial of Aaron Burr. He later served as United States Attorney General for twelve years (1817–29) during the administrations of James Monroe and John Quincy Adams. At least one reviewer of Wirt's *Memoirs* praised him as an ideal example of the "rise of the common man," describing him as "one of those instances of successful talent so often seen in this country. The son of a tavern-keeper at Bladensburgh, he rose to high rank in the profession . . . enjoyed personal friendships with Jefferson, Madison, and Monroe, and became Attorney General of the United States.[1]

John Pendleton Kennedy (1795–1870), the editor of Wirt's *Memoirs,* served in the House of Representatives with Millard Fillmore in the twenty-seventh Congress and was later appointed secretary of the navy by Fillmore. In addition to compiling the *Memoirs,* he published two fictional works, *Swallow Barn* (1832) and *Horse-Shoe Robinson* (1835), both of which the Fillmores owned in their personal library. On March 17, 1851, Kennedy sent a presentation copy of Wirt's *Memoirs* to President Fillmore as a token of their friendship enclosed with the following note: "I beg you to receive this work as a grateful remembrance of a comrade in that happy and glorious Twenty Seventh Congress which was no less distinguished for its service to the nation than for the occasions it furnished to many warm and enduring friendships."[2] Prior to receiving this personal gift, Fillmore had purchased a copy of the *Memoirs* for the White House collection.

105,133 voucher 5: Kennedy's Life of Wirt 2 vols. 8vo $4.00.
Purchased from Charles Welford on December 13, 1850.
Roosevelt Catalogue: Kennedy, John P. *Memoirs of the Life of William Wirt.* Philadelphia, Lea
    & Blanchard, 1849, 2 vols.

TITLE PAGE
MEMOIRS I OF I THE LIFE I OF I WILLIAM WIRT, I ATTORNEY GENERAL OF THE UNITED STATES, I BY I JOHN P. KENNEDY. I [thin wavy rule] I IN TWO VOLUMES. I VOL. I. [II.] I [thin wavy rule] I PHILADELPHIA: I LEA AND BLANCHARD. I 1849.

PAGINATION
Vol. I. 1–418.
Vol. II. 1–452.

CONTENTS
Vol. I. 1 half title, 2 blank, 3 title, 4 copyright statement and printer's imprint, 5 dedication
    to the young men of the United States, 6 blank, 7–11 contents, 12 blank, 13–14 introduc-
    tion, 15–417 text, 418 blank.
Vol. II. 1 title, 2 copyright statement and printer's imprint, 3–7 contents, 8 blank, 9–450 text,
    451 errata, 452 blank.

PLATES
Vol. I.
Engraved portrait frontispiece of William Wirt, engraved by A. B. Walter from a portrait by
    Charles B. King, Lea and Blanchard, 1849.
Vol. II.
Facing title, folding facsimile of a letter to William Wirt from John Adams.

REFERENCES
Hayes p. 312; Roosevelt p. 24; Putnam p. 73, cf. 174; Roorbach p. 591; cf. Fillmore Packing Lists p. 4; cf. Fillmore ca. 1858 p. 70; cf. Fillmore 1861 p. 226.

COPY DESCRIBED
DLC: E 340 W79 K29. *Leaf.* 230 × 140.

---

1. *The American Quarterly Register and Magazine (1848–1849),* December 1849, available at *APS Online,* http://www.proquest.com/products_pq/descriptions/aps.shtml.

2. John Pendleton Kennedy, letter to President Fillmore, March 17, 1851, Millard Fillmore Papers, BECHS.

APPENDIX A

A List of the Books Purchased for the
First White House Library, 1850–1853

A double asterisk (**) indicates a title for which the original Executive Mansion copy of the book has been located. A dagger (†) indicates a title that President Fillmore ordered apart from Charles Lanman's purchasing trip. A double dagger (‡) indicates a book recommended to the president by Edward Everett.

1. Abbott, Charles. *A Treatise of the Law Relative to Merchant Ships and Seamen.* Ed. J. C. Perkins. [5th or 6th American ed.] Boston: Little and Brown, [1846 or 1850].
2. Adams, John. *A Defence of the Constitutions of Government of the United States.* London: John Stockdale, 1794.
3. *Aesop's Fables; A New Version Chiefly from Original Sources.* Trans. Thomas James. Illus. John Tenniel. New York: R. B. Collins, 1850.
4. Aikin, John. *The Works of the British Poets Selected and Chronologically Arranged.* 3 vols. Philadelphia: A. Hart, 1850.
5. Alison, Archibald. *History of Europe from the Commencement of the French Revolution to the Restoration of the Bourbons in MDCCCXV.* 14 vols. Edinburgh and London: William Blackwood and Sons, 1849.
†6. *American Almanac and Repository of Useful Knowledge.* 22 vols. Boston: Gray and Bowen, 1830–51.
†7. *American Quarterly Register and Magazine.* Ed. James Stryker. Philadelphia, 1848–53.
8. *The American Review: A Whig Journal.* New York: Wiley and Putnam, 1845–47; *A Whig Journal Devoted to Politics and Literature* (1847–50); and *The American Whig Review* (1850–52).
9. *The Annual Biography and Obituary.* 21 vols. London: Longman, et al., 1817–37.
10. *Arabian Nights.* Ed. Edward Lane. 3 vols. London: Murray, 1850.
†11. Atcheson, Nathaniel. *Report of a Case Recently Argued and Determined in His Majesty's Court of the King's Bench.* London: Butterworth, et al., 1800.
12. Bacon, Francis. *The Works of Francis Bacon.* Ed. Basil Montagu. 3 vols. Philadelphia: Carey and Hart, 1848.
†13. Bancroft, George. *History of the United States.* 4 vols. Boston: Little and Brown, 1850–52.
**14. Barthélemy, Jean Jacques. *Travels of Anacharsis the Younger in Greece.* 6th ed. 6 vols. London: Rivington, Clarke, Longman et al., 1825.
———. *Maps, Plans, Views, and Coins, Illustrative of the Travels of Anacharsis the Younger in Greece.* 6th ed. London: Rivington, Clarke, Longman et al., 1825.
†15. *Bible.*

†16. Blackstone, Sir William. *Commentaries on the Laws of England.* Ed. John Wendell. 4 vols. New York: Harper, 1847.

†17. *Blackwood's Edinburgh Magazine.* Edinburgh: Blackwood, 1817–51.

18. Boswell, James. *Life of Johnson.* Ed. John Wilson Croker. London: Murray, 1848.

19. Bouvier, John. *A Law Dictionary.* 3rd ed. 2 vols. Philadelphia: T. and J. W. Johnson, 1848.

20. *British Essayists.* London: Jones, 1825–29.

21. Brougham, Henry Lord. *Speeches.* 4 vols. Edinburgh: Adam and Charles Black, et al., 1838.

22. ———. *Political Philosophy.* 3 vols. London: Knight and Co., 1846.

†23. Browne, Arthur. *A Compendious View of the Civil Law, and of the Law of Admiralty.* 2nd ed. 2 vols. London: Butterworth, 1802.

24. Burke, Edmund. *Works of Edmund Burke.* 9 vols. Boston: Little and Brown, 1839.

†25. Burns, Robert. *The Works.*

26. Burton, Robert. *The Anatomy of Melancholy.* London: [Blake or Tegg], 1849.

‡†27. *Cabinet Library of Scarce and Celebrated Tracts.* Edinburgh: Thomas Clark, 1837.

†28. Calhoun, John C. *A Disquisition on Government and a Discourse on the Constitution and Government of the United States.* Ed. Richard K. Cralle. Columbia, S.C.: Johnston, 1851.

**29. Campbell, John Lord. *The Lives of the Lord Chancellors and the Keepers of the Great Seal of England.* 3rd ed. 7 vols. London: Murray, 1848.

30. ———. *The Lives of the Chief Justices of England.* 2 vols. Boston: Little and Brown, 1850.

31. Campbell, William W. *Life and Writings of De Witt Clinton.* New York: Baker and Scribner, 1849.

32. Carey, Henry Charles. *Principles of Political Economy.* 3 vols. Philadelphia: Carey, Lea & Blanchard, 1837–40.

33. Catlin, George. *Illustration of the Manners, Customs, and Condition of the North American Indians.* 2 vols.

‡†34. Chalmers, George. *Opinions of Eminent Lawyers.* 2 vols. London: Reed and Hunter, 1814.

35. Chambers, Robert, and William Chambers. *Chambers's Miscellany of Useful and Entertaining Tracts.* 20 vols. in 10. Edinburgh: Chambers, 1847–48.

36. Chase, Lucien B. *History of the Polk Administration.* New York: Putnam, 1850.

37. Chillingworth, William. *The Works.* 3 vols. Oxford: Oxford University Press, 1838.

‡†38. Chitty, Joseph. *A Practical Treaty on the Law of Nations.* London: Clarke and Son, 1812.

†39. Clarke, Mary Cowden. *The Complete Concordance to Shakespeare.* London: Charles Knight, 1845.

40. Colton, Calvin. *The Life and Times of Henry Clay.* 2 vols. New York: A. S. Barnes and Co., 1846.

41. ———. *Public Economy for the United States.* 2nd ed. New York: A. S. Barnes and Co., 1849.

42. Cooper, James Fenimore. *The History of the Navy of the United States of America.* 2 vols. London: Bentley, 1839.

†43. Curran, John Philpot. *The Speeches of the Right Honorable John Philpot Curran.* Ed. Thomas Davies. London: Bohn, 1847.

44. Cuvier, Georges. *Animal Kingdom.* 8 vols. London: G. Henderson, 1834–37.

45. Davis, Matthew L. *Memoirs of Aaron Burr.* 2 vols. New York: Harper, 1836.

46. Dodd, Charles R. *A Manual of Dignities, Privilege, and Precedence.* London: Whittaker, 1844.

47. Domat, Jean. *The Civil Law in Its Natural Order.* Ed. Luther S. Cushing. 2 vols. Boston: Little and Brown, 1850.

48. Dwight, Theodore. *History of the Hartford Convention.* New York: N. & J. White, 1833.

49. Eaton, John Henry. *The Life of Andrew Jackson.*

50. Edgeworth, Maria. *Tales and Novels.* 9 vols. London: Whittaker and Co., et al., 1848.

51. *The Edinburgh Review, or Critical Journal.* Edinburgh: A. and C. Black, 1802–46.

52. *Encyclopaedia Americana.* Ed. Francis Lieber and E. Wigglesworth. 14 vols. Philadelphia: Lea and Blanchard, 1849.

53. Erskine, Thomas. *The Speeches of the Hon. Thomas Erskine.* 2 vols. New York: Eastburn, Kirk, and Co., 1813.

†**54. Fisher, Richard S. *The Book of the World.* 2 vols. New York: J. H. Colton, 1849.

55. Fleming, Charles, and J. Tibbins. *Royal Dictionary English and French and French and English.* 2 vols. Paris: Didot, 1844.

    Franklin, Benjamin. *The Works of Benjamin Franklin.* 10 vols. Ed. Jared Sparks. Boston: Tappan, Whittemore, and Mason, n.d.

    See Sparks, Jared, entry 162.

†56. Fynn, Robert. *British Consuls Abroad.* London: E. Wilson, 1851.

57. Garland, Hugh A. *The Life of John Randolph of Roanoke.* 2 vols. New York: Appleton, 1850.

**58. Gibbon, Edward. *The History of the Decline and Fall of the Roman Empire.* Ed. H. H. Milman. 2nd ed. 6 vols. London: Murray, 1846.

59. Goldsmith, Oliver. *The Miscellaneous Works.* Ed. James Prior. 4 vols. New York: Putnam, 1850.

60. Goodman, Godfrey. *The Court of King James the First.* 2 vols. London: Bentley, 1839.

†61. Grahame, James. *The History of the United States of North America.* 2 vols. Philadelphia: Lea and Blanchard, 1850.

62. Gray, Asa. *The Botanical Text-book.* 3rd ed. New York: George P. Putnam, 1850.

63. Greenleaf, Simon. *A Treatise on the Law of Evidence.* 3rd ed. 2 vols. Boston: C. C. Little and J. Brown, 1844–46.

64. Griswold, Rufus Wilmot. *The Prose Writers of America.* 3rd ed. rev. Philadelphia: Carey and Hart, 1849.

65. ———. *The Poets and Poetry of America.* Philadelphia: Carey and Hart.

**66. Grote, George. *History of Greece.* 2nd ed. 12 vols. London: John Murray, 1849.

‡†67. Grotius, Hugo. *The Rights of War and Peace.* Ed. J. Barbeyrac. London: W. Innys, et al., 1738.

68. Guizot, François. *The History of Civilization from the Fall of the Roman Empire to the French Revolution.* Trans. William Hazlitt. Ed. Caleb Sprague Henry. 4 vols. New York: Appleton, 1846.

†**69. Hallam, Henry. *The Constitutional History of England from the Accession of Henry VII to the Death of George II.* 2 vols. London: Murray, 1846.

70. ———. *View of the State of Europe During the Middle Ages.*

71. Hamilton, Alexander, John Jay, and James Madison. *The Federalist.*

72. Hammond, Jabez. *The History of Political Parties in the State of New York.* 4th ed. 2 vols. Cooperstown, N.Y.: Phinney, 1846.

73. *Harper's Classical Library.* 36 vols. New York: Harper, 1844–48.

†74. Haskell, Daniel, and J. Calvin Smith. *A Complete Descriptive and Statistical Gazetteer of the United States of America.* New York: Sherman and Smith, 1850.

†75. Haydn, Joseph. *Book of Dignities.* London: Longman, Brown, Green, and Longmans, 1851.

‡†76. Heineccius, John Gottlieb. *A Methodical System of Universal Law.* Ed. and trans. George Turnbull. 2 vols. London: George Keith, 1763.

77. Herschel, John F. W. *Outlines of Astronomy.* London: Longman, 1849.

†78. Hildreth, Richard. *The History of the United States of America.* 6 vols. New York: Harper and Brothers, 1849–52.

79. Hope, Thomas. *Costume of the Ancients.* 2 vols. London: Bohn, 1841.

†80. Hume, David. *The History of England.* 6 vols. New York: Harper, 1850.

†81. *Index to Review.*

82. Irving, Washington. *The Works of Washington Irving.* 15 vols. New York: Putnam, 1849–51.

83. Jefferson, Thomas. *Memoir, Correspondence, and Miscellanies, from the Papers of Thomas Jefferson.* Ed. Thomas Jefferson Randolph. 4 vols. Charlottesville, Va.: Carr, 1829.

84. Jenkins, John S. *The Life of Silas Wright.* Auburn, N.Y.: Alden and Markham, 1847.

†85. ———. *The New Clerk's Assistant, or, Book of Practical Forms.* 4th ed., revised and enlarged. Auburn, N.Y.: Derby and Miller, 1850.

†86. *The Jesuit.*

87. Johnson, Samuel. *The Works of Samuel Johnson, LL. D.* Ed. Arthur Murphy. 2 vols. London: Jones, 1825.

†88. Johnston, Alexander Keith. *The National Atlas of Historical, Commercial and Political Geography*. Edinburgh: Blackwood, 1850.

89. ———. *Dictionary of Geography, Descriptive, Physical, Statistical, and Historical, Forming a Complete General Gazetteer of the World*. London: Longman, Brown, Green, and Longmans, 1851.

90. Junius. *Letters by the Same Writer, Under Other Signatures*. 3 vols. London: Rivington et al., 1812.

†91. Keily, James. *A Map of the City of Washington*. Camden, New Jersey: Lloyd Van Derveer, 1851.

‡†92. Kent, James. *Commentaries on American Law*. 6th ed. 4 vols. New York: Kent, 1848.

†93. Klapka, György. *Memoirs of the War of Independence in Hungary*. 2 vols. London: C. Gilpin, 1850.

94. Lafayette, Marie J. P. Y. G. M., Marquis de. *Memoirs, Correspondence and Manuscripts*. 3 vols. London: Saunders and Otley, 1837.

†95. Lamartine, Alphonse de. *History of the French Revolution of 1848*. Boston: Phillips Sampson & Co., 1849.

†96. Linden, Johannes van der. *Institutes of the Laws of Holland*. Trans. Jabez Henry. London: J. and W. T. Clarke, 1828.

97. Lingard, John. *A History of England from the First Invasion by the Romans*. 5th ed. 8 vols. Paris: Baudry, 1840.

98. Locke, John. *Essay on Human Understanding*. London: Tegg, [1828, 1841, 1846, or 1849].

99. Lockhart, John Gibson. *Memoirs of the Life of Sir Walter Scott*. 4 vols. Paris: Baudry, 1838.

†100. Lolme, Jean Louis de. *The Rise and Progress of the English Constitution*. Ed. A. J. Stephens. 2 vols. London: Parker, 1838.

101. Lyell, Charles. *Principles of Geology*. 8th ed. London: Murray, 1850.

102. Macaulay, Thomas Babington. *History of England*. 2 vols. New York: Harper, 1849.

103. McCullagh, W. Torrens. *The Industrial History of Free Nations*. 2 vols. London: Chapman and Hall, 1846.

104. McCulloch, John Ramsay. *A Dictionary, Practical, Theoretical, and Historical of Commerce and Commercial Navigation*. Ed. Henry Vethake, LL.D. 2 vols. Philadelphia: Carey and Hart, 1849.

†**105. MacGregor, John. *Commercial Statistics*. 5 vols. London: Whittaker and Co., 1847.

106. ———. *Progress of America to 1846*. 2 vols. London: Whittaker and Co., 1847.

†107. Machiavelli, Niccolò. *The History of Florence with the Prince*. London: Bohn, 1851.

108. Malthus, Thomas Robert. *An Essay on the Principle of Population*. 4th ed. 2 vols. London: J. Johnson, 1807.

‡†109. Manning, William Oke. *Commentaries on the Law of Nations*. London: S. Sweet, 1839.

‡†110. Martens, Georg Friedrich von. *The Law of Nations: Being the Science of National Law*. 4th ed. London: Cobbett, 1829.

111. Martin, Montgomery R. *British Colonial Library*. 10 vols. London: Bohn, 1844.

112. *The Merchants' Magazine and Commercial Review*. Ed. Freeman Hunt. New York: 1840–50.

113. Michelet, Jules. *Historical View of the French Revolution*. Trans. C. Cocks. London: Bohn, 1848.

114. ———. *History of the Roman Republic*. Trans. William Hazlitt. 1847. [Either London: Bogue, or New York: Appleton.]

115. Mill, John Stuart. *Principles of Political Economy*. 2 vols. Boston: Little and Brown, 1848.

†116. Mills, Abraham. *The Literature and the Literary Men of Great Britain and Ireland*. 2 vols. New York: Harper, 1851.

117. Milton, John. *The Poetical Works of John Milton with Notes and a Life of the Author*. 2 vols. Boston: Little and Brown, 1845.

118. ———. *The Prose Works of John Milton: With a Biographical Introduction*. Ed. Rufus Wilmot Griswold. 2 vols. Philadelphia: Herman Hooker, 1845.

†119. Mitchell, Samuel Augustus. *New Universal Atlas Containing Maps of the Various Empires, Kingdoms, States and Republics of the World with a Special Map of Each of the United States*

Plans of Cities &c. Comprehended in Seventy Sheets and Forming a Series of One Hundred and Seventeen Maps Plans and Sections. Philadelphia: Thomas Cowperthwait and Co., 1850.

120. Murray, Hugh. *Encyclopaedia of Geography.* 3 vols. Philadelphia: Lea and Blanchard, 1848.

121. Niebuhr, Barthold Georg. *Lectures on the History of Rome.* Ed. Leonard Schmitz. 3 vols. London: Taylor, Walton, and Maberly, 1850.

122. Niles, Hezekiah. *The Weekly Register.* Baltimore: Niles, 1811–49.

123. *North American Review and Miscellaneous Journal.* Boston: Wells and Lilly, 1815–50.

†124. *Official Opinions of the Attorneys General.* 5 vols. Washington: Farnham, 1852.

†125. Paget, John. *Hungary and Transylvania.* 2 vols. Philadelphia: Lea and Blanchard, 1850.

126. Paley, William. *Paley's Works.* London: Bohn, 1847.

127. Pardoe, Julia. *Louis the Fourteenth and the Court of France in the Seventeenth Century.* 3rd ed. 3 vols. London: Bentley, 1849.

128. *The Penny Cyclopaedia.* 16 vols. London: Charles Knight, 1833–43.

129. Phillips, Charles. *Curran and His Contemporaries.* New York: Harper, 1851.

†130. Phillips, Samuel. *Essays from the London Times.* 1st ser. New York: Appleton, 1852.

131. Prescott, William H. *The History of the Reign of Ferdinand and Isabella, the Catholic.* 3 vols. New York: Harper, 1849.

132. ———. *History of the Conquest of Mexico.* 3 vols. New York: Harper, 1849.

**133. ———. *History of the Conquest of Peru.* 2 Vols. New York: Harper, 1848.

134. Prichard, James Cowles. *The Natural History of Man: Comprising Inquiries into the Modifying Influence of Physical and Moral Agencies on the Different Tribes of the Human Family.* London: H. Baillière, 1848.

‡135. Pufendorf, Samuel. *Law of Nature and Nations.* 5th ed. Trans. Basil Kennet. London: J. and J. Bonwicke, et al., 1749.

†136. Pulszky, Theresa. *Memoirs of a Hungarian Lady.* Philadelphia: Lea and Blanchard, 1850.

137. Putnam, George P. *The World's Progress: A Dictionary of Dates, with Tabular Views of General History, and a Historical Chart.* New York: Putnam, either 1850 or 1851.

‡†138. Reddie, James. *Inquiries in International Law.* Edinburgh: Blackwood and Sons, 1842.

139. Robertson, William. *The Works.* London: William Ball, 1840.

‡†140. Robinson, Christopher. *Collectanea Maritima.* London: White and Butterworth, 1801.

141. Russell, William. *The History of Modern Europe.* 3 vols. New York: Harper, 1849.

‡†142. Rutherforth, Thomas. *Institutes of Natural Law.* 2 vols. Cambridge: Thurlborn, Beecroft, and Innys, 1754–56.

143. Sabine, Lorenzo. *The American Loyalists.* Boston: Little and Brown, 1847.

144. Sage, Alain René Le. *The Adventures of Gil Blas of Santillane.* Trans. Tobias Smollett. 2 vols. London: Dubochet, 1836.

145. Sanders, Francis Williams, George Williams Sanders, and John Warner. *An Essay on Uses and Trusts: And on the Nature and Operation of Conveyances at Common Law: And of Those Which Derive Their Effect from the Statute of Uses.* 2 vols. London: A. Maxwell, 1844.

146. Sanderson, John. *Biography of the Signers of the Declaration of Independence.* 9 vols. Philadelphia: Pomeroy, 1823–27.

‡†147. Schlegel, Johan Frederik Vilhelm. *Neutral Rights, or, an Impartial Examination of the Right of Search of Neutral Vessels under Convoy and of a Judgment Pronounced by the English Court of Admiralty, the 11th June, 1799, in the Case of the Swedish Convoy : With Some Additions and Corrections.*

148. Schömann, George Fredrich. *A Dissertation on the Assemblies of the Athenians.* Cambridge: Grant, 1838.

**149. Scott, Walter. *Waverley Novels.* 20 vols. Edinburgh: Cadell, 1847–50.

†150. Semmes, Raphael. *Service Afloat and Ashore.* Cincinnati: Moore, 1851.

†151. Shakespeare, William. *The Dramatic Works of William Shakespeare.* 7 vols. Boston: Phillips, Samson and Co., 1849.

152. Sheridan, Richard Brinsley. *The Speeches of the Right Honourable Richard Brinsley Sheridan.* 3 vols. London: Bohn, 1842.

153. Sismondi, Jean-Charles Léonard de. *Political Economy, and the Philosophy of Government.* London: Chapman, 1847.

154. Smith, Adam. *An Inquiry into the Nature and Causes of the Wealth of Nations.* Ed. J. R. McCulloch. Edinburgh: Adam and Charles Black, and William Tait. London: Longman and Co., 1846.

155. Smith, William. *Dictionary of Greek and Roman Antiquities.* Boston: Little and Brown, 1849.

156. ———. *Dictionary of Greek and Roman Biography and Mythology.* 3 vols. Boston: Little and Brown, 1849.

†157. The Society for the Diffusion of Useful Knowledge. *Maps for the Society for the Diffusion of Useful Knowledge.* New ed. 3 vols. London: C. Knight, 1846–47.

158. Southey, Robert. *Common Place Book.* Ed. John Wood Warter. Vol. 1. London: Longman, 1849.

**159. Sparks, Jared, ed. *The Library of American Biography.* 1st ser. 10 vols. New York: Harper Brothers, n.d.

160. ———. *The Library of American Biography.* 2nd ser. 15 vols. Boston: Little and Brown, 1848.

161. ———. *The Writings of George Washington.* 12 vols. New York: Harper, 1847.

162. ———. *The Works of Benjamin Franklin.* 10 vols. Boston: Tappan, Whittemore, and Mason, n.d.

†163. Stephen, Henry J. *New Commentaries on the Laws of England.* 4 vols. New York: Halsted and Voorhies, 1841–46.

‡†164. Story, Joseph. *Commentaries on the Constitution of the United States.* 2nd ed. 2 vols. Boston: Little and Brown, 1851.

165. ———. *Commentaries on the Conflicts of Laws.* Boston: Little and Brown. London: A. Maxwell, 1846.

†166. ———. *Commentaries.*

†167. Supreme Court Reports.

†168. Taylor, John. *Summary of the Roman Law.* London: T. Payne, 1772.

169. Taylor, Richard Cowling. *Statistics of Coal.* Philadelphia: J. W. Moore, 1848.

170. Taylor, W. Cooke. *The Life and Times of Sir Robert Peel.* 3 vols. London: Fisher and Son, [1846].

†171. Terrestrial Globe.

172. Thiers, Louis Adolphe. *The History of the French Revolution.* London: Whittaker and Co., n.d.

173. ———. *The History of the Consulate and the Empire of Napoleon.* London: Bohn, 1850.

174. Tocqueville, Alexis de. *Democracy in America.*

†175. *United States Digest: Digest of the Decisions of the Courts of Common Law and Admiralty in the United States.* Vols. 1–11. Boston: Little and Brown, 1840–52.

176. *United States Magazine and Democratic Review.* Washington, D.C.: Langtree and O'Sullivan, 1837–50.

177. Ure, Andrew. *A Dictionary of Arts, Manufactures, and Mines.* 11th American ed. New York: D. Appleton and Co., 1848.

‡†178. Vattel, Emmerich de. *The Law of Nations.* 5th American ed. Philadelphia: T. & J. W. Johnson, 1839.

———. *The Law of Nations.* Ed. Edward D. Ingraham. Philadelphia: T. & J. W. Johnson, 1852.

179. Walpole, Horace. *Memoirs of the Reign of King George the Third.* Ed. Denis le Marchant, 4 vols. London: Bentley, 1845.

‡†180. Ward, Robert. *An Enquiry into the Foundation and History of the Law of Nations in Europe.* 2 vols. London: Butterworth, 1795.

‡†**181. Warden, David Bailie. *On the Origin, Nature, Progress and Influence of Consular Establishments.* Paris: Smith, 1813.

†182. Warren, John Esaias. *Para; Or, Scenes and Adventures on the Banks of the Amazon.* New York: G. Putnam, 1851.

†183. *The Washington City Directory and Congressional, and Executive Register, for 1850.* Comp. Edward Waite. Washington, D.C.: Columbus Alexander, 1850.

Washington, George. *The Writings of George Washington.* Ed. Jared Sparks. 12 vols. New York: Harper, 1847.

See Sparks, Jared, entry 161.

184. Webster, Daniel. *Speeches and Forensic Arguments.* 8th ed. 3 vols. Boston: Tappan, Whittemore, and Mason, 1850.

†185. ———. *The Works of Daniel Webster.* Ed. Edward Everett. 6 vols. Boston: Little and Brown, 1851.

†186. Webster, Noah. *A Dictionary of the English Language.* Springfield, Mass.: G. and C. Merriam, 1850.

†187. Wharton, Francis. *State Trials of the United States During the Administrations of Washington and Adams.* Philadelphia: Carey and Hart, 1849.

‡188. Wheaton, Henry. *Elements of International Law.* Philadelphia: Lea and Blanchard, 1846.

‡189. ———. *History of the Law of Nations in Europe and America.* New York: Gould, Banks, and Co., 1845.

‡†190. Whewell, William. *The Elements of Morality.* 2 vols. London: John W. Parker, 1848.

‡†191. Wicquefort, Abraham de. *The Embassador and His Functions.* London: Lintot, 1716.

‡†192. Wildman, Richard. *Institutes of International Law.* 2 vols. London: Benning, 1849–50.

193. Wilkes, Charles. *Narrative of the United States Exploring Expedition, During the Years 1838, 1839, 1840, 1841, and 1842.* 5 vols. Philadelphia: Lea and Blanchard, 1845.

†194. Wilks, Washington. *The Half Century: Its History, Political and Social.* London: Gilpin, 1852.

195. Wirt, William. *Memoirs of the Life of William Wirt.* Ed. John P. Kennedy. 2 vols. Philadelphia: Lea and Blanchard, 1849.

APPENDIX B

A Subject Index of Books in the
First White House Library Catalogue

ART

79. Hope, Thomas. *Costume of the Ancients.*

BIOGRAPHY

AMERICAN

31. Campbell, William W. *Life and Writings of De Witt Clinton.*
36. Chase, Lucien B. *History of the Polk Administration.*
40. Colton, Calvin. *The Life and Times of Henry Clay.*
42. Cooper, James Fenimore. *The History of the Navy of the United States of America.*
45. Davis, Matthew L. *Memoirs of Aaron Burr.*
49. Eaton, John Henry. *The Life of Andrew Jackson.*
57. Garland, Hugh A. *The Life of John Randolph of Roanoke.*
82. Irving, Washington. *The Works of Washington Irving.*
83. Jefferson, Thomas. *Memoir, Correspondence, and Miscellanies, from the Papers of Thomas Jefferson.*
84. Jenkins, John S. *The Life of Silas Wright.*
143. Sabine, Lorenzo. *The American Loyalists.*
146. Sanderson, John. *Biography of the Signers of the Declaration of Independence.*
150. Semmes, Raphael. *Service Afloat and Ashore.*
159. Sparks, Jared, ed. *The Library of American Biography.* 1st ser.
160. ———. *The Library of American Biography.* 2nd ser.
161. ———. *The Writings of George Washington.*
162. ———. *The Works of Benjamin Franklin.*
195. Wirt, William. *Memoirs of the Life of William Wirt.*

BRITISH

9. *The Annual Biography and Obituary.*
18. Boswell, James. *Life of Johnson.*
29. Campbell, John Lord. *The Lives of the Lord Chancellors and the Keepers of the Great Seal of England.*
30. ———. *The Lives of the Chief Justices of England.*

35. Chambers, Robert, and William Chambers. *Chambers's Miscellany of Useful and Entertaining Tracts.*
60. Goodman, Godfrey. *The Court of King James the First.*
82. Irving, Washington. *The Works of Washington Irving.*
99. Lockhart, John Gibson. *Memoirs of the Life of Sir Walter Scott.*
116. Mills, Abraham. *The Literature and the Literary Men of Great Britain and Ireland.*
129. Phillips, Charles. *Curran and His Contemporaries.*
143. Sabine, Lorenzo. *The American Loyalists.*
170. Taylor, W. Cooke. *The Life and Times of Sir Robert Peel.*
179. Walpole, Horace. *Memoirs of the Reign of King George the Third.*

FRENCH

94. Lafayette, Marie J. P. Y. G. M., Marquis de. *Memoirs, Correspondence and Manuscripts.*
127. Pardoe, Julia. *Louis the Fourteenth and the Court of France in the Seventeenth Century.*

GEOGRAPHY

54. Fisher, Richard S. *The Book of the World.*
74. Haskell, Daniel, and J. Calvin Smith. *A Complete Descriptive and Statistical Gazetteer of the United States of America.*
88. Johnston, Alexander Keith. *The National Atlas of Historical, Commercial and Political Geography.*
89. ———. *Dictionary of Geography, Descriptive, Physical, Statistical, and Historical, Forming a Complete General Gazetteer of the World.*
91. Keily, James. *A Map of the City of Washington.*
119. Mitchell, Samuel Augustus. *New Universal Atlas Containing Maps of the Various Empires, Kingdoms, States and Republics of the World with a Special Map of Each of the United States Plans of Cities &c. Comprehended in Seventy Sheets and Forming a Series of One Hundred and Seventeen Maps Plans and Sections.*
120. Murray, Hugh. *Encyclopaedia of Geography.*
157. The Society for the Diffusion of Useful Knowledge. *Maps for the Society for the Diffusion of Useful Knowledge.*
171. Terrestrial Globe.

GOVERNMENT

107. Machiavelli, Niccolò. *The History of Florence with the Prince.*
127. Pardoe, Julia. *Louis the Fourteenth and the Court of France in the Seventeenth Century.*
191. Wicquefort, Abraham de. *The Embassador and His Functions.*

AMERICAN

2. Adams, John. *A Defence of the Constitutions of Government of the United States.*
28. Calhoun, John C. *A Disquisition on Government and a Discourse on the Constitution and Government of the United States.*
31. Campbell, William W. *Life and Writings of De Witt Clinton.*
36. Chase, Lucien B. *History of the Polk Administration.*
40. Colton, Calvin. *The Life and Times of Henry Clay.*
45. Davis, Matthew L. *Memoirs of Aaron Burr.*
48. Dwight, Theodore. *History of the Hartford Convention.*
49. Eaton, John Henry. *The Life of Andrew Jackson.*

57. Garland, Hugh A. *The Life of John Randolph of Roanoke.*
71. Hamilton, Alexander, John Jay, and James Madison. *The Federalist.*
72. Hammond, Jabez. *The History of Political Parties in the State of New York.*
83. Jefferson, Thomas. *Memoir, Correspondence, and Miscellanies, from the Papers of Thomas Jefferson.*
84. Jenkins, John S. *The Life of Silas Wright.*
143. Sabine, Lorenzo. *The American Loyalists.*
146. Sanderson, John. *Biography of the Signers of the Declaration of Independence.*
159. Sparks, Jared, ed. *The Library of American Biography.* 1st ser.
160. ———. *The Library of American Biography.* 2nd ser.
161. ———. *The Writings of George Washington.*
162. ———. *The Works of Benjamin Franklin.*
164. Story, Joseph. *Commentaries on the Constitution of the United States.*
174. Tocqueville, Alexis de. *Democracy in America.*
181. Warden, David Bailie. *On the Origin, Nature, Progress and Influence of Consular Establishments.*
183. *The Washington City Directory and Congressional, and Executive Register, for 1850.*
184. Webster, Daniel. *Speeches and Forensic Arguments.*
185. ———. *The Works of Daniel Webster.*
193. Wilkes, Charles. *Narrative of the United States Exploring Expedition, During the Years 1838, 1839, 1840, 1841, and 1842.*
195. Wirt, William. *Memoirs of the Life of William Wirt.*

BRITISH

21. Brougham, Henry Lord. *Speeches.*
22. ———. *Political Philosophy.*
24. Burke, Edmund. *Works of Edmund Burke.*
29. Campbell, John Lord. *The Lives of the Lord Chancellors and the Keepers of the Great Seal of England.*
30. ———. *The Lives of the Chief Justices of England.*
43. Curran, John Philpot. *The Speeches of the Right Honorable John Philpot Curran.*
46. Dodd, Charles R. *A Manual of Dignities, Privilege, and Precedence.*
56. Fynn, Robert. *British Consuls Abroad.*
60. Goodman, Godfrey. *The Court of King James the First.*
69. Hallam, Henry. *The Constitutional History of England from the Accession of Henry VII to the Death of George II.*
70. ———. *View of the State of Europe During the Middle Ages.*
75. Haydn, Joseph. *Book of Dignities.*
90. Junius. *Letters by the Same Writer, Under Other Signatures.*
100. Lolme, Jean Louis de. *The Rise and Progress of the English Constitution.*
129. Phillips, Charles. *Curran and His Contemporaries.*
143. Sabine, Lorenzo. *The American Loyalists.*
152. Sheridan, Richard Brinsley. *The Speeches of the Right Honourable Richard Brinsley Sheridan.*
170. Taylor, W. Cooke. *The Life and Times of Sir Robert Peel.*
179. Walpole, Horace. *Memoirs of the Reign of King George the Third.*

HISTORY

137. Putnam, George P. *The World's Progress: A Dictionary of Dates, with Tabular Views of General History, and a Historical Chart.*
139. Robertson, William. *The Works.*

AMERICAN

13. Bancroft, George. *History of the United States.*

28. Calhoun, John C. *A Disquisition on Government and a Discourse on the Constitution and Government of the United States.*

45. Davis, Matthew L. *Memoirs of Aaron Burr.*

48. Dwight, Theodore. *History of the Hartford Convention.*

49. Eaton, John Henry. *The Life of Andrew Jackson..*

57. Garland, Hugh A. *The Life of John Randolph of Roanoke.*

61. Grahame, James. *The History of the United States of North America.*

71. Hamilton, Alexander, John Jay, and James Madison. *The Federalist.*

72. Hammond, Jabez. *The History of Political Parties in the State of New York.*

78. Hildreth, Richard. *The History of the United States of America.*

83. Jefferson, Thomas. *Memoir, Correspondence, and Miscellanies, from the Papers of Thomas Jefferson.*

94. Lafayette, Marie J. P. Y. G. M., Marquis de. *Memoirs, Correspondence and Manuscripts.*

139. Robertson, William. *The Works.*

143. Sabine, Lorenzo. *The American Loyalists.*

146. Sanderson, John. *Biography of the Signers of the Declaration of Independence.*

150. Semmes, Raphael. *Service Afloat and Ashore.*

159. Sparks, Jared, ed. *The Library of American Biography.* 1st ser.

160. ———. *The Library of American Biography.* 2nd ser.

161. ———. *The Writings of George Washington.*

162. ———. *The Works of Benjamin Franklin.*

ANCIENT

14. Barthélemy, Jean Jacques. *Travels of Anacharsis the Younger in Greece.*
   ———. *Maps, Plans, Views, and Coins, Illustrative of the Travels of Anacharsis the Younger in Greece.*

58. Gibbon, Edward. *The History of the Decline and Fall of the Roman Empire.*

66. Grote, George. *History of Greece.*

68. Guizot, François. *The History of Civilization from the Fall of the Roman Empire to the French Revolution.*

114. Michelet, Jules. *History of the Roman Republic.*

121. Niebuhr, Barthold Georg. *Lectures of the History of Rome.*

148. Schömann, George Fredrich. *A Dissertation on the Assemblies of the Athenians.*

155. Smith, William. *Dictionary of Greek and Roman Antiquities.*

156. ———. *Dictionary of Greek and Roman Biography and Mythology.*

BRITISH

29. Campbell, John Lord. *The Lives of the Lord Chancellors and the Keepers of the Great Seal of England.*

30. ———. *The Lives of the Chief Justices of England.*

35. Chambers, Robert, and William Chambers. *Chambers's Miscellany of Useful and Entertaining Tracts.*

43. Curran, John Philpot. *The Speeches of the Right Honorable John Philpot Curran.*

53. Erskine, Thomas. *The Speeches of the Hon. Thomas Erskine.*

60. Goodman, Godfrey. *The Court of King James the First.*

69. Hallam, Henry. *The Constitutional History of England from the Accession of Henry VII to the Death of George II.*

70. ———. *View of the State of Europe During the Middle Ages.*

80. Hume, David. *The History of England.*

97. Lingard, John. *A History of England from the First Invasion by the Romans.*
100. Lolme, Jean Louis de. *The Rise and Progress of the English Constitution.*
102. Macaulay, Thomas Babington. *History of England.*
129. Phillips, Charles. *Curran and His Contemporaries.*
139. Robertson, William. *The Works.*
143. Sabine, Lorenzo. *The American Loyalists.*
179. Walpole, Horace. *Memoirs of the Reign of King George the Third.*
194. Wilks, Washington. *The Half Century: Its History, Political and Social.*

CENTRAL AND SOUTH AMERICAN

132. Prescott, William Hickling. *History of the Conquest of Mexico.*
133. ———. *History of the Conquest of Peru.*

EUROPEAN

5. Alison, Archibald. *History of Europe from the Commencement of the French Revolution to the Restoration of the Bourbons in MDCCCXV.*
68. Guizot, François. *The History of Civilization from the Fall of the Roman Empire to the French Revolution.*
70. Hallam, Henry. *View of the State of Europe During the Middle Ages.*
107. Machiavelli, Niccolò. *The History of Florence with the Prince.*
131. Prescott, William H. *The History of the Reign of Ferdinand and Isabella, the Catholic.*
139. Robertson, William. *The Works.*
141. Russell, William. *The History of Modern Europe.*

FRENCH

68. Guizot, François. *The History of Civilization from the Fall of the Roman Empire to the French Revolution.*
94. Lafayette, Marie J. P. Y. G. M., Marquis de. *Memoirs, Correspondence and Manuscripts.*
95. Lamartine, Alphonse de. *History of the French Revolution of 1848.*
113. Michelet, Jules. *Historical View of the French Revolution.*
127. Pardoe, Julia. *Louis the Fourteenth and the Court of France in the Seventeenth Century.*
172. Thiers, Louis Adolphe. *The History of the French Revolution.*
173. ———. *The History of the Consulate and the Empire of Napoleon.*

INDIAN

139. Robertson, William. *The Works.*

HUNGARY

93. Klapka, György. *Memoirs of the War of Independence in Hungary.*
125. Paget, John. *Hungary and Transylvania.*
136. Pulszky, Theresa. *Memoirs of a Hungarian Lady.*

LAW

1. Abbott, Charles. *A Treatise of the Law Relative to Merchant Ships and Seamen.*
11. Atcheson, Nathaniel. *Report of a Case Recently Argued and Determined in His Majesty's Court of the King's Bench.*
16. Blackstone, Sir William. *Commentaries on the Laws of England.*
19. Bouvier, John. *A Law Dictionary.*
21. Brougham, Henry Lord. *Speeches.*

23. Browne, Arthur. *A Compendious View of the Civil Law, and of the Law of Admiralty.*

24. Burke, Edmund. *Works of Edmund Burke.*

27. *Cabinet Library of Scarce and Celebrated Tracts.*

34. Chalmers, George. *Opinions of Eminent Lawyers.*

38. Chitty, Joseph. *A Practical Treaty on the Law of Nations.*

43. Curran, John Philpot. *The Speeches of the Right Honorable John Philpot Curran.*

47. Domat, Jean. *The Civil Law in Its Natural Order.*

53. Erskine, Thomas. *The Speeches of the Hon. Thomas Erskine.*

63. Greenleaf, Simon. *A Treatise on the Law of Evidence.*

67. Grotius, Hugo. *The Rights of War and Peace.*

76. Heineccius, John Gottlieb. *A Methodical System of Universal Law.*

92. Kent, James. *Commentaries on American Law.*

96. Linden, Johannes van der. *Institutes of the Laws of Holland.*

109. Manning, William Oke. *Commentaries on the Law of Nations.*

110. Martens, Georg Friedrich Von. *The Law of Nations: Being the Science of National Law.*

124. *Official Opinions of the Attorneys General.*

135. Pufendorf, Samuel. *Law of Nature and Nations.*

138. Reddie, James. *Inquiries in International Law.*

140. Robinson, Christopher. *Collectanea Maritima.*

142. Rutherforth, Thomas. *Institutes of Natural Law.*

145. Sanders, Francis Williams, George Williams Sanders, and John Warner. *An Essay on Uses and Trusts: And on the Nature and Operation of Conveyances at Common Law: And of Those Which Derive Their Effect from the Statute of Uses.*

147. Schlegel, Johan Frederik Vilhelm. *Neutral Rights, or, an Impartial Examination of the Right of Search of Neutral Vessels under Convoy and of a Judgment Pronounced by the English Court of Admiralty, the 11th June, 1799, in the Case of the Swedish Convoy: With Some Additions and Corrections.*

152. Sheridan, Richard Brinsley. *The Speeches of the Right Honourable Richard Brinsley Sheridan.*

163. Stephen, Henry J. *New Commentaries on the Laws of England.*

164. Story, Joseph. *Commentaries on the Constitution of the United States.*

165. ———. *Commentaries on the Conflicts of Laws.*

166. ———. *Commentaries.*

167. Supreme Court Reports.

168. Taylor, John. *Summary of the Roman Law.*

175. *United States Digest: Digest of the Decisions of the Courts of Common Law and Admiralty in the United States.*

178. Vattel, Emmerich de. *The Law of Nations.*

180. Ward, Robert. *An Enquiry into the Foundation and History of the Law of Nations in Europe.*

184. Webster, Daniel. *Speeches and Forensic Arguments.*

185. ———. *The Works of Daniel Webster.*

187. Wharton, Francis. *State Trials of the United States During the Administrations of Washington and Adams.*

188. Wheaton, Henry. *Elements of International Law.*

189. ———. *History of the Law of Nations in Europe and America.*

190. Whewell, William. *The Elements of Morality.*

191. Wicquefort, Abraham de. *The Embassador and His Functions.*

192. Wildman, Richard. *Institutes of International Law.*

LITERATURE

DRAMA

  59. Goldsmith, Oliver. *The Miscellaneous Works.*

  87. Johnson, Samuel. *The Works of Samuel Johnson.*

151. Shakespeare, William. *The Dramatic Works of William Shakespeare.*

POETRY

American

  65. Griswold, Rufus Wilmot. *The Poets and Poetry of America.*

British

   4. Aikin, John. *The Works of the British Poets Selected and Chronologically Arranged.*

  25. Burns, Robert. *The Works.*

  35. Chambers, Robert, and William Chambers. *Chambers's Miscellany of Useful and Entertaining Tracts.*

  59. Goldsmith, Oliver. *The Miscellaneous Works.*

  87. Johnson, Samuel. *The Works of Samuel Johnson.*

117. Milton, John. *The Poetical Works of John Milton with Notes and a Life of the Author.*

Classical

  73. *Harper's Classical Library.*

PROSE FICTION

American

  64. Griswold, Rufus Wilmot. *The Prose Writers of America.*

  82. Irving, Washington. *The Works of Washington Irving.*

British

  25. Burns, Robert. *The Works.*

  35. Chambers, Robert, and William Chambers. *Chambers's Miscellany of Useful and Entertaining Tracts.*

  50. Edgeworth, Maria. *Tales and Novels.*

  59. Goldsmith, Oliver. *The Miscellaneous Works.*

  87. Johnson, Samuel. *The Works of Samuel Johnson.*

144. Sage, Alain René Le. *The Adventures of Gil Blas of Santillane.*

149. Scott, Walter. Waverley Novels.

French

  14. Barthélemy, Jean Jacques. *Travels of Anacharsis the Younger in Greece.*

    ———. *Maps, Plans, Views, and Coins, Illustrative of the Travels of Anacharsis the Younger in Greece.*

144. Sage, Alain René Le. *The Adventures of Gil Blas of Santillane.*

Classical

   3. *Aesop's Fables; A New Version Chiefly from Original Sources.*

  73. *Harper's Classical Library.*

Middle Eastern

  10. *Arabian Nights.*

ESSAYS

20. *British Essayists.*
    Johnson, Samuel. *The Rambler.*
    Johnson, Samuel. *The Idler.*
    Town, Mr. *The Connoisseur.*
    Addison, Joseph, and Richard Steele. *The Spectator.*
    Hawkesworth, John. *The Adventurer.*
    Steele, Richard, and Joseph Addison. *The Guardian.*
    Steele, Richard, and Joseph Addison. *The Tatler.*
35. Chambers, Robert, and William Chambers. *Chambers's Miscellany of Useful and Entertaining Tracts.*
64. Griswold, Rufus Wilmot. *The Prose Writers of America.*
73. *Harper's Classical Library.*
87. Johnson, Samuel. *The Works of Samuel Johnson.*
118. Milton, John. *The Prose Works of John Milton: With a Biographical Introduction.*
130. Phillips, Samuel. *Essays from the London Times.*
158. Southey, Robert. *Common Place Book.*

NATIVE AMERICANS

33. Catlin, George. *Illustration of the Manners, Customs, and Condition of the North American Indians.*

PERIODICALS

7. *American Quarterly Register and Magazine.*
8. *The American Review: A Whig Journal.*
17. *Blackwood's Edinburgh Magazine* (September 1817–80).
51. *The Edinburgh Review, or Critical Journal.*
112. *The Merchants' Magazine and Commercial Review.*
122. Niles, Hezekiah. *The Weekly Register* (1811–14).
123. *North American Review and Miscellaneous Journal* (May 1815–April 1821).
130. Phillips, Samuel. *Essays from the London Times.*
176. *United States Magazine and Democratic Review* (1837–52).

PHILOSOPHY

12. Bacon, Francis. *The Works of Francis Bacon.*
26. Burton, Robert. *The Anatomy of Melancholy.*
98. Locke, John. *Essay on Human Understanding.*
107. Machiavelli, Niccolò. *The History of Florence with the Prince.*
126. Paley, William. *Paley's Works.*
190. Whewell, William. *The Elements of Morality.*

POLITICAL ECONOMY AND COMMERCE

32. Carey, Henry Charles. *Principles of Political Economy.*
41. Colton, Calvin. *Public Economy.*
103. McCullagh, W. Torrens. *The Industrial History of Free Nations.*
104. McCulloch, John Ramsay. *A Dictionary, Practical, Theoretical, and Historical of Commerce and Commercial Navigation.*
105. MacGregor, John. *Commercial Statistics.*
106. ———. *Progress of America to 1846.*

108. Malthus, Thomas Robert. *An Essay on the Principle of Population.*
112. *The Merchants' Magazine and Commercial Review.*
115. Mill, John Stuart. *Principles of Political Economy.*
153. Sismondi, Jean-Charles Léonard de. *Political Economy, and the Philosophy of Government.*
154. Smith, Adam. *An Inquiry into the Nature and Causes of the Wealth of Nations.*
169. Taylor, Richard Cowling. *Statistics of Coal.*
177. Ure, Andrew. *A Dictionary of Arts, Manufactures, and Mines.*

PSYCHOLOGY

26. Burton, Robert. *The Anatomy of Melancholy.*

REFERENCE

6. *American Almanac and Repository of Useful Knowledge.*
15. *Bible.*
39. Clarke, Mary Cowden. *The Complete Concordance to Shakespeare.*
46. Dodd, Charles R. *A Manual of Dignities, Privilege, and Precedence.*
52. *Encyclopaedia Americana.*
54. Fisher, Richard S. *The Book of the World.*
55. Fleming, Charles, J. Tibbins, *Royal Dictionary English and French and French and English.*
56. Fynn, Robert. *British Consuls Abroad.*
75. Haydn, Joseph. *Book of Dignities.*
81. *Index to Review.*
85. Jenkins, John S. *The New Clerk's Assistant, or, Book of Practical Forms.*
128. *The Penny Cyclopaedia.*
137. Putnam, George P. *The World's Progress: A Dictionary of Dates, with Tabular Views of General History, and a Historical Chart.*
155. Smith, William. *Dictionary of Greek and Roman Antiquities.*
156. ———. *Dictionary of Greek and Roman Biography and Mythology.*
169. Taylor, Richard Cowling. *Statistics of Coal.*
177. Ure, Andrew. *A Dictionary of Arts, Manufactures, and Mines.*
181. Warden, David Bailie. *On the Origin, Nature, Progress and Influence of Consular Establishments.*
183. *The Washington City Directory and Congressional, and Executive Register, for 1850.*
186. Webster, Noah. *A Dictionary of the English Language.*

RELIGION

15. *Bible.*
37. Chillingworth, William. *The Works.*
126. Paley, William. *Paley's Works.*

RHETORIC

21. Brougham, Henry Lord. *Speeches.*
24. Burke, Edmund. *Works of Edmund Burke.*
43. Curran, John Philpot. *The Speeches of the Right Honorable John Philpot Curran.*
53. Erskine, Thomas. *The Speeches of the Hon. Thomas Erskine.*
152. Sheridan, Richard Brinsley. *The Speeches of the Right Honourable Richard Brinsley Sheridan.*
184. Webster, Daniel. *Speeches and Forensic Arguments.*

SCIENCE

  26. Burton, Robert. *The Anatomy of Melancholy.*

  35. Chambers, Robert, and William Chambers. *Chambers's Miscellany of Useful and Entertaining Tracts.*

  44. Cuvier, Georges. *Animal Kingdom.*

  62. Gray, Asa. *The Botanical Text-book.*

  77. Herschel, John F. W. *Outlines of Astronomy.*

101. Lyell, Charles. *Principles of Geology.*

134. Prichard, James Cowles. *The Natural History of Man: Comprising Inquiries into the Modifying Influence of Physical and Moral Agencies on the Different Tribes of the Human Family.*

193. Wilkes, Charles. *Narrative of the United States Exploring Expedition, During the Years 1838, 1839, 1840, 1841, and 1842.*

TRAVEL

  14. Barthélemy, Jean Jacques. *Travels of Anacharsis the Younger in Greece.*

  ———. *Maps, Plans, Views, and Coins, Illustrative of the Travels of Anacharsis the Younger in Greece.*

  18. Boswell, James. *Life of Johnson.*

  82. Irving, Washington. *The Works of Washington Irving.*

111. Martin, Montgomery R. *British Colonial Library.*

150. Semmes, Raphael. *Service Afloat and Ashore.*

182. Warren, John Esaias. *Para; Or, Scenes and Adventures on the Banks of the Amazon.*

193. Wilkes, Charles. *Narrative of the United States Exploring Expedition, During the Years 1838, 1839, 1840, 1841, and 1842.*

APPENDIX C

Edward Everett's Recommendations for
the First White House Library

&⁘⁘⁙⁙⁘⁘&

On September 23, 1851, President Fillmore wrote to Edward Everett requesting recommendations for books about international law for the library. Everett replied with a lengthy list of recommendations on September 29. Although Fillmore had already purchased some of the books that Everett recommended, he bought fourteen of the books from the list the following December.[1] That order included the following three books that were not on Everett's list:

Brown, Arthur. *A Compendious View of the Civil Law, and of the Law of Admiralty.* 2nd ed. 2 vols. London: Butterworth, 1802.
Linden, Johannes van der. *Institutes of the Laws of Holland.* Trans. Jabez Henry. London: J. and W. T. Clarke, 1828.
Atcheson, Nathaniel. *Report of a Case Recently Argued and Determined in His Majesty's Court of the King's Bench on the Validity of a Sentence of Condemnation by an Enemy's Consul in a Neutral Port, and the Right of the Owner of the Ship to Call upon the Underwriters to Reimburse Him the Money Paid for the Purchase of the Ship at Sale by Auction.* London: Butterworth et al., 1800.

Everett's list of recommendations has been transcribed below. The punctuation of titles has been standardized and abbreviations have been spelled out. If no edition or publisher is specified, Everett did provide this information. Likewise, if no format (4to, 8vo, or 12mo) has been included, he did not indicate one. Any additional comments that Everett made about these books has been placed in a note following the appropriate title. Approximate transcriptions have been provided in brackets for words that are unintelligible in the original. Those books that Fillmore had already purchased before consulting Everett have been marked with a double asterisk (**). A single asterisk (*) indicates books that Fillmore purchased from Little and Brown in December 1851.

Admiralty Reports by Robinson, Dodson, and Haggard.
> *Note.* Of great importance for the opinions of Sir William Scott.
Armed Neutrality: A Collection of Publick Acts and Papers Relating to the Principles of the . . . 8vo. London, 1801.
> *Note.* This volume contains Lord Mansfield's celebrated reply to the manifesto of the Pompean Government Relative to the Silesian loan.
Baring, Alexander (The late Lord Ashburton). *An Inquiry into the Causes and Consequences of the Orders in Council.* 8vo. London, 1808.

Bunge, William. *Commentaries on Colonial and Foreign Laws Generally, and in Their Conflict with Each Other and the Law of England.* 4 vols. 8vo. London, 1810.

Burlamaqui, J. J. *Principis du Droit de la Nature et des Gens.* Translated by Thomas Nugent and often reprinted in London and America, 1763.

Bynkershoek, [Cornelius van]. *Quaestionum Juris Public Libri Duo.*
  Note. The first book was translated by the late [M. der Pinceau] and published at Philadelphia in 1810 in 8vo.

*Chalmers, George. *Opinions of Eminent Lawyers on Various Points of English Jurisprudence, Chiefly Concerning the Colonies, Fisheries, and Commerce of Great Britain,* 2 vols. 8vo. London, 1814.

———. *Collections of Treaties Between Great Britain and Other Powers.* 2 vols. 8vo. London, 1790.

*Chitty, Joseph. *A Practical Treatise on the Law of Nations.* 8vo. London, 1812.

Cumberland, R. A. *A Treatise on the Law of Nature.* Translated from the original Latin by [Tower]. London, 1729.

Duane, W. J. *The Law of Nations Investigated in a Popular Manner.* 8vo. Philadelphia, 1809.

Eden, Frederic. *An Historical Sketch of the International Policy of Modern Europe as Connected with the Principles of the Law of Nature and Nations.* 8vo. London, 1823.

Fulbecke, William. *The Pandectes of the Law of Nations.* 4to. London, 1642.

Gales and Seaton [United States Congress] *American State Papers.* 21 vols. Washington: Gales and Seaton.

Gardner, Daniel. *A Treatise on International Law and a Short Explanation of the Jurisdiction and Duty of the Government of the United States.* 12mo. Troy, 1844.

**Grotius, Hugo. *De Jure Bellis ac Pacis.*
  Note. The last English translation, I believe, is that of A. C. Campbell in 3 vols. 8vo [Pontefract].

Hay, George. *A Treatise on Expatriation.* 8vo. Washington, 1814.

Hay, George. *An Essay on Naturalization and Allegiance.* Washington, 1816.

*Heineccius. *Elementa Juris Natura et Gentium.* Translated by George Turnbull under the title of *A Methodical System of Universal Law.* 2 vols. 8vo. London, 1763.

International Law Tracts. 8vo. Edinburgh, 1837.

**Kent's, J. *Commentaries on American Law.* 4 vols. 8vo.
  Note. The last (6th?) edition. The first volume contains a valuable summary of the law of nations.

Mackintosh, Sir James. *A Discourse on the Study of the Law of Nature and Nations.* 12 mo. London, 1835. Boston 8vo. 1843.

[Madison, James]. *An Examination of the British Doctrine, Which Subjects to Capture a Neutral Trade not Open in Time of Peace.* 8vo. 1806.
  Note. This most able tract was published anonymously, but a copy was sent to each member of Congress.

*Manning, W. O. *Commentaries on the Law of Nations.* 8vo. London, 1839.

*Martens G. F. *A Summary of the Law of Nations.* Translated from the French by William Cobett. Philadelphia 8vo. 1795. With additions London 1802.
  Note. The later editions in the original of which the 4th appeared at Paris in 1831 are much enlarged. Latest edition of all.

———. *An Essay on Privateers, Captures, and Recaptures.* Translated from the French by T. H. Horne 8vo. London, 1801.

**Puffendorf, Samuel. *Law of Nature and Nations.* Translated from the Original Latin by Basil Kennet with the notes of Barbeyrac. 5th edition. fol. London, 1749.

*Reddie, J. *Enquiries into International Law.* 8vo. Edinburgh, 1842.

———. *Researches Historical and Critical in Maritime and International Law.* Edinburgh, 8vo. 1844.

*Robinson, Christopher. *Collectanea Maritama: A Collection of Public Instruments etc. Tending to Illustrate the History and Practice of Prize Law.* 8vo. London, 1801.

*Rutherforth, T. *Institutes of Natural Law.* 8v. 2 vols. Cambridge, 1754.

*Schlegel, J. F. W. *An Examination of the Sentence in the Case of the Swedish Convoy.* Translated from the Danish, 8vo London, 1800.

Selden J. *Mare Clausum.* Translated into English by M. Nedham, 2nd Ed. London fol. 1662.

Sparks, Jared. *Diplomatic Correspondence of the United States during the Revolutionary War.* 12 vols. 8vo. Boston: 1829–30.

————. A continuation of the same work by a different editor to the adoption of the Constitution of the United States. 7 vols. 8vo, Washington 1833–34.

**Story, Joseph. *Commentaries of the Conflict Laws Foreign and Domestic.* 2nd edition. 8vo. Boston, 1841.

**Vattels. *Law of Nations.* Translated from the French by J. Chitty. 8vo. London. 1834 6th American.

Stephen, James. *War in Disguise or the Frauds on Neutral Flags.* London, 1806, 8vo, and New York the same year.

————. *Answer to* [*the*] *Hon. Rufus King.* 8vo. New York, 1806 (Anonymous).

*Ward, Robert. *An Enquiry into the Foundation and History of the Law of Nations in Europe.* 2 vols. 8vo. London, 1795.

————. *Treatise on the Relative Rights and Duties of Belligerent and Neutral Powers.* 8vo. London 1801.

*Warden D. B. *The Origin, Nature, Progress and Influence of Consular Establishments.* 8vo. Paris, 1815.

Wheaton, Henry. *A Digest of the Law of Maritime Captures and Prizes,* 8vo. New York, 1815.

————. *Inquiry into the Validity of the British Claim to a Right of Visitation and Search of American Vessels.* London and Philadelphia, 8vo, 1842.

**————. *Elements of International Law, with a Sketch of the History of the Science* 3rd edition.

**Wheaton, Robert. *The History of the Law of Nations in Europe and America from the Earliest Times to the Treaty of Washington.* 8vo. 1842.[2]

**United States Supreme Court. The Reports of Cranch, Dallas, Wheaton, Peters and Howard.

————. *Laws of.* Little and Brown edition.

Note. The 8th volume contains treaties with foreign powers.

*Whewell, William Dr. *Elements of Morality Including Polity.* 8vo. 2 vols. 1845 and 12 mo. 2 vols. 1848, London.

*Wicquefort M. de. *The Rights and Privileges of Ambassadors and Public Ministers.* Translated from the French by John Digby fol. London, 1740.

*Wildman's *International Law* 2 vols.

NOTES

1. See "White House Collection," 22–23, for a discussion of the Cuban filibuster and Everett's recommendations.

2. This book is by Henry, not Robert, Wheaton.

SELECTED REFERENCES

Print Resources

Bartlett, John Russell. *Autobiography of John Russell Bartlett (1805–1886)*. Edited by Jerry E. Mueller. Providence: John Carter Brown Library, 2006.

Bode, Carl. *American Life in the 1840s*. Garden City, N.Y.: Doubleday, 1967.

Bowers, Fredson. *Principles of Bibliographical Description*. 1949. New York: Russell and Russell, 1962.

A Catalogue of the Law Library of Harvard University. Cambridge, Mass.: Metcalf and Co., 1846. (Harvard)

Cohen, Morris. *Bibliography of Early American Law*. 6 vols. Buffalo, N.Y.: William S. Hein and Co., 1998. (*BEAL*)

Colman, Edna M. *Seventy-Five Years of White House Gossip from Washington to Lincoln*. Garden City, N.Y.: Doubleday, 1925.

"A Course of Historical Reading." *Universalist Quarterly and General Review*, January 1850. Available at *APS Online*.

"A Course of Historical Reading, Part II: Modern History." *Universalist Quarterly and General Review*, April 1850. Available at *APS Online*.

Fleeman, J. D. *A Bibliography of the Works of Samuel Johnson*. Oxford: Clarendon, 2000. (Fleeman)

Greenleaf, Simon. "Greenleaf's Select Law Library." In *A General Catalogue of Law Books*, x–xix. Boston: Little, Brown and Co., 1850. (Greenleaf)

Hoffman, David. *A Course of Legal Study, Addressed to Students and the Profession Generally*. 2 vols. Baltimore: Joseph Neal, 1836. (Hoffman)

Hoganson, Kristin. "Abigail (Powers) Fillmore." In *American First Ladies: Their Lives and Their Legacy*, ed. Lewis L. Gould, 99–106. New York: Garland Publishing, 1996.

Holloway, Laura C. *The Ladies of the White House; Or in the Home of the Presidents*. 1869. Philadelphia: A Gorton, 1882. Facsim. ed. New York: AMS, 1976.

Irving, Pierre Monroe. *The Life and Letters of Washington Irving*. Vol. 3. New York: Putnam, 1869.

Kelley, Mary. *Private Woman, Public Stage: Literary Domesticity in Nineteenth-Century America*. New York: Oxford University Press, 1984.

Larned, J. N. *The Literature of American History: A Bibliographical Guide*. 1902; repr., New York: Unger, 1966. (Larned)

"The Lincolns Redecorate the White House." *Daily Alta California* [San Francisco], May 12, 1862.

Little and Brown (firm). *A Catalogue of an Extensive and Valuable Collection of Books, Ancient and Modern, in Every Department of Literature, for Sale by Little & Brown*. Boston: Little and Brown, April 1850. (L and B 1850)

———. *A Catalogue of Law and Miscellaneous Books Published and for Sale by Little and Brown*. Boston: Little and Brown, January, 1852. (L and B Law 1852)

———. *A Complete Catalogue of the Extensive and Valuable Collection of Ancient and Modern Books in Several Languages, and in Every Department of Literature*. Boston: Wilson and Son, 1853. (L and B 1853)

———. *A General Catalogue of Law Books; Including All the Reports*. Boston: Little and Brown, 1853. (L and B Law 1853)

———. *A General Catalogue of Law Books Published During the Present Century: And Including All the Reports from the Earliest Period*. Boston: Little and Brown, 1850. (Land B Law 1850)

———. *Little, Brown and Company, General List of Works*. Boston: Little and Brown, July, 1852. (L and B 1852)

The London Catalogue of Books Published in Great Britain with Their Sizes, Prices, and Publisher's Names, 1816–1851. London: Thomas Hodgson, 1851. (*LC 1816–1851*).

Low, Sampson, comp. *The British Catalogue of Books Published from October 1837 to December 1852; Containing the Date of Publication, Size, Price, Publisher's Name, and Edition*. London: Sampson Low and Son, 1853. (*British Catalogue*)

———. *The English Catalogue of Books Published from January, 1835, to January, 1863*. London: Sampson Low, Son, and Marston, 1864.

Marvin, J. G. *Legal Bibliography, or a Thesaurus of American, English, Irish, and Scotch Law Books*. Philadelphia: T. and J. W. Johnson, 1847. (Marvin)

Mott, Frank Luther. *A History of American Magazines, 1741–1850*. Cambridge: Harvard University Press, 1939.

———. *A History of American Magazines, 1850–1865*. Cambridge: Harvard University Press, 1957.

National Union Catalog, Pre-1956 Imprints. 754 vols. London: Mansell, 1968–81. (*NUC*)

Nourie, Alan, and Barbara Nourie. *American Mass-Market Magazines*. New York: Greenwood Press, 1990.

Peddie, Robert Alexander, and Quintin Waddington, eds. and comps. *The English Catalogue of Books, 1801–1836*. London: The Publisher's Circular, 1914.

Ponko, Vincent, Jr. *Ships, Seas, and Scientists: U.S. Naval Exploration and Discovery in the Nineteenth Century*. Annapolis: Naval Institute Press, 1974.

Pulszky, Francis, and Theresa Pulszky. *White, Red, Black*. 1853. New York: Johnson Reprint Corporation, 1970.

Putnam (firm). *The Book Buyer's Manual*. New York: Putnam, 1852. (Putnam)

Rayback, Robert J. *Millard Fillmore: Biography of a President*. Buffalo, N.Y.: Henry Stewart for the Buffalo Historical Society, 1959.

Richardson, James, ed. *A Compilation of the Messages and Papers of the Presidents, 1789–1897*. Vol. 5. Washington, D.C.: GPO, 1897.

Roorbach, Orville A., comp. *Bibliotheca Americana: Catalogue of American Publications, Including Reprints and Original Works, from 1820 to 1852, Inclusive. Together with a List of Periodicals Published in the United States*. New York: Orville A. Roorbach, 1852. (Roorbach)

Ryan, Francis de Sales. "Centennial of the White House Library." Photocopy, Office of the Curator, White House, Washington, D.C., 1950.

Scarry, Robert. *Millard Fillmore*. Jefferson, N.C.: McFarland and Co., 2001.

Seale, William. *The President's House: A History*. 2 vols. Washington, D.C.: White House Historical Association, 1986.

Severance, Frank H., ed. *Millard Fillmore Papers*. 2 vols. Buffalo, N.Y.: Buffalo Historical Society, 1907.

Singleton, Esther. *The Story of the White House*. 2 vols. New York: McClure, 1907.

Thacker-Estrada, Elizabeth Lorelei. "The Heart of the Fillmore Presidency: Abigail Powers Fillmore and the White House Library." *White House Studies* 1, no. 1 (2001): 83–98.

Walsh, S. Padraig. *Anglo-American General Encyclopedias: A Historical Bibliography, 1703–1967*. New York: Bowker, 1968.

The Washington City Directory and Congressional, and Executive Register, for 1850. Comp. Edward Waite. Washington: Columbus Alexander, 1850.

Wharton, Anne Hollingsworth. *Social Life in the Early Republic.* 1902. New York: Benjamin Blom, 1969.

White House Library List. August 9, 1963, n.p.

Whitton, Mary Ormsbee. *First First Ladies, 1789–1865: A Study of the Early Presidents.* 1948. Reprint, Freeport, N.Y.: Books for Libraries Press, 1969.

Archival Resources

Buffalo Erie County Historical Society, Buffalo, N.Y. Millard Fillmore Papers.

Charles E. Young Research Library, University of California Los Angeles. Charles Lanman Papers (collection 728).

Herbert Hoover Presidential Library, West Branch, Iowa. Lou Henry Hoover Papers.

———. Presidential Papers.

Library of Congress, Manuscript Division. Library of Congress Archives. Washington, D.C. Central File.

Massachusetts Historical Society, Boston. Edward Everett Papers.

National Archives and Records Administration, College Park, Md. Records of the Accounting Offices of the Department of the Treasury. Record Group 217.

———. Records of the Bureau of Accounts (Treasury). Record Group 39.

Penfield Library, SUNY at Oswego, Oswego, N.Y. Millard Fillmore Papers.

Princeton University Library, Rare Books and Special Collections, Princeton, N.J. George Palmer Putnam Collection.

———. John Story Gulick Collection of American Statesmen.

Rutherford B. Hayes Presidential Center, Spiegel Grove, Fremont, Ohio. Rutherford B. Hayes Papers.

University Archives, University Libraries, University at Buffalo, SUNY, Buffalo, N.Y. Millard Fillmore Papers.

Online Resources

American National Biography. American Council of Learned Societies, Oxford University Press, 2005. http://www.anb.org/articles/home.html.

American Periodical Series (APS) Online. Proquest. http://www.proquest.com/products_pq/descriptions/aps.shtml.

America's Historical Newspapers, 1690–1922. Readex, NewsBank. http://www.newsbank.com/readex.

Congressional Globe. Washington, D.C.: Blair and Rives, 1834–73. http://memory.loc.gov/ammem/amlaw/lwcg.html.

Dictionary of American Biography (DAB). Base Set, American Council of Learned Societies, 1928–36. Reproduced in *Biography Resource Center.* Farmington Hills, Mich.: Thomson Gale, 2007. http://galenet.galegroup.com/servlet/BioRC.

Hayes, Rutherford B. *Diary and Letters of Rutherford B. Hayes,* Vol. 3. http://www.ohiohistory.org/onlinedoc/hayes/Volume03/Chapter38/Christmas1880.txt.

Keeler, Lucy Elliot. "Excursion to Baltimore, Md. and Washington, D. C., January 18–February 15, 1881." The Rutherford B. Hayes Presidential Center. http://www.rbhayes.org/online texts.

Officer, Lawrence H. "Exchange Rate Between the United States Dollar and the British Pound, 1791–2005." Economic History Services, EH.Net, 2006. http://eh.net/hmit/exchangerates/pound.php.

Oxford Dictionary of National Biography (ODNB). Ed. H. C. G. Matthew and Brian Harrison. Oxford: Oxford University Press, 2004. http://www.oxforddnb.com.

Proquest Historical Newspapers. Proquest. http://www.proquest.com/products_pq/descriptions/pq-hist-news.shtml.

The Public Statutes at Large of the United States of America. Boston: Little and Brown, 1845–67. http://memory.loc.gov/ammem/amlaw/lwsl.html.

RLG Union Catalogue. Eureka, 1993–2005. http://eureka.rlg.org/eureka/zgate2.prod.

West, Lucy Scott. "Journal of Lucy Scott West at the White House During the Hayes Administration." The Rutherford B. Hayes Presidential Center. http://www. rbhayes.org/online texts.

Williamson, Samuel H. "Six Ways to Compute the Relative Value of a U.S. Dollar Amount, 1774 to Present." MeasuringWorth, 2008. http://www.measuringworth.com/uscompare/.

WorldCat. Online Computer Library Center (OCLC). http://www.oclc.org/worldcat/default.htm.

INDEX

The following abbreviations have been used in the index:

art.	artist	eng.	engraver	pub.	publisher
comp.	compiler	MF	Millard Fillmore	trans.	translator
ed.	editor	prtr.	printer	WH	White House

Since the occupations of bookseller and publisher were not as clearly defined in the eighteenth and nineteenth centuries as they are today, no distinction is made between individuals introduced in the imprint by phrases like "and sold by" and those who are named without any introductory phrase. Many "publishers" also sold books to retail customers and many "booksellers" often shared the publishing costs. All have been identified in this index with "(pub.)" following their name. Page numbers in italics refer to photos or illustrations. Numbers enclosed in parentheses refer to the book entry number.

Jones, A. (comp.), 234
Jones, A. (eng.), 350
Jones, William, 278
Jones & Company (pub.), 14, 121, 210, 211
Jordan and Halpin (eng.), 349, 350, 351
Junius, 76, (90) 215–17, 228

Kame, Lord, 247
Kay and Brothers (pub.), 226
Kearny, E. (eng.), 283
Kearny, F. (eng.), 286
Keats, John, 265
Keeler, Lucy, 25
Keily, James, (91) 217–18
Keith, George (pub.), 196
Kemble, Fanny, 42
Kemble, W. (eng.), 116
Kennedy, Jacqueline, renovation of WH Library, 29–30, 33 n. 37
Kennedy, John Pendleton, 27, 47, 105 n. 2, 203, 355
Kennet, Basil (trans.), 271
Kent, James, 11, 20, 97, (92) 218–19, 240, 342
Kent, William (pub.), 218
Kettell, Thomas Prentice (ed.), 328
Key, Francis Scott, 328
King, Charles (pub.), 346
King, Charles B. (art.), 355
Klapka, György, 22, (93) 219–20
Knight, Charles and Co. (pub.), 123, 124, 144, 145, 263, 264, 298
Knox, Dr., 192
Kombst, Gustaf, 213
Kossuth, Louis, 47, 52 n. 52, 219
  visit to WH, 5, 22, 52 n. 50, 259, 272
Kyd, Thomas, 247

labels. *See* bookplates; spine labels
Lacery(eng.), 210
Lacey, Dan, 29
Lafayette, Marquis de, (94) 220–21, 254
Lamartine, Alphonse de, 4, 16, (95) 221–22
Lamb, Charles, 130
Lane, Edward (ed. and trans.), (10) 106–7
Langtree, S. D. (ed.), 328
Langtree and O'Sullivan (pub.), 328
Lanman, Charles, 32 n. 19, n. 20, 64, 67 n. 13
  as Fillmore's agent, 4, 11–13, 14, 19, 62, 63, 65–66, 77, 78, 79, 114, 190, 313
Larned, J. N., 177, 300
law, 4, 13, 19–20, 62, 83 n. 10, 122, 207
  admiralty, 11, 108, 125, 130, 143, 276–77, 287, 326

British, 11, 21, 115, 138, 185, 232, 281–82, 310
  of conflicts, 312–13
  Dutch, 222–23
  European, 241, 333, 342–43
  of evidence, 179
  French, 153
  international, 23, 108, 130, 138, 143, 185, 196, 240, 271–72, 274–75, 277, 330, 347
  maritime, 11, 97, 108, 276–77, 287
  of nations, 130, 143, 185, 196, 240, 241–42, 271–72, 330, 347
  natural, 18, 130, 196, 271–72, 279
  references sources for, 80–81, 120
  Roman, 153, 317
  U.S., 11, 24, 132, 218, 257, 312–13, 326, 341–43
Law (pub.), 100
Lawrence, Sir Thomas (art.), 120, 150, 320, 321
Lea and Blanchard (pub.), 162, 177, 251–52, 259, 273, 343, 348, 352, 355
Leland (trans.), 193
Lennon, Mark, 100
Leslie, Frank, 56
libraries, 69, 71
  nineteenth-century home, 14–18, 23–24, 30–31, 31 n. 7, 43, 156, 322
  state and territorial, 10, 32 n. 13, n. 15
Library of Congress (L of C), 2, 4, 10, 77, 84 n. 31
  exchange of books with WH Library, 25–28, 36 n. 79, 37 n. 85, 71
Lieber, Francis (ed.), 161, 162
Lincoln, Abraham, 25
Lincoln, Mary Todd, 25, 289
Lind, Jenny, 45, 49
Lindbergh, Charles A., 29
Linden, Johannes van der, (96) 222–23
Lingard, John, 18, (97) 224–25
Lintott, Bernard (pub.), 346
Lippincott Grambo and Co. (pub.), 156
literature, 5, 13, 16–17, 140
  British, 13, 160, 172–73, 209–10, 247, 248
  classical, 192–93
  French, 166, 281
  U.S., 24, 104–5, 180–82, 203, 256, 327–28
Little and Brown
  as bookseller, 61–62, 66, 67 n. 2, 79, 81, 97, 127
  as publisher, 110, 134, 138, 145, 153, 179, 246, 249, 280, 297, 300, 306, 307, 308, 312, 313, 314, 326, 327, 338, 339
Liverpool, Lord, 131
Locke, John, 5, 100, 142, (98) 225–26, 260
Locken, John (pub.), 128

Lockhart, John Gibson, 16, 117, (99) 226–27

Lolme, Jean Louis de, 11, 215, (100) 227–29

London Times, 265

Longacre, J. B. (eng.), 283, 285, 286

Longfellow, Henry Wadsworth, 25, 144–45, 180

Longman (pub.), 299, 329

Longman, Brown, Green, and Longmans (pub.),
    161, 195, 198, 231, 251

Longman, Hurst, Rees, Orme, and Brown
    (pub.), 106, 216

Longman, Hurst, Rees, Orme, Brown, and
    Green (pub.), 112, 113

Longman, Orme, Brown, Green, and Longman's
    (pub.), 123

Longman, Rees, Orme, Brown, and Green
    (pub.), 106

Longman, Rees, Orme, Brown, Green, and
    Longman (pub.), 106

Longman, T. N. and Rees, O. (pub.), 161

Longman & Co. (pub.), 296

Lopez, Narciso, 22, 46

Louis XIV (king, France), 15, 261

Lowell, James Russell, 105, 328

Lucas, J. (art.), 321

Lyell, Sir Charles, 16, (101) 229–31, 271

Lytton, Bulwer, 117

Macaulay, Thomas Babington, 15, 16, 161, (102)
    231–32

MacGregor, John, 21, 66, 72, 78, (105) 235–38,
    (106) 235–38

Machiavelli, Niccolò, (107) 238–39

Mackie, R. (pub.), 157

MacKintosh, Sir James, 131

Madison, Dolley, 44, 47–48, 52 n. 57

Madison, James, 43, (71) 189–90, 254, 355

Maea, J. (art.), 267

Malby and Sons (pub.), 322

Malthus, Thomas Robert, 21, 146, (108) 239–40,
    246, 260, 296

Manning, William Oke, (109) 240–41

manufacturing, 232, 329

maps, 58, 76, 211–12, 217, 250–51, 298–99, (171)
    322–23. *See also* geography

Marchant, Sir Denis le (ed.), 332

Marsh, George P., 105

Marshall, John, 342

Martens, Georg Friedrich von, (110) 241–42

Martin, Montgomery R., (111) 242–43

Marvin, J. G., 81, 97, 115, 120, 125, 143, 179, 185,
    196, 218, 240, 279, 282, 310, 326, 343

Mason, F. (pub.), 112, 113

Matchett, H. Vicary (pub.), 156

Maverick, P. (eng.), 164

Mawman, J. (pub.), 112, 113, 216

Maxwell, A. (prtr.), 281

Maxwell, A. and Son (pub.), 314

Maxwell, J. (prtr.), 283

McCarty and Davis (pub.), 156

McClelland, D. (eng.), 337

McCullagh, William Torrens, 21, (103) 232–33

McCulloch, John Ramsay, 21, 162, (104) 233–34,
    251, 296, 329, 341

melancholy, 16, 129–30

Melville, H. (eng.), 321

Merriam, G. and C. (pub.), 62, 341

Metcalf, Theron, 256, 326, 327

Mexican-American War of 1846, 290–91

Mexico, history of, 15, 266. *See also* United
    States and Mexico Boundary Survey
    Expedition

Michelet, Jules, 4, (113) 244–46, (114) 244–46

Michelin, F. (art.), 191, 192

Michelsen, Leopold, 224

Middle Ages, 187–88

Middleton, T. (art.), 286

Mignard, Pierre (art.), 262

Mignet, M. (ed.), 295

Mill, John Stuart, 21, 27, 146, (115) 246–47, 296, 344

Miller, John (pub.), 136

Miller, Julia, recollections of, 24, 44

Miller, R. (eng.), 191

Miller, Robert L., 217

Miller, William (pub.), 201

Milliken, Andrew (pub.), 343

Milliken and Son (pub.), 241

Mills, Abraham, (116) 247–48

Milman, Henry Hart (ed.), 15, 170, 171

Milton, John, 5, 17, 33 n. 35, (117) 248–50, (118)
    248–50

mining, 317–18, 329

Missouri Compromise of 1820, 145. *See also*
    Compromise of 1850

Mitchell, Samuel Augustus, 11, 217, (119) 250–51

Monroe, Elizabeth, 44

Monroe, James, 44, 57, 354, 355

Montagu, Basil (ed.), 109

Montagu, Lady Mary Wortley, 247

Montesquieu, Baron Charles-Louis de Secondat,
    239

Montgomery (pub.), 335

Moore, J. W. (pub.), 130, 318